DEMOCRACY

AND THE

ORGANIZATION OF POLITICAL PARTIES

DEMOCRACY

AND THE

ORGANIZATION OF POLITICAL PARTIES

BY

M. OSTROGORSKI

IN TWO VOLUMES

VOL. I

TRANSLATED FROM THE FRENCH
BY

FREDERICK CLARKE, M.A.

FORMERLY TAYLORIAN SCHOLAR IN THE UNIVERSITY OF OXFORD

WITH A PREFACE BY

THE RIGHT HON. JAMES BRYCE, M.P.
AUTHOR OF " THE AMERICAN COMMONWEALTH "

HASKELL HOUSE PUBLISHERS LTD.

Publishers of Scarce Scholarly Books

NEW YORK. N. Y. 10012

1970

First Published 1902

HASKELL HOUSE PUBLISHERS Ltd.
Publishers of Scarce Scholarly Books
280 LAFAYETTE STREET
NEW YORK, N. Y. 10012

Library of Congress Catalog Card Number: 72-122620

Standard Book Number 8383-1003-6

Printed in the United States of America

To My Father

M. O.

CONTENTS OF THE FIRST VOLUME

FIRST PART

FIRST CHAPTER

SECOND CHAPTER

SECOND PART

FIRST CHAPTER

SECOND CHAPTER

I. The political parties who were aimed at by the extra-constitutional organizations in pursuit of reforms, have recourse to extra-parliamentary organizations themselves. Before 1832 they had no organization outside Parliament, and had

SIXTH CHAPTER

THIRD PART

FIRST CHAPTER

SECOND CHAPTER

THIRD CHAPTER

FOURTH CHAPTER

PREFACE

ALTHOUGH political parties are as old as popular government itself, their nature, their forces, and the modes in which they have been organized have received comparatively little attention either from historians or from writers on what is beginning to be called political science. Something has been said, and by no one perhaps so well as by Edmund Burke, upon the theory and aim of Party, and the functions which it ought to discharge; and historical accounts, though seldom either full or philosophical, have been given of the development and career of the two great parties in England and in the American Union. But no one has, so far as I know, produced any treatise containing a systematic examination and description of the structure of parties as organizations governed by settled rules and working by established methods. Even in the United States, where party organization early attained a completeness and effective power unapproached in any other country, I could not find, when in 1883 I began to study and was seeking to portray the institutions of that country, any account of the very remarkable and well-compacted scheme of organization which had been at work there for forty or fifty years; and noted that among even the best-educated men there were few who had mastered its details. The historical action of the parties, their principles or tenets, their local distribution, the social influences that pervaded them, the characters of the men who had led them, — these were the matters on which attention had been fixed, to the neglect of the less attractive and less conspicuous questions connected with the machinery by which they worked. There was no book on which one could draw,[1] and the persons whom I interrogated usually seemed surprised that a stranger should feel interested in enquiries of the kind. Still less has any

---

[1] I note with interest that M. Ostrogorski says in his preface that he was struck by the same fact when he began to study the subject.

attempt been made in Europe to handle the topic as a whole. There is room, therefore, for a treatise which shall take Party Organization and Party Machinery for its specific subject, and shall endeavour to treat these phenomena of modern politics with a fulness commensurate to the importance of the part which they play to-day in popular governments.

They have indeed now become so apparently essential a part of democratic institutions in the country which has seen their most complete development that the traveller in the United States is disposed to ask how it happens that they are of such recent appearance in history, and how democracies in other ages and countries got on without them, seeing that in all popular governments there have been active and often extremely fierce and violent parties. The answer is that popular governments have within the last hundred years entered upon a new phase, which is marked by two remarkable facts. The number of participants in the business of government is immensely greater, and the method of participation is much more pacific. The republics of antiquity, as well as those of mediæval Germany (including Switzerland) and Italy, were each of them with few exceptions composed of an exceedingly small number of citizens participating in the control of the state as compared with those modern democracies which we see in the United States, in Britain and in her self-governing colonies, in France, in Belgium, in Norway. And in the second place, these republics consisted of men accustomed to the use of arms, and ready to resort to arms on slight occasion, so that when party feeling rose above a certain temperature, physical force settled the dispute. Modern democracies consist of hundreds of thousands or even millions of voters, and their method of action is by dropping into boxes pieces of paper bearing the names of candidates. These absolutely new conditions required new methods, and the inventive genius of man was not long in devising the methods.

In England, the oldest example in the modern world of a large community whose government, though far from democratic, had, at any rate since the seventeenth century, a sensible infusion of the popular element, parties had existed for some two hundred years before the great extensions of the suffrage which came in 1867 and 1884. But the parties had little or no organization in the sense we now give to the term. The members of a party were linked together by ties of religious sympathy, or of economic interest, or of belief in a few broad ideas, or of attachment to particular families. The only occasions on which parties could act together by pacific methods were afforded by parliamentary elections. Down till 1832, the number of voters in nearly all the boroughs was so small, and the control of one person, or a few persons, was so effective in most of those boroughs, that no organization of the voters was needed, while in the counties the influence of a few great landowning families supplied the necessary leadership when an election arrived. Political clubs, which after all touch only a small number of voters, were little known and unimportant before the Reform Bill of 1832. Local party associations are practically the growth, in their present activity and power, of the last thirty-five years.

In the United States the need of collecting and disciplining the voting power in which the strength of the parties lay, was sooner felt, first, because the number of voters was, in proportion to the total population, much larger than in England, and elections were much more frequent; secondly, because there existed a completely popular elective system of local government; thirdly, because elections of all kinds came oftener; and fourthly, because the number of offices given by popular election was larger. Yet in the United States it was not till the extensions of the electoral suffrage in the several States, which mark the period between 1810 and 1840, together with the corresponding democratization of the administrative and judicial machinery of State government, had greatly increased the number and power of voters and the number of elective offices that the portentous fabric of party organization which we see to-day began to be built up. Its foundations were laid between 1820 and 1830. Its completion can hardly be placed earlier than 1860. And it rose so quietly and gradually that the keen eye of Tocqueville, whose philosophic study of American democracy was published in 1834, had not noted its appearance, much less foreseen the tremendous power it was destined to exert. Nor indeed do I know of any European visitor to the United States down to very recent times who seems to have been struck by it, or to have appreciated its importance. It has now grown to be a second ruling force in the country, in some respects fully as powerful as the official administrations which the Constitutions of the Nation and of the several States have established. It has become a sort of link between the legislative and the executive departments of the Federal Government, and may (in some aspects) almost be called a second and parallel government, directing that which the Constitution creates. Its unit, the Primary meeting, has in some States obtained a statutory recognition which astonishes English lawyers.[1]

This system of party organization in America, and the incomparably simpler, ruder, and less effective system which the last thirty-five years have created in Great Britain, have now found in M. Ostrogorski a singularly painstaking and intelligent student. He is both scientific in method and philosophical in spirit. He has examined the facts with exemplary diligence. He has described them with a careful attention to the smallest details of the structure and working of the two systems, the English and the American. He has brought to the investigation of their phenomena a breadth of view which recognizes the large historical causes by which institutions are moulded, as well as an impartiality which shows no more leniency to the faults of the Republicans than to those of the Democrats in the United States, to the errors of the Tories than to those of the Liberals in England. Leniency is indeed the last thing he shows to any party; and it is only in respect to the Rhadamanthine attitude he preserves throughout that I feel bound to utter a note of mild dissent. It is for American readers rather than for an Englishman to say how far his picture of the party machinery of the United States is overcharged with gloom, for gloomy it unquestionably is. As regards Great Britain, I can hardly doubt that his description, a minute, and on the whole accurate, as well as fair description, — though here and there his generalizations seem to me open to question, — will make upon a reader in some other country an impression darker than the realities of the case warrant. Taken one by one, the particular facts and incidents he states

---

[1] This side of party government has been ingeniously and instructively handled by Mr. Henry Jones Ford in his *Rise and Growth of American Politics* (1898).

are (so far as I can judge) almost always correctly stated. It is the tendency to assume these facts and incidents to be more generally typical of English political methods as a whole than I believe them to be, and the omission of qualifying considerations, such as perhaps only an Englishman can fully appreciate, that may make his account suggest to those who do not possess an independent knowledge of England a judgment too unfavourable. I am myself an optimist, almost a professional optimist, as indeed politics would be intolerable were not a man grimly resolved to see between the clouds all the blue sky he can. But apart from all professional optimism, and allowing for the natural tendency of a citizen to view even the deficiencies of his own country with indulgent eyes, I cannot but think that M. Ostrogorski exaggerates the power and the poison of what he calls the Caucus in England, and that he does not quite sufficiently allow for the healthy influences that are at work to correct whatever dangers its growth may involve. Party organization is a totally different thing in England from what it is in the United States. It is in the hands of a different class of men. It is almost wholly free from the more sordid elements which may enter into the interest men take in their party. M. Ostrogorski knows this, and indeed says it. But he seems, when he comes to judge English phenomena as a whole, and when he pronounces that English party organization is on the road to becoming what American party organization has become, to have been scarcely sufficiently influenced by it.

It is chiefly to readers in America and in the British Colonies that this word of caution needs to be addressed. Englishmen will judge for themselves with how few or how many deductions they must take what M. Ostrogorski says of them. They will all be the better for knowing what a diligent, careful, and eminently honest foreign observer thinks of their party system, and they may find in his description warnings far from unneeded of the mischiefs which a wider and ranker growth of that system may breed. Yet they may draw some encouragement from the reflection that in the British self-governing colonies, including those Australasian colonies which seem to have gone farther towards a pure democracy than any other communities, the party system has not developed upon American lines.

Popular governments do not in all countries follow the same paths, nor show the same evils in equal measure. M. Ostrogorski has wisely chosen to concentrate the attention of his readers upon the forces rather than the forms of democracy, since it is the forms that have hitherto been more largely discussed. He has made a valuable contribution — perhaps the most valuable we have had in recent years — to what may be called the pathology of party government. But there are other maladies also to which democracy is liable. When the time comes for a scientific study of democratic government in general, the phenomena of Switzerland, of the British self-governing colonies, and of France will throw much additional light upon the problems which free countries are, so far with imperfect success, endeavouring to solve.

To estimate the chances that those mischiefs will arrive, or to discuss the means of averting them, is no part of my duty in this preface, which is meant solely to call attention not only to the merits of these volumes, but also to the high significance of their subject, as being at once an interesting branch of political science and also an important branch of politics as an art. It is, moreover, a branch likely to receive further development in Europe, for in the United States it has been already pushed so far that one can hardly imagine what more even American ingenuity can effect. Whatever may be thought of its value, — and I suppose that most sensible men would have preferred to leave parties unorganized, since their organization involves enormous labour and expenditure of an un-reproductive kind, — Party Organization is a logical and inevitable consequence of party government in a large democracy. Where votes rule, and where great issues turn on the results of voting, and most of all where (as in America) a party victory means pecuniary gain or loss to a multitude of men, every effort will be made to attract the voters to the party flag, to keep them united under it, to bring them up to vote when the polling day arrives. The extent to which it becomes necessary to do this is, in the case of each political community, measured by the degree in which that community falls below the level of the ideal democracy. In the ideal democracy every citizen is intelligent, patriotic, disinterested. His sole wish is to discover the right side in each contested issue, and to fix upon the best man among competing candidates. His common sense, aided by a knowledge of the constitution of his country, enables him to judge wisely between the arguments submitted to him, while his own zeal is sufficient to carry him to the polling booth. Though it is usually assumed in platform speeches that the audience addressed are citizens of this attractive type, everybody knows that in all communities, not only in Chicago, but even in Liverpool, let us say, or in Lyons, or in Leipzig, a large proportion of the voters are so indifferent, or so ignorant, that it is necessary to rouse them, to drill them, to bring them up to vote. The party leader who first sees what the new circumstances of the time call for gains an advantage, and the other party is obliged to follow suit. Once the business of organization is entered upon, each party has the strongest motive for endeavouring to make its own system effective, and to form its adherents into disciplined battalions. But this carries the community still further away from the democratic ideal of the intelligent independence of the individual voter, an ideal far removed from the actualities of any State.[1] Organization and discipline mean the command of the leaders, the subordination and obedience of the rank and file; and they mean also the growth of a party spirit which is in itself irrational, impelling men to vote from considerations which have little to do with a love of truth or a sense of justice. These are deviations from the democratic ideal which are bad enough; and if the motive of pecuniary advantage is added, a widely spread motive where the so-called Spoils System of the United States prevails, the state of things will evidently become still worse.

If it is impossible to arrest the development of party organizations, what can be done to check their incidental evils ? The most drastic remedy would be to get rid of party government altogether, but though many political philosophers have called for this change, none has shown how it can be effected. M. Ostrogorski feels the importance of the question, and essays to answer it in the concluding chapters of his book. I have not the space to summarize or to examine the interesting suggestions which he puts forward on this topic. Practical poli-

---

[1] I may perhaps be permitted to refer upon this point to an essay on Obedience in a book entitled *Studies in History and Jurisprudence* (1901).

ticians will, as he himself foresees, be disposed to think his
scheme either impossible to introduce, because too much opposed to existing notions and habits, or impossible to work,
or perhaps open to both these objections. Nevertheless, the
suggestions made ought to be read and considered, for no
one who is sensible of the evils that exist will lightly dismiss
what comes from a writer whose acuteness and knowledge he
will have recognized when he has perused the earlier descrip-
tive parts of the treatise.

Few books of our time show equal appreciation of the problems democracy has to solve, or bring more useful materials
and more acute criticism to their discussion. Reverting to the
general question, let it be noted that there are three kinds of
influence which an organization may employ to attract and hold
voters. One is the sordid inducement of personal gain, whether
in the form of a money bribe, or in the hope of obtaining a place.
From this our English party organizations are happily free, and
it should be a prime aim of those who work them to avoid the
least lapse towards such a dangerous quagmire. Another is
social pressure, whether in the form of a coercion by the landlord or the customer on the one hand, or in that of an appeal
to snobbishness on the other. M. Ostrogorski finds this kind
of influence largely used in England, and what he says of it
deserves to be pondered. The third is an appeal to the intellect and conscience of the voters through speeches and literature. The making of such appeals bears a larger ratio to the
total work done by political organizers in Great Britain than
it does in America, though of course it is done there also on a
large scale. It is obviously the safest channel into which the
efforts of party workers can be turned, and if organizations
made it their chief business, and did it with reasonable fairness, they would justify their existence and render a service
to that diffusion of an intelligent interest in public affairs on
which the welfare of democratic governments depends. There
is perhaps no way of reducing the evils that necessarily flow
from organized partisan activity so effective as that the public
opinion of the community and the sense of public honour and
duty in the chiefs of the parties should guide the subordinate
workers of an organization towards this form of activity, and,
as far as possible, away from the two other forms.

I have referred to public opinion. After all, it is public

opinion which must keep the party organizations in check. There has happily been always, both in Britain and in America, a large body of voters who refuse to be "roped in" by the "workers" of the organizations, and who retain sufficient independence, not only to think for themselves, but also to vote as they please and not as their party bids them. The love of truth, the disposition to apply moral standards to public questions, the unselfish preference of national to sectional or party interests, are always to be found in a certain number of independent citizens, and the tone of public opinion depends upon the influence which such citizens exert. Others are not keenly interested in politics, nor perhaps very intelligent, yet they prefer to follow their own impressions rather than submit to party dictation. These independent citizens (of both types) are sometimes the victims of error, and are, of course, like all citizens, liable to be misled by the press, which cannot, even in the freest countries, be trusted to present both sides of a case with fairness, because one side may have a far larger command of the social and economic forces which — not perhaps in any corrupt way, but by the necessities of the case — affect the press, and because writers in the press, like other men, are naturally disposed to say what will please their readers, to fall in with and intensify the passion of the moment, and to extol their country even where they would serve her better in pointing out her mistakes. Still, it is among these independent citizens that the reaction against the misdeeds of a dominant party begins to be effective. It is they who keep the parties in order by casting their weight, now on the side of one party, now on the other, according to their judgment of the merits of each. It is they who at all times hold in check, not only the spirit of faction, but also the tendency of party organizations to push to excess methods with which, used in moderation, modern democracies seem unable to dispense. In the United States, formidable as the organizations are, the independent citizens are, I think, more active and more sensible of their duty at this moment than they were thirty years ago. In England, happily for England, the organizations have not ceased to be controlled by men occupying a position which makes them amenable to public opinion, nor have they as yet departed far from those traditions in which the strength of English free government resides.   JAMES BRYCE.

NOTE BY THE TRANSLATOR

THE difficulties of this translation have been lightened by the kind co-operation of the author, who has not only responded most readily to all my requests for information and help, but has also been good enough to read the proofs of the translation and to favour me with a number of observations and suggestions which, owing to his grasp of the subject and remarkable knowledge of the English language, have proved of great service. Many of the knotty points have been carefully discussed between us, and in no instance has he failed to make his meaning perfectly clear to me. For this valuable assistance I desire to express my warm acknowledgments.

F. C.

AUTHOR'S PREFACE

" Il faut une science politique nouvelle à un monde tout nouveau.

" Mais c'est à quoi nous ne songeons guère ; placés au milieu d'un fleuve rapide, nous fixons obstinément les yeux vers quelques débris qu'on aperçoit sur le rivage, tandis que le courant nous entraîne et nous pousse à reculons vers les abîmes."[1] — TOCQUEVILLE, *De la Démocratie en Amérique*, Introduction.

IN this book I investigate the working of democratic government. But it is not institutions which are the object of my research : it is not on political forms, it is on political forces that I dwell. Hitherto attention has been too exclusively directed to the study of political forms. The method of observation itself, introduced into political science with the *Esprit des Lois*, was practised more on institutions, on laws, the concrete individuals who create and apply them being, for a long time, wholly neglected. The very idea of political forces as distinct from political forms was not sufficiently clear to men's minds. Concealed at first by the relative simplicity of political life, in which forms and forces appeared to blend into one another, it had some difficulty in emerging even after the great outburst of political thought and the advent of liberty in the eighteenth century ; that century was too much dominated by the metaphysical notion of man in the abstract, considered as the universal and unchangeable basis of the political order, and by the mechanical conception of the moral order. Again, the experience and the practice of liberty were needed for the part played by active wills and by their varied combinations in political life to assert itself and stand out in

[1] " A new political science is wanted for an entirely new world.

" But this is what we think very little about : placed in the middle of a rapid stream, we fix our gaze obstinately on a few débris that are seen upon the bank, while the current is sweeping us along and driving us backwards towards the abyss."

clear relief. In proportion as democratic government developed and made political life more complex, the free play of political forces also developed and gained in complexity, and it became more and more necessary, for the best fulfilment of the objects of the body politic, to acquire an exact knowledge of the working of these forces.

How is this knowledge of political forces to be acquired? In the same way that the forces of nature are ascertained; both of them are apprehended only in a state of motion which must be observed. The method of observation must be applied to political action, the manifestations of this action must be watched, and they will disclose to us the moods, the mental tendencies, the workings of the wills which set political society going. These observations will increase in value as they are brought to bear on acts which occur under more or less regular aspects, in a more or less methodical manner. In other words, the best way to study political forces is to study political methods. Of course, to be successful, this investigation cannot be confined to a purely formal investigation of those methods. In that case it would scarcely have an academic interest, and, from a practical point of view, would at the most be serviceable only to political wire-pullers in search of useful notions. To really understand the character of social action, its modes of procedure must be studied in the light of the character of those who apply them, and of the social and political conditions in which their wills are formed and manifested. It is only in this sense that the investigation of political methods will have, in addition to a philosophical value, a genuine practical value. It is a study of the methods of democratic government conceived in this spirit, a study of social and political psychology, based on observation, that I have tried to undertake, and it is that which is the aim of this book.

To accomplish this purpose it was necessary in the first place to find in political life a field where the modes of action are in a way concentrated and systematized, a field offering a clearly defined sphere for observation and a firm vantage-ground for the observer. These seemed to me to be presented by the life of organized political parties. I mean parties organized not only inside Parliament, which is henceforth merely the great stage on which the action prepared elsewhere is unfolded, but organized in the country itself on a more or less wide and comprehensive basis. Wherever this life of parties is developed, it focusses the political feelings and the active wills of the citizens; it is essentially the continuous application of the methods of action of political society. The material organization of parties appeared to me to offer the required post of observation, and its historical growth the landmarks for tracing the development of the political tendencies and forces themselves, which would enable me to ascend from the present to the past, from the effects to the causes, and to consider the working of democratic government as a whole, not in the inanimate fabric of political forms, but in the midst of living society.

The various countries living under the democratic régime were not all equally suited for this study of political forces within the sphere of organized parties, because the life of the parties and their organization do not everywhere exhibit the same fulness and the same regularity. In almost every country of the European continent the organization of parties working regularly outside Parliament is still but little developed; the *cadres* of the parties are formed on the eve of the elections, and break up soon afterwards, their contingents often present only floating masses. Two countries are in advance of all the others in this respect. They are England and the United States, which the greater development that liberty has attained there has already placed at the head of political humanity on other grounds. The study of political phenomena which I had in view could consequently be pursued with most advantage in those two countries, and in truth could not be pursued with the desired comprehensiveness save in those countries. It is they in fact which have provided me with the materials of my investigation. Yet the range of this investigation is not confined to the countries of the Anglo-Saxon world; *mutatis mutandis* it extends also to the other countries under a democratic form of government. To admit this, there is no need to accept in all its strictness the theory of Auguste Comte, according to which, at every moment of history, the people whose evolution is most advanced represents the whole of humanity. The variety of national characters and of historical antecedents ought not to be ignored, but the traits common to different countries predominate in existing civilization, where political institutions are nearly everywhere framed on the same model, where the social conditions produced by the economic evolution are the same, and where, consequently, men are subjected to similar influences and move on parallel lines.

Owing to the nature of the investigation which I undertook, the greater part of the materials had to be gathered from real life and not from libraries. If the organization of parties has blossomed abundantly in the Anglo-Saxon world, this was not the case with the documents on the subject, either as regards the present or the past of that organization. In this respect I found myself confronted with a void when, about fifteen years ago, I began my work. The facts relating to it were evidently not deemed worthy of the attention of historians and political thinkers. In the press they were relegated to unimportant paragraphs, unless they happened to be connected with political scandals or abuses. Comprehensive writings on the subject were non-existent. The information which might have been discovered in the files of old newspapers, in magazine articles, in pamphlets, or even in more or less important works or official documents, had never been treated scientifically. What had to be done was to bring all this category of facts for the first time within the purview of science. After having cast a glance at the organization of the English parties, I turned my attention to America, where the already lengthy career of the democratic régime and of the popular organization of parties promised more abundant sources of information and a more extensive view of the phenomena which I wanted to observe. I approached the subject on its historical side, and endeavoured to trace the development of the régime of parties and of their organization in the country, during the first century of the American Republic. The result of my labours was given to the public in the form of a series of articles inserted in the *Annales des Sciences Politiques* of 1888–1889. Just as the publication of these articles was coming to an end, Mr. Bryce's monumental work, *The American Commonwealth*, appeared, containing the first methodical description of the existing party system, which was a revelation, not only to readers in the Old World, but to the Americans themselves.

In England the organization of parties founded on a popular basis was of very recent creation, and its study presented far greater difficulties than that of the American parties. To obtain the data for it, I have had to engage in a long and minute enquiry, carried out in England itself, and based to a great extent on personal testimony and on direct observation of political life in general and of the working of party organization in particular. I have often had to collect by my own exertions the raw material that was to serve for generalizations, to search for it in one town after another, to make enquiries on both sides in order to elicit the truth, which was obscured by political strife or simply by local rivalry. The facts and the impressions as well as the few documents which I obtained led me to generalizations which I constantly verified by putting myself in touch with men and things. I broke up my generalizations into concrete and often very matter-of-fact questions which I put to my interlocutors, whom I treated not only as witnesses, but also as subjects of direct observation, whether they belonged to the staff of the party organization or to other classes of the community. Then I recast my generalizations by adding to them or pruning them in accordance with my new impressions. After operating in this way for years in various parts of the country, without neglecting the literary research required for the historical part of the subject, I seemed to have arrived at conclusions worthy of being presented to the public. I mention these details because I hold that I owe the public an account of my method, to enable it to fix my responsibility, which is certainly a heavy one. I can seldom shelter myself behind authorities, quote my authors, in the contemporary part of my work; all the information which has been given me, all the impressions which have been conveyed to me, have been accepted by me for what they were worth; I made what appeared to me the best use of them, in all liberty and, I venture to say, in all honesty. I alone am responsible for all the comments on the facts which I have put forward, and often for the authenticity of the facts themselves, for in my turn I appear as a witness before the public. I acknowledge the responsibility

which rests upon me, and I accept it in its entirety. What I
have just said of course applies also to the American part of
my enquiry, which I undertook after having exhausted my
subject in England. Having mastered the method which I
tested in my English researches, I began the study of America
over again and pursued it on that method in the United States.

In this way I have succeeded in putting together a whole,
which, under the form of a scientific investigation, alike historical and critical, of the régime of organized parties, is in
reality an investigation of the working of government in democracy and of the vital problems which it puts before existing
society, and which involve the whole future of our political
civilization. The miscellaneous facts which hitherto have
been disdainfully thrown into the rubbish-heap of history and
of the political news of the day have enabled me to rise step
by step to the highest generalizations of political speculation
and of the political art. If the well-nigh religious respect
with which we are accustomed from our youth to surround the
names of those who have made their mark as thinkers allowed
the current use of the forms of language which they employed
to describe their works, if it were permissible to apply their
formulas to a modest undertaking, I might have recalled the
expression, *Proles sine matre creata*. I do not say this by way
of boast: a student of political phenomena, having observed
them in real life, amid the perpetual flux of things as difficult
to grasp as the running stream, I have received many a lesson
of humility. I do not say it either by way of excuse, to ex-
tenuate the divergence which there is between my design and
the execution of it: I have honestly done what I could.

The object of my ambition being a scientific investigation,
that is to say a calm, unbiassed one, my chief concern was
absolute independence of mind in observation and perfect sincerity in the statement of its results. I have said all that
appeared to me to be true, without allowing myself to be influenced by any extraneous consideration, without being afraid
of the constructive charges which might be brought against
me, without fearing either to be *inconsistent*, in pointing out
the good and the bad in the same community, in the same sets,
in the same category of political conceptions or aspirations.
The only fear which I might have felt on this score was that

of becoming, or at least of appearing to be, the mouthpiece of a party, the spokesman of a sect. But I hope that I have escaped this danger, and it is with conviction that I borrow the words of a celebrated writer who was also a man of action : " I send this book into the world with the hope that it will displease all political sects." [1]

Before laying down my pen I must refer to the help which I have received from many persons, in England as well as the United States, in the performance of my task. It could never have been brought to a satisfactory conclusion without this assistance, which I have met with on all sides and which has been extended to me both liberally and straightforwardly, and in the most varied forms, such as personal interviews, communication of documents, written answers to lengthy interrogatories, notes written specially for me on certain questions, etc. As the names of all the persons who have been good enough to place themselves at my disposal would have made a very long list, I am obliged, to my great regret, to mention only a few of them here. Several of these persons I have been grieved to see pass away, and I can only pay a grateful tribute to their memory. First and foremost among them comes Thomas Nicols Roberts, Esq., formerly chief agent of the Liberal party in England. A veteran of the Liberal organization, who supervised the electoral registration department of the Anti-Corn Law League, he placed at my disposal his professional knowledge and his connections in the country with a kindness only equalled by his simplicity. I am glad to be able to tender my thanks to several other persons whose assistance was not less valuable to me. I am under great obligations, in England, to Arthur G. Symonds, Esq., M. A., of the National Reform Union. I also owe warm acknowledgments to R. W. E. Middleton, Esq., of the Central Conservative Office, to George Lane-Fox, Esq., of the Primrose League, and, last but not least, to several members of Parliament of the different parties, among whom I am anxious to mention Mr. James Bryce and Sir John Gorst, who initiated me into several points of English political life and gave me valuable introductions.

The persons from whom I have received help in the United

---

[1] " Ich schicke ihn mit der Hoffnung in die Welt, dass er allen politischen Secten missfallen werde." — F. C. DAHLMANN, *Die Politik*, Erster Band, 1835.

States and from whom I continued to receive it after leaving the great American Republic were not less numerous. I would like to mention a few names with the expression of my warmest gratitude: R. R. Bowker, Esq., Roger Foster, Esq., Hon. Frederick William Holls, George McAneny, Esq., Hon. John de Witt Warner, of New York City; Hon. Andrew D. White, of Ithaca, N.Y.; Hon. William F. Harrity, Herbert Welsh, Esq., Hon. Clinton Rogers Woodruff, of Philadelphia; Moorfield Storey, Esq., and Edmund M. Wheelwright, Esq., of Boston; Roger W. Cull, Esq., of Baltimore; Edwin Burritt Smith, Esq., of Chicago; Frederick W. Dewart, Esq., of St. Louis, Mo., now at Spokane, Wash.; Hon. James M. Allen, of San Francisco; Professor Henry Dickson Bruns, M.D., of New Orleans; Hon. P. W. Meldrim, of Savannah, Ga.; the Secretaries of State of thirty-five States of the Union and the United States Civil Service Commission, who have sent me important official documents.

While I was writing the last chapters of this book and it was passing through the press, events occurred in the political sphere and in the domain of legislation which naturally could not be commented on here or mentioned. But as these new facts do not alter the conclusions at which I have arrived, there is no need, either for the reader or for me, to trouble about them.

M. O.

PARIS, March, 1902.

FIRST PART

THE advent of democracy shattered the old framework of political society. The hierarchy of classes and their internal cohesion were destroyed, and the time-honoured social ties which bound the individual to the community were severed. As the old fabric had to be replaced by a new one, the problem was to find out how the individual could be reunited to society, in what new organization both could be incorporated, so as to assure form and permanency to their existence. The supremacy accorded to numbers in the State complicated matters by raising the question how the promiscuous crowd of old and young, of learned and unlearned, of rich and poor, who were all declared collectively arbiters of their political destinies, would be able to discharge their new function of "sovereign." The representative form of government adopted by modern democracies simplifies the problem in appearance only without touching its essence, for after all national representation proceeds from the great mass of the people.

Without, perhaps, having considered this problem in its general aspect, or having defined all its factors, some modern democracies have endeavoured to solve it amidst the march of events and in a somewhat empirical fashion. This solution consists in a methodical organization of the electoral masses, by extra-constitutional means and in the form of disciplined and permanent parties. The experiment has been carried to considerable lengths in the Anglo-Saxon countries of Europe and America, and the experience gained incontestably possesses great importance. Under what conditions has it been inaugurated ?   What has been its progress and development, and its influence on political life ?   Does it bring us nearer the possibility of embracing the political society which issued from the democratic revolution in a new synthesis ?   In a word, what are the results which it has given or which it holds out ?   The answer to these questions will be as interesting to the historian as to the political thinker and the thinking politician.

Both the historian and the politician, the former in order to bring this answer into distinct relief, and the latter in order to arrive at a better comprehension of it, must begin by forming a clear idea of all the factors of the problem in their successive development.   This can be done more easily in England than in any other country with a democratic government, France not excepted.   In the French democracy, which sprang from the Revolution, the new order of things has been more than once called in question and its progress violently interrupted.   These interruptions, with the disappointments and hopes to which they alternately gave rise, made the old order appear far more remote from us on the stage of history than it was in reality.   And as, in addition to this, it underwent a long agony before it succumbed, the break-up of the old society and the evolution of the new one do not always exhibit a direct and distinct connection of cause and effect to the investigator.   In this respect the England of our days presents incomparable advantages.   Hardly two generations back she was still an aristocratic and feudal society ; at the present moment she is completely drawn into the democratic current, with no inclination to retrace her steps or to wrangle about the results obtained.   Compressed into a more limited space of time and uninterrupted in its progress, the democratic evolution of England pursues its course before the spectator, working out its logical development under his eyes and presenting an orderly sequel of premise and conclusion.

This is especially the case with the problem which we propose to study.   We shall begin with England for this reason, and, in accordance with the plan sketched out, start by considering the unity of the old English society with its spontaneous connection and, so to speak, organic cohesion; we shall take note of its disintegration and then deal with the endeavours to restore unity to it in the sphere of politics; this will bring us eventually to the attempts to create a methodical organization of the electoral masses; we shall make a special study of that organization and pursue its evolution as far as possible; arrived at its extreme limit, we shall return to the starting-point in order to survey the horizon and ascertain from this vantage-ground the direction of the paths opened in the country traversed, with the view of discovering, if possible, the line of the main road leading to the goal.

FIRST CHAPTER

THE OLD UNITY

I

THE state of political society in England on the eve of its transformation may be summed up in a single sentence: it was the absolute domination of an aristocratic class. The English aristocracy did not exercise its power by virtue of caste privileges, it was not divided from the rest of the population by any legal barriers. Its authority rested almost entirely on its property and its social influence. As owner of the soil, it concentrated the public wealth in its own hands, personal property being still very far from possessing the importance which it has since attained. The invention of the steam-engine and the other mechanical discoveries of the second half of the eighteenth century only helped at the outset to consolidate the economical supremacy of the gentry, the money made in the early days of manufacturing industry being employed in buying up small estates, which were thus eventually lost in the great mass of large holdings. Thanks to its wealth, the landed aristocracy monopolized all the approaches to public power. Public functions were mostly honorary posts, carrying no salary. Besides this, a considerable income was necessary to qualify for them. A property qualification varying from a few pounds to several hundreds was required for the parliamentary vote, for a seat in Parliament, for the appointments of magistrate, coroner, and sheriff, for serving on a jury, for a commission in the army or even in the militia. Legislation, local administration, and armed forces were thus under the exclusive control of men of leisure and fortune.

As the towns were few in number, and as a rule without importance, being inhabited for the most part by traders and artisans, the leading type of these men of leisure and fortune was the great rural proprietor, the squire. The Court and the capital did not attract him as they did the corresponding class in France under the *ancien régime.* He lived on his estate for the greater part of the year, and consequently had not the same opportunities of impoverishing himself as the French nobility. Being exempt by law from seizure for debt and protected from possible caprices of its owner by the practice of entail, landed property was handed down intact from generation to generation. This stability, while it secured the owner uninterrupted enjoyment of the property, enhanced his prestige and was alone sufficient to make him the centre of attraction for the whole neighbourhood. He farmed out his estate to a more or less considerable number of tenants, generally without a lease. They might receive notice to quit at any moment, but as a matter of fact they stayed with him all their life and left their children in their place. A farm would hardly change hands once in the course of half a century. The ties which were formed between landlord and tenant under these circumstances made them a sort of family, with a feeling of paternal regard, kindly but at the same time autocratic, on the one side, and of devotion and respect on the other.

This influence of a private nature was very frequently reinforced by an extensive authority of a public kind, due to the squire's participation in local administration, in the government of the county entrusted to the local notables as an honorary function by the Crown. Police powers for keeping the King's peace, the right of issuing warrants of arrest and of trying persons guilty of misdemeanours or even of felonies, preparation of criminal cases coming within the jurisdiction of the Assizes, inspection of prisons and of work-houses, administration of the rates, power to deal with appeals in assessment cases and to try offences against the revenue, inspection of roads, supervision of the public health, relief of the poor, church patronage, — were all exercised or controlled by the squires in their capacity of magistrates, within the sphere of self-government. To deal with the business of general administration, the magistrates of the locality met once a fortnight in petty sessions or in special sessions. Once every three months they assembled in greater numbers to hold the Quarter Sessions in the chief county town, attended by all the functionaries of self-government, the sheriff or the under-sheriff, the coroners, the high-constables of hundreds, the district bailiffs, the governors of prisons and the masters of work-houses, and the members of the grand jury and the special jury.   It was the regular rendezvous of a ruling class. *Coram populo* it could feel a consciousness of its individuality, of its rôle in public life, and of its rank.

The sentiments which the position of this class inspired were transported by it into its every-day life, and from them it took its ideas of politics and society and its rules of conduct in matters small and great.   The fact of sharing these ideas and following these rules qualified for membership of the class and was the passport for admittance into it, or, what amounted to the same thing, constituted the gentleman.   Incapable of exact definition, the notion of gentleman was the social charter of the ruling class, an unwritten charter like the constitution of the Realm.   Gentle birth gave a good claim to the title but property and the *noble* use made of it were indispensable to make the gentleman.   He was supposed to possess an independent income derived from his estate and not from speculations or from a salary.   The landed proprietors were considered the only people really interested in the welfare of the country, they alone had a stake in it.[1]   People who had no estate or who only possessed personal property might at any moment shake the dust off their feet and leave their locality or their country with its permanent interests; they were only adventurers.   Thus the landowners, considering themselves as the only gentlemen, formed a society apart, or rather *the* society.   A man who was in business, even if he was a banker, did not belong to it.   In the country people were not on visiting terms with him, in town he could not obtain admittance into a club.   The case was the same with persons belonging to liberal professions, excepting those at the summit of the hierarchy.   Literary men and artists were not admitted into society as a matter of course.   But if a man of the middle

---

[1] "The landed interest alone has a right to be represented; as for the rabble who have nothing but personal property, what hold has the nation of them?" said the Lord Justice Clerk in his summing-up to the jury in the High Court of Justice at Edinburgh, at the famous trial of Muir in 1793 (*Collection of State Trials*, by Howell, XXIII, 231, L. 1817).

class rose in the social scale by his intelligence and his industry, or through his connections, and if he lived like a gentleman, there was nothing to prevent his being admitted into the circle of the ruling class, the reason being that there were no legal barriers between the various classes. And if he knocked at the door, it was opened but shut again immediately behind him, and in this way the members of the ruling class always kept to themselves.

There was no jostling, however, on the threshold. The English middle class of those days was not afflicted with the vanity of the French race, and experienced none of the humiliations to which the *tiers état* was a martyr. It was by no means on a level with the gentlemen as regards enlightenment, and still less was it their superior in point of fortune, as was the case with the *tiers* in France. Besides, it had none of the social brilliancy of the French bourgeoisie in the eighteenth century; its tastes were unrefined, its existence was dull, not to say vulgar. Hard-working and full of the vigorous instincts of home life, it enjoyed its modest pleasures in peace and quiet and kept its aspirations within due limits. To rise a step in the social scale, to better one's self, this was an ambition which might be indulged in, and not unfrequently it was realized by dint of industry and perseverance. But as for assuming the rank and position of the gentry, nobody wasted his time in bestowing a thought on such a thing. The noblemen and gentlemen, who seemed to occupy their exalted position by virtue of the natural order of things, were only regarded with feelings of reverence and admiration. Even up to a somewhat advanced period in this century, at the county ball, which took place in the winter in the county town and was attended by the local gentry and the leading middle class people, the gentlefolk danced among themselves in a separate part of the room, and the rest of the company in their own corner, but the latter were all the time flattered at the idea of being under the same roof with these superior beings and almost in physical contact with them, and their wives were only too glad to be able to gaze at the grand ladies with their splendid dresses and their aristocratic partners.

Sentiments of this kind as well as the absence of enlightenment were not calculated to make the middle class acquire a consciousness of its importance and consider itself as a social group antagonistic to the gentry in its interests and aspirations. It did not contain the element of agitation supplied in France by the lawyers. The lawyer class never rose to political importance in England. The work of legislation and central administration was performed by the members of the landed aristocracy in Parliament. The members of the same class also undertook the gratuitous discharge of all the important functions of local government and of the administration of justice. In so doing they cut the ground from under the feet of the lawyers in the sphere of public life. In the sphere of private life, that is to say in the practice of their profession, the lawyers were actually dependent on the gentry for their livelihood, for this was the propertied class with all the transactions and disputes to which property gave rise and which required the assistance of men learned in the law. Deeds of entail of real property, marriage settlements, leases for tenant-farmers and the disputes arising out of them — the attorneys and solicitors were ready to perform all this kind of work. In important cases a higher class of lawyers, the members of the Bar, assisted them. Thus the lawyers in England only served to swell the landlord's train and never dreamed of undermining his privileged position, or of fomenting animosity and rancour against him and his order and of constituting themselves the mouthpiece of these feelings, as was the case in France.

Nor was parochial self-government in a position to encourage tendencies of this description, for it had long ceased to be a reality. In boroughs which had obtained a charter of incorporation municipal government was the appanage of a small hereditary oligarchy. In places which had not received a charter and in rural districts, the self-government of the parish was in a languishing condition since the concentration of the land in the hands of the gentry and the disappearance of the small proprietors, who are the materials of which really free communities are constituted. The gentry took care not to arouse public spirit in the lower strata of the nation; they were not inclined to part with their power.

There remained the clergy, but they were the least capable of standing in the way of the ruling class. The Church of

England was simply a branch establishment of this class. The clergymen often came of the same stock, being younger sons or relatives or dependents of good families. Associating with the gentry as magistrates in local self-government, they were still more ready to join in the social life of the landlords, participating even in their pleasures and amusements. The clergyman was not unfrequently an ardent sportsman, a bold rider, a keen fisherman, a bit of an epicure, and a good hand at the bottle.

The power and the social homogeneousness of the ruling class were thus complete.

II

The structure of the political organization presided over by this class contributed another element of unity. The village was linked to the capital, and the local to the central administration, by an unbroken series of living ties and not by the fetters of a centralized bureaucracy. In the country the justice of the peace, who is the principal functionary of the system of self-government, combines the offices of administrator and judge. His jurisdiction extends to every part of public life in the locality. Independent of a central bureaucracy, this self-government possesses its own hierarchy, but each superior grade is only an amplification of the living elements which form the lowest one, and in spite of the ascending scale they all remain, at each stage, at the same distance from the men and the things with which they have to deal. The ladder leads directly to the supreme power in the State and throughout presents the same optical impression. Three-fourths of the Members of Parliament have taken part in the self-government of the county, or still do so. The peers of the realm, the leaders of the aristocracy who constitute the House of Lords immediately below the King, occupy the position of Lord-Lieutenant in the counties, command the militia and discharge other honorary functions belonging to local self-government. Finally, the government of the Church itself is drawn into this endless administrative network. The bishops, as heads of the clergy, meet the leaders of the aristocracy in the House of Lords and there vote with them on temporal as well as spiritual matters.

Thus, from whatever point of view it is regarded, the whole political fabric always presents itself in all its grandeur, and the ruling class seems to rise from it as from a pedestal composed of a single huge block.

The vast impression of unity conveyed by this spectacle gains in breadth and height when we have cast a glance at the internal arrangement of the political structure. The same leading idea emanates from each of its parts.

The monarchy, which is at the apex, is the first to exhibit this unity. With the triumph of the parliamentary régime the King is reduced to impotence. The centre of gravity in the government is transferred from the *King in Council* to the *King in Parliament*, but this centre is always the King. The ministers, who owe their appointment to the favour of the Houses of Parliament, are his Privy Councillors. In local administration, all the unpaid functionaries representing society hold their power from him and not from the people. Thus the monarchy always appears as the one point in which all the rays of the life of the State are focussed. And the more the royal power dwindles in reality, without losing a single prerogative as a matter of right, the more it assumes an impersonal character, the more strikingly does it symbolize the moral conception of the supreme power which in its unity pervades all the manifestations of public life without dominating them, from which all authority proceeds but only to converge on the one object which is the *raison d'être* of a political society.

The real power is in the hands of Parliament, with the always implied sanction of the Crown. As direct representative of the nation, it exercises every attribute of sovereignty on its behalf. Legislative and executive functions meet and are blended in it. The body which has received the name of the Cabinet is only a committee of the two Houses. The power of making laws, regulations and orders, is not entrusted to a separate authority in each case. Every high act of government proceeds from the Lords and Commons united to the Crown, from the *King in Parliament*, that is to say, from society and the State fused into a single whole.

Local administration with its self-government is only a fresh

manifestation of this whole. Besides the local business transacted nowadays by elective assemblies such as municipalities,
district councils, etc., the self-government of the county includes judicial and administrative powers, in other words,
attributes of political sovereignty. The great landowners who
combine all these varied functions do not derive them from
any hereditary right nor from any mandate conferred on
them by this or that group of the population under their
jurisdiction. They are chosen from the ranks of the society
whose habits, needs, and aspirations they more or less faithfully reflect. But they are appointed by the Crown which
represents the State. Holding their powers from this source,
they simply exercise as delegates the authority entrusted to
them by the chief of the State, the supreme depositary of its
sovereignty.

The mark of the one and indivisible State is thus stamped
on every organ of public life, however great its distance from
the centre; the State covers the whole ground occupied by
the political fabric, and to complete the unity it absorbs the
spiritual province by making religion a State religion. It
adopts its dogmas and professes them as not only the truth
but the whole truth; it makes adhesion to them the criterion
of a sound judgment and an upright heart, and rejects all who
do not admit them. Public posts, elective offices, whether in
Parliament or in local assemblies, can only be filled by members of the Established Church. The Universities are open
only to those who formally embrace the State religion. Even
secondary education is practically denied to the children of
Catholics and Dissenters, for all the grammar schools are in the
hands of the Anglican clergy. Thus identifying itself with
the Church, the State sets the crowning seal of moral unity
on political society.

III

What was the position of the individual in this State and
society? The experience we have just gained conveys the
idea that it was not an exalted one. As a matter of fact, the
whole public life of the England of old days, from one end
to the other, marks the subordination of the individual to
society. A member of the House of Commons, "elected to

serve in Parliament," cannot resign before the legal expiration
of his mandate; even ill health is not accepted as an excuse,
and he is obliged to have recourse to an expedient in order to
retire into private life — to apply for the post of steward and
bailiff of the Chiltern Hundreds.[1] In the county the sheriff,
who is the acting representative of public authority, cannot
decline to serve. In the administration of the parish offices
are conferred by election, but acceptance of them is obligatory
on the persons elected. The other parishioners are also often
reminded that they are only anonymous items of a whole. The
whole attitude of the revenue department towards the taxpayer
makes him feel this. It ignores the individual and never
addresses him. Taxation is not personal but real. The revenue authorities never consider the relations of properties with
persons; the rates are demanded not from the owner but from
the occupier, from whoever happens to be in possession. The
moral personality of the rate-payer is treated with just as little
consideration; payment of the rates for the Established Church
is demanded from the Dissenters on the same grounds as from
the members of the Anglican Church. The religious scruples
of this or that individual are of no consequence, he has property in the parish, and that is a sufficient reason for making
him pay the Church rates as well as the other rates assessed
on the parish.

It is not only in the discharge of obligations that the individual suffers in this way for the benefit of the community.
The social and political constitution bears traces of the same
spirit in regard to the exercise of rights. First of all in the
family. Among the gentry, as soon as a man attains his majority and comes into his property, he renounces his right in
favour of his eldest son by a deed of substitution. This child
is perhaps not yet born, but that is of no consequence; it is
not his personality which is in question, but the new generation

[1] Several centuries ago the Chiltern Hundreds, a district in Buckingham-
shire, were infested with brigands, and an officer was appointed to provide for
the security of the inhabitants of the locality. The brigandage was soon put
down, but the office remained, and as it was a post of "honour and profit
under the Crown," the member of Parliament who accepted it lost his seat
eo ipso. Since then members of the House who wish to retire obtain the
stewardship of the Chiltern Hundreds, and resign it the same evening, to
make way for another member.

of which he will become the representative. He, in his turn, will waive his rights in the same way, with the same object of keeping the property intact and thereby preserving in future ages the prestige of the family, of which he is only a fraction in the march of time.

When he exercises his rights of citizenship, it is also not on his own account. He belongs to a free country governed by a representative assembly, but it is not he who is primarily represented. The assembly is not the "Chamber of Deputies" but the "House of Commons," of the counties and boroughs, living members of the State. As they alone possess political individuality, they are represented without reference to population, just as human bodies, be their stature great or small, perform the same vital functions. And it is only as a part of the electoral entity that the individual obtains representation in Parliament. No doubt the act of election can only be accomplished by individuals who inhabit the county or borough, but when it is on the point of taking place they are detached from their own conscience by being made to record an open vote, under the watchful supervision of their neighbours, and, so to speak, as their representative and agent.

Even the sphere of private life does not escape the tendency to subordinate the individual. This is difficult to reconcile with accepted notions, for it is in this sphere above all that the Englishman is supposed to enjoy complete freedom. He possesses, as Blackstone says in the jargon of the eighteenth century, "natural liberties." "These were formerly the rights of all mankind; but in most other countries of the world, being more or less debased or destroyed, they at present may be said to remain, in a peculiar and emphatic manner, the rights of the people of England. And they may be reduced to three principal or primary articles: the right of personal security, the right of personal liberty, and the right of private property." Chatham emphasizes the same point in magnificent language: "The storm and rain may beat into the cottage of the poor man, but the King cannot enter it." Beyond a doubt, these "natural liberties" of the individual existed and were respected so long as they did not directly or indirectly interfere with the community. As soon as this conflict of interests appears, human individuality is crushed, and occasionally with refine-

ments of cruelty. Under the Settlement Act[1] the inhabitant
of a parish cannot leave it for the term of his whole life ; he
remains in it like a bondsman attached to the soil, because if he
were free to go where he liked he might move into another locality, where, if he found no means of livelihood, he would have
to be maintained by the parish. Poor people coming into another parish conceal themselves like criminals hunted by the
police. When discovered, they are sent back at once into their
parish, even if they are suffering from a dangerous illness
which unfits them for the journey. A poor man who will not
work is made to do so by force, for here again the parish would
be obliged to keep him from starvation. He is confined in a
work-house for the whole of his life, on the mere order of an
overseer of the poor. His children are taken from him and
apprenticed in another parish, perhaps at the other end of the
country, where they will remain separated from him as if by
the grave. The persons with whom these apprentices are
placed are obliged to take them and keep them. If a workman left the country, there would be no fear of his coming on
any parish, but he would inflict injury on the larger community
to which he belongs, on his country, by taking his professional
skill abroad with him ; consequently the law forbids artisans
to leave the Kingdom. Workmen are not allowed the right of
combination. Freedom of contract is not complete ; wages are
fixed by the authorities.

Being treated with such scant consideration by the community in the lawful course of his existence, the individual
forfeits all claim to the respect due to him as a human being
directly he comes into conflict with the law. Under the bank-
ruptcy law the insolvent debtor is thrown into prison on the
simple application of the creditor. The same treatment is
meted out to a man who is accused by a woman with child of
being the cause of her pregnancy.[2] The persons called vaga-
bonds and beggars by the law — and their number is a large
one[3] — are publicly whipped until, as the old statutes say,

---

[1] Act of 1662, 14 Chas. II, c. 12; its severity is to a certain extent mitigated
by the Act of 1795, 35 Geo. III, c. 101, and of 1809, 49 Geo. III, c. 124.

[2] Bastardy Acts of 1733 (6 Geo. II, c. 31) and of 1809 (49 Geo. III,
c. 68).

[3] The Vagrant Act of 1744 (17 Geo. II, c. 5).

"their body becomes bloody." [1] If after this they do not go
back to their parish they are whipped in every place consecu-
tively until they are brought home.[2] A theft of five shillings
is punished with death, and protracted efforts of philanthropists were required to raise the price of human life to forty
shillings and afterwards to five pounds. The law becomes less
rigorous when the vindication of human personality is concerned; the severest penalties of the code apply to offences
against property and not to those against the person.

So much for the legal sphere. In the domain of social life
the importance of the individual is relatively still further
diminished. Here a man can never "be himself." Society
forces on him a crowd of obligations from which he cannot
escape without prejudicing his claim to the title of gentleman.
Invisible and pervading every corner of life, the notion of
gentleman brings every member of society under the yoke of
a general and uniform law, and subjects him to a pitiless discipline, leaving no field for his personal preferences, from his
religious opinions down to his dress. It is ungentlemanlike
to be a Dissenter, just as it is ungentlemanlike to wear a white
hat, as those Radical fellows are so fond of doing.

The cult of the individual, the apotheosis of man in the
abstract, were consequently very far from ever having existed
in England.

IV

But if in the political society of England the individual was
only an atom in the general mass, he was not always an atom
isolated in space. Apart from the representative institutions,
in every-day life many an Englishman was led by local self-
government to work for a common object possessing a general
interest. By this continual co-operation in the sphere of the
immediate needs of the population men learned to know each
other, to come to an understanding and to pursue in concert
an aim which rose above their own personal concerns. The

---

[1] "Till his body be bloody by reason of such whipping" (22 Hen. VIII,
c. 12, an. 1530–31).

[2] "Be openly whipped until his or her body be bloody" . . . "in every
place to be whipped till such person be repaired to the place limited" (39 Eliz.
c. 4, an. 1597–98).

independent fortune and the social rank of the magistrates who took part in the self-government of the county made their public labours more an affair of honour and social duty. In discharging their functions they very often displayed class prejudice and a domineering spirit; still they gave their time and their money to the service of the public. In doing so they set a daily example which showed that private persons had duties towards the community, and that it was not right for the individual to hold aloof from public life. Service on the grand jury and on special juries very often brought together people of lower social position and made them feel a common bond of union. Moreover the system of taxation of real property in the counties kept the members of the parish in close contact, the total required being fixed in a lump sum for each parish and then apportioned amongst each other by the parishioners themselves.

In this way a social current was formed which, starting from the heights of political society, penetrated low enough to reach the level ground occupied by the mass of the population and parching, so to speak, under a restricted parliamentary franchise, an oligarchical municipal administration, and an anemic system of parochial self-government. The power and the range of this social force have no doubt been exaggerated by the retrospective enthusiasm of writers who have sung the praises of the England of old days, such as Gneist and others, who readily ascribed to it the merit of having completed the organic unity of English society and of having once and for all secured the co-ordination of its component parts. It was impossible to complete the organic unity in question, because it never existed. We have just seen, merely from the lot of the individual in this society, that he was too much repressed to be really an organic part of it, and that the moral entity of the community was too often identified with a single class, to which the rest of the nation was only adjusted, in many cases even simply by a turn of the screw. But narrow as was the social current in the England of old times, it was not dammed up by barriers of privilege like those which divided the nation into small isolated groups in France, and it could flow unchecked through the whole English community, while gradually shrinking in volume. In this way it concealed the lines of cleavage in political society, and readily conveyed the impression of a complete organic unity. This social current was sometimes a perception of the common welfare and a reasoned determination to advance it, not without an admixture of selfishness; at others a vague and spontaneous idea of the duties prescribed by the general interest; very frequently the necessity or social propriety of not separating from the leading men; still more often a sort of traditional, almost automatic, adhesion to the chiefs whom the public was always accustomed to see in the front rank; but whatever its aspect, the current, within its narrow bed, continually carried the members of the community along with it, and made them unite in the psychological order just indicated. This process, unceasing in its nature like the formation of solid strata under the waves of the sea, ensured the cohesion of the body politic and brought its dominant organs into relief. Their position as leaders of society made them leaders of men in the State. Their political authority was simply another expression for their social power, which rested on the attachment of man to man. Since the primitive period of the Middle Ages, which produced the lord and his vassal, the relations of life had become far more complicated, but they had not become differentiated in the same proportion, partly in consequence of the large infusion of social feeling which pervaded the English community. Powers had increased in number, but the necessity of a corresponding division of functions made itself but slowly felt. And even close upon the period of reforms not only was society an avenue to politics, but people combined political power and social functions even of the purely fashionable kind. Thus the great Lord Chesterfield was leader of fashion and political leader at the same time.[1] Political and social life met and blended once more in the leadership; society was completely reflected in its leaders.

V

Under these circumstances the political system worked with extreme simplicity. For parliamentary elections the most

---

[1] Wellington, when discussing, in 1837, the chances of the Tory party, drew attention to the disadvantage at which it was placed owing to its leaders: " Peel has no manners and I have no small talk."

influential squires in the county met in an informal manner
and selected a candidate. All the members of their class
accepted him from motives of confidence or propriety. The
other electors, who were few in number owing to the high
qualification, and accustomed all their life to gravitate in the
orbit of the great landlords, could only follow their habitual
tendency. The urban constituencies also were subject to the
influence of the landed aristocracy. Many boroughs were
under the direct patronage of the great proprietors in their
capacity of owners of the soil on which the urban agglomerations had arisen. They obtained control of other boroughs by
making their tenants become members at their expense of the
municipal corporations which possessed a monopoly of the
franchise. In case of need the electors in the towns could be
secured by bribery ; the votes of freemen were openly bought,
not to mention the pocket or rotten boroughs, by which a seat
in the House could be purchased right out. In one way or
another the members nearly all belonged to the aristocratic
class, being sons of lords or their near relatives, or other persons on whom the magnates who procured them admittance
into Parliament could depend. According to a table prepared
about 1815, the House of Commons contained 471 members
who owed their seats to the good-will and pleasure of 144
peers and 123 commoners, 16 Government nominees, and only
171 members elected by popular suffrages.[1]

Having gained a seat in Parliament through the same influences, and belonging nearly all to the same social sphere, they
brought with them the same habits of mind and feelings, and
were perfectly ready to obey the instinct which impels men to
form a group and accept the control of a chief. Social *esprit
de corps* compelled each member to follow his set, his party.
To desert it, even for a moment, was an act of treachery,
or, what was perhaps still worse, ungentlemanly. And why
should he take a line of his own ? The voice of his conscience might prompt such a course, but did not the other
and louder voice of his surroundings and his party bid him
follow his leaders ? Was a fraction to set itself above the

---

[1] T. H. B. Oldfield, *The Representative History of Great Britain and
Ireland*, Lond. 1816, Vol. VI, Appendix: Correct tables of parliamentary
patronage.

whole? "You go with your family, sir, like a gentleman; you are not to consider your opinions like a philosopher or a political adventurer," says Lord Monmouth to his grandson in one of Disraeli's novels.[1] Independent members were consequently very rare. Social discipline enforced discipline in Parliament. The House was "the best gentlemen's club," and if any one of its members took it into his head to disturb the general harmony, he was disposed of in the same way as a bore in a drawing-room. To accuse a member of this was equivalent to telling him that he was not a gentleman. Pitt, when Prime Minister, in 1798, was obliged to fight a duel with Tierney because he had reproached him with obstructive conduct. The feeling of members towards their leaders was not only the professional devotion of a soldier to his chief, but even more the respect and absolute confidence inspired by men of honour. Confidence in their wisdom and in their experience of affairs occupied the second place. These sentiments constituted the atmosphere of the House for years after 1832. On one occasion during the discussion of the Reform Bill Croker moved an amendment which he supported in an able and conclusive speech. Lord Althorp rose and simply said that he had made calculations and arrived at results which told against the amendment, that unfortunately he had mislaid the papers, but that if the House would leave it to him they would reject the amendment. And the House voted against the amendment, for the reasons which Lord Althorp had forgotten but which had seemed to him conclusive at the time.[2] A Minister, as Robert Lowe stated in 1867, defeated a motion to appoint a parliamentary committee by simply saying: "I cannot grant such a committee."[3] "When I first entered Parliament," once remarked Sidney Herbert, who was a member of Peel's and Palmerston's Cabinets, "the House of Commons was divided into two camps. A leader guarded both; a leader whom no man questioned, and whom every man on his side followed. His party acquiesced in everything he thought best; and five minutes after his decision was announced to them, they were heart and soul engaged

[1] *Coningsby, or The New Generation*, Bk. VIII, ch. 3.
[2] *Memoir of J. C. Viscount Althorp*, by Sir Denis Le Marchant, Lond. 1876, p. 400.
[3] *Speeches and Letters on Reform*, Lond. 1867, p. 91.

in it, clamorous that it was the only one that could be arrived at." [1]

The division into political parties in no way impaired the homogeneousness of the whole body, it only facilitated the formation of the two groups and preserved cohesion in the ranks. Subdivisions as they were of the same society, separated by rivalries and grudges and to a slight extent by principles, Whigs and Tories in Parliament were animated by the same spirit and the same passions. It was a struggle of Capulets and Montagues. Social discipline made each party into a living chain which nothing could break: afflux of ideas, pressure of public opinion, revolts on the part of individuals, were not strong enough for the purpose. A very considerable number of members of the House were anything but "philosophers." Younger sons of peers, and as a rule young men, principally attracted by the pleasures and amusements of society and the clubs, country gentlemen who accepted a seat because it had become the fashion to spend a few months each year in London, they took but a slender interest in the debates, and seldom came to the House, except on the great field-days when every member of the party was whipped up to make a majority, and even then they only arrived at the last moment, just in time to learn how they should vote. Members of a more serious turn of mind were not likely to be much troubled with ideas. The questions in dispute were few in number and not of recent date; in those days people were slow in raising problems and a long time in solving them.[2] A man could make up a programme to last all his life at the outset of his political career. It was seldom that he was taken unawares by an unforeseen question which would oblige him to adopt a fresh attitude on the spur of the moment.

The pressure of public opinion, apart from exceptional cases, was still less felt by the politician. There hardly existed any opinion outside parliamentary circles and the drawing-rooms

---

[1] The *Times* of Oct. 29, 1858. Speech at the Warminster Athenæum.

[2] Lord John Russell once remarked in the House of Commons that Lord Chatham, the most powerful Minister of the eighteenth century, had not passed a single legislative measure. During the twenty years which followed the Reform Bill many more important laws were enacted than during the hundred and twenty preceding years (quoted by Bagehot, *Essays on Reform*, Lond. 1883, p. 169).

connected with them. Outdoor opinion had no means of ex-
pressing itself; the platform and public meetings scarcely
existed; the means of communication were difficult; the
Press, which was crushed by heavy duties, had a very limited
circulation. The price of a copy of a newspaper rose as high
as seven pence (in 1815 after the new stamp duties). At the
beginning of the century (1801), the yearly sale of newspapers
was less than a copy and a half per head of the population, and with a few variations it remained at this figure up
to 1835.[1] The general public paid little heed to politics. It
was the pet hobby of a select group, the sport of an aristocracy.
And it was only in this latter capacity that it interested the
English masses. who were full of a deferential admiration for
all the doings of their nobility. There were a few eccentric
individuals who followed and discussed the policy of the Government, but they were looked on as armchair strategists, who
spend their time in criticising the commanders-in-chief. The
knowledge of what went on in Parliament was slight and
inaccurate; the reports of the proceedings were of the most
summary description; the division-lists were never published,
except on great occasions, when private copies of them were
circulated. It was consequently difficult for the constituents
to follow the conduct of their members, even if they wished to
do so. The latter, for their part, were by no means anxious to
be under control, and opposed the publication of their votes in
the House, being of opinion that secrecy was essential to their
independence.

The further removed they were from the control of public
opinion, the more close became the ties which bound them to
their party and its leaders. Independent tendencies in a private member died out of themselves. The only alternative
was to go over to the other side. In what quarter could he
have found even moral support when the door of public opinion was closed? Consequently there was no field for the
formation of a third party holding the balance between the

[1] In the United States the circulation of the Press rose during the same
period from 2½ copies per head to 5 or 5½. It is true that in addition to the
stamped newspapers, the statistics of which are the basis of these calculations, many contraband journals were circulated in England at certain
periods.

two great parties, and they always remained compact and in perfect discipline.   A Cabinet supported by the majority was sure of the immediate future, the policy of the Government was marked by continuity, and the State enjoyed the advantage of stability.

SECOND CHAPTER

BREAK-UP OF THE OLD SOCIETY

I

SOLID and coherent as the political and social fabric of England was, it was too narrow to contain the national life. Everything in it was cramped : the private individual, beginning his career with a fairly sound but very incomplete education; society, drawn from a limited circle, its every-day life ruled by conventions and prejudices, its mental culture derived from a literature modelled on the formal lines of classic art, its spiritual sustenance supplied by a religion free from mysticism but also devoid of enthusiasm, and reduced by the homilies of the pulpit to arguments in which the existence of God was demonstrated by his utility ; the Church a branch of the State ; the State reposing solely on a single class supposed to be the only one with a stake in the country. The great mass of the nation received hardly a ray of light or warmth from this society of gentlemen, from this aristocratic Church, from this State religion embodied in paragraphs, from this exclusive political system. True, the individual was not molested as in continental countries ; the restrictions on freedom of labour were falling into disuse ; the fundamental rights of the citizen were under the protection of the tribunals ; the administration, invested with a judicial character in the person of the magistrates and controlled by settled laws, was not exposed to the arbitrary proceedings of a bureaucracy and was free from the shifting influences of parliamentary parties ; the material condition of the people was not unbearably wretched before the industrial revolution ; the feelings of the ruling class towards the lower classes were characterized by anything but ill-will. But this ruling class did nothing to lift the masses out of the slough of ignorance in which they were sunk, to enlarge their mental horizon, to make them feel that they, too, had a stake in the country; it took no step to enroll the masses in the political and social system of England, to admit them to a sphere of civic action in which the individual might find scope for his energies and rise to higher things. The Church treated them with equal indifference both in the matter of general instruction and religious edification. The representatives of the Established Church, who were ecclesiastical officials rather than servants of God, seldom penetrated to the hearts of the people, and the people went their own way, combining with their torpid existence a state of complete irreligion. "They live precisely like brutes to gratify the appetites of their uncultivated bodies, and then die, to go, they have never thought, cared, or wondered whither."

Thus the larger nation, still more than the small nation composed of the ruling class, presented the aspect of a confused and colourless mass, in which the individual was hardly perceptible and the soul had no consciousness of its existence. But the human being created in the image of God was still there, with all its needs and instincts, not dead but only sleeping, and when, towards the middle of the eighteenth century, John Wesley's appeal to the human soul rang through the Anglo-Saxon world, a thrill passed over the masses. " Overwhelmed with misery, laden with sin, doomed to perdition, you can obtain your deliverance at once by descending into your soul, to perceive the living God by faith. As soon as you feel this faith you are purified." " But what is faith? It is not an assent to any opinion or number of opinions. A man may assent to three or three-and-twenty creeds, he may assent to all the Old and New Testament, and yet have no Christian faith at all. . . . It is the internal evidence of Christianity, a perpetual revelation directly from God into the believing soul." If all do not possess it, that is because it is a free gift of God. But there is no need of merit or virtue to obtain it from Him. " His pardoning mercy supposes nothing in us but a sense of mere sin and misery." . . . " This justifying faith implies not only the personal revelation, the inward evidence of Christianity, but likewise a sure and firm confidence in the individual believer that Christ died for *his* sins, loved *him* and gave His life for *him*." [1] But who or what

[1] R. Southey, *Life of Wesley and the Rise and Progress of Methodism*, 2d ed. Lond. 1820, II, 175 seq.

will show that the individual has attained to faith, that he has
risen above the herd of sinners, that he has become " perfect " ? He will feel it himself, he is himself judge of his
own soul. The Protestant dogma of justification by faith,
which had become obsolete in England, is thus revived, and,
pushed to its extreme conclusions, is launched .into general
circulation. Freed from all trammels, given up to his impulses, the Wesleyan becomes intoxicated with spiritual pride
and not unfrequently loses his moral equilibrium. A shock
is felt in society and in family life; the new doctrine leads to
antinomianism, to the belief that the moral law as such is not
binding on the Christian.[1] Soon, however, the individual becomes once more a prisoner. Puritanism, revived by Wesley,
disparages all the pleasures of life which give expansion to
human personality. Continually directing the thoughts towards
the examination of the soul, Wesleyanism isolates man from
the external world, and closes the avenues to social and political life. At the same time Wesley, who has appealed to the
individual conscience to draw men from their evil mode of
life, to make things doubly sure bids his followers walk together in the new faith, for mutual aid and supervision and
in order not to swerve from the path. Weekly meetings,
" classes," are instituted, to which each member comes to confess his thoughts and actions. He lays bare the state of his
soul, and there is not a corner left in which he can be alone
with himself. He is surrounded day and night by a system
of mutual espionage, and can only elude the vigilance of his
co-religionists by assuming a conventional mask and becoming
the slave of an abject hypocrisy.

But the appeal to the individual conscience, which Wesley
was the first to put forth, had time to spread and find an echo.
People belonging to the middle and upper classes were also
touched with emotion, and, without separating from the Established Church, took upon themselves to bring back to it in
triumph the creed of the Gospel, the religion of the heart. To
the frigid and well-bred morality of the Church, the Evangel-

---

[1] See the dialogue, quoted by Lecky (*History of the Eighteenth Century*, II,
p. 596), between Wesley and the antinomianist preacher of Birmingham, who
assures him that man, being no longer under the laws, is the heir to all things,
and can take whatever goods and lie with whatever woman he pleases.

icals, as they were called, opposed personal piety, the individual responsibility of each soul to its Creator. Passing from feeling to practice, they inaugurated a great philanthropical movement in the England of the second half of the eighteenth century. Founding a number of pious institutions, establishing missionary and Bible societies, for the greater glory of Christ, the Evangelicals were also full of compassion for the misery in the social system. The ignorance in which the masses were plunged, the barbarous provisions of the penal code, the pitiable state of the prisons, in which men rotted away alive, and above all, man enslaved by his fellows touched their hearts. They set on foot a vast public agitation. For this purpose they systematized and almost invented the methods of propaganda employed to influence opinion in modern times — pamphlets, public meetings, platform speeches, monster petitions to Parliament. At all times and in all places they appealed from the miserable reality to the human conscience. In the criminal they pointed out the man, and in the negro the brother. A new character — the fellow-creature, the "man" — was ushered from the platform into the social and political world of aristocratic England, and was destined to remain there. "Man born free and in chains," as J. J. Rousseau puts it, begins to take hold of the English imagination in the person of the negro. Societies for the suppression of the slave-trade and for preaching the Gospel to the negroes spring up on all sides. More than one humble family — old and young together — experience a delightful emotion in contributing the contents of their money-box. Three hundred thousand persons pledge themselves to abstain from the use of sugar, to avoid tasting a product due to slave labour. The Evangelicals make their way into Parliament, and their voice rises louder and louder in the halls of Westminster to vindicate the claims of outraged humanity. Although few in number, they possess great influence in the House. Belonging nominally to the Tory party, they separate from it whenever their conscience does not permit them to vote with it, for they fear the living God. This novel spectacle of the individual conscience taking its own course in politics commands respect; they are not styled "philosophers" or "adventurers," but "the party of saints."

II

Simultaneously with the spread of the philanthropic movement another stream from a different quarter flows into it and
swells its volume. Religious emotion is reinforced by the
emotion of thought. Good society has grown weary of con-
ventionalism and longs to experience genuine sensations.
And as it has sufficient time and money to indulge in the luxury of fine sentiments, its principal object is to enjoy emotion.
The man of feeling makes his appearance and is welcomed
on all sides. " The literature of the day may be called the
library of the man of feeling." [1] The heroes of the fashionable novels of Richardson, Sterne, and Mackenzie have a soul,
they shed tears at everything and nothing, " they give way to
emotion five or six times a day, and fall into consumption
through excess of sensibility." [2] Then comes J. J. Rousseau
with his fervid and emotional pæans to nature. Society is
touched and begins to sigh for " the return to nature." It
goes into ecstasies over beautiful scenery, which can now be
easily admired, the recent introduction of post-chaises having
facilitated travelling. People take pleasure in the thought
that they have sentiment and a heart, and let their imagination range beyond their native country in order to find subjects
of emotion. Public sensibility goes out to savages, to the
heathen, to the ill-treated Caribees in the island of St. Law-
rence ; the public conscience arraigns Warren Hastings for his
oppression of the rajahs of India. Subscriptions are collected
in aid of the Corsicans, who are defending their independence
against the French, assistance is sent to the Poles, who are
trying to protect the last shreds of their political existence
from rapacious neighbours. For they too are fellow-creatures,
just like the negro, the protégé of the middle classes, the concrete object by means of which the latter have obtained a
clearer grasp of the conception of " man," a conception of too
abstract a nature, in its metaphysical nudity, for the English
mind.

For the same reason, perhaps, the political and social conclusions which ideologists in France developed from this

---

[1] Taine, *Histoire de la lit. angl.* IV, 227.   [2] *Ibid.*

conception do not strike the English at the first blush; but people arrive at them in England just as in France, only by another route, or rather by a lateral path which soon leads into the main road followed by ideology.

III

By making man look into his own soul the religious revival and sentimentalism bring him face to face with the problem of his duty. He has not far to seek. Christian piety and the dictates of the heart at once prescribe the path to be followed — that of "morality." But does this "morality" exhaust all the duties of man? No, replies the most popular moralist of the century, Paley: "The part a member of the commonwealth shall take in political contentions, the vote he shall give, the counsels he shall approve, the support he shall afford, or the opposition he shall make, to any system of public measures, — is as much a question of personal duty, as much concerns the conscience of the individual who deliberates, as the determination of any doubt which relates to the conduct of private life."[1] The subject of politics is consequently identical with that of morality; in both cases it is man interrogating his conscience. Nor is their object different; it merely expands in proportion to the new limits prescribed. On the one side, in the restricted sphere of morality, the peace of the individual soul is concerned; on the other, within the province of a morality conceived on a larger scale, the happiness of man living in society is at stake. "All people," says Priestley, "live in society for their mutual advantage, so that the good and happiness of the members, that is, the majority of the members of any state, is the great standard by which everything relating to that state must finally be determined."[2] And who is the judge of the good of the members? But this is equivalent to asking who knows his own interest best. The answer is obvious, — the members themselves, each member. It was the inevitable conclusion. Aided by the force of events, it was destined to alter the political and social aspect of England. Half a century elapsed

[1] W. Paley, *Moral and Political Philosophy*, Preface.
[2] *Essay on the First Principles of Government*, 1768, p. 17.

before the transition from theory to practice took place. During this interval English thinkers were incessantly engaged in defining and developing the terms of Priestley's proposition and in drawing conclusions from it both in the domain of speculation and practice.

Several other factors contributed to the same result. First of all, the new science of political economy acting as the spokesman of new interests. Towards the middle of the eighteenth century England was stirred by an extraordinary development of commerce and industry. It had been preceded, at a much earlier date, by a number of isolated and independent efforts, which marked out the line of the future individualist régime in the economical life of the nation, and which succeeded by their own strength, so long as they were not trammelled by State regulation. The mercantile genius of the nation, which had shed such a lustre on the two hemispheres in the reign of Elizabeth, now awoke with fresh vigour. The reserve of moral force accumulated for centuries in the Anglo-Saxon race supplied it with tenacity of will, indefatigable energy, and bold initiative. Give us elbow-room and the world will be ours! This idea, which was fermenting in the caldron of national energies, took definite shape under the pen of Adam Smith. Without actually stating the French formula of "laissez faire laissez passer," Adam Smith propagated it in all his writings. Taking his stand on facts, he pleaded for freedom of trade and commerce, pointed out all the mischief caused by State interference with economic activity, and exposed all the narrowness of Colbert's system of tutelage, "so opposed to the generous policy enjoined by equality, justice, and liberty of letting every man manage his own business as he thinks proper." He attacked the customs of entail and primogeniture and everything which weakened or fettered the individual in his natural aspirations towards well-being. Society, he argued, could only gain by the economic liberty of the individual, for their interests are identical, and free trade could not fail to become a source of wealth for each and all.

These ideas, which were so nearly akin to the general conception of natural liberty, a kinship which Adam Smith was far from disavowing, produced a still greater effect by their eminently practical English character; they were couched in the language of interests and appealed to interests. They penetrated into the public mind, and in time grew into a current of opinion which carried "the individual" forward with constantly increasing force.

In grander and loftier accents the genius of France pleaded the same cause of the oppressed individual before the bar of assembled humanity, appealing to natural right, to reason, and to justice.

The founding of the American Republic and the French Revolution converted the idea into a reality. The *Declaration of the Rights of Man* proclaimed it to the world. The good tidings were received with enthusiasm in more than one quarter in England. Thomas Paine expounded them in "The Rights of Man," which obtained an enormous circulation and remained for many years the text-book of the élite of the working classes. The rights of men all equal by nature, the State owing its existence to their free consent, the superiority of a democratic republic, the moral deformity of kings and priests, who are the source of all the misfortunes of mankind — all these doctrines were stated in vehement language which appealed rather to the passions than to the intelligence.

In William Godwin deductive rationalism found a much more powerful advocate. His book on "Political Justice" develops it with a pitiless logic which does not shrink from the most extreme conclusions, and reaches a point which Rousseau himself did not arrive at. Man, as conceived by Godwin, a being of pure reason, is compelled by his very nature to follow the eternal decrees of justice; all constraint is therefore useless; laws and government are only an encroachment on the liberty of the individual, and on these grounds Godwin declines to recognize the validity of the *contrat social*. In spite of its exaggerations Godwin's book took hold of the public mind by its intense feeling of individualism, by its hatred of every obstacle to the expansion of human personality, by its faith in man and in reason. The excesses of the French Revolution supplied a refutation of this optimism and stirred up a violent reaction against "French ideas" in English society, developed to the point of paroxysm by the long implacable war waged by Pitt against France. But "French ideas," *i.e.* ideas of liberty, found a resting-place in the very heart of England; they penetrated thither under cover of the utilitarian philosophy, so well-suited to the positive English mind as regards its principle but so highly revolutionary in its application. It is in vain that its representatives from Paley onward endeavour to refute the *contrat social* and deny the existence of natural rights; it is of no use their filling their writings with a profusion of judicious and sensible maxims, a collection of which would make an admirable hand-book if good sense in politics were a branch of instruction; their utilitarianism is destined to make a formidable breach in the old political fortress. Priestley and Paley began this work of destruction; Bentham gave the finishing touches to it.

IV

Combining a rare power of analysis with consummate skill in classification and a passion for detail, Bentham subjected several departments of English legislation to a minute examination. He took each institution to pieces as a clockmaker does the works of a clock. Applying the criterion of utility in every case, he contrasted the end with the means, and, guided solely by logic, pronounced his sentence of condemnation; for the province which he was exploring presented a vast chaos of enactments heaped together at random and placed one on the top of the other without method or guiding principle. Bentham "laid bare this mass of rubbish and called on mankind to throw off the tyranny of authority and to reject the wisdom of our ancestors in the sphere of law."[1] Then, by means of the same principle of utility which he had used for his analysis, Bentham constructed a synthesis of morals and of politics culminating in the individual conscience sovereign judge of all things and in each citizen "his own legislator."

The moral conscience of man to which philanthropy appealed, as well as the justice springing from natural right to which the French philosophers had recourse, seemed to Bentham inadequate and dangerous supports for propping up the social system. For what is natural right or the law of nature? A fiction, a metaphor which each man can interpret as he likes. And

[1] Preface to the *Fragment on Government*, 2d ed.

moral conscience ?   Simply an arbitrary distinction between
good and ill, resting in reality on unreasoning feelings of
sympathy or antipathy.   Bentham rejects *a priori* rationalism
and claims to have discovered in experience that nature has
placed man under the sway of pleasure and pain, that we owe
all our ideas to them, that we refer to them all our judgments
and all the decisive steps of our life.   This tendency to seek
for pleasure and avoid pain, both of a physical and moral description, being, as it is, eternal and irresistible, constitutes our
rule of conduct : each man must follow his interest and take
utility for the criterion of his actions, arriving at the value of
their results by a simple arithmetical calculation which strikes
the balance of pains and pleasures.   " No subtlety, no metaphysics ; no need to consult Plato or Aristotle.   Pain and
pleasure are felt as such by every man, by the peasant as well
as the monarch, by the unlearned man as well as the philosopher." [1]   As each man possesses the common measure of utility,
so " each is judge of his own utility ; this is and must be so,
otherwise man would not be a rational agent."   The only thing
to do is to let him alone.   To apprehend a *bellum omnium contra
omnes* is to mistake the real motives of human actions ; given
the mutual dependence of men in a social state, not only for
the satisfaction of their material wants, but also for the equally
natural enjoyment of the esteem and affection of their fellow-
creatures, egoism is necessarily converted into altruism.   " Society is so constituted that in working for our own happiness
we work for the general welfare." [2]   What is the use of interference by the State ?   And Bentham is never weary of saying
to the legislator : "leave us alone, be quiet, get out of my light."
The dictates of prudence will suffice of themselves in the case
of actions which only concern the individual.   The law should
only intervene to prevent men from injuring each other.   Its
aid is necessary in cases of this sort because the majority of
mankind are not sufficiently enlightened to grasp the connection between personal and general interest.   Every law is an

[1] *Principes de législation*, Ch. I. (N.B. Most of the passages quoted here
are taken from the French edition of Bentham's works by Dumont; being to
a great extent compiled from Bentham's manuscripts and having been published before the English edition, the French version is thus sometimes the
real original edition).   [2] *Ibid*. Ch. X.

evil in itself, because it is an infraction of the liberty of the individual, and it can only be justified when it serves to prevent or restrain a larger infraction of liberty than it constitutes in itself, that is to say, when the safety of individuals is endangered. "It is in this way that poisons administered in proper doses come to be remedies."

How can we ensure the administration of the proper dose of poison, how ought government to be constituted? Approaching this question after having spent years in defending the individual against the importunities of the legislator, Bentham retains his principle of personal interest as a motive for action only in its strict sense of pure egoism. The persons who rule, being men, are necessarily egoists; they therefore inevitably pursue their own interest and not that of the ruled. In fact, the object of government in all its forms has always been not the greatest happiness of those for whom but that of those *by* whom it is carried on, the happiness of the few (the ruling interest), and not of the many. The Monarchy, the House of Lords, the Established Church, are all examples of the ruling interest which is hostile to the interest of the many. To prevent this clashing of interests in the future, power must be placed in the hands of the greatest number. It is only by this means that we can ensure *the greatest happiness of the greatest number*, which is the aim and object of morals and politics. Accordingly Bentham demands the introduction of universal suffrage, vote by ballot and annual parliaments into England.

These conclusions are the same as those which French ideology had arrived at, and, as a matter of fact, they were obtained by the same method. Although wearing the English garb of empirical moralist, Bentham, in constructing his synthesis (which must not be confounded with the analytical portion of his work, as is usually done), adopts the same mode of procedure as the French metaphysicians, that of *a priori* reasoning.[1] Discard-

---

[1] In fact Bentham's premises, that pleasure and pain are man's only sensations, and that utility is the mainspring of human actions, are in no way derived from experience. Even supposing that utility *is* the only motive of human actions, how does it follow, as a matter of experience, that it *ought* to be the rule of conduct? Evidently this conclusion, which has been arrived at by an abrupt mental transition, is only a postulate. And in that case how can the principle of utility serve as a universal and infallible criterion? If

ing, like them, the teaching of history, because "the past is of no use" (Bentham's own remark made in the course of a conversation with Philarète Chasle, and related by the latter in his Memoirs), and seeing in social man only " what essentially appertains to man," according to the expression of Rousseau, to wit, human nature in general, he completely identifies him with one of his attributes. Bentham's man never follows his impulses or his habits; he is always deliberating, always engaged in calculation, just as the personage of the ideologists does nothing but indulge in abstract reasoning. Consequently, in his system men appear perfectly like each other in all latitudes. The government suited to them is the same everywhere — a representative democracy. Humanity is one and indivisible for Bentham, just as for the French ideologists.

it is a question of utility in its ordinary sense, then the consequences of actions considered from this point of view will always fall below their real scope; for in the moral world acts are prolonged by their effects, and owing to the reactions caused by the phenomena with which they come in contact on their path they continually form new combinations producing new effects, which combine in their turn. If the criterion of utility rises higher than the immediate consequences, if it is meant to include every possible consequence, to consider acts done by men living in a state of society in the light of a remote future (People, observes Bentham, who have not a clear idea of the useful often quote the remark of Aristides: "Themistocles' plan is very advantageous but it is very unjust." Aristides might have said: Themistocles' plan would be useful for the moment and detrimental for future ages, what it offers us is nothing in comparison with what it deprives us of. — *Principles of Legislation*, Ch. V), then it borders on the infinite, and is on a par with every ideal standard set up by the intellect for judging things *sub specie æternitatis* — the *just*, the *good*, the *beautiful* — in short with every term by which the mind can conceive of the absolute. Bentham himself declares that the useful viewed in its larger application and not in the vulgar sense is in no way opposed to the just, that it even coincides with the just. But Godwin, the authorized representative of ideology, makes no scruple of admitting that justice coincides with utility. Bentham therefore did not do away with the absolute; he only rejected all the other forms of it as false gods; he repudiated them in order to proclaim that his absolute was the only true one and that the world was governed by it. No doubt, every one claims this attribute for his god; but who has seen these gods? Do they not exist only in the imagination of those who worship them? Whereas Bentham's sovereign principle, according to him, can be touched, so to speak, and be seen at work. We cannot estimate the value of the *just*, but we can estimate the value of the *useful*; in other words, Bentham's principle is alone susceptible of a scientific method in its application. The objection will be made that pleasures and pains are not homogeneous quantities. Be it so, but as they eventually take the form of sensations, all that you have to do is to compare the sensations. It is true that they vary according to the character of the person who feels them and accord-

For Bentham, too, patriotism is bound to give way to it. "I should repudiate with horror," he declared, "the imputation of patriotism, if being a friend of my country involved being an enemy of the human race," — because, as the French ideologists would have said, the human race is composed of the same "men," because, says Bentham, the permanent interests of all peoples are identical.[1]

This synthesis of Bentham's, obtained by the same logical process as the synthesis of the French ideologists, was, like it, doomed to failure, but not because it originated in an ideal conception. Bentham's attempt, if it were a final one, would alone suffice to show how difficult or even impossible it is to discover a governing principle of life in the facts supplied by experience. Starting from a tangible fact and obliged to take

ing to the external circumstances which react on his sensibility. Nevertheless, every sensation contains an objective element which can be separated from the others. Science might make lists of these objective elements obtained by means of analysis, and so compile general inventories of sensations which would show us how to act with certainty, and even how to reduce the most difficult problems involved in the choice of acts conducing to happiness to a sort of mechanical operation.

Bentham, however, while recommending a mathematical appraisement of sensations, admits that of "two categories of circumstances" which react on the sensibility only one can be observed in all its particulars, that the "circumstances of the first order," such as temperament, strength, constancy of mind, natural and acquired habits, etc., are beyond the reach of calculation, and that we must therefore be content with "circumstances of the second order," such as age, sex, rank, etc. But how can the total lay claim to correctness if we are obliged to omit several items, and those the most important ones, from the account? In that case is not the value of these items left to the arbitrary and varying estimate of the person who makes the valuation? Bentham's criterion is consequently no more experimental in its application than in its origin. The scientific conscience which was to take the place of the moral conscience is no scientific conscience at all, and yet it preserves the authority with which Bentham had invested it on the strength of its imaginary qualities; it is made the sovereign judge of good and evil, just like the judge installed by the right of nature. In both cases an unconscious ideal transition from the relative to the absolute has given the appearance of a reality to what after all was only a conception of the intellect. The criterion of utility which at one time takes into consideration the immediate consequences and nothing more, as we are in the habit of believing, and at another weighs all the consequences of actions, as Bentham pretends, is a fallacy which only facilitates the step from the relative to the absolute. It is the sop thrown to the positive mind of England, to that of Bentham himself and his fellow-countrymen, in order to lull them into security.

[1] Dumont's "discours préliminaire" prefixed to the *Tactique des assemblées délibérantes.*

the road of ideology in spite of himself, Bentham repeated
the error of the French ideologists, who, having set up an ideal
controlling principle of social life, made no allowance for the
counter-operation of social facts, but drew on it *ad infinitum*,
like a universal legatee taking a mistaken view of the rights
conferred on him by his legal title.   In like manner Bentham
took for his starting-point man not in the relative aspect which
he bears in real life but in his abstract nature, and transformed
him into a being complete in itself.   Society consequently was
reduced to an aggregate of atoms, to a sum total of interests
requiring only to be left to themselves.   The *raison d'être* of
a power set over individual interests was nothing but the
protection of their unfettered development.   Henceforth the
State was bound to be only a watch-dog, and not an active
factor in the moral development of society.   To prevent the
dog from biting those whom he is set to guard, he must have a
good strong muzzle on; the powers of the State must be strictly
limited; the freedom of the individual can only be obtained
on this condition.

V

All these doctrines — political economy, empirical utilitarianism, the rights of man in their French dress or in their
English garb of Bentham's utilitarian philosophy — converge
on one centre and tend to form a new social cosmogony, in
which the starting-point as well as the goal is the individual
and not society, in which it is not the community which im-
parts light and heat to the individual, but the latter which is
the source of both.   Attaining its final expression in Bentham,
this idea constantly ran through English thought since man
and his rights and duties had become a subject of study.
Writers frequently stated it in language of great precision
without realizing its political significance.   "Although," remarks the highly conservative Paley, "we speak of communities as of sentient beings ; although we ascribe to them
happiness and misery, desires, interests, and passions; nothing
really exists or feels but individuals.   The happiness of a
people is made up of the happiness of single persons. . . .
The riches, strength, and glory of nations, the topics which
history celebrates, and which alone almost engage the praises

and possess the admiration of mankind, have no value farther than as they contribute to this end " (to the greater happiness of individuals).[1] Godwin denies that society has any existence of its own. " Society is an ideal existence and not on its own account entitled to the smallest regard. The wealth, prosperity, and glory of the whole are unintelligible chimeras. Set no value on anything but in proportion as you are convinced of its tendency to make individual men happy and virtuous." [2] " Let there be no doubt about it," cries Bentham; " the interests of individuals, it is said, must give way to the public interests. But what is the meaning of that? Is not each individual as much a part of the public as any other ? Individual interests are the only real interests. Take care of individuals. Don't meddle with them, and don't allow any one else to meddle with them, and you will have done enough for the public."

These notions, which were so opposed to the spirit of the traditional order of things, could not have forced themselves on the public mind if that order itself had not been vehemently assailed from several points at the same time. A social idea, however great its intrinsic upward force, can only advance in proportion as a vacuum is formed in front of it by the psychological action of material or moral facts. English society in the first quarter of the century came under the influence of both kinds of reaction. The first was brought about by the industrial revolution to which I shall refer later on. In the moral sphere it was Bentham again who most contributed to the formation of a state of mind ready to welcome new ideas. By making a detailed examination of English institutions, and showing what a quantity of refuse had accumulated in them for centuries, he broke the charm of historical continuity, shattered people's belief in the perfection of those institutions, and lowered the insular pride of his fellow-countrymen. These results were obtained as much by Bentham's personal action as by that of his disciples who propagated the master's doctrine, the original sources of which were little known to the great mass of the public. These disciples, a small group of remarkable men, who called themselves

---

[1] *Principles of Moral Philosophy*, Book VI, Ch. XI.
[2] *Enquiry concerning Political Justice*, 2d ed. Lond. 1796, II, 139.

"Philosophical Radicals," "offered an uncompromising opposition to many of the generally received opinions."[1] Under their direct inspiration "an incessant fire" was opened in the daily Press "against the wretched superstition that the English institutions were models of excellence, exposing the absurdities and vices of the law and the courts of justice, paid and unpaid, until they forced some sense of them into people's minds."[2] In the *Westminster Review*, "which made considerable noise in the world," the Philosophical Radicals attacked the landed aristocracy, the unpaid magistracy, the Established Church, and every institution which promoted the domination of a class, the happiness of a few as opposed to the "happiness of the greatest number." They sang the praises of personal property and of the middle class which held it. The economists, especially Ricardo, joined in the strain and glorified capital, wealth which passes to the bearer, to "man," and depreciated property in land, the aristocratic form of wealth which domineers over man and keeps the individual in a subordinate position. Confining the sphere of the State to the protection of persons and the security of property, the Philosophical Radicals were indefatigable in agitating for the liberty of the individual in every department and against every one, even going so far as to reject the system of co-operation in the economical sphere. In conjunction with the Economists they vehemently opposed protection and advocated free trade. Finally, as the principal article of their political creed, they demanded a democratic suffrage, protesting at the same time that their demand for it was not based on the rights of man, but that it was claimed "as the most essential of securities for good government."[3]

These ideas made a breach in the public conscience which grew wider and wider as time went on. Young men of a thoughtful turn of mind, the rising generation who were entering into public life and embracing liberal professions, discussed the radical doctrines with ardour.[4] All classes were affected by them in the long run, not with the result that political partisans were converted and went over to the opposite side, but

---

[1] John Stuart Mill, *Autobiography*, Lond. 1873, p. 100.
[2] *Ibid.* p. 90.   [3] *Ibid.* p. 107.
[4] *Personal Life of George Grote*, by Mrs. Grote, Lond. 1873, p. 24.

that, while "retaining their old distinctive names, men reasoned after a new fashion and according to principles wholly different from those to which they had been previously accustomed."[1]

The movement was accentuated by contact with foreign countries, which became much closer after the war. When the ports of the kingdom were opened on the conclusion of the peace, travellers thronged to the Continent in never-ending crowds. A constant traffic to and fro arose between the two shores of the Channel, and every vessel which brought travellers home brought with them feelings of commiseration for insular institutions and ideas.

With the commencement of the century another force, less obtrusive but extremely penetrating, appears on the scene to give a new impulse to thought — literature, already invaded by the spirit of revolt, by romanticism. Classic formalism is discarded, and henceforth inspiration is sought in the depths of the soul, and not in the outside world, the routine of which weighs like lead on the individual. The mere contact with this atmosphere of cant, the pestilent fumes of which stifle all personal initiative, is sufficient to scare away the choicer spirits, and the leaders of the new literary movement, the Southeys, the Coleridges, and the Wordsworths, take refuge in the North, in the Lake country, to probe the depths of their hearts amidst the tranquillity of nature. Byron begins by frequenting the fashionable world and leading its empty, frivolous life, only to end by regarding it with increased contempt and disgust. Each of his poems which reaches the shores of his native country from the distant scenes of his voluntary exile fills the air with doubt and fans the flame of revolt in the hearts and minds of his fellow-countrymen.

When we arrive at the second quarter of the century every principle is called in question, and every department of life is invaded by the spirit of doubt and negation. The system of which England was the embodiment is doomed to destruction.

VI

About the same time that the revolution in the sphere of ideas was taking place, another revolution of a material kind

---

[1] Roebuck, J. A., *History of the Whig Ministry* of 1830 to the passing of the Reform Bill, Lond. 1852, Vol. I, p. 344.

was in full swing, which had run a parallel course with the
first, starting from the middle of the eighteenth century —
the industrial transformation of the country effected by the
great mechanical inventions, the spinning-jenny, with its numerous improvements, and the steam-engine. It shook the ancient
edifice from top to bottom, and produced a general shifting of
positions throughout it. Industry, which up to this time had
been carried on at home by workmen dispersed throughout the
country districts and in small towns, was concentrated in large
factories and carried on by machinery which gave work to hundreds and thousands of hands. Country life and agriculture
were deserted for the towns. In the north of England, hitherto
sparsely populated, but abounding in coal suitable for feeding
the furnaces, huge agglomerations of men engaged in industrial labour sprang into existence. The raw material was transformed as if by the wand of the magician,[1] the manufacturers
turned out goods incessantly, daily displaying fresh resources,
securing the markets of the world and flooding them with their
products.[2]

In this marvellous outburst of industry individual effort and
the spirit of enterprise met with unexampled success. Men
belonging to the lower strata of society rose to high positions
in the world. Personal initiative was constantly stimulated,
and daring action often found its reward. It seemed as if
everything might be within the reach of all; every man tried
to rise and to extend the circle of his activity. These aspirations eventually assumed a morbid, feverish character; the
wild speculation of the years 1824–1825 supplied striking
proof of this; in fact the passion for individual expansion was
not a less powerful factor than the greed of gain.[3] However
this may be, a considerable number of men managed to rise
from the ranks. Some took the lead in producing fresh
wealth, others helped to develop it, others again benefited by

[1] Thus Sir John Throgmorton was able to wear at dinner a suit the cloth of
which came from wool which had been on the backs of sheep that very morning (Past and Present State of the Country, *Quarterly Review*, 1825, Vol. 32,
p. 174).

[2] In less than half a century the value of cotton exported increased more
than fifty-three times over, from £864,000 in 1785 to £46,000,000 in 1833.

[3] " It was not altogether rapacity, with many the charm was in the excitement, — in the pleasure of sympathy in large enterprises, — in the rousing of

it — manufacturers, factory managers, traders, contractors, professional men who made fortunes. They acquired new tastes and new ideas, and above all new desires and new ambitions. The monotonous and colourless existence of the middle class, of which we have caught a glimpse in the last century, was replaced by a more refined mode of life. Members of the new aristocracy of capital, whose wealth rivalled and often surpassed that of the old aristocracy of race, were anxious to mingle with the latter. At the close of the Napoleonic wars, in which immense fortunes were made, a great struggle took place; several of the new men managed to force their way into "society," and its ranks were thrown into confusion. It was in vain that society endeavoured to entrench itself behind the barriers of aristocratic exclusiveness. It was assailed at another point, that of its position of ruling class in the State. Here it held power by its monopoly of the parliamentary suffrage, which was in the hands of certain fixed groups. All the new-comers, and especially the inhabitants of the great towns created or developed by the rise of industry, were consequently excluded from the franchise. The contrast between their real power in the new society and their legal position in the State flashed upon them. Like their first parents in the Bible, they eat of the fruit of the tree of knowledge and knew that they were naked. They demanded their share of power, for they too were men and Englishmen: "We claim the birthright of our sires, by union, justice, reason, law." [1] The aspirations of the new social strata, their consciousness of their strength, were reinforced by a conviction of their right. The ideas which had been fermenting in England since the middle of the eighteenth century now had the material power

the faculties of imagination and conception when their field of commerce extended over the Pampas and the Andes, and beyond the farthest seas and among the ice-rocks of the poles." (*History of the Thirty Years' Peace*, by H. Martineau, I, 352.)

Cf. Mr. Bryce's remarks on the halo of idealism which the imagination of the Americans of the far West throws around their mad race for wealth: "It is not really or at least it is not wholly sordid. These people are intoxicated by the majestic scale of the nature in which their lot is cast, enormous mineral deposits, boundless prairies, forests which, even squandered, will supply timber to the United States for centuries . . . " (*The American Commonwealth*, 3d ed. Vol. II, Ch. CXVII, The Temper of the West.)

[1] From the reformist hymn sung at Birmingham and elsewhere by the members of the popular organizations known as Political Unions.

of the urban populations as their ally, and the old ruling class surrendered. By the Bill of 1832 the franchise was conferred on every inhabitant of a borough with a certain property qualification, and the monopoly of parliamentary representation was thus taken out of the hands of the aristocracy. The reforms which followed that of 1832 had the same tendency; their effect was to break up the old system and sever the traditionary bonds which united society. The ties which bound the Established Church to the State were loosened in 1828, and gradually relaxed still further as years went on. The repeal of the Test and Corporation Acts, in 1828, opened the public offices and Parliament to Dissenters. The Emancipation of the Catholics, in 1829, admitted the detested Papists to political life. The reformed Parliament completed these measures by authorizing the Dissenters to celebrate marriages in their chapels, and by making the registration of births and deaths a purely civil function independent of ecclesiastical ceremonies. The municipal reform of 1835 abolished the oligarchical corporations under the control of the territorial magnates, and entrusted the government of the towns to the great body of ratepayers. The relief of the poor, which had been managed by the landlords in their capacity of magistrates, was reorganized by the introduction of representatives elected by the population and of a large staff of salaried officials under a central board in London. The reform of the Poor Laws, by which these changes were effected, diminished the importance of the " great unpaid " in the principal branch of local self-government. The successive formation of new administrative departments, as that of public health and others, with officials controlled by boards in London, deprived the gentry still more of their sphere of action in local public life and of their opportunities of daily contact with the population. The abolition of the protectionist system, begun under Huskisson and completed by the repeal of the Corn Laws in 1846, gave the finishing stroke to the landlords' ascendancy, not only from the economic but also from the social point of view. It weakened their feudal power with the rights and duties involved in it. Sir Robert Peel, before he became a convert to free trade, opposed the repeal of the duties on corn for the very reason that the landowners, when reduced to commercial competition and forced to adopt a purely business line of conduct, would no longer be able to cultivate the moral and social relations which had existed for centuries between landlords, farmers, and labourers, and that the measure " would alter the character of the country." [1] The reduced incomes of the landlords prevented them from displaying their old hospitality and liberality, and their attractive power ceased to exist in the same degree. The new means of locomotion and of communication, introduced in the years 1830–1840, altered the old relations between the different classes still more. In the relative state of isolation which prevailed before the era of railways, the great landlords irradiated the whole neighbourhood and made it gravitate with all its interests in their orbit. The shopkeepers and artisans of the neighbouring town lived on their custom. Their entry into a town with a string of coaches and carriages was an event which set all the population agog. These relations, with their element of prestige on the one side and of dependence on the other, came to an end when, owing to the construction of railways, people could travel with less expense to the great centres of population, where they found all that the most capricious taste could desire. The moral effect which increased facility of communication produced by revealing new worlds and opening up fresh horizons proved a still stronger dissolvent.

VII

The successor to the system which was thus perishing bit by bit, a result which the representatives of ideology had demanded for half a century, was the very personage of whom they had constituted themselves the champions — the individual. The religious revival had told him that he had a soul of his own; the laws of religious emancipation acknowledge the fact. Political economy and philosophy had declared that he had his own interests and consequently his own rights; the Bill of 1832 recognizes them by placing the electoral qualification on an elastic and rational basis and thus making the franchise a security payable " to bearer." The reform of the Poor Laws introduces the same principle in the administration of relief to the poorer classes. The abolition of restrictive duties

[1] *Hansard*, 3d series, Vol. CXXXI, p. 376.

delivers man from all impediments to his activity and starts
him on the wild career of free competition. Railways, the
telegraph and the penny-post, by uniting and separating people
and things at will, complete the emancipation of the individual. Formerly, when means of communication were difficult,
slow, and irregular, every one was confined within the narrow
range of his own home and compelled to submit to all its
material and moral servitudes; people resigned themselves
to it beforehand, and considered themselves at the mercy of
an inevitable destiny which baffled all human combinations.[1]
But now the obstacles of space and time seemed to melt away
before them; they had only to express a wish, and they were
transported with rapidity to a distance of a hundred miles;
they could hold a conversation with the antipodes; the forces
of nature were always at hand ready to obey their behests.

It is true that this exaltation of the individual had found
scope mostly in the middle class, and that some of the very
phenomena which had contributed to his emancipation soon
began to impose restrictions on it. The development of industry did much to open a field for the individual, but the same
movement created the industrial serf side by side with the industrial baron. The workmen who flocked into the factories,
uprooted from the soil, obliged to give up work in their own
homes, bound like slaves to the machinery, fell into a state of
complete dependence on the capitalist class, which constituted
a new sort of feudalism in the transformed social system. The
railways which destroyed the old local relations of vassalage
substituted for them a new kind of dependence by centralizing
the markets of the country and the circulation of wealth. The
post-office and the telegraph, by contributing to centralization,
also helped to make the individual a satellite of the system of
which the capital or the great provincial town was becoming
the centre.

In more than one way then man was once more caught in

---

[1] Sydney Smith says, recalling his travels in the good old days: "In going
from Taunton to Bath I suffered between 10,000 and 12,000 severe contusions,
before stone-breaking Macadam was born . . . and whatever miseries I suffered, I had no post to whisk my complaints for a single penny to the remotest corners of the empire; and yet in spite of all these privations, I lived on
quietly, and am now ashamed that I was not more discontented." (*Modern
Changes*, Works, p. 678.)

the toils; another hierarchy, and with it a new species of subordination, arose in the industrial world. But the new ties,
being of a purely mechanical kind, and having none of the
binding force which held the old society together, not only did
not check the movement but accelerated it. They revealed the
process of individualist expansion which was at work in England in a new light, and showed how, the traditional relations
between man and man having ceased and the social horizon
being enlarged, the individual was becoming isolated in the
society which had undergone transformation. When manufacturing industry took the place of domestic labour, direct
intercourse between the owners of factories and the shifting
masses of workmen became impossible; henceforth their only
points of contact were work and wages, governed by the stern
law of supply and demand; they became anonymous abstractions one to the other; they came together and parted without
seeing each other. The workmen, herded together in the factories, had no bond of union but that of chance promiscuity;
their only approach to an organic existence was an ephemeral
combination for purposes of revolt, such as that of the Chartists,
for instance. Agricultural labour itself was also affected by
the new order of things; it assumed a nomadic impersonal
character. The introduction of machinery in agricultural
operations by substituting work in gangs for individual labour
led to farming on a large scale, just as it had created industry
on a large scale in towns. Conducted on the same principle of
division of labour, agricultural production, to which nature has
set bounds in point of quantity, ceased to provide continuous
employment; there was no need to spend the winter in thrash-
ing by hand the corn which had been reaped; everything could
be done by the machine almost at the same time. It was no
longer necessary to engage men permanently, and so the agricultural labourer was hired by the week instead of by the
year. Wandering troops of labourers provided by contractors
or agents travelled from county to county (gang system), just
like the factory-hands who migrated from town to town. The
changes in the world of commerce also altered the relations
between man and man by substituting fluctuations in custom
for the old fixity of connection between buyer and seller.
Even in the staff of commercial houses, offices, and shops, men

were too often strangers to each other; the time had gone by
when, as before the second half of the eighteenth century,
master and workman, employer and employee, formed a single
family. They now belonged to different strata of society. The
more refined mode of life which grew up in the middle class in
consequence of the industrial revolution was marked by distinctions which varied according to the income of its members,
and each distinction constituted a new line of demarcation and
separation.

Thus the second stage in the movement which broke up
English society was completed: by destroying the old hierarchy it set free the individual; in setting him free it isolated
him. But the change did not stop there; the process of isolation and separation gave rise in its turn to a fresh development of the individualist movement, which formed, as it were,
its synthesis: it became a levelling process as well. In de-
composing the concrete, the logic of facts as well as that of
ideas, opened the door to the general. Here as elsewhere
industrialism gave the first impulse. In the eyes of the manufacturer the mass of human beings who toiled in the factory
were only *workmen*, and the workman associated the factory-
owner only with the idea of *capitalist* or *master*. Not being
brought into immediate contact, they formed a conception of
each other by mentally eliminating the special characteristics
of the individual and retaining only what he had in common
with the other members of his class. In proportion as the
new conditions of existence enlarged the social horizon in
the sphere of life, just as it expanded by means of thought,
the process of abstraction extended to all social relations.
The rapid growth of large towns destroyed the old neigh-
bourly intercourse, or at all events, its intimate character. The
extension of markets again stripped buyers and sellers of their
concrete individuality, and resolved them into the general categories of *tradesmen* and *customers*. Railways, by bringing together for half an hour men who saw each other for the first
and perhaps the last time, reduced them to the general notion
of *travellers*, all placed on an equal footing by a uniform ticket,
a piece of pasteboard printed wholesale for all present and
future travellers. In great industrial enterprises creative
energy and active will associated in the form of *shares*, negoti-

able securities, transferable to an infinite series of potential entities existing only as *shareholders*. Even the feelings which take their rise in the depths of the soul, such as the love of one's neighbour and pity, were obliged, when projected over a larger area, to conform to abstract notions; the familiar figure of the wretched Jim or Tom, who had been the regular recipient of relief, gave place to the idea of the poor man, the *poorer classes*.

The change of ideas involved a change in principles of conduct. It is difficult, in fact, to feel a regard for a number of workmen whom one hardly knows by sight; you cannot be on cordial terms with all your fellow-travellers in a railway carriage; you can be charitable to poor individuals but not to the poorer classes. They can only be enveloped in a more general sentiment. Being henceforth confined to particular cases only, the feelings of regard, of cordiality, of charity, as they assumed a general character, resolved themselves into an inclination to be correct and just towards all, and to respect the human element with its material and moral needs in the humblest and most wretched members of society.[1] This applied equally to the moral sanction of the duties of man in a social state which consists of the feeling of responsibility to his fellow-creatures. Confined hitherto to the narrow range of his social circle, it now spread further and further beyond these limits; the tribunal of public opinion sat in judgment wherever cognizance could be taken of the individual's conduct; at the bar of his conscience man became responsible not only to his own society in the restricted sense of the word, but to society in general, to his country, to the nation, even to humanity. Thus a readjustment of forces took place in man's social existence between the particular which constituted nearly all his being and the general which occupied but a small portion of it. Destined as he is

---

[1] In cases where the moral obligations of social intercourse are supplemented by those of the law, as in the relief of the poor, the legislature soon intervened to divert the legal obligations of their concrete character. A poor man was entitled to relief only when he belonged to the parish. An Act of Sir Robert Peel, passed in 1846, prescribes that every poor person who happens to be living in the parish shall be relieved, wherever he comes from. Subsequent legislation on this subject only develops this principle by " investing the relief of the poor more and more with the character of an abstract obligation."*

* Aschrott, *Das Englische Armenwesen*, p. 148, Leipz. 1886.

by his finite and limited frame to cling to the concrete and
the particular as his starting-point and strongest support, man
nevertheless launched on all sides into the general, with the
result that henceforth his social relations were bound to be
guided not so much by sentiment, which expresses the perception of the particular, as by general principles, less intense in
their nature perhaps, but sufficiently comprehensive to take in
the shifting multitudes of which the abstract social groups were
henceforth composed, groups continually subject to expansion
by reason of their continual motion. In a word, in passing
from the concrete to the abstract, social relations exhibited a
natural tendency towards the principle which is commonly
designated by the name of equality.

The psychological process which social relations were undergoing led therefore to the same conclusions as rationalism and
by the same logical path — that of abstraction and generalization. But while the latter moved in the untenanted world
of speculation, the former operated in a living society, amid
inveterate habits, traditions, prejudices and interests constituting so many centripetal forces which check and often
neutralize the most powerful centrifugal movements. Consequently each of the various stages of the former process was
destined to be completed with a slowness which will often
leave the actual situation a long way behind its logical postulates. The divergence that will thus arise between the decom-
position of the old society and the generalization of the new
social relations will constitute the drama of the history of
modern English society and of the State which is its political
embodiment.

VIII

Naturally united to society by the closest ties, the State in
fact was passing through the same crisis. At one time serving
as a target for the ideas and facts which assailed society, at
another reflecting the movement which operated directly within
it, the State underwent every phase of the logical process
which we have just been considering in the case of society and
the individual. The Reform of 1832 took the State out of the
narrow groove of a single ruling class. The series of Acts of
a secularizing tendency which were passed from and after the

year 1828 dissolved the compound existence of Church and State and restored to the State its proper function. The numerous administrative reforms which followed the Bill of 1832 defined the sphere of the State and the powers and operation of its organs, and made it clearly distinguishable from the old representatives of self-government recruited from the ranks of society. The State ceased to be a spirit pervading every manifestation of public and social life; its figure began to assume a distinct outline; it became more human, more personal. But as it was no longer one and indivisible with society, which constituted alike its foundation and its cohesive power, it ceased to be one and indivisible itself. Its own cohesion and that of its constituent parts became impaired. Local self-government was no longer linked to parliamentary government by the unbroken chain of a single and united ruling class. Henceforth each of them had its own existence with its own special authorities, its means and method of action which tended to isolate it in the great world of national life. Severed one from the other, local self-government and parliamentary government lost their homogeneous character in the new conditions under which they had to work; they crumbled away in their turn, thus establishing in the second degree the great fact of the separation of the emancipated State and society.

Self-government was the first to supply the demonstration of this. It lost its consistency and was subjected to a systematic process of dismemberment. The habit of piecemeal legislation which prevails in England no doubt had a great deal to do with this result. The movement of reform which triumphed in the Bill of 1832 did not abolish government by the gentry in local administration, it merely curtailed it: side by side with the magistrates, elective offices were created for certain branches of local self-government. But even this qualified homage paid to the democratic principle only went half way: in the constituencies which elected the local officers, the rich electors were given an increasing number of votes in proportion to the amount of the rates paid by them. This double moral *enclave*, however, was as nothing compared with the material *enclaves* created by the multiplicity and variety of the elective bodies imported one after another into the system of self-government, without a shadow of a plan and irrespective of all unity of conception.

The reform of the Poor Laws divided the country, for purposes of Poor Law administration, into Unions (composed of so many parishes), which each elected a Board of Guardians. The fourteen thousand parishes of England and Wales were distributed into about six hundred Unions, without the slightest consideration for the old historical and economic divisions, so that a Union was often in two counties and included urban and rural parishes, etc. What was done for Poor Law administration has been repeated at different intervals, whenever the need of reforming a public service or creating a new one made itself felt : new electoral powers were conferred (for the maintenance of roads, for sanitary matters, etc.) with new districts, the boundaries of which in no way coincided with the other divisions of local government. The districts carved out for the various elective authorities sometimes met, sometimes diverged, sometimes overlapped and sometimes intersected each other. Each authority taxed those within its jurisdiction separately, and had its independent budget of receipts and expenditure. "It prevents the possibiiity of anything like a local budget. It is impossible to make out what is the total expenditure for any given locality. The ratepayer who essayed the task could only give it up in bewildered disgust." [1] The inevitable result was that interest in local affairs and habits of co-operation were discouraged. There was no fixed unit of local administration with a centre in which all the good-will and energy of the locality could be focussed. The old administrative unit, the parish, was swamped in the chaos of districts, authorities, and assessments. The vestry, which was composed of the ratepayers of the parish, continued to exist, but its most important functions were transferred little by little to the new elective bodies. Even in the privileged towns described as "municipal boroughs," in which the reform of 1835 gave all the ratepayers a share in the administration of the borough, the sphere of action conceded to the municipalities was not an extensive one. On the other hand, the Unions, which gradually monopolized several departments of local government besides the relief of the poor, were too large to serve as a field for the discharge of civil duties. In the rural districts the difficulties were still

[1] M. D. Chalmers, *Local Government*, Lond. 1883, p. 29.

greater; there the Union presented a still more bloated and the parish a more emaciated appearance. There was hardly anything left to keep the public interest alive. The village vestry ceased to meet, for want of current business, and the villagers, as a farmer put it, never had "a chance of looking into each other's mind." [1]

At the same time the growing complexity of modern civilization multiplied the functions of local administration and led to the introduction, as in industry, of the principle of the division of labour. To meet the new requirements of the situation, the Legislature thought fit to introduce into the local departments a large staff of salaried officials, and for the sake of greater security it placed them under the control of the authorities in London, the Poor Law Board, etc. In this way officialism and centralization penetrated into local government and pushed the representatives of society out of it. The latter made no resistance, either because self-government in its new aspect, as we have just seen, did not offer a suitable field for action, or because they were indifferent on the subject. In his famous speech on the Chartist petition, Disraeli demonstrated with impassioned eloquence that the Chartists were the victims of the new political and social system, which had placed in power a new governing class which did not govern. "The old constitution invested a small portion of the nation with political rights. Those rights were entrusted to that small class on certain conditions — that they should guard the civil rights of the great multitude. It was not even left them as a matter of honour, society was so constituted that they were entrusted with duties which they were obliged to fulfil. They had transferred a great part of that political power to a new class, whom they had not invested with those great public duties. Great duties could alone confer great station, and the new class which had been invested with political station had not been bound up with the great mass of the people by the exercise of social duties. For instance, the administration of justice, the regulation of parishes, the building of roads and bridges, the command of the militia and police, the employment of labour, the distribution of relief to the

[1] Rev. T. W. Fowle, "The Decay of Self-government in Villages," *Fortnightly Review*, April, 1879.

destitute — these were great duties which ordinarily had been confined to that body in the nation which enjoyed and exercised political power. But now they had a class that had attained that great object that all the opulent desired — political power without the conditions annexed to its possession and without fulfilling the duties which it should impose. What was the consequence ? Those who thus possessed power without discharging its conditions and duties were naturally anxious to put themselves to the least possible expense, they were anxious to keep it without any appeal to their pocket and without any cost of their time. To gain this object they raised the cry of cheap government that served the first, to attain the second they called for the constant interference of the government." [1]

In point of fact, when the middle class had obtained political power its civic ardour soon cooled down. The remnant of its enthusiasm was spent in the struggle against the Corn Laws, in which its material interests were involved. Having carried the day against the landed aristocracy, the middle class stood aside from the game of politics and devoted all its energies to amassing wealth and enjoying it. Thus both the substance and the spirit of the old self-government died away.

In the centre of political life, in Parliament, the old springs of action soon began to give way as well. The ominous date of 1846, which marked the eclipse of the old society, brought this fact into strong relief. In thrusting the repeal of the Corn Laws on his followers, Sir Robert Peel shattered the historic Tory party. That party represented the opposition of the landed interest, which was the embodiment of the old England, to the new industrial classes. The abolition of the Corn Laws, following on so many other reforms, obliterated this antagonism. At the same time a considerable section of the Tory party, faithful to its traditions and its feelings,

---

[1] *Hansard,* 3d series, Vol. **XLIX,** p. 248 (Sitting of the 12th of July, 1839). Cf. Gneist's views on the process of destruction which the old basis of the English State (die innere Cohärenz der Communitates) was undergoing. The learned argument of the illustrious jurist is on the same lines as the fervid language of Disraeli. Recently Gneist has once more stated his favourite argument (Die heutige Lage der Englischen Verfassung nach den drei Reform-bills 1832, 1867, 1885, *Deutsche Revue,* 1887, t. 1.). His last work, *Die natio-nale Rechtsidee von den Ständen,* Berlin, 1894, contains several passages giving expression to identical views.

refused to follow Peel in his evolution and formed an independent group, equally hostile to Peel and to the Whigs.   The
dual system of party government at once lost its historical *raison
d'être* and its material basis.   Henceforth there was no homogeneous majority in Parliament.   The House of Commons continued to split up into groups.   The irreconcilable Tories, the
" Protectionists," could not forgive Peel for his "great treason."
The Peelites, divided by a great gulf from the bulk of the Tory
party, remained in a suspended state between it and the Liberal
party.   The latter was torn by internal dissensions which had
been gathering ever since 1832.   Forming a coalition of aristocratic Whigs, of representatives of the middle class, of Benthamite Radicals and Manchester Radicals, they had united
in a fashion to lay siege to the Tory fortress, but when once
the stronghold was taken, the allies had no reason for conciliat-
ing each other, and their divergencies of origin, of temperament,
of habits and aspirations were allowed full swing.   Soon the
traditional party ties slackened all along the parliamentary line ;
discipline ceased to exist, and no one could depend on his followers.   This became a subject of general complaint.   " I am
told," writes to Croker one of his correspondents, " that the
House of Commons is becoming more unmanageable every session, that no division can be calculated upon, that so many of
the town members owe no allegiance and vote for popularity."[1]
Croker himself writes to Lord Brougham : "Phrase it as you
will, — a House of Commons unmanageable or the country un-
governable, — the indisputable fact is that our representative
system is not only, as you say, likely to be brought into disre-
pute, but is actually so, and will every session become more
and more notoriously incompatible with what was called our
constitution."[2]   This is not merely the peevish utterance of a
splenetic Tory.   The Greville Memoirs are full of observations
of the same kind.   Greville sums up the session of 1854 as follows : " The whole conduct of the session and the relations of the
government with the House of Commons presented something
certainly very different from what had ever been seen before
in the memory of the oldest statesman, implied a total dissolution of party ties and obligations, and exhibited the Queen's

---

[1] *The Croker Papers*, edited by L. J. Jennings, Lond. 1885, III, 327.
[2] *Ibid.* 340 (letter of the 21st of July, 1854).

government and the House of Commons as resolved into their separate elements and acting towards each other in independent and often antagonistic capacities." [1] In 1855 Greville notes: " Nobody owes allegiance or even any party ties or seems to care for any person or anything." [2] The Journal of 1856 repeats Graham's remarks to the effect that " there is not one man in the House of Commons who has ten followers, neither Gladstone, nor Disraeli, nor Palmerston." [3]

Every day, in fact, the difference between the two great historical parties grew less marked. You could not tell a moderate Tory from a Whig. [4] Personal considerations inevitably became factors of importance in parliamentary combinations. A policy was combated one day and adopted the next by the victorious coalition; ministers left office by one door and crept in at another. Members of Parliament transferred their allegiance to another leader without being false to their political convictions, because they had none to speak of; others withheld their support because they entertained opinions which they were not disposed to sacrifice to calculations of parliamentary strategy. From one motive or another the individual asserted his independence within the halls of Parliament as well as elsewhere.

Political veterans deplored the perversity of the new generation, and were at a loss for words to denounce the inconsistency and insincerity displayed by members of all parties. These censors, like all *laudatores temporis acti*, little dreamed, in clinging to their traditional ideas, that they were applying old principles to a new society, or at all events to a society in course of transformation. However much the decline in political force of character and the weakening of political con-

---

[1] *The Greville Memoirs,* Longmans' edition in 8 vols., Lond. 1888, VII, 182.
[2] *Ibid.* 247.   [3] *Ibid.* VIII, 41.
[4] A foreign observer who has since acquired a certain celebrity, Herr Lothar Bucher, defined the two parties as follows: A Whig is a man who descends from John Russell's grandmother, a Tory one who sits behind Disraeli (*Der Parlamentarismus wie er ist*, 1854, p. 113). A few years later an analogous definition was given by an old English parliamentarian. " What is a Liberal? A gentleman who, if Lord Derby were to issue a circular requesting all those members who were disposed to accord to him any confidence would do him the favour to meet in St. James' Square to hear his programme, would not respond to the invitation. Other test I know none." (Sir John Walsh, *The Practical Result of the Reform Act*, Lond. 1860, p. 85.)

victions may have contributed to the result, the relaxation of discipline and the break-up of parliamentary life were not due to them alone. Parliament ceased to exhibit its old consistency because society had lost it. The constant multiplication of degrees in the social scale, the variety of new aspirations, the change of social relations from the concrete to a generalized standard, all found their way into the House, narrow as the entrance to it was at that time. Many a member of Parliament had to reckon, not with this or that magnate who disposed of a seat in his own dining-room, or with the small clique which enjoyed a similar power, but with a constituency composed of varied elements. He could no longer follow the advice of the Duke of Monmouth: "You go with your family, sir." Political duties and responsibilities, just like the rules for private conduct, were passing out of the concrete stage into that of the abstract and the general. In the old days political virtue consisted of loyalty to a chief; the oath of fealty taken by the vassal to his lord was an epitome of this ideal. There was nothing dishonouring even in fighting against one's native country, as long as it was a loyal combat under the banner of the accepted chief; it was impossible to be untrue to one's country if one remained faithful to one's chief. Great captains have been often known to offer their sword to one country after another. Condé and Turenne take up arms against France; during the Revolution the *émigrés* join the enemies of their country without a shadow of scruple, because they are fighting for their *Roy*. In England the King is soon eclipsed by Parliament. A corporate body representing the community gradually becomes supreme, but its exercise of power is really based on the old idea. There are only two rival chiefs followed by their retainers who contend for the mastery, euphemistically described as two parties representing the natural dualism of political thought and alternately taking the helm of the State. When the new generalized social relations widened the circle of duty and responsibility, the loyalty of the vassal ceased to be a virtue for the politician, and the inelastic fabric of government by historical parties, which were supposed to contain between them every political tendency and aspiration, became too narrow for the varied and varying relations of political life, while too large for the old order of things which had shrunk under the pressure of events.   The break-up of the old English society was therefore logically bound to culminate in the downfall of party government, which was its highest expression in the sphere of politics. Henceforth the political life of the nation, which had been identified with parliamentary institutions, demanded, like society, a more comprehensive guiding principle and a wider channel.   In both cases the question at issue was whether this result would be obtained with more or less prolonged friction between the old habits and the new requirements, and more or less violent collisions between particular interests and the general interest; whether the break-up in society and Parliament would only be a period of transition, a sort of wilderness between Egypt and the land of Canaan, leading to the adoption of principles, rules, and forms capable of reuniting society and the State in a new synthesis.   The solution of this twofold problem was reserved for the future, but one thing was clear: the exodus had commenced, the English people were on the march.

THIRD CHAPTER

ATTEMPTS AT REACTION

I

THE exodus had commenced. But whether it was that the mountain from which the promised land could be descried was too distant and too lofty for some, or that others saw the paths leading to the new Canaan blocked by the rising torrent of individualism and were afraid of perishing in the wilderness with their kith and kin, cries of alarm and distress were raised in various quarters, and retrograde movements were attempted after several stages of the journey had been passed.

The first attempt at reaction came from the Church. It was the Church which, identified with the State and inextricably bound up with the ruling class, best symbolized the old one and indivisible order which covered the whole surface of society. And it was against the Church that was directed the first revolt of the repressed individual, of the individual conscience bent on asserting its relations with the Creator. From the second half of the eighteenth century the contending sects and the spirit of doubt and negation which invaded educated society worked continual havoc in the Church. When the State itself was obliged, from and after the year 1828, to sever one by one the legal ties which bound the citizen to the Church, the illusion even of external conformity was destroyed, and the confusion in the spiritual sphere became only too visible. It was then that champions of the Church arose at Oxford who sought to restore the old unity, men like Newman, Pusey, Keble, and Froude, subtle theologians and refined and tender poets. Their ardent imagination made them see the vast structure of the Established Church totter to its base, the crash of its falling ruins seemed to smite upon their ears, and they recoiled in mental affright, like a rider who reins in with a jerk on the brink of

a precipice. Leaving out of consideration the secular process
which was differentiating and individualizing the religious idea,
a process which they would fain have regarded as a disagreeable
incident, as a bad dream, the Oxford group took a single step
back to the first three centuries of Christianity. They performed wonders of theological casuistry to prove that in spite of
the Reformation, the Anglican Church differed in no way from
the primitive Church, that it would only be resuming possession
of its heritage in reverting to the tradition of the Catholic universal Church, to the apostolical body of doctrine as transmitted
by the Fathers of the Church, with belief in the regenerating
virtue of baptism, in the Real Presence of Our Lord in the Communion, in the sacraments which convey grace, in the power of
the priests who administer them to lead the soul to salvation
and pronounce the absolution of sins. Exhorting men to return
to dogmas of this kind, which appeal to the believer's imagination and stir his feeling for the marvellous, the authors of
the Oxford movement surrounded public worship with ritual
and ornament which flatter and lull the senses and through
them cast a spell over the soul. For reason they substituted
sentiment; to the inward faith which justifies they opposed
the visible Church, communion with which, by means of observance of external and uniform rites, suffices to obtain salvation; between the individual conscience and God, whom it
beholds face to face, they interposed the priesthood as the
depository of the traditions and the authority of the Church,
and mercifully spared man the use of reason and all the
mental distress which it involves.

To ensure the acceptance of their doctrines, however, they
too were obliged to appeal to public opinion, and they impressed their views on every thinking mind by means of small
pamphlets called " tracts," to which they owe their name of
Tractarians. They who aimed at placing restrictions on or
even suppressing individual judgment were forced in the end
to admit its jurisdiction. The State, with its intervention in
the affairs of the Church for the purpose of withdrawing this
or that privilege, appeared a tyrant in their eyes, and they
were reduced to plead the cause of liberty against authority
on behalf of the Church as opposed to the State. When their
doctrines were published to the world, a storm arose; the

exercise of private judgment which they had provoked rent
the Church itself asunder, — one party taking their side and
another declaring against them.   The Tractarians, when attacked, and Pusey at their head, took their stand on the
right of free discussion.   The whole controversy made religious unity more remote than ever, but at the same time it
stimulated the ardour of the combatants and intensified the
religious life of the various groups into which believers were
divided.   The Oxford sect was the first to derive vital force
from the movement, although it had failed in its ambitious
attempt to restore religious unity.   Having started under the
banner of authority and tradition, the Tractarians only succeeded in proving that liberty is, after all, the safest principle
of conduct in modern society.

II

The agitation against latitudinarianism in religion promoted
by the Oxford movement had hardly calmed down when
another campaign was started against "political infidelity,"
to combat the destruction of the old political creed which knit
classes and individuals together.   Disraeli, who was then at the
threshold of his career, placed himself at the head of this
movement.   By descent a stranger to the traditions of English
society, but profoundly imbued with the genius of his own race,
in which the idealist element struggles for mastery with the
realist, he declared war against the social atomism which he
saw supreme on all sides.   In his eyes, all was disorganization
and demoralization: "a mortgaged aristocracy, a gambling
foreign commerce, a home trade founded on a morbid competition, and a degraded people."   The Queen of England reigns
over "two nations, the rich and the poor."   Class is set against
class.   "In the manufacturing districts there is no society but
only an aggregation."   "How, Disraeli asked himself, are the
elements of the nation to be again blended together?"   By a
new distribution of political power?   No, this would be a repe-
tition of the old error which consists in believing that national
content can necessarily be found in political institutions.   A
political institution is only a machine; the motive power is
the national character.   The character of the English nation
was declining, and it is this which must be worked upon.   But

in what way ?   Since the Peace there had been an attempt to
reconstruct society on a purely rational foundation, on a basis
of material motives and calculations, on the principle of utility.
The experiment had failed, as it was bound to do, for the power
of reason is limited.   " We are not indebted to the Reason of
man for any of the great achievements which are the landmarks
of human action and human progress.   Man is only truly great
when he acts from the passions; never irresistible but when
he appeals to the imagination.   Even Mormon counts more
votaries than Bentham.   The surest means to elevate the
character of a people is to appeal to their affections."

Disraeli, therefore, looking at the English society of his day,
came to the conclusion that it was necessary to rekindle the
old feelings in men's hearts — attachment to the Throne and
to the Church, and social sympathy between the people and
its natural leaders.   The Whigs, in setting up an oligarchy for
their own benefit, had turned the King into a Doge, and had
separated the sovereign from the people, and two great exist-
ences had been blotted out of English history — the Monarch
and the Multitude.   The new class which had been invested with
political power in 1832 was not linked to the masses by the
performance of social duties as under the old "territorial
constitution," in which the fulfilment of great public duties
alone conferred a great position.   Wealth had been allowed
to accumulate on a principle which ignored "the duty to
endow the Church, to feed the poor, to guard the land and to
execute justice for nothing."   "I see no other remedy," concluded Disraeli, "for that war of classes and creeds which
now agitates and menaces us but in an earnest return to a
system which may be described generally as one of loyalty
and reverence, of popular rights and social sympathies."   In
this system "the Venetian oligarchy " and plutocracy would
be eliminated to make way for a king acting as real leader of
the nation, and for a people cherished by their betters and
repaying them by devotion and affection.   Salvation lies in a
return to these ideas which are identical with the old Tory
principles upheld by the great Tory statesman Bolingbroke
and revived by that other great statesman, Pitt.   Modern conservatism, which gathered round it a selfish coalition of interests and was itself the offspring of latitudinarianism, was

powerless to give England a political creed which should be a permanent source of inspiration.

To turn this programme of popular Toryism to account, the "Young England" party was formed, in which Disraeli was joined by several young men of good family full of romantic ideas. Under their inspiration solicitude for the humbler classes became the fashion among the landed aristocracy, in an autocratic and sentimental form. The landlords provided generously for the wants of *their* peasants, promoted their welfare, and organized popular fêtes; largess was distributed at fixed times at the doors of baronial halls; daughters of noble houses made "pilgrimages of charity" through the villages; young lords played at cricket with the villagers. In return for this kind treatment the peasants were expected to be docile and submissive to their landlords in every relation of life. The movement did not go very far beyond these idyllic proceedings. The old flame which Young England wished to rekindle proved simply a display of fireworks. Sentiment was no match for facts, imagination was powerless to alter reality. English society was no longer in the feudal condition characterized by the class relations which Young England wished to see re-established. England had, so to speak, passed out of the phase of sentiment and entered on that of general principles. And Disraeli, who stood up for the Chartists, whom he regarded as victims of the social atomism, might have read the answer to his policy on the banners which they carried in their processions and which bore among others the motto: "We demand justice before charity." The problem with which society was confronted was to know "how are the elements of the nation to be again blended together; in what spirit is that reorganization to take place," it being admitted that the spirit of feudalism was dying, and that a breath of liberty and independence was passing over society. Ignoring this main factor of the problem, the solution proposed by Young England was, to use a logical term, simply a *petitio principii*, which left things as they were.

III

A far greater measure of success attended another champion, who also waged war against the new social system bred

of Benthamism and industrialism — Thomas Carlyle. Like
Disraeli, he deplored the loss of the old social creed, considered constitutional changes as only paltry expedients, and
saw no hope of reform but in the re-establishment of a social
leadership based on a conviction of duty in governors and
governed. But unlike Disraeli, the man of action, Carlyle, a
hermit centred in himself, his mind steeped in Scotch Puritanism, lived the whole crisis of his time in his inward soul.
His heart welled over in vehement invective and solemn warnings addressed to his fellow-countrymen. For many a year
his utterances were an endless recitative on the theme " Ah
nation of sinners, people laden with iniquity," after the
fashion of the prophets of Israel, always excepting their
style, for that of Carlyle, when it was not entirely incom-
prehensible, was more like the language of the Apocalypse.
Carlyle, too, had his beast with seven heads and ten horns,
which was Mechanism : " The huge demon of Mechanism
smokes and thunders, panting at his great task, in all sections
of English land; changing his *shape* like a very Proteus, and
infallibly at every change of shape *oversetting* whole multitudes of workmen, and as if with the waving of his shadow
from afar, hurling them asunder, this way and that, in their
crowded march and course of work or traffic, so that the
wisest no longer knows his whereabouts." . . . " Cash payment
had grown to be the universal sole nexus of man to man." . . .
" It is said that society exists for the protection of property.
And now what is thy property ? That parchment title-deed,
that purse thou buttonest in thy breeches pocket ? Is that thy
valuable property ? Unhappy brother, most poor insolvent
brother. I, without parchment at all, with purse oftenest in
the flaccid state, imponderous, which will not fling against
the wind, have quite other property than that! I have the
miraculous breath of life in me, breathed into my nostrils by
Almighty God. I have affections, thought, a God-given *capa-
bility* to be and do; rights, therefore — the right, for instance,
to thy love if I love thee, to thy guidance if I obey thee . . .
rights stretching high into Immensity, far into Eternity."
Opposing the spiritual nature and requirements of man to
the materialist tendencies of a "mechanical age," asserting
the need of an ideal for every society which aspires to **live,**

Carlyle urged his fellow-countrymen to imbue themselves with the sentiment of duty. The rest, that is to say the practical solution of the social crisis, will come of itself, as in the Gospel.

The new conception of the State placidly adopting the doctrine of "*laissez-faire*," was the principal obstacle to improvement as well as the source of all the mischief in Carlyle's eyes. It was a "false, heretical, and damnable principle, if ever aught was." Society and the State have no right to remain indifferent to the welfare of their members. The masses cannot live without being *really* led and governed. "What are all popular commotions and maddest bellowings from Peterloo to the Place-de-Grève itself? Bellowings, inarticulate cries as of a dumb creature in rage and pain; to the ear of wisdom they are inarticulate prayers: Guide me, govern me! I am mad and miserable and cannot guide myself. Surely, of all rights of man this right of the ignorant man to be guided by the wiser, to be, gently or forcibly, held in the true course by him, is the indisputablest. Recognized or not recognized a man *has* his superiors, a regular hierarchy above him; extending up, degree above degree, to heaven itself and God the Maker, who made His world not for anarchy but for rule and order." Before cash payment had grown to be "the universal sole nexus of man to man," the lower classes had a guide and a ruler in the aristocracy. "It was something other than money that the high then expected from the low, and could not live without getting from the low. Not as buyer and seller alone, of land or what else it might be, but in many senses still as soldier and captain, as clansman and head, as loyal subject and guiding king, was the low related to the high. With the supreme triumph of Cash, a changed time has entered; there must a changed aristocracy enter." This aristocracy must not be an aristocracy of birth or privilege, but of the mind and the heart. How are we to distinguish it, by what token are we to recognize the real aristocrats in order to entrust them with the government? — to this question Carlyle vouchsafes no answer. He contents himself with pouring out his sarcasm on the suffrage and giving vent to his contempt for and hatred of democracy. "The English people are used to suffrage; it is their panacea for all that goes wrong with them; they have a fixed idea of suffrage. . . . House-

hold Suffrage, Ballot Question, 'open' or not: not things but
shadows of things; Benthamee formulas; barren as the east-
wind!'" "The thing everywhere passionately clamoured for at
present is Democracy," what is called 'self-government' of the
multitude by the multitude." But "democracy is by the nature
of it a self-cancelling business, and gives in the long run a net
result of *zero*." A strong man, a despot, yes, even a despot,
would be better able to cope with the task than the anarchic
multitude.

The effect produced by Carlyle's denunciations was immense.
The English soul, with its religious fibre and its reserve of
repressed emotion, is never insensible to the appeals addressed
to it; only they must be couched in a loud and forcible tone,
and convey the impression that the person who makes them
feels what he says. Appeals of this kind are more likely to
find a hearing at certain seasons than at others. The state of
mind produced by indifferentism — brought to a pitch either
by the moral apathy which plunges men into a sort of torpor,
or by the atrophy which attacks a community sunk in
materialism or again by the scepticism which scatters to the
winds what until lately was the general creed and rule of
conduct — offers the most favourable psychological moment
for thrilling the soul of a community, and of Englishmen
in particular, with the accents of a commanding voice. The
middle of the eighteenth century, in which Wesleyanism and
Evangelicalism made their appearance, was an epoch of this
kind, and so was the period from 1830–1840, which combined
the two last-named aspects of social indifferentism. It was
then that Carlyle stepped on the scene and produced a sort of
nervous crisis in society, and especially among the younger
members of it, who in their emotion repeated his own words:
"Guide me, govern me! I am mad and miserable and cannot
guide myself." The new prophet, however, did not vouchsafe
any revelation or point out the right path, but only continued
to rouse the heart and stir the inner man. His appeals powerfully impressed the imagination, but hardly touched the reason,
and the nervous tension soon relaxed. To arrest the movement
which was drawing society into the current of individualism,
it was after all not enough to cry in a voice of thunder that the
Benthamite formulas were "barren as the east wind."

IV

The only positive proposal which was made for restoring organic life to society came from certain reformers who had been particularly struck with the effects of the industrial régime on the material existence of the working classes. They saw that the principle of free competition, so dear to political economy, increased the power of the strong and diminished that of the weak, with the result that the latter were at the mercy of the former, who knew neither justice nor pity;[1] and they conceived the idea of combating competition on practical lines. The campaign was opened by Frederick Denison Maurice and Charles Kingsley, clergymen of the Established Church, but generous-hearted and large-minded men, to whom Christianity was the equivalent of humanity. Their belief was that in the universe as it had issued from the hand of God selfishness was not the ruling principle, and that the spirit of devotion, self-sacrifice, and co-operation could alone reconcile the conflict of interests. Applying this idea to the economic system of the day, they arrived at the conclusion that competition, which divides man and sets him against his fellow, must be opposed by association. In their own country Robert Owen had already endeavoured to put the idea of industrial association into practice. In France, also, the various socialistic schools had advocated this method.[2] But "the Parisian *ouvrier* so often forgets Him whose everlasting Fatherhood is the sole ground of all human Brotherhood, whose wise and loving will is the sole source of all perfect order and government." Association, however, could never defeat competition without fraternal co-operation, without self-sacrifice, without subordination of

[1] " Sweet competition! Heavenly maid! Nowadays hymned alike by penny-a-liners and philosophers as the ground of all society — the only real preserver of the earth! Why not of Heaven too? Perhaps there is competition among the angels, and Gabriel and Raphael have won their rank by doing the maximum of worship on the minimum of grace! We shall know some day. In the meanwhile ' these are thy works, thou parent of all good!' Man eating man, eaten by man, in every variety of degree and method! Why does not some enthusiastic political economist write an epic on the 'Conservation of Cannibalism'?" (*Cheap Clothes and Nasty*, by Charles Kingsley.)

[2] The principal collaborator of Kingsley and Maurice, J. M. Ludlow, was well acquainted with the associations of French workmen and followed the movement of 1848 on the spot, after having passed his youth in France, where he was brought into close association with the doctrines of Buchez.

the individual, and Christianity alone had the power to communicate this motive force, — not dogmatic Christianity, but moral Christianity, the Christianity of Christ. Undertaking the emancipation of the poorer classes on the basis of Christianity, Kingsley, Maurice, and their friends themselves accepted the name of Christian Socialists. The association of Christianity and socialism seemed to them natural and imperative; in their eyes, the one was only the development and the expression of the other. The Bible was the book of the poor, of the downtrodden, the voice of God against the oppressor; and the most sacred duty of the representatives of the Church was to raise the condition of the poor and not to preach to them obedience and resignation. The socialism of the Christian Socialists, however, had nothing revolutionary about it: "We are teaching them . . . that true socialism, true liberty, brotherhood, and true equality (not the carnal, dead level equality of the Communist, but the spiritual equality of the Church idea, which gives every man an equal chance of developing and using God's gifts, and rewards every man according to his work, without respect of persons) is only to be found in loyalty and obedience to Christ." [1] Nor did the Christian Socialists call for the intervention of the State; they considered it a delusion and a snare to look to legislative enactments for social reform. To the Chartists, who demanded universal suffrage and the other "points" from Parliament, they said: "Do you believe that the Charter will make you free? The Charter is good if the men who use it are good." Society cannot be reconstructed by Acts of Parliament; everything depends upon man himself finding his path in God. Let all who are convinced of these truths unite, and they will be invincible.

In this spirit the Christian Socialists founded the co-operative tailors' association in London, in which wages were paid in proportion to the work done and in accordance with the capacity of the workman, but profits shared equally among all so long as each member had worked his best in the opinion of his comrades. The success of this association led to the formation of several others. Kingsley, Maurice, and their friends laboured devotedly for them, and were unremitting in their

[1] *Charles Kingsley, his Letters and Memories of his Life,* 3d edit. Lond. 1877, I, 248.

endeavours to propagate the idea of co-operation by means of lectures, pamphlets, newspapers, and works of fiction. Prejudices and animosities arose against them on all sides, from the ranks of the Church, from the orthodox school of political economy, from the middle class, who were frightened at the word "socialism" and alarmed by the events of June, 1848, in Paris. They met every attack with unshaken courage and pursued their labours. They obtained the legal recognition of co-operative societies from Parliament. Associations multiplied under the auspices of the central society managed by Kingsley and his friends. Their dream was to gradually cover the whole country with co-operative associations and make a reality of the principle inscribed at the head of their constitution:[1] "The human society is a body consisting of many members, not a collection of warring atoms." The results obtained by the societies brought about a reaction in their favour. But before long they began to decline, especially those formed for the purposes of production, and they eventually ended in a complete fiasco. The egoism inherent in human nature showed itself there as elsewhere; jealousy and rivalry broke out among the members; every one followed his own selfish impulses. The associations fell to pieces, some passing into the hands of a master spirit, others disappearing or splitting up into smaller bodies controlled by the detested principle of competition.

The experiment made by the Christian Socialists forms a touching episode in the social history of England, which will never fail to evoke feelings of admiration and gratitude towards the men who did not despair of humanity. But in making association the sovereign and absolute principle of social organization in despite of the selfish propensities of mankind, and in believing that Christianity, which had ceased to be the general creed, could supply the requisite motive power, they turned their backs upon the reality and doomed their plan of social synthesis to inevitable failure.

The four movements of revolt against individualism or latitudinarianism which I have just described took place

---

[1] Article I of the constitution of the "Association for promoting Industrial and Provident Societies."

about the same time.[1] Proceeding from different sources and acting on different sections of society, they exhibited a close affinity with one another, not only in the aim which they pursued but in their spirit and methods of action, which conducted them to the same negative result. Taking their rise in a nation considered the most practical and positive-minded on the face of the earth, they were marked by a disregard of the reality of things and a tendency in the direction of the absolute, as indeed was Benthamism against which they waged war. Inspired, not by pure reason like Bentham, but by imagination and inward impulse, their adherents also ignored the primary factor of the problem before them: some held that salvation could only be found in a return to theocracy, although the emancipation of the religious conscience had become an accomplished fact; others proposed to reunite the separate atoms of society by means of feudal sentiment, although the feudal spirit had passed out of it; others launched into violent invective against democracy and proclaimed that it was a "zero" when it was already beginning to manifest its power; others again met the absolute principle of self-interest as the basis of social equilibrium with the no less absolute principle of self-sacrifice and abnegation in order to bring about the same equilibrium. One and all imagined that they were prescribing an antidote for the malady, whereas they were only putting forward its antithesis. The synthesis was still to be discovered.

Coming straight from the heart, the appeals of Carlyle, Kingsley, Dickens, who preached to the public in his novels, and numbers of others found an echo in the heart, and contributed in no small measure to raise the moral tone of society, to soften class prejudices and animosities, to fill the gulf between rich and poor; on the whole, they influenced the feelings of the community, but did not modify its ideas, which had already taken the definite impress of individualism.

---

[1] The Oxford movement may be placed about 1833–1845; the Young England movement in the years 1837–1846; Carlyle's action extended over the same period and went beyond it; and the Christian Socialist movement covers the years 1848–1853.

FOURTH CHAPTER

DEFINITIVE TRIUMPH OF THE NEW ORDER OF THINGS

I

NEVERTHELESS the times were undoubtedly critical for the new conception of social order of which we have traced the origin and development; for the sentimental reaction provoked by the excesses of industrialism had left deep down in the heart one of those uneasy states of feeling which, however vague, daily and hourly preys upon the mind, and prepares the way for new and it may be still undefined convictions by undermining the old ones. Yet man is only too pleased to be reassured on the subject of his opinions, and a single word uttered with authority is often sufficient to dispel his doubts. The England of the years 1848–1860 received more than this; it obtained, or thought that it obtained, convincing proof that it was on the right path. The abolition of the duties on corn in 1846, and the other great free trade measure, the repeal of the Navigation Laws, passed in 1849, were followed by an unprecedented rise of commerce and industry.[1] The enthusiasm produced by this upward movement of the economic forces of England infected even for-

[1] The exports doubled in five years; their total rose from 50 to 100 millions sterling a year. Profits increased with still more surprising rapidity. "In the ten years from 1842 to 1852 the taxable income of the country increased by 6 per cent, but in the eight years from 1853 to 1861 the income of the country increased by 20 per cent. That is a fact so singular and striking as to seem almost incredible. . . . Besides the development of mechanical power and of locomotion, there is another cause which has been actively at work during the lifetime of our generation, and which especially belongs to the history of the last twenty years. I mean the wise legislation of Parliament which has sought for every opportunity of abolishing restrictions upon the application of capital and the exercise of industry and skill, and has made it a capital object of its policy to give full and free scope to the energies of the British nation. To this special cause appears especially to belong most of what is peculiar in the experiences of the period I have named so far as regards the increase of the national wealth" (Speech of Mr. Gladstone, Chancellor of the Exchequer, on the Budget of 1863, *Hansard*, CLXX, p. 244).

eigners,[1] and the prosperity which it diffused in every section of the community, the working classes included, allayed discontent and proved the value of a system based on the unfettered play of interests.

Theory in its turn supplied a doctrinal consecration of the facts. The Manchester School undertook to bring this home to the middle class. The "Manchester men" belonged to the trading and manufacturing classes, and were by no means given to abstract ideas; but the economic aspect of the doctrine of "laissez-faire" recommended it to them, and being under the impression that this maxim supplied a general solution of all practical wants they made it their exclusive theory of life. According to the Manchester School unrestrained competition the abstention of the State from all interference with the production and distribution of wealth, whether in favour of the rich or the poor, in other words free trade between citizens and nations, was in the nature of a divine law,[2] extending its beneficial influence to the material and moral sphere, to the internal life of a country and its international relations. By allowing every man to make the most lucrative use of his abilities, free competition would foster self-confidence, manly independence and self-respect in the individual. In directing human effort toward a pacific rivalry in the field of industry, free trade would ensure peace between the nations to the greater glory of civilization and its uninterrupted development.[3] The policy

1 Léon Faucher, in his *Études sur l'Angleterre*, indulges in these transports as follows: " It is said that when Montbrun's cuirassiers poured through the breach into the redoubt of Borodino, which the Russians had defended so desperately, an English officer, who was looking on at the carnage as an amateur was so carried away by his admiration that he forgot the horrors of the scene and the intensity of the struggle, and exclaimed, ' Well done, Frenchmen this is a sight one only sees once in a lifetime.' And we too may lay aside the rivalry of war and industry in order to heartily applaud this expansion of commercial genius which has exacted tribute from every nation. There is a sympathetic force in the great and beautiful which fascinates the mind in spite of itself, and makes man feel that he belongs to humanity first, and to his country afterwards" (Vol. I, p. 190).

2 The "international law of the Almighty," according to Cobden's expression.

3 "Free trade! what is it? Why, breaking down the barriers that separate nations; those barriers behind which nestle the feelings of pride, revenge hatred, and jealousy, which every now and then burst their bounds, and deluge whole countries with blood; those feelings which nourish the poison of war and conquest, which assert that without conquest we can have no trade, which

of States was therefore clearly prescribed, and might be summed up in the words "peace, retrenchment, economy": to live in peace with one's neighbours; not to meddle with the affairs of other countries on the high-sounding pretext of national dignity and international rank; not to crush the subject with taxation and to let him grow rich in his own way.[1]

A philosophy of sordid manufacturers and shopkeepers, according to the opponents of the Manchester School, it was less narrow than people are generally inclined to admit in our day. Its exaggerated faith in the moral force of industry was shared by idealists and lofty dreamers like the Saint-Simonians, who looked on industry as a religious function and applied the word "cult" to its organization. "Everything by and for industry" was Saint-Simon's motto. In his view, as well as in that of his adherents, industry emphasized the law of progress and established the reign of work in place of idleness, privilege, and brute force. It was therefore natural that the Manchester School should agree with the formulas of Saint-Simonism: "to each man according to his capacity, to each capacity according to its work;" "organization of industry and consequently no more war." The two schools differed as to the best method of organizing industry, the Saint-Simonians advocating universal association founded on love and the Manchester School looking to universal competition; but the final result was intended to be the same, — the happiness of mankind. Full of love and good-will towards men in general, a sworn enemy of national chauvinism, waging war against aristocratic privileges and the "landlord spirit" in the political and social life of England, in order to set the free development of the individual on an impregnable basis, the Manchester School was, on the whole, far more of a democratic than a "bourgeois" movement.[2] Its doctrines were, in fact, the vul-

foster that love for conquest and dominion which sends forth your warrior chiefs to scatter devastation throughout other lands, and then calls them back that they may be enthroned securely in your passions, but only to harass and oppress you at home" (*Cobden's Speeches*, edit. in one vol., by John Bright, Lond. 1878, p. 401).

[1] " I don't feel sympathy for a great nation or those who desire the greatness of a people by the vast extensions of empire. What I like to see is the growth, development, and elevation of the individual man" (*Ibid.* 467).

[2] Cobden writes (in a letter of the 5th of January, 1849, addressed to J. Combe): "It is this moral sentiment more than the £ *s. d.* view of the

gate of the gospel of rationalist individualism for the use of traders and manufacturers.[1]

II

About the same time a fresh version of that gospel was put forth which seemed like a new revelation. From the lofty realms of thought came a message, delivered in a tone which seemed to brush aside all doubt for the future, that the independence of the individual in the State was an eternal verity reposing on the foundations of reason. The intellectual élite of the nation, who had been somewhat unsettled by Carlyle and others, recovered or rather were confirmed in their creed, and hailed the man to whom they were indebted for this relief, — John Stuart Mill. For more than a quarter of a century he kept them under the spell of his eloquence and logic, and having once acquired a hold on their mind he influenced it for many years to come.

Mill's doctrine was in substance the same as Bentham's. He started with the same utilitarian theory of life, and took his stand on the same method of observation and experience. In his eyes too man can only desire and pursue what is pleasant to him. But, he maintains in opposition to Bentham, to arrive at a correct estimate of pleasures they ought not to be valued only by their quantity, but by their quality as well. It is better to be a discontented man than a satisfied hog. The most perfect pleasures being those which are the most elevated in their nature, the path which the individual must take to attain his own happiness is that which leads to the welfare of the human race. In this sense personal happiness can only be fully

matter which impels me to undertake the advocacy of a reduction of our forces. It was a kindred sentiment (more than the material view of the question) which actuated me on the Corn Law and free trade question. It would enable me to die happy if I could feel the satisfaction of having in some degree contributed to the partial disarmament of the world " (*Life of Cobden*, by J. Morley, II, 42).

[1] " Cobdenism was an intruder in the line of legitimate succession " of the Radicalism which has been continually driving in an anti-" laissez-faire " direction if we are to believe an English publicist of the "Fabian socialist " school ("Socialism in English Politics," by W. Clarke, *Polit. Science Quarterly*, N.Y., December, 1889). It is hardly necessary to point out the incorrectness of this assertion, which merely supplies a fresh instance of the mania which parvenus have for providing themselves with a line of ancestry.

realized in the general welfare, and egoism to become a reality must identify itself with altruism.   There is nothing impossible in this; for a state of society is so natural, so indispensable, and so habitual to man that, by virtue of the psychological process of association of ideas peculiar to him, he cannot help linking the conception of his own destiny to that of society, and eventually feels a sort of intellectual inability to keep them apart.   This association, of which man's intelligence is at once the seat and the instrument, grows stronger and stronger in proportion as mankind progresses.   " In the comparatively early state of human advancement in which we now live, a person cannot indeed feel that entireness of sympathy with all others, which would make any real discordance in the general direction of their conduct in life impossible."   But this state of civilization is only a step in the scale which mankind will ascend in its continual progress towards perfection. .

Pending the arrival of the millennium, in which the individual will consider his own happiness as inseparable from the general welfare, what line of conduct should society pursue with regard to the individual ?   Society, replies Mill in his essay on *Liberty*, must leave the individual to himself in all that concerns him; it can only interfere with his freedom of action on the ground of self-protection ; his own good, either physical or moral, is not a sufficient warrant for interference; " over himself, over his own body and mind, the individual is sovereign."   The reasons for restricting individual liberty which might commend themselves to society can only be used as arguments for reasoning with and persuading the individual, but not for compelling him.   It is all the same whether the compulsion is moral and not material.   Again, liberty does not consist only of political liberty, as we have been accustomed to understand it; that is only one aspect of liberty.   Side by side with the despotism of the State there is another tyranny of a not less oppressive kind, that of opinion and of manners and customs, and it is from the undue pressure of their yoke just as much as from the bondage of institutions that Mill wishes to deliver the individual.   And he puts forward these demands not on the ground of abstract reason, of some categorical imperative, but on that of interest.   Just as the mere operation of satisfying the individual desire for pleasure ought to make for the general happiness, so liberty ought to be vouchsafed to the individual on account of its utility : " Mankind are greater gainers by suffering each other to live as seems good to themselves, than by compelling each to live as seems good to the rest."

If the independence of the individual determined by his interest in all that concerns him is the proper basis of the moral and social existence of man, there is at least equally good reason for treating it as the guiding principle of his material existence in the pursuit of wealth and its production and distribution. As an economist Mill, while he pays far more attention than his predecessors to society, to the whole community, and to the sacrifices which the individual owes to it, none the less sets up as a matter of principle that " letting alone should be the general practice : every departure from it, unless required by some great good, is a certain evil." Mill considers competition as " not pernicious, but useful and indispensable." He is opposed to large properties, to entail, and generally to every institution in the economic sphere which is a hindrance to the individual and impedes the free play of activity in the humblest members of society.

The principle which thus prescribes the relations of men in a state of society makes the political form of that society, the form of its government, a foregone conclusion. If " each is the only safe guardian of his own rights and interests," it is clear that all ought to have a share in the sovereign power. If any members, whoever they may be, are excluded therefrom, their interests are left without the guarantee accorded to the others, and they themselves have less scope and encouragement for their energy and fewer opportunities for displaying their individuality. But as the whole population cannot personally take part in public affairs, it follows that the ideal type of a perfect government is representative government.

The method adopted by John Stuart Mill in arriving at these conclusions, which bear the stamp of the purest Benthamism, was in reality precisely, as in Bentham's case, that of abstract reasoning. The tendency of all men towards a happiness realized in the general welfare is simply a postulate foreign to all experience. The bridge of association of ideas which connects the happiness of the individual with the general welfare,

however ingeniously constructed, is nevertheless entirely built
of ideal pieces of timber, intended to support imaginary pas-
sengers. In point of fact, perfect association of ideas implies
a perfect intelligence. The appeal to a more advanced state
of civilization, required for the complete realization of these
hypotheses, is merely a fresh development of abstract reasoning, speculating on man not as he is but as he may be some
day. He will indubitably become so, according to Mill, thanks
to education which is all-powerful and, like a seal with melting
wax, can mould man to any shape required. But is this, again,
an induction supplied by experience ?

Not only in the domain of morals, but in the political sphere,
which from one end to the other is pre-eminently that of the
relative, Mill's subject is invariably man, viewed through the
optimist medium of infinite perfectibility, whom free discussion suffices to enlighten in the pursuit of his own happiness,
and whose aptitude for seeking it gives him the right to independence in society. Composed, therefore, of individual interests coexisting in a somewhat mechanical combination, but too
numerous to be directly adjusted to each other, Mill's political
society ends by being a joint-stock company provided with an
electoral machinery ·for its government, just as individual
morality is brought by Mill under a mechanism of ideas which
effects their association and "constitutes the moral faculty in
man." The better the association of ideas, the nearer man will
be brought to his moral aim. In the same way, the more perfect the electoral machinery, the more perfect will be the government of States. This is why Mill was overjoyed when the
improvement of the electoral machinery proposed by Hare, the
author of proportional representation, was brought to his notice.
The very destiny of mankind was involved in his eyes : "This
great discovery," he relates, "inspired me with new and more
sanguine hopes respecting the prospects of human society."

Thus John Stuart Mill, while rejecting the notion of right
as a basis for society, so as to avoid falling into the error of
the French ideologists, none the less constructed a system
which resembled theirs. It could hardly be otherwise, for in
both cases the materials used were the same. Mill's French
predecessors in utilitarianism. the Helvetiuses and the Hol-
bachs, who had also adopted personal interest as the social

principle, arrived at the same political conclusions as Rousseau
and his followers, from whom they were separated by a gulf
in morals and psychology; for both schools reasoned by way of
deduction on "man," on the human monad. The co-ordination
of all particular interests with the general interest, demanded
by the materialists, or the absorption of all individual wills
into one general will, advocated by Jean Jacques, came to the
same thing for the constitutional legislator, there being only
one person in whom the "particular interests" and the "individual wills" are vested, that is "man," the human monad.
Bentham, therefore, who operated on the same subject, and
used the same method of abstract reasoning, found himself
after all, in spite of his protests, in complete agreement with
the French rationalists of the eighteenth century, and his dis-
ciple, John Stuart Mill, who had criticised the "geometric or
abstract method" so sharply, was in his turn landed in the
same result.

While thus reproducing Bentham's doctrine with absolute
fidelity, Mill tempered it with certain elements which, without
taking from it much of its essence and practical significance or
remedying its defects, gave it an aspect which was of supreme
importance for its success with the public. Taking the desire
for pleasure as the starting-point of human actions, Mill imports
into it the loftier standard of *quality*, justifies it by the "sense
of *dignity* all human beings possess in one form or other," and
ends by placing the criterion of utilitarian morality not,
like Bentham, in the agent's own greatest happiness, but in
the greatest amount of happiness altogether, and this not because the general welfare is the concomitant of the welfare of
the individual, because there is a material identity between
them, so that man has only to follow his inclination and harmony will come of itself, but because man himself enthrones
this harmony in his own intelligence, because he creates the
association of the individual's happiness with the general welfare in his own mind.

Inheriting all the doctrines of individualist political economy,
Mill inaugurates his succession by throwing the doors wide
open to his opponents, without, however, allowing them to take
up their abode within the precincts; he tones down the strictness of the principle of "laissez-faire"; he goes beyond all

his predecessors in admitting exceptions to the dogma of the orthodox economists, and comes forward himself as the exponent of them. He even goes so far as to embrace the heresy which denies the sanctity of property; he declines to recognize it in the case of land, but admits it spontaneously in the case of income derived from labour and from capital; the *rent* of land, the unearned increment of the soil, due to social causes independent of man, ought, according to Mill, to be used for the good of the community, whereas income derived from labour and capital is created by man's efforts and is a manifestation of human personality. Finally, as a crowning indulgence to his adversaries, the socialists, he admits that private property is only one of the possible types of distribution of wealth, and that it may disappear *some day or other.*

Mill is more uncompromising in regard to the ideal form of government; for every people that has passed the stage of infancy representative democracy is the best possible government, but he himself admits its "infirmities and dangers," and tries to discover remedies for them.

In every department, in politics, in morals, in political economy, Mill makes extensive concessions to his adversaries, and by these very inconsistencies in his doctrine he accentuates its success; he not only conveys to the public the seductive impression of impartiality and sincerity, of boldness and openness of mind, but he allays discontent and silences the misgivings aroused by the uncompromising character of Bentham's doctrine, and wins the sympathy which was being attracted towards his opponents.

In spite of all the concessions and advances made by Mill, which were more in the nature of embroidery on the surface of the Benthamite pattern, his criterion in the moral, social, and political sphere still remained the individual; all social and political relations are viewed by Mill with reference to their power of acting on the individual; [1] but the interest of the indi-

---

[1] The individual pursues the general welfare in his own happiness, because this is the path which will conduct him to an "ideal nobility of will and conduct." Liberty ought to be the leading principle in society, for "it is only the cultivation of individuality which produces or can produce well-developed human beings." And when Mill advocates the intervention of the State, as for instance to enforce on parents the obligation of educating their chil-

vidual is presented in a new light, far more attractive than
Bentham's, the taint of selfishness which clung to it disappears,
and Bentham's rude fetish [1] appears henceforth encircled with
a halo of idealism.

The transformation thus wrought in the body of the doctrine
is still further set off by a charm peculiar to the writer, by a
spirit glowing with generous affection for the masses, for
obscure and humble folk.   All Mill's writings are permeated
by a deep sympathy for the working classes, and an intense
desire to raise them in the material and the moral scale.   As
the Bible was the book of the poor and oppressed in the eyes
of the Christian Socialists, so under Mill's pen political economy
became the worker's book, instead of being a cold and unrelenting exposition of "general laws," under which the weak
were to be crushed as under the car of Juggernaut.   Everywhere between the lines of Mill's writings, under the smooth
and tranquil surface of his logic, there is the same sympathetic
and loving spirit flowing like a strong current.   The imagination is at home in them as well as the reason.   The treatise
on *Utilitarianism* may be called the philosophic hymn of a
mystery resembling the Christian Sacrament of Transubstan-

---

dren, it is with a view to the final result; for "instruction, when it is really
such . . . strengthens as well as enlarges the active faculties: in whatever
manner acquired, its effect on the mind is favorable to the spirit of independence." Mill allows unrestricted competition in the economic sphere, because
"to be protected against competition is to be protected in idleness, in mental
dullness." He condemns the aristocratic form of property because it checks
the expansion of individuality; and he extols the system of small landed
properties because it makes men, and inspires the peasant proprietor with
the consciousness that "he is a free human being, and not perpetually a
child, which seems to be the approved condition of the labouring classes
according to the prevailing philanthropy." The various forms of government
are appraised by the same standard.   "The first question in respect to any
political institution is, How far they tend to foster in the members of the
community the various desirable qualities, moral and intellectual." The
answer to this question is decisive as to the merits of democracy.   Under
a system of absolute government what sort of human beings can be formed,
in what way can their faculties of reflection and action be developed?   "The
maximum of the invigorating effect of freedom upon the character is only
obtained, when the person acted on either is, or is looking forward to becoming a citizen as fully privileged as any other."

[1] "No subtlety, no metaphysics; no need to consult Plato or Aristotle.
Pain and pleasure are felt as such by every man, by the peasant as well as
the monarch, by the unlearned man as well as the philosopher" (quoted
above, p. 34).

tiation: just as the Christian communicates with Christ, with
His soul and His godhead by means of the elements of bread
and wine which satisfy the gross bodily appetites, so man following his own interests ends, by means of the association of
ideas, in realizing the general happiness, the welfare of mankind. The essay on *Liberty* is another hymn, and, like the
Song of Solomon, an anthem of love, in which the lover and
his beloved are man and freedom of thought, and certainly the
attractions of this freedom are not set forth with less eloquence
in Mill's syllogisms than are the charms of the Shulamite in
the stanzas of the royal poet. But to enjoy the happiness
proffered by Mill there is no need of Christian grace or of the
favour of the daughter of Jerusalem; it is sufficient to be man.
Mill invariably speaks as a cosmopolite; his subject is "man
and his fellows," "man," and "mankind."

The entire formula of the French Revolution — Liberty,
Equality, and Fraternity — was expressed by Mill's writings,
but in the old English fashion, without pathetic gestures, or
loud tones, or sentimental outpourings; simply arguments
presented with all the semblance of scientific exactness, language remarkable for lucidity and distinctness, and with nothing metaphysical about it; general propositions always linked
to reflections taken from the sphere of reality and plentifully
supported by facts, and a constant attention to practical considerations, to results. In a society which prides itself, or at
all events used to pride itself, on controlling its emotions by
reason, and verifying reason by experience, Mill's language
proved the best conductor of the new social and political fluid.
The feelings awakened by Carlyle, Dickens, and others were
led by Mill into the channels of logic and science. This was
his great achievement, and this was what gave him his power
over opinion, and in particular his influence with the rising
generation, which combines the enthusiasm of the intellect and
of the heart, or, to put it in another way, thinks it is following
reason while it is really only obeying its emotional impulses.
Mill sustained and exalted its impulses by providing food for
its reason, and *vice versa*. "The younger generation," as a
contemporary observer remarks, "were a good deal stirred by
Carlyle; but Carlyle, after all, woke people up, and made them
look out of the window to see what was the matter, after which

most of them went to bed again and slept comfortably. His cries were rather too inarticulate to furnish anything like a new gospel, and he never took hold of the intellectual class. But Mill did." [1] With induction for his sail, and catching the humanitarian breeze which was "moving upon the face of the waters," he brought abstract rationalism with faith in reason and confidence in theory safely to their moorings, and he made English society renew its alliance with radical individualism, thus forcing it still further in the direction whither this individualism was tending, that is, towards disbelief in the traditional order of things and a general levelling of political and social conditions.

III

Everything conspired to give an impulse to this intellectual movement. Contemporary thought produced no doctrines to compete with those of Mill, and individualism was left without a rival in the domain of speculation. The only opposition which it encountered came from sentimentalism in its various aspects, ecclesiastical, feudal, and social. The weapons used by the latter had a sharper edge, but were too short to reach its powerful adversary, entrenched behind a rampart of ideas and facts. Slightly touched, but in no way overcome by these appeals to sentiment, public opinion barely paid them an occasional tribute, of which the factory legislation was the most important practical manifestation. These emotional outbreaks and legislative enactments were only exceptions confirming the rule. The English mind was engrossed by individualism, and remained inaccessible to all other teaching for years to come. Profound disillusions and terrible shocks produced by events in the outer world were required to make English society probe its conscience afresh. [2]

[1] English correspondent of the New York *Nation*, 1873, Vol. 16, p. 350.
[2] It is not till after 1868, when the early years of the official reign of Liberalism have disappointed the sanguine hopes of radical enthusiasm which preceded them, — it is not till after the war of 1870 that John Stuart Mill's political doctrines and the philosophy of individualism are seriously disputed, and "the paltry commonplaces (of liberty, equality, and fraternity), which are so popular amongst us" (in England), are contrasted with "the well-regulated, disciplined energy which planted the German flags on the walls of Paris." This is the way in which Sir James Stephen, who made the first vigorous attack on Mill in his *Liberty, Equality, and Fraternity* (Lond. 1873),

Enjoying a monopoly in the province of thought, individualism was no less free from counteracting forces in the practical sphere. The latter were suppressed or prevented from operating by the lukewarmness which characterized public life after the triumph of the middle class and by the want of political education in the country. Instead of impeding the rise of rationalist individualism, as might be supposed at the first blush, this state of things rather assisted it than otherwise: the moral vacuum which it created supplied a field for abstract ideas.

The political education of the masses in fact was not in a much more advanced condition than it had been before the Reform Bill. While displaying more intelligence and generosity in this respect than the aristocracy, the middle class which attained power after 1832 did not modify the general aspect of things. From the second quarter of the century private initiative no doubt made laudable efforts to diffuse instruction among adults by means of Mechanics' Institutes and other agencies for organizing classes and lectures as well as by cheap publications. But when they were not paralyzed by the clergy or the orthodox folk whom it stirred up, these efforts missed their mark in two ways: they did not reach the mechanics and the masses for whom they were destined, it was the lower middle class alone which benefited by them; besides this the teaching provided was often too technical, too utilitarian, with too slight an admixture of real mental culture and no political instruction at all. As for the latter, there was no one anxious to promote it, nor was the ground sufficiently prepared for it by general instruction. In 1807, when the Whitbread Bill, which proposed to establish a system of popular instruction, was being debated, the least reactionary of its opponents said: "The increase of this sort of introduction to knowledge would only tend to make the people study politics and lay them open to the arts of designing men."[1] The Whigs, who filled the political stage after 1832, did not propound maxims of this kind, but they certainly were not disinclined to believe in the mischief which would result if the people took to "studying

comments on his own book in a letter to his German translator (published in the German edition *Die Schlagwörter Freiheit, Gleichheit, Brüderlichkeit* in ihrer ethischen, socialen, und politischen Anwendung, Berlin, 1874).

[1] *Hansard*, IX, 548, Speech of Mr. Windham.

politics." Several of them, it is true, talked from time to time
of the political education of the masses,[1] but took scarcely any
steps to carry out the idea.[2] A small élite of workingmen in
the towns succeeded, by dint of individual energy, in reaching
the tree of knowledge, from which they hastily plucked the
unripe fruit of general ideas and flung them at the governing
classes, whose rule was attended by so much misery among the
people : " All men are born free " — " God has given men equal
liberties and equal rights " — " We demand justice before
charity."[3] The masses had no opportunity of acquiring even
elementary knowledge. There were not many schools in the
country, and they were attached to the Churches or kept
by private individuals. The State paid as good as no heed
to public instruction ; its intervention was confined to grants
amounting to £20,000 a year, since the year 1833. The few
schools which existed were in a wretched state, both as regards
housing and teaching.[4] Public instruction did not form part

[1] Lord Brougham said : " Why should not political, as well as all other
works, be published in a cheap form, and in Numbers ? . . . It is highly useful to the community that the true principles of the constitution, ecclesiastical
and civil, should be well understood by every man who lives under it " (*Practical Observations upon the Education of the People*, Lond. 1825, pp. 4, 5).
Thirty years afterwards Lord Aberdeen, alarmed at the dictatorial power
assumed by the Press over the public, returned to the charge : " We must
educate by all the means in our power, and we shall be able to trust the
people more safely with their own concerns " (Letter of the 6th of January
1855, to Croker, *Croker Papers*, III, 350). Just as twelve years later, Robert
Lowe, alarmed in his turn by the admission of the urban populations to political power, exclaimed : " We must educate our masters."

[2] Owing to Lord Brougham's efforts, assisted by leading Whigs, a great
" Society for the Propagation of Useful Knowledge " was founded, for the
publication and circulation of short popular treatises. The numerous volumes which it published related to physics, chemistry, mechanics, astronomy
but not to politics, past or present, " on which it was impossible to touch
without provoking angry discussion." A long time afterwards and solely at
the request of its president, Brougham, it decided to bring out a politica
series, inaugurated by a work of Lord Brougham himself. This was his
Political Philosophy (Lond. 1842), which, apart from the intrinsic value of
the book, presents a curious example of an error common to many educators
of the lower classes, which consists in addressing them as if they had received
a literary training, with the result that the teaching is entirely lost upon them
The " political series " did not get beyond this work.

[3] These were the mottoes on the banner under which the Chartist procession
marched to Parliament with the monster petition.

[4] The following is taken from a description of the state of the elementary
schools about the year 1840 : " A minimum education has been given at a

of the traditions of the Tory party. The Whig party, who claimed to be the friend of the people and of enlightenment, was largely composed for the most part of Nonconformists, divided into rival sects. Not being able to agree as to what religious education should be given, that is to say, whether the Bible should be read with or without commentary, they preferred not to open any schools at all. Here and there one or two public men, who were not blinded by party passion and spite, were deeply pained by this state of things, but their isolation rendered them powerless. "The greatest of all causes," exclaimed Richard Cobden, "has no *locus standi* in Parliament."[1] A few years afterwards, when the Liberal party was again agitating for the extension of the suffrage, Cobden, who was in favour of a radical reform, wondered what would be the result in view of the ignorance of the masses. "Without the cordial sympathy and the co-operation of the masses, our electoral system will become as soulless a thing as that which lately existed in France."[2]

Nor was the practical school for learning this co-operation, that supplied by institutions, within the reach of the general public or frequented by those who had access to it. The old local self-government, as we have seen, had been taken to pieces and had not been reconstructed or completely recast. The middle class rather turned away from public life. Not only munici-

---

minimum cost. Babies of eight and ten years old were set to teach other babies of the same age ; . . . writing-desks were few, scanty, and fixed to the walls. . . . Of apparatus there was little but a few slates ; of maps there was perhaps one, a meagre map of Palestine ; of books there were scarcely any but the Holy Bible. In the Holy Bible used as a primer, little children were drilled in spelling and reading ; and their arithmetic was too often drawn from the same source. . . . In order to give the children a reverence for sacred things, the sums set were drawn from historical statements of numbers in the Holy Scriptures. 'There were 12 patriarchs, 12 apostles, and 4 evangelists ; add the patriarchs and evangelists together ; subtract the apostles ; what is the remainder?' 'Solomon had so many wives and so many concubines ; add the concubines to the wives, and state the result.' . . . The buildings were low, thin, dingy, ill-drained, often without means of warming, often without proper conveniences ; with no furniture but a teacher's desk, a few rickety forms, a rod, a cane, and a fool's cap. The floor was almost invariably of brick, the worst kind of floor" (*Address on National Education* by Harry Chester, quoted in J. Hole's "*Light! more Light!*" On the present state of education amongst the working classes of Leeds. Lond. 1860).

[1] Letter from Cobden to J. Combe, dated Nov. 5, 1850 (Morley's *Life*, II, 84).

[2] Letter from Cobden to John Bright, dated Nov. 9, 1853 (*Ibid.* p. 147).

pal business, but parliamentary elections, had little interest for
them. This was particularly the case with the higher strata
of the new ruling class, — the upper middle class. Abstention from voting, which was very common in the constituencies, increased in proportion to the wealth of the voters.
"They" (the rich), we read in an official inquiry, "think it
beneath their dignity to go and vote."[1]   And why should they
trouble their heads ?   Did not the Palmerston Ministry, under
which parties were grouped in a sort of truce, provide them
with "a strong government" and "a safe government," which
would take care not to start schemes of reform or raise other
awkward questions worthy of philosophers and theorists ?   To
prevent the calm degenerating into stagnation, there was the
foreign policy of Palmerston, who had long become a passed
master in the art of addressing arrogant challenges to neighbouring countries and tyrannizing over the weak.   There was
enough to stir the blood of the Briton and flatter "the egre-
gious vanity of the beast," as Cobden said.   With the refrain
of *Civis Romanus sum* resounding in their ears, the ruling
classes of England sat quietly under their vines and their fig-
trees.   The House of Commons enjoyed a calm and peaceable
existence.   Nothing was taken tragically or seriously in it, as
befits an assembly of well-bred people, of "gentlemen," of
whom Palmerston was the perfect type and model.   The
debates led to no loss of temper, and very often the sittings
came to an end for want of a quorum; "counting out has now
become a regular institution," said Sir W. Molesworth in 1862.
Even the advanced Radicals laid down their arms and waited
for the death of Palmerston, who appeared to incarnate in his
person the England of the past and in whom it seemed to
survive itself.

IV

These intervals of apathy and indifference in the life of a
nation are the most favourable of all for "philosophers and
theorists," who fill the unoccupied space, which they find
before them, with their philosophy and their theories, what-

[1] From the evidence of an election agent before a committee of the House
of Lords (*Blue Books*, 1860, Reports from Committees, XII, 174).   Other evidence to the same effect was given before the committee (*Ibid.* pp. 72, 240).

ever the intrinsic value of these may be; the *horror vacui* is
still more true of the moral than of the physical world. Just
as in the latter the force of penetration of a body is in the
direct ratio of its mass, and in the inverse ratio of the consistency of the substance which it enters; so the greater the
weakness of the mind the greater the facility with which it
admits an idea, and the more comprehensive the idea the more
easily it takes possession of the mind. Accordingly in the
social sphere the less firmness there is in the public mind and
the less intensity in public life, the more society is exposed to
the invasion of general ideas, provided that there is sufficient
motive force behind them. This force is often created by the
very condition of stagnation which it is about to attack; for
want of action the élite of the nation turns to the world of
thought, and there prepares and gathers the explosive material
destined to produce a more or less marked upheaval of society.

This was the very process at work in England during the
years 1846–1865, and under particularly favourable conditions.
Although the boundaries of the political system had been considerably extended since 1832, although it occupied a much
larger area, public spirit, as we have seen, had not expanded
in proportion. The result was that with a greater number
of persons brought into political life, there was relatively
less political activity than in the former period. The State
was no longer uppermost in the thoughts of society. The
sphere of social influence covered by politics was contracting,
and at the same time the importance of the principles at stake
in political warfare, as well as its emotional attraction, dwindled in proportion as the grave questions which had exercised
the minds of succeeding generations, such as parliamentary
reform, religious liberty, and free trade, were disposed of.
The élite of the community, relieved so to speak of their
functions, had recourse to thought. Consequently when
John Stuart Mill entered the field with his great writings, he found a far more numerous public to listen to and
applaud him than the Philosophical Radicals of five-and-
twenty or thirty years back could have addressed. A Young
England party was in process of formation, but different to
that imagined by Disraeli, with aspirations turned not towards
the past but towards the future, with faith in the vivifying

power, not of social traditions, but of the "Reason of Man," which really indicates the "landmarks of human action and human progress." A new spirit passed over the old Universities, their mediæval atmosphere underwent a change, the outer air of philosophy, of criticism, of true science entered by their Gothic windows. Oxford, till lately the stronghold of orthodoxy, the home of Tractarianism, became a hot-bed for the new ideas. Young men of good family were among their most zealous devotees. The influence of philosophy and of the new science of sociology readily accepted as such was reinforced by natural science with its methods of exact observation and uncompromising analysis, which rejected every authority and every idea incapable of making good its title, and of allowing it to be verified at any moment before the permanent tribunal of reason. John Stuart Mill and Professor Goldwin Smith, Darwin and Huxley, Herbert Spencer, who was on the threshold of his great philosophical career, Buckle, and many other thinkers of less eminence conjointly exercised an intellectual dictatorship over English society. Foreign influences, notably Positivism and its religion of humanity, added their quota. Each working in his own sphere, they all helped to discredit the past, to substitute the power of reason for that of tradition, to diffuse enthusiasm for ideas with belief in a continual advance towards a better state of things, and in the final triumph of the cause of progress in spite of the obstacles which tend to block its path. The new spirit of investigation and criticism invaded regions which seemed forever closed to it, as for instance that of theology. Members of the University, Doctors of Divinity, clergymen of the Established Church, Bishops even applied the canons of scientific criticism to the Scriptures as to any other book. In vain did scandalized orthodoxy protest and call for punishment of the destroyers of the faith, the representatives of the secular power itself either refused to interfere or treated them with sarcasm and contempt.[1]   Very

---

[1] The case which made the most stir in this respect was that of the collection of *Essays and Reviews*, written by several clerical and lay members of the University of Oxford. The freedom and broad-mindedness of their theology created a sensation. The champions of orthodoxy took legal proceedings against some of these writers in the ecclesiastical courts, but were defeated on appeal to the Judicial Committee of the Privy Council. Eventually they

soon nothing was safe from doubt.   Every principle was impugned, every subject discussed.   British phlegm invested this
intellectual process with something of the impassive sternness
which attends the operations of the dissecting-room.   The
existence of God was put to the vote without fuss and without
animation.   The spirit of tolerance appeared in society to an
extent hitherto unknown; the boldest flights of thought, the
most daring speculations of the intellect, ranged unmolested.
For the bulk of society this freedom was attributable far more
to the decay of the old faith than to the progress of the new
one, as is generally the case in situations of this kind, which
are characterized by a sort of moral truce of God, due not
so much to the elevation as to the relaxation of the public
mind.   In England after the year 1855, as in France a century
before, the doubt and negation produced by the earnest medi-
tations and settled convictions of a small group of leading
spirits spread over society like a noxious vapour, blighting
the old creeds which had lost the vivifying principle of true
faith.   Lacking the strength of mind to discard its old ideas
and prejudices, and without the force of character to uphold
them, society let them slumber on, while assuming to outward appearances an air of conventional indifference.   The
facetious and frivolous tone of which Palmerston set the
fashion in Parliament and which extended outside its
walls, contributed to that atmosphere of amiable scepticism
which constitutes the charm of periods of transition, and
which gave rise to Talleyrand's saying: " Celui qui n'a pas

---

succeeded in getting the book condemned by Convocation, the representative
assembly of the Established Church.   The decisions of Convocation being
subject to the approval of the Crown, the Government was interrogated in the
House of Lords as to the course which they proposed to pursue.   The Lord
Chancellor, who is the "keeper of the King's conscience," of the conscience
of the "defender of the faith," replied that the excommunication launched
by Convocation did not so much as deserve the attention of the Government.
"There are three modes," he explained, "of dealing with Convocation when
it is permitted to come into action and transact real business.   The first is,
while they are harmlessly busy, to take no notice of their proceedings: the
second is, when they seem likely to get into mischief, to prorogue and put an
end to their proceedings; and the third, when they have done something
clearly beyond their powers, is to bring them before a court of justice and
punish them."   The "synodical condemnation" of a work, pronounced by
Convocation, appeared to the Lord Chancellor to belong to the category of
harmless acts of which no notice need be taken.

vécu dans les dernières années de l'ancien régime n'a pas connu la douceur de vivre."

The fashionable scepticism which invaded society and the stagnation arising from the decrepitude of political parties weakened the leading section of the ruling classes just as the increase of wealth enervated the rank and file. While their strength of character departed and their capacity for resistance declined, the tide of radicalism continued to mount. The untoward events and the disappointments of the Crimean War provoked a series of attacks on the existing régime and the spirit which it embodied. The public demanded that full light should be thrown on the military administration, that the reign of aristocratic favouritism should come to an end, and that personal merit, irrespective of birth, should be recognized as the sole qualification for public honours and appointments. The language of the Press became unusually violent; it attacked everything and everybody in the most unsparing manner.[1] The repeal of the paper duties, in 1860, gave a considerable impulse to the growth of the cheap Press and at the same time to the spirit of opposition and criticism. Literature reflected the same tendency. "It is incontestable," notes Montalembert, "that bitter and violent abuse of aristocratic ideas and habits is gradually becoming the dominant note in political discussion and historical study." [2] "We must not disguise the fact," insists the same observer, "that a whole literary and political school is endeavouring to imbue the English people with a dislike for their time-honoured institutions and with a desire to ape Continental democracy." [3]

Tinged as they are with bitterness, these impressions of the famous Catholic champion none the less faithfully reflect the intellectual movement of the time. A feeling entered men's minds, like a thorn penetrating the flesh, that England was far behind other nations, that from head to foot there was something antiquated and mouldy about her. It made no difference that this or that old institution was working well, *expediency*

---

[1] Greville, alarmed at the attitude of the Press, exclaims: "The Press, with the *Times* at its head, is striving to throw everything into confusion. . . . They diffuse through the country a mass of inflammatory matter" (*Memoirs*, VII, 247).

[2] *De l'avenir politique de l'Angleterre*, Paris, 1856, p. 51.

[3] *Ibid.* p. 56.

was no longer the national divinity to whom exclusive honours were paid, the people had run after " strange gods," and their eyes were opened to the perception of *anomalies*. A new tone became observable in the language of politics. At one time, under the influence of the scientific methods of the day, the jargon of science was applied to politics. At another time, writers in the Press and speakers at public meetings affected the style of natural right. " Men of Birmingham, if I can call you men, who do not possess the suffrage," were the words with which John Bright began one of his speeches in 1859. Mr. Gladstone himself, who was at that time a sort of hostage of the advanced Liberals in the Palmerston Ministry, spoke in similar terms: " Every person," he declared, in 1863, " not presumably incapacitated by some consideration of personal unfitness or political danger, is morally entitled to come within the pale of the Constitution." Three years afterwards, he was more outspoken in combating those who opposed the grant of the suffrage to the working classes: " They are our fellow-Christians, and of the same flesh and blood as ourselves."

Pending their admission into the inner political life of England, the ideas of Radical individualism penetrated its approaches; they found their way into colonial government and international relations. The colonies, it was asserted, were entitled to manage their own affairs; and all that England had to do, for her own honour and their advantage, was to recognize their individuality, and treat them as responsible communities. People even went so far as to contest England's right to her possessions beyond the seas, on the ground that she had acquired them by violence, by fraud, and by crimes against justice and humanity. These ideas, so closely related to the doctrines of the Manchester School, especially as regards their premises, were propagated with the greatest energy by philosophical Radicals, and especially by Goldwin Smith, who at that time almost rivalled John Stuart Mill in influence on the rising generation. They created quite a current of opinion, and made their power felt by the Government. One colony after another received autonomy on the pattern of the system of responsible government introduced for the first time into Canada in 1847. The same individualist principle, transported into the international sphere under the name of the principle of nationalities, made the English Government take a step which was without precedent in British annals: it restored the Ionian Islands to Greece spontaneously and without compensation. A little more, and Gibraltar would have been sacrificed on the same altar.

In their heart of hearts, the ruling classes clung to their old opinions, which occasionally showed themselves in the crudest form. Thus, when civil war broke out in the United States, they took the side of the slave-holding South against the North, and, believing that the American Republic was doomed, were overjoyed at the idea that democracy had thus, as they thought, proved its impotence. This attitude of the ruling classes, as well as the general state of dull immobility in which the political world gathered round Palmerston remained, far from cooling the radical ardour of the rising generation, gave it an additional stimulus. The idea prevailed that it was impossible to strike too hard in order to overcome this inert mass, upheld by aristocratic tradition and sentiment, and fed by a spirit of privilege and selfish domination, and that it was therefore useless to count the blows, or select the points suitable for attack. Most of the English institutions, thought the Radicals, were fit only for destruction. They became confirmed in this view, and indulged in anticipations of the most sanguine kind, all the more easily because it was not necessary to begin the process of demolition at once, or calculate the force of resistance which might have to be encountered. Palmerston's immense prestige in Parliament and in the country and his dogged opposition to reform alone sufficed to render all attempt at change abortive. The popular minister having become, so to speak, the embodiment of the existing order of things, the reformers, in their turn, ended by making Palmerston the incarnation of all the obstacles which blocked their path.

V

Consequently when Palmerston died in 1865 the advanced school thought that their time had come, and that now, at last, the flood-gates of progress could be opened. But which direction was progress to take? How were they to set about realiz-

ing the new social and political ideal ? In point of fact, there
was more enthusiasm than clearness of views on the subject of
the new ideals and the mode of converting them into practice.
Since the days of the Chartists, who naïvely advocated universal suffrage as a remedy for the sufferings of the people,
advanced opinion was bent on the extension of the parliamentary franchise. Radical enthusiasm, without looking further afield, now took up this question and devoted all its
energies to it. The anti-reforming tendencies of the ruling
classes were the same as ever; they were still opposed to
all fresh extension of the suffrage. At the general election
which had just been held (in 1865) they had returned much
the same men to Parliament. The people themselves were
indifferent; except in the industrial centres of the north there
was now none of the enthusiasm which animated the masses in
1832. But beneath the surface a profound change had taken
place. Reforming zeal, confined for years to the sphere
of speculation, had acquired consistency, and now that the
period of grace seemed to have expired with Palmerston's
death, it demanded payment of its account. The ruling classes,
who were sunk in stagnation, had no resistance to offer; they
were without ideas, without strong convictions, and consequently
without strength. Resistance pure and simple is never a force
in itself; it can only derive power from the spirit and from the
inward faith of the combatant. To proclaim one's hostility to
an idea, without being able to meet it on equal terms, only
gives it a fresh stimulus. It is just as useless to ignore it; if
you do ignore it, or retire from it, it advances; if you halt
before it in a neutral attitude, it fixes and hypnotizes you; if
you pay it the formal tribute of recognition, you at once become its slave. While the ruling classes sank deeper into their
selfishness, Reform crept in imperceptibly; very soon its presence was felt. "It was in the air." And many a politician,
penetrated with the amiable scepticism of the time, had no
objection to giving Reform a Platonic adhesion, with the mental rider that nothing serious was involved thereby. After a
time several Whig members of Parliament, in addition to the
earnest reformers, found themselves committed to it, and were
extremely embarrassed as the agitation for the extension of
the suffrage grew more vehement. Before long even the most

old-fashioned Whigs came to the conclusion that it was difficult, if not impossible, to avoid a new measure of Parliamentary Reform.

The same events and the same intellectual movement made a breach in the Tory party, in·a different way, but quite as effectively. After the catastrophe of 1846 the Tories, who had been "betrayed" by their leader, had lost confidence in every-body and everything. They gave way to a profound discourage-ment, and to a fear so intense and so little concealed that those who witnessed it must have been divided between compassion and amusement. The rising tide of new ideas convinced the Conservatives that all hope was lost, that a relentless fatality was dragging England towards the abyss of radicalism and democracy, and they went so far as to repeat the line of Homer which the blind child recited to Mummius. after the taking of Corinth, "Happy are those who are in the tomb." [1] Tories of a less imaginative stamp gave themselves up prosaically to despondency and apathy. Parliamentary life, with its sterile contests and the simulated warmth of its debates, only served to nourish and intensify these sentiments. It was in vain that Disraeli tried to restore the failing courage of his fol-lowers by incessant attacks on the governments of the day. Even his successes were ephemeral. He was "compelled to fight battles without profit, and to take office without power," as a devoted biographer admits.[2] It is true that the Conserva-tive party had increased in size to a certain extent; the great prosperity of the country since the year 1846, which had created in the urban middle class a large category of prosper-ous people contented with things as they are, had driven many of them into the Conservative camp. This accession

[1] Wellington when bidding farewell to Croker, whom he believed to be at the point of death (but who survived him by a few weeks), said to him: "But at least, my dear Croker, it is some consolation to us who are so near the end of our career that we shall be spared seeing the consummation of the ruin that is gathering about us" (*Croker Papers*, III, 363). The whole corre-spondence collected in these three volumes betrays the same mental preoccu-pation in the Conservative ranks. Lord Strangford writes, in a letter of the 21st October, 1854: "Chateaubriand sometimes speaks truth, and never more so where he says: 'Nous sommes sur les bords d'un monde qui finit et d'un autre monde qui commence.' What a frightful thing this 'commence-ment' will be!" (*Ibid.* 343).

[2] T. E. Kebbel, *Life of Lord Beaconsfield* (1888), p. 92.

of strength from the middle class, while widening the basis of Conservatism throughout the country, also acted as a dissolvent. The Tories of the old school had lost faith in the strength of their cause, and the new men had never possessed it. The crowd of wealthy manufacturers, merchants, and shop-keepers who called themselves Conservatives had no traditions to cling to or defend with resolution. But in return they brought with them the business mind which urged that the customer must be kept in a good humour; that it was more prudent to come to terms, and save what could be saved from the wreck — in a word, the complete philosophy of the counting-house.

Between these two states of mind — of demoralization on the one hand, and aggressive enthusiasm on the other — an arbiter interposed under the pretext of bringing about a settlement, but in reality with the object of seizing the property in dispute, like the third thief in the fable. This arbiter was the political parties. Having exhausted, from the year 1846, all the great questions which divided them, they were living from hand to mouth and wasting their existence in sterile conflicts devoid of all principle. They played with every political question which circumstances brought to the front or which they invented themselves for the requirements of the game which was henceforth their sole resource. Not that public life no longer presented a field for genuine activity; on the contrary, the transitional state of society issuing from a feudal condition created pressing needs which imperiously demanded the attention of the legislator: the education of the masses, "the greatest of all causes," according to Cobden; the recasting of local self-government for the repair of the civic machinery which brought citizens together in the discharge of a daily task undertaken for the furtherance of common interests, which invited and to a certain extent compelled them to study the general interest and to feel themselves live in it. The parties in the State were indifferent to these reforms; for they were not "political questions," which by means of the natural or artificial antagonism created by them give the victory to this or that side. Being in their nature unconnected with party interests, the great measures of social reconstruction would only have benefited the country at large. Things however, were not going smoothly for these exhausted factions; there was no vigour, no cohesion, especially in the Liberal party. The advanced section, which alone had ideas as representing the views of the Philosophical Radicals and the radicalism professed by the élite of the workingmen in the towns, became more and more refractory. Harassed by the Tories on one side and by the Radicals on the other, the old Whigs agreed with the latter to reopen the question of a fresh extension of the suffrage. They complied reluctantly and without the faintest wish for the success of the reform, which inspired them with more fear than hope for their future. From 1852 onward plan after plan was brought forward, but all were still-born. When the Tories came into power in 1858 with no particular policy, they took up the question of the suffrage on their own account, but with as little sincerity and success as the Whigs. For both sides Parliamentary Reform was a good pretext for overthrowing the government of the day in order to take its place. When the truce of Palmerston, "the Tory chief of a Radical Cabinet," was established in the House of Commons, the two sides came to the conclusion that the farce had lasted long enough, and the question of Reform was dropped. But after the death of the illustrious statesman broke the spell which kept parties in a state of immobility and the latter had to resume their position, the problem of the electoral franchise was taken up again and with it that of the future of political parties. Worn-out, well-nigh ruined, they had lived on Palmerston's credit for the last few years. What were they to live on now? Feeling, in spite of the bluntness of their perceptions, — as is the case with all ultra-moderate parties, — that "Reform was in the air," the Whigs thought that the extension of the suffrage might after all contain an element of good; that it might be a sort of plank thrown out in the shipwreck of historical parties; and that if the new electors were indebted to the Whigs for the right of voting they would swell their train, strengthen their position in the country, and give the effete Whig party, as it were, a renewal of youth. But it was just this probability which threw the Conservatives into despair; it seemed to sound their death-knell. Thereupon their ingenious leader Disraeli resolved as a last resort to dish his opponents: his plan was to offer the franchise to the masses on behalf of the Conservative party after having previously fash-

ioned it in a conservative spirit. "You cannot," he explained
to his followers, "form a party of resistance pure and simple,
because change is inevitable in a progressive country; the
question is whether Reform shall be carried out in the spirit of
the national customs and traditions, or whether you will follow
abstract principles and general doctrines." The dilemma was
well stated; as in the time of the *Young England* party, a
quarter of a century before, Disraeli had a luminous vision of
the situation, of the causes which had conduced to it, and of
the conflicting elements; but on this occasion too he miscalcu-
lated their respective forces by imagining that Reform would
be carried out "in the spirit of the national customs and traditions" if the Tory party were entrusted with the preparation
of the Bill. These customs and traditions were mere phantoms,
and at the first summons of Radicalism Disraeli himself con-
signed them to the nether world. The popular demonstrations
in favour of Reform, which were got up soon after the Conservative government came into office, created a regular panic in
the Tory ranks. The country as a whole remained tranquil
and almost indifferent. Even the disturbances in Hyde Park,
where the agitators had assembled a monster meeting, did not
exceed the limits of the kind of riot which the London mob
liked to indulge in. But this display of physical force was
enough to intimidate the members of Parliament who were
opposed to Reform. Believing that the triumph of Radicalism
was inevitable, both Tories and Whigs rushed to meet it half-
way, in a wild race in which each tried to outstrip the other.

In bringing in his Reform Bill Disraeli expressly stated that
Parliament ought to represent not numbers but interests; that
to give a faithful reflection of the country the dominant characteristic of the suffrage should be not uniformity but variety
of electoral qualifications; that England was and would remain
a country of classes which balanced each other, and that each
class was entitled to an influence in Parliament corresponding
not to the number of heads which it counted, but to its social
worth, its intelligence, and its wealth, so that no class should
be able to crush the others by mere numerical superiority.
To carry out these ideas Disraeli's plan, while lowering the
rating electoral qualification, gave votes irrespective of the rating franchise to various groups of individuals who had proved

their capacity either by their education or their practical activity (for instance to graduates of universities and others, to depositors of £30 in the savings-bank, to persons possessing £50 in the public funds or paying 20s. in direct taxes). If the 20s. taxpayers occupied a dwelling which gave a right to the suffrage, they were to have a double vote. In the towns the rating qualification was to be lowered from £10 to £6, but the payment of a rent of £6 would not secure a vote unless the occupant of the dwelling paid the poor-rate himself, so that the "compound householders" would have been excluded from the franchise. On the other hand, the Bill rejecting all "artificial symmetry" in the arrangement of the constituencies, only gave seats to a few large towns which had remained unrepresented, while preserving all the unimportant boroughs which already had the right to return a member.

Not one of these "checks and balances" against democracy conceived by Disraeli withstood the assault of parties. The Liberals, who had not the slightest intention of being taken in tow to pass a reform which they considered a patent of their own, maintained that all the "safeguards" provided by the Bill were unjust and vexatious. They threatened to give up the question of the extension of the suffrage rather than accept it under such conditions. The Tories, in their turn, did not wish to throw up the game and were afraid of alienating the new electors by a too uncompromising attitude. "Educated by events," according to Disraeli's expression, they made one concession after another under the guidance of their adroit chief. "We have no longer," as Robert Lowe pointed out, "a party of attack and a party of resistance. We have instead two parties of competition, who, like Cleon and the sausage-seller of Aristophanes, are both bidding for the support of Demos." All the safeguards were abandoned. The special franchises, contemptuously styled "fancy franchises," were given up without a struggle. The double vote shared the same fate. Disraeli spontaneously threw over the £6 qualification for urban electors in spite of the adverse opinion of several Liberals who inclined towards a £5 qualification, and household suffrage pure and simple was adopted. The condition of personal payment of the poor-rate, which was the backbone of the Bill, was simply dropped. The franchise was granted not only to all householders in towns, but also to lodgers paying a yearly rent of £10. In the redistribution of seats the criterion of population was applied on a much more extended scale than in the original Bill, which was a protest against "artificial symmetry."

Whatever may have been the motives and calculations which mingled in the brains of Conservatives and Liberals, the spirit which presided over their legislation was from one end to the other a levelling one. The variety of electoral qualifications was sacrificed and as much uniformity introduced as possible; instead of maintaining the traditional "balance of power" by emphasizing the distinctions between the constituent elements of the electoral body, they were well-nigh obliterated. Property qualifications being almost abolished for electors in towns, and the suffrage being extended to lodgers, Parliament ceased to reflect interests and became simply the representative of numbers; the urban masses obtained the largest share of political power, and England became a democracy. It was of no consequence that one or two more stages had to be passed before universal suffrage was reached; those who were not admitted to the franchise were bound in logic to obtain it sooner or later, as there was no longer an immovable limit to keep them out of it. The Reform Bill of 1832 had already pushed it back, by adding a rational qualification for the franchise to the historical electoral right. People endeavoured to minimize the significance of that Bill and to persuade themselves that it had only readjusted the "balance of power" without making any "concession to the principle of numbers." This was not the case; there was no longer a balance, but an incline, which, when once stepped upon, had to be descended to the end. The Bill of 1867 supplied a demonstration of this, and by establishing the fact in an emphatic manner it opened the era of democracy in the English State.

The "abstract principles and general doctrines" to which Disraeli wished to oppose "national customs and traditions" were consequently triumphant all along the line. We have followed their victorious progress in these pages for a century, and have seen how, with the powerful aid of circumstances, one success after another led them to a decisive triumph. A time-honoured prejudice insists that the English are inaccessible to general ideas, as if these ideas were a sort of contagious malady against which the robust Anglo-Saxon constitution is proof. On the other side of the Channel the English were often congratulated on this, they became objects of envy, and they themselves were only too ready to believe that they could not catch the "French complaint." If this had really been the case, the English would have been outside humanity and would not have shared in its greatness and its wretchedness. Driving individuals and nations from sublimity to folly, the power of an idea strikes indiscriminately and takes possession of the whole being. The outward semblance alone varies. One people embraces an idea with rapture, another tries to bargain with it, like the countryman who, in order to beat down the price, pretends not to care about the article which he is sure to buy in the end, as he has left home for that very purpose. From the moment when the individual soul awoke and claimed to assert itself before God and society, the conception of "man" entered the social and political life of England once and for all. It penetrated into England by the path of morality as it did into France by that of logic. An idea finds its way into the intelligence by the door which is easiest to open, here by one and there by another; but this does not make it change its character or its postulates, and if these latter are developed by similar methods and under similar circumstances, they are bound to assert themselves with equal force. In England, as in France, the individual was for a long time repressed and sacrificed to the community, or rather to what usurped its place. At last he demanded justice. Opinion on both sides of the Channel advancing towards him could see nothing but him; absorbed in its task of emancipation, it rushed straight on without looking to the right or to the left. As soon as it had brought its protégé out of the crowd, it gave him and each of his fellows the power of governing themselves, with the result that the community which they formed became the sum total of their persons and their powers, a democracy as it is generally called, an arithmocracy, as it has been more accurately described. To become realities these conceptions needed the co-operation of events, and this was not denied them. What the destroyers of the Bastille did in France was accomplished by the spinning-jenny and the steam-engine in England; both gave a helping hand to the conclusions of philosophy. The fact that the new ideas did not find vent in England by means of a violent explosion, but made their way little by little, rendered their effect on the public mind all the more certain. Their conversion into practice having devolved on the political parties in the State, the latter in their passionate rivalry only thrust them deeper into the narrow channel marked out by thought. All forms of mental narrowness, whether in the sphere of speculation or that of action, conspire together. Like the "geometric theory of society,"[1] which recognizes only one cause of all social phenomena and only one property of human nature, and disregards all the others, so political parties in their undeviating pursuit of the object which secures them a brief period of power compress into it as into a sort of Procrustean bed all the phenomena of the political and social situation with their causes and their consequences. In their anxiety to carry Reform over the heads of their opponents, English politicians not only brought their legislative enactments to the level occupied by the postulates of ideology, but unconsciously agreed with its arguments and its inmost thoughts. "Not till this question of Reform has disappeared amongst the subjects of controversy," said Mr. Gladstone in 1866, "can we hope to see the people of England what they once were, and what we ought to be desirous they should ever continue to be, — a united people."[2] Subsequently, after the passing of the Bill of 1867, John Bright in calling attention to its merits remarked: "The Bill of 1832 was a great Bill; but still it left two nations among the people — a small minority included, and a large majority excluded."[3] Reverting to the division into two nations of Disraeli's "Sybil," Gladstone and Bright evidently suggested the inference that the extension of the suffrage put an end to it, that this reform had the power to restore the moral unity of a disintegrated society, that it was the bearer of the long-expected synthesis. But if equal right

---

[1] To use the term of J. S. Mill (*System of Logic*, Bk. VI, Chap. VIII, of the geometrical or abstract method).

[2] *Hansard*, 3d series, Vol. 185, p. 248.

[3] *Public Addresses of John Bright*, ed. by J. E. Thorold Rogers, Lond. 1879, p. 193.

of voting is enough to make a nation united, it is because society is simply the arithmetical total of the individuals who compose it. Neither Bentham nor his French predecessors of the eighteenth century went farther than this.

VI

At the moment therefore when the Reform Bill of 1867 was about to become law, Benthamism might have repeated to itself: *Nunc dimittis servum tuum.* Its most illustrious representatives, J. S. Mill and G. Grote, lived to witness the triumph of rationalist individualism in the sphere of politics. But their satisfaction was very far from being without alloy. For a long time their minds, especially that of Mill, had been gravely preoccupied with the future destiny of the individual in society. They demanded the political emancipation of the individual, but if, by virtue of the right on which they took their stand, it was granted indiscriminately to all members of society, if the whole body of individuals was invested with it, how would the particular individual be able to preserve his independence against them; would not the freedom become a delusion and a snare and the individual be at the mercy of a tyranny just as oppressive as that from which he was liberated? The result then was to create a Frankenstein — to adopt the illustration of which the English are so fond — like the hero of the celebrated story,[1] the young student Frankenstein who plunged so deep into the study of alchemy that one day a quasi-human creature stepped out of the crucible in his laboratory, but inasmuch as divine skill had not been vouchsafed to the human artificer, instead of a man he created a frightful monster to which he himself fell a victim after protracted agony. The emancipated individual crushed by individualism, what a prospect! Grote, who throughout his whole life advocated the ballot, or system of secret voting, to insure the independence of each elector, contemplated with feelings akin to melancholy the approaching accomplishment of the reform of which he had constituted himself the champion. He thought that the advantages conferred by the ballot would be lost with the enormous exten-

[1] *Frankenstein, or the New Prometheus,* by Mrs. Shelley, the wife of the poet. Lond. 1816.

sion of the electorate introduced by the Bill of 1867. For "the English mind," said the illustrious historian, "is much of one pattern, take whatsoever class you will,"[1] and with great masses of electors the tendency to advance in one direction and to crush by weight of numbers would only increase. Even a republican form of government, which was his ideal, was no longer a safeguard in his eyes. "I have outlived," said Grote in 1867, à propos of the United States, "my faith in the efficacy of republican government regarded as a check upon the vulgar passions of a majority in a nation, and I recognize the fact that supreme power lodged in their hands *may* be exercised quite as mischievously as by a despotic ruler like the first Napoleon."[2] Mill did not wait till the end of his life to indulge in similar reflections. They began in his case with the perusal of "Democracy in America" by de Tocqueville, just as in his early days another French book, the life of Turgot by Condorcet, inspired him with the faith in the infinite perfectibility of man which made him adopt Bentham's theories of democracy. "In that remarkable work" (of de Tocqueville), says Mill himself, "the excellences of democracy were pointed out in a more conclusive, because a more specific, manner than I had ever known them to be, even by the most enthusiastic democrats; while the specific dangers which beset democracy, considered as the government of numerical majority, were brought into equally strong light, and subjected to a masterly analysis."[3] The more Mill's mind outgrew the narrow formulas of the Benthamism of Bentham and of his father, James Mill, the more uneasy he became about the individual confronted by numbers. Examining his master's doctrine, Mill asked himself "is it at all times and places, good for mankind to be under the absolute authority of the majority of themselves," and he came to the conclusion that Bentham had not turned his genius to the best account when, "not content with enthroning the majority as sovereign by means of universal suffrage without King or House of Lords, he exhausted all the resources of ingenuity in devising means for riveting the yoke of public opinion closer and closer. . . . Wherever all the forces of society act in one single direction, the just claims of

[1] *Personal Life of Mr. Grote,* by Mrs. Grote, Lond. 1873, p. 313.
[2] *Ibid.,* p. 314.   [3] *Autobiography,* p. 191.

the individual human being are in extreme peril. The power of the majority is salutary so far as it is used defensively not offensively, as its exertion is tempered by respect for the personality of the individual, and deference to superiority of cultivated intelligence." [1] But how is the majority to be armed for the defensive and to be made powerless for the offensive? Mill thought that " Montesquieu with the lights of the present age would have done it; and we are possibly destined to receive this benefit from the Montesquieu of our times, M. de Tocqueville." [2]

The years rolled on, and there was no sign of a remedy in the direction of France. At last Mill thought that he had discovered it in the plan of his fellow-countryman, Thomas Hare, for personal representation. " I saw in this great practical and philosophical idea the greatest improvement of which the system of representative government is susceptible; an improvement which, in the most felicitous manner, exactly meets and cures the grand, and what before seemed the inherent, defect of the representative system; that of giving to a numerical majority all power, instead of a proportional power to its numbers, and enabling the strongest party to exclude all weaker parties from making their opinion heard in the assembly of the nation, except through such opportunity as may be given to them by the accidentally unequal distribution of opinions in different localities. To these great evils nothing more than very imperfect palliations had seemed possible; but Mr. Hare's system affords a radical cure. This great discovery, for it is no less, in the political art, inspired me, as I believe it has inspired all thoughtful persons who have adopted it, with new and more sanguine hopes respecting the prospects of human society; by freeing the form of political institutions towards which the whole civilized world is manifestly and irresistibly tending, from the chief part of what seemed to qualify, or render doubtful, its ultimate benefits. Minorities, so long as they remain minorities, are, and ought to be, outvoted; but under arrangements which enable any assemblage of voters, amounting to a certain number, to place in the legislature a representative of its own choice, minorities cannot be suppressed. Independent opin-

---

[1] *Dissertations and Discussions*, I, 381.   [2] *Ibid.*, p. 382.

ions will force their way into the council of the nation and make themselves heard there, a thing which often cannot happen in the existing forms of representative democracy ; and the legislature, instead of being weeded of individual peculiarities and entirely made up of men who simply represent the creed of great political and religious parties, will comprise a large proportion of the most eminent individual minds in the country placed there, without reference to party, by voters who appreciate their individual eminence." [1]

Hare's idea was not an entirely new one,[2] but as conceived and stated by him and expounded by Mill it was really a great landmark in the history of political thought and in the art of political legislation. It was the first and still remains the most important practical attempt that has been made to organize numbers in democracies. It was the first proposal which grasped the new material and moral conditions under which representative government would have to work in the future, which recognized the necessity of replacing the old social ties now snapped asunder by spontaneous and deliberate ones, of protecting the individual against his new master, the sovereign people, of establishing politics on an ethical basis by paying attention to justice in the distribution of power among the units of the sovereign, and of introducing a moral criterion in the choice of the men appointed to govern the State by lifting electoral life out of the narrow and corrupt

---

[1] *Autobiography* of J. S. Mill, pp. 258, 259.

[2] As early as the debates on the first Reform Bill we find germs of it,* which were subsequently developed in some writings,† and incorporated in a clause of Lord John Russell's Reform Bill of 1854. On the continent Victor Considérant, the celebrated Fourierist, raised the question as far back as 1834. At Geneva, where he was living, he pointed out at public meetings the defects of the system of majorities, and recommended the substitution of a method of election based on a preliminary grouping of electors in "constituencies of opinion" and even submitted his plan to the Grand Council of Geneva in 1846.‡

In America the question of minority representation was broached for the first time in a pamphlet of Thomas Gilpin on "The representation of minorities of electors to act with the majorities in Elected Assemblies." *Philadelphia*, 1844.

* Praed's motion in 1831 (*Hansard*, Vol. 188, p. 1075).

† J. G. Marshall, *On Minorities and Majorities*, Lond. 1853 ; *Spectator*, 1853 ; *Edinburgh Review*, July, 1854.

‡ His very interesting circular on this subject, addressed to the members of the Grand Council, and entitled "De la sincérité du gouvernement représentatif ou exposition de l'élection véridique," has been reprinted at Zürich, in 1892 (Imprimerie de la Société suisse du Grütli).

groove of traditional parties. Unfortunately there was a dis-
proportion between the end in view and the means suggested.
The improvement proposed in the electoral machinery, ingenious as it was, could not of itself alone supply the moral
force of which the new political society stood in need; the
justice which it claimed to secure in political relations was
chiefly an arithmetical justice; the psychological reaction
which the new electoral system was intended to produce in the
electors, however probable and salutary, could only be of a very
indirect and consequently very limited kind, in any event too
limited to cover the whole field of political life and become
its motive power. Viewed with reference to the effect which
it held out, the plan of "personal representation" inevitably
laid itself open to the criticism which Mill himself passed on
Bentham in a sentence pregnant with meaning in spite of its
apparent truism: "Nobody's synthesis can be more complete
than his analysis."[1] Confined to electoral arrangements, the
political synthesis which it was supposed to offer was not a
synthesis at all. Mill was all the less able to see the weakness of his position because there was no other alternative
open to him. Led by the principle of utility to install numbers as the supreme power in the State, and perceiving subsequently that the individual ran the risk of being crushed
by numbers which had become master, the philosopher had
nowhere to look for protection for his unfortunate client; for,
laden with the original sin of Benthamism, he had repudiated
the sovereignty of right in politics just as he had rejected that
of duty in the moral sphere. As only material forces remained
to be brought into play, there was nothing whatever to interfere
between the individual interest and the multiplied interest of
numbers, unless some new dynamical combination could be devised to enable the weak to hold its own against the strong. In
proportional representation, Mill believed that he had at last
hit on this undiscoverable combination, and hence his delight
("this great discovery inspired me with new and more sanguine hopes respecting the prospects of human society"),
which under the circumstances strikes us as excessive for such
a powerful intellect. He fastened on it with all the resources
of his genius, as a shipwrecked man clings with all his strength
to the plank that comes within his reach. He made Hare's

---

[1] *Dissertations and Discussions*, I, 350.

plan his own, laid it before public opinion, enforced general attention to it by the prestige of his name, brought the question within the category of the great problems of politics, and finally submitted it to Parliament, to which he had in the meanwhile been elected.

When the debates on the Reform Bill were drawing to an end, Mill moved the insertion of a clause relating to personal representation. According to the amendment which he brought forward with this object, in the sitting of the 30th May, 1867, the total number of votes recorded throughout the Kingdom in the same election, divided by 658 (the number of members to be elected), was to determine the minimum of votes necessary for the election of a candidate, and all the votes given to a candidate, even in more than one constituency, having been added up and credited to him, any candidate who received the above-mentioned quotient of votes, whether in his own constituency or in several taken together, would be declared elected. The electors were to have the power of specifying several candidates in the order of preference which they assigned to them, but an elector's vote would only count for one candidate; if the candidate had already obtained a number of votes exceeding the quotient necessary to secure election, the surplus would be transferred to the candidates who had not attained the quotient at the first start, always following the order of preference indicated, until the number of 658 members was completed. In the speech which Mill delivered in support of the amendment, he pointed out with much force that the proposed enactment was not inspired by any considerations of party; that far from allowing one party to lord it over all the others, its result would be to save those which were in danger of being overwhelmed; that it would remedy the inherent defect of representative government, which is that minorities defeated in elections are left without any representation and that local majorities themselves are not faithfully represented, the voter being obliged to choose between the candidates of the two great parties, who are often selected by intrigue and thrust upon the constituency by corruption. The exclusion of minorities on the pretext that the opinion of the minority defeated in one constituency is successful in another is not in accordance with the representative system,

the object of which is to insure the representation not of
parties, but of citizens. Every opinion entertained by a reasonable number of electors ought to be directly represented,
and the sentiments, opinions, and interests of a community
must not be subordinated to party considerations. The option
which the electors would be allowed of giving their votes to
persons other than local candidates, far from destroying the
local character of representation, would enable it to express
itself with greater deliberation. The plan proposed would
suit the Conservatives, who are anxious that variety in representation should be maintained, and it is just as much in
harmony with democratic principles, which demand that every
one should be represented and to an equal extent. The plan
would allow the representation of the working classes, but it
would be a safeguard against the predominance of these
classes as well as that of any other class, and in this way
the principles of spurious democracy would be opposed by
the principles of genuine democracy.

This speech of Mill's was lost on the House, the Liberal
members included, and the observations presented by the
greatest thinker of the time were on the point of being passed
over amid general silence, when a young member, who already
held a prominent position in Parliament, rose from the Tory
benches to support Mill's amendment. This was Viscount
Cranborne, who has since become Prime Minister of England
under the name of the Marquis of Salisbury. He agreed that
the danger pointed out by Mill really existed; that the result
of conferring the suffrage on the multitude would be to swamp
local influence and substitute for it that of committees and
professional politicians, although he could not refrain from
observing that the mischief, as well as the remedy proposed,
was due to a certain extent to Mill himself and to the school
to which he belonged. The philosophers had led them into
the difficulty; if the country was landed in household suffrage,
it was not in order to meet a practical necessity, but to comply
with philosophical arguments. Noting that power was after
all about to be entrusted not to philosophers, but to persons
who were anything but philosophers, the speaker viewed with
the greatest apprehension that, after the non-philosophical English mind had been carried a certain distance, people shrank

from adopting the remedies which the philosophers recommended for preventing the evils inherent in the advanced political condition of society. They were putting new wine in old bottles. Household suffrage had just been granted on purely theoretical principles; why then should they reject a purely theoretical cure for evils due to the extension of the suffrage on the ground that it was utterly unpractical? Mill's amendment therefore deserved most serious consideration.

This agreement of a high-and-dry Tory like Lord Cranborne with the apostle of Radicalism was piquant enough, but nevertheless logical. Mill was preoccupied with the fate of the abstract individual who was in danger of being overwhelmed by numbers; the Tories were thinking of their old constituents, that is, of the concrete individuals who would probably be swamped by the new mass of voters. Since electoral reform had come to the front again, they had exercised their ingenuity in trying to discover some means of partially neutralizing the consequences of the extension of the suffrage. Their efforts were directed to two points, — the variety of the franchise and secondly and especially the homogeneity of the constituencies, in order to preserve as much as possible of the old unity and social cohesion on which the power of the old ruling class had rested. As early as the Bill of 1859 Disraeli had endeavoured to keep the country electors separate from those of the towns, and on this point Mill found himself in agreement with the Tories when he too declared for the exclusion of urban voters from the county constituencies in order "to enable the agricultural population to hold its fair share of the representation."[1] During the debate on the Reform Bill of 1866 the Tories took up the same attitude with regard to the introduction of urban agglomerations into the old county constituencies and denounced "the urbanizing tendency which ran through the whole of this Bill."[2] The Conservatives offered an equally determined opposition to the grouping of boroughs, which had hitherto been independent constituencies, into more or less equal electoral districts, for the result would be to destroy the individuality of these boroughs and put an end to the time-honoured social and political relations which had grown up

[1] *Thoughts on Parliamentary Reform*, Lond. 1859, p. 15.
[2] *Hansard*, Vol. 183, p. 1829.

with them.   With unerring instinct the Tories discerned that
the break-up of the old society, with all its political consequences, would be consummated by an electoral reform which
tended in the direction of a uniform suffrage and equal electoral districts.   "Such a system was about the most destructive
surgical operation you could put a country through; it would
be a severing of the limbs from the trunk, and cutting through
the muscles and sinews of the body politic." . . . "If they left
the people under their natural leaders, and if they had naturally selected districts, there was no fear that the people would
choose improper men, and there would be no need of checks or
counterpoises to defend the minority."[1]   Lord Cranborne saw
clearly that all these pious wishes could be nothing but wishes
in a society with its old unity gone and with its traditional
relations irrevocably destroyed, and that the old political weapons had grown rusty; consequently he boldly laid his hand on
the armour forged by Mill for the use of the abstract individual
in order to arm his own followers with it.

Lord Cranborne's speech made a considerable impression,
and he was thanked for having saved the House from a great
disgrace by his intervention, but in view of the hostile attitude
of Parliament, Mill withdrew his amendment.

A month later the question came before the House again in
consequence of an amendment moved by Robert Lowe, who
proposed that in every constituency with more than one seat
the elector who had to record a number of votes equal to the
number of seats might give them all to one candidate or distribute them among several candidates.   In the debate, which
on this occasion was a lengthy one, the speakers on one side
dwelt on the necessity of giving minorities the means of making
themselves heard in Parliament, of defending themselves and
of protecting their interests, and at the same time of insuring
a certain variety in the national representation; while on the
other side every measure for the representation of minorities
was regarded as a spoliation of the majority and an attack on
the true principles of representative government.   This last
position was upheld by John Bright, the famous orator and at
that time one of the leaders of advanced Liberalism.   Warmly
protesting his devotion to "the ancient ways of the Constitu-

[1] *Hansard*, Vol. 186, pp. 575, 576.

tion," a devotion of which people hardly suspected him capable, he adjured the House not to allow itself to be led away by "new-fangled ideas." The amendment was rejected. But the friends of minority representation were more successful in the House of Lords. On the motion of Lord Cairns the Upper Chamber inserted a clause in the Reform Bill enacting that in the twelve three-cornered constituencies the elector could not vote for more than two candidates, and in the city of London, which returned four members, for more than three; then the remaining seat was bound to revert to the minority if it amounted to one-third (or to one-fourth in the city of London) of the constituency. When the Bill was sent back to the House of Commons, the new clause inserted by the Lords was strongly attacked. John Bright once more exerted himself vigorously and undertook to move its rejection. The effect might be, he asserted, not to confer a representation on minorities, but to curb the democracy, to defraud the population of the large towns of a part of their representation; by guaranteeing a seat to the minority beforehand, the contest was nullified for the majority and stagnation introduced into political life; the side which had a majority was cheated not only by withdrawing a seat from it, but by neutralizing the vote of a member of the majority by that of the member for the minority; henceforth each constituency would have two voices, of which one will say white and the other black, like a conjuror who produces port, champagne, milk, or water out of the same bottle; it was difficult to imagine a principle more calculated to destroy the vitality of the elective system. Every plan of this kind would enfeeble and finally destroy the authority and strength of the executive government. Some of these arguments had already been used by Disraeli in the debate on Lowe's amendment.

In 1832, when the rotten boroughs were about to be abolished, Wellington asked with naïve dismay: "How will the King's government be carried on?" Bright now said much the same thing: How could you have your snug majority if you took so much care of the minority. It was the cry of the old party system, which had been suffering from an acute internal malady since 1846, and was now touched to the quick by the proposed scheme of personal representation. That a great party leader like Disraeli should join in this outcry was natural enough. But that Bright should constitute himself the mouthpiece of it was perhaps somewhat inconsistent with the reputation of political icono-clast which his opponents had conferred on him during the first half of his public career. In reality he was nothing of the kind. When Bright protested his attachment to the "ancient ways of the constitution," he was perfectly sincere, more so even than he imagined himself. In spite of his de-meanour of a tribune of the people, Bright was never a demo-crat; his generous and passionate temperament gave him a certain affinity with the people, but he was a thorough *bourgeois* in mind. Unlimited freedom for trade and labour, endless de-velopment of manufactures, the destruction of the landlords' "hereditary privileges," and the permanent exclusion of the Tory party from power was enough for his ideal. In Bright's eyes democracy was a party, the good and the right party, to which he belonged and for which he laboured, and which now, thanks to the extension of the franchise, would be placed on a solid basis throughout the country. Any measure tending to limit the power of the majority would undermine this founda-tion, would be an unfair blow levelled at the democracy, a dodge of the Tories brought to bay, and an invention of the philosophers. The great mass of members, whose political horizon was not wider than Bright's, were only too ready to adopt this point of view, that of party interests.

Thus as England was about to cross the very threshold of democracy a singular antagonism broke out: on the one side people wanted to protect the individual from the oppression of numbers which owed their supremacy to the individual-ist movement, while on the other side they were anxious to defend numbers in order to maintain the old system of party government which the same movement was breaking up. Each of these propositions presented a problem of the utmost gravity for the future of England. If the individual had to defend himself against democracy, and if democracy could only be founded on the uncontrolled dominion of numbers, would it not be like a new Saturn devouring its children? If in order to consolidate itself it clung to the old party system which had decayed under the action of the very forces which had given democracy life, would it not impair the vigour of this life and perhaps dry up its source, or, to apply Lord Cranborne's homely simile in a wider sense, would not the new wine be irretrievably spoiled by putting it in old bottles ? Whatever was destined to be the outcome of the impending conflict, the first act of a stirring drama was evidently beginning on the political stage of England.

The opposition of Bright and of several other members to Lord Cairns' clause was not successful in Parliament; the House of Commons, after an animated debate, agreed to the amendment voted by the Lords. The principle of the representation of minorities obtained the sanction of the law, although in a qualified form and to a limited extent. But the opposition which it aroused did not come to an end. Bright, in particular, was irreconcilable. He appealed to the electoral body with all the vehemence of which he was capable, and this was considerable. "An odious and infamous clause," "the most outrageous heresy against a popular representative system which was ever propounded in the legislature," "a clause which ought to have come not from the honest representation of the people, but from Bedlam or a region like that " — these were the terms in which Bright described the minority clause to his constituents in Birmingham. This town was one of those to which the new system of voting was to be applied. "Every Liberal throughout the United Kingdom," said Bright, "is asking: 'What is Birmingham going to do with the minority clause ? '"

Birmingham was not long in returning an answer. It created the " Caucus," a permanent electoral combination for fighting the battle of majorities under the banner of the democratic Liberal party. The new institution, which was soon extended to the whole country, became the starting-point of a movement which is still far from being exhausted, and which will perhaps exercise a decisive influence on the destinies of English democracy. Started in opposition to the minority clause, which was a partial attempt at organizing electoral opinion, the more successful Birmingham movement has in point of fact undertaken, in a fashion, the organization of the electoral masses. Arising at the very moment when the great extension of the suffrage made the need for it peculiarly felt, it has put forward a solution of the problem stated at the commencement of this work, and of which we have just finished analysing the historical factors. What is the economy, the efficacy, and the bearing of this solution? To form a proper estimate of them we must turn to the movement inaugurated at Birmingham and follow its evolution closely. We shall therefore quit the high road of English history and enter the side-path of extra-parliamentary electoral organization.

SECOND PART

FIRST CHAPTER

THE ORIGINS OF POLITICAL ASSOCIATIONS

THE form of the combination started at Birmingham for fighting the battle of democracy — *political association* and its basis — *party organization*, were already familiar to English public life. A short survey of the precedents of extra-constitutional political organization in England may therefore assist us in following its subsequent development.

I

Before liberty had become the basis of government, popular opposition and discontent found vent in riots and civil wars. In proportion as the régime of opinion took the place of that of brute force, internal conflicts assumed another character. The adjustment of differences was henceforth left to the free play of the moral forces of the nation; conspiracies were to give way to a union of convictions, and revolts to the manifestation of these convictions. But the transition was a long one. England succeeded sooner than other nations in creating a constitutional organ for making the voice of the country heard. Nevertheless she had to struggle for centuries, and often sword in hand, in order to convert constitutional government into a reality. The Crown, defeated in its duel with the nation represented by Parliament, endeavoured to obtain control of Parliament by corruption, and succeeded. But public opinion rose up once more against it for a final struggle. This is the drama which occupies the first half of the long reign of George III. The beginning of this reign was particularly disturbed. The populace, injured in its immediate interests, which were neglected by Parliament, or affected by the general grievances of the country, whether real or imaginary, resorted to riots, in the old fashion.[1] The élite of the nation, on the other hand, were so convinced of the justice of their cause that they deemed it sufficient to combat the corruption of Parliament with the moral force of opinion.

But as this very Parliament happened to be the constitutional mouthpiece of opinion, it was necessary to look about for another instrument to give general expression to popular aspirations. The Press, still in its infancy, was deficient in authority. The right of petitioning, one of the glorious conquests of English liberty, has generally been used, — except during the period of the Revolution, — as a means of obtaining redress for individual or local grievances. To make an impression on the Government, in the general interest, the co-operation of the masses was necessary. Public meetings are destined to supply the first weapon for securing this. The resolutions voted in them will be transmitted to Parliament by means of petitions. But, in order that these petitions should carry weight, they must be numerous, and agree in their demands. This result can only be achieved if the movement is organized and controlled. Committees and associations will therefore be formed for this purpose.

The disturbances caused by Wilkes' case gave the signal for these manifestations. The House of Commons expelled Wilkes, a journalist and pamphleteer who was obnoxious to Ministers, and then, although he was re-elected several times in succession, declared his election null and void each time, and finally gave his seat to a rival candidate, who had been brought forward against him, but who had been defeated at the polls. Indignant at the expulsion of their member, Wilkes' constituents subscribed large sums to defray the expense of a fresh election, and forwarded petitions and remonstrances to the King. In several counties meetings were organized to support the protest against the violation of law committed by Parliament. From this time forward the holding of public meetings became a regular practice in England, and they soon developed into a national institution. At one of the meetings held in London in consequence of the invalidation of Wilkes' re-election, those who took part in it, people of note, formed themselves into a " Society for support-

[1] Weaver's riots in 1765, riots about Wilkes in 1768, Gordon riots in 1780, etc.

ing the Bill of Rights." [1] In this way the first political association was founded. The significance of the new institution which was making its way into political life was appreciated at once. " This was deemed," we read in the " Memoirs " of one of the principal promoters of the Society, Horne Tooke, " a favourable conjuncture to organize a new as well as formidable species of opposition, and by means of political associations to concentrate the hitherto unheeded resentments and influence of a number of scattered individuals into one formidable mass which, without either the forms or restraints of a body politic, should produce all the spirit, zeal, and effect of a great corporation." [2] The Society proposed to assist every one affected by the arbitrary conduct of the authorities, and by its meetings, its speeches and its pecuniary sacrifices, it did a great deal to keep the public mind on the alert and to reassert the discredited principles of law and public liberties in more than one individual case. The famous author of the " Letters of Junius," in bearing testimony to the services which the Society was rendering to the common weal, recommended the formation of similar societies throughout the Kingdom. The " Society for supporting the Bill of Rights " soon fell to pieces owing to the action of Wilkes' friends, who wanted to make it an instrument for securing his personal ends. The other members parted company with Wilkes' friends, and founded a new society (Constitutional Society), which was shortly followed by other associations of small importance. [3]

A few years later, in consequence of the shock given to the public mind by the secession of the American colonies, the movement gathered force. When the expenses of the war which was still going on increased the waste of money caused by bribing members of Parliament and keeping up the numerous sinecures by which their creatures were maintained, public opinion arose and demanded that the scandals connected with the administration of the finances should be put an end to. It was resolved to get up a number of petitions to demand economic reforms, to which was soon added the reform of parliamentary

---

[1] *Memoirs of John Horne Tooke*, by Alex. Stephens, Lond. 1813, Vol. I, p. 161; *The Correspondence of John Wilkes and Memoirs of his Life*, by John Almon, Lond. 1805, Vol. IV, pp. 7–14.

[2] *Memoirs of Horne Tooke*, I, 161.   [3] *Ibid.* I, 175.

representation, which was considered the surest means of effecting the suppression of abuses and preventing their recurrence. A "corresponding committee" was appointed in each county, with power to control the movement. Yorkshire set the example. At a great meeting of the gentry, clergy, and freeholders of the county a petition was drawn up and a committee appointed with the duty of corresponding on the subject of the petition and of "preparing a plan of an association, on legal and constitutional grounds, to support the laudable reform and such other measure as might conduce to restore the freedom of Parliament."[1] The zeal of the reformers was great; the baneful influence of the Crown was denounced in all quarters; petitions were covered with signatures. In some counties, however, doubts arose as to the expediency of the committees. The mere term "corresponding committee" evoked unpleasant memories, for it was the name of the popular organizations which had prepared the revolution in the American colonies. These organizations had arisen at Boston, through the efforts of a group of influential men who had taken up public affairs and who formed themselves into a small informal body styled "Caucus."[2] When the relations with the mother-country became

[1] *Annual Register*, 1780, p. 85.

[2] This word has been adopted in American political terminology from the 18th century onward, to denote a small committee of men who settle electoral affairs privately beforehand. The nickname "caucus" has had a wonderful success. It has become the synonym for a political system, and a name for extra-parliamentary party organizations, brought about by the advent of radical democracy in the United States, and, in our day, in England. In this sense the expression "caucus" will often recur in this book.

The origin of this word which has come into such general use is very uncertain. Several theories have been advanced on the subject. According to some the term "caucus" is supposed to come from the North American Indians, from the word *kaw-kaw-was*, which in their language meant to talk, to give advice, to instigate, and by a transition denoted the persons who performed these acts as well; substantives with the same root are also quoted, *cawcaw-wassoughes*, used to denote the elders of a tribe or family, and *caucorouse*, which was the equivalent of "chief" or "captain." Another theory, backed by the authority of well-known lexicographers, such as Webster, Worcester, and Pickering, derives "caucus" from the English word "calker" or "caulker," the proper pronunciation of which is supposed to have been altered in the expressions "caulker's meeting" or "caulker's club." According to some it referred to the calkers in the Boston dockyards, who, when seeking redress against the English soldiers with whom they came in conflict, assembled in meetings at which, as it would appear, delegates were chosen to bring their grievances before the authorities. Pickering, who in his

particularly strained, the members of the Caucus, in order to
stimulate the spirit of resistance, procured (in 1772) the appointment by the people of Boston of a corresponding committee of twenty-one members, whose duty was to enter into
communication with the inhabitants of all the other places in
Massachusetts. This example was followed by Virginia and
other colonies. The consequence was that in England, in 1780,
many persons who had great sympathy for the petitioning
movement against the Crown and a venal Parliament, were
afraid that the committees and associations, when once formed,
might be launched on an incline which it would be difficult to
reascend; and in four counties no committees were appointed.
While the petitions from the counties which had been lodged
in the House of Commons were awaiting their turn to be
examined, and Burke was delivering his famous speech on the
plan of economic reform, the chairmen of several committees
who had come up to London invited the county associations to
send delegates to deliberate on the best mode of ensuring the
success of the petitions and on other matters of importance.
A letter enclosed with the convening circular expressed the
hope that " each county, city, and town, having first associated
separately and apart, on grounds which have received the
general approbation, the whole body of the petitioners in due
time may be collected and firmly consolidated in one great
'National Association.' The obvious consequence of which
must be certain and complete success to the constitutional
reform proposed by the people." [1] The delegates arrived and
by a considerable display of energy succeeded in creating
alarm in more than one quarter. " The Committees of Association began to give great alarm. They voted themselves a

---

Dictionary also derives " caucus " from the calkers, explains that, according
to a version transmitted to him by persons living at the time, the term
" caucus " was applied to political meetings in an invidious sense in order to
connect them with the lowest class of men in the social scale who attended
the meetings of calkers, or met in the *calking house* or *caulkhouse*. According to others the nickname of " caucus " is supposed to have been given to
private gatherings of politicians in Boston, in this case also by a modification of the word " caulker," because they held their meetings in the *caulker's
club*, or in a room which had formerly been used as a meeting-place for the
calkers (cf. Ripley and Dana's *American Cyclopædia*, and a discussion on
the subject in *Notes and Queries*, 1885, Vol. XI, pp. 309 and 451; Vol. XII,
pp. 54, 194, and 336). [1] Chr. Wyvill, *Political Papers*, York, 1796, I, 114.

right of considering and deciding on questions pending in
Parliament, and of censuring or approving the part taken
by particular members," writes Horace Walpole in his
"Journal." [1]   The attitude of the delegates was anything but
conducive to the success of the petitions, which in the end were
put on one side.   But the county associations would not give
up the struggle, and in the following year, under a new Parliament, they returned to the charge.   On this occasion several
members of Parliament on the Opposition side of the House,
such as Fox and General Burgoyne, were among the delegates.
When the plan of economic reform proposed for a second time
by Burke was rejected by the House of Commons, the delegates, or rather a section of them, appeared on the scene in
person with a petition to Parliament.   Many of the delegates recoiled before the apprehensions which had already
been aroused by the presence in the capital of a representative delegation deliberating side by side with Parliament.
To allay these misgivings, the other delegates who had signed
the petition presented it in their own name, dropping the title
of delegates.   In spite of this precaution, the legality of the
petition gave rise to a very animated debate in the House.
Besides the Ministerial majority, which of course vehemently
denounced the committees and the delegates, several independent members expressed the opinion that the associations and
the meetings of the delegates were unconstitutional; that the
members of the House were the proper delegates of the people;
that all plans of reform should emanate from the House; that,
apart from the extremely laudable object of the petition and
the undoubted respectability of the delegates, the bolder course
would be to take the earliest opportunity of resisting an extra-
constitutional intervention of this kind rather than allow the
creation of a dangerous precedent. [2]   Fox, in a show speech, delivered a panegyric on the associations, by connecting them with
the time-honoured struggles for liberty, and pronounced the
action of the delegates not only legal but highly meritorious considering the circumstances under which it had taken place.   Addressing himself to the legal aspect of the case, he asked to be

[1] *Journal of the Reign of King George III.*, Lond. 1859, Vol. II, p. 378.
[2] See the speeches of Coke, Powys, Sir Horace Mann, Rolle (*Parliamentary
History*, Vol. XXII, pp. 144. 157, 196).

shown the law which prohibited the people from appointing delegates to live in London for the purpose of watching the conduct of their representatives. We are told, he remarked, that the committees, the associations, and the delegates want to overthrow the Constitution, but the contrary is the truth; for are not the delegates rendering homage to the Sovereign and to the omnipotence of Parliament by applying to them for the redress of their grievances?[1] The reply was an adroit one, but it was obviously somewhat beside the real question, which was not whether the extra-constitutional organization was contrary to or in conformity with the letter of the law, but whether, in view of its consequences, and of the reaction which it might bring about in political life, it was compatible with the regular working of the representative system. General Burgoyne, without specifying the point in this way, bluntly took his stand on political ground: he declared that there were moments when resistance to the supreme power was a duty, that cases of the kind had existed in times when the encroachments of the Crown were avowed and obvious, that in the present case the Crown was aiming at absolute power by clandestine methods, and that the only point to be considered was whether the delegates conscientiously believed that they were doing their duty in promoting the plan of associations.[2] The great lawyer Dunning (afterwards the first Lord Ashburton) summed up the debate. In his opinion, the right of forming associations was a corollary of the right of petitioning; if the citizens had the right of forwarding petitions to the Legislature, they were entitled to unite for this purpose. To descend to particular cases, this or that association was lawful or not according to the intention with which it had been formed or the aim which it pursued. There might of course be illegal or criminal associations, but even these latter might under certain circumstances be justifiable. If the House of Commons, forgetful of its origin and of its duty, became the slave of the Crown and the Lords or of one of these powers, it would be perfectly legal for the people of Great Britain to resume their just share in the Legislature; and the means employed for this purpose, whether associations, remonstrances, or force, would be not only lawful but meritorious. On this particular occasion

[1] *Parliam. History*, Vol. XXII, pp. 144, 176. [2] *Ibid.* p. 157.

all the proceedings had been conducted with calm and dignity; the sole object of the members of the associations was to support, by legal and constitutional measures, the contents of the petitions presented to Parliament for the redress of grievances. As for the delegates, their action was confined to the mission entrusted to them, namely that of maintaining the definite objects of the petition; if they went beyond this they would exceed their powers and lose their character of delegates.[1]

II

Parliament refused to examine the petitions promoted by the "corresponding committees," and the latter soon vanished from the scene. But when the triumph of the Revolution in France revived ideas of liberty, the movement for the Reform of the House of Commons reappeared, and associations were again formed for the purpose of carrying it to a successful issue. These societies, composed chiefly of workmen, soon became the organ of the extreme section of opinion, and the instrument of a democratic agitation throughout England. They spent a good deal of their time in exchanging congratulatory addresses with the French Convention, the Commune of Paris, and the French clubs. The English associations imitated the French revolutionists in everything. Their members took the name of "citizens," and they manufactured the word "citizeness" in order to give the same appellation to women.[2] Their programmes and their declarations were couched in the same highflown style, decked with the flowers of the political language of the day: tyranny, national will, humanity, nature, etc.[3] The

---

[1] *Parliam. History*, Vol. XXII, p. 198.

[2] In the United States, where the same republican masquerade was then still more freely indulged in, the variation *citess* was introduced ("Both men and women seemed for the time to have put away their wits and gone mad with republicanism. . . . At Boston every man was soon calling his neighbor Citizen and his wife Citess." — J. B. McMaster, *A History of the People of the United States*, N.Y. 1893, Vol. II, p. 94).

[3] The following is a specimen taken from the manual of the "Birmingham Society for Constitutional Information" (Printed for the Society, MDCCXCII): "In order to do away with privilege and oppression, the intention of our meeting is to establish a brotherhood of affection with the whole human race for the promotion of knowledge, and to establish love and goodwill among all men, the free citizens of the earth. . . . We . . . call to mind the sentiments which nature has engraved in the heart of every citizen,

avowed object of these organizations was still parliamentary reform, but they declined to admit it on any basis other than that of universal suffrage.[1] The moderates, whose views were becoming more and more disregarded in the reformist camp, did not, however, abandon the cause of reform. They founded the " Society of the Friends of the People " on their own account, but refused to co-operate with the democratic organizations which invited them to join a national convention. The extreme moderation of the " Friends of the People" did not protect them from the general disapproval incurred by the political associations. Fox himself repudiated them from his seat in Parliament, while remaining faithful to the reform of the representation. They were all the more strongly denounced by Pitt and Burke, who waged war against " French principles." The extravagant and occasionally somewhat seditious language of the " corresponding societies " alarmed the ruling classes and contributed not a little to make them plunge headlong into reaction. The Government adopted a repressive policy; it commenced proceedings against the members of the societies and directed prosecution after prosecution against the Press. After an enquiry into the societies, conducted by a secret committee of the House of Commons, Pitt obtained the suspension of the Habeas Corpus Act from the House (1794). In the following year the Government carried a Bill restricting the liberty of public meeting.[2] The popular organizations, hampered in their operations by this law, took refuge in mystery. A network of secret associations spread over England. They maintained an active correspondence, organized a secret system of publication, distributed writings clandestinely, and posted up seditious placards. Pitt passed a bill suppressing some asso-

and which take a new force when solemnly recognized by all; for a nation to love liberty it is sufficient that she knows it, and to be free it is sufficient that she wills it."

[1] In the Parliament thus reformed, declared the " London Corresponding Society," " there would be no party debates, the interests of the people being one; long speeches much diminished, honest men seeking reason not oratory." The rest is on a par with this.

[2] No meeting of more than fifty persons (except county and borough meetings duly called) should be held for considering petitions and addresses, for alterations of matters in Church and State, or for discussing any grievance, without previous notice to a Magistrate, who should attend to prevent any proposition or discourse tending to bring into hatred or contempt the Sovereign or the government and constitution (Seditious Meetings Act, 36 Geo. III, c. 8).

ciations by name and declaring illegal all societies the members
of which had to take an oath not required by law, all those
with members or committees unknown to the whole society and
not entered on its books, and all those which were composed of
distinct sections or branches.

When, towards the close of the war with Napoleon, and in
the years which immediately followed it, the distress produced
by the fall in wages and the high price of corn rekindled discontent among the masses, they took it into their heads that
the remedy lay in the introduction of universal suffrage and
annual Parliaments.   To obtain these reforms, a vast organization was set on foot in the form of clubs which were started
in almost every village, " Hampden clubs," " Spencean clubs,"
etc.[1]   The Legislature intervened once more, and the repressive
measures directed against the " corresponding societies " were
followed (in 1817) by new ones placing obstacles in the way of
the appointment and the co-operation of delegates of various
societies.[2]

III

The political organizations were not rooted out.   The movement retired below the surface, but only until the next occasion
for popular disturbances.   When the price of bread was rising,
the starving masses began to move, the demands for parliamentary reform reappeared, and with them the secret associations.   In 1830, a great economic crisis broke out.   The middle
class, having become conscious of its importance through its
wonderful success in the field of industry, on this occasion
joined the masses in the agitation for reform.   Organizations
were formed in broad daylight, the membership of which was
no longer confined to workmen, and which boldly confronted
monopoly and aristocratic privileges with right and justice.
Their idea was that "they may have the reform which has
been proposed, if they will show that they really desire to
have it; and to show this desire they must form themselves
into unions, and endeavour to procure as many petitions
to Parliament and memorials to the King as they can."[3]

[1] Report of the Secret Committee of the House of Commons, of the 19th
February, 1817 (*Hansard*, XXXV, 439–445).   [2] 57 Geo. III, c. 19.
[3] Letter of Francis Place to G. Grote (*Personal Life of Mr. Grote*, p. 69,
Lond. 1873).

Birmingham became the centre of the agitation. It was there that arose, in 1830, the first "general political union between the lower and the middle classes of the people," which was soon imitated in all the large towns of the Kingdom. The Birmingham Union repudiated all notion of violence, it simply claimed to "produce the peaceful display of an immense organized moral power, which cannot be despised or disregarded."[1] The Union sent up petitions to the King; it asked him to dismiss the Ministry, which was hostile to reform. During the discussion of the Reform Bill in Parliament it organized demonstrations in which members marched in procession wearing their special badges, and preceded by bands of music. The Unions kept up the agitation in every quarter with the greatest energy. At a meeting held in London it was resolved, in order to bring the various Unions in the country into line, to form a confederation, the "National Political Union," with a political council sitting in the capital. But the central organization, which was controlled by representatives from the working classes, speedily fell into the hands of men of extreme opinions, and they very soon seriously compromised it. The Government became alarmed, and a Royal proclamation (of the 22d November, 1831) declared as illegal and unconstitutional all "political associations composed of separate bodies with various divisions and subdivisions under leaders with a gradation of rank and authority and subject to the general control and direction of a superior committee or council."[2] The Unions then gave up their system of affiliation, but none the less continued their agitation until the Lords had yielded and the Reform Bill had become law. At one moment the Birmingham Union threatened to march on London, if the Lords persisted in their opposition.

After the victory the middle class hastened to leave the Unions, and they soon died out. Their atmosphere was too democratic for the middle classes, who, moreover, had obtained their object. The great Whig leaders now spoke of their old popular allies, the "Birmingham fellows," with a touch of disdain,[3] and they turned up their noses when reminded of the

---

[1] J. A. Langford, *A Century of Birmingham Life*, Lond. 1868, II, 536.
[2] *Annual Register*, 1831, p. 297.
[3] *Greville Memoirs*, 4th ed. Vol. II, p. 215.

organizations which had helped to secure for them Reform and power.[1] The working classes having been left out of the franchise, found themselves, moreover, in no better material condition. Their sufferings were intense, and, with a naïve belief in political panaceas, they recommenced the agitation for universal suffrage. A "Workingmen's Association" was started, and, with the aid of the Radical members of the House of Commons, they framed "The People's Charter," and carried the agitation into the country. The movement assumed enormous dimensions, and has become famous under the name of "Chartism." The political Union of Birmingham, as well as those of several other towns, was revived. The Chartists sent delegates to London from all the great manufacturing centres; they formed themselves into a national convention (in 1839) and the "People's Parliament," as it was styled, held its sittings side by side with the Parliament of the Realm. The convention eagerly got up the great petition with 1,200,000 signatures. In 1840, the Chartist organization underwent a fresh development; at Manchester the "National Charter Association" was founded, which was soon joined by four hundred affiliated societies, with a very large number of members. However, the triumph of the extreme party and its violent propaganda had alienated public opinion from Chartism; the movement had no effect whatever on the constituted authorities, and wasted its strength in futile efforts. The success of the Revolution of 1848 in France gave for a while fresh life to the hopes of the Chartists. They played their great card of the monster petition with 6,000,000 signatures, the ignominious failure of which is a matter of history. After Parliament had refused to take it into consideration, the Chartist convention, which was sitting in London, moved to Birmingham. Soon afterwards it disappeared in the break-up of the Chartist movement.

But the agitation for a fresh extension of the franchise survived, Birmingham still remaining the prime mover in it. A network of societies for keeping up the propaganda spread from this centre. Under the titles of "Household Suffrage

---

[1] See the conversation between Lord Grey and the painter Haydon, who proposed to paint a picture of a public meeting held by the political Union (*Life of B. Haydon*, Vol. II, p. 344, quoted in Bunce, *History of the Corporation of Birmingham*, I, 130).

Societies," "Complete Suffrage Societies," "Reform Associations," etc., these organizations existed in various places, with more or less vitality. But they were very far from possessing the importance of the "Political Unions." Their influence was not very great, except in some parts of the North. Eventually the Reform Act of 1867 deprived them of their *raison d'être*.

IV

The reformers had not been alone in using the weapon of association; their opponents had done the same on more than one occasion. About 1793, when the democratic propaganda was in full swing, many societies had been formed for assisting the Government in discovering and punishing seditious writings or speeches. They acted by means of spies and informers. The first of these associations was the "Society for the Protection of Liberty and Property against Republicans and Levellers."[1] In 1820, the "Constitutional Association" was founded for a similar object.[2] Subsequently, when the agitation assumed a more peaceful character, there arose "constitutional associations" which opposed the extension of the franchise by less reprehensible methods.

It was chiefly religious passions, however, which supplied a pretext for reactionary organizations. In consequence of an Act of Parliament which conceded a certain amount of toleration to the Catholics (in 1778), fanatical Protestants started an agitation for obtaining the repeal of the law. A large number of Protestant associations and committees were formed. They became a hotbed of an odious propaganda among the lower orders, carried on by speeches, sermons, and incendiary handbills. It was as if political association, which had barely sprung into life, was anxious to show that, if it could serve as the mouthpiece of enlightened opinion, it could still more easily become the tool of base passions and of a malignant fanaticism. The Protestant associations formed a sort of confederation, with Lord George Gordon at its head, and spread over the whole country. After a meeting of the Association in

[1] J. Adolphus, *History of England from the Accession of George III to 1783*, Lond. 1802, Vol. V, p. 225.

[2] Spencer Walpole, *History of England*, II, 19; Erskine May, *The Constitutional History of England*, Lond. 1865, II, 206.

London, at which Gordon presided, a frenzied mob marched on the Houses of Parliament, broke into the lobbies, and nearly forced its way into the House of Commons while it was sitting. Then for the space of a week the rioters made barbarous havoc in the capital, burnt the chapels of the Catholic embassies, broke open the prisons, and destroyed private houses.

A few years later a similar movement arose in Ireland. Bands of Protestants, over-zealous for their religion, took up arms against their Catholic fellow-citizens. After defeating their opponents they kept up their organization and formed themselves into societies for maintaining Protestant ascendency. These associations, known as "Orange Lodges," spread into England and multiplied there to a great extent.

The Irish Catholics in their turn resorted to organization, and after many attempts, which were continually hampered by the English Government, created a formidable organization for upholding the disregarded and violated rights of their nation and their religion. This was the "Catholic Association," formed in 1823. Possessing ramifications throughout the country, it set up as a rival power to the Government and assumed all its powers. Its ascendency over the Catholic population was complete, and it openly defied the English authorities. The latter were finally obliged to yield, and the Act of Emancipation was carried in 1829.

V

This was the first time that a great legislative measure was forced on the country through the pressure of a political organization. But it had only achieved this result by a demonstration of the material strength which it had succeeded in bringing into the field: the English Government had yielded when confronted by the prospect of a civil war. Three years afterwards, in the agitation for the Reform Bill, the Political Unions were an important factor, and, like the Catholic Association, helped to incline the scale towards their own side by intimidation, by a display of physical force. It was only in the agitation which led to the third great reform, the repeal of the Corn Laws, that the political Association which took the lead in the movement used moral force as its main weapon, the power of convictions which it brought home to the mind. In the field of philanthropy, association had already succeeded in winning peaceful victories. The " Anti-Slavery Association," one of the greatest ever known in England, had converted public opinion and the constituted authorities simply by its indefatigable propaganda. It was this body which brought about the abolition of the slave trade and afterwards of slavery itself. But in the sphere of politics, the Anti-Corn Law League was the first and is still the greatest example of a political association contributing to the legislative triumph of an idea by instilling it into the national conscience. The masses remained indifferent to the movement during the early years of its existence. The workmen, still engrossed in the pursuit of the panacea of universal suffrage, looked on all other agitation as an unfair competition. The leaders of the League, on their side, although very favourable to the introduction of universal suffrage in principle, deemed it expedient to limit the agitation, to keep the question of economic liberty distinct before the public mind. Consequently the League, not having the passions of the masses at its disposal and not making any appeal to them, was obliged to lean, materially and morally, on the middle class, which was directly interested in the question of commercial freedom, and to conduct the campaign by means of discussion alone. It was this last point which gave the League its distinctive character. In fact, its labours constituted an immense *persuasive agitation.* It sent forth a body of public speakers to carry on the free-trade propaganda, who traversed the country in all directions. Cobden, Bright, and the other leaders of the League were indefatigable; they travelled unceasingly from one end of the country to the other, wherever there were minds to be convinced or consciences to be won. At the instigation of the League associations were formed in all the manufacturing centres, meetings of delegates were held in every district, the question was discussed in all its aspects and on every occasion. At the same time, the League was engaged in conducting a vast economic enquiry. Its agents and adherents had to collect information on the state of trade, the rate of wages, the growth of pauperism, and generally on everything which affected the means of subsistence. As this information poured unceasingly into headquarters, an immense provision of facts and arguments accumulated at Manchester, which the League took care to turn to the best account in its propaganda. The more stubborn the resistance of the Protectionists, the greater became the zeal of the Leaguers in their missionary effort. They undertook "a campaign against every elector in the Kingdom" by literature distributed from house to house,[1] and by lectures. From the towns they passed into the country districts, and there they endeavoured to drive the idea of free trade into the heads of the farmers. The Protectionists tried to counteract the League by the same methods, by founding associations, but they lacked vitality and spontaneity; the farmers attended the meetings of these associations as if by compulsion; the stewards and agents of the landlords used to come to their houses and fetch them to the meetings.[2]

The landlords, entrenched behind the majority in Parliament, continued to resist; but the mind of the country was made up, thanks to the League, and only a shock was needed to make the fruit drop from the tree. The bad harvest which supervened in Ireland supplied this. The inevitable famine and the determination of the League not to dissolve until the duties on corn were abolished made the Protectionists give way, and legislative sanction was accorded to the measure which had already been approved by the national conscience.

VI

Thus the three great reforms which have renovated England, religious freedom, parliamentary reform, and economic liberty, were obtained under pressure from extra-constitutional organizations. On each occasion their interference with the legislature assumed the aspect of an exceptional case justified by the quasi-revolutionary features of the situation[3]: that is that public

---

[1] In 1843, 500 agents were engaged in distributing pamphlets throughout the towns; they visited 24 counties and 187 towns, and distributed more than 9,000,000 printed papers.

[2] A. Prentice, *History of the Anti-Corn Law League*, II, 218, 219.

[3] And even those who led the struggle or rallied the masses to it were the first to plead extenuating circumstances. We are already acquainted with the observations submitted to Parliament on this point in 1780. Fifty years later, when extra-parliamentary agitation had had time to become familiar to English political life, in 1832, the champions of Reform admitted that the formation of the Political Unions was unconstitutional, but that the reformers

opinion was not allowed to assert itself freely and fully within the boundaries of the constitution. The object of each movement was the redress of a grievance; its aim was specified and limited; and the combination formed was consequently a provisional organization destined to come to an end with the triumph of the particular cause which had called it into life. The organization of opinion in the country did not tend to supplant its constitutional organ. On the contrary, the object of the first attempts at extra-constitutional organization was to make Parliament more independent; and the latter, when once rehabilitated and raised to its ideal level, was to remain undisputed master of the situation. The movement of opinion was directed, not against Parliament and constitutional government, but against the factions which had monopolized them. In fact, at the first awakening of opinion under George III, combination is resorted to as a means of forming a patriotic party with the object of reminding the coterie which has a majority in Parliament and a monopoly of power, of their duty. Corruption disappears from Parliament; the basis of national representation is widened by the Reform Act of 1832, but the approaches to Government, to the Legislature, are guarded by parties which do not reflect opinion with its unceasing aspirations towards an improved moral and material existence, but are more in the nature of traditional sets, stereotyped in their petty ideas and their paltry passions, against which every new current of opinion is powerless. The struggle for economic liberty brought out this situation in all its clearness, and all the efforts of the League, from the very first day, were in the direction of keeping the question outside parliamentary parties, of lifting it above them. The organ of the League, the "Anti-Corn Law Circular," roundly declared that all political factions were equally dishonest and corrupt, that the adherents of the abolition of the duties on corn would never allow their great cause to be converted into an official cry, that they would continue, without swerving from their path, to appeal to the na-

had been provoked. See with reference to this the *History of the Thirty Years' Peace* of H. Martineau, whose position in the Reform camp is well known ("There was no question about the fact but only about the justification of it. No one denies that occasions may and do occur when the assertion of a nation's will against either a corrupt government or a tyrannical party is virtuous and absolutely required by patriotic duty." Vol. II, p. 25).

tion at large, convinced as they were that the repeal of the protective duties would never be granted by the one or the other set of "pettifoggers," of whom the country was alternately the victim.[1] Cobden held identical opinions. While fighting the Tory Government with the utmost energy, he wrote to his brother, in 1842: "The worst danger is of the Whigs coming in again too soon. The hacks would be up on their hind legs, and at their old prancing tricks again, immediately they smelt the Treasury crib."[2] The fall of the Ministry might have put the country on the wrong scent, whereas it would only have been the substitution of one coterie for another; and the object was to strike a blow at cliques in general. John Bright had the same preoccupation.[3] Cobden was never weary of declaring that he was just as ready to accept reform from the hands of Sir Robert Peel as from Lord John Russell. And when Peel was on the point of yielding, and the Whigs broke out into exultation, Cobden could not help exclaiming: " What a bold farce it is now to attempt to parade the Whig party as the Free Traders *par excellence!* I will be no party to such a fraud as the attempt to build up its ruined popularity upon a question in which the Whig aristocracy and proprietors in the counties either take no interest, or, if so, only to resist it. I see no advantage, but much danger, to our cause from the present efforts to set up the old party distinctions."[4]

In the end the law for the complete abolition of the corn duties was passed. It was a triumph of extra-constitutional organization over parliamentary parties representing a small fraction of the nation. As the special object of the League was attained, its dissolution was at hand. But Cobden saw with regret that the fountain-head of the abuse which he had striven against would be untouched if the old party system survived. He applied to Peel, his enemy of the day before. He approached him for the first time in his life. In an urgent appeal, he implored him to put an end to party government by placing himself at the head of the whole middle class: "There must be an end of the juggle of parties, the mere representatives of tradition."[5]

[1] J. Morley, *Life of R. Cobden,* Lond. 1881, Vol. I, p. 151.
[2] *Ibid.* p. 241.   [3] Prentice, *History of the Anti-Corn Law League,* II, 25.
[4] J. Morley, *Life of Cobden,* I, 363.   [5] *Ibid.* 395.

SECOND CHAPTER

THE BEGINNINGS OF PARTY ORGANIZATIONS

I

THE parties, however, had laid hands on the very weapon which was being used against them, extra-parliamentary organization. The movement had begun somewhat late. For a long time parties had no distinct life of their own save in Parliament; in the country they barely existed as moral entities independently of the personages or families which were the embodiment of them. The language of the day only testified to the facts in using, instead of " Tory " and " Whig," such expressions as " the Rutland interest," " the Bedford interest," etc. The voters simply represented the personal following of the rivals who fought the electoral duel; they were their retainers or sold themselves to them on the polling-day for money. In the counties the tenant followed his land-lord. When the estate changed hands, all the tenants changed their political complexion, if the new landlord did not belong to the same party as his predecessor. This occurred very often, even after the parliamentary reform of 1832.[1] The rural free-holders, who were more independent, generally gravitated in the orbit of the great nobleman who irradiated the neighbour-hood. Of the boroughs, several were directly dependent on territorial magnates, who owned them as private property or exerted a hereditary influence over them. Most of the other towns sold themselves at the elections, wholesale or in lots. The operations of sale and purchase were often conducted through the agency of organized bodies, sometimes public

[1] Even after 1832, the custom of asking the landlord's permission to canvass his tenants had been continued. This permission was seldom granted (Report from the Select Committee on Bribery, 1835, Blue Books of 1835, Vol. VIII. p. 228).

bodies, such as municipalities, which made money out of their boroughs, sometimes voluntary organizations, which acted in the guise of non-political societies or even as societies without any legal existence.[1] Side by side with these juntas there sprang up occasionally, in a sporadic fashion and with an ephemeral existence, *bona fide* political organizations, in the form of clubs or committees, for supporting a particular candidate.

But whatever the organs of electoral action, secret or avowed, municipal corporations, clubs or private agents, they represented local divisions and rivalries more than anything else. The only party organization on a basis approaching a national basis was in Parliament. Its efforts were felt essentially within the walls of Parliament itself. The members who had secured election through the territorial influence or that of their patrons, or who bought their seats for ready money, were practically independent of their constituencies. The parliamentary parties would therefore have wasted their time in trying to influence the electors. It was the members that the Government or the Opposition had to make sure of at all hazards. When the parliamentary cliques did not supply a sufficient number of followers to the Government or the Opposition, the latter bought parliamentary boroughs directly on their own account, or assisted political friends engaged in electioneering with their own money. It is in this way that party organizations confined within the walls of Parliament came to extend their action, in a subsidiary fashion, over the country. After 1832 their intervention increased to a considerable extent. It helped to cover the country with a network of organizations which were destined to completely alter the balance of power inside the parties themselves.

[1] Thus the first committee to enquire into electoral matters appointed in virtue of the Grenville Act (of 1776) disclosed the existence in a certain town of a *Christian Club*, formed ostensibly for purposes of charity, but which was really engaged in selling the borough at election times to the highest bidder, and which afterwards divided the money amongst its members. Another instance discovered during the electoral enquiry of 1835, is the *Blue Club* or *Committee*, at Bristol, which, in return for votes, used its influence with the Government to obtain favours, appointments, and even pardons for offences against the revenue (Report on Bribery, 1835, p. 377).

II

The study of party organization in Parliament must therefore engage our attention in the first place. It was represented at that time, as in our own day, by the " Whips " which each party has in the House of Commons. In fox-hunting language "Whip" denotes the huntsman's assistant who whips in the pack of hounds; applied by analogy to the parliamentary hunting-field, this sporting term has in political language acquired a more complicated meaning, and one which is not so easy to explain. The shortest and most accurate definition of "Whips" would perhaps be the following: stage-managers of companies who unite in acting the parliamentary play; stage-managers, and not directors. This last office is filled by the leaders, the Prime Minister or one of his colleagues, if he does not sit in the House of Commons himself, and the leader of the Opposition. The two chiefs act in broad daylight, and are responsible to the public; the Whips work in the dark, and are unknown to the mass of the public. The leaders lay down the main line of action, and exert themselves actively on great occasions. The Whips, who are initiated by the leaders into all the secrets of the plan of action, see that it is carried out, and keep an eye on the actors so as to ensure that each man is at his post and ready to play the part which has been allotted to him, whether it is a minor part or even that of a supernumerary. Being constantly in touch with the members in the lobbies, etc. of the House, the Whip is in a position to follow the current of opinion in the party; he reports thereon to the leader, nips incipient revolts in the bud, retails the leader's views to the members of the party, and communicates to them the plans into which the leader thinks it expedient or necessary to initiate them. The authority of the Whip is of a purely moral nature; it is derived solely from the prestige of his position and from his tact. He must be acquainted with each member, know his weak and strong points, be able to talk him round, to coax him by smiles, by exhortations, by friendly remonstrances, by promises or other devices, such as invitations to the entertainments of the dukes and marquises of the party which he gets for members and their wives. Every day he must perform wonders of affability, of patience, and of firmness, in view of the object which is the dream of a Whip's whole existence: to keep the party united, compact, and in fighting order.

When state policy and party strategy do not demand the attention of the Whip, he has his daily drudgery to perform, which is to mount guard over his men from one sitting to another. If he is the Government Whip, he is specially responsible for the regular working of the parliamentary machine. He must take care "to make a House" and "keep a House," so that the Government bills or motions of the day can be discussed. He must have a reserve of members in the lobbies or in the smoking-room to take the place of those who have left the House, so as to stop the attempts of the other side to count it out. Still more necessary is it for him to have all his followers ready for the divisions. For the enemy is treacherous, and may plan a surprise and call a division unexpectedly. The Whip must act as watch-dog, and not allow members who want to dine out to leave the House. In any event he must know where to find them in case of need, and be able to warn them by telegram or special messenger. The fate of a ministry sometimes depends on the accuracy of his information of this kind, and on his rapidity of action. To prevent the debate from languishing the Whip must have a reserve of fluent speakers who can talk by the clock to enable those who are late to come in time for the division. The Whips of both parties often have to come to an understanding, as the parliamentary play is a piece with two *dramatis personæ*. On great field-days they settle the order in which speakers are to address the House, fix the number of sittings to be devoted to the debate, etc.

The performance of these duties requires uncommon suppleness, but is compatible with perfect honesty in our day. In the beginning, on the other hand, this quality was a fatal objection; for the post was created for the corruption of members in the criminal sense of the word. Ministers bought their majority by payment of actual cash; they had a window in the House itself where members came to be paid for their votes after the division. The First Lord of the Treasury, having too much to do, created, in 1714, the office of political secretary to the Treasury to aid him in these financial operations. This official was called the Patronage Secretary, because, in his capacity of agent of corruption, he disposed of the patronage, that is to say, of appointments to Government offices. Places in the Custom House, the Post Office, and the Excise were the small electoral change which the Government distributed at the request of members to their electors. The Patronage Secretary had another name — that of "Secretary for Political Jobs." This was in fact his principal business. "It is rather a roguish office," as Wilberforce remarked in the presence of Steele, just as the latter was about to take up the appointment. Distributing their allowance among the members of the party, the Patronage Secretary brought them up to the vote like a flock of sheep, goaded them on, and had become their "Whipper-in." The opposite party had to adopt a similar mode of discipline, and it also introduced the office of Whip or Whipper-in. The Patronage Secretary had to supply the Government with a majority as cheaply as possible. For a long time, at any rate up to Pitt's accession to power, he worked directly on the members, and bought each of them individually. When, owing to the improvement in Parliamentary manners, these transactions perceptibly diminished or disappeared altogether, the Patronage Secretary and his *vis-à-vis* on the other side, the Opposition Whip, bought constituencies, that is, seats in Parliament, for friends who were to vote as they were told. The Whippers-in negotiated with corporations or private individuals who had seats to sell, or, in "contested" elections,[1] sent down their candidates well supplied with the sinews of war. The Government Whip was in the best position for operations of this kind. He had secret service money at his disposal. George III contributed largely to it from his civil list. The amelioration of manners made itself felt here, too, and, after the elections of 1806, Lord Granville was able to publicly announce that not a guinea of public money had been spent on the election campaign. The Patronage Secretary had discovered another expedient. He had bought boroughs cheap, below the market price, from friends of the Government, paying them the difference in titles or other favours at the disposal of the Government. Then he

---

[1] A vote is not always taken at elections; if there is only one candidate, he is declared elected without a poll. A poll is held only when there is more than one candidate for the seat. In the former case, the election is called "uncontested"; in the latter, it is styled "contested."

had resold his seats at the price of the day, and with the well-understood obligation for the buyers to vote with the Government. The money made in this speculation was used to buy additional seats or to help friendly candidates engaged in contested elections. As long as the purchase and sale of seats in the market and the traffic with corporations lasted, the Patronage Secretary and the Opposition Whip took an active share in it on behalf of their respective parties. This is how the organization of parliamentary parties as represented by the Whips worked outside Parliament.

III

It was not till after the Reform that regular party organizations arose in the country. The Act of 1832 was the direct occasion of them. The Reform Bill, which had altered the constitutional machinery, also prescribed new methods for its working; but in spite of all the care bestowed on the point, several gaps were left, especially as regards the preparation of the electoral lists. Before 1832, there was no register of electors at all, and no documents of any kind to prove their qualification. The official who presided over the elections (returning officer) checked the claims of persons who came forward to vote at the poll itself. Consequently the polling for the election of a member to Parliament lasted for months. But as this procedure became impossible with the increase in the number of electors entailed by the Reform Act, the Legislature, when sanctioning the extension of the suffrage, made arrangements for the formation of electoral lists. This matter having been settled in great detail, the Act of 1832 left the execution of the provisions to the representatives of parochial self-government. The parish overseers of the poor, who were selected annually from among its inhabitants by the justices of the peace, for the assessment and collection of the poor rate of the locality, were entrusted by the law with the duty of keeping the electoral lists. The Legislature thought they would be able to discharge this duty satisfactorily, because in their capacity of local taxation agents they had information concerning every person entitled to the vote by his property qualification.

This was only partly the case. True, every holding situated in the parish being ratable to the poor, the occupiers of holdings of the letting value of at least £10, to whom the Reform Bill had just granted the suffrage, necessarily figured on the overseers' lists. But the occupation of a holding was not the sole condition attached to the right of voting; there were other electoral qualifications besides. To find out the holders of them, the overseer had to call on them by public notice to make themselves known. The electoral register having been prepared in this way, on the strength of information which reached the overseers from various sources, was corrected by the representations of private individuals if the latter thought fit to make them. Each elector had the right to lodge with the overseer a claim, if his name had been left out, or an objection to the admission on the register of the fellow-citizens who appeared to him not to possess the necessary qualifications. The disputes to which this gave rise were referred to the Revising Barrister, a member of the Bar appointed annually by the judge of the circuit to hold the registration court, in which the parties appeared as in a court of law for a civil suit. The Revising Barrister was empowered to settle the register by admitting well-founded claims and objections.[1] An appeal lay from his decision to a parliamentary committee, and since 1843 to the Court of Common Pleas.

This system, which rested to such a large extent on private initiative, was evidently framed on the assumption that this initiative would be sufficiently active to secure the regular preparation of the electoral register. In practice, the electors displayed the most complete indifference on the subject. The electioneering manners and customs before 1832 were little calculated to develop a sentiment of electoral duty or the habit of spontaneous action in the voter. The rank and file of the voters, ignored and slightly despised by the ruling classes, became all at once an object of their solicitude when election time came on. Then they were canvassed, wheedled, or intimidated on behalf of some *grand seigneur* or of a wealthy candidate who spent money lavishly. As soon as the voting was over, the voter sank back into political obscurity, until he

---

[1] Before Reform was carried, the returning officer who had to examine the qualifications of the voters at the poll used to consult a barrister on doubtful points. The Act of 1832 only legalized the intervention of lawyers in a way by providing for the appointment of revising barristers.

was once more fetched to be dragged to the poll. The mere promulgation of the Reform Bill could not alter manners and customs on the spot. All that the new electoral machinery could do and ought to have done, was to make the material conditions attached to the right of voting easy of fulfilment. The Act of 1832 did just the contrary by letting the State remain a stranger to the preparation of the register and leaving the duty to private individuals. A voter who had not known how to comply with the required formalities, who had not replied in good time to the objection which a fellow-citizen took it into his head to lodge against him in the overseer, or who had not thought fit to waste a day in supporting his claim before the Revising Barrister lost his right of voting *ipso facto*, for the year. And the following year he had to begin over again. In addition to this, the law had prescribed a registration fee of one shilling, and many electors objected to it.

The State had trusted to private initiative; private individuals did not trouble their heads about the matter; so the only persons left to take an interest in the register were the members of Parliament or the candidates who were contesting the constituency. Clearly, it would have been of no use to them to make converts, to recruit adherents if these latter were prevented from voting for them because they had not established their right to vote in good time, owing to the complicated procedure of registration. It was therefore in the interest of the rival candidates to help the electors to get over the formalities which lay between them and the vote. In doing so they not only secured the attendance of their thick-and-thin partisans at the poll, but also made recruits among the lukewarm, who naturally were inclined to give their vote to those who had procured it for them. Politicians soon grasped the new situation created by the Act of 1832, and from and after this time party spirit fastened on the electoral register. Left to itself by the constituted authorities, registration became, so to speak, a gap through which the parties, hitherto confined to Parliament, made their way into the constituencies and gradually covered the whole country with the network of their organization.

The party machinery which was started for this purpose after 1832 was not of a uniform character. In some places the

business of registration was for a long time left to the intervention of private individuals, under the hap-hazard operation
of local circumstances, generally at the instigation and on behalf
of members or interested candidates. But in several districts
" Registration Societies " made their appearance. There were
some of them in various places as early as 1832. These societies were composed of adherents of the party who paid a
subscription to defray the expenses of registration operations.
The bigwigs of the party of course headed the list, and it was
they who supplied the greater part of the funds. The staff of
the Registration Societies collected information relating to the
legal qualifications of the electors, placed themselves in communication with the overseers and appeared before the Revising
Barristers to support the claims of their friends and oppose
those of their political antagonists. The earliest Registration
Societies do not seem to have had a very large number of
members. A good many electors, especially those engaged in
trade, did not like to parade political preferences for fear of
losing customers belonging to the opposite party. The threat
of withdrawing custom from shop-keepers if they voted for *the
other* side was one of the commonest and most effective weapons of political propaganda at that time. This was why the
Registration Societies had secret members who paid the subscription, but who were not entered on the lists.[1] For the
same reason, a good many electors declined to be placed on the
electoral register and chose to forego their right of voting.[2]

IV

The period which immediately succeeded the Reform Bill
was also marked by the appearance of central party organizations, the influence and activity of which were destined to
radiate from London over the whole country. The first of them
was the Carlton Club, founded by the Conservatives. Political
clubs were not unknown in England before this. Their origin
goes back to the seventeenth century ; it is almost contemporary
with the introduction of the use of coffee into England and with
the establishment of coffee-houses, which speedily became places
for social meeting and for political and other intercourse. In

---

[1] Report on Bribery, 1835, p. 183.   [2] *Ibid.* p. 400.

1659 the club "Rota" was founded in one of these coffee-houses; its frequenters, Republicans bent on free discussion, indulged in regular political debates followed by voting by ballot. Harrington, the author of "Oceana," was a leading figure at these meetings, and apparently it was his favourite scheme of rotation in office which gave the club its name. This club as well as those of other shades of political opinion (the "Rump Clubs" of the Jacobites, the "Calf's Head Clubs" of the Whigs, etc.) did not live long. But at the beginning of the eighteenth century, in the great outburst of clubs under Queen Anne, political clubs reappeared. They were composed of a knot of political friends who met in certain taverns to dine well and drink hard. During the second half of the eighteenth century they assumed a more definite political character on the pattern of party divisions in Parliament. One famous tavern was frequented by the Opposition, another was a resort of the Ministerialists. Gibbon, who belonged to the latter, has left a not very edifying description of the convivial gatherings of the Tory club which met at the "Cocoa Tree Tavern" in St. James' Street. These clubs, however, like the non-political clubs, had no separate existence in the present sense of the word "club"; they had no premises of their own, and no fixed number of members paying a subscription in order to procure the advantages of a decent common establishment. They were meetings of a more or less open and casual character. Real clubs, as we understand them nowadays, that is, clubs on the basis of subscription and formal admission of members, did not make their appearance till the nineteenth century. Established in the first instance to meet the requirements of sociability and the demand for comfort in a permanent fashion, clubs in this new aspect were soon destined to supply a base of operations for politicians.[1]

During the Reform Bill agitation, when the advanced Reformers started their "Political Unions," the Tories felt the need of closing their ranks and uniting for a common object.

---

[1] Cf. E. F. Robinson, *The Early History of Coffee Houses in England*, Lond. 1893; W. C. Sidney, *Social Life in England* from the Restoration to the Revolution, Lond. 1892, pp. 409–424, 433; W. C. Sidney, *England and the English in the 18th Century*, Lond. 1891, Vol. I, p. 218; W. Fraser Rae, "Political Clubs" (*Nineteenth Century*, May, 1878).

With this view, a number of leaders of the party, ex-Ministers and ex-ambassadors, assisted by several Tory country notables, founded the Carlton Club, in 1831, which was intended to combine the purpose of a social club and of a centre for rallying the party and for political action in general.

The plan of the club succeeded. Members of Parliament belonging to both Houses, from the leaders down to the most obscure members, met at the Carlton, laid their heads together there, and gave or received the word of command. The local leaders, the provincial notables who came up to London and wished to see the great men of the party, were sure to find them at the Carlton, and there they could approach them on a footing of equality and even of intimacy. The relations to which this gave rise and the influences resulting therefrom linked the constituencies to the Carlton all the more strongly because the tie was invisible. The note struck at the Carlton Club was invariably and faithfully re-echoed in the country, because there too, in every locality, the local leaders and the mass of electors were united by the same imperceptible ties of social influences. A political committee formed in the club itself kept up constant relations with the local associations or agents, and stimulated the work of electoral registration. The Liberals were not long in discerning the part played by the Carlton Club, and about 1836 they founded a similar institution with the name of the Reform Club, which in its turn soon became the headquarters of the Liberal party. It also had its political committee, which discharged the same duties as that of the Carlton.

In both clubs the threads were held by the party Whips. There they had all their parliamentary following ready to hand, and from there too they could work the provinces. They could no longer do it as in the days when they bought parliamentary boroughs and sold and resold them; the market had ceased to exist; but a sort of electoral labour exchange grew up in the clubs. The aspirants to parliamentary honours generally belonged to the Carlton or the Reform Club, — the politicians were not so very numerous, — and the Whips knew them all, their ambitions as well as their abilities. Provincials who had no candidates could recruit them in London, at the clubs, with the aid of the Whips.

V

The Whip was assisted by a general agent of the party whose special business was to watch the electoral situation in the constituencies. This chief agent had correspondents throughout the Kingdom. In places where there were associations their secretaries communicated with him. The information being concentrated in his hands, he in his turn was in a position to assist the Whip and the leaders of the party in general with his suggestions. At a time when the provincial Press possessed but little importance, and when it was credited in London with much less than it really possessed, local life was imperfectly known. Besides, public feeling on politics had few opportunities for displaying itself in the intervals between the elections. Consequently the electoral situation in different parts of the country appeared somewhat hazy, even to politicians. The general agent of the party was supposed to be able to see through it, and he enjoyed the same respect in party circles as country folk have for the local bone-setter. A Prime Minister, before risking a dissolution of Parliament, closeted himself with the agent of the party to consult him on the chances of a general election. When he appeared in the lobbies of the House, at times when a dissolution was in the air, people pressed round him; journalists hung upon his utterances as if they were those of the Delphic Oracle.

As time went on, this somewhat empirical fashion of managing electoral matters became inadequate; the necessity for more methodical action made itself felt, and, at the same time, it became inconvenient to attend to party business in the club itself, over one's wine, so to speak. The Liberal Whip Brand (afterward Viscount Hampden) thereupon started about 1861 an independent central organization called the "Liberal Registration Association," composed of members[1] elected by the committee and paying a subscription of a few pounds. Its principal business, as its name indicates, was to see after the register. It promoted the formation of Registration Societies, sent them instructions and circulars, gave them opinions on

---

[1] " Of gentlemen of known Liberal political opinions," in the words of the Statutes of the Association drawn up in March, 1861 (Art. I).

knotty points of law, and looked up non-resident electors (out-voters) throughout the Kingdom and sent them to the poll in their respective constituencies. The residence qualification in England is different for voters in boroughs and for those in counties. While the former, in order to exercise their right of voting, must reside within a radius of not more than seven miles from the borough, persons qualified to vote in counties may vote at an election even if they never live in their county. They can reside abroad, and yet preserve their right of voting if they like to exercise it. Non-resident electors were always a valuable contingent in electoral contests. Before 1832, when the suffrage was extremely restricted and the relative value of a vote was much greater, voters were occasionally fetched from abroad, from Holland and France.[1] The reimbursement of the outvoters' travelling expenses was one of the regular forms of electoral corruption; the real expense was exaggerated. The Legislature was obliged to intervene, and in 1858 the payment of travelling expenses, whether in cash or in any other shape, was prohibited; the law only allowed the candidate or his agent to supply the voter with the conveyance required to take him to the polling station.[2] The Registration Societies and the election agents thereupon undertook to treat with the carriage proprietors or the railway companies. The negotiations with the various railway companies were no easy matter for a local Association. But the difficulties did not end there; the great thing was to get hold of the absent voter, to persuade him to undertake the journey, and then supply him with the carriage or the railway ticket. And these outvoters were very numerous, at least fifteen per cent of the total number of electors.[3] The central organization which had just been formed in 1861 was destined to render signal service to the local organizations in all these matters. The Liberal Registration Association centralized all the work relating to outvoters. Being in posses-

---

[1] Report on Bribery, 1835, p. 123: Report from the Commissioners on Municipal Corporations in England and Wales, 1834. Appendix, Part IV, p. 2310 (Blue Books, 1835, Vol. XXXIV).

[2] 22 and 23 Vict. c. 87, s. 1.

[3] The following are some figures by way of example: the division of West Kent had, in 1858, out of 9000 electors, 1500 outvoters dispersed throughout the Kingdom: for the county of Middlesex, out of 14.500 voters on the register of 1866, 3000 lived out of the county.

sion of the electoral registers of the whole Kingdom it made separate lists of all persons who were entered on them as residing elsewhere, and, with the aid of its local correspondents, placed itself in communication with the outvoters in each locality and offered them railway tickets.[1] The railway companies received the fares on returning the tickets which had been used [2] to the Central Association, and the money was refunded the Association in its turn by the candidate on whose behalf the outvoters had made the journey.

Besides the management of registration and of the outvoters, the Association also undertook the recommendation of parliamentary candidates. Men who wished to stand for Parliament applied to the Association. The Whip took note of their political opinions, if they had any, and especially of the pecuniary sacrifices which they were disposed to make for the electoral struggle. He entered them in the candidates' book and classed them. A good Whip, after a talk with a candidate, could see at once whether he would do for any constituency, and fixed on the constituency which would probably suit him. Then, when there was an application for a candidate, the Association sent down a name to its local agent. The agent, who was frequently the secretary of the Registration Society, called a meeting of the party leaders, the most influential men, and submitted the candidate's name to them. Very often a deputation came up to London, and an interview was arranged between it and the candidate in the office of the Association. If they did not come to terms, the Association offered another candidate; it always had a supply of all shades of opinion and suited to all tastes. The Association did not put pressure on the constituencies in the choice of candidates, it only acted the part of honest broker. The Association did not spend any money on the elections, it was the candidate who had to defray all the expense. If he was a poor man and if his presence in Parliament was desirable in the interest of the party, the Whips supplied him with money ; they had funds subscribed by the wealthy men of the party which they used at their discretion. That a portion of these

[1] A first-class ticket was always given, even to workmen ; the voter considered it beneath his dignity to travel second or third on this occasion.

[2] As a rule, about fifty per cent of the outvoters consented to undertake the journey.

funds was employed in bribing voters when the candidate was not rich enough to do it himself, is not improbable. The intervention from London haunted people's minds in the provinces, even when it never took place; and, in accordance with the old tradition, it was attributed to the Carlton Club or to the Reform Club. In reality, the clubs had no share in it, they had lost their influence, especially the Reform Club; all the electoral operations of the party were henceforth managed from the office of the Central Association. The Conservative party founded one on the same basis as the Liberal organization which I have just described. After having been, at its start, under the control of a well-known firm of solicitors, it was soon placed in the hands of special agents. Devoting itself particularly to the cultivation of social relations, which were the electoral mainspring of the Conservative party, the central Tory office kept in close touch with the Carlton Club; if they had not the same body, they were animated by the same spirit.

The local correspondents of the central associations were generally solicitors. They were at the same time the moving spirits of the Registration Society, if there was one in the locality. They were not paid for these services, but it was to their interest to render them; either because their activity on behalf of the party gave them a connection and increased their practice, or because this activity marked them out beforehand for the appointment of election agent, who conducted the election campaign for a candidate, and this was an extremely lucrative employment. Besides the very ample remuneration which he received directly, the agent made a good deal of money out of the election expenses, which in the old days reached an enormous total and all passed through his hands.[1]

VI

The movement set on foot after the Reform Bill for the formation of local party associations continued with a strength which varied according to the times and the localities. The

[1] The accounts which the agent sent in after the election to the candidate for whom he had been working, were almost always of a fanciful and occasionally of a humorous description. Thus one agent entered among the various election expenses: "mental anxiety, £500."

Liberals set the example. The Conservatives followed when they had shaken off the torpor in which they had been plunged by Reform. Their leading statesman, Sir Robert Peel, more than once called the attention of his party to the importance of registration. "The battle of the Constitution," he said, "will be fought in the registration courts." Consequently, he exclaimed on another occasion, the watchword of the day should be: "Register, register, register!"[1] Following this advice, the Conservatives also set to work to form societies for attending to the registration and giving cohesion to the party. The principal scene of their activity was Lancashire, where, thanks to the assiduity with which their organizations devoted themselves to the register, the Conservatives succeeded in making up their lost ground in the county constituencies.[2] One feature which must be noticed and borne in mind in connection with these Lancashire organizations, is that they were divided into two categories, one for gentlemen and the other for the lower orders who had their own associations, under the name of "Conservative Operatives' Societies." The Liberal organizations were generally called "Liberal Registration Societies" or sometimes "Liberal Associations." The Conservative organizations were partial to the title of "Loyal and Constitutional Associations."[3] The agitation against the duties on corn gave a great impulse to the formation of Registration Societies. When the campaign of persuasion undertaken by Cobden and his friends was in an advanced stage, the League set about transforming the accumulated moral force into political force by preparing the mobilization of the electoral army for the next general election. But, as the exercise of the suffrage depended on the correctness of the electoral register, and the preparation of this register was left more or less to private initiative, the lists were in a state of great confusion in many places.[4] The League decided to intervene for the purpose of

[1] Speech at the Tamworth election dinner, 7 Aug. 1837, 28 July 1841, etc.

[2] *The Tory Reform Act*, by a member of the Council of the National Union of Conservative and Constitutional Associations, Lond. 1868.

[3] The first traces of a Conservative organization in the metropolis which I have discovered relate to the Loyal and Constitutional Association of the borough of Marylebone, about the year 1834 (Report on Bribery, 1835, p. 423).

[4] See in connection with this Prentice, *History of the Anti-Corn Law League*, II, 221.

placing all its adherents on the register. A registration department was instituted in the offices of the League at Manchester; it started committees and registration societies in the constituencies, which, assisted by legal advice and other instructions from headquarters, devoted their efforts to getting the followers of the League on the register. Several of the Registration Societies founded on this occasion outlived the free-trade agitation and became instruments of the Liberal party.

After 1846, the contests in the registration courts became less keen. Owing to the indifference of the voters and the insufficiency of funds, a good many associations fell into a languishing state. Sometimes also a sort of truce grew up between parties, and then they disbanded their forces; they dissolved the Registration Societies, and left the register to its fate.[1] Or, again, when one side had an overwhelming majority in a constituency, the other side gave up the struggle, and Registration Societies were considered of no use.[2] But in constituencies where parties were evenly balanced, or where the opponent's prospects were improving, the Associations still confronted each other. The member and his agent did not always like to be encumbered with an Association; in that case they did not encourage, or discouraged, its formation; the agent took sole charge of the register, and collected subscriptions to meet the expenses of registration proceedings.[3] Lastly, in certain districts, especially in the counties, a territorial magnate would order one of his dependents to look after the register, and would defray all the expenses himself.[4]

VII

In the electoral proceedings which followed the settlement of the register, viz. in the selection of candidates, and in electioneering operations, the part played by the Associ-

[1] Select Committee on Registration of Voters in Counties (Blue Books of 1870, Vol. VI, p. 99, § 2156).

[2] Report from the Select Committee of the House of Lords (Blue Books of 1860, Vol. XII, p. 65).

[3] Select Committee on Registration of County Voters (Blue Books of 1864, Vol. X, p. 87).

[4] Committee on the Corrupt Practices Act (Blue Books of 1860, Vol. X, p. 250).

ations varied in importance.   In the choice of candidates their share was slight.   It was more the play of living social forces, still highly important, that marked men out and thrust them upon the public.   The Associations or their committees examined the names submitted by the central organization in London, or by a few private individuals, or even by the candidates themselves who came forward, and laid them before the electors.   Strictly speaking, the committee only represented itself; its members had no mandate conferred on them by formal vote but held it by the tacit acquiescence of the electorate. The whole Association also only represented the subscribers who had thought fit to combine together.   The Associations and the committees had no mandate and did not lay claim to one.   They merely recommended the candidates, and their recommendation carried the same weight as the personal influence of their members and no more.   This influence was derived from their social rank, their wealth, their intelligence, or their adroitness.   Good or bad, they were the natural leaders of the society of the time.   Their small number of course made them an oligarchy, and encouraged the formation of coteries and of "hole-and-corner management."   But in spite of this, the selections of candidates were not at all bad, while not unfrequently open to criticism.   These leaders were not devoid of a sense of responsibility.

A candidate rejected by the Association did not consider himself, and was not considered, bound by this decision; the committee did not take the place of the electorate.   A candidate who did not accept the decision of the committee came before the electors supported by a committee of his own.   To ensure union in face of the enemy, the whole party was sometimes consulted beforehand upon the rival candidates.   The procedure employed to take the sense of the electors varied: a circular was forwarded to the electors asking them to state in reply by post which of the candidates they preferred;[1] or the agents of the rival candidates called on each voter and took down the replies, then they compared their lists and the less favoured candidates withdrew; sometimes again a preliminary vote was arranged, a non-official, full-dress rehearsal of

[1] Report from the Select Committee on the Corrupt Practices Prevention Act (Blue Books of 1860, Vol. X, p. 159).

the polling.[1]   Another mode of preventing the multiplication of candidatures, by which the opposite party could benefit, was arbitration.   The arbitrators weighed the chances of the rivals, and decided which should retire.   The party Whip also took up cases of this kind; by dint of tact and skilful argument he would induce one of the competitors to withdraw.

VIII

The operations during election time for winning the seat were conducted in accordance with the old traditions and centred chiefly in the canvass.   The canvass consisted of the visits which the candidate and his friends who possessed influence in the locality paid to each voter in the district just before the poll, to get him to promise his vote.   In the rural districts, where territorial influences were firmly established and made the elections a foregone conclusion, a canvass was not very necessary.   But in urban constituencies these visits were indispensable.   They were a duty from which the *grand seigneur* himself could not escape.   At a time when political convictions counted for little or nothing with the great mass of voters, the art of canvassing, of talking a voter over, was of paramount importance in electioneering contests.   Like every art, canvassing had its great masters.   But they were not formed in a school, they *were born*, like poets.   Among the fine old types of canvassers produced by the eighteenth century, the Marquis of Wharton is the most famous.   His biographer relates how he canvassed on behalf of one of his candidates in the borough of Wicomb: "Wharton was going up and down the town with his friends to secure votes on their side.   Entering a shoemaker's shop he asked 'where Dick was?'   The good woman said her husband was gone two or three miles off with some shoes, but his lordship need not fear for him, — she would keep him tight.   'I know that,' says my lord, 'but I want to see Dick and drink a glass with him.'   The wife was very sorry Dick was out of the way.   'Well,' says his lordship, 'how does all thy children?   Molly is a brave girl, I warrant, by this time.'   'Yes, I thank ye, my lord,' says the woman, and his

[1] Report on Parliamentary and Municipal Elections (Blue Books of 1868-9, Vol. VIII, p. 524).

lordship continued, 'is not Jemmy breeched yet?'" A friend of the rival candidate, who had slipped into Wharton's train, could stand it no longer; he rushed off to his friends and told them that the contest was hopeless, that nothing could make way against a great peer who knew the age of Molly and Jemmy so well.[1]

The poet Cowper has left a curious description of a canvassing visit which Grenville had paid him: " We were sitting yesterday after dinner, the two ladies and myself very composedly . . . when, to our unspeakable surprise, a mob appeared before the window, a smart rap was heard at the door, and the maid announced Mr. Grenville. In a minute the yard, the kitchen, and the parlour were filled. Mr. Grenville advancing towards me shook me by the hand with a degree of cordiality that was extremely seducing. As soon as he and as many more as could find chairs were seated, he began to open the intent of his visit. I told him I had no vote, for which he readily gave me credit. I assured him I had no influence, which he was not equally inclined to believe, and the less no doubt, because Mr. Ashburner, the draper, addressing himself to me at this moment informed me that I had a great deal. Supposing that I could not be possessed of such a treasure without knowing it, I ventured to confirm my first assertion by saying that, if I had any, I was utterly at a loss to imagine where it could be or wherein it consisted. Thus ended the conference. Mr. Grenville squeezed me by the hand again, kissed the ladies, and withdrew. He kissed likewise the maid in the kitchen, and seemed upon the whole, a most loving, kissing, kindhearted gentleman." [2]

Ladies also occasionally joined in the canvass and they were just as expansive when it was a question of securing a vote. There is the well-known story of the beautiful Duchess of Devonshire who, when canvassing for Fox, allowed a butcher to give her a kiss in return for a promise to vote for the great Whig orator.

---

[1] *Memoirs of the Life of the Most Noble Thomas, late Marquess of Wharton*, Lond. 1715, p. 34.

[2] Quoted in the article of the *Quarterly Review* of 1857, Vol. CII, " Electioneering," apparently written by Thackeray (see Jos. Grego, *A History of Parliamentary Elections and Electioneering in the Old Days*, Lond. 1887).

The Whartons, the Duchess of Devonshire, who introduced artistic touches of one kind or another into their canvassing, were rare; and as time went on, especially after the extension of the franchise, canvassing lost, so to speak, its poetry, its picturesqueness; but it none the less remained the great electioneering weapon. People still continued, and probably rightly so, to rely more on direct personal influence than on principles and programmes. Only, owing to the increase in the number of voters, it was necessary to bring this action to bear with more method, to have an organization. The Registration Societies supplied the framework of it. Having made their way into the political life of the nation through the gap left by the defects in the registration laws, the Societies and Associations acquired a fresh hold on the electorate by means of the canvassing system.

The canvassing machinery was set in motion whenever the period of electioneering commenced. The most important members of the Associations formed themselves into a central committee, into which they also admitted persons who did not belong to the Association but whose connections might make them of use. Then they established committees in the various districts composed of persons who were full of energy and resource in electoral matters. The district committees conducted the canvass, each member separately or in groups. The canvassers of the rival candidates made their expeditions at the same time, one party in one street, the other in the next; it was considered fair to agree as to the opening day of the electoral shooting season, and the two armies of canvassers started simultaneously. The canvassers visited all the voters indiscriminately, even those who notoriously belonged to the opposite side. They noted down all the replies of the voters, and were in a position to forecast the probable result of the polling before the election. After the canvass, the next great business of the committees was to get the voters to the poll. Besides these official, acknowledged duties, the committees were more or less engaged in the work of electoral corruption. The district committees generally sat in the public-houses. It was here that people came to receive the password, and here, too, they were supplied with food and drink gratuitously, that is to say, at the candidate's expense, during the whole canvass.

IX

In all this the party associations only continued the old practices; they had simply followed up the electioneering system created in the old days and developed by the manners and customs of the nation. Where the motive power really emanated from the Associations, as was the case with the registration operations, it was not long before they incurred a grave responsibility. Their activity in this important department of electoral life was marked by exclusive party spirit to such an extent as to warp the electoral machinery far more than keep it in proper working order. The defects in the system of registration established by the law of 1832 set a premium on party manœuvres. True, the Legislature had tried to remedy them; it had abolished the registration fee of one shilling, it had empowered the Revising Barristers to allow costs for unfounded objections. But these slight attempts at reform could not overcome the indifference of the electors who did not care whether they were on the register or not, nor the ignorance and carelessness of the tradesmen appointed overseers for the year, nor the dishonesty of the parties represented by the organizations. The latter set to work to strike properly qualified persons off the register, or to prevent their opponents from being entered on it, and to get their own followers who had no right to vote admitted. Every year the Registration Societies started thousands of objections to the claims lodged by the electors. They calculated, and rightly, that many of those who were opposed would not or could not appear in the registration court to uphold their right to vote, or even that they would receive no notice of opposition owing to removal, etc; and the legal consequence of the non-disallowance of an objection was that the name was struck off the list. By these manœuvres they could easily manage to transfer the majority from one side to the other. The Associations had therefore made a regular business, "a trade,"[1] of lodging objections. At the same time they started unfounded claims, which had to be allowed if no one objected to them; the overseers

---

[1] Select Committee on Registration of Voters in Boroughs (Blue Books of 1868–9, Vol. VII, p. 134).

had not the means or the wish to check them, and the Revising
Barristers had no right to do so if an appeal was not made to
them. "Improper claims originate chiefly with the Registration Societies. Voters very seldom make claims of their own
head; they are generally got to do so by the agent of the Registration Society."[1]

It is true that the societies of the rival parties, in supervis-
ing and controlling each other, helped, as they maintained, to
purify the register. But, out of the mass of objections and
claims with which the parties assailed each other, a good many
unfounded ones slipped through and well-founded ones were
unsuccessful. In any event, the methods by which the recti-
fication of the register was effected destroyed all the benefit
of the result. An elector whose right was unjustly attacked
by one party association reasserted it by the help of another,
which had an eye on his vote, and always at the cost of wasted
time and of trouble to the persons engaged in the proceedings.
The special parliamentary committee, appointed in 1868 to
inquire into the registration of electors in boroughs, took a
quantity of evidence on Registration Societies and came to the
conclusion that "the action of such associations is necessarily
prejudicial to the independence of a constituency, and not only
affords the means, but supplies a grave temptation to illegitimate practices and corrupt inducements, whilst at the same
time the imperfect operation of the responsible registration
authority justifies their existence and forms an excuse for their
operations."[2]

It is remarkable that this opinion was shared by representatives of the organizations themselves. There were enlightened men among them who did not hesitate to denounce
the intervention of associations in political life. And they did
so under circumstances which gave their statements a peculiar
importance, especially in the great parliamentary enquiries into
electoral matters during the years 1860–1870. The secretary of
the Liberal Association of the City of London, when giving
evidence before the Committee of the House of Lords, said

[1] Select Committee on Registration of Voters in Counties (Blue Books of
1870, Vol. VI, p. 122, § 2687).
[2] Report from the Select Committee on Registration of Voters in Boroughs
(Blue Books of 1868–9, Vol. VII, p. 6).

that the abandonment of registration to associations "was a very great political evil. Of course I ought not to speak against that which employs myself; but I think it a most unconstitutional thing. . . . If the suffrage were extended, an election would depend to a much greater extent than it does at present (and it does too much now) upon political organizations. It would increase the power of those political Associations . . . and would *pro tanto* disturb the natural expression of public opinion."[1]

Before the Select Committees on registration, many representatives of the organizations expressed the opinion that an official system of registration should be instituted, in order to cut the ground from under the feet of the "Societies."[2] The founder of the central Association of the Liberal party, Mr. Brand (raised to the peerage with the title of Lord Hampden for his signal services as Speaker of the House of Commons), at a committee of enquiry of which he was a member, also emphatically condemned the associations which he had himself helped to develop to meet the exigencies of the party. He considered that the party associations had an unhealthy effect.[3]

[1] Blue Books of 1860, Vol. XII, pp. 76, 226.

[2] Evidence of Mr. Temple before the Committee of 1869 (Blue Books of 1868–9, Vol. VII, p. 134), of Mr. T. N. Roberts before the Committee of 1870 (Blue Books of 1870, Vol. VI, § 762).

[3] The Blue Book on the parliamentary enquiry of 1870 contains a curious dialogue between Mr. Brand and a witness, a clerk of the peace. The clerks of the peace had to work at the electoral register in the counties, but, as the parties had taken possession of the registration, the clerks trusted to the Associations. The clerk who was giving his evidence before the parliamentary committee considered the Associations useful.

Mr. Brand. The character of the legislature depends on the registration, the component parts of the House of Commons depend for their character on registration, do they not, and the registration depends for its success in the counties on the activity of certain wealthy partisans on each side — is it a desirable state of things? You gave it as your opinion that registration associations had a healthy effect on the constituencies.

Witness. Yes.

Mr. Brand. I have been trying to prove to you that they have not; do you still consider that registration associations have had a healthy effect on constituencies?

Witness. I do consider that Registration Societies have a healthy effect on the purity of the register . . . I think the political parties on each side are the best check.

Mr. Brand. You are thoroughly enamoured with political associations. (Committee on Registration 1870, Blue Books of 1870, Vol. VI. p. 119, 120.)

X

Yet the activity of the party associations, which gave rise to these criticisms, was only a beginning of interposition between the electorate and the Constitution. The extension of the sphere of action and of the influence of party organizations was often viewed with apprehension. It was one of the aspects under which people considered the probable consequences of the many electoral reforms which had stirred public opinion from and after the second half of the century: of the extension of the franchise, of the representation of minorities, of the introduction of the ballot. The extension of the suffrage was opposed because "with a widely enlarged suffrage the candidate would find himself less and less able to come face to face with his constituency, and would be compelled in consequence" . . . "to rely more and more on the aid of the election agent, and, as in America, of that of committees and canvassers whose mouthpiece and delegate he would have to make himself."[1] Secret voting, in the opinion of some of its opponents, was bound to entail the same untoward consequences: with open voting the electors could follow the fluctuations of the poll and during its progress make up their minds how to vote; with the absolute secrecy of the ballot, they thought, it would be necessary to trust to the previous arrangements of organizations to make sure of the success of the party candidate.[2] When the idea of the representation of minorities was put forward by Hare and supported by J. S. Mill, protests were raised against this innovation because it was likely to lead to the formation of a powerful party organization with ramifications throughout the country.[3] This argument was reverted to when the discussion of proportional representation was resumed, either in Parliament,[4] or in the Press.[5] The adherents of Hare's plan, on the other hand,

[1] *Hansard's Parliam. Debates*, Vol. CLXXXVII, p. 811. Cf. the observations to the same effect in the *Quarterly Review*, Jan. 1869, "Politics as a Profession," p. 285.

[2] Cf. E. Maitland, "Misrepresentation of Majorities," *Fortnightly Review*, Vol. VIII, 1870.

[3] G. O. Trevelyan, "A Few Remarks on Mr. Hare's Scheme of Representation," *Macmillan's Magazine*, April, 1862.

[4] *Hansard*, Voi. CLXXXIX, p. 458 and elsewhere.

[5] Leslie Stephen, "The Value of Political Machinery," *Fortnightly Review*, Dec. 1875, p. 844.

were convinced that when once this electoral reform was realized, party organizations would lose their power. " They may
return, but they will come as suppliants to beseech, instead of
as masters to command." [1]

The increased activity of the party organizations which had
been apprehended, came to pass. The movement was carried
out under the auspices of the Radical democracy of Birmingham in consequence of the campaign against the representation of minorities undertaken in that city.

[1] L. Courtney, " Political Machinery and Political Life," *Fortnightly
Review*, July, 1876.

THIRD CHAPTER

THE ESTABLISHMENT OF THE CAUCUS

I

THE Birmingham Radicals who regarded the minority clause of the Reform Bill of 1867 as antidemocratic, were very anxious to nullify its effect. Their idea was, that this might perhaps be accomplished by means of an electoral scheme adopted beforehand, but that a formidable organization would be necessary for the purpose. The old organization of the Liberal party seemed to them too lax, too feeble. The Registration Societies, the Reform or Liberal Associations which had sprung up since 1832, were groups of subscribers, of amateurs, and were in the hands of traditional leaders incapable of getting at the masses who had just been brought on the political stage by the extension of the franchise. Birmingham received 30,000 new electors. The opponents of the minority clause believed that to ensure the victory, the party organization ought to reach all these voters, to make them feel that they were about to fight *pro aris et focis*, that the Liberal party was their own party, the party of each one of them. To meet these views, one of the Radical leaders, Mr. W. Harris, architect, man of letters, and secretary of the Birmingham Liberal Association, proposed a plan of organization according to which all the Liberals of the locality were to meet in every ward, and elect representatives to manage the affairs of the party. Being nominated directly by the people and keeping in constant communication with the inhabitants of the wards, the delegates would be able to decide authoritatively on the general direction to be given to the party, as well as on all the important questions of the day, and especially on the choice of candidates for the elections. For this latter purpose in particular "a more popular body must be provided — a body which should not only be a reflex of popular opinion, but should be so manifestly a reflex of that opinion that none could doubt it." The representatives appointed with this object, "elected openly and freely by the burgesses, without dictation or suggestion from the central body or anybody else," will select the candidates. "Gentlemen aspiring to the honourable position of representing Birmingham must abide by the vote of the selecting body, and the Liberal electors must do so." [1]

This plan, which was indefatigably urged in every ward and at one meeting after another, was adopted. The Liberal committee formed in consequence selected candidates for all three seats in view of the impending general election (in 1868). But as each elector could only vote for two candidates, owing to the minority clause, the committee hit upon the following device: by a preliminary canvass the central committee ascertained the exact number of Liberal electors in each ward and the minimum of votes necessary to obtain the majority at the poll, then distributed the three candidates by twos among the electors of the ward, in such fashion that each candidate would only receive the number of votes strictly necessary to obtain the majority at the poll, and the votes over and above this would be given to one of the two other candidates so that each of them should eventually have a majority. One ward voted for A and B, another for A and C, a third for B and C, a fourth for A and B, etc. The voter, who had left the selection of the three candidates to the general committee, was also to renounce the privilege of selecting from among them the two which he preferred. "Vote as you are told" was the password. This was the price which had to be paid for the victory over the foes of democracy. Each voter received a ticket with the two names which he had to declare at the poll. Some Conservatives were ill-advised enough to counterfeit and circulate tickets with the same names of Liberal candidates, but differently distributed among the wards. If any number of electors had voted in accordance with these forged tickets the Liberal committee's game would have been completely spoilt. The fraud was discovered in time, and the tendency to vote in implicit obedience to orders only grew all the more marked in the Liberal camp. The

[1] *Birmingham Daily Post*, 21 December, 1867.

enthusiasm, however, was not unanimous; a workingman's party, small in numbers and with no influence, distrusted the champions of the vote-as-you-are-told democracy. Some Radicals of the old school, survivors of the "glorious days" of 1831–1832, who had fought for the extension of the suffrage, were grieved to see that their fellow-citizens were about to exercise it not as free men but as puppets.[1] But the immense majority of the electors "voted as they were told," and the three Liberal candidates were elected in spite of the restricted voting clause passed for the benefit of minorities.

II

The "enemies of democracy" and the "philosophers" who introduced the limited voting system, refused to profit by the lesson which Birmingham had given them, and they took the first opportunity of extending the application of the principle of minority representation. The law of 1870 on primary education, which placed the management of schools supported by the ratepayers in the hands of elected Boards, provided that the elections should be held on the cumulative voting system.[2] The Birmingham Radicals once more started a campaign to nullify the cumulative vote as they had done with the limited vote. But the elaborate distribution of votes among the candidates, which was too complicated on this occasion, did not succeed; and instead of capturing the whole Board, as they intended, the Radicals were left in a minority.

The prestige of the Liberal Association suffered from this; its organization broke up, but only to reunite soon afterwards with fresh strength and enter upon a career of striking inter-

---

[1] A friend and companion of Atwood in the Political Union of 1831, wrote: "You must vote as you are told! We who have flattered and petted you when you had no vote — stating over and over again our entire confidence in your ability rightly to use it — now cannot trust you! I say it is an insult, and the securing of any end, no matter how desirable, will not justify it. I, even, the bosom friend of Atwood, have had this degrading proposition put to me. . . ." (*Birmingham Daily Gazette*, 27 Oct. 1868.)

[2] The system of cumulative voting consists in allowing the elector who has to vote for several candidates, for five or ten for instance, to give five or ten votes to a single candidate, so that a small group of electors concentrating their votes on a single person can ensure his election and make their voice heard in the teeth of the dominant majority.

est and pregnant with consequences for the political life of the whole country. This was in 1873. About that time two men appeared on the scene at Birmingham. Very dissimilar in personal weight, in ambition, and in abilities, and destined to very different futures, they helped more than any one else to alter the character of extra-parliamentary political life. One was Mr. Schnadhorst, the new secretary of the Liberal Association, and the other Mr. Joseph Chamberlain, who became the inspirer of the organization. Elected mayor of Birmingham in 1873, Mr. Chamberlain was the most brilliant representative of a group of remarkable men whom chance brought together there. They were all very advanced Radicals. Their Radicalism had nothing speculative about it. For the most part active and intelligent men of business, they were not much encumbered with reading. They had a few men of literary education among them, but little inclined to philosophic doubt. The picture of the Athenian democracy drawn by G. Grote had imbued them with a Radical enthusiasm of an uncompromising stamp; they did not understand the scruples of a John Stuart Mill, who tried to discover counter-checks for democracy; for, they believed, if democratic government is a good thing, it is so, without restriction, without reserve. A very important position in this group was held by some Unitarian ministers, animated with a generous and overflowing enthusiasm which lifted every question into the higher regions of morality and civilization. The humanitarian zeal and public spirit of one section as well as the desire of others to make their mark in public life after having succeeded in business, found a sphere of activity in the municipality of Birmingham. A quarter of a century ago the capital of the Midlands was anything but a well-ordered city. It still bore the stamp of the great manufacturing centres which had developed with extraordinary rapidity in the north of England and which exhausted their energies in huge buildings with tall chimneys vomiting forth clouds of smoke from dawn to sunset; absorbed in the task of production, the inhabitants were not only little open to intellectual and artistic ideas, but were even indifferent to the material well-being of their city. In spite of the growing prosperity of Birmingham, everything in the town was in an unsatisfactory state, from the street pavements to the sanitary condition of the dwellings. The men who gathered round Mr. Joseph Chamberlain conceived the ambition, under the special inspiration of the Unitarian ministers above-mentioned,[1] of taking in hand the improvement of the town; and to accomplish this object they decided to make themselves masters of the Town Council. After a vigorous electoral campaign they carried the day.

Once installed in the Town Hall, Mr. Chamberlain and his friends undertook a whole series of public works for the sanitation and embellishment of Birmingham. Their activity was of the Haussmann order. Like the famous prefect of Napoleon III, the new municipality opened new streets; demolished the slums in the heart of the town; erected magnificent buildings; organized a system of drainage and sanitary inspection and paved the streets; founded public libraries, baths, hospitals; opened out squares; made the town owner of the gas and water supply. The cost of the transformation was considerable, but the results were still more so.[2]

III

In the execution of this work Mr. Chamberlain and his friends were supported in the Council by a compact and devoted majority. This was provided by the organization of the Liberal party, which was brought to a rare degree of perfection by the efforts of Mr. Schnadhorst, a born organizer, a master in the art of "wire-pulling," to use the political language of the day. Every inhabitant of the town, whether a voter or not, could join the Association. Payment of a subscription was not absolutely required. It was fixed at a minimum of a shilling a year, but might be dispensed with by "signifying adhesion to the objects and to the organization of the Association." All the members of the Association in each ward appointed a committee of as many persons as they liked in public meeting. These elected members could add to their number

[1] Cf. *Henry W. Crosskey, His Life and Work*, by R. A. Armstrong, Birm. 1895, for the position of the Rev. George Dawson and the Rev. Henry Crosskey among the municipal reformers of Birmingham.

[2] On this last point cf. Fred. Dolman, *Municipalities at Work*, Lond. 1895, Chap. I.

to an unlimited extent. Above the ward committees was an *executive committee* for the whole town, composed of the chairmen and secretaries of the ward committees as *ex officio* members, plus three delegates for each ward chosen *ad hoc* in public meeting; that is to say, each ward was represented on the executive committee by five delegates, which made eighty members for the sixteen wards of the city of Birmingham. These eighty had the right of adding thirty persons to their number. Side by side with this executive authority there was a deliberative assembly, the *general committee*, which was composed of all the members of the executive committee $(80 + 30)$ and of thirty members for each ward, elected *ad hoc* in public meeting $(30 \times 16 = 480)$. Finally, to crown the pyramid, the general committee appointed a committee of four persons, to which the executive committee added seven of its members, forming the managing sub-committee of eleven persons. This body of 594 persons became popular under the name of the " Six Hundred." They were supposed to be the embodiment of the democracy of Birmingham. The management of the Liberal party was said to be entrusted to them because there was confidence in the people. In reality the confidence was not so boundless as they tried to make out. The elaborate constitution of the Association even contained some precautions against the "people." The constituted authorities of the Association did not emanate directly from the people. The "Six Hundred" only appointed four members out of eleven of the managing committee, and two-thirds of this latter were nominated by the executive committee, which was itself in part a *co-optative* body. In fact, thirty of its members were chosen by the eighty elected members, and of these latter two-fifths owed their appointment to the ward committees in which the co-opted members were unlimited in number. No doubt, if the ward meetings which were at the base of the organization elected delegates of intractable independence, all attempts at manipulating them from above would have failed. The adroitness of the leading organizers consisted precisely in obtaining control of the ward meetings and in making them elect delegates who could be relied on. In addition to all kinds of influences employed to bring about this result the Association also introduced practices such as the use of travelling companies, who went from one ward to another to attend the public meetings in which the delegates were elected, and who ensured the success of certain candidates by the aid of their votes. This manœuvre was all the more easy of execution because the elections of delegates in the various wards did not take place simultaneously but were spread over a period of four, five or even six weeks.[1] The final upshot was that the " Six Hundred " consisted of men devoted to Mr. Chamberlain and his friends, and who worked for them at the elections.

IV

Having obtained control of the Association, Mr. Chamberlain and his friends did not, however, convert it into a mere instrument of personal domination; they imparted to it a real and fairly vigorous life. Following their lead and especially at the entreaties of Mr. Chamberlain, the best men of the Liberal party joined the Association, consented to serve as delegates to the " Six Hundred." They maintained uninterrupted relations with the masses by means of public assemblies, informal meetings, and personal communications on questions of general interest, and thus kept up a current of public spirit. The schemes and measures which were coming before the Town Council were often explained at meetings of the Association with the best results for the political education of the citizens. Mr. Chamberlain set the example. At the meetings of the " Six Hundred " and at other gatherings he displayed the style of oratory which has since, in a larger sphere of action, placed him in the front rank of debaters, a style marked by clearness, incisiveness, and an inexorable logic which goes straight to the point and opens out wide vistas in the driest and most complicated subjects, as the backwoodsman's axe hews a path through the tangle of a virgin forest. The speeches and personal communications on municipal affairs were supplemented by articles and pamphlets which were widely distributed among the public. The members of the Association were equally active in promoting several other matters of general interest which were outside the province of the Town Council.

The knot of men who were working together under Mr. Cham-

---

[1] In 1885 the Liberal organization thought itself strong enough to abandon this mode of election.

berlain not only made all these personal sacrifices, but were just as ready to make pecuniary sacrifices as well. In every public subscription they invariably headed the list and with considerable sums. All schemes for the public good were sure to meet with their sympathy and interest. In this way they supplied striking proof that the social leadership which had been the greatness of the England of former days could be exercised for the general welfare by others as well as landlords, and in a spirit differing widely from the paternal condescension of an aristocracy. It is true that of all the large manufacturing towns Birmingham was the most favourably situated for the establishment of relations of this kind between the upper middle class and the masses. Thanks to the special character of its industrial life Birmingham did not exhibit the usual contrast and antagonism between enormously wealthy employers of labour and a wretchedly poor manufacturing population, it was not inhabited by the "two nations" of Disraeli's "Sybil." This fact, which was peculiar to this manufacturing centre, attracted the attention of observers at an early period. Léon Faucher, who had visited the district during the agitation against the Corn Laws, remarked that Birmingham was a "manufacturing democracy in a great city, this being the case even in the workshops where steam is the motive power. . . . While in Great Britain generally the tendency of capital is towards concentration, in Birmingham it is more and more in the direction of subdivision. The manufacturing industry of this town, like the cultivation of the soil in France, is parcelled out into small divisions. There are few large fortunes and hardly any big establishments. . . . This industrial organization is due to the actual nature of the work. . . . At Birmingham labour is purely manual. Machines are used as an accessory to manufacture, but everything depends on the skill and the intelligence of the workman." [1] If this state of things has more or less changed during the quarter of a century which followed the repeal of the Corn Laws, it was nevertheless true that the gradation of classes

---

[1] *Études sur l'Angleterre*, Paris, 1856, I, 502, 503.

Quite recently (in 1894) Mr. Joseph Chamberlain has recalled the fact that when he came to Birmingham as a young man, there were only three private carriages in the whole town, and that when one of them passed in the streets everybody could give the name of its owner.

in the manufacturing community of Birmingham remained a gentle one, and that consequently it was easy for the leaders to reach the masses. The statutory meetings of the Association and its branches only supplied an opportunity or a pretext.

But as the Liberal Association was, so to speak, the firm under which Mr. Chamberlain and his friends carried on their operations, it reaped the benefit of the legitimate and well-deserved influence which they had acquired. The persons who stood behind the Association having assumed the direction of every public enterprise, in the Town Council and elsewhere, a confusion readily grew up in the public mind. Everything seemed to be focussed in the Association and its organs, they were appealed to on every occasion, their intervention was solicited in things small and great. Mr. Chamberlain and his friends, far from clearing up this misunderstanding, tried to give currency to the idea that the Association was the source and the necessary instrument of the public prosperity.

In politics the identification of the interests of the town with the work carried on by the Association had a much more serious effect. The Association being a Liberal organization, could only invite the co-operation of those who belonged to the Liberal persuasion. Hence, the Conservatives were excluded from public life in Birmingham. It is true that they had themselves been clumsy enough to supply the Radicals with a pretext for making the local administration a party affair. Ousted from representation in Parliament by the vote-as-you-are-told arrangement, from the share of it which the minority clause would have given them, the Conservatives tried to storm the political stronghold of Birmingham by means of the municipal elections; they fought the battle on political lines but were defeated. Long after they had been reduced to impotence in the Town Council, the Liberal Association continued to oppose them with the utmost bitterness at the annual municipal elections. The majority obtained by the Liberals became an overwhelming one; eventually they won nearly every seat on the Council; but their rancour against the Conservatives was not appeased. The latter were dislodged from every position in the local government, from every representative body even of an entirely non-political character, from charitable institutions, from the governing boards of schools. Ignored and thrust out of public life, the Conservatives in their turn soon came to identify the interests of Birmingham with those of the Liberal party, and to regard the former with lukewarmness, almost with complete indifference. The Liberals of the Association, who were for making a clean sweep of the Conservatives, of course disclaimed all responsibility for this: it was the electoral body which preferred Liberals to Conservatives, the Liberals could not be expected to start and support Conservative candidates. And then, they argued, the transformation of the town could only have been accomplished by a municipality sure of an overwhelming majority, with no fear of having its grand plans thwarted by petty cliques.[1] The real truth was that the overwhelming majorities in the elections for the Town Council were required by the prompters of the Association for something else as well, for the parliamentary elections. The conversion of their Conservative fellow-citizens to their municipal schemes would not have quite suited them. The conciliatory spirit which would have resulted therefrom would have diminished the keenness of the political contests for the parliamentary seats, all of which they meant to keep for themselves.

Driven out of the common abode, the Conservatives were pursued into their own ground. Referring to them invariably as "the enemy," the Liberals set the populace at them and made it resort to violence. Bands of adherents of the Liberal Association broke into the Conservative meetings and created disturbances in them. This was carried on so methodically that the Conservatives were obliged to give up holding public meetings in Birmingham. These rowdies did not receive formal orders from the Liberal Association, but the latter did nothing to stop them; and it was considered an accomplice in, if not an instigator of the disorderly proceedings of which its opponents were the victims. The Conservatives of course were greatly exasperated. Years passed on, the irony of political fate converted the old enemies into allies at the time of the

---

[1] This fear was perhaps exaggerated, for Mr. Chamberlain himself has admitted that the great things accomplished by the municipality were done with the cordial approval of the bulk of the population, including a large number of Conservatives ("The Caucus," by J. Chamberlain, M.P., *Fortnightly Review*, November, 1878).

Unionist coalition against the Gladstonian Home Rulers, but in the breasts of the Conservatives the injuries rankled as deeply as ever.

V

The political services which the Liberals expected from the Association were faithfully performed: its candidates came in at the parliamentary elections with flying colours. Mr. Chamberlain himself was returned in 1876. The discipline in the electoral body was perfect, " the forces at the disposal of the Liberal Association were not hordes of wayward free lances: they were armies of disciplined men, well accustomed to stand side by side and to move in unbroken battalions," as the leaders of the organization declared with satisfaction. But Birmingham was not to be the only city to benefit by this highly perfected instrument. Its advantages were to be extended to the whole country for the greater triumph of the Liberal cause. A campaign of propaganda was started with this object by the Birmingham group. Their Association was proposed as a model which had only to be imitated. Did not the results obtained by its aid speak volumes for it: " This Association has succeeded in rendering municipal and political life a consistent, earnest, true and enthusiastic life among the vast population in which it labours, instead of a spasmodic electioneering impulse." By the introduction of politics into all local affairs, "by this extension of the idea of Liberalism the Association connected itself with the development of the general life of the town." There is no town in which democracy has been so largely interpreted as " *the life of the people as an organized whole*," and " to the Liberal Association the acceptance of this interpretation is chiefly due." " The Association is an agency through which men who believe in the possibility of a higher state of civilization than now exists — who have faith in realizable ideals — have attempted and are attempting to carry out clear and definite plans for the culture, happiness, and prosperity of the community." [1]

Mr. Chamberlain and Mr. Schnadhorst, especially the latter, visited the important towns of the Kingdom one after another

[1] " The Liberal Association — ' the 600 ' — of Birmingham," by H. Crosskey (reprinted from *Macmillan's Magazine*, February, 1877).

to propose the "Birmingham plan." After holding small private meetings composed of the most influential, or the most active, people of the locality, they explained the plan in public meetings. The propaganda was carried on with great activity. Along with prominent members of the Association the latter despatched emissaries who kept their mission a secret so as to work with greater freedom. The Association had a small band of them, recruited from among persons such as are found knocking about great towns, men who dislike the routine of regular work and prefer a varied existence, or who have seen better days and so fallen out of the ranks. There were not very many of them, barely twenty, and they were well paid. All of them had the gift of the gab, some of them could wield a pen, compose a good "letter to the editor" of a newspaper, or at a pinch even write a pamphlet. They worked sometimes at Birmingham, sometimes in the other towns, always of course preserving their *incognito*.

For the rest, the Birmingham propaganda found the ground pretty well prepared in the country. The introduction of the ballot in 1872, shortly after a considerable increase in the number of electors who were henceforth left to their own inspirations on the day of the poll, made it very difficult to manage the elections without preliminary arrangements, without a more or less closely knit organization. But a still stronger argument for the "Birmingham plan" was the defeat sustained by the Liberals at the general election of 1874, which had returned an enormous Conservative majority to the House of Commons for the first time since 1841. The Liberals, who imagined that the country had given them a perpetual lease of power, could not get over it; and, as generally happens to beaten parties, they looked outside their own conduct for the cause of the electoral catastrophe and found it chiefly in the fact that they *were badly organized*. The "Birmingham plan" claimed to supply a perfect remedy for this deficiency. The defeated candidates took a special interest in it, they accepted it with the naïve confidence of certain gamblers who swallow puffs of an "infallible method of winning" at *rouge et noir*. They did not realize the peculiar situation of Birmingham, nor the potency of the social leadership exercised by Mr. Chamberlain and his friends in that city : they thought that the whole secret lay in the patent Association of Birmingham. Consequently there was a rush to create "hundreds" on the Birmingham pattern in a good many towns, the "Three Hundred," the "Four Hundred," etc.

VI

Profoundly impressed with the importance of their part, the "hundreds" took the earliest opportunity of performing it. This was given them by foreign politics. The Eastern question, having come to the front again in consequence of the insurrection in Herzegovina, was engrossing the attention of Europe, and of England in particular. Disraeli's government, following the then traditional policy of England, was in favour of Turkey against Russia, who had taken up the cause of her oppressed Slav co-religionists. The news of the Bulgarian atrocities aroused a loud cry of horror in England, and the country resounded from one end to the other with vehement protests against Turkish barbarity. The new Liberal organizations eagerly made themselves the instrument of this agitation, which they turned at the same time against their political opponents in power. They accused the Conservative government of moral complicity with the Turks. The chiefs of the Liberal Opposition in the House of Commons, who according to the rules of the game ought to lead every assault on the rival party, were more guarded in their attacks on the Government. Whether it was that their patriotic anxiety made them think that foreign politics was not a proper field for the display of the usual party animosity, or that their (perhaps exaggerated) feeling of responsibility as statesmen as well as their unsanguine temperament prevented them from rushing into decisive action, they held back. The enthusiasts and busybodies outside Parliament only bestirred themselves all the more energetically. The "hundreds" were indefatigable in holding anti-Turkish meetings, and in voting resolutions hostile to the Ministry. The Birmingham Association encouraged and even incited them. At its instigation the other Associations got up more than a hundred and fifty "indignation meetings" in a few days. It was also on its initiative that delegates from several Associations met in conference at Sheffield and Birmingham to bring about a National Convention on the Eastern question. No convention took place, but a monster meeting was held in London with the co-operation of many provincial delegates.

The unanimity with which the Liberal Associations joined in all this movement gave a vague impression of what their action might attain if it was always combined and if it obeyed a single impulse. Ideas of this kind were germinating in the minds of the Birmingham leaders, who had already on one or two occasions promoted collective action on the part of the Associations. And when the "plan" had been adopted in a sufficient number of localities, Mr. Schnadhorst thought that the time had come to link the Associations together by permanent ties and assure unity of action by a central organization. All the Liberal organizations formed on a "representative basis" were invited by a circular from the Birmingham Association to send delegates to that town for the purpose of considering the plan of a federation. A hundred Associations responded to the appeal, and on the 31st of May, 1877, the conference was opened at Birmingham under the presidency of Mr. Joseph Chamberlain. In an able speech, which led off the discussion, he vindicated the utility and necessity of the new organization, and showed how it was about to open a new chapter, nay a new era in the destinies of English Liberalism, by establishing a new basis and introducing new methods of action. In the new conditions of politics, "it has become necessary, as, indeed, it was always desirable, that the people at large should be taken into the counsels of the party, and that they should have a share in its control and management." . . . "Hence the new constitution upon which the Liberal Association of Birmingham is founded, according to which every Liberal in the town is *ipso facto* a member by virtue of his Liberalism, and without any other qualification. The vote of the poorest member is equal to that of the richest. It is an Association based on universal suffrage." After reminding his audience of the success of the Association and indulging in a few hits at his opponents, — Liberals "ignorant of what are the first elements of Liberalism, and whose lingering distrust of the good sense and the patriotism of the people has found expression in machinery — cumulative vote, minority representation, and I know not what of the same kind, which tends to divide the party of action in face of the ever united party of obstruction," — Mr. Chamberlain held out the prospect of a number of new associations founded on the same basis and all united by a central organization which would form a truly Liberal Parliament outside the Imperial Legislature and elected not as it is elected, but by universal suffrage. Its duty would be not so much to lay down a new Liberal creed, as to make the Liberal policy more definite and Liberal action more decisive. The events of the last few years had shown only too clearly that the official leaders were the last persons to realize public opinion. The object and the merit of the new organization would be to lend expression and force to opinion and obtain for it a better hearing than it had hitherto enjoyed.

The two main points of this speech — the right of the " people " to a direct initiative in the selection of men and measures and the deposition of the traditional leaders — were emphasized more strongly in the fiery harangue delivered by the next speaker, Mr. W. Harris, the author of the " Birmingham plan," who reflected the sincere but aggressive enthusiasm with which several of the leading members of the Association were inspired. Now that the suffrage has been extended to the urban masses, it was, urged Mr. Harris, no longer possible for the leaders in London to draw upon the people of the country and say two months after date pay to our order in the country for an agitation on a particular purpose. The people themselves ought to decide what the agitation should be and when it should begin. The people have shown their power by forcing the Government, over the heads of the official leaders of the Liberal party, to stop short in its iniquitous and scandalous philo-Turkish policy. But if a special agitation were set on foot for each political question, what an enormous waste of energy, of time and abilities, would be entailed. Instead of having an Educational League to promote national education, a Reform Union to secure Parliamentary reform, a Liberation Society to obtain religious equality, instead of all these organizations would it not be better to form once and for all a federation which by focussing the opinions of the majority of the population in great centres of political activity would be able to speak on any question that might arise, with all the authority of the

voice of the nation.   The organization proposed by the speaker
and his friends would supply this very instrument.

Such were, as expounded by the principal authors of the
scheme, the spirit, the character, and the aim assigned to the
federation. The great extra-constitutional organizations, which
have made their appearance at different intervals on the political
stage of England, were now about to enter on a new departure
with the Birmingham federation : a "Parliament outside the
Imperial Legislature" was being created on a permanent footing, confronting the national power established by the constitution and founded on a basis wider even than that of the House
of Commons elected by a restricted suffrage.   At one time the
mouthpiece, at another the instigator, of opinion, the free Parliament was taking up the general business of political agitation
on all questions present and to come ; to the organs of government and legislation it was adding a new organ — that of agitation — in the political constitution of the country.

The scheme of organization which involved such profound
changes in the working of the constitution, was hardly discussed at all.   The delegates had only been made acquainted
with the scheme and the statement of objects and reasons on
that very morning. However, as soon as it was propounded
and explained by its authors, a section of the delegates intimated that their only feeling for it was one of admiration, that
their adhesion was given already.   They bore witness to it as
persons taking part in religious meetings testify with abundance of asseverations, for the edification of the audience, how
they have found salvation.   In the same tone delegates bore witness to the conference how elections were won, "simply by
trusting the people."   Thus one delegate had innumerable
powers, all the powers of darkness, arrayed against him at the
election: "a Lord-Lieutenant whose land surrounded the place
for miles; and there was magisterial influence, aristocratic
influence, legal influence, and nearly all influences against him
(the speaker); but it was simply by trusting to the people that
he was successful. . . . And without a farthing of any legal
expense, simply by throwing himself upon the people, they not
only secured the seat, but they secured it by a majority of
nearly 100 votes.   He was only telling them this in order that
they might never be disheartened in fighting for Liberalism

if they trusted to the people. In nine cases out of ten the people were right, and they would not trust in the people in vain."

This note of enthusiasm was not the only one heard at the conference. In the course of the debate or rather of the remarks of the delegates, some exceptions were taken. While giving their full adhesion to the federation scheme, several of them nevertheless betrayed apprehensions lest the Federation would encroach on the independence of the local Associations. Besides the legitimate preoccupations inspired by this subject, many of the delegates felt a touch of parochial jealousy of Birmingham taking the lead. The statement of objects and reasons of the Federation anticipated these misgivings by declaring that "no interference with the local independence of the Federated Associations is proposed or contemplated." Several delegates took note of this with eagerness and emphasis. It was mentioned by way of illustration that they did not intend to submit to the Birmingham practice of turning all the local elections into political contests. The admission of all comers to membership of the Association without any subscription also gave rise to an exchange of observations. One delegate demanded that, in conformity with the principle of consulting the people, invoked at the conference itself, the scheme should be submitted in the first instance to the local Associations which were to be brought within the Federation. But the authors of these proposals were not allowed to dwell on the subject, and the proposals were summarily rejected. Finally the scheme was adopted, and the "National Federation of Liberal Associations," known since under the shorter title of "National Liberal Federation," was founded. Its object was according to the statutes, firstly, to assist in the organization throughout the country of Liberal Associations based on popular representation, and secondly, to promote the adoption of Liberal principles in the government of the country. The constituted authorities of the Federation were: a council formed of delegates of the local Associations, which each nominated five to twenty of them, — according to the population, —and a general committee composed of a smaller number of delegates, plus twenty-five members to be added by the committee itself. Being entrusted with the realization of the "objects" of the Federation, the special duty of the committee was to "submit to the Federated Associations the political questions and measures as to which united action might appear desirable."

VII

The formalities of the constitution of the Federation were completed, but this was only the first part of the programme. The chief piece was to be given that very evening, as the circular which summoned the delegates to Birmingham took care to announce: a public meeting with Mr. Gladstone as principal orator. The illustrious statesman was coming himself to stand godfather to the Federation. The sponsorship derived special importance from the exceptional position which Mr. Gladstone held at that time.

Soon after the defeat of the Liberal party at the general election of 1874, Mr. Gladstone gave up the leadership of it, having decided to bring his long political career to a close and to employ the rest of his days in preparing for the great moment when he would appear before the Eternal Judge. A successor was given him, Lord Hartington, who formally assumed the control of the Liberal party. But with the rigid organization of English parliamentary parties each led by a single chief for the term of his natural life, toward whom all eyes are constantly directed, it was by no means easy for one who had for years filled the office of leader in a brilliant fashion, to retire into political obscurity. For the Liberal party and the country he always remained Mr. Gladstone, as a king who has abdicated always remains His Majesty, Sire! Besides he himself had some difficulty in becoming reconciled to his self-imposed effacement; penance and prayer could no more fill up his existence than they could that of Charles V in the monastery of St. Juste. His tempestuous soul, haunted by the memories of a thousand battles, only required an opportunity to burst forth. The opportunity came: the Bulgarian atrocities drew Mr. Gladstone from his retreat. Overflowing with wrath and indignation he denounced, in a series of fiery harangues which stirred the English people to its depths, the cruelties of the Turk and the wretched system of government which left Christians a prey to the violence of savage hordes. In this oratorical campaign Mr. Gladstone, who has passed through so many successive and simultaneous incarnations, asserted himself once and for all and with more emphasis than ever in that of popular leader. The temperament of demagogue (in the etymological meaning of the word) which contended with many others in this complex nature, had at last, after long years of growth, found its fullest expression. At the moment when Palmerston's death was closing one epoch and ushering in another in the history of England, a shrewd observer referring to Mr. Gladstone as future leader of the Liberal movement in spite of some reactionary tendencies displayed by him, foreshadowed that if he did attain that position, it would be not as a party favourite but as a popular leader, and added: "From the time I first heard Gladstone speak when carried beyond himself by the passion of debate, I came to the conclusion that nature meant him for a popular demagogue, and that the scholarlike moderation that his University training had imparted to his habitual utterances was a matter of education, not of instinct." [1]

His generous and impulsive instincts and strong religious temperament readily inclined him towards all aspirations which were derived from an ideal sense of goodness and justice, and which at the same time served his political ends. He embraced them with ardour directly events brought them across his path. His imagination conjured them up as facing him when he walked straight before him, as turning to the left when he turned to the left, and to the right when he turned to the right. But why should they prevent him from advancing, asked an inward voice. Was he their enemy? No; they even had a place deep down in his heart, — beyond a doubt they had a place there and a legitimate place ; — does not reason itself in fact plead their cause? And thereupon the marvellous flexibility of Mr. Gladstone's intelligence suggested to him one argument after another which converted the gratification of these unsatisfied aspirations into an irresistible postulate of the logic of men, an imperious command of the logic of things. But as his dialectic, which was often too admirable, succeeded in carrying conviction to his own mind rather than to that of others, he turned by an unconscious impulse towards the source of his opinions, towards the

[1] New York *Nation*, 1865, Vol. I, p. 586, "Letter from England."

impetuous feeling which brought him in closer touch with the
people's hearts. Placing himself in unison with them he
evoked cries of approbation which mounted like furious waves,
surging against each other, rising above one another, and finally
blending in a mighty roar of the ocean. With a single stroke
he loosed the wallet of Æolus, and if the foolish and the
blind did not choose to take the same course as the liberated winds, so much the worse for them. He called the
people to witness, he made them the judge, the supreme judge
supposed to have a sound judgment because endowed with an
upright heart. Logicians might wrangle about the lines of demarcation between politics and ethics, the people were delighted
with the confusion of the two or the identification of the one
with the other which Mr. Gladstone made in form as well as in
substance. The tone of his harangues, always pitched in the
key of uprightness, of justice, lifted his hearers into a region
in which the people, perennial victim of injustice, likes to be
transported, if only in imagination. The respectful intimacy
with the Almighty which Mr. Gladstone was in the habit of
affecting stamped him in the eyes of the people as the blessed
man of the Psalm who walketh not in the counsel of the un-
godly, but whose delight is in the law of the Lord, and in his
law doth he meditate day and night. Merely listening to him
one felt as it were brought nearer to the face of the Lord.
The tone of profound emotion and the fiery passion which ran
through all Mr. Gladstone's speeches, supplied the masses with
the strong sensations which they thirst for, and his fighting
temperament, which found free vent in his eloquence, flattered
even the less elevated instincts of combativeness common to
all crowds and to English crowds more than any others. Thus
he came to hold the people by a power almost hypnotic, and
to him might be applied the saying in the East anent a celebrated *imam*, a military and religious leader: "by his mere
breath he aroused a tempest in the soul, and the heart of a man
hung upon his lips."

The prestige arising from this immense power was bestowed
on the Federation by the patronage which Mr. Gladstone extended to it, and that too at the moment when his popularity
had reached its climax, in consequence of his campaign against
the Bulgarian atrocities. The inauguration by him of the new

organization imparted to this provincial association a national significance, and, what was not less essential under the circumstances, gave it the stamp of authentic Liberalism. In setting up an organization for the general supervision of Liberalism, independently of those who controlled it by virtue of a formal delegation from the Liberal members of Parliament, the creators of the Federation practically denied the authority of the official leaders of the party; but with Mr. Gladstone on their side they had with them the real leader of Liberalism. Mr. Gladstone's peculiar situation after his abdication of the leadership alone enabled the Birmingham Radicals to get into this fortunate position. Thus in this as in every other respect the visit of Mr. Gladstone, arranged by Mr. Chamberlain and his friends, was a master-stroke on their part.

Addressing an enormous meeting estimated at 30,000 persons, Mr. Gladstone commended the new organization and eulogized the popular principle introduced at Birmingham. "As the law of popular election," he said, "is the foundation of the British House of Commons, so, if I understand you aright, it is the principle and practice of your great town that local organization shall be governed by the same principle, and that free popular choice shall be its basis and its rule. I rejoice not merely that you are about to inculcate this lesson, but that the large attendance here to-day of many hundreds of representatives of the constituencies of the country, met together to consider this subject and to join in counsel with you, testifies to the disposition which exists to adopt this admirable principle of which you have given the example, and of which, if it be freely and largely adopted, I, for one, am sufficiently sanguine to predict with confidence the success." After having pointed out that the Liberal party stood in greater need of organization than the Tories, who represented immobility in politics, Mr. Gladstone recalled in eloquent language the share of Birmingham in carrying the Reform Bill and complimented the town on having once more "raised the banner of order in the Liberal party." On the part to be played by the Federation which he had come to inaugurate, on the programme which it was framing, on the sphere of influence which it assigned to itself, on the attitude which it was assuming towards the leaders of the party and towards the Constitution in general, Mr. Gladstone vouchsafed no explanations. He turned to the Eastern question, and soon the whole audience forgot itself in the wild enthusiasm which each of his speeches habitually produced.

For the Federation there remained the great fact that the leader of English Liberalism had come forward as its sponsor.

Public opinion soon directed its attention to this organization and to the whole political situation which it entailed; and before long an animated discussion arose in the Press and on the Platform. It was perfectly natural that party polemics should be among the first to seize on the subject. The authors of the Birmingham system claimed for it the power of making the Liberal party victorious and put it forward as an engine of war against the Conservatives. This was enough to make the latter look upon it with very unfavourable eyes. Lord Beaconsfield in a sarcastic attack on his opponents flung the American nickname of "Caucus" at the new organization, a word which had long been associated in the history of American parties with the intrigues and devices of unscrupulous electoral wire-pullers and with political corruption. Launched by the Prime Minister, a master of epigram, the appellation of "Caucus" at once passed into general use in England and became the ordinary designation of the new Liberal organizations. The Birmingham politicians, after exhibiting some signs of ill-humour on the point, thought it would be "better frankly to accept the word while trusting to time and experience to attach new and more attractive meanings to it."[1] They flattered themselves that it might become a glorious epithet like that of Whig and Tory. I shall follow their example here and in future use the word "Caucus," if only for the sake of its brevity, to denote the representative party organizations started at Birmingham.

[1] *The Caucus*, by J. Chamberlain, quoted above.

FOURTH CHAPTER

THE GROWTH OF THE CAUCUS

I

HOWEVER great may have been the stir made by the appearance of the Federation on the stage, and imposing as was the ceremony of giving the finishing touch to the work of popular organization, its solidity and its duration were to depend on the broadness of its basis in the country. The Associations of 93 places which sent delegates to the Birmingham function evidently did not present an adequate support. Consequently the leaders of the Federation zealously kept up the propaganda *extra muros.* Mr. Schnadhorst continued to travel about the country to advertise the model association and recommend the adoption of it, which he did in the most inviting terms: "No subscription. No opinion, creed, or position shut a man out. So long as the minority are content to submit to the majority, no matter what opinion upon any particular question a man held, he was not excluded. Free discussion was granted to all so long as perfect loyalty to each other existed. The object of their meetings was that they should be thoroughly representative in their character. The next business was the election of committees in each ward; every man was qualified, and those who were willing to serve were elected."[1] Mr. Gladstone, too, was inexhaustible in praise of the Birmingham system. "I venture to say it is admirable, it is sound, it is just, it is liberal, it is popular. . . . A man is not bound by the Birmingham plan to subscribe to any list of political articles. That is one of the rocks on which we have split. At Birmingham you know they are tolerably advanced, but they don't attempt to exclude the most moderate."[2]

[1] Speech of Mr. Schnadhorst at the Cambridge Reform Club, January, 1878.
[2] Speech of the 27th September, 1877, at Nottingham. Cf. his speech at Southwark, of the 20th July, 1878, and his letter of the 10th September, 1878, about the election at Newcastle-under-Lyme.

The Caucus spread from one town to another, that is to say, representative Associations were established in them in due form. Very often they were started amid complete indifference on the part of the masses. Sometimes the latter did not care for the direct participation of the people in the affairs of the party, or for the grand speeches in which it was claimed; sometimes they looked on the "plan" with suspicion, having no confidence in the sincerity of the "bourgeois" who had undertaken the conduct of it. But in several places the system was well received by the masses and they hastened to turn it to account. The attitude of the traditional leaders who belonged to the old ruling classes also varied a great deal. Some, considering the new Associations a real means of restoring the fortunes of the party, gave them their unqualified adhesion. Others, although with little enthusiasm for democratic Organizations, thought it wiser not to make a fuss and joined the new Associations or actually helped to establish them, and naturally became their leaders. Others, again, were averse to abdicating in favour of the masses and opposed the formation of the "hundreds." Sometimes a compromise was arrived at which was highly characteristic of the English political temperament. The masses offered to divide the power with the traditional leaders. For instance, instead of electing all the "300" by the people, as they would have liked to do, they were satisfied with 200 delegates chosen directly in the ward public meetings, and allowed the leaders to appoint the remaining 100 delegates themselves.[1] In so doing the masses acknowledged in a way that the representatives of the old ruling classes possessed vested interests in the exercise of political power and influence, and consented to the mixed form of government which was the ideal of the classic theorists of the art of politics. Lastly, in several towns the old leaders offered an energetic resistance to the introduction of the Caucus. In places where their influence was not paramount they were disregarded, and an Association was founded on the Birmingham plan, but this was not always sufficient to anni-

[1] The example quoted here refers to the Liberal Association of Chester, the circumstances attending the formation of which are related in a parliamentary electoral enquiry (*Blue Books*, 1881, Vol. XXVI,—Report of the Commissioners).

hilate the leaders, nor to do away with the old Registration Societies or Liberal Associations which existed in the locality, and in more than one case the constituency was left with two rival Associations each having its own special adherents.

In the central organization the same dualism was still more strongly accentuated. The Birmingham Federation claimed to control the affairs of the party, but the old institution of parliamentary Whip with its offices (Central Liberal Association) still subsisted. Great as was its confidence in its traditional authority, it could not help seeing that a new rival power had sprung up, and instinctively it retreated before it as before the rising tide. By a tacit agreement it abandoned to the Federation all the Midland counties of which Birmingham is the capital; it had also given up London, but the Federation had no idea of being confined within this line of demarcation, it invaded the other parts of the Kingdom, hoisted its flag in them, and left its garrisons in them in the form of representative Associations. Closely pressed by the Caucus, the parliamentary Whip's organization retired within its shell, and subsided more and more into the essentially Whig character which the very history of the English Liberal party has stamped on it. Every step in advance taken by the Birmingham system was so much ground won from the old Liberalism; every gesture, every act of the new Organization, was a threat or an attack directed against the venerable figure of Whiggism. The Birmingham movement everywhere brought out the more or less latent or patent antagonism between Whigs and Radicals and accentuated it.

II

The differences within the Liberal party were not of recent date. It has never been a homogeneous party and it could not be so considering that it represented the party of movement, of changes which are conceived or displayed in a thousand different ways. United in attack against the common enemy, it was always destined by its very nature to relax its discipline after the victory was won. As soon as the Parliamentary Reform of 1832 brought a certain number of frankly Radical members into the House, friction began between them and the Whigs. The quarrels and reconciliations which fill up the existence of every disunited household brought the historic Liberal party to the ominous date of 1867. The extension of the suffrage to the urban masses effected by the second Reform Bill inspired the Radicals with great hopes; they would no longer be dragged at the heels of the Whigs, plunged in political languor as under Melbourne, or in torpor as under Palmerston; on the contrary, it would be they, the Radicals, who would give the tone to the policy of the Liberal party, and that policy would assume a frank, definite character, free from pusillanimous hesitation and compromise. Great disappointments were in store for them. The new reformed Parliament, elected in 1868, contained an enormous Liberal majority, but it was very far from being a Radical one. The Gladstone Ministry, which came triumphantly into power, soon wore out its prestige. It dissatisfied everybody, alarmed the Conservatives, and irritated its Radical adherents. Toward the close of its administration, in 1873, the advanced section of the Liberal party was almost in a state of revolt. It was in vain that Mr. Gladstone, to coax it into submission, took John Bright into the Cabinet. The discontent was not confined to the halls of Parliament, it was very strong in the country itself where, owing to the extension of the suffrage, Radicalism henceforward had a broader base of operations than it has ever possessed in England. And it was from this quarter, from the provinces, that protests proceeded. One of the most violent was made by Mr. Joseph Chamberlain. As yet quite unknown outside Birmingham, he delivered a regular attack on the leaders of the party, not sparing Mr. Gladstone himself. He accused the Liberal Government of refusing to grapple with reforms, of amusing the democracy by bringing forward insignificant Bills, of producing half-measures, of ignoring the just demands of the working classes, etc.[1] The collapse of the Liberal majority at the general election of 1874, lent a melancholy tone to these recriminations,[2] but they were far from coming to an end. The substitution of Lord Hartington for Mr. Gladstone as head

---

[1] "The Liberal Party and its Leaders," *Fortnightly Review*, September, 1873.

[2] Cf. the article by Mr. Chamberlain, "The Next Page on the Liberal Programme," *Ibid.*, October, 1874.

of the party, a genuine representative of aristocratic Whiggism, filled the young Radicals with suspicion and apprehension, which soon developed into vehement and indignant protests in consequence of the attitude adopted by Lord Hartington and his colleagues on the front bench with regard to Eastern affairs.

It was at this moment that the popular Liberal Associations appeared on the scene. Having rushed at once and with great ardour into the anti-Turkish campaign, and having thus taken up an attitude distinctly opposed to that preserved by the leaders of the party and their moderate followers, their intervention was forthwith invested with a significance which was out of proportion to the affair which had been the pretext or occasion of it. While the moderates remained calm and apathetic, the Associations stormed and raged throughout the country. " You see," exclaimed the Radicals, " it is there in the meetings, in the Associations that the pulse of true Liberalism beats." The formation of the Associations, in the midst of the anti-Turkish agitation, having set in motion the ardour, the enthusiasm, the advanced political feeling of each locality, these manifestations gave the impression, to the Radicals at all events, that a numerical majority of the nation was behind them. " You see," they said, " that all the real Liberals are on our side." The visible organization of the Associations even presented, for the first time in the history of the party, the illusion of a tangible line of demarcation, of a boundary. Those who were outside it, the moderates, the lukewarm, were no longer real Liberals. This was the great conclusion which required a practical solution, a solution concisely expressed by the demand that they should clear out. Such indeed was the cry which resounded through the Radical camp. Never had the Whigs had to face such a formidable Radical onslaught, nor had such direct aim ever been taken at the very heart of their being and of their whole existence, which was identified with the destinies of English political society as moulded and fashioned by them. In fact, it was no longer a conflict of two rival factions, it was a collision of two worlds — the one composed of old and more or less dried up strata, the other rising from the waves after the democratic storm of 1868 and consolidating itself in the Caucus.

III

In the first of these, in the world of old Liberalism, there were two fundamental strata, — parliamentarism and individualism. The one was contributed by the historic Whigs, the other was due to political economy, to philosophy and to the industrial revolution. In combating the absolute power of the Crown, the Whigs had strengthened the fabric of parliamentarism, with the support of their aristocratic followers, who were arrayed behind them and kept in good order by social discipline. When the middle class, being desirous of a share of power, joined their ranks, the Whigs had to come to terms with them, to compromise with their character and the tendencies of their mind trained in ideas or notions of individual liberty and commercial freedom. The Whig aristocrats renovated their old historic claims with these " principles," while the Liberal middle class acknowledged their traditional position of leaders, and readily confiding in their political experience and prestige, also insensibly fell within the sphere of their social influence. This fusion gave rise to a body of opinion and to a political temperament which, extending in numerous successive shades almost to the confines of Toryism on the one side and of Radicalism on the other, presented an average type equidistant from both extremes, free from their defects but sometimes also devoid of their virtues.

The fundamental creed of Whiggism elaborated in the contests with the Crown, that is to say that no person, no body has absolute power, justified in the mind of the Liberal his admiration for the balanced and harmonized government which he called the " English Constitution," and filled him with disgust for the Jacobin spirit. Authoritarianism, in all its forms and all its consequences, whether they affected the State or the individual, was an abomination to him. It offended not only his ideas but his sensibility still more. His love of liberty being derived from education and habit, he was not so much a passionate lover, like the classic Radical, as a dilettante one. Liberty appealed more to his æsthetic sense as a man of refinement than burst into a flame within his heart. The fire which gave warmth to his soul was a slow fire, well kept up because covered with embers, never a red-hot one. Reflective without being exactly a thinker, but above all sedate, he was not easily carried away. Calm and reserved, he often appeared cold and frequently haughty with all the haughtiness of his aristocratic pedigree or of the fortune which he had amassed in business. Endowed in addition to this with a robust confidence in sound principles, especially those of political economy, " some of which are susceptible of mathematical demonstration," he combined with aristocratic haughtiness or plutocratic arrogance the intellectual pride of the doctrinaire or the dull conceit bred of a little knowledge. These sentiments, joined to a genuine spirit of individual independence, made him little accessible to the mobile influences of " opinion." In any event he did not admit its absolute power, for this he refused to concede to any one. All the more was it repugnant to him to look for inspiration or to pretend to take it in the street, in the market-place. The feeling of personal dignity which kept him back was mingled also with a shade of contempt for and fear of the crowd, of the mob. On the other hand, being trained in the proprieties of society or in the compromises of business life, he naturally fell in with party combinations and readily submitted to party exigencies. The mild and somewhat vague tolerance which constituted the groundwork of his character, thoroughly imbued him with the opportunism and the flexibility which are, as it were, the essence of old parties. But at the same time this easy sluggish temper surrounded him, so to speak, with a rampart against attacks from outside, a sort of slope which he could descend with ease, but which did not permit every one to come to close quarters with him, so that while following others he could honestly say to himself that he was not dragged along by them. Balance of mind, self-possession, moderation, a taste for or a habit of compromise, all these valuable political qualities — which alone had been able to raise the fabric of liberty on the aristocratic soil of England, bristling with privileges, monopolies, selfish interests, traditions, and class prejudices — the Whig Liberal was only too conscious of having them, and he was in consequence only too much disposed to consider himself born for the work of government and to look on power as a right and a duty at the same time. In order to enjoy the right he indulged in concessions which he readily viewed as sacrifices to duty, and being naturally anxious to spare himself the sacrifices, he guarded the enjoyment with a jealousy, with a spirit of exclusiveness, which tended to keep bores and intruders at a distance.

But this barrier with which Whig Liberalism surrounded itself rather invited attack, and instead of serving as a defence it exposed it to danger. The Birmingham Radicalism, which broke through it, engaged the old Liberalism along the whole line. All the gods which the old Liberalism venerated and adored, the other was ready to burn; everything which was abhorred and feared by the former was extolled and exalted by the latter. Proclaiming the deposition of leaders of every kind and transferring to the masses the immediate duty of governing themselves, demanding for the "people" the right of deciding without appeal on the policy to be adopted, of marking out the lines of it themselves, the new Liberalism repudiated the whole Whig doctrine which holds that in a free country no one, no individual nor body however numerous, wields an absolute, undivided, direct power; it overthrew the imposing and ingeniously constructed fabric of government in which all the parts balance each other and are carried forward in a harmonious and unbroken movement; it made the people not only the primary source of power, but the authority which prescribed the acts of the supreme government, following only its own will and obeying only its own inspirations of the moment; for the regular working of established organs, controlled by principles and traditions supplied by experience, it substituted the irregular action of extra-constitutional bodies, on which the former would only have to model their movements. In one word, it laid sacrilegious hands on the holy ark of parliamentary institutions which contained the whole Whig law.

Rejecting the principles of the Whigs as too narrow and unbending, Radicalism condemned their conduct as too fainthearted; for the latitudinarianism of their political conscience it substituted a jealous and exclusive creed expressed in the formula, "trust in the people"; those who would not confess the faith of "confidence in the people" had no place in the fold of the new Liberalism; and the sincerity of the believer's faith was proved only by following the numerical majority of the "people," or those who were supposed to represent it. With little relish for the discipline which was demanded in consequence, the Whigs had a still greater dislike to the uninterrupted stream of enthusiasm turned on by the "hundreds" and their meetings. The sentimental note on which Mr. Gladstone played with a skill which was all the more masterly because it was natural to him, did not vibrate within them; they mistrusted sentimentalism in politics, or, as their detractors asserted, they ignored the influence of moral sentiment in the sphere of politics. The loud tones, the noisy ways, the exuberant gestures of the Caucus people were quite enough to jar on them; by their placid temperament and their social relations they were, or considered themselves, too much of gentlemen to be able to put up with the "want of sobriety in language and of dignity in demeanour" which offended them in the advanced section of the party. The old Whig Liberals were thus attacked in their principles, in their conduct, in their habits and their ideas of decorum. They were wounded in their faults as well as in their virtues. And there was no chance of the latter securing forgiveness for the former; in politics virtues are often expiated even more than faults.

The Whigs received notice to quit, they had held their position only too long; they had been, they were told, simply a clique engaged in the selfish pursuit of power, they were out of sympathy with all the aspirations of the nation, they did not understand its requirements, they were incapable of directing it. In vain did the moderates protest that they still had a great part to play; that the leadership in the Liberal party was their natural function; that no proof existed that the democratic spirit had developed to a point which justified the placing of Radicalism in power. It was of no avail, they said, hoisting the red flag of democracy; the old social conditions had not disappeared and England was still, politically speaking, a nation of traders governed for the most part by landed proprietors, or of shopkeepers whose one ambition was to be raised to the class of landed proprietors. England, to quote the saying applied to France, was Left Centre, equally hostile to Tory stagnation and to the utopias of men of extreme opinions. The divergent attitude of the leaders and of the masses in the Eastern question, which had been triumphantly turned to account against the moderates, in no way marked the difference between aristocratic tendencies and democratic aspirations; it was not Whiggism but statesmanship and good sense to keep cool in times of popular excitement, to distrust the capacity of indignation meetings to conduct foreign policy. The crime of the moderates or of the Whigs, as their opponents affected to call them, consisted in holding fast to principles, in looking beyond the democratic passions of the moment and fixing their attention on the liberties and the permanent interests of the nation. "For us the question is not to know what is popular, but what is reasonable and just, and we consider it one of the duties of statesmen to combat popular illusions even at the sacrifice of place and power."[1] All these grounds of defence pleaded by the Whigs were so many confessions of guilt in the eyes of the Radicals, they seemed to them only to corroborate the charge that the official leaders were no longer in touch with the feelings and ideas of the nation, and as the leaders were moderates and representatives of moderates, both were confounded in one common reprobation. The war-cry raised by the "Birmingham plan": *down with the leaders, and up with the people*, being converted in these circumstances into the cry: *down with the Whigs, war on the moderates, up with the Radicals*, the popular movement inaugurated in the Midlands inevitably turned against the moderates with redoubled force. And for hurling its shafts the permanent Organizations on a representative basis supplied it with a perfected and hitherto unknown engine of war.

IV

The Eastern question remained to the end up to the Berlin Congress, the sheet-anchor of the Caucus. Its central organ, fastening on the foreign policy of the Government, deemed it necessary to take up an attitude, whether of blame or approval,

---

[1] Among the numerous writings to which this controversy gave rise in the Press, may be quoted, besides the two articles by Mr. Chamberlain already mentioned: "Whigs and Liberals," by Goldwin Smith (*Fortnightly Review*, 1878, vol. 23); "Liberals and Whigs," by Geo. Brodrick (*Ibid.*); "A Word for Indignation Meetings," by Goldwin Smith (*Ibid.* vol. 24); "The Government and the Opposition" (*Edinburgh Review*, January, 1879); "Whigs, Radicals, and Conservatives" (*Quarterly Review*, 1880, vol. 150).

in all the incidents of the crisis; at one time with reference to
the summoning of troops from India, at another in regard to
the participation of England in the Congress.   In the local
Associations the anti-Turkish movement, which was tolerably
spontaneous and genuine at the start, soon lost this character; the emotion aroused by Mr. Gladstone's agitation had time
to calm down, and the meetings and demonstrations of the
caucuses were kept up rather by *vis inertiae* and at the instigation of Birmingham.   But this did not make them display
greater wisdom.   For the inauguration of the direct influence
of the masses on public affairs it was if anything to be regretted that their first appearance should have been in the province of foreign policy, in which popular emotion, the ardour,
and the enthusiasm, nay even the excellent intentions of the
multitude, are not indispensable or useful factors.   It is therefore not surprising that in their anti-Turkish campaign the
Associations should have given striking proof of their want of
discernment on more than one occasion.   The speeches made and
the resolutions adopted were often characterized by extrava-
gance and ignorance of the first conditions in which the English
political system works, as, for instance, the resolutions relating
to the impeachment of Lord Beaconsfield and other moves of
the same kind.

It is beyond a doubt that in several localities the new Organizations, apart from the Eastern question which appealed to
the generous instincts of the masses, had called forth a great
deal of civic enthusiasm and of honest and genuine interest
in the public weal.   But it is no less true that these impulses
stood in need of guidance, and that this guidance was very
often non-existent.   It was easy enough to copy the Birmingham Organization, but it was not so easy to reproduce the
merits of the men who controlled it, the public spirit which they
contrived to create and maintain.   The Radical leaders who
joined in the movement lacked, as a rule, the first quality of
leaders — a sense of the fitness of things, and more than one
extravagant act of the Associations, during the Eastern crisis
for instance, and afterwards, must be attributed wholly to
them.   On the other hand, the men with more balance who
possessed influence in the locality, and who hastened to accept
the Caucus, often had not sufficient enthusiasm or sincerity to

exercise a beneficial influence on the masses. Belonging for
the most part to the old ruling classes, they were more anxious
about preserving the reality of the power which they had had
to relinquish in appearance.   In any event their mind, imprisoned in the narrow circle of party ideas, could not take
in the real grandeur of the work implied in the political education of the masses, and even if they could do so, these traders
or manufacturers who thought themselves Liberals because they
swore by Mr. Gladstone were incapable of taking the lead in it.
In the most favourable circumstances, the old leaders who had
joined the Caucus succeeded by dint of moderation and tact in
restraining the aggressive zeal of the enthusiasts and in keeping
the peace between the different sections of the party. In places
where this was not the case, where men of this kind were not
forthcoming, or the new electors were of a less conciliatory temper, the Caucus, which rallied round it the advanced and ardent
spirits of the party, soon became the stronghold of a faction
imbued with a sectarian spirit and all the more intolerant and
imperious because the popular form of its constitution gave it
a pretext for putting itself forward as the only true, legitimate
representative of the Liberal party

V

In the Caucus, this spirit speedily displayed itself in the
discharge of its first duty, which was the choice of candidates
for the parliamentary elections. Conformably to the Birmingham doctrine, no candidate could henceforth stand for Parliament irrespective of the Caucus. In order to be true to the
democratic spirit, the caucuses did not make a selection in the
real sense of the word, but organized a sort of public competition among the candidates by requiring from them complete
submission beforehand. The members whom the Caucus found
in possession had to submit to the same process if they
aspired to re-election. The fact that the Caucus often represented only a fraction of the party, and that the most
passionate, the most ardent, was not calculated to secure it
adhesion in every quarter, and the pretensions of the new
Organizations aroused vehement protests. One of these cases
made a great stir throughout the country, owing to the emi-

nence of the protesting party. The conflict arose at Bradford between the Caucus and one of the members for the town, W. E. Forster, the well-known statesman.

Forster had represented Bradford in Parliament for eighteen years. Having been returned in consequence of his local notoriety, he was not long in achieving a considerable position in the House, and soon rose to the first rank of statesmen in the Liberal party. The brilliance of his political career, being reflected on the town which he represented, accentuated the feelings of devotion and affection which had bound him to his constituents from the very first. But for some time past, a small fraction of the constituency, inspired by religious passions, had pursued Forster with unrelenting animosity. It could not forgive him the part which he had played in the creation of a system of popular instruction. When Forster became Minister of Education in Gladstone's first Cabinet (1868–1874), England was still without a system of primary instruction, the introduction of which, as will be remembered, ran counter to the fanaticism of the various religious sects, especially of the Nonconformists, who could not agree as to what religious teaching should be given. Forster boldly grappled with the question and passed, by way of compromise, an organic law of primary education which made instruction obligatory and undenominational to the extent that all religion was excluded wherever the population so desired it, and which allowed the reading of the Bible in the schools, without any dogmatic instruction or a catechism, in cases where the School Boards elected by the ratepayers did not prohibit all religious teaching. The law also provided that the Treasury should continue its grants to the establishments for primary education by distributing them among the Board schools as well as the denominational schools, on condition, however, that they should submit to Government inspection, and that religious instruction should only be given before or after school hours and be optional for the schoolchildren.

Hardly was the law passed (in 1870) when the extreme Radicals denounced it as contrary to "logic" because it only permitted the introduction of obligatory instruction, but did not enforce it against the will of the population. Again, the provisions of the law relating to the denominational schools

exasperated an important section of the Liberal party, — the
Nonconformists, who considered that the Act showed too
much favour to the Established Church by keeping up the
grants to its schools while not prohibiting them from giving
religious instruction.   In reality, it was not hostility to religion which inspired the opposition of the Dissenters, far
from it: as a general rule, the adherents of the various
Nonconformist sects can vie with the followers of the Established Church in bigotry and fanaticism, but being separated
from their great rival by an irreconcilable jealousy and by the
memory of the persecutions which it has inflicted on them in
the past, their one object is to " écraser l'infâme."   Joining the
extreme Radicals, the militant Nonconformists began an agitation against the law of 1870 and its author throughout the
country.   The agitation was directed from Birmingham by
the same men who were destined to lead the Caucus two or
three years later, — Mr. Chamberlain, Mr. Schnadhorst (who had
entered public life as secretary of the " Central Nonconformist Committee"), and other Radical Dissenters.   The connections which the Birmingham group formed on this occasion
were subsequently of great assistance to them for the Caucus,
for it was precisely the Nonconformists brought into the field
against Forster's Act who nearly everywhere formed the rank
and file of the caucuses.

The mode of election of the School Board established by the
law, especially the cumulative vote, which gave minorities the
power of getting on the Board, also met with an unfavourable
reception from the opponents of the Act of 1870, and they devoted their energies to nullifying it by devices of electoral
organization.   We have already seen the Birmingham group
at this work; the tactics of "vote as you are told" failed on
this occasion, but met with success in other places where the
calculations were more accurately made, at Leeds for instance.[1]
Although in more than one case, especially in London, the oppo-

---

[1] Forster was much distressed by this.   " We do not want party lines in
these elections," he said; " we want everybody, whether he belongs to a big
party or to a little one, to have his fair say in the choice of the people who
are to manage the education of his children; and I think you Liberals of
Leeds have behaved very badly in upsetting the original intention of Parliament when it passed the Bill " (T. W. Reid, *Life of W. E. Forster*, Lond.
1888, I, 517).

nents of Forster's Act had been among those who had obtained a seat on the Board by means of the cumulative vote, they none the less made a grievance of it against Forster.[1]

After Gladstone's retirement Forster was, next to the new leader of the party, Lord Hartington, the most conspicuous statesman on the Liberal staff, and in this capacity he shared in the policy of reserve which the chiefs of the Liberal Opposition in Parliament maintained during the Eastern crisis, and which brought on them so many attacks from the Radicals.

VI

Such was Forster's situation when Bradford was provided with a proper Caucus, which was at once filled with fanatical Nonconformists and Radicals of more enthusiasm than sober-mindedness. In the statutes which it adopted in 1878 it incorporated the whole Birmingham doctrine, written and unwritten. It took up the provision which placed candidates and members under the orders of the Caucus, and it hastened to demand from Forster recognition of this rule. Article 15 of the statutes, which soon became quite famous throughout England, provided that it should be "required from the proposer of any intending candidate for the representation of the borough in Parliament, that he should, before the time of making such proposal (having previously obtained the consent of such intending candidate), give an assurance to the General Committee of the Association that the candidate he proposes will abide by their decision." The Chairman of the "300" of Bradford, a Nonconformist of a highly militant type, who had opposed Forster tooth and nail at his last re-election (in 1874), now held out the olive-branch to him by offering to propose him to the Caucus as candidate, only he mildly added as a condition that Forster should undertake to submit to the Caucus. Forster refused, he was not prepared to be adopted by the Caucus at this price. "I cannot bind myself to a rule which even theoretically enables any Association to stand between me and the constituency I have so long represented. I am a member for the borough, and I cannot think it right to make myself the nominee or the delegate of

[1] Cf. Forster's letter of the 7th March, 1871, to John Bright (*Ibid.*, 527–529).

any organization within the constituency, however important that organization or however I may agree with it in political opinion." Criticising the rule of Article 15 from a general point of view, Forster pointed out how little it was in accordance with good sense : "it might be that the committee might be mistaken in the grounds of their decision. It is possible that the member might be able to persuade not merely the majority of the constituency, but the majority of his party, that he is right, and yet the condition to which this rule would bind him would prevent him from appealing to his constituents or to his party or even to second thoughts of the committee. If such a rule became general, it would greatly injure the political life of the country. Imagine a wave of prejudice overwhelming the constituencies, as for instance, at the time of the Crimean War ;[1] would it be desirable that the Cobdens and Brights and Milner-Gibsons of the future should be bound not to offer themselves for re-election, and should be forced to hold their tongues and submit to ostracism in silence because they had undertaken not to stand if the majority of a committee disagreed with them ? " The Chairman of the "300" replied in an arrogant tone that with a candidate who ventured to ignore or thwart the decisions of the party in order to follow his personal interest, his own duty was to support the Association; that a candidate had no right to appeal to the whole constituency; that he owed obedience to his party and to its committee appointed in due form ; and that if Forster respected himself he would bow to the rule laid down in Article 15. This attitude of the Caucus was aggravated by the fact that the Chairman of the Bradford "300" had himself admitted that there was no difference of opinion between Forster and the Association at that time. If this was so, if there was no doubt as to the views of the constituents and the member being in unison, what was the object and the meaning of the ordeal to which he was being subjected? There could be only one : to make Forster pass under the yoke of a committee which claimed to represent the people, to assert the power of

[1] The Crimean War aroused the combative instincts of the nation, and in the first general election which followed it (of 1857) the members who protested against the aggressive foreign policy of Palmerston were defeated at the polls. In this disaster of the peace party Cobden and Bright themselves lost their seats.

the Caucus over every one who desired to take part in public life, however high the position conferred on him by his character and talents and however honourable his past.   Mr. Schnadhorst himself, with the authority which belonged to him in these particular matters, had propounded this maxim when explaining the "Birmingham plan": "John Bright himself," he said, "would have to be nominated and stand or fall by the voting."[1]

The publication in the newspapers therefore of the correspondence between the Chairman of the Caucus and Forster produced a great impression throughout the country.   The public grasped the fact that it was not a merely local matter, that a new tendency was seeking admittance into political life and degrading the representative of the people in Parliament to the status of a clerk at the mercy of a committee taking the place of the whole body of electors and usurping its rights and its powers.   The *Times* only expressed the views of a considerable section of opinion when it said that this correspondence was a warning which ought not to be disregarded. If a public man like Forster could be forced to submit to the yoke of the Association, what must be expected from less conspicuous and less independent politicians?   "We have to thank the Bradford '300,'" said the great newspaper, "for giving us clearly to understand the conditions to which, in the opinion of the 'organizing' party, public life in England must henceforward be subject."[2]

In the meanwhile the town of Bradford was plunged in profound agitation.   Forster possessed many friends and admirers in his constituency.   The Caucus set to work to detach his adherents, to estrange the masses from him and to isolate him.   A violent campaign was started, he was denounced from house to house, and stigmatized in meetings as a traitor to the cause of Liberalism.   The watchword given by the leaders of the Caucus was taken up in the ward meetings by worthy folk who thought that the triumph of the popular cause was really at stake, and each tried to shout his loudest against Forster.[3]

[1] *Cambridge Independent Press*, 12th of January, 1878.
[2] *Times*, 12th of August, 1878.
[3] In the course of the enquiry into the Caucus which I undertook at Bradford one of these ward orators, who had learnt wisdom by time and events, said to me in a deprecatory tone: " I was one of these shouters."

His firm attitude won him sympathy all over the country; politicians belonging to all parties congratulated him and thanked him for fighting the good fight. Mr. Gladstone thought fit to interpose in the conflict and offered his services to his old colleague in order to put an end to it. Forster intimated to Mr. Gladstone that there was nothing to arbitrate about under the circumstances, but that he would have been very glad to see him express his opinion on the question of the organization in general, because, he wrote to him, "I think the advocates of some such rule as the Bradford one have a lurking hope that you are on their side. The Birmingham people disavow this rule;[1] but I am not quite sure that I have as much faith as you have even in the Birmingham system, mainly for the reason that I doubt any permanent committee, or any committee annually elected in quiet times, thoroughly representing the party when an election is imminent. Birmingham itself may be an exception, political interest, not to say excitement, there being both strong and abiding; but generally I suspect the men who elect the committees are themselves but a small part of the party. And is not this likely to happen — either that, being thus small, they would degenerate into wire-pullers, as in the States; or, as in Bradford, represent the agitation for disestablishment, or some such special question? In either case there is a chance of the committee being disavowed by the party when the election really comes. . . . I therefore rather prefer the old system of our towns; namely, a permanent committee to look after the registration, but a choice of candidates by the whole party just before the election. It seems to me one of the best safeguards against the wire-pullers — that is, against the real danger besetting large constituencies — is to so frame the machinery as to keep members as much as possible in communication and contact with the whole constituency, and candidates as much as possible with the whole party."[2]

The Bradford Caucus, which did not expect that its preten-

<hr />

[1] The disavowal was more formal than real. Mr. Schnadhorst was of opinion that "the objection to the Bradford rule seems to be that it embodies in a law a principle of the very greatest value but which should be applied with moderation and discretion, and with a due regard to circumstances and persons" (Letter to the *Times*, 23d of August, 1878).

[2] *Life of W. E. Forster*, II, 213.

sions would give rise to protests in the whole country, was at last obliged to make a concession which put an end to the conflict, for the moment at all events: the wording of the famous paragraph 15 as to the undertaking to be demanded from the candidate was altered in an optional sense, " may be required" being substituted for the imperative " shall be required." Forster thereupon agreed to be nominated by the Association. In reality the concession made by the Caucus, being almost entirely one of form, was not very great, and if any one it was Forster who gave way. All his firmness was spent in solemn protests and high-sounding declarations.[1]

The struggle between Forster and the Bradford Caucus gave a most powerful impulse to the controversy raised by the Birmingham system and definitively made the Caucus one of the questions of the day for a long time to come.[2]

The discussions on the Caucus started in the Press did not produce a great effect on the life of the new Organizations.

---

[1] W. M. C. Torrens, the distinguished Liberal member of Parliament, remarks on this subject in his Memoirs (*Twenty Years in Parliament*, Lond. 1893, p. 358) : " After the passing of the Education and the Ballot Acts, Mr. Forster believed himself strong enough to set the Caucus at defiance, but by degrees the instinct of expediency which was strong within him, though sedulously kept out of notice by his bluntness of manner, prevailed, and to the regret of all who respected him, he consented to be put up with others as a candidate at the next election, on the suppressed assurance that no attempt would be made in reality to oust him in favour of a stranger."

[2] Cf. Edw. D. J. Wilson, " The Caucus and its Consequences " (*Nineteenth Century*, October, 1878) ; Geo. Howell, " The Caucus System and the Liberal Party " (*New Quarterly Magazine*, October, 1878) ; W. Frazer Rae, " Political Clubs and Party Organizations " (*Nineteenth Century*, May, 1878) ; Geo. Brodrick, " Liberal Organization " (in the collection of articles published under the title *Political Studies*, Lond. 1879) ; Th. Hare, " The Reform Bill of the Future " (*Fortnightly Review*, 1878, vol. 23) ; L. Courtney, Speech in the House of Commons of the 8th May, 1878 (*Hansard*, CCXXXVIII, 1010) ; *Times*, 31st of July and 12th of August, 1878 ; " The Government and the Opposition " (*Edinburgh Review*, January, 1879) ; Montague Cookson, " The Nation before Party " (*Nineteenth Century*, May, 1879) ; Goldwin Smith, " Decline of Party Government " (*Macmillan's Magazine*, July, 1877) ; Joseph Chamberlain, " A New Political Organization " (*Fortnightly Review*, July, 1877) ; " The Caucus " (*Ibid.*, November, 1878) both reprinted in pamphlet form, Birmingham, 1879 ; H. W. Crosskey, " The Birmingham Liberal Association and its Assailants " (*Macmillan's Magazine*, December, 1878) ; Speeches of J. Chamberlain at the annual meetings of the Council of the National Liberal Federation, of the 22d January, 1879, and 3d February, 1880; Letter from him to the *Times*, 1st August, 1878; Letters of Mr. Schnadhorst to the *Times* of the 20th and 23d August, 1878.

They followed the impulse given them from Birmingham without paying heed to the attacks of the opponents of the system.
The lesson conveyed by the Forster incident was almost lost on
the Associations, and in other places besides Bradford the candidates or the old members who sought re-election were summoned to undertake beforehand to submit to the decisions of
the Caucus.[1] These tactics, perhaps, in some places, as at
Bradford, served to conceal, by means of general principles
and rules, the hostility of a section of the party towards certain candidates and groups of electors who supported them.
But it is possible that they were adopted in all sincerity, as
the logical result of the "plan" of popular organization, and
cases occurred in which, at the request of the candidates con-

[1] It may not be amiss to quote the case of Mr. (since Sir) John Simon, member for Dewsbury, who, like Forster, refused to submit to the demands of the
Caucus. Anticipating the reproaches levelled at Forster of wishing to be
returned with the help of Tory votes, Simon declared himself ready to withdraw his candidature in case a majority of the Liberal electors, consulted
beforehand, decided against him; but he refused to recognize any authority
other than that of the Liberals themselves. The reasons which he gave for
this completed in some points the arguments already used by Forster and his
friends. "I object to it," he said, "as an infringement of the electoral
freedom of the constituency. It would virtually transfer from them the
whole electoral power of the borough, so far at least as the Liberal electors
are concerned, to the Association or its committee. It would, in effect, restore the old system of nomination boroughs. . . . For a body of gentlemen
to form themselves into an association, in order to introduce a candidate of
their choice, and to use all lawful influence to secure his return, is a perfectly
fair and legitimate object; but it is quite another thing for them to call upon
a candidate to bind himself beforehand to a possible ostracism, and by so
narrowing the field of choice, to deprive a whole constituency or a whole
political party, of the opportunity of exercising their undoubted right to
return the man they would most prefer." And what, according to Mr.
Simon, increased the impropriety of the pretension put forward by the Caucus, was that the engagement required from the candidate was not a reciprocal
one; the Association could not guarantee him the votes of all its members.
In fact, the statutes of the Association of his constituency, as well as those
of several others, provided that if the members did not wish to vote for
the candidate adopted by the Caucus, they were to abstain from voting or
resign before taking any hostile step against the candidate selected by the
committee. While this rule made the support to be given to the candidate an
optional matter, whereas the candidate bound himself unconditionally, on the
other hand it increased the servitude of the electors. "I unhesitatingly
declare it as my opinion, that a rule binding electors to vote, or to abstain
from voting, in a particular way, or practically compelling them to make
known how they vote is a violation of the spirit and object of the Ballot Act.
That Act was intended by *means of secrecy* to secure to the elector complete
freedom in the exercise of the franchise " (*Times*, September, 1879).

cerned, the chiefs of the Organization, Mr. Chamberlain for instance, intervened and advised the local caucuses to adhere less
strictly to principle and not to insist upon the submission of
the candidates. At the approach of the general election in
which the combined forces of the Liberal party were about to
deliver the final assault to dislodge the Tories from power, the
attitude of the caucus leaders became somewhat more conciliatory, and Mr. Chamberlain was anxious to give assurances that
"there was no intention of ignoring their moderate friends, that
though out of sight they were never out of mind." "The Radicals," Mr. Chamberlain remarked, "are, I venture to say, the
majority of the Liberal party. Yet sufferance is the badge of
all our tribe, and we have conceded — we are conceding — we
will concede to our moderate friends, to their convictions, even
to their prejudices, if they will meet us somewhere on the road
in a similar spirit." "We feel we want the aid of every man
who is opposed to the policy of the present government." [1]

[1] Speech at Darlington, on the 3d of February, 1880, at the meeting of the
Council of the National Liberal Federation.

FIFTH CHAPTER

THE CAUCUS IN POWER

I

SHORTLY afterwards Parliament was dissolved, electioneering began, and Mr. Gladstone commenced his famous Midlothian campaign. The Tory seats went down one after another, and finally the Conservative majority was replaced by an enormous Liberal majority. Mr. Chamberlain thereupon uttered a shout of triumph and defiance: "By this token know ye the power of the Caucus and bow before it!" This was the purport of the proclamation which he issued in the form of a letter to the *Times*. Mr. Chamberlain pointed out that in almost every borough which possessed representative Liberal Associations, "sometimes called the 'Caucus' by those who have not taken the trouble to acquaint themselves with the details of the Birmingham system," the Liberal candidates had been victorious. "This remarkable success is a proof that the new Organization has succeeded in uniting all sections of the party, and it is a conclusive answer to the fears which some timid Liberals entertained that the system would be manipulated in the interest of particular crotchets. It has on the contrary deepened and extended the interest felt in the contest, it has fastened a sense of personal responsibility on the electors, and it has secured the active support, for the most part voluntary and unpaid, of thousands of voters, who have been willing to work hard for the candidates in whose selection they had for the first time had an influential voice." The candidates chosen were Liberals of a firmer and more decided stamp; a well-filled purse was not a sufficient passport; preference was accorded to candidates who had won their spurs in political contests and had given proof of loyalty to their principles and of capacity to uphold them. "Altogether," concluded Mr. Chamber-

lain, "for good or for evil, the Organization has now taken firm
root in this country, and politicians will do well to give it in
future a less prejudiced attention."[1] Mr. Schnadhorst proclaimed in his turn that "it could be no longer denied that the
Caucus was a great fact."

A few days afterwards Mr. Chamberlain went straight into
the new Gladstone Ministry, with a seat in the Cabinet,[2] without having ever held a subordinate ministerial office, and with
barely four years of parliamentary life behind him. Among
the comments to which this rapid elevation gave rise, some
accounted for it by the services which Mr. Chamberlain had
rendered to the Liberal party by the introduction of the Caucus, and which Mr. Gladstone was anxious to acknowledge.
This was supposed to be the opinion of Mr. Chamberlain himself.[3] In reality, there was not much foundation for Mr.
Chamberlain's remarks on the glorious part played by the Caucus, and still less for the view that Mr. Gladstone so far
admitted the truth of them as to feel bound to give the leader
of the new Organization a place in his Ministry. Mr. Chamberlain's elevation was due to considerations unconnected
with his electoral activity.[4] As to the part which the Caucus
was supposed to have played in the elections of 1880, it was
very far from having been as important as Mr. Chamberlain
tried to make out. The factors which had brought about the
defeat of Lord Beaconsfield were many and various. First of
all came the immense popularity of Mr. Gladstone, his passionate eloquence which stirred the masses as in the time of
the agitation against the "Bulgarian atrocities"; the adventurous foreign policy of Disraeli which kept the country continu-

---

[1] *Times*, 13th of April, 1880.

[2] In England, as is well known, the Ministry or *Administration* is distinguished from the Cabinet. The latter contains only the most important
members of the *Ministry*, selected by the Premier, so that not only the
Under-Secretaries of State and the great officers of the Royal Household
who change with the Ministry, but even some heads of departments, are or
may be outside the Cabinet.

[3] Cf. Frazer Rae, "The Caucus in England," *International Review*, N.Y.,
August, 1880.

[4] It appears that Mr. Gladstone, wishing to take a representative of the
advanced section into the Ministry, selected Mr. Chamberlain by a process
of elimination, all the other candidates having been rejected for various
reasons.

ally in an unsettled state and affected the stability and security
of the immediate future, so necessary to a mercantile nation,
had lost the Conservative Ministry a good many votes; many
moderates had voted for the Liberals not so much from a wish
to bring them into power as with the object of turning out
the too enterprising Disraeli. The economic crisis of the preceding year also weighed very heavily in the balance against
the Tories; for however limited may be the sphere of influence
of the Government, the lower-class voter is always ready to lay
the blame on it, to make it responsible for a bad harvest and for
bad times. Not that he is sure that " the other side " will bring
good times with them, but the experiment can always be tried.
This line of argument, which is very familiar to the English
elector, caused a displacement of many votes in the elections of
1880. And what finally turned the electoral scale was the altogether extraordinary number of new voters who took the
Liberal side.[1] The Caucus seized on these voters in the large
towns. There it rendered real service by stimulating their
enthusiasm and bringing them up in compact battalions to the
poll. But the electoral arrangements made by the Liberal Whip
were, as the other side admitted, not less effective; the well-
known Whip Adam, who had grown grey in office, succeeded
in bringing the whole strength of moderate Liberalism into the
field.[2] As regards the rural constituencies, the Caucus could
not even put forward any pretensions, the Birmingham system
was only just being introduced into the counties, and yet the
success of the Liberals was not less marked in that quarter;
they won about fifty seats in the counties. As for the claim
that the Caucus had ensured the triumph of a new class of
candidates by curbing the power of the " well-filled purse," the
Caucus did not succeed in this, to judge by the fact that the
elections of 1880 rank in the electoral annals of England as
among those most tainted with corruption. The trial of election petitions even disclosed the fact that certain Associations
of " hundreds " had been privy to acts of corruption : the old

[1] Cf. for the statistics of the elections *Political Parties, their Present Position and Prospects*, an argumentative comparison of the figures of the last
two general elections, by Galloway Rigg, Lond. 1881.

[2] Cf. the speech by Sir H. Stafford Northcote, the illustrious Conservative
leader, of the 4th October, 1882, at Glasgow.

political manners and customs were stronger than the fine
programmes and the professions of faith of the Caucus.   The
powerful contingent contributed by the moderate Liberals
in the electoral battle to a certain extent again confirmed
the view of the Whigs, who maintained that the old social
conditions of England and the old influences had not disappeared.

Nevertheless the audacity and noisy assurance with which
the power of the Caucus was paraded, did, under the circumstances, make an impression on public opinion and give it a
greater idea of the importance of the Birmingham system than
the latter really possessed.   The Tories, who were loud in
attributing their defeat to the Caucus, naïvely did their best to
contribute to the system of advertisement with which the Birmingham group were indefatigably and boldly pushing their
Organization, and which became one of their great weapons.
If I refer here to these tactics of the leaders of the Caucus, it
is not so much to convict them of resorting to the methods of
puffery employed by modern business men as to draw attention
to the appearance with the Caucus in English political life of
a conventional force confronting real, living forces; and it is
in order to point out the distance which separates the former
from the latter in this particular case that I have examined the
various factors which decided the elections of 1880.   Presenting all the appearance of real forces, conventional forces act
like them on the conscience and the will; we admit that they
have an existence of their own, we take this into account, we
attach importance to it, and shape our conduct accordingly.
Just as in the financial market bills issued, endorsed, and
discounted, though possessing no real value, nevertheless discharge all the functions of exchange, at all events until the
next settlement or the first crash.

II

After the accession to power of the Liberal Ministry a good
many Liberals thought that the work of the Organization was
at an end, now that the power of the Tory party was destroyed
and that Parliament contained an enormous Liberal majority
which faithfully reflected the feeling of the country.   This was

not the opinion of the leaders of the Caucus, on the contrary they believed that its career was only beginning.[1] Considering itself to be the most genuine depository of the wishes and ideas of English Liberalism, the Organization held that it was its duty to bring them to the knowledge of the Government and to aid it in carrying them into effect. The first part of this mission, which was undertaken by the central organ of the Caucus, the National Liberal Federation, did not present much difficulty and was of little use. The legislative reforms recommended by the Federation (the extension of the suffrage to rural populations, the reform of the land laws, more stringent measures against electoral corruption) had long been before the Liberal party, and the only practical object of the resolutions of the Caucus, voted at intervals with much pomp, was to call the attention of the Government to the legislative duties incumbent on it, to serve as a reminder to it, and at the same time to invest these reforms with popular sanction, or, at all events, to convey the impression of this by constantly setting in motion the machinery of extra-parliamentary organization.

If the Caucus did in fact possess the power and the authority to give the Government these hints or this sanction, how could it discharge the second duty which it assumed, that is, help the Ministry to make these measures go down with the majority ? According to the traditional notions of English parliamentary government, the co-operation of the Ministry with the majority is based on mutual confidence, and if this is non-existent, no power on earth can create it; there remains only the heroic remedy of separation, of an appeal to the country by means of fresh elections. The Caucus held that between the Government and its supporters there was room for a third body. The parliamentary situation which grew up soon after Mr. Gladstone's accession to office seemed to it to demand this intervention. The Liberal majority of 1880, like that of 1868, was not homogeneous, and Mr. Gladstone's legislative proposals soon created alarm among his moderate followers. To pacify Ireland, he proposed a sweeping reform of the land laws, which, to a certain extent, upset the received ideas regarding rights of

---

[1] Cf. the speech of Mr. Jesse Collings at the annual meeting of the National Liberal Federation, at Liverpool (*Times*, 26th of October, 1881).

property and freedom of contract, by empowering the judicial authorities to fix a fair rent for the land, in spite of the land-lords and of existing contracts. This measure opened a door to all kinds of apprehensions on the part of the moderates; it seemed to them to create a most dangerous precedent for England itself. On the other hand, the Irish members led by Parnell demanded Home Rule and made all progress in Parliament well-nigh impossible by systematic obstruction. In these circumstances the Caucus considered that it "had an obvious duty to discharge" in inviting the local Organizations of the party to bring the refractory members, who did not follow the Government with sufficient docility, to their senses. The Committee of the Federation sent out a circular to all the federated Associations, in which it vehemently denounced the lukewarm members of the majority. "Within a few weeks of their accession to office," ran the document, "it became apparent that among the members of the House of Commons who had secured Liberal seats, there were some who were not heartily loyal to their leaders. . . . During the present session the same disloyalty has reappeared and has threatened the Government with very serious embarrassments. . . . Liberal members recently supported an amendment hostile to the Irish Bill of the Government or intentionally abstained from voting against it." Declaring such a state of things to be intolerable, the Committee of the Federation called on the Associations to take the measures required by the situation.[1]

"This circular produced the effect which the Committee hoped to secure," it soon announced with satisfaction. Telegrams or letters from the local Associations poured in on the members ; in more or less courteous terms they were ordered to vote for the Irish Bill as it stood, not to move or support amendments, to co-operate more loyally with the Government. At Birmingham, in a formal meeting of the " 800," notice was given that all the disloyal Liberal members would be turned out of their seats. Some of them accepted the warning and obediently fell into line behind the Government. Encouraged by this success, the Caucus took the reins and especially the whip firmly in hand. As soon as the Ministry met with resistance or with a display of hostile feeling in either House,

Circular of the 29th June, 1881.

the managers of the central Caucus let loose the Associations, urged them to hold meetings, to send monster petitions to Parliament, to vote resolutions of protest or indignation, to remonstrate with their members or even to give them direct orders. "We ask you," ran the Birmingham circulars sometimes, "to put yourselves at once in communication with your representatives in the House of Commons, strongly urging them to be in their places on . . . next and to vote for. . . ." As the legislative measures in regard to which this intervention was demanded seemed in themselves worthy of support to a large section of opinion, the Associations had no difficulty in complying with the proposals which came from Birmingham; without exactly wishing to honour or obey the Committee of the Federation, they co-operated in a common cause. The mode of action recommended to them provoked all the fewer scruples because the Associations were chiefly composed of militant politicians, and then it invested them with a power, with an authority, the exercise of which is always welcome. Every little Peddlington Association liked to indulge in the idea that the fate of great measures depended on the energy of its attitude, that the great departments of the State had to reckon with it.

By force of habit the co-operation of the local Associations with Birmingham became, so to speak, automatic; those who were jealous of their independence asserted it by paraphrasing the resolutions sent from Birmingham, but they voted them all the same, convened public meetings, inveighed against the members who were not loyal to Mr. Gladstone, etc. A mere telegram from the bigwigs of the Caucus was enough to set the Associations in motion throughout the country, and the lion growled, screamed, roared, with pleasure or with anger, as occasion required. It will be recollected that when the Federation was inaugurated, in 1877, one of its founders, when giving a glimpse of the new vistas which this Organization opened to the democracy, exclaimed: "It is no longer possible for the leaders in London to draw upon the people of the country and say two months after date pay to our order in the country for an agitation on a particular purpose." The Caucus, in fact, had changed matters; henceforth, the bill was drawn at Birmingham on behalf of the people and

at two days' sight instead of two months'.[1]　The rapidity
with which the demonstrations of the caucuses followed the
parliamentary events that served them as a pretext was alone
sufficient to prove how little they were due to spontaneous
movements of opinion.　Mr. Chamberlain's remarks on people
who "assume, without rhyme or reason, the existence in this
country of manufactories of political opinion, where zeal and
unanimity are produced to order"[2] sounded less sarcastic as
they came to correspond more and more with the facts.　The
whole process of agitation which was methodically applied
throughout the country, all the resolutions, circulars, etc.,
emanated from three or four persons in the offices of the Federation.　It was supposed that Mr. Chamberlain was acting with
these persons or rather standing behind them, that it was he
who was pulling the strings : being a member of a government
which needed the support of public opinion as well as head of
the extra-parliamentary Organization engaged in setting this
opinion in motion it was evidently he who touched the springs
from his place in the Cabinet, for the benefit of the latter.
Plausible as this conclusion seemed, Mr. Chamberlain protested against it; he asserted that since he had joined the
Ministry, his connection with the Caucus had ceased; that he
was only a subscriber to the Birmingham Liberal Association;
that he paid his subscription and that was all.[3]

[1] With regard to Mr. Gladstone's Irish Bill the House of Lords ordered an
enquiry which was viewed by a good many Liberals as a manifestation of
hostility against the Ministry.　Hardly had the decision of the Upper House
been taken when the Caucus convened a meeting by telegraph, of delegates of
Associations throughout the Kingdom for the next day but one; their protest
against the enquiry was intended to intimidate the House of Lords, and check
its tendencies towards independence.　The delegates flocked to the meeting
from all quarters, and the Caucus boasted that its summons had been obeyed
with such alacrity that the Scotch members had not hesitated to do violence
to their Presbyterian scruples by travelling on Sunday, in order to get to
the meeting in time.

[2] *The Caucus*, p. 21.

[3] "The noble Lord (Randolph Churchill) says I am the Birmingham caucus.
Again I am much flattered by this description of my influence and ability,
but it is a total mistake.　Except that I am a subscriber, although I believe
not one of the largest subscribers. . . ." (*Hansard*, Vol. CCXCIII, p. 573,
30th October, 1884).

III

Among the many questions by means of which the Caucus interfered in the working of the Constitution, none gave it an opportunity of appearing in so many aspects, of showing how far-reaching and penetrating its intervention could become, as the reform of the Procedure of the House of Commons undertaken in 1882. Party tactics in Parliament had long since introduced habits of obstruction in debate in order to hamper the Government, to impede their work of legislation by starting useless and futile discussions which simply wasted the time of the House. After the extension of the suffrage, which brought into Parliament representatives of a more democratic stamp who were anxious to keep themselves before the public, the loquacity of the members of the House perceptibly increased and contributed in no small measure to the useless prolongation of debate. This obstruction, which was sometimes deliberate, sometimes spontaneous, reached its climax when the Irish Home Rulers led by Parnell converted it into a system and began to practise it with extraordinary zeal and skill. It was impossible to stop them, for the old Procedure allowed the debate to go on as long as there were orators ready to speak and able to command an audience large enough to form the quorum required by the rules. If the speaker could only secure thirty-nine indulgent listeners, it was impossible to silence him. To put down the obstructionists, Mr. Gladstone proposed a new Procedure which imposed serious restrictions on the unlimited freedom of speech in parliamentary debate, the most important being the introduction of the closure. In future the majority was to be empowered on certain conditions to close the debate when it thought fit. This proposal created great excitement not only among the Tory Opposition but in the ministerial ranks. Several Liberal members, including representatives of the extreme Radical section, held that too little discussion was still more fatal than too much, that the "right of free speech was more valuable than all the measures in the ministerial portfolio." Besides, three years had not elapsed since Mr. Gladstone himself, under the Beaconsfield Ministry which had to put up with a good deal from the obstructive tactics of its opponents, defended obstruction as a legitimate weapon for minorities and as a necessary evil. " The House of Commons," he said, "is, and we must hope will continue to be, above all and before all a free assembly ; and if this is the case, it must submit to pay for its freedom." [1] The obstructionist practices of the Irish in 1880–81, which passed all bounds, had made Mr. Gladstone change his mind. Nor did the Liberals and the old Radicals refuse to take them into account, but they deemed it necessary to surround the discretionary power which the Ministry demanded for its majority with serious guarantees.

Hardly had the opposition to the plans of the Ministry broken out within the walls of Parliament than the Caucus intervened. An imperious circular from Birmingham denounced it to the federated Associations and urged them to declare to all whom it might concern " in the most energetic form and without the slightest delay " that they expected the Government to be supported by the whole of the Liberal party in this conjuncture. The central Caucus pointed out that the closure was indispensable for getting the various measures in which the Federation was interested passed by the House. These explanations only confirmed the apprehensions and suspicions as to the real significance of the proposed Procedure. Rightly or wrongly, people feared that it was to be used more for paralyzing the Opposition than for preventing obstruction; that in deference to the militant Radicals a whole series of measures would be placed before Parliament and that they would be forced through the House, by means of the closure. The idea prevailed that the latter was " part of a vast scheme of political manipulation " set on foot by the Birmingham group, that it would be the counterpart of the Caucus in Parliament, and that it would enable the former to control the latter and transform it into a chamber for registering the decrees of the Caucus and of the Press of the party. To dispel these apprehensions, Mr. Gladstone stated in the House that the Liberals would never make a party weapon of the closure; that they would not use it against the constitutional Opposition. On the contrary, rejoined a spokesman of the " young Radicals,"

---

[1] " The Country and the Government," *Nineteenth Century*, August, 1879. **Cf.** Mr. Gladstone's speech against the closure delivered in the House of Commons on the 27th of February, 1880 (*Hansard*, Vol. CCL, p. 1593).

Mr. Labouchere, if this were so, it would not be worth while coming down to the House to vote for the ministerial proposal. In "stating the views of the democracy on this point," Mr. Labouchere expressed the hope that the Government would consider it its first duty to use the closure in the interests of the party. This pleasing contingency was supplemented in his mind by the prospect of elections held as frequently as possible, in which measures would be submitted to the people, and after the people had come to the conclusion that they ought to be adopted and that the Ministry representing the majority had an imperative mandate to pass them, all discussion in the House would be needless, for it would have taken place beforehand. By proceeding in this way the Liberal party would very soon bring the country into harmony with the "spirit of the age." [1]

If the apprehensions of old Radicals, who thought that the closure meant the end of liberty of speech, were as exaggerated as the hopes of "young Radicals," who considered it the beginning of the "Radical democratic Millennium" in which the functions of Parliament would be reduced to those of a registrar of the people's decrees, the attitude of the Caucus justified the one and encouraged the other. The appeal issued by the central Caucus found a hearing, all the Associations complied with its request and gave notice to their members to discontinue all opposition to the ministerial plan, and members who had already taken up a position in public against the closure eagerly recanted and informed their Associations that they would not fail to vote for the Government. When the debate on the new Procedure began, a Liberal member (Marriott) moved an amendment hostile to the principle of closure by a simple majority. He was immediately summoned to appear before the Liberal Association of the borough which he represented in the House to justify his conduct. A considerable number of his Liberal colleagues approved of the amendment. But the Ministry threatened to dissolve if it was carried. If a dissolution took place, members would have to run the risk of a new election, with the Caucus lying in wait for those who were not *loyal* to the Ministry. Placed between two fires, most of the Liberal members surrendered,

[1] *Hansard*, Vol. CCLXXIV, pp. 678 seq.

and the hundred or so of members of the majority who were
supposed to be in favour of Marriott's amendment dwindled
to five on a division, without counting sixteen who took refuge in abstention.   Although the amendment was rejected,
the Government was still far from having won the day; it was
only a negative victory.   The united forces of the Conservatives, independent Liberals, and individualist Radicals continued to attack the Government plan.   Mr. Gladstone made
some concessions in favour of minorities.   But the Caucus
considered them inopportune; it insisted on the majority
pure and simple.   The Associations spent the parliamentary
recess in stirring up the country on behalf of the closure;
they organized meetings, voted resolutions, got up a quantity
of petitions.   Thereupon Mr. Gladstone, believing that public opinion was on his side, withdrew the concessions he had
made, demanded the closure by a simple majority and carried
it by the vote of almost the whole of the Liberal members.

   Whether the ministerial measures on behalf of which the
party Organization exerted itself so actively were excellent
and necessary or dangerous and useless, — we have not to
discuss the point in this work, — the fact of the intervention
of the Caucus and the circumstances under which it took
place threw a very crude light on the Caucus itself: they
revealed, so to speak, its nature, its tendencies, its methods
of action.   Conceived with the design of opposing minorities in the constituencies and having from its birth adopted
as a maxim that a minority is made to be domineered over if
not crushed by the majority, the Caucus now interposed between the majority and the minority in Parliament and set
one against the other.   Within the ranks of the majority
hesitation is expressed, several of its members scrutinize their
opinions, examine their conscience to see if they can follow
the leaders of the party.   "What an idle question," exclaims
the Caucus; "as members of the majority you owe obedience
to its chief; look sharp or I'll dismiss you as unfaithful servants!"   A parliamentary party leader is thus converted into
a party dictator.[1]   But how is he to assert his dictatorship?

[1] " When Mr. Gladstone and the Government met the House of Commons
and said it was impossible for them to conduct the business with the present
antiquated rules . . . there was only one course open to every loyal member

The members of the party are not appointed by him; they derive their authority from the free choice of the electors. "No doubt, but I am the electors, the constituency," rejoins the Caucus, "and it is me that you will have to deal with." But after all, cannot the Ministry and the majority, the Government and the House, come to an understanding by means of mutual concessions, which are the essence of all parliamentary life? "Sheer waste of time," observes the Caucus; "we have already voted resolutions on the point in our meetings; no haggling, it's a case of Hobson's choice." Relations between majorities and minorities, of the leader of the party with its members, of a member of Parliament with its constituents, between Parliament and outside opinion — in all these the Caucus intervened as an arbiter if not as a master.

IV

In interfering on all important occasions, for the purpose of supporting the Government, the Liberal Associations controlled by the Birmingham Caucus considered that they were simply discharging their duty of serving as the organ of public opinion. Devoting themselves to it with such zeal that occasionally some of them gave their approval to Government measures of which they did not even know the main features, the Associations nevertheless kept in the background in cases in which it would have been not less important to know the public feeling of which they were supposed to be the mouthpiece. This abstention was most remarkable in connection with the highly dramatic incidents of the foreign policy of the Gladstone Ministry. As is well known, this policy was not attended with success. Drifting from indecision to hesitation, from weakness to feebleness, the Cabinet met with one disaster after another, in every quarter, in the Transvaal, in Egypt, in the Soudan, in Afghanistan. The Liberal Associations and the Birmingham Federation, which during the Eastern crisis fretted and fumed throughout the country and denounced the Turcophil attitude of Disraeli as an insult to civilization

of the Liberal party, to *sacrifice his personal convictions in order to support Mr. Gladstone*" — said Mr. Schnadhorst at a meeting in Brighton, **Mr.** Marriott's constituency, on the 6th of June, 1882.

and a disgrace to Christianity, what were they doing now in face of all the carnage in which the British armies were engaged? They remained silent "in order not to embarrass Mr. Gladstone." When the tragic death of General Gordon, who was sent by the Government to Khartoum and afterwards left to his fate, extorted a loud cry of indignation from the public, some members of Liberal Associations in the north of England wished to unburden themselves. They met in the city of York and having considered the situation came to the conclusion that it was expedient to provoke a general manifestation of public feeling on the affairs of the Soudan. They applied to the official organ of the party, to the National Liberal Federation, asking it to summon a conference of representatives of the federated Associations. The Federation refused, "in order not to embarrass Mr. Gladstone." Those who had taken part in the meeting at York threatened to leave the Federation. Before this threat the Birmingham Caucus gave way and convened a conference in which after much discussion a mongrel resolution was voted protesting the confidence of the Liberals in Mr. Gladstone and his government, assuring him of their support in the future and regretting that military operations had been deemed necessary.

Thus the body ostensibly created for giving regular and free expression to opinion, for making the voice of the country heard by its rulers, proved powerless to discharge its function in circumstances of the most critical kind. It was fit only to stand guard over a party in power.

V

The Birmingham Federation was not the only central Organization of the Liberal party. Besides that of the Whip with his correspondents in the provinces there was another popular Organization with Manchester for its headquarters. Among the many Associations founded in former days for obtaining the extension of the parliamentary franchise (Reform Societies, Reform Associations, etc.), one had been formed at Manchester, in 1864, on a national basis, that is to say with numerous branches in the country, under the name of the *National Reform Union*, with the co-operation of several old and leading members of the famous Anti-Corn Law League. While it never attained to the importance of Cobden's League, the *National Reform Union* had a fairly large share in the reformist agitation which preceded the Reform Bill of 1867. As soon as the extension of the suffrage was carried, the members of the *National Reform Union* were of opinion that its task was at an end. Nevertheless it was not formally dissolved and several members tried to keep it alive after 1868 by taking up great questions of current politics, such as for instance the Disestablishment of the Irish Church. But they were stopped by the indifference of their old adherents, and the traditional aversion to permanent organizations on a national basis. Consequently the *National Reform Union* had become extinct after 1870. After the Liberal defeat in the general election of 1874, when Birmingham uttered the cry: "Organize! organize!" several Lancashire Liberals, uneasy at seeing that "the tree of political life appeared to be transplanted to Birmingham," and anxious that Manchester should not be too late in the field, thought that the organization of the *National Reform Union* might be made use of and decided to resuscitate it. The plan was submitted to John Bright, whose name had become a household word in Lancashire since his exploits at the time of the Anti-Corn Law League. He approved the idea of the *Union*, but insisted that it should confine its programme to one point, to a single reform, and recommended the reform of the land laws. In this he adhered to the old conception of popular Organizations formed for the realization of a distinct and specified object; in the pursuit of which men differing in opinion on other points might unite, resuming complete liberty of action as soon as the object was attained. A great conference of delegates of several Liberal Associations, clubs, and societies held at Manchester sanctioned the reorganization of the *Union*, adopting a programme of four specified points, four reforms to be carried.[1] The new Organization thus became a society of propaganda and agitation in favour of certain reforms. Its principal mode of action consisted of distributing pamphlets and books, of sending lecturers into different

---

[1] The extension of the suffrage to the rural populations; disestablishment of the Church of England; reform of the land laws; regulation of the sale of liquors by the people.

parts of the country, of organizing meetings for the discussion of questions relating to the programme of the *Union*. From the very commencement of its new existence (from 1876) it had the good fortune to secure the services as manager of a University man, a gentleman of literary training who gave a powerful impulse to the work of the political education of the masses undertaken by the *Union*.

When, in 1877, the Birmingham group also started a *national* Organization in their town, the *National Reform Union* declared that they were in no way offended, the sphere of action of each being distinct although directed towards the same ultimate object: "the task of reorganizing the Liberal party is now divided into two parts, both tending to the same end; and while the *Union* continues to teach the people *what* to fight for, the *Federation* will instruct them *how* to fight. Each is necessary to and supplements the other."[1] Nevertheless the *Union* was gradually tempted beyond its programme; the Birmingham laurels evidently disturbed its repose, and it began to imitate its rival by agitating on a large scale, first of all on the Eastern question and then on other problems of the day. The programme which confined it within the "four points" grew irksome to it and, after the victory of 1880 which the Caucus attributed to *organization*, it exchanged them for the following general vague definition: "The *Union* shall have two objects, viz.: 1. the dissemination of political knowledge, and the furtherance of organization, especially in the county constituencies; 2. the promotion and agitation of any leading question which the Government, or any important section of the party, may from time to time place before the nation, and in regard to which it may be thought desirable to move and instruct the members of the party throughout the country." The meaning of this change in the constitution of the *Union* was well explained by an authorized interpreter: "The Union is so constituted that it can do any amount of needful work. It can organize the party — instruct the party — arouse the party — guide the party."[2] It was simply the programme of the Caucus. The *Union* was very anxious not to be confounded with

[1] Report of the Executive Committee of the National Reform Union for the year 1877.

[2] *The Northern Pioneer*, 3d of March, 1880, "The National Reform Union."

it and proclaimed that it was not "a caucus in the narrow and vulgar sense of the term"; that it had no leanings towards dictatorship; that it did not wish to turn the members of Parliament into delegates. Several of the most influential members of the Union however considered that the Organizations "ought to act as political barometers which members could consult and by which they might to a certain extent steer their course"; that "it was useful that there should be some organization which should from time to time, not put the screw on, but use a certain amount of influence, or else there might be more Marriotts and more Cowens[1] than there were at that moment"[2] — which in plain English meant that there would be more independent members than there were already. Beyond a doubt, the Birmingham spirit was "moving upon the face of the waters" of English Liberalism.

In fact, apart from the work of *political education* which it continued to carry on very zealously, the *Reform Union* was falling into line behind the Birmingham Federation; it took part in all the agitation initiated by the latter; like it sent circulars to the local Organizations and to the members, enjoining the one to convene meetings, to get up petitions, and urging the others to be in their place in the House and to vote with the main body of the party. It was the same tune which was sung at Birmingham, only the voice was a different one; it was of no use for the *Reform Union* to force it; it could never hit off the arrogant and comminatory tone of the real Caucus and it did not produce the same effect. It was well known that there were no important party personages, let alone Cabinet Ministers, behind the *Union*, and that its direct influence on the local Associations was more or less confined to the radius of Manchester. To sum up, as long as it was engaged in diffusing ideas throughout the country by means of its lecturers and its publications, the *Union* occupied the position of well-behaved women who are not talked about, and when it tried

[1] Messrs. Marriott and Cowen, the one a moderate Liberal, the other an advanced Radical, were the members of the House of Commons who had declared with energy against the closure by a simple majority proposed by the Gladstone Ministry.

[2] Chairman's speech at the annual meeting of 1883. Cf. also the other speeches, especially those of Russell, Agnew, and Richards (*Manchester Examiner*, 24th of January, 1883).

to make a noise the Caucus shouted twenty times as loud and made more impression on the gallery. It was therefore natural that the *Reform Union*, far from attaining the popularity of the Birmingham Federation and its influence in the management of the party, was if anything effaced by it.

This effacement extended also to the principles on which the *Reform Union* had been founded, and it is in this point that lies the interest which its history possesses for us in the movement of party organization. Having adopted the realization of one or more well-defined legislative measures as its object, and the methodical enlightenment of public opinion thereon as its means of attaining that object, the *Reform Union* presented as it were the counter-current of the tendencies embodied in the Caucus. On the one side was the conception of the old Liberalism and Radicalism with its firm belief that ideas and principles constituted the rallying-point in party strife; that all the combatants ought to know beforehand *what* they were going to fight for and when they would lay down their arms; and that the real struggle consisted in instilling these ideas into unconverted minds, in achieving the conquest, slow and laborious perhaps, but all the more durable, of convictions, of consciences. The tendency of the new method was to confine opinion for good and all within fixed limits under a general and unchangeable banner; to impart strength to it by the permanence of the organization and the unlimited duration of the term of enlistment; to bring would-be stragglers into line by pressure from the whole body; to form an army which would follow its leaders in measured step, subject to the formality of preliminary ratification of the appointment of these leaders by popular choice; to teach this army only to fight, to charge the enemy at the first signal, on the general conviction that it is fighting and will always fight for a glorious cause whoever is or may be the enemy. The effacement of the *National Reform Union* behind the Caucus, the attempts which it made to adapt itself to the methods and procedure of the Caucus, to walk in its footsteps, meant that the counter-current which it represented in its early days was being more and more driven out of the political life of England and was making way for the new stream issuing from the rock of Birmingham.

Highly instructive proof of this was also supplied by another Organization which, amid different social conditions, attempted to establish Liberalism on the basis of principles similar to those on which the *National Reform Union* took its stand. This was the *London and Counties Liberal Union*, created after the elections of 1880 for London and the neighbouring counties. The southern counties were and still are one of the most backward parts of England. An agricultural region, the principal abode of large landed proprietors, the south remained to a certain extent untouched by the social revolution brought about by the rise of industry, which derived all its impetus from the north. The electoral qualification being still pretty high in the counties, up to 1885, the great mass of the rural population was not only deprived of the suffrage but also destitute of all political culture. The farmers in these parts followed the lead of the landowners more submissively than elsewhere, and the latter were bound to the Conservative party by tradition and to some extent by their interests. Consequently if the Liberal candidates ventured into these counties (known as the Home Counties), they were generally defeated. In the general election of 1880 of the 28 members returned for these counties only one was a Liberal, and he owed his seat to the minority clause of the Reform Bill of 1867. London, on the contrary, had a Liberal past. But in proportion as the metropolis enlarged its area with the alarming rapidity familiar to us, it lost its sense of individuality, its *esprit de corps;* indifference to the public welfare took permanent root, aided by the growth of comfort which swells the ranks of materialism; and the immense agglomeration of London slipped away more and more from Liberalism. Caucuses were no doubt established in most of the metropolitan boroughs, but they did not much advance the cause of the Liberal party. In the neighbouring counties the organization was a good deal weaker, although there were here and there Associations with a more or less permanent organization, but practically their operations were reduced to those of the committees in the old days, which were formed on the eve of the elections and dissolved soon afterwards. Social influences were, as in the past, the great organizing power in these districts. The Birmingham Federation which, especially in its early days, worked chiefly the urban agglomerations, had not included the Home Counties in its sphere of action; it reached them indirectly by the Liberal oases which were scattered over them, without devoting itself specially to their organization, a somewhat thankless task owing to the social condition of the country. The *London and Counties Liberal Union* was intended to fill this gap by supplying a great local Organization which would bring all its strength to bear on this part of England.

But for the founders of this Union the gap did not consist of "bad organization," but in the fact that the population was ignorant, imprisoned within a narrow horizon, without capacity for public life. To bring light into this darkness, to open the mind of the rural population, to awaken in it an interest in the public welfare, became the great object of the *Union* from the very beginning. Organization was on the second plane, and formed a subsidiary means of action. The *Union* endeavoured to drag the existing Associations from their lethargy and to bring about the formation of new ones, but it wished them to have a spontaneous life of their own. It repelled interference in the affairs of the local Associations with energy and almost with indignation.[1] Its notion was that it was to be not the master but the servant of the local Organizations by offering them the advantages of concentrated action for obtaining lecturers, publications at reduced rates, information and advice, on legal points connected with electoral registration matters so full of intricacy in England, etc. Lectures on political and historical topics and the distribution of small publications — pamphlets and leaflets — became the great weapons of the *Union*. The tone in which its representatives as well as those of the local Associations addressed the masses often contrasted with the habits of violent controversy and of abuse of opponents by which the Caucus was distinguished.[2] Undertaking

---

[1] "Interference was not in the least degree contemplated. They held it to be nothing less than impertinence to attempt to enter into any district where their co-operation would not be thoroughly welcome" — said the Chairman at the opening meeting.

[2] At one of the general conferences in which the delegates of the local Associations exchanged their views and impressions, one of them characterized the mode of action adopted in his locality as follows: "We have aimed, not at stirring up party strife and ill-feeling among neighbours by violent attacks upon our political opponents, but rather at setting forth the positive

the political education of the masses, the *Union* held that the business of its own staff in their turn was to make a constant study of the political questions which came or were shortly about to come before public opinion, and to do so in a spirit absolutely free from all party preoccupations. A result was the formation in London, which was the seat of the *Union*, of a sort of club for mutual improvement, in which the members read papers on problems of legislation or politics which they had investigated, followed by a discussion intended solely to enlighten the audience and not to end in a vote. Distinguished men who had already or have since made themselves a name in politics or literature took a very active part in these meetings.[1] The idea had also been started of making these discussions at head-quarters find an echo in the other localities : the representatives of the local Associations who attended the meetings in London were in their turn to reopen discussion in the local meetings on the topics debated, inviting to the conferences not only members of the Association but neutrals and Tories, so that every one could take sides on the question after due reflection and not before it.

The *Union* occasionally, although in a discreet fashion, joined in the agitation promoted by Birmingham (for instance, that in favour of the extension of the franchise to the rural population). One clause in its statutes, which brought it nearer to the programme of the Caucus, imposed on it the very general obligation of " securing the adoption of Liberal principles in the government of the country." But in practice the *Union* was very anxious not to preserve a vague and ambiguous attitude, and being preoccupied with its " chief duty of stimulating and promoting political education and organization," it was convinced " that this end would be most effectually attained by the advocacy of some definite objects as the immediate goal of their efforts." It adopted two : the reform of local self-government and that of the land laws, and made them a platform at

advantages which flow from Liberal government, and the *substantial gains* to be hoped for from these changes for which the country is now ripe " (London and Counties Liberal Union, Report of the Conference of officers of Liberal Associations, 7 Nov. 1882, p. 22).

[1] For instance, H. Arnold-Forster, Geo. Brodrick, James Bryce, Sydney Buxton, W. S. Caine, Arthur Cohen, Q.C., A. V. Dicey, Sir John Lubbock, H. S. Tremenheere, and others.

the general election of 1885. These elections were the first and also the last in which the *Union* took part. Its work and its methods of action were not properly appreciated. It was badly supported and always short of funds; the magnates of the party opened their purses only just on the eve of the elections, not understanding that a long preparation of the public mind is required to win votes by honest means. In vain did the *Union* proclaim that " political education is the life-blood of Liberalism." Such an ungrateful soil as that of the southern rural counties demanded not only a special kind of cultivation, but also the patient work of years before it could yield a crop. Party spirit, engrossed in the present and never bestowing a thought on the future, was incapable of comprehending this simple truth, and when the general election of 1885, in which the *Union* took part for the first time, resulted unfavourably for the Liberals within its sphere of operations, the verdict was that the *Union* had not gone the right way to work; it was dissolved and not long after the Home Counties were annexed to the Caucus so that the latter might bring its superior methods to bear on them.[1]

Thus the counter-currents represented by the other central Organizations receded before that identified with the Birmingham Federation. The latter soon drove into the background or took in tow all its rivals. The *London and Counties Union* in the south was still dragging out its existence and the *National Reform Union* in the north continuing its own, as it was destined to do for years to come, when the Birmingham Federation came to the front. Claiming to be the direct depository of the will of the people and the regular mouthpiece and supporter of the Ministry, it identified itself officially with the Liberal party and Government. Always occupying the stage of extra-parliamentary political life, it assumed the air of being the chief actor. The signal for all agitation in the country emanated from it; every great question before the public served it as a pretext for manifestations; to every Gov-

[1] The following answer was given to a question put to a member of the staff of the National Liberal Federation as to the causes of the want of success of the London and Counties Union: " Perhaps it may be ascribed to the fact that the limits of its work were too confined, and to an overwhelming desire not to have the slightest appearance of interference with the local Associations."

ernment measure it affixed its *imprimatur*. Its resolutions were proclaimed *urbi et urbi* in general meetings of delegates, either periodical or extraordinary, which were intended to represent, as it were, the Grand Assizes of English Liberalism. The Federation held them in different towns in turn. Great as the stir made by them might be, the significance of these meetings was not a real one, they lacked spontaneity. Everything was cut and dried by the Birmingham group, the resolutions to be voted, the orators who were to speak. It was more of a grand orchestral performance than a gathering of representatives of opinion assembled for the purpose of throwing light upon or putting forward their views on the questions of the day or their aspirations. The Birmingham set could not brook contradiction or divergence of views. Those delegates who chanced to become the mouthpiece of it were looked on as wet blankets. They were greeted in the lobbies with ironical remarks: "How do you do, you have brought with you an amendment to the resolutions, have you not?" Sometimes these delegates happened to be the representatives of very large towns which had a history. Intoxicated with their success, the Birmingham leaders were not careful to avoid wounding susceptibilities. The National Liberal Federation aspired not only to influence in the party but to power.

SIXTH CHAPTER

THE CAUCUS IN POWER (*continued*)

I

AFTER having followed the movements of the Federation on the political stage, let us transport ourselves for a brief space amid the local Associations. Since we became acquainted with them at the time of their first appearance under Disraeli's government, we have seen them on more than one occasion in the train of the central Caucus, contributing to its impressiveness by their numbers and swelling the noise which it made. Following the lead of Birmingham, they tried their hand at politics on a large scale, and interfered demonstratively in the work of Parliament. But they could only carry out their will in Parliament through their members. The question, therefore, of the relations between the member and the party Association soon assumed a prominent position as that of the relations between the Association and parliamentary candidates had previously done. The solution which the Caucus gave to the new problem was still more decisive. It did not consider the general authority with which it had invested the member by the fact of nominating him as sufficient; it held that in the actual discharge of his duties he was bound to follow the opinions of the party Organization on every occasion. We have already seen the caucuses, in the agitations got up by Birmingham, send their members communications, resolutions, and injunctions to vote in such and such a way, to support this and oppose that. As in the case of those standing for Parliament, most of the members preferred, to avoid making a fuss, not to insist on the question of principle raised by this attitude of the caucuses. Some hastened with exemplary docility to assure their Caucus that they were quite ready to vote in the manner required; others complied in silence, whether they yielded to the demands of the Caucus or that these demands coincided with their own convictions. The division lists in the House showed few Liberal votes recorded in opposition to the policy of the Caucus, and when such a thing took place it seldom forgave the members who assumed this independent attitude. It called on them imperiously for explanations, or still more often, without having heard them, the Association passed a vote censuring or branding the delinquent. The independent members adhered firmly to their attitude, and the Caucus persisted in its own while continuing to "brand" the recalcitrants. In some cases these conflicts became extremely acute and produced an extraordinary sensation. This time again, that is to say in the relations between members and the party Organization just as in regard to the latter's dealings with the candidates, it was reserved for W. E. Forster to be in the front rank of those who asserted their independence as against the Caucus.

After the period of his conflict with the "400" of Bradford on the subject of Article 15, Forster once more had an opportunity of being one of the official leaders of Liberalism; with the return of Mr. Gladstone to power, he entered the Cabinet as Chief Secretary for Ireland. But two years afterwards, in 1882, disapproving the new policy adopted with regard to the Irish Home Rulers, he left the Ministry. This act of independence isolated him in his own party, and although as a rule he freely gave it his support he became a "suspect." Thereupon the Bradford Caucus laid hands on him as an executioner does on a man under sentence of death. It indulged in the most violent attacks on Forster, abused him at gatherings and meetings, and branded him with resolution after resolution, at one time with regard to his attitude on a specified question, at another with reference to an expression which he had used in speaking of the policy of the leader of the party, or again on account of "his conduct during the present session, not only for withholding his support from the Government in the recent vote of censure, but in making speeches on more than one occasion which could only have the effect of damaging their position and strengthening the hands of the opposition." Forster remained calm and unmoved in face of the storm, while not ceasing to assert the right of a member to speak and vote in accordance with his conscience. Between Forster and the

Bradford Caucus it was not even, properly speaking, a question of divergence of views; for if Forster had ideas on the question of the day, the Caucus had none. "But the committee may tell me," remarked Forster to the 400, "your opinion on this Egyptian question is not ours, in this matter you do not represent us, and of this fact we must inform the electors of Bradford and of the country. Certainly this would be both their right and their duty, but I must venture most respectfully to state that the committee have not given me their opinion."[1] What was demanded from him was not a particular policy, but to abide by that which the leader of the party would eventually adopt. Forster's crime, therefore, was that he would not follow him blindly. Those electors of Bradford who were devoted to Forster were quite convinced that it was the central Caucus which was pulling the strings throughout the whole of this affair. Apart from the old accounts which the Birmingham group had to settle with the author of the *Education Act* of 1870, Mr. Chamberlain, who had entered the Gladstone Cabinet, was supposed to have conceived an aversion for his moderate colleague who was curbing the Radical tendencies of the inspirer of the Caucus. Consequently Forster's friends at Bradford imagined that the whole campaign against him was planned at Birmingham, and they saw the hand of the central Caucus everywhere. Its hand was not everywhere, but it was a fact that Birmingham inspired and approved the campaign of the Bradford Caucus, and that the latter to a great extent derived its power of defying independent opinion from this support of the Organization.

When, in pursuance of the Redistribution of Seats of 1884–1885, the borough of Bradford was divided into three divisions, the local Caucus was converted into three associations on the same pattern, but this did not put an end to the opposition to Forster. On the eve of parting from his constituents of the whole borough, whom he had represented in Parliament for more than a quarter of a century, Forster wished to give them an account of his stewardship. The Caucus did all in its power to prevent him from meeting his electors face to face.[2] How-

[1] *Times*, 22d May, 1884.
[2] Cf. the *Times*, 16th November, 1885 " Political Organizations ": Leeds and Bradford, and T. W. Reid, II, 516.

ever the meeting took place and Forster concluded his speech with the following words, the last which he uttered in public: " I thank you for this more than for anything else, — that for the long time I have been your member, the time that I have taken part in the government of the nation or in the deliberations of Parliament, I have been not your mere delegate, not your mere mouthpiece; but your representative, doing what I thought to be right; and upon no other condition will I serve you in the future." [1]   The passionate cries of approval, the enthusiasm of the enormous crowd which filled the building, proved that in the heart of the people there was plenty of room for admiration of and respect for political uprightness and honesty, for men who, instead of flattering the masses, tell them the truth.   But it soon appeared that the people were not complete masters of their actions.   Forster stood for one of the three new divisions. The Caucus set to work to defeat him, and its influence proved too great to be disregarded.   Stricken with a mortal disease, Forster left his election in the hands of friends.   The latter, being anxious to spare him the bitterness of a last struggle, opened negotiations with the Caucus and arrived at a compromise which put a stop to hostilities.   Beyond a doubt they would have soon broken out again if Forster's death had not supervened a few months later and terminated the contest; for, in spite of the weaknesses which have been referred to above, Forster was, as Mr. Gladstone said in the funeral oration on his old colleague delivered in the House of Commons, " a man upon whom there could be no doubt that Nature had laid her hands for the purpose of forming a thoroughly genuine and independent character." [2]

II

But, after all, was the war which the Bradford Caucus had waged for years against Forster, really a war on the independence of members ?   Was it not more a contest of opinions, Forster being a moderate, almost a Whig, whereas the Caucus represented the advanced Radicalism which was daily gaining

[1] T. W. Reid, *Ibid.*
[2] Sitting of the House of Commons of the 6th April, 1886 (*Hansard*, Vol. CCCIV, p. 976).

ground in the country ?　If there had been a Radical in Forster's place would there have been any pretext or cause for opposition ?

A peremptory answer was returned to these questions at Newcastle-on-Tyne, where the local Caucus was confronted by a Radical, a real Radical, if ever there was one, — Joseph Cowen.

Devoted, body and soul, to the cause of the people from his youth upwards, he laboured incessantly for their moral and material elevation, lavishing on them the resources of his high culture acquired by severe study and by meditation, of his energy, of his ardent democratic faith, and also of his large fortune. Full of solicitude for the workmen of the factories owned by him, Cowen extended it to the whole hardworking population of the Tyne district; introduced co-operative societies among them; organized libraries, classes, lectures; turned lecturer, schoolmaster, secretary himself; took part in every social movement tending to the welfare of the people. An intimate friend of several Chartist leaders, he resumed the political propaganda in the north by his speeches and his writings, in the Palmerston days; that is to say, at a juncture when, in consequence of the defeat of Chartism and the success of a prosperous middle-class, the political pulse had almost ceased to beat in the nation. Assisted by a group of friends recruited chiefly from among intelligent workmen, Cowen carried his propaganda into every little town and village of the district, appealing to workmen in the towns, to the labourers in the fields, and to the toilers underground, not in order to cry up revolt to them, but to enlighten their minds, to awaken the human being in them, and to prepare them for civic life. An ardent lover of liberty, Cowen longed for and laboured for its triumph in other countries besides his own. When still a young man, he formed a connection with Mazzini and through him with other leaders of the European Revolution who had taken refuge in England after the victory of reaction in 1848 and the *coup d'État* of the 2d of December. Kossuth, Louis-Blanc, Ledru-Rollin, Pierre Leroux, Alexander Herzen, and many others penetrated into the far north to visit the young English democrat whose overflowing enthusiasm and invincible faith consoled their aching hearts. He also assisted them actively to continue the struggle. Bred in the school of the old masters of rationalist individualism, from Godwin and Paine onwards, and inspired by their descendants, the "Philosophic Radicals," Cowen had the passion for individual liberty in the highest degree, without, however, falling into the narrow views of the Manchester school,[1] and a veneration for "principles" without being infected with doctrinaire fanaticism.[2] He was profoundly convinced that spontaneous individual effort, ensuring independence of thought and energy in action, was the sole basis of really strong communities, while principles supplied ideas which alone gave a meaning to the existence of communities, and provided a conductor and a proper aim for the policy of States. He had a horror of the opportunism which seeks inspiration in the interest of the moment, in the passions or the follies of the day, in the prejudice in vogue, or in the complicity of hatred, animosity, or greed. "Every man," he said, "must act according to his convictions. They are his safest and ought to be his only guide. Upon matters of detail he may subordinate his opinion to his associates. The majority in such cases may guide him, but upon questions of principle he must stand firm even if he be as one against one thousand." "The working classes have achieved their personal independence, they must now," said Cowen to them, "devote themselves to their intellectual emancipation; let them think for themselves and not be put in swaddling-clothes or leading-strings by crafty advisers."[3] Democrat to the backbone, he was for a "robust, high-spirited, magnanimous Democracy,— the Democracy of Pericles, not of Cleon."[4]

After a quarter of a century of work on the banks of the Tyne, Cowen was asked to represent Newcastle in Parliament, and he entered the House in 1874. There he soon proved one

---

[1] "I am not and never was an adherent of what is popularly known as the Manchester school. . . ." (Speech of the 31st January, 1880, at Newcastle, *Life and Speeches of Joseph Cowen*, edited by E. R. Jones, Lond., 1885, p. 153.) "I am a free-trader and always have been. I have no superstitious regard for the principles of political economy, however. . . ." (Speech of the 24th November, 1885, at Newcastle, *Speeches at the General Election 1885*, Newcastle-on-Tyne, 1885, p. 203.)

[2] "In the application of a principle there may be opportunity and necessity for concession. Legislation is a practical science, and it is modified by traditions, customs, and institutions" (Speech of the 3d January, 1881, at Newcastle, *Life and Speeches*, p. 180).

[3] *Life and Speeches.*   [4] *Life and Speeches*, 279.

of the greatest orators that contemporary England has produced. But at the same time he showed himself incapable of
following the lead of a party or of any one whatever. Sometimes he opposed the Disraeli Ministry with the utmost vigour,
sometimes he gave it the support of his great abilities; an
advanced Radical, he occasionally came to the rescue of the
Tories, especially in the Eastern question in which the Liberals
seemed to him to be influenced by party considerations, by the
wish to embarrass the Tory government, when they vented
their rage against Turkey and encouraged the autocracy of
Russia, which, in his eyes, was as wretched a government as
that of Constantinople. When the Conservatives seemed to
him in the wrong, he disagreed with them; when he thought
they were in the right path, he agreed with them. That right
should always be on one side of the House and wrong always
on the other appeared to him a false and often pernicious convention. After the fall of the Tories he observed the same
independent attitude with regard to the Liberal government;
he gave it his support, but not on all occasions. Whenever he
thought it infringed the principles of Liberalism, Cowen had
no hesitation in opposing it. The policy of coercion adopted
by Mr. Gladstone towards Ireland found in him an unrelenting
opponent. He had the whole Liberal party against him, but
he none the less continued to defend the cause of Ireland. He
opposed the restriction of free speech in Parliament, and predicted that the undeniable evil of obstruction would be in no
way prevented by it. Sympathizing with the movement of
national regeneration attempted in Egypt by Arabi Pasha on the
basis of Egypt for the Egyptians, Cowen feared that the interference of a European power would lead to bloodshed, to much
bloodshed. He also warned the Government that if the English, after having entered the land of the Pharaohs, hesitated
to defend it against the Mahdi, they would expose themselves
and the country to disaster. Most of the Liberal members,
unlike Cowen, thinking themselves bound to silence and discipline by party ties, followed their leader. Lines of conduct
of the most opposite character were approved with docility in
accordance with the orders of the day. And having sowed
the wind, they reaped the whirlwind. " Principles," which are
so contemptible in the eyes of " practical politicians," were in

the right as against them and the " party interests " which the latter claim to serve.   But as a rule parties leave the task of gleaning the lessons conveyed to them by events to history; no one opposed to them is ever right.   Cowen was; consequently he was in the wrong.

The position of an independent member in the House of Commons had for some time past become a delicate one, since the ranks had closed up on both sides after the appearance of the masses on the political stage, in 1868.   Two great armies reformed into line with two powerful leaders, Gladstone and Disraeli, the contest between whom assumed the character of a duel, of an epic struggle.   But if a man of great force of character were to maintain an independent position in Parliament, would it not be possible for him to hold his own by relying on the confidence of his fellow-citizens merited by a genuine devotion to the popular cause, by leaning on the very masses who supply the fighting material of politics, by appealing, so to speak, from the weakness of the democracy to its strength ?   Cowen's attitude raised this question.   The Caucus undertook to answer it.   The reply was in the negative.

III

The branch of the Caucus established at Newcastle, as in other towns, began a merciless opposition to Cowen.   The latter had not welcomed the introduction of the Caucus, which had no distinctive creed or recognized principles, but which required simply " adhesion to the Organization," and he took no notice of the new institution.   The Caucus on its side, having set up from the outset as the defender of Liberal orthodoxy, was offended with Cowen's attitude in the Eastern crisis.   Nevertheless, being aware of his immense influence in the Tyne country, it did not venture to oppose him at the general election of 1880, but tried to make him accept his seat from them, as was the wont of the " representative Organization."   Cowen did not fall in with this, and explained that as a divergence of views had broken out between himself and the " organized Liberals," he was anxious to respect their opinions by coming before the electors on his own responsibility. When in the new Parliament Cowen showed that he meant to preserve his independence under the Liberal government as he had done under Disraeli's, the rage which had been smouldering in the breasts of the Caucus leaders at Newcastle, burst forth. They almost got it into their heads that Cowen's sole preoccupation was to create obstacles for the Liberal government. For what other explanation is there of his conduct? He defends these Irish, these Home Rulers who prevent Mr. Gladstone from governing. Not only does he speak, but he even occasionally votes against the Ministry. It is all very well his being out of sympathy with the aristocratic composition of the House of Lords and regretting its reactionary conduct, but he none the less maintains that it is acting on its rights, although with little wisdom, and he censures the violent language and the threats directed against it in this respect. Was this the attitude of a Liberal? Certainly not. It was not official Liberalism. And thereupon the Newcastle Caucus set itself up as a sort of Holy Inquisition with the mission of watching every word that fell from Cowen and examining into its motives. The most unfriendly construction for him was invariably placed upon them before the electors. The old inhabitants of Newcastle, who had witnessed his whole life and were almost sharers in his labours, knew the rights of the matter, but the rising generation or the new-comers, who knew nothing of Cowen's past, listened more readily to the insinuations of the Caucus.

The prestige attaching to Cowen's personality remaining considerable in spite of this, the Caucus thought that as a new love drives out an old one, another eminent man introduced into the political life of Newcastle might be the means of ousting Cowen. And when one of the two parliamentary seats assigned to the borough became vacant in 1882 owing to the resignation of the sitting member, the Caucus offered it to Mr. John Morley. A brilliant writer, an eminent thinker, a journalist of talent and knowledge, well versed in political questions, a man of lofty character, Mr. Morley undoubtedly was a member of a stamp which is unfortunately too rare in the English Parliament as well as in all Parliaments. But being introduced to Newcastle by the Caucus, he was unlucky enough to serve as a screen for its manœuvres. The very manner of his nomination seemed rather suspicious to independent opinion and had the appearance of being directed against it. In the morning the telegram announcing the, to the public at all events, unexpected resignation of Mr. Cowen's colleague arrived at Newcastle; in the evening Mr. Morley, who had been summoned from London by telegraph, was on the spot, and all the formal proceedings for the selection of a candidate — consideration of his claims by the executive committee, discussion of its report in the meeting of the "hundreds," and finally the introduction of the candidate to a special meeting of elec-tors — was got through by the next day. For the candidature of a stranger, even a distinguished one, in a place where local feeling is highly developed, and where there were possible candidates who were well-known and respected in the neighbourhood, this rapid action was certainly extraordinary. The desired effect of the *fait accompli*, intended to discourage any other serious candidature, was produced, and the candidate of the Caucus was elected. Encouraged by this success, the Caucus became still more intolerant and intractable with regard to its grievances against the too independent member. These grievances were many: Mr. Cowen was not loyal to the Liberal party; he would not admit the authority of the Organization representing local Liberalism in its relations with the electors; he paid no attention to it in his votes in the House; and lastly he repelled all interference of the Caucus in the policy of the newspaper which he published at Newcastle (*Newcastle Chronicle*). The Caucus held that in its capacity of official representative of local Liberalism it ought to control all the political utterances of the Liberal members of the locality, whether on the platform or in the Press. Subsequently, at the time of the enquiries made by the author of this work, the leaders of the Caucus observed not without bitterness: "Why, Mr. Morley assured us that he was responsible to us for what appeared in his newspaper, and he (Cowen) declined all responsibility." The *Newcastle Chronicle*, a pioneer of English democracy (it had existed for more than a century) had never been the servant of any party, and Cowen took care to keep up the tradition. To compete with him in this line as well, the Newcastle Caucus started an orthodox paper with a subsidy from the headquarters of the party. In its war against Cowen the Caucus made extensive use of public meetings, of

gatherings of the "hundred," in which the charges just referred to were constantly brought against him, and in which
resolutions of censure, of indignation, of denunciation, were
invariably voted. At the same time they secretly worked on
the electors by means of the old but always successful device,
that if you only throw enough mud, some of it is sure to stick.
Cowen was in league with the Tories — this was the awful
truth revealed to the electors who in the ingenuousness of
their hearts had placed their confidence in a traitor. Cowen
paid no heed to the attacks of the Caucus and did not even
condescend to reply to them as did Forster for instance, who
met the Liberal Association of Bradford with courteous explanations " due to so important a section of the constituency."

At the general election of 1885 the Caucus made a final effort
against Cowen while affecting a complete neutrality with regard
to him. The minions of the Caucus scoured the district, appealing to every susceptibility, to every prejudice, to every malignant feeling. " What," they said to the electors, " you are
going to vote for this sworn friend of the Irish, of the Papists,
the enemies of our Protestant religion and of the English
race ! " The Catholics were addressed in another fashion :
" Just consider what this man is, a friend of Garibaldi,[1] of
the tormentor of the Pope." " He assumes," they went on, " the
attitude of an independent politician who only follows his convictions and listens to the voice of his conscience, but it is only
a mask for hiding his disloyalty to Liberalism." At the election meetings they turned up with scores of questions prepared
beforehand and requested Mr. Cowen to answer them on the
spot, in the hope that in the shower of questions he would
lose his balance and commit himself. He replied with calm-
ness and dignity. In a series of admirable speeches,[2] full of
facts and ideas, he initiated his audiences, as in fact he always
did, into the political questions which had come before Parliament. While pointing out the solution which he thought they
required and for which he had voted, he left the electors to de-

[1] Cowen had been a friend of Garibaldi who paid him a visit at Newcastle and he gave the Italian patriot much help in his efforts on behalf of
Italian unity.

[2] They have been published in book form : *Speeches delivered by Joseph
Cowen as Candidate for Newcastle-upon-Tyne at the General Election 1885.*
Newcastle-on-Tyne, 1885.

cide on his conduct. Avoiding all controversy, all recrimination against the Newcastle Caucus, he touched on all the questions of principle which were at stake in the conflict with the elevation of views, the dignified language, and the manly frankness which distinguished him, — questions of the relations between a member and his constituents, of party ties, of political organizations. Referring to his own particular case, he said: "I will in a sentence or two summarize my grounds of difference. I put first Liberal principles. They put first the Liberal party. I care most for measures. They care more for men. In this lies all the quarrel. . . . Party is simply a means to an end. It is not *the* end. Leaders are all very well in their place, but none of them are infallible, and I will surrender my judgment in matters of principle to no man, however powerful, and to no body of men, however numerous."[1]

This bold attitude, if it did not convert the masses roused to fanaticism by the Caucus, filled Cowen's old electors with pride, extorted the admiration of his Tory opponents, and found an echo outside Newcastle in Radicals of the old school. Cooper,[2] the last survivor of the great Chartist leaders, wrote to Cowen: "I am delighted to see your noble determination to have no committee and to defy the hateful Caucus. Here my heart grieves to see what they have done" (here follows an account of the doings of the Caucus of the locality, which had ousted a veteran of the democracy from the seat, to bring in a big manufacturer whose *employés* were among the leaders of the Caucus). "Go on, my dear friend, keep your noble and independent way, and may you conquer every foe. Alas! for the poor 'workies,' they *do* so fail in gratitude. But we must not heed that. They are *ours*, my friend. We are sworn to their cause, let the sacrifice be what it will — only we will not be their *slaves*."[3]

The caucuses of the whole northern district were anxiously

---

[1] *Speeches*, p. 136.

[2] Thomas Cooper, who paid for the part which he played in the Chartist movement by long years of imprisonment, preserved up to the close of his life the pure and ardent love for the people which animated him, and was an example of one of the noblest types which militant democracy has produced in our age. He was the author of a remarkable poem entitled *The Purgatory of Suicides*, but, as was observed on the occasion of his death (in 1892), his life was his best poem.   [3] *Speeches*, p. 201.

awaiting the issue of the conflict at Newcastle. Each of them considered Cowen as a personal enemy. They gave the Newcastle Association their moral support and even more. The Caucus of the town of Sunderland, to help in exhorting the electors, sent it a gang of energetic and roughish men who accentuated the tone of the electoral campaign in their own fashion. Things reached such a pitch that Cowen was mobbed in the streets, and had mud and stones thrown at him. On hearing of this outrage, the leader of the Caucus, a man respected and respectable in his private capacity, was much distressed. He and his lieutenants, at least those who stood nearest to him, were far from having provoked not only the personal violence, but even the abuse of which Cowen was the victim, but they had let loose the party fanaticism of the mob, had stimulated it to fury by means of organization, and eventually they were overborne.

At the election Cowen headed the poll, but the number of electors who would not vote for him was enormous. There could be no doubt about it, his position was to a great extent undermined. He felt the blow and when thanking his supporters for having returned him once more he declared that he would never stand for Newcastle again. And when the Parliament elected in 1885 was dissolved (in 1886), Cowen did not come forward. In reply to invitations to stand, he explained that it was impossible for him to accept the position which the Caucus imposed on a member. He reminded his constituents that he readily submitted to party requirements except when his conscience bade him take up an independent attitude, and pointing out how this claim to think for himself, and vote in accordance with his convictions, had drawn upon him the hatred and the persecution of the Caucus, he said: "This conduct did not concern me greatly while it was confined to a body of bilious party zealots, but at the last election their proceedings were endorsed by upwards of 7000 Liberal electors, who not only voted against me, but some of them accompanied their opposition by acts of personal violence which I have certainly not forgotten, and (I fear) not forgiven. After such a demonstration, there was no other course but retirement open to an honourable and independent man. I am willing to do my duty in any sphere, however high or however humble, to which my fellow-citizens call me; but I am under no obligation to become a party slave, or subject myself to spiteful persecution for no useful purpose. What the Caucus wants is a political machine. I am a man, not a machine. . . ." [1]

Joseph Cowen retired from political life.

The Caucus had won the day.

IV

The defeat which it inflicted on Cowen was more than a personal defeat; it marked in a striking way the overthrow of the political tendency which Cowen personified, of the old Radicalism which relied solely on principles as a motive of action, for which private judgment was not only the first of rights but even the first of duties, in the eyes of which all subjection, all dependence, whether it came from above or from below, was equally contemptible, and which, deaf to the seductions of power, had too much faith in the influence of well-propagated ideas to take unfair advantage of the material strength of the masses and too much moral and intellectual pride to win them by flattery and cajolery. The representatives of the old Radicalism left standing after the advent of the Caucus felt and saw that the latter was scattering their ideals, their political and moral conceptions to the winds, and they shouted a warning to all within hearing. The pretext that the Caucus was serving the cause of Liberalism did not allay the anxiety even of such of these Radicals as were closely connected with official Liberalism. Thus Mr. Leonard Courtney was not stopped by his position as Under-Secretary of State in the Gladstone Ministry from putting the democracy on their guard against the new tendencies. Addressing his electors on the occasion of the inauguration of a political Association of workmen, he pointed out that the first care of such societies should be to make their members think. "Teach them," he said, "to discuss and examine and criticise and probe to the bottom the different problems set before them. Do not bring working-men together simply for the purpose of passing a prearranged vote." While warning them against those who pretend that Working-men's Associations have no concern with education, but that

1 *Times*, 2d of July, 1886.

the object of them is "to make use of the force that working-men possess, to bring it into play, to prevent its being wasted, to use it in the most powerful manner when occasion arises for its employment," Mr. Courtney observed that machinery was useless if it lacked motive power, that it was idle if it did not preserve and develop individual force, and that it might even become dangerous by reducing men to the level of automatons. "Now you may ask," added Mr. Courtney, "why is it I have suggested these things for your reflection to-day ? Is there any danger that the Association we are inaugurating to-night or corresponding Associations that have been established throughout the country may be affected in this manner? I think there is. I think we see in our country a tendency of machinery to supersede individuality, and a tendency on the part of the people to trust to machinery instead of maintaining individual activity. There are creeping among us some of the signs of a detestable demagogism . . . so that we are in danger through the popularization of our institutions of degrading our political life." [1]

Exhortations of this kind did not find much echo in the country nor men to bestow them on the public. Those who uttered them, those who still confessed and professed the creed of old Radicalism, daily appeared with more distinctness, both to themselves and to others, like the survivors of an extinct race. Mr. Joseph Cowen noted it with melancholy : "Radicalism as expounded by these Fathers of the Faith has become a tradition merely. . . . Here and there a Radical of the old type may be found, but he lives in the midst of a population that does not understand him. A Fifth-monarchy Man would hardly be more out of place. . . . When the 'dew of youth was fresh upon me,' I espoused the principles and became enamoured of the teachings of these apostles of philosophic democracy. Amidst every vicissitude of fortune and life, I have striven to be faithful to their traditions and to uphold — I only know too well at how great a distance — their policy and to expound their creed. But a generation has arisen that 'does not know Joseph.' They conceive all independent thought heresy, all generosity to opponents weakness, and are puzzled and alarmed when praise or blame is dispensed

[1] Speech at Liskeard, *Times*, 25th of November, 1881.

discriminately, when a man's principles don't turn with the tide and the times, when more regard is shown for measures than for men, for truth than for victory." [1]

Divided by a gulf from the Liberal middle-class, from the plutocracy with the Liberal trade-mark, the old Radicals were just as unable to appeal to the militant elements of Liberalism, to the progressives. The Caucus, with all the tendencies which it embodied, absorbed most of these elements, except a few groups of irreconcilables and extremists, and the classic Radicals remained, so to speak, in the air. There was no longer room for them under the Caucus. Cowen's case showed with startling clearness that there could be no exception to the general rule; it was no use trying to combine the thoughtful and independent Radical with the tribune and the man of action capable of rousing the masses; the one excluded the other.

The old Radicalism was dead, quite dead.

V

Classic Radicalism was already breathing its last when the Caucus came into power, and the latter in reality was only its undertaker and its grave-digger. The case was not the same with moderate Liberalism, which the Caucus found still erect and on which it fastened in a special way. Of less purer metal than classic Radicalism, with a considerable admixture of alloy, it stood wear and tear better. It was not dead toward the end of Gladstone's second Ministry, but it also was hard hit, and in its best points. The old Liberalism was not represented merely by aristocratic Whigs of reactionary tendencies and plutocrats engendered by the successful middle-class. It included a good many men who without attaining to the moral grandeur of the classic Radicals, whose spirit had the temper of steel, were sterling characters, with genuine popular sympathies, with a broad-minded faith in mankind and in liberty, of manly independence allied to wise moderation. They did not represent so much a caste or a class, as a real political temperament, the moderate temperament in the best, that is to say, in the true sense of the word. Forster's case proved that they too

[1] Speech to the electors of Newcastle, 3d of January, 1881 (*Life and Speeches*, p. 182).

could not find favour in the eyes of the new Radicalism, and
as it happened, not because of the failings of the aristocratico-
plutocratic Whiggism, from which they were more or less free,
but owing to their qualities of firm and sober moderation and
independence of mind, which were particularly odious to the
new Radicalism. Even if it had a liking for them, its machine,
the Caucus, with its rigidly uniform action, was not suited for
the logical or ethical operations of sorting or selection; it
crushed or threw out everything that did not fit into its
mould.

There was a collision and an explosion when men of great
force of character like Forster were in question; the process
went on more quietly in the immense majority of instances
in which the material was more malleable, as is generally the
case with men of moderate opinions; they were assimilated or
eliminated without much friction or noise. This double operation, which we have been able to observe from the first appearance of the Caucus Associations, was perceptibly accentuated
by the victory of 1880 and by the impression which it gave,
rightly or wrongly, of the strength of the new Radicalism
represented by the Caucus. In reality, as has been proved
above, the Whig contingents had not fought this battle with
less success, or demonstrated their existence in a less conclusive fashion. Mr. Gladstone made allowance for this. Often
as he exerted himself to evoke the democracy, he none the
less remained, owing to his education and the connections of
his early career, as it were a Conservative brake on the new
Liberalism, especially in regard to forms handed down by tradition which left a deep impression on his character. Consequently when he returned to power he felt bound to give the
Whigs their proper share in the government, and he adorned
his Ministry with a goodly number of lords, half of whom had
seats in the Cabinet. The Whigs were not much better off for
this. In the Cabinet the Radicals were in a small minority,
but in the country they soon managed to reverse the proportions, chiefly by means of the new Organization.

The equilibrium between the moderate and the Radical element in the "hundreds," which at first was preserved after a
fashion, was destroyed after 1880. The advanced element began to press the moderates closely, being excited by the victory

at the general election and by the decisive tone of the policy of
the Gladstone Ministry, which seemed to show that the tide
was flowing on the side of the militants. Their propelling
force was at the same time considerably increased by a change
of seeming insignificance, in the external conditions of the
Associations, — the abolition of the subscription. According to
the " Birmingham plan " it was optional, but in several Associations, especially in those which had been formed out of the elements of the old registration societies, it was still compulsory.
The extreme smallness of the sum — two shillings or one shilling a year — could not, it would appear, keep any one out; it
was not, strictly speaking, a qualification. However, it did not
find favour, and after 1880 the subscription was no longer demanded in almost all the caucuses. The Associations were
soon filled with members who paid nothing but held forth a
good deal. Being swamped by numbers, the members who
belonged to the old political staff carried a rule in several localities that no one could be on the council or the committee without paying a trifling subscription, but this remained a dead
letter. A moderate and conciliatory spirit was not the distinguishing mark of the non-paying members; they were rather
inclined to display the contrary, if only for the purpose of
asserting their equality with those who paid. Among the
moderates some, of a politic turn, let them act or rather shout
as they pleased, in the expectation, which was correct up to a
certain point, that they would expend their energy in vehement
language and demeanour. Others, less Machiavellian or less indulgent, feeling more and more out of their element in the Associations, left them without, however, breaking with the party.
The Caucus, or what came to the same thing, the militant element which made the Caucus its stronghold, only assumed
greater authority in consequence; it spoke in the name of the
party, and appeared all the more entitled to do so because it
invariably supported the policy of the great leader of the
party, of Mr. Gladstone, at whose shrine all the Liberals wor-
shipped. All of them more or less, therefore, followed the
skirmishers. The timid and sulky ones grumbled, but nevertheless followed, as did their representatives in the House.
Others again, and there were a great many of them, let themselves go with their eyes shut, buoyed up by their faith in Mr.

Gladstone. Finally the rest, more critical or more timorous, would have much liked to resist, but what were they to do? They had no organization of their own. The Associations of the old type (Registration Societies and others), which survived and which supplied the old-fashioned Liberals with a base of operations, hastened after 1880, in order to comply with practical requirements or with fashion, to remodel themselves on the "Birmingham plan," and after having changed their skin they soon worked themselves up to Caucus pitch. Then what flag were the moderate Liberals to hoist, or what cry could they adopt? Were they to proclaim themselves the real and only depositaries of historic Liberalism? This was perhaps a demonstrable proposition for the learned in history, but the bulk of the party flocked towards the sign, and this was outside the door of the Caucus, brand-new and with flaming letters: The Liberal 500, the Liberal 600, the Liberal 800! and all "representative," "strictly representative" of the Liberal party, all recognized and quoted on the great exchange of Liberalism where their bills were readily accepted and they themselves were drawn upon even more readily. No doubt, the moderates always had the resource, so important in English electoral life even in our own day, of fortune and social relations. But they could only avail themselves of it in exceptional cases; for their own plutocrat relatives, following the bent of their opportunist temperament, had gathered round the new sign in order to have a second string to their bow, just as on the turf a man backs two horses in the same race to make more certain of winning. Consequently, if the moderates would not follow, they were bound to keep in the background. Under either alternative the organization of the Caucus, because it was the organization of the Liberal party commanded by Mr. Gladstone, disqualified them as Liberals.

As Liberals, yes, but you can preserve the grace of the moderate state as Conservatives; why don't you join us then, cried the Conservatives. Since the Gladstone Ministry (of 1880) had set to work and had adopted a Radical policy by its reform of the land laws in Ireland, the Tories had not ceased to warn the Whigs, to point out the depth of the abyss into which they were plunging after the Radicals, who were carried away by the demon of subversion and destruction. By way of apologue they quoted Voltaire's story of the two philosophers who when ordering a dish of asparagus at an inn could not agree as to whether it should be cooked with butter or plain. While they were waiting for the dish and beguiling their hunger with a discussion of high metaphysics, one of the two philosophers, being heated by the dispute, had a stroke of apoplexy, whereupon the other rushed into the kitchen crying out: The whole of it plain! The same thing would happen to the Whigs and the Radicals feasting together; the end would be the death of Liberalism dressed with melted butter, and Radicalism would be served up quite plain.

" Cut yourself adrift " — the advice was easy to give but not so easy to follow. They were tolerably near the Conservatives in point of feeling, no doubt; but what a gap was placed between the two by the memory of long struggles and of rivalries, of traditional and hereditary grudges; by the *amour-propre* of a man with a house of his own, to whom it would be worse than death to take up an abode in a lodging in his old age. His old-fashioned mansion is heavily mortgaged, it seems to sink under the weight of encumbrances and lawsuits, but it still bears his name, and it is there that everybody comes to see him. If the worst comes to the worst, if fate is inexorable, well then . . . in any event there will always be time to leave the old home. The Whigs, therefore, in great perplexity and demoralized by the sight of the tide of Radicalism submerging their venerable principles and their habits, did not flatly reject the advances made to them, but replied that the time had not yet arrived and perhaps would never arrive, that the advent of a revolutionary party was not at present a sufficient reason for discarding the good elements of Liberalism, and that their position was not so desperate; that Whigs and Radicals could still fight side by side for many years to come; that it could not even be otherwise, for "they (the Whigs) could do nothing without the Radicals, and the Radicals, in spite of all their bluster, could do nothing without them." [1] And if, they said

[1] " The Whigs," *Nineteenth Century*, July, 1883, by Lord Cowper (who had just left the Gladstone Ministry with W. E. Forster, in consequence of the " Kilmainham treaty " made with Parnell). Cf. also " The Revolutionary Party," by Lord Dunraven (*Ibid.*, August, 1881) ; " The Liberal Victory from a Conservative Point of View," by Alfred Austin (*Fortnightly Review*, 1st

to themselves, there is a dissolution of partnership, what is to become of the firm, and how are the customers to be kept? This, in fact, was the great preoccupation of the Whigs, which made them follow with many a grumble or groan. It was still the question of the sign, though looked at from another point of view. And it was not only considerations of interest that were involved for them; responsibility and duty were also at stake. The authority of the Whig partners was impaired in the establishment and even disregarded by a great number of customers, but still they were able to sign for the firm; thanks to the delicate attention of Mr. Gladstone, they had a numerical majority in the Cabinet. This contradictory position of the Whig leaders made them repress the anxiety and the apprehension aroused by Radicalism with its great engine of war, the Caucus, and even check tendencies towards resistance among their followers.

Tendencies of this kind showed themselves here and there in the provinces. Liberals of sincere convictions but thoroughly moderate temperament came to the conclusion that the game was up, and they wished to have an open rupture with the Caucus and start a moderate Organization against it. The great Whig chiefs in London to whom the scheme was submitted replied that they quite sympathized with the views of their moderate friends, that they shared their opinions only too strongly, but in the end they pronounced against the plan of a new Organization in order not to break up the Liberal party.[1] It was still the question of the firm that preoccupied them. This advice was deferred to, and the scheme for an independent Organization of moderates was given up. It is very doubtful moreover, for the reasons stated above, whether they would have succeeded in stemming the Caucus. They were too doctrinaire, too sober for the masses, as may be seen from the analysis of one of these draft schemes which has been communicated to me, the programme of a *Moderate Liberal*

June, 1880) ; "Whigs, Radicals, and Conservatives" (*Quarterly Review*, Vol. CL, 1880) ; "The Position of the Whigs," by C. M. Gaskell (*Nineteenth Century*, December, 1881) ; "A Whig Retort" (*Edinburgh Review*, January, 1882) ; "Future of Parties and Politics" (*Quarterly Review*, Vol. CLVI, 1883).

[1] I have been made acquainted with a correspondence exchanged on this subject, in 1884, between some moderate Liberals of one of the largest towns in Lancashire, and Lord Hartington and Mr. Goschen.

Union. Paragraph 2 of this document ran as follows: "Since it is a fact that in political contention only those triumphs are enduring which result in an admission by the conquered of the justice of the victor's cause, and that political action can only be permanently successful where reaction is barred, this Association shall rather strive to undermine and slowly extirpate adverse opinion and convert its professors than attempt to stifle utterance and imperiously coerce its professors." Stipulating that the Association would be open to every Liberal, however radical his views, the scheme declared that the very fact of his joining the Association would mean on their part "both a readiness to accept compromise and an abandonment of all effort to force on premature measures by violent language and fanatical agitation;" "the Association does not pledge itself to support any definite Liberal principle nor to uphold or seek to establish any definite Liberal political system; but it is a confederacy of Liberals of a particular temperament and cast of mind to support the political action of other Liberals of the same moral and intellectual character. For such as these there is no need to lay down principles or formulate political creeds; for from where Liberals assemble to consult for the public good and moderation prevails, Truth, Reason, and Justice cannot be absent." [1]

Prevented, in spite of their inmost feelings, from leaving the ranks of official Liberalism, the moderates were anything but reassured. And before long, on the eve of the general election (of 1885) when the principal representative of the new Radicalism and the creator of the Caucus, Mr. Chamberlain, issued his "unauthorized programme," a panic took place among the

---

[1] The printed copy of the draft scheme placed at my disposal was annotated by its authors with a freedom of language and style which reflected the inmost thoughts of their political co-religionists much better than the stale and prosy document which we have just analyzed, and for this reason some interest may attach to the reproduction of these annotations. Paragraph 1, which proclaims that the object of the Association will be the defence of Liberal principles, the diffusion of Liberal ideas, and the maintenance of the Liberal party in power, is commented on by the remark: " Avoid accusation of Toryism." The other paragraphs analyzed above are accompanied by the following annotations: " Liberal party used to be the party of freedom; now Liberals are becoming a party of coercion; " " The chief character toleration — even Chamberlain admissible if he were not so violent and domineering; " " No horse ought to be ridden to death; " " Temperament the bond of union."

moderate Liberals.   It was no longer from benevolent Tories, it was from their own camp that a cry went forth that the time had come, that there was only one thing to be done, — to go over to the Conservatives.

The Conservatives might take *them* in, but could they offer a shelter, a real shelter for their principles and their habits ? Was the ground which was quaking beneath their feet in the old abode of Liberalism more solid in the not less old-fashioned dwelling of Conservatism ? What was going on behind the door at which the fugitives would demand admittance ? This is what I propose to investigate by returning to the Organization of the Conservative party, which we have left at the moment when the great democratic Reform of 1867 was about to take place.

SEVENTH CHAPTER

I

THE extension of the parliamentary suffrage to the urban masses conceded by the Act of 1867 looked very threatening for the Conservative party. The boroughs, which had always been the stronghold of Liberalism, were now about to throw the counties definitively into the shade. When taking the "leap in the dark," or rather after having taken it, the Tories, and Disraeli in particular, entertained the hope that the populations of the towns would supply them as well as the other side with an electoral contingent, that they could not be deaf to Tory influences and principles. Whether this calculation was a fanciful one or not, it was clear that the future of the Conservative party would henceforward depend on the urban voters. To lay hands on them forthwith became the main preoccupation of the Conservatives. They hastened to form organizations for enlisting the new electors. As after the year 1832, it was Lancashire which took the lead. In several manufacturing towns of this county the old "Constitutional Societies" were revived, or new ones were founded. This example was followed in various other places, but not to any very great extent. The organizing movement thus inaugurated, which was in a way a new and enlarged edition of that which had been started thirty years before, in consequence of Sir Robert Peel's cry of "Register, Register, Register!" was characterized by a novel and highly significant feature: the Conservative Associations scattered throughout the country were combined into a confederation, entitled the *National Union of Conservative and Constitutional Associations*, represented by a body of delegates to be renewed from year to year. The business of the *Union* was to stimulate and direct the organizing movement in the country, by bringing about the formation of new Associations, by helping the existing Organizations with advice and information, providing them with lecturers and speakers for their meetings, publishing pamphlets and reprinting speeches delivered on important political questions.

The part assigned to the new institution was, to be sure, not of high political importance, while the local Associations which formed the basis of the *Union* were only voluntary combinations of partisans, devoid of a representative character, modelled on the usual pattern of Registration Societies. None the less the fact remained that a new central authority, invested with an elective mandate and representing, although in an indirect and incomplete fashion, Conservative opinion in the country, was taking its place in the organization of the Conservative party side by side with the Whip appointed by the parliamentary leader of the party. The power of the new authority could not become a reality so long as Conservative opinion had no independent existence in the true sense of the word. The body of Conservative opinion which represented all that was left standing after the break-up of the old society — traditions, interests, prejudices — the whole knit together by ties of social subordination, continued as in the past to look for and obey the word of command proceeding from above, from the great chief of the party. The Whip and his colleagues of the Central Conservative Office, who managed the electoral business of the party, had therefore nothing to fear from the *Union* which had been set up towards the end of 1867. They looked on it, with some condescension, as an auxiliary which might render service to the cause. A few years later, to prove their good-will to the *Union*, they accommodated it in the rooms of the head office of the party. But the new Organization took care not to forget its place. " The Union has been organized rather as a handmaid to the party than to usurp the functions of party leadership,"[1] as the president of the Union (H. Cecil Raikes) said at one of its first annual meetings. Although representative in point of form, the organization of the Union was profoundly imbued with the aristocratic spirit which was the essence of the old Toryism. Apart from the usual hierarchy of President, Vice-President,

[1] *Report of Proceedings at the Seventh Annual Conference*, 1873, p. 10.

etc., it had Patrons and Vice-Patrons, who were generally noblemen and often of the first rank, dukes. The Council, which wielded executive power, contained in addition to the delegates of local Associations a considerable number of non-elected members.

The formation of the local Associations, which at first proceeded somewhat slowly outside Lancashire, received a marked impulse after the year 1870, when Disraeli entrusted the task of organization to a young barrister who has since become one of the most conspicuous of the Tory statesmen, Mr. (now Sir) John Gorst. Devoting himself zealously to the discharge of his duties, he looked out for the energetic men of Tory views in the constituencies, formed them into groups, stimulated them to action, started Associations, and in a few years succeeded in considerably extending the system in the towns. Great pains were taken to attract the masses to the Organizations. The men of action in the party admitted that they had " outlived the time of great family influences, and also that period which succeeded the first Reform Bill, which might be called the period of middle-class influence in boroughs," and that they were " living in a day in which the people were to be applied to in a much more direct, clear, and positive manner than was the case under the old forms of the constitution." [1] Besides, had not the line of the new route been marked out by the great leader of the party, by Mr. Disraeli ? Was it not he who had long ago raised the standard of popular Toryism ?

II

Popular Toryism was in fact the bridge which Disraeli built for himself when he passed from Radicalism to Conservatism at the beginning of his career. Throwing in his lot with the latter, he set to work to clear Toryism, in his own mind, from the stigma of being the reactionary party which was generally held to attach to it. His subtle reasoning, aided by a powerful imagination, supplied him with the historical theory that hostility to progress and to civil and religious liberty was the outcome of a degenerate Toryism, demoralized by a long spell of power under exceptional circumstances ; that the old Toryism,

[1] *Report of Proceedings* quoted above.

that of the beginning of the eighteenth century, far from being
an exclusive party, was anxious to take in the whole nation in
all the variety of its constituent elements from the Throne
down to the lowest strata of the people, that it was Whiggism
which had monopolized power for the benefit of an aristocratic
oligarchy and thereby warped the institutions of England, the
basis of which is equality, not a levelling and destructive but an
elevating and constructive equality, not like that of France
where the law invests every citizen with equality to prevent
the elevation of his neighbour, but one which allows every
subject to rise if he has claims to distinction. Every Englishman in fact, Disraeli found, is born to civil equality and can
aspire to the highest positions. With democratic liberties
England seemed to him to have combined the advantages of
monarchy, by having set up a popular throne, and the security
of an aristocracy, by having invested certain orders of citizens
with legislative functions without conferring on them exclusive privileges.

The very genuine sympathy for the people which ran in the
veins of Disraeli the plebeian, the descendant of outcasts, and
the admiration for grandeur and magnificence in which his
imagination indulged, combined in him to produce the odd
conception of a popular throne and an unprivileged aristocracy. The romanticism of the day sanctioned, if it did not
contribute to inspire, the theory of primitive Toryism; and
reinforced by the sentiments of revolt which the triumph of
the Liberal middle class in the state, and of individualism in
the economic life of the nation, had aroused in feeling minds,
this theory acquired consistency and found expression in the
Young England movement. The aroma of sentimentalism
exhaled by *Young England* soon evaporated, but Disraeli retained his conception of popular Toryism. It remained his
creed up to the end of his life, although he did not put it into
practice.

To the man of romance, living by imagination, he united the
fighting politician, contending amid the realities of life. For
years an isolated gladiator, then after endless ordeals leader
of a group, and finally a great *condottiere*, he had but one preoccupation — to parry blows and to deliver them; he observed
but one rule of conduct, that which led to success, even if it

entailed leaving his professions and his engagements behind him. Dragging his party along with him, Disraeli brought it, by a succession of steps, by one leap after another, to the very threshold of democracy, and in the course of this wild race made it discard its reactionary ways. The new departure, far from being a development of "popular Toryism," which was only an idealization of the old days, was entirely due to the opportunism introduced by Disraeli. It was by swerving from the creed, by teaching the Tories not to stand on ceremony with the "institutions" which, according to the orthodox doctrine, ought to form the unassailable foundations of Toryism, that Disraeli rejuvenated the decrepit Tory party and procured it a fresh lease of power.

But while making the Conservatives wheel in the direction of a levelling type of democracy, Disraeli, in his anxiety to justify his opportunism, placed this evolution under the auspices of his old aristocratico-popular creed. From it as from a sacred spring he drew the holy water with which he besprinkled his career of *condottiere*. Taking good care not to use the language of the democrat pure and simple, or of the demagogue, not to convey the idea that the government for the people which he prized ought to be also a government by the people, he maintained that the reforms carried by the Tories were in the spirit of the national traditions, that the apparently hazardous measures which he had passed were really in harmony with the venerable institutions of England and the conceptions of primitive Toryism. And taking himself, so to speak, at his word, the *condottiere* disappeared in the man of romance, reverting to his doctrine of a sublimated Toryism embodying the old national character. "The Tory party," repeated Disraeli, "is nothing if it is not a national party. It is not a confederation of nobles, nor is it a democratic mob, it is a party composed of all the numerous classes in the Kingdom." The principles of which the Tory party is the champion because they alone can give security to England, the principles of liberty, of order, of law, and of religion, cannot be abandoned to private judgment or to the caprices or passions of the masses. In Disraeli's eyes the bulwark of English liberty remains the landed interest, which supplies the community with its natural leaders. "The liberty of England rests upon the fact that there is a class which bids defiance alike to despots and to mobs, and round which the people can always rally," declared Disraeli, forgetting that the author of the Reform Act of 1867 had himself helped to supplant these "natural leaders of the people."

Thus the "popular Toryism" of Disraeli, viewed as a sincere and consistent doctrine, had nothing really popular or democratic about it within the ordinary political meaning of the words, and when his policy did contain these elements he denied it. In the long run, then, "popular Toryism" rested on an illusion or a verbal juggle which could hardly be dispelled or explained away by the fact that from 1868 onwards Disraeli and his lieutenants were fond of giving a prominent place to the "improvement of the condition of the people" in the Tory programme side by side with the "maintenance of institutions" and the "preservation of the Empire"; for devotion to the material welfare of the masses can be practised under any political régime, including those of the most reactionary or even despotic character. Lacking political substance, the "popular Toryism" which was brought out under Disraeli's auspices was in reality only a name. It is true that in politics a name is often of greater importance than the thing, and that of "popular Toryism" was destined to furnish a fresh proof of this.

III

The interpretation which the organizers of the party gave to the notion of "popular Toryism" was as simple as its real meaning was vague and undiscernible. For them to enter on the path of popular Toryism marked out by Disraeli meant to run after the votes of the multitude for the Tory candidates; to appeal to the people signified for them to enlist it directly in the electoral army of the Tory party. In the days of restricted suffrage when a committee of local notables was formed for the occasion just before the election, to attract the popular voter one or two artisans were added to it, or a special "committee of workingmen" was even created, without, however, allowing them the slightest influence in the choice of candidates or in the management of the electoral campaign.

This tradition was reverted to, and the provisional arrangements were replaced by a permanent organization, in which as many workingmen as possible were enrolled, and no longer merely isolated individuals to represent their class. The Associations which were thus formed were often, in reality if not in name, clubs which had not much that was political about them except the fact that their members bound themselves to vote at elections for the Tory candidate. The ways of English society and particularly of the Tory section of it not being favourable to daily intercourse between men of different classes on a footing of equality, the popular element was left to itself in those clubs. Besides, very often the organizations of the Conservative party derived this exclusive character from their official constitution under which the workingmen were grouped separately in Conservative Workingmen's Associations or Clubs, just as in the old days, in the early organizations of Lancashire which were constructed in two compartments, one for the gentlemen and the other for the common herd brought together in the Conservative Operatives' Societies.

This creation of electoral regiments, composed exclusively of workingmen, did not exactly correspond with Disraeli's grand theory, according to which the Tory party was the national party, embracing all the elements of society with all the variety of their respective conditions and of their aspirations in one organic coexistence. Consequently Disraeli could not help disavowing, on the first opportunity, the way in which "popular Toryism" had been applied in the organization of the party. In 1873, at Glasgow, when receiving the representatives of the Association of Conservative Workingmen among many other deputations, he began by telling them that he had never consented to meet any separate body entitled "Conservative workingmen." "I have never," he said, "been myself at all favourable to a system which would lead Conservatives who are workingmen to form societies merely confined to their class. In the Church and in the polling-booth all are equal, and all that concerns Conservative workingmen and interests them concerns and interests the great body of Conservatives of whom they form a portion. Therefore, it is to the Conservative Association I see before me, of whom a very considerable majority consists of workingmen, it is to that

Association that I address myself." [1] The Conservative Workingmen's Associations none the less continued to exist, and more new ones were founded. The organizers evidently thought that theory was one thing and practice another, that the best way of imparting cohesion to the electoral forces was to arrange the voters in the order in which they were grouped in daily life, where classes were very deeply divided. The community of interests and even of political views subsisting between the different social strata of the Conservative party was however insisted on with much emphasis. This was the great argument advanced by Disraeli, who affirmed that the Reform of 1867, of which he was the author, had been framed with the conviction that the majority of the nation and the workingmen in particular were Conservatives. He never wearied of repeating that the workingmen were undoubtedly Conservatives, that they understood that the "greatness and the Empire of England were due to the ancient institutions of the country." The Liberals greeted these assertions with a merry scepticism, and they had all the more difficulty in forming an idea of the lower-class Tory because he had not come to the front in the general election of 1868; for it was precisely in the towns where the masses voted for the first time that the Conservatives were defeated. The Associations which the Tories founded in and after 1868, succeeded however in enlisting a good many artisans who joined with a will in the electoral contest in which the Conservatives won a brilliant victory (in 1874). To the delight of the Tories and to the dismay of the Liberals, the fact appeared to be proved that the Conservative workingman was not a myth, but a reality. The winning side in their transports ascribed all the honour to Disraeli, who with his gift of divination had discerned the Conservative workingman, who, like a Cuvier, had discovered this unknown genus, this new political species. [2]

---

[1] Speech to the Workingmen's Conservative Associations, at Glasgow, 22d November, 1873.

[2] On this subject the *Times*, when Lord Beaconsfield's statue was inaugurated, on the second anniversary of his death, rising to the level of the occasion, used the following language: "In the inarticulate mass of the English populace he discerned the Conservative workingman as the sculptor perceives the angel prisoned in a block of marble" (leading article of the 18th April, 1883).

The triumph of the Conservatives naturally reacted on the local organization of the party and gave a stimulus to the creation of Tory Associations and Clubs in places where none existed. But the activity and the influence of the Organizations did not increase with their number, it declined rather than otherwise. Without spontaneous life of their own, having been set up as electoral machinery, they began to languish as soon as victory had deprived them of the incentive to effort. "The National Union of Constitutional and Conservative Associations" exhibited just as little vitality, its annual meetings were dull and insignificant. The profound calm of the early years of the Tory administration was followed by the Eastern question, which made the whole country hang on the doings of Disraeli (now Lord Beaconsfield). He himself, absorbed in great affairs of State, lost sight of the local life of the party and of the Associations. He was not reminded of them until his triumphal return from the Berlin Congress, when nearly fifteen hundred delegates of "Constitutional and Conservative Associations" and of "Conservative workingmen" came to London to pay him their respects. The language in which he addressed them threw a somewhat crude light on the part which the leaders of the party assigned to Associations supposed to represent the free opinion of English Conservatism in which the Government sought its inspirations. The gist of Lord Beaconsfield's harangue amounted to a single sentence: your duty is to supply us with fighting material for the elections, mind you do not forget it. The actual expressions which he used were not much more toned down. He borrowed his arguments and his metaphors from military history, which in his eyes embodied for the occasion "the experience of mankind in all ages." "All men have agreed," he said, "that in the conduct of public affairs there is nothing more precious than discipline, and it is a great mistake that discipline is incompatible with the deepest convictions and even with the most passionate sentiments. Whether we look into military affairs in ancient or modern times, we see many illustrations of that principle. I suppose there never was a body of men animated by a higher degree of patriotism or who extended their influence through a longer period than the Roman legion; and the Roman legion was a model of discipline.

So again when the Macedonians contemplated conquering the world, they formed their phalanx; and though they were animated by so great an idea, still no one can deny that it was the discipline of the Macedonian phalanx which contributed to the conquest of Asia." Passing from antiquity to modern times, the speaker dwelt on the discipline of Cromwell's soldiers and Wellington's troops. Then, turning his attention to the universe, he discerned that even there discipline was the sovereign law: "Nature herself is organized; and if there were not a great directing force which controls, guides, and manages everything, you have nothing but volcanoes, earthquakes, and deluges. In public life without discipline — organization — similar effects would be produced." Breaking off in this discourse on military history and cosmic philosophy to which he was treating the "Conservative, Constitutional, and Workingmen's Associations," he said: "I wish to say one word upon Workingmen's Associations. I favoured them from the beginning [he had evidently forgotten his own speech at Glasgow in 1873], and always had confidence in their future, though they have been subjected, as many have been in their infancy, to taunts about their character and influence. I have been asked often why should workingmen be Conservatives? And I reply, — of all men, workingmen should be most Conservative. It is no light thing to belong to a nation where liberty and order coexist in the greatest degree. That must benefit all classes, and most particularly it must benefit the workingmen." Then, after this digression, he reverted to the necessity of discipline. "It is for you now," he said to the delegates, "the assembled officers of the great constitutional army that you have formed, to feel convinced of these views. . . . Act upon these views of organization. . . . It is only by encouraging discipline that you will be able to maintain yourself in that power which you have obtained."[1] Perhaps Lord Beaconsfield's speech was accentuated in consequence of the challenge proceeding from the opposite camp, where the Caucus was being noisily established. The day after his return from Berlin, when the frenzied shouts of the crowd which had dragged him in triumph like a victorious general through the streets of London had scarcely died away, the

[1] *Times*, 7th of August, 1878.

mighty voice of his illustrious rival, Mr. Gladstone, was heard, summoning the Liberals to organize themselves on the "Birmingham plan," for an attack on the Tory position.[1] Disraeli's first impulse was to reply by sarcasm, by the nickname of the Caucus. Then, bethinking himself of the contest, the old *condottiere* spoke of discipline. The day of battle arrived, and in spite of the discipline of his troops, they were beaten and routed. Evidently there were forces still more powerful than the Roman legion and the Macedonian phalanx.

IV

The day after the defeat, the Tories were confronted with the usual question : who is to blame ? The simplest explanation which occurred to many minds was, exactly as with the Liberals in 1874, that the Conservatives had been beaten because they were badly organized, while their opponents possessed the perfected weapon of the Caucus. The Tories unhesitatingly rejected even the idea of borrowing this institution from the latter, they had repudiated it with virtuous indignation from its first appearance. In fact, at the beginning of the year 1878 the Central Conservative Office unburdened its conscience in a circular to the adherents of the party which held up the Birmingham system to their reprobation. Then at the height of the discussion aroused in the country by Forster's conflict with the Bradford Caucus the Tory headquarters took advantage of it to point out to the public, through the medium of the *Times*, that the Conservative party did not resort to the odious practices of the Caucus, so derogatory to the freedom of members of Parliament, that the Tory Organization did not impose its authority by force, but left complete liberty to all, etc.[2] Having become still more hostile to the Radical Caucus after their rout in 1880, the Tories none the less thought that they needed an equally strong Organization, and they were very anxious to create one, to hit upon a sort of caucus which however would not be the Caucus.[3]

While these views and wishes, of a more or less definite or

[1] The Southwark speech mentioned above, p. 183, note.
[2] *Times*, 10th of August, 1878.
[3] Cf. the article " Conservative Reorganization " (*Blackwood's Magazine*, June, 1880), one of the first of the many expressions of opinion of this kind.

vague character, were agitating the Conservatives, the death of Lord Beaconsfield supervened, in 1881. The confusion in the Tory camp became complete. Lord Beaconsfield seemed to have carried to the grave all the courage and hope with which he had managed to inspire the Tory party during their long years of wandering in the wilderness of opposition. Discipline became relaxed, and a mutiny broke out among the rank and file. Flying in the face of all the proprieties of Tory society and its traditions of discipline and of deference to its leaders, the malcontents openly defied their authority, treated them with contempt, charged them with being the cause of the distress of the party. This revolt against the chiefs was produced by the mingling of two currents — the impatience of the hot-blooded younger members and the ambition of the plebeians of the party. The old leaders seemed to the former too feeble, too easy-going, nay, actually incapable of heading a victorious attack on the Liberal Ministry. Resolution and repeated doses of audacity were wanted, they thought, to revive the drooping courage of the Tories, and to strike terror into the hearts of their rivals. The leader of the Opposition, Sir Stafford Northcote, a parliamentary statesman of the old school, and a genuine Conservative in the best sense of the word, did not consider a reckless dare-devil policy the best suited for restoring the fortunes of a party or the most worthy of the Conservative party in particular. The rebels, four in number, formed themselves into a group of free-lances, called the "Fourth Party," and waged a pitiless war alike against the Liberal Ministers and the official leaders of the Conservative party. The audacity and the violent language of the assailants more than made up for their small number, and the two front benches had much to put up with from the Tory guerilla. The position of Sir Stafford Northcote and his lieutenants, continually attacked on their own flank, was very like that in which Lord Hartington, the leader of the Liberal Opposition after the defeat of 1874, was placed by Mr. Chamberlain and his friends. The analogy was destined to become more complete. The Tory rebels were not content with harrying the leaders in the discharge of their duties: they fastened on the leadership, and just as the Birmingham Radicals charged the Liberal leaders with the original sin of Whiggism, so the

young Tories held up their chiefs to public reprobation as
aristocrats.

This grievance which, stated by Tories and to Tories, was
certainly extraordinary and well-nigh inconceivable, had its
hidden source in the recent events of the inner life of the
party. Disraeli's last Ministry, like all the preceding Tory
Cabinets, was composed almost entirely of *grands seigneurs*.
In the House of Commons there were a good many men of
plebeian origin belonging to the party, especially among the
borough members. But the old Tory tradition made them
rank somewhat as an auxiliary force of the great Conservative
army supplied by the counties, where the electors, who were
not numerous before the year 1885, voted obediently for the
great landlords. The urban constituencies, which were more
difficult to carry, were left to the "new men," while the counties remained a sort of preserve for the aristocrats, for the
gentlemen of England. It was the latter too who generally
divided the spoils of office, without however shocking anybody
thereby; it was in the nature of things. It was all very well
for the Reform Bill of 1867 to act as a readjustment of political power between the boroughs and the counties for the benefit of the former, and for the Tory majority of 1874 to be
indebted for part of its strength to the borough constituencies
which had just been wrested from the Liberals, thanks to the
efforts of the organizers referred to above; in spite of this,
when the Ministry was constituted and the subordinate offices
distributed, the plebeians of the towns were forgotten, including
even those whose energy had helped to win the victory. This
inspired some of them with keen resentment against the "aristocratic clique" which "monopolized all the places," which
"took to themselves all the good things," and in their heart of
hearts they swore a sort of Hannibal's oath against them. On
the eve of the elections of 1880 Lord Beaconsfield remembered
the forgotten ones, and having sent for one of them said to
him: "Why didn't you come and see me and remind me of your
existence? It is impossible for me to think of everybody,
especially when there are so many who are pushing themselves."
The offer of reparation came too late, there was too much bitterness in the hearts of the plebeians, and they were not slow
in giving vent to it after the disappearance of the great leader

for whom they had retained affection and respect in spite of all their grievances. The attitude which the malcontents were about to take up was fraught with important consequences for the fortunes of the Tory party and even for the future of Conservatism in England. One might perhaps parody the *mot* of Pascal that if Cleopatra's nose had been longer the face of the world would have been changed, and say that if the "good things" had been more widely distributed in 1874, the movement caused by the Young Tory revolt which broke out after Lord Beaconsfield's death would not have arisen till later, some years later; but at the pace at which things have been going in England since the year 1867 a few years means a very long stage. Discontented plebeians, or at all events persons who entirely shared their views, were the very men who formed the "Fourth Party," "taking as a sign" a young nobleman who had broken with his own class, Lord Randolph Churchill. From the House of Commons the campaign was carried into the country, at first by the agency of the Press. Under the somewhat transparent veil of "Two Conservatives" (who were Mr. Drummond Wolf and Mr. Gorst), the malcontents published a sort of manifesto which from one end to the other was a violent indictment of the Tory leaders in general. "If the Tory party," they declared, "is to continue to exist as a power in the State, it must become a popular party. . . . Unfortunately for Conservatism, its leaders belong solely to one class; they are a clique composed of members of the aristocracy, landowners, and adherents whose chief merit is subserviency. The party chiefs live in an atmosphere in which a sense of their own importance and of the importance of their class interests and privileges is exaggerated, and to which the opinions of the common people can scarcely penetrate. They are surrounded by sycophants who continually offer up the incense of personal flattery under the pretext of conveying political information. They half fear and half despise the common people, whom they see only through this deceptive medium." The Associations which had been formed throughout the country during the years 1868–1874 "complained that they were not patronized by the aristocratic members of the party. It was fortunate that they were not. There was no temptation to waste time and energy in organizing demonstrations to which no great man would come. They were thus driven to devote themselves to registration and the machinery necessary for an election contest. The victory of 1874, which was totally unexpected by the aristocratic section of the party, was the result. As soon as success was achieved, the men who had stood aloof since 1868 rushed in to share the spoils. A ministry was formed composed almost exclusively of peers and county members. Those by whom the campaign had been planned and fought were forgotten. . . . The distinction between county and borough members was revived. . . . Social influence became predominant. Independence of political thought was visited with the severest punishment. . . . In legislation the interests of boroughs were subordinated to those of the counties. . . . The Conservative Associations as a natural consequence steadily declined; those by whom the work was performed gradually withdrew to make way for noisier partisans whose main purpose was to recommend themselves to the leaders of the party. Defeat was not long in coming. . . . Some constituencies doubtless still possess associations composed of earnest workers, with unselfish leaders, who labour for the good of the cause. . . . The entire organization of the Tory party must undergo a radical revolution before it can afford ground for any well-founded satisfaction. In its existing shape it is managed by a committee in London whose names are unknown to the people at large, and who act without any mandate from the constituencies. The complaint of the individual Associations prior to 1874 that they were not patronized by the privileged class can no longer be made. They are corrupted by patronage and few escape its baneful influence. The object for which a great number of the Associations exist is to hold periodical demonstrations at which some member of the late Cabinet may exhibit his oratorical talents before the admiring crowd. When this has been accomplished, when the local leaders have had the satisfaction of shaking hands with the great man, their zeal collapses and the Association languishes until there is a fresh opportunity of catching a lion. . . . In the great person's speech the masses catch no word of sympathy for themselves, nothing to show that it is their rights, their privileges, their liberties that he is jealous to maintain. He is a being made of a different clay and living in a different atmosphere from theirs. If these are the means on which the Conservative leaders rely for bringing themselves back to power, they have a long time to wait." [1]

Such language as this in the mouth of Tories astonished and perhaps delighted people by its audacity, but it was too deeply tainted with acrimony and personal rancour to be a true picture of the real state of things. The aristocratic devil, although doubtless of a very deep hue, was perhaps not so black as they painted him; in any event it was not the fact that it was his contact with the Associations which threw a spell over them. They were not wholly destitute of aristocratic patrons before the year 1874; the "Union of Conservative and Constitutional Associations" owned a fairly good collection, while the local Associations, created somewhat recently, had not had the opportunity nor the time to acquire the importance which procures relations with and visits from persons in a prominent position. And if "admiring crowds" thronged round "great men" from London, it was not so much to gratify the latter as for their own enjoyment; for the "multitudes" took a pleasure and always do take a pleasure in gazing on a lord or a great personage. As a matter of fact, the great majority of the Tories in the country were far from sharing the passion for equality and the rancour of the revolted plebeians. Their appeal, therefore, did not produce the effect of the tocsin of a Saint Barthélemy. But it did not die away in space; other cries which met it soon blended with it and swelled its volume.

V

The deposition of the aristocratic leaders demanded by the members of the "Fourth Party" involved the "radical revolution" in the organization of the party, and that in a popular direction. This last point coincided with the preoccupations which had engrossed attention from the very day after the elections of 1880, and it presented in a way the solution of the problem. Whether from reasons unconnected with or akin to the motives which inspired the Fourth Party,

[1] "Conservative Disorganization," *Fortnightly Review*, 1882, Vol. 32 (new series).

several Tories occupying different positions in the social scale joined or agreed with them in their proposals relating to the organization of the party. The view began to prevail even among the aristocratic members of the party, who were more enlightened, that the party machinery was antiquated, quite unsuited to the "spirit of the times." "Mr. Chamberlain," they pointed out, "introduced a system of organization founded on a popular basis, and greatly benefited his party and himself. It is true he also inflicted great damage on the nation, but that is owing chiefly to the manner in which the machinery is worked, not to the nature of the machine. I am far from recommending the Birmingham Caucus as a model to be closely followed by the Tory party. But they must take it as a model, accepting what is good and discarding what is bad in it. The idea is good. Organization to be successful must originate in the people. The people must be made interested in party politics. The active, pushing local men must be utilized, must be given an outlet for their energy and a field for the exercise of their talent. . . . The people must be interested and taught to feel that they can do something more than merely record their votes." [1]

So far as they were addressed to the bulk of the party, these exhortations often reached the ears of people already half convinced of their truth. In more than one great manufacturing town the Tories were already engaged in extending the party organization, or in creating one on a wide basis, in order to cope with the Radical Caucus. The home of the latter, Birmingham, was among the first of the towns which imparted this movement to the Tory party. Prostrated by the organization of Messrs. Chamberlain and Schnadhorst, the Birmingham Tories gradually recovered themselves and set to work with much patience and method to form an army. They created a permanent organization in every district and ward in the form of local Associations and district committees, which by a successive delegation of authority eventually merged in the central Association. Its leaders sought opportunities for making the personal acquaintance of the prominent people in the wards, and by means of meetings, lect-

[1] Lord Dunraven, "The Future Constitutional Party," *Nineteenth Century*, April, 1883.

ures, banquets, and picnics they endeavoured to bring the electors together as much as possible, and to accustom them to close their ranks and keep step with one another. Contesting every municipal election under the party flag, the Conservative Association trained its forces to warfare. In a word, the Conservatives set about following the methods of their opponents very closely.

And it was not only the needs of the party, the practical requirements of the struggle for existence, which drove the Tories into this path. As in most human affairs, personal interest, ambition, or vanity were not wanting here too. The great manufacturing towns which had always been the seat of Liberalism, witnessed the gradual formation of a Tory society in their midst. In former days there had been no Tory society in the industrial centres, but only a Tory following recruited almost entirely among the populace and attracted by the two-fold power of "beer and Bible." In proportion as the political and commercial claims of the middle class were satisfied and it had to defend its own position against new assailants, its Liberalism evaporated and it became Conservative; it joined the Tory party. In this way there were many manufacturers, doctors, barristers, and other professional men who hoisted the Tory flag. Inhabiting large towns not subject to the territorial influences around which gathered the traditional Tory society, and made more independent or more proud by their social status, they were not so ready as the classic Tory to submit tamely to external influences. Shaking hands with the big-wigs of the party who occasionally visited their town was not enough for them; they aspired to gratifications of a less ephemeral kind. The hole-and-corner management of the affairs of the party, so long in vogue with the Tories as with the Liberals, if it offered a prospect of real and continuous influence, procured it only for a handful of persons who formed the small managing coterie, but this latter was materially and morally too narrow to afford scope to all the ambitions which were now coming to the front. To penetrate within the charmed circle it was necessary to show one's credentials, and a good many Tories who wanted to have a share of influence had no other title than their personal qualities. In a word, the Tory party, which had hitherto been composed mainly of the aristocracy

and the populace, henceforth possessed a *tiers état* in the large
towns, and this "third estate" wished to be of importance like
its historic namesake. The local autonomy entailed by the reorganization of the party on popular lines held out the desired
sphere of influence to the Tory *tiers;* while at the same time the
representative machinery of the new organization with its elections, public meetings, and speeches helped to a certain extent
to satisfy the desire for publicity inseparable from the life
of large agglomerations of individuals. Led by these varied
motives, the Tories, someti nes reluctantly, sometimes with a
good grace, borrowed their model of organization from the
Liberals, while continuing to revile the Caucus in public.
Without making too much fuss, they set up representative
Associations in one town after another, which bore a considerable resemblance to the genuine Caucuses. Beginning during
the period of 1880–1885, this evolution was destined to become
more and more marked. It coincided with the movement of
the mutineers of the Fourth Party, and both of them helped
each other to a considerable extent. Entering on a path which
Tory foot had never trod, the provincial movement had need to
be reassured as to the course which it was taking, to be encouraged, nay to be roused. The "Fourth Party" and especially
one of its members, Lord Randolph Churchill, supplied it with
the required stimulus.

VI

Lord Randolph Churchill had speedily eclipsed his colleagues
in the eyes of the great mass of the public. He had forced
himself on their attention by his extraordinary conduct in the
House. The son of a Tory duke, of a Marlborough, he broke
his political allegiance; setting every one at defiance, he took
up a position by himself and, what was still more remarkable,
he did wonders in it. Full of imperturbable self-confidence,
with a vehement audacity under perfect control, always in the
breach, he laid about him with the ferocious resolution of an
inverted Decius Mus, devoting his opponents to the infernal
gods. Quickwitted and going to the point, he combined fairly
close reasoning with incisive and caustic language, which,
however, had no resemblance to the poisoned irony of Lord
Salisbury or the biting sarcasm of Disraeli. Churchill's elo-

quence was not so much stinging as burning, of a coarse combustible matter like the bitumen, the darting flames of which are thought a grand sight by the crowds at country fairs. This was just the effect which his virulent style produced on the small townspeople who were the mainstay of the new party organization, commercial *employés*, clerks, newspaper-reading artisans. They applauded him frantically. The young lord talking Billingsgate impressed their imaginations; the champion of the people's cause, in which character he posed, won their hearts. His temperament was a wonderful help to him in achieving, almost without loss of sincerity, this success with the Tory lower class; for he was unquestionably endowed with a popular instinct genuine enough to place him in sympathy with the masses although not deep enough to take him out of the traditional surroundings of Toryism which he made his base of operations. To the classic type of popular aristocrat so familiar from the Gracchi downwards, Churchill united the feeling of religious respect of his race for " property " and the cant of his caste with regard to " institutions." The history of English Toryism even presented a precedent, of a somewhat vague resemblance it is true, for a similar anomalous political combination which brought success to its author. Thus, his mind haunted by the recollection of Lord Beaconsfield's wonderful career, and dreaming of " Elijah's mantle " [1] falling on him, Lord Randolph adopted for his own use Disraeli's youthful methods as well as his creed of popular Toryism. But he discarded the reservations of the great deceased leader which wrapped the latter's doctrine in obscurity; his would-be successor threw light on it in his own fashion. In an oratorical campaign which he made in the country, during 1883–1884, he went about proclaiming that Radicalism was nothing but humbug; that the Tories whom he, Churchill, represented were the most genuine democrats in existence, and the best friends of the people. " The well-known proverb ' *Vox populi, vox Dei* ' is to the Whig as sounding brass and tinkling cymbals, for they have always existed by corrupting and deceiving the people. To the Radicals it is a fetish of the lowest order, for they exist by driving and

[1] Cf. the article by Lord Randolph Churchill, " Elijah's Mantle," *Fortnightly Review*, 1883, Vol. 33.

tyrannizing over the people. But to the Tories ' *Vox populi,
vox Dei*' is an ever-springing faith, a vivifying principle, an
undying truth, without which their politics would be as naught,
without a future and without a hope. . . . The Tory party
of to-day exists by the favour of no caucus, nor for the selfish
interests of any class. Its motto is — Of the people, for the
people, by the people." [1] " I have long tried to take as my
motto the phrase used recently by Mr. Gladstone, ' Trust the
people.' There are few in the Conservative party who have
still that lesson to learn, and who do not yet understand that
the Tory party of to-day can no longer be dependent upon the
small and narrow class identified with the ownership of land;
but that its strength must be found and developed in our large
towns as well as in our country districts. Trust the people,
and they will follow us in the defence of the Constitution
against any and every foe." [2] Up in London, at the party
headquarters, "they regard with some apprehension the popular voice, but I have no doubt the popular voice will soon sub-
side. I look to the Associations to popularize the organization
of our party. Our object is to obtain a representative executive who will hold itself responsible to the electors who appoint it. In fact my idea, and it is the idea of my friends,
is that the Tory party shall be like the English people —
a self-governing party." [3]

This language was a spur to the young Tories in the large
towns. Lord Randolph Churchill and his friends of the Fourth
Party felt in their turn that they had support in the country;
in their struggle with the leaders of the Tory party they
could count upon public opinion organized in and identified
with the popular Associations. The latter thus supplied the
Neo-Tories with an engine for overthrowing the stronghold of
the official leaders just as the Neo-Radicals had found one in
the Birmingham Caucus, which, moreover, inspired Lord Randolph with great admiration.[4] It was the same game, the same
methods, and the same style.

---

[1] Speech delivered at Blackpool, 24th January, 1884.
[2] Speech at Birmingham, 16th April, 1884.   [3] *Ibid.*
[4] As he acknowledged afterwards, in his speech the 30th of June, 1886, at
Manchester, " I must confess to having always had a sneaking admiration
for the [Birmingham Liberal] Organization."

They were destined, however, to be reinforced by an inno-vation of an original kind. In Lord Beaconsfield's political inheritance Lord Randolph Churchill and his fellow-workers had found, among a number of valuable examples and pre-cepts, the maxim that to secure victory the imagination of the people must be acted on, that the appeal must be made to its sentiments, to its emotions. Disraeli had himself endeav-oured to give shape to these ideas in *Young England*, without much success, however. His successors and continuators de-cided to go to work in a more practical way. Coming down from the dreamland in which the young Disraeli dwelt, their idea was to adapt themselves to the conditions of society as it was. Breaking loose from the landlords who were the princi-pal personages in the drama of *Young England*, they aspired to bind all classes of the nation in a sentimental alliance, by appealing to popular emotions which would be converted into political energy by the impulse given to the imagination. The modern method of organization would provide a form for the alliance, would supply it with its framework and secure the play of its forces. By placing the alliance on a wide national basis political energy would be made to circulate through the Tory party like the blood throughout the body, and the leaders would be reduced to impotence, the haughty, selfish aristocrats who monopolized power and bestowed all the good things on their friends and relations. Having planned this new *coup* against the chiefs, the Fourth Party were much afraid that the latter would get wind of it and frustrate it. Its authors, therefore, wrapped it in the deepest secrecy. It was in a corner of the Carlton Club itself, the whole atmosphere of which is saturated with respect for the leaders, that they met to mysteriously lay the foundations of a new political cult for the Tories. Wor-shipping at the same shrine of personal honour and national pride, the members of the new Association were to form a new chivalry. Just as mediæval chivalry, animated by the senti-ment of honour, made itself the champion of every good cause, so the members of the Tory brotherhood were to devote themselves to the defence of Conservative principles, to the maintenance of religion, of the Estates of the Realm, and of the imperial supremacy of the British Empire. They were to bind themselves by an engagement and to form companies

which they would enter first as *squires*, rising afterwards to
the rank of *knights*. The favourite flower of the illustrious
departed chief, of Lord Beaconsfield, the primrose, was to be
the symbol of their alliance, which would take the title of
"The Primrose Tory League." The romanticism of the Middle Ages did not supply any appropriate methods for making
the league known and for enlisting members, and its founders
were obliged to resort to those of our own day and to insert
advertisements in the newspapers. The future squires and
knights were asked to send in their names to a bank at which
Lord Randolph Churchill kept his account. The appeal issued
in this manner was anonymous, none of the promoters of the
league signed it, to prevent the secret being discovered. The
plan met with the support of a few Tory members of Parliament who did not belong to the Fourth Party, and also of the
leading men of the Tory *tiers état* in the provincial towns.
Very unpretending at the beginning, the movement in a short
time developed to an extraordinary extent. While departing
from the lines laid down for it by its founders, the Primrose
League achieved an unprecedented success, and soon became,
as we shall see, a most powerful factor in the organization of
the Tory party.

EIGHTH CHAPTER

THE CONSERVATIVE ORGANIZATION (*continued*)

I

WHATEVER were the hopes placed in the Primrose League by its initiators, the movement was yet in its infancy, and their principal resource in the way of organization still remained the Associations. Encouraging and stimulating, therefore, the democratization of the local Associations which were to serve as a lever for the Neo-Toryism, the Fourth Party thought that the fulcrum of this lever might be supplied by the Council of the "National Union of Conservative and Constitutional Associations." Not in its actual condition, however; for it lacked vitality, had no material resources or moral authority, and was simply a show institution, a shadow of a representative body of Conservative opinion side by side with the small coterie of official leaders who wielded real power in the party. Immediately after Lord Beaconsfield's death, before the leadership had been filled up, an attempt was made to transfer the supreme authority to the "Council of the National Union." It was proposed that the Council should appoint Lord Beaconsfield's successor to the leadership of the party in Parliament. The plan was a bold one, it was equivalent to forcing a chief for life on the Tory members of both Houses from outside. But it fell through, and the peers and members elected their respective leaders themselves — Lord Salisbury for the Upper House and Sir Stafford Northcote for the House of Commons. When the movement of the democratic Associations acquired consistency in the country and Lord Randolph Churchill's ascendancy grew more marked, the Fourth Party returned to the charge. At its instigation, in the annual meeting of delegates of the Associations, held at Birmingham in 1883, the Conference gave instructions to the Council

of the *Union* to " obtain for this body its legitimate share in the
control of the organization of the party." Elected President
on the first renewal of the Council, Lord Randolph Churchill
demanded the exclusive management of the affairs of the party
for the *Union*. The official leaders were called upon to resign.
They had their own Organization which, as in the old days on
the Liberal side, was a development of the office of Whip —
that is to say, the Whips and some other members of the party
appointed for this purpose by the leaders formed a small *Central Committee* which disposed of the party funds, looked after
parliamentary candidatures and other matters connected with
the organization of the party in the country. The *Union of
Associations* demanded the dissolution of the Central Committee, and the transfer to itself of all the latter's powers. The
official leaders, Lord Salisbury and Sir Stafford Northcote, were
naturally not much inclined to part with their influence, especially in favour of the Fourth Party, which had seized on the
Union. They negotiated; and, while declaring their readiness
to enter into the *Union's* views, demanded that the Whips
should be made *ex officio* members of the Council of the
Union with the right of voting, but Lord Randolph Churchill
insisted on the Council being a strictly representative body.
The Marquis of Salisbury at last broke off the negotiations rather abruptly. He gave the *Union* notice to quit
the rooms which it was occupying in the office of the head-
quarters of the party, and intimated that the leaders declined all further responsibility for the acts of the *Union*.
Lord Randolph replied to the Marquis in a very determined letter, for which he obtained the approval of a majority of the Council, and in which he reproached him with
wishing that " the Council of the Union should be completely
and permanently reduced to its old position of dependence on
and servility towards certain irresponsible persons who found
favour in his [Lord Salisbury's] eyes." " It is quite clear to
us," remarked Lord Randolph, "that in the letters we have
from time to time addressed to you, and in the conversations
which we have had the honour of holding with you on this
subject, we have hopelessly failed to convey to your mind
anything like an appreciation either of the significance of the
movement which the National Union commenced at Birming-

ham in October last, or of the unfortunate effect which a neglect or repression of that movement by the leaders of the party
would have upon the Conservative cause. The resolution at
the Conference at Birmingham . . . signified that the old
methods of party organization, namely, the control of parliamentary elections by the leader, the Whips, the paid agents
drawing their resources from secret funds, which were suitable to the manipulation of the ten-pound householder, were
utterly obsolete, and would not secure the confidence of the
masses of the people who were enfranchised by Mr. Disraeli's
Reform Bill, and that the time had arrived when the centre
of organizing energy should be an elected, representative, and
responsible body. The delegates at the Conference were evidently of opinion that if the principles of the Conservative
party were to obtain popular support, the organization of the
party would have to become an imitation, thoroughly real and
bona fide in its nature, of that popular form of representative
organization which had contributed so greatly to the triumph
of the Liberal party in 1880, and which was best known to the
public by the name of the Birmingham Caucus. The Caucus
may be, perhaps, a name of evil sound and omen in the ears of
aristocratic or privileged classes, but it is undeniably the only
form of political organization which can collect, guide, and control for common objects large masses of electors." Alluding
to the negotiations which had taken place, Lord Randolph
Churchill said: "The Council committed the serious error of
imagining that your lordship and Sir Stafford Northcote were
in earnest in wishing to become a real source of usefulness to
the party. . . . The Council has been rudely undeceived."

The orthodox Tories were scandalized at this attitude of Lord
Randolph, and accused him of wishing to make the *Union* a
caucus not only in the sense of a representative organization
but for the purpose of dictating to members of Parliament
and to local Associations like the Birmingham Caucus. The
Tory instincts of deference, or, to adopt the language of Lord
Randolph Churchill, of servility toward the leaders, reasserted
themselves even among the members of the majority of the
Council of the *Union*, and retracing its steps it decided to seek
a *modus vivendi* with the leaders. Interpreting this decision
as a vote of censure on himself, and thinking that he was left

in the lurch, Lord Randolph resigned the chairmanship of the
Council and gave out that he was going abroad for a time.   For
the moment he seemed to have the worst of it, but in reality
his position was an excellent one; for whatever may have been
his personal motives, in the eyes of the public he embodied,
at this particular juncture, the popular principle as against the
domineering spirit of aristocratic exclusiveness, the very real
need for a wider basis of party organization which the interested adherents of the old " hole-and-corner " style of management refused to satisfy.   The excitement produced by Lord
Randolph Churchill's resignation was very great in the Tory
party in general and especially among his admirers, the representatives of popular Toryism in the provinces.   The Associations of the great towns set to work at once, their Chairmen
met in London and drew up a declaration of principles which
put forward the basis of a compromise between Lord Salisbury
and Randolph Churchill, between the traditional leadership
and the voice of the people aspiring to be master of its destinies, and at the same time dispelled the apprehensions that
the Union might become a tyrannical caucus like the Radical
machine.   The memorandum declared the following to be
" fundamental principles in any Conservative organization ":
" non-interference on the part of political associations with
the direction of matters incident to the duties and policy of
our members in Parliament; " the right of every Association
to " full independence of action in the management of its local
political matters "; the necessity of having a " thoroughly
representative central elective council sitting in London."
Pointing out that the National Union presented the outline of
such a Council, the memorandum demanded that a reorganization of this body on a wider basis, which would make it
thoroughly representative of the Conservative party in the
country, should be taken in hand at once.   But at the same
time the authors of the Declaration agreed to admit two representatives of the leaders on the Council, as *ex officio* members,
and left the finances of the party, the questions of general
policy, and the selection of candidates in cases in which the
constituencies desired it, entirely in their hands.   Lord Salisbury, lowering his tone, consented somewhat ill-humouredly to
the proposed compromise.   Lord Randolph Churchill accepted

it much more enthusiastically,[1] and was eventually elected Chairman by a unanimous vote.

This *dénoûment* was undoubtedly a considerable success for the principle of popular Organization, for it was to this principle that Lord Salisbury bowed; it was in its favour that he relinquished some of the pretensions of the leadership which he had hitherto maintained with uncompromising haughtiness. It is not very likely that, as some people thought, it was a wish not to divide the Opposition forces in the House and to present a united front in the impending conflict with the Liberals, which overcame the Marquis of Salisbury's resistance, for the influence of the Fourth Party in the House itself was extremely slight. Great as was the valour of these doughty knights, they were only four in number — no more and no less. It was more their position outside Parliament, their popularity in the country, the enthusiasm with which Lord Randolph Churchill inspired the members of the democratic Organizations, which forced Lord Salisbury's hand. The domestic quarrel which had just ended showed that the Associations would have to be reckoned with in the future, although they represented only a section of Conservative opinion, and that with them a new factor was gaining admittance into the daily life of the Tory party. The space assigned to it was still limited, as the compromise proposed by the representatives of the local Associations themselves proved: in spite of all their jealousy of the leaders who were accustomed to exercise autocratic power, they gave up to the latter a fairly extensive sphere of influence of their own free will. Evidently Tory society was not yet ripe for democratic self-government, from the lowest to the highest rung in the ladder; the prestige of the aristocratic chiefs was still a power among so many other social forces which Tories submitted to as to those of nature. Not making allowances for this state of things, and remembering only their oath to be revenged on the leaders, Lord Randolph Churchill's colleagues of the Fourth Party were, it would appear, highly dissatisfied with the solution given to the conflict; they thought that Lord Randolph was wrong

---

[1] Cf. the letters written in reply to the memorandum which was submitted to them by Lord Salisbury, Sir Stafford Northcote, and Lord Randolph Churchill (*Times*, 19th May, 1884).

in not fighting the matter out and in not pinning Lord
Salisbury to the wall of the democratic organization of the
party; that he had left them in the lurch, and that, in fact, he
had "gone over to the other side." It is quite possible that
Churchill may have been guided by personal considerations in
making peace with the aristocratic leaders, and that if he had
not been in such a hurry to return to the aristocratic fold, he
might have been able to get more, for people soon come to
terms with the popular spectre. But the compromise was so
little of a failure that the adherents of the leaders were burning to take their revenge, and at the first annual meeting of
delegates of the Associations, which took place at Sheffield,
they gave battle to Lord Randolph Churchill and the democratic section. With signal clumsiness they ostentatiously displayed their motto of "loyalty and unity of the Conservative
party under its recognized leaders." They were beaten in
every encounter,[1] and the principle of democratic organization
issued from the struggle more triumphant than ever. With
the complete local autonomy which the leaders themselves had
conceded to the Associations, and with an elective and representative central organ,[2] it was now for them to assert themselves, and even to try and supplant the leaders in the latter's
own preserve. Theoretically at least it had been established
that the Conservative party was a "self-governing body"; no
more "natural leaders" of whom Disraeli used to dream, no
more landlords round whom, according to him, the people
could always rally. At last one distinct point, clearly visible
to the naked eye, could be made out through the haze of
"popular Toryism": the "popular" character of the Tory
party was showing itself in the democratic organization which
it adopted.

II

But was the new Toryism to stop there? Was it enough
to provide the Tory party with a popular organization to make
it a popular party?

[1] Cf. the report of the Conference in the *Times*, of the 24th July, 1884.
[2] The Council of the Union had only 24 elected members, who added 12 to
their number. At the Sheffield Conference it was decided that "co-optation"
should be abolished and that all the 36 members of the Council should be
chosen by the general meeting of delegates.

When the Tory party set to work to interrogate itself directly after the defeat of 1880, it was recognized that besides the reform of organization the party also needed a new clearly defined policy, of a positive and not merely negative character, a progressive policy capable of solving the rising problems of the day. The Tory party, it was said, ought no longer to be a party of resistance, but it should acquiesce in and promote all the timely reforms for which society is already ripe. This is the traditional function of the Liberal party, but true Liberalism has no place in the Liberal party as it now exists; the organization of this party is in the hands of the Radicals and they are not likely to lose control of the "machine." The spirit of true Liberalism is not extinct, but it is a spirit without a body. The body of Conservatism exists, but it lacks a soul. Would it not be possible to blend the two into one vigorous whole and form a constitutional party taking in both Tories and Liberals, which would be the champion of liberty and the opponent of equality, which would recognize that despotism is always despotism whether it is exercised by an individual or by a mob? It was a programme of enlightened Conservatism, clearly outlined and logical, which assigned an extremely honourable if not a brilliant rôle to the Tory party. But it did not suit the young Tories; they wanted their party to be, not the buffer or the safety-valve of the steam engine, but its furnace and boiler. And so far as they were concerned, they boldly adopted *democratic Toryism* as their programme. As in the case of Disraeli's "popular Toryism," the question arose — What would it consist of, what would be the fruit of the union of Toryism and democracy? The town of Liverpool conceived the ambition of bringing the new political species into the world. "Birmingham has taken the lead in the country of the party aiming at revolutionary changes; in like manner the Conservatives of Liverpool aspire to head the phalanx of men, who, while sound upon constitutional principles, are yet alive to the necessity for such national progress as the growing intelligence of the age demands."[1] As in the home of the Caucus, here, too, it was the municipality, and especially the mayor, the author of the passage just quoted,

---

[1] "Democratic Toryism," by A. B. Forwood, *Contemporary Review*, February, 1883.

who headed the movement. The principles which he professed for himself and on behalf of his political coreligionists were those of the stereotyped creed of Toryism, — Throne, House of Lords, Church and State, unity of the British Empire. The Tories of Liverpool met the progress demanded by the enlightenment of the age, chiefly by introducing and keeping up pleasant relations with the masses. Any one who had business with the municipality was received in the most amiable way, services were rendered most obligingly on all sides, the leading Tories had no objection to taking part in popular gatherings, they were "not the least proud," they mingled unaffectedly with the "people," and did not even take offence at the turbulence which it too often exhibited, — a natural characteristic of the populace of a great seaport town.[1] This attitude was all the more successful in winning the people's hearts, because the Whigs of Liverpool were one of the most disagreeable types of the species; merchant princes of three or four generations, with a positively dynastic dignity, stiff, stuck-up, they were cordially detested.[2] Their political rivals, the Tories, on the other hand, had "confidence in the people," and the people "reciprocated the sentiment." They urged the "leading citizens" of the great towns to follow their example, and to make some exertions to meet the wish of the workingmen for "common political association" with them. For the experience of the promoters of Tory democracy in Liverpool made them believe and assert that the "workingmen are far from sympathizing with the radical shibboleth for abolishing class distinctions; nor are they advocates of the doctrine of equality and fraternity in a republican sense." They understood the need of being governed by men of a superior stamp, and their only complaint was: "the leaders do not come amongst us sufficiently often."[3]

Lord Randolph Churchill developed the same views with all the authority which now attached to his name; on behalf of

[1] Later on when, at Liverpool as well as elsewhere, the Liberal Unionists joined the Tories, owing to the Liberal split on the Home Rule question in 1886, they were astonished and even scandalized at the turbulence displayed by the lower-class Tory voters at political meetings and at the tolerance shown by the leading Conservatives in these circumstances.

[2] Their demeanour got them the nickname of "red currant jelly."

[3] Cf. the article "Democratic Toryism" just quoted.

the Tory democracy he proclaimed his "reverence and affection for the institutions of the country which the Radicals regard with aversion"; [1] he would not abate one jot of the political inequalities which they enshrined; the House of Lords, for instance, was "the nucleus of the Tory party" in his eyes; "the existence of the party is inseparable from the existence of an hereditary Chamber; as inseparable as the latter is from the existence of an hereditary monarchy." [2] Without troubling himself to provide formulas, he repeated after Disraeli: "Rally the people around the Throne, unite the Throne to the people, a loyal Throne and a patriotic people — this is our policy and this is our creed." [3] "The social progress of the people by means of legislative reform in the lines and carried under the protection of the (ancient) institutions . . . that must be the Conservative cry, as opposed to the foolish scream for organic change by the Radicals, who waste their time in attacking institutions whose destruction would only endanger popular freedom." [4] This programme of social reform or rather these protestations of devotion to the material welfare of the masses were interspersed with compliments paid to the latter. They had all the virtues, they were the fountain-head of political wisdom, their judgment was infallible: "*Vox populi, vox Dei* — that is only too common;" "governments will go wrong, parliaments will go wrong, classes will go wrong, London society and the Pall Mall clubs always go wrong; but the people do not go wrong." [5]

III

Loading the people in this way with attentions, the promoters of *Tory democracy* nevertheless refused to concede to them what is the very essence of democracy, viz., political equality; they withheld it inside the Constitution while granting it outside the Constitution in the form of a democratic organization of the party. There was a contradiction in this which, if it might be used as a basis for the particular species of "Tory

[1] Speech at Birmingham, 16th April, 1884.
[2] "Elijah's Mantle," *Fortnightly Review*, 1883, Vol. 33.
[3] Speech at Birmingham quoted above.   [4] *Ibid.*
[5] Speech at Blackpool, 24th January, 1884.

democracy," not only undermined the foundations of Toryism but still more those of Conservatism, of real Conservatism. When numbers were proclaimed the sole arbiter, when their shifting will was the only guide of the party's existence, how would the party be able not only to keep the "ancient institutions" intact, but to regulate or check the political progress of the nation in accordance with the dictates of reason and experience, while opposing the reactionary prejudices or unreflecting impulses of the mob? how would the party be able to withdraw this or that institution, which is to be maintained or abolished, from the clamour of the market-place, after having made it the seat of all power? Were not the "Tory democrats" unsettling even the theoretical foundations of Conservatism which Disraeli, to whose authority they were continually appealing, was anxious to preserve throughout all his twists and turnings? Although his popular sympathies were far deeper than those of the Churchills, he did not contrast the "classes" who always go wrong with the "masses" who do not go wrong, he did not offer their nostrils the savour of a holocaust of leaders, he did not identify the nation with the "people" whose voice is the voice of God, but regarded it, in conformity with true Conservative ideas, as a spontaneous union of classes placed side by side. Having driven the Tory party into the arms of democracy, Disraeli vehemently denied the fact, from a remnant of scrupulousness, in order to keep up appearances. His would-be successors noisily paraded the irregular union of Toryism and democracy. Even if, as the "Tory democrats" asserted, it were intended only to make the old home safer, yet they were setting up there in the place of Conservatism a new kind of plebiscitary Cæsarism exercised not by an individual but by a huge syndicate: by means of well-adjusted legislation the people will get its *panem* (the *circenses* will soon follow) and in return will allow the Tory party to govern with its Lords, Established Church, and landed interest; the Tory party will not assume this mandate itself, the aristocratic leaders will not be allowed to invest themselves with it, but the people assembled in the gatherings of the party, in the caucuses, will confer it on the men of its choice.

But suppose the people is not satisfied with delivering the

mandate, suppose it takes it into its head to alter the tenor thereof, can it be prevented from doing so? In demanding a Radical revolution in the organization of the party, had not the "Tory democrats" themselves declared that "rights of property, the Established Church, the House of Lords, nay even the Crown, could only be maintained in so far as the people considers them necessary and useful for the preservation of liberty?"[1] The existence of the Tory party however, being bound up with political inequalities, according to the "Tory democrats" themselves, how would the latter be able to preserve them and at the same time retain the favour of the masses who are continually being tempted by alluring offers coming from the other side? Being powerless to hold the balance between these conflicting exigencies, they will have nothing but expedients of equilibrists to fall back upon. In order not to be beaten by Radical competition, they will part with the political inequalities one after another, in the fashion inaugurated by Disraeli. This will be their connecting link with him. On the opportunist Toryism, of which he was the founder, they will have grafted, by means of the Caucus borrowed from the Radicals and of fervent professions of popular faith, the democratic, and, to a certain extent, demagogic Toryism, which by the power of *sic volo sic jubeo* inherent in the nature of democracy will sanction every kind of tergiversation and every change of front with more authority than all the arguments of Disraeli.

IV

This evolution was not long in coming: it showed itself immediately in a startling way, in the first political crisis brought on by the question of the extension of the suffrage to the rural population. This question was before Parliament during the whole of 1884, the same year in which democratic Toryism definitively gained a footing in the country. The Tory leaders, who had been so terribly scandalized by the democratic attitude of the Neo-Tories, soon adopted it on their own account. Being unwilling, for fear of the rural voter, to oppose the actual principle of extension of the suffrage in the counties which

---

[1] "Conservative Disorganization," quoted above.

seemed to them inevitable, they concentrated their resistance on the question of the *redistribution of seats*. As had been the case at every preceding electoral reform, the creation of new categories of electors was to be accompanied by a rearrangement of the constituencies to amend the old distribution of seats which had been settled in a rather arbitrary way, and not in accordance with the importance of the population. In the interest of their party, the Tories were very anxious that the traditional constituencies, which varied greatly in area and population, should be preserved, with their old social influences, to as great an extent as possible, while the Liberals wished to swamp them in electoral districts carved out in a uniform manner according to the population. The Tory minority of the House of Commons, supported by the majority of the House of Lords, declined to vote for the extension of the suffrage before seeing the schedule of new constituencies, which would be submitted for their consideration when too late. The conflict between the two Houses looked very threatening for a moment; but when, in order to terminate it, the leaders of both parties agreed to negotiate, the concessions spontaneously made by the Tory leader threw the Liberals into a state alike of jubilation and stupefaction; their rivals unhesitatingly accepted a plan of redistribution of seats on an almost arithmetical basis.[1]

When the conflict about the redistribution of seats was in full swing, the Radical Caucus set all its machinery in motion to excite public opinion against the Tories by making the Associations pass angry resolutions, by organizing meetings of protestation and processions, etc. Lord Salisbury could not find words strong enough to denounce this way of settling the differences between the two branches of the legislature. "They descend into the streets," he exclaimed; "they call for processions. They imagine that 30,000 Radicals going to amuse themselves in London on a given day expresses the public opinion of the country. This is not the way in which a pro-

---

[1] A publicist who had occasion to see one of the Liberal negotiators, a leading Minister, in privacy on the following day said: "The Minister's mood will always remain in my memory as a measure of the vast change effected by Lord Salisbury's sudden adoption of the democratic principle" ("The Electoral Future," by Edward R. Russell, *Contemporary Review*, February, 1885).

gressive, cultured, and civilized State determines the opinion of its citizens. . . . They appeal to the streets; they attempt legislation by picnic. But that has its dangerous side. There is no more hopeless condition in which a popularly governed State can be plunged than when its policy is decided by demonstrations held in the streets of the metropolis."[1] On the following day, in Sheffield itself, where these words were uttered, at the meeting of the National Union of Conservative Associations, was fought the battle between the followers of the leaders and the disciples of democratic Toryism. The latter, as we have seen, won the day. The Conservative organization, in its turn, set its machinery going to retort upon the Radical Caucus, and Lord Salisbury hastened to co-operate in this campaign of "picnics." A fortnight after his speech at Sheffield he paraded his connection with Randolph Churchill, and, appearing on the same platform[2] with him, before an enormous crowd, which had flocked together from "the streets," took democratic Toryism and its boldest champion to his bosom. Before long he honoured them with a still more emphatic recognition: when a parliamentary surprise brought him into power, in 1885, he offered Lord Randolph Churchill a leading place in his Cabinet; and to crown his attentions to the "Tory democrats," he sent the illustrious Sir Stafford Northcote, whose truly Conservative conduct had a knack of exasperating them, to the House of Lords. The Ministry in which Lord Randolph Churchill and his friends took their places launched out at once into a policy of State Socialism, so that Mr. Chamberlain was able to say, with some degree of truth, that "the Tories were in office, but the Radicals in power."[3] At the same time, the "Tory democrats" and Lord Randolph Churchill kept on proclaiming that Radicalism, if it had its way, would plunge England into the abysses of demagogism, and they called to the moderate Liberals to come over and join them. "It is possible," replied Lord Hartington, "that there are some subjects upon which there exists less difference of opinion between some members of the Conserva-

[1] Speech of the 22d July, 1884, at Sheffield.
[2] At the great public demonstration of the 9th August, 1884, in the Pomona Gardens at Manchester.
[3] Speech of the 31st July, 1885, at Hackney.

tive party and myself than between myself and some of the more irresponsible and advanced members of my own party. But I confess that I still find some difficulty in understanding what Conservative policy is, and what I am invited to come over to help the Conservative party to do. . . .   I am obliged to confess, in reply to that invitation addressed to me by Lord Randolph Churchill, that in the leaders of the Conservative party I feel no confidence whatever." [1]   The moderate Liberals, who were swamped by the Radicals, and were asking themselves in despair if the moment had not come to shake the dust off their feet, were bound to ponder Lord Hartington's words.   The same wind, in fact, was blowing from the Tory side as on the heights of Radicalism : it was tearing the leaves from the old trees, and by sweeping along their trunks was dooming them to speedy destruction.   And as a climax, in the large gaps which were already appearing at intervals on Tory ground, the Caucus was seen to rise, — the same Caucus which had done so much to make the position of the moderates in the old abode of Liberalism untenable.   If they were to go over to the other side, would they not be exchanging Charybdis for Scylla ?   A thunder-clap which burst in the political sky suddenly relieved them from the perplexity in which they were plunged.   This was the crisis brought on by the question of Home Rule for Ireland.

[1] Speech of the 10th October, 1885, at Rawtenstall.

NINTH CHAPTER

I

IRELAND, which had long been like a thorn planted in the body
politic of England, had at last worked its way into the heart of
her parliamentary system. The representatives of irreconcilable Irish opinion had gradually become so numerous in the
House of Commons that they stopped the regular working of
the old party system by interposing between the two parties, or
even paralyzed the activity of Parliament by their systematic
obstruction. The price which they demanded was Home Rule,
the political autonomy of their country. But nearly the whole
of English opinion and English statesmen, Conservative and
Liberal, would not hear of it. Mr. Gladstone, therefore, at the
general election of 1885 asked the country to return a Liberal
majority strong enough to deal with the Conservatives and the
Irish together, and thus make the latter powerless. This wish
was not gratified; the Irish Home Rulers came back in greater
numbers than ever, and it was only by the aid of their votes that
the Liberals would be able to overcome the Conservatives and
dislodge them from power, which they had held for some time.
Mr. Gladstone then took a sudden resolution in which, as was
always the case with him, the calculations of a parliamentary
tactician and of a party *impresario* coincided with the impulses
of a generous nature and the aspirations of a lofty mind : he
decided to offer the Irish Home Rule in order to secure a
majority and put an end to the enmity between the two nations.
But would he be followed in this abrupt change of front ?
Would his great authority and the wonderful prestige of his
name be strong enough to carry with him the whole body of

those who up to this point followed him inside and outside
Parliament?

The vague rumours as to Mr. Gladstone's plans which began
to circulate directly after the elections were quite enough to
produce such a deep impression in the Liberal camp that a
split seemed inevitable. The Conservative Ministry, which
had not obtained a majority at the elections, was placed in a
minority in the House on the first opportunity, and Mr. Gladstone was entrusted with the task of forming the new Administration. The moderates, the Whigs, declined for the first time
to join it; Lord Hartington, Mr. Goschen, Sir Henry James,
all refused to take office; they had a presentiment that the
time was drawing near when they would be obliged rather
to cut themselves adrift.[1] In fact, directly Mr. Gladstone produced his Home Rule scheme the moderate Liberals, led by
Lord Hartington, parted company with him. In face of what
they considered as endangering the unity of the Empire and
the very foundation of the English constitutional system, they
no longer hesitated to combine with the Conservatives against
the man who had been the great representative of Liberalism,
but who, in their eyes, had become simply the leader of a destructive type of Radicalism. The situation became strangely
complicated, owing to the fact that Mr. Gladstone was unable
to obtain the unanimous approval of his own Ministers for his
new Irish policy. In spite of their proved Radicalism, two of
them, of whom Mr. Chamberlain was one, taking up a purely
Imperial standpoint, preferred to forego power rather than co-
operate in a measure which, in their opinion, made for the
disintegration of the Empire. Mr. Gladstone then had to face
a resistance within his own party which was all the more formidable because he could not set up the will of the electorate
against it to justify the granting of Home Rule, for the question was not laid before the constituencies. An appeal was
now to be made after the event to Liberal opinion, but the
latter was for the most part identified with the caucuses which
acknowledged and obeyed the leadership of Mr. Chamberlain.
The party Organization which had been constructed with so

---

[1] The caucus of the town which Sir H. James represented construed this
refusal as an act of "insubordination" against Mr. Gladstone and passed a
severe censure on the member who declined to take office.

much labour was about to undergo a terrible ordeal. Was it to forsake the man who had, so to speak, called it into existence, and who was the most authoritative representative of the democratic Radicalism to which it appealed; or was it to follow the old chief of the Liberal party in his struggle for a measure which was in the strict logic of Radicalism? If it revolted against Mr. Chamberlain, would it not run the risk of shattering its fabric, by causing a split in its own ranks? If, on the other hand, it took sides against Mr. Gladstone, would it not be exposed to the same danger? Or, to put the question in another way, would the authority of the illustrious statesman be strong enough to deprive the Caucus of its followers? would the traditional leadership embodied in Mr. Gladstone prevail against the representative Organization which was introduced on the pretext of destroying the power of the leaders, however great and influential they might be? Thus side by side with questions of persons and of circumstances, the fundamental problem of the Organization itself was being debated.

On the eve of the Home Rule debate in the House of Commons the Liberal Federation Committee requested all the affiliated Associations to consider the question and to forward it the resolutions which they might adopt, after which a general meeting of delegates was to decide on the Bill on behalf of the Liberal party. Opinion was much divided in the Associations; the members had or still wished to have confidence in Mr. Gladstone, but on the subject of Home Rule there was a good deal of wavering and irresolution which Mr. Chamberlain's resistance by no means helped to dispel. The perplexity of the Associations was further enhanced by the fact that the Federation, realizing the division of opinion, confined itself on this occasion, contrary to its usual practice, to a simple statement of the problem without suggesting to the local Associations what answer should be given. Left to their own inspiration. the Associations for the most part did not know what line to take. They who were supposed to have the power of giving expression to public opinion and of pointing out the policy to be pursued by their rulers, could do nothing but stammer. True, they voted resolutions, and lengthy ones, but without giving a plain answer: Yes or No, for or against the Home Rule Bill. And it was left to Mr. Chamberlain to utter the feeling cry: "Why are you here? Why are you formed? Why do you remain an Association for Birmingham?"[1] After having been drilled into being only a *claque*, it was no easy matter for them to blossom suddenly into art critics.

II

While in Parliament preparations were being made for the great battle between those who had followed Mr. Gladstone's example in becoming converts to Home Rule and those who adhered to the old views of the Liberal party on the Irish question, the country was in a state of suppressed agitation. Mr. Gladstone's mighty voice was making its way into the national conscience, and in face of the Gladstonian flood which began to rise in the Associations, a good many of their members withdrew from them or were ready to go. In the midst of all this the delegates of the Liberal Associations met in London and there, at the Westminster Palace Hotel, was fought the first battle between Mr. Gladstone and Mr. Chamberlain. The encounter was a desperate one, and ended disastrously for Mr. Chamberlain and his friends. The veneration with which Mr. Gladstone was regarded, the belief which had taken root among his admirers that he could not do wrong or swerve from the right path, the divergence of opinions on the merits of the question of Home Rule, were reinforced by all the animosity, jealousy, and rancour which had gathered round the Birmingham set during the period of their omnipotence. As was remarked above, they had not been able or willing to spare the *amour-propre* of the other towns; they were too prone to display dictatorial tendencies, and by means of the Federation which they had called into being, they established the supremacy of Birmingham over the provinces. The pride of the other great towns, however, was hurt; they were always jealous of each other, and in a fashion which had no resemblance to the feeling which made the cities of Greece contend for the honour of being the birthplace of Homer. Being all of recent origin and prosperity, all *parvenus*, they possessed the dignity and the aspirations peculiar to *parvenus*. To cut out their neighbours,

[1] Speech of Mr. J. Chamberlain to the Birmingham Association, *Times*, 22d April, 1886.

if only by the dimensions of their town hall, was the aim and object of every one of them. Birmingham, therefore, had political rivals. At one of these — Leeds — important meetings of delegates of the Liberal Associations were occasionally held, but this was not much of a consolation. When Mr. Chamberlain refused to countenance the new Irish policy of the great leader of the party, the rivals of Birmingham felt that the Lord had delivered it into their hands. At the general meeting of delegates convened to give their verdict on Home Rule, the Leeds contingent opened fire. They roundly declared Mr. Chamberlain a traitor to the Liberal cause, although it was not yet known which side the bulk of the Liberal party would take, the Irish question being still in suspense. In vain did the officers of the Federation, who were Birmingham men, propose by way of compromise a resolution accepting the principle of Home Rule for Ireland, but urging Mr. Gladstone not to insist on the exclusion of the Irish representatives from the House of Commons, an exclusion which in the eyes of a good many Liberals denoted a complete separation of the two countries. The Chairman of the meeting, a Leeds man, refused to put this resolution, which had been drafted by the officers of the Federation Committee, and declared purely and simply, without reserve or exception, for Mr. Gladstone's plan. A heated debate ensued; the Birmingham party was worsted, and the Caucus pronounced for Mr. Gladstone by a very large majority. The consequences of this rupture were, as we shall see, of decisive importance for the future of the Organization and of the Liberal party.

As soon as the word of command had been issued from above, the local Associations threw aside all their doubt and hesitation and plunged into the fray with their usual ardour. The resolutions which they now voted had nothing ambiguous about them. They called on their members to support Mr. Gladstone's Bill in its entirety. When letters and telegrams did not attain their object, delegations from the caucuses came up to London to ply their representatives with arguments *ad hominem*, and the lobbies of the House were the scene of a very active campaign on these lines. The unanimity and enthusiastic energy displayed by the caucuses made, as it would appear, an impression specially on Mr. Gladstone. He inferred that the whole Lib-

eral strength of the country was with him and that all he had
to do was to overcome the resistance of the members who had
been led away by Lord Hartington, John Bright, and Mr. Chamberlain. In the meanwhile the second reading of the Bill and
the division were delayed in an unusual way. Lord Hartington
maintained that the Government was adopting these dilatory
tactics in order to give the caucuses time to carry out their conversions among the members opposed to the Bill. Mr. Gladstone emphatically repudiated this charge. However this may
have been, the caucuses managed to convert a certain number
of Members, but not enough to ensure the success of the Home
Rule Bill. Many Liberal Members remained deaf to the remonstrances and threats of the caucuses. They voted with the
Conservatives and threw out the Irish Bill. Mr. Gladstone
would not accept his defeat, and dissolved Parliament in order
to appeal to the country.

The rejection of the Home Rule Bill in the House of Commons, by separating the *Gladstonian Liberals* once and for all
from the *Liberal Unionists*, completed the dismemberment of
the Liberal Associations which had begun when the crisis broke
out. Several of them lost their Chairmen or Secretaries, who
did not want to be borne away by the current which was driving all the caucuses in the direction of Home Rule. The
vacancies caused by these resignations were quickly filled, and
the Organization drew up in battle array with a united front.
Mr. Chamberlain and his friends, who had already withdrawn
from the Federation after their defeat at the Westminster
Palace Hotel, hurriedly started a new Organization to conduct
the impending electoral campaign, entitled the "Radical Union,"
with its headquarters at Birmingham and a certain number of
branches in the country. It adopted as its programme the
single question of local government, which it proposed to extend on a very large scale to every part of the Kingdom, not
excepting Ireland, which would thus enjoy exactly the same
amount of autonomy as England, Scotland, and Wales. The
Caucus Organization, which was left in the hands of the Gladstonians, refused to follow it on to this ground; in taking up
the cudgels for Home Rule it held, and in this it was backed
by the parliamentary chiefs of the Gladstonian party, that
the divergence brought about by this problem was a general

test of Liberalism; in other words, that it was not a difference of opinion between Liberals which the country was asked
to decide upon, but a conflict between Liberals and men who
were no longer such. In so doing the Caucus at one blow
drove out of the party all the Liberal Unionists, led by such
men as John Bright, Joseph Chamberlain, Leonard Courtney,
etc. In refusing to recognize them as Liberal belligerents, the
Caucus treated the Liberal members who had voted against
Home Rule more as rebels. The Associations condemned them
beforehand without allowing them to come to an explanation
with their constituents, whose business it now was to give the
verdict, or they sent them imperious summonses to appear before the Caucus.[1] The mere fact of appealing to the voters over
the heads of the caucuses was viewed by the latter as an act of
high treason against Liberalism. Their great and legitimate admiration for Mr. Gladstone made them forget that he himself
was defending a cause and not his own person or his power; and
making Mr. Gladstone's glorious name a sort of shibboleth, they
converted the great national deliberation in which the country
was invited to take part into a personal plebiscite. The methods
of warfare, the character of the campaign, could not help being
influenced by this, contests conducted on personal lines being
always marked by a greater display of acrimony and intolerance against the opposing side. The policy pursued by the
caucuses drew the following remarks from John Bright: "The
action of our clubs and associations is rapidly engaged in making delegates of their members, and in insisting on their forgetting all principles if the interests of a party are supposed to be
at stake. What will be the value of party when its whole
power is placed at the disposal of a leader from whose authority
no appeal is allowed?"[2] It was only too natural that counsels
of moderation and appeals to tolerance should not be listened
to in the thick of the fight. Having, so to speak, taken the
bit between their teeth, the caucuses were bent on one thing,

---

[1] A Radical veteran, Peter Rylands, who had voted against the Home Rule
Bill, was summoned on the following day to appear before the Association
within forty-eight hours. Afterwards the Caucus thought better of it and
graciously allowed the member up to the end of the parliamentary session
(which was drawing to a close).

[2] Letter to Mr. Caine, *Times*, 24th June, 1886.

to overthrow and trample on every one that crossed their path. The Liberal Unionists were not always able to argue their case; on more than one occasion they were not allowed a hearing in electoral gatherings, their voice was drowned by the clamour of packed meetings. The caucuses therefore gave the Liberal Unionists a plausible reason for exclaiming against the tyranny of official Liberalism and for saying with Mr. Goschen that "they were fighting for the right of private judgment and the right of independent action." [1]

The final result of the elections was unfavourable to Mr. Gladstone and to Home Rule. He resigned at once, without waiting for the meeting of Parliament. The victory of the Conservative and Liberal Unionist coalition was in fact complete. A large number of Liberals voted against Mr. Gladstone, and a still greater number of old adherents of the Liberal leader abstained from voting, and in so doing greatly helped to turn the scale in favour of the opponents of Home Rule. This result showed only too clearly that the Caucus was far from representing the opinions of the bulk of English Liberalism, as the Chairman of the executive committee of the Federation had the good grace to admit by saying, after the event, it is true, that "the enthusiasm for Mr. Gladstone and his measure in the Associations was in reality not a correct reflex of the attitude of the whole mass of the party." [2] The Caucus Associations therefore misled Mr. Gladstone, confirmed him in his attitude by their noisy demonstrations, and made him pull the string so tight that it snapped asunder.

Nevertheless Mr. Gladstone showed his appreciation of the services rendered by the Caucus in the campaign which had just terminated. On leaving office, he made the President of the Caucus a baronet and conferred a knighthood on the Chairman of the executive committee of the Liberal Federation. In so doing he was more just than the bulk of the party, who, in trying to discover the reasons of their defeat, attributed it to the inadequate arrangements of the Caucus: it had been thrown out of gear by the split and had not done what was expected

---

[1] *Times*, 7th July, 1886.
[2] Letter from Sir B. Walter Foster in the *New Liberal Programme* edited by Andr. Reid, Lond. 1886, a collection of opinions on the causes of the Liberal defeat in 1886 and on the new policy to be adopted.

of it. The contrary was nearer the truth. Although it lost a certain number of distinguished members, the Caucus had kept all the machinery of organization, and what was just as important, the head machinist, Mr. Schnadhorst, the only one of the Birmingham group who went over to the other side. All the threads of the Organization being in his hands, the machine worked on without a moment's interruption. In the same way the local Associations, which were now Gladstonian, kept all the books, the lists, the funds, and, above all, most of the agents who were used to manipulating the constituencies. The majority of the leading people, the men of wealth and culture, and, generally speaking, most of the "influences," having left the Gladstonians, the voters who had voted for Mr. Gladstone and Home Rule belonged to the masses and to the lower middle class, many of whom were brought to the poll by the exertions of the Caucus. And these exertions were so far from being of no avail that in the English boroughs, for instance, where the Gladstonian candidates suffered most, their minorities were more than respectable. Next to the magic of Mr. Gladstone's name, the Caucus was undoubtedly the most powerful influence, and it would be by no means rash to affirm that without the support of the Caucus the defeat of the Gladstonians would have been an utter rout.

III

If the assistance rendered by the Caucus was very useful to the Gladstonians, it must be admitted that from the point of view of the Organization the Caucus was very well advised in taking Mr. Gladstone's side. It may be that, as was generally supposed, Mr. Chamberlain, in parting from Mr. Gladstone, hoped to have the last word, thanks, among other things, to the Caucus, of which he was the master and the guiding spirit. If this was so, the calculation was a mistaken one. The Caucus had been called into being on behalf of the sovereignty of the people; it was based on the formal application of the principle of local autonomy; and its machinery was kept going not so much by sober-minded persons, as by the enthusiasm and political ardour which naturally follow the direct lines of political thought. The solution of the Irish problem put forward by Mr. Gladstone, combining as it did all these logical and psychological elements, exactly suited the intellectual and political temperament of the contingents of the Caucus, and if the latter had tried to force them in an opposite direction, it would have broken its mainspring. The result would have been such a dismemberment, not only of its staff (which actually did take place), but of the rank and file, as to break it up, reduce it to the level of an organization of a Liberal fraction (as was the case with the Organizations started by the Liberals opposed to Home Rule), and prevent it from keeping up even the appearance of being a more or less complete representative of the party. Mr. Gladstone being still the official chief of the Liberal party, the head of orthodox Liberalism, the Caucus was able to preserve this appearance by following in his wake. In so doing it also escaped the danger of having its representative authority contested by that of the supreme leader, of the anointed of the party. If things had reached this point, the old political factor of the leadership which the Caucus had taken on itself to supplant, but which was still a living force in English life, would have risen up against it with a power all the more formidable, because on this occasion the leader appeared as a Radical champion. On the other hand, by walking in the footsteps of the great chief, the Caucus was strengthened with all his strength and enhanced by all his importance.

Whether all the consequences involved in the decision taken by the Federation were clearly realized or not, its immediate and personal effect was easily grasped, viz. the deposition of the powerful master of the Caucus. The defeat inflicted on Mr. Chamberlain at the Westminster Palace Hotel was hailed with delight by many Liberals. They held that the Federation had rescued the freedom of the Liberal Organization which was in the hands of a single man, and more than this, that the democracy of England had won its spurs on this occasion. The rising generation in particular was infected by these views. Having arrived at the age of discretion under Lord Beaconsfield's government, its political opinions were formed under the special influence of that period. The unexpected return of the Tories to power with an enormous majority after a long Liberal reign which seemed destined to last indefinitely, had affected people's imaginations, and with the exaggeration of language peculiar to party polemics, Beaconsfield was represented as a sort of political Antichrist, and the Liberal victory of 1880 as a victory over the forces of darkness.[1] The political ardour which young Liberals imbibed under these circumstances was marked not so much by a rationalist enthusiasm, like that which grew up in the latter years of the Palmerston epoch, as by a jealous and irritable belief. The attacks which were being made by the Tories on Mr. Chamberlain and the Caucus, which they liked to describe as a tool of an ambitious and unscrupulous politician, gave a painful shock to the minds of youthful Radicals and inspired them with grave suspicions. The spectacle of Members of unquestioned Radicalism swelling Mr. Chamberlain's train, and of Liberal Associations at his beck and call, filled many young men with apprehensions as to the destiny of the English democracy, not yet arrived at maturity, but with the springs of its existence already poisoned. Consequently when Mr. Chamberlain was thrown over by the Federation, they thought that the English democracy had recovered itself, and that the Caucus, in its odious aspect, was a thing of the past. The young, ardent democrats, moreover, were not alone in attaching this importance to the crisis which the Federation had just gone through. There were still a certain number of Associations in the country which held aloof from the Birmingham Federation and had refused to join it, for fear of losing their independence. Mr. Chamberlain's fall overcame their scruples, and, one after another, they gave in their adhesion.

To remove all the apprehensions of the local Associations, the Federation hastened to modify its statutes in a decentralizing direction. In the Council of the Federation they were given a representation proportioned to the number of voters, and in the general committee three delegates to each Association whatever its importance, just as in the federative republics,

---

[1] Edward Freeman, the historian, for instance, actually compared the elections of 1880, which brought Mr. Gladstone into power in place of Disraeli, to the conquest of Magna Charta, and, alluding to Beaconsfield's foreign policy, added that the advent of the Liberals would be a source of joy " wherever the name of Christ is named in the lands where the misbeliever still holds the Christian as his bondsman " (*Contemporary Review*, 1880, Vol. 37).

in the United States, or in Switzerland, the States or Cantons are represented in proportion to their population in the lower chamber, whereas in the other branch of the federal Legislature they all have the same number of representatives. The new statutes of the Caucus also allowed the creation of District federations with representatives in the central bodies of the Organization. But the most important point, the point most pregnant with consequences, of the constitutional revision adopted by the Caucus, was the transfer of its head office. It was impossible to stay at Birmingham, for Mr. Chamberlain's influence was still all-powerful there; and the Federation was now, so to speak, in the middle of a hostile camp. It being necessary to move somewhere else, Leeds was proposed as headquarters; but the Leeds politicians, who had done all they could to overthrow Mr. Chamberlain, declined the offer, being afraid of inspiring the great provincial centres with the jealousy which had caused the downfall of Birmingham.[1] Thereupon London was clearly marked out as the home of the Liberal Organization. Installed in the capital of the Empire, the Federation at once rose in public estimation. Divested of its provincial origin, which was a drawback to it in spite of all the influence which it wielded in the Birmingham period of its existence, it now shed its rays over the whole country from the centre of political life. The dream of its founders to make it a Liberal Parliament side by side with the Imperial Legislature was realized in a material sense now that it had its offices in Parliament Street. The popular association of ideas which magnifies and exalts all that goes on in the capital, even in countries which are not highly centralized, forthwith clothed the Federation with a new authority. This authority was speedily enhanced, and to as great an extent, by the fact that the Federation became the regular organ of the chiefs of the party, with Mr. Gladstone at their head. The alliance of the popular Organization with the leadership, contracted during the electoral crisis of 1886, was thus placed on a permanent footing, and its effect, as analyzed above, only became more striking and more fruitful in consequences for the Federation. It could no longer be said that it obeyed the inspirations of a single

---

[1] " We did not care to make fools of ourselves," as was said afterwards by one of the Leeds men who led the attack at the Westminster Palace Hotel.

man, that it ministered exclusively to his interests, as Mr. Chamberlain's victorious adversaries retrospectively, but perhaps somewhat tardily, made out.[1] It was now supposed to unite all the elements of Liberalism, to be, as it were, its visible, catholic, universal church. The poor young men who in the innocence of their hearts rejoiced over Mr. Chamberlain's fall as betokening the end of the Caucus had no idea that its power was only beginning.

Nor did the commotion created in the local Associations by the Home Rule crisis prove disadvantageous to them. True, they had lost some members, whose importance was due not so much to their number as to their position, their wealth, and their influence in the locality. *Respectable* people as they were for the most part, their respectability was of use to the Associations which they had joined out of party loyalty; they went bail, so to speak, in the popular Organizations for the too impulsive and noisy elements, not to mention the more or less large subscriptions which their means enabled them to contribute. Their departure was no doubt a serious blow to the Liberal Associations. But their respectability was not infrequently accompanied by the haughtiness and arrogance with which a certain class of Whigs treated people of small means or low birth. In this respect, therefore, the retirement of these personages from the Liberal Associations was more a gain than a loss to the latter; their moral atmosphere was decidedly cleared by it. Then, the presence of the moderates in the Associations having acted as a check and a counterpoise, or, as the ardent spirits of the Caucus termed it, as an impediment, an obstacle to the advance of the party in the path of progress, their departure had the effect of removing the friction between the moderate and the Radical element and of enhancing the propelling force of the latter by bringing more cohesion into the ranks of the Caucus, by introducing greater unity of views and aspirations among its members, for a while at least, until the inevitable growth of conflicting opinions and feelings would once more give birth to a group of " reactionaries." In the meanwhile the cau-

---

[1] " They had no longer a one-man society. . . . Attempts were made to use that Organization for the purposes of one man " . . . (Speech of the President of the Caucus, Sir James Kitson, at the annual meeting of the Federation, Oct. 18, 1887).

cuses obtained more elbow-room.   Just as great a mistake was therefore made by those who, at the opposite political pole to the "stalwarts" and to the rising generation which hailed Mr. Chamberlain's fall as the fall of the Caucus, held with Mr. Goldwin Smith that the retirement of the men who lent respectability to the Caucus had dealt this "political devil-fish" a fatal blow.[1]   The real upshot was that the circum-stances which had the appearance of weakening the Caucus — the separation from its creator and prompter, Mr. Chamberlain, the compulsory desertion of its stronghold at Birmingham, the loss of many of its important members — all conspired, on the contrary, to enhance its power and extend its influence.

IV

But the very incidents which contributed to this result soon thrust new duties upon the Organization, and imposed on it new obligations.   The first marked effect of the altered situ-ation appeared in the relations of the Organization with the party chiefs.   Being indebted for its accession of prestige to its closer connection with the parliamentary leaders of the party, it speedily fell under their direct influence.   These leaders — it is enough to mention a single name, that of Mr. Gladstone — held too exalted a position for the representatives of the Caucus, who, after all, were unimportant people, to be able, when brought into continual contact with them, to resist them and take up an independent, let alone a divergent, attitude in regard to the common cause, of which the parliamentary chiefs of the party were the devoted and indefatigable champions. This state of things, which grew up after the transfer of the headquarters of the Caucus to London, was not altogether unforeseen.   When the Federation was obliged to move from Birmingham, after the disastrous general election of 1886, the proposal to transport the Organization to London met with opposition among its members for the very reason that the independence of the popular Organization might be exposed to danger.   Without actually pointing out the leaders of the

---

[1] " The Caucus has lost most of the men who lent it respectability, and we may hope that this political devil-fish has received a severe wound " (" Elec-tion Notes," *Macmillan's Magazine*, August, 1886).

party, — which no one would have ventured to do, — fears were expressed that the official atmosphere of the capital would rob the Organization of the popular spirit which animated or ought to animate it; cut off from the provincial centres, it would no longer be able to interpret their political views with ease and accuracy. Mr. John Morley (who at that time was not connected with Liberal official circles by the close ties since formed in the course of years of common struggles) dwelt with much force on these considerations, but they were disregarded. The anxiety to uphold the independence of the Organization as opposed to the official leaders of the party was also very great among the managers of the Caucus who had joined the Gladstonians, and they came up to London with the firm intention of keeping as much as possible aloof from these leaders. But they were very soon caught in the official toils.

One special fact contributed greatly to this result. It will be remembered that long before the creation of the Caucus the Liberals had a central office managed by the Whips (the Central Liberal Association). The Whip himself was only an agent of the leader of the party; the Organization which he controlled had no policy of its own, it obeyed that of the party chief. The *Central Association*, therefore, although it had a long Whig past, followed Mr. Gladstone in the Home Rule campaign of 1886, but without making a great impression or achieving much success. Being gradually driven back by the rising tide of the popular Organization of Birmingham, the Association which represented the leaders lost its vitality and energy with the ground which was slipping from beneath its feet. After the defeat of 1886, the leaders of the Liberal party wanted to bring some fresh blood into it, and considered this all the more feasible because it was now as Radical as the representative Organization. They thought of Mr. Schnadhorst as the man to conduct this delicate operation. But he preferred to remain at the head of the Caucus, especially as its headquarters were about to be transferred to London, where a fresh era of activity awaited him. Being unable to entice away the skilful organizer, the leaders discovered another means of obtaining his services: as he was taking up his abode in London on behalf of the Caucus, why should he not, while continuing to look after it, keep an eye on their Organization, which was close by. Mr. Schnadhorst yielded to these entreaties and accepted the title of Honorary Secretary to the Central Liberal Association, that is, he added it to his office of secretary of the National Liberal Federation. As sole manager of both Organizations, he became their maid-of-all-work: as secretary of the Central office, he was the factotum of the leaders; as secretary of the Caucus, he was the servant of the popular Organizations. The field of action of both being the same, a fusion of the two Organizations practically took place.

Of course the influence of the official leaders on the affairs of the Federation was brought into play behind the scenes so to speak, but it was none the less real. The Caucus continued to hold its Grand Assizes *coram populo;* thousands of delegates representing all the constituencies in the country flocked to these meetings; but the proceedings were arranged beforehand down to the minutest details. The items of the programme, measures or demands to be submitted to the Legislature, resolutions approving or censuring the policy of the day, were discussed and drafted in private by the leaders of the party and the managers of the Caucus. The list of business of the Federation meetings being fixed by them beforehand down to the names of the speakers, independent utterances had great difficulty in obtaining a hearing. In the first place, the mere proposal of a motion not anticipated or eliminated by the authorities was a piece of courage or audacity on the part of a small provincial delegate. In the hall which was still resounding with the loud cheers evoked by the appearance of Mr. Gladstone, where *he* was going to speak or had spoken, where the accents of his magic voice was still vibrating in every ear and in every heart, how was a humble delegate to rise and oppose the persons who surrounded Mr. Gladstone on the platform and whom he addressed as his dear friends, whom he described as the pillars of Liberalism, of the great cause for which they were doing battle? And if any one had the hardihood to do it, the President was there ready to rule the delegate's motion or amendment "out of order" without further ado, and to refuse him a hearing, while making up for this treatment by retrospective denunciations of the unholy dictatorship which Mr. Chamberlain wielded over the Federation before it had regained its freedom in the crisis of 1886.

No great amount of perspicacity was required to perceive that under these circumstances the Federation had become a quasi-official institution, that it represented only official Liberalism, that of the regular leaders, and in no way the aspirations of the masses. The managers of the Caucus took offence at remarks which began to be made on this point and protested vehemently against all imputation of officialism. "The Federation," they declared, "embodies and expresses the profound and unshaken loyalty of the Liberal party to its great chief, and the confidence felt in his colleagues. At the same time the Federation has never been, and if it be consistent with the principles upon which it was established can never become, a merely official organization. It receives its inspiration from the people."[1] The authors of these words were so impressed with them that they took them for a motto, which they reproduced on the first page of their annual reports. A good many influential representatives of local Associations, however, prominent members of the central committee of the Caucus, were not so profoundly convinced of the absolute independence of the Federation, and in the confidences in which they indulged before foreign enquirers they pointed out with some bitterness that the Federation was too much under the thumb of this or that big-wig of the party. As for what went on at the great annual meetings of the Caucus, they let drop the singularly piquant admission that "there was much more liberty at Birmingham."

Each succeeding year brought fresh confirmation of this state of things. Many a member of the Liberal party realized it and grumbled; but they did not dare to protest out loud; this was left to the *enfants terribles* of the party, to men like Mr. Henry Labouchere, who said bluntly: "A feeling is growing amongst Liberals that the wire-pullers of the National Liberal Federation are taking too much on themselves, and that the Federation does as much harm as it does good. A great meeting of delegates is annually held. A programme is submitted to it, but by whom the programme is framed is shrouded

[1] Proceedings in connection with the eleventh annual meeting of the Federation held in Birmingham on Nov. 6 and 7, Lond. 1888, p. 26.

in mystery. The delegates are asked to accept it or to reject it. All amendments and all additional 'planks' are ruled out of order. This deprives the meeting of any real representative character. Some things that they might desire to see in the programme are not there, others which they — or a good many of them — deem of doubtful acceptance by the entire party are pushed into the front." [1] To the rejoinder of the Caucus officials, who referred him to the statutes of the Federation, Mr. Labouchere replied: " Yes, this is all very well, but it does not alter the fact that there is a growing feeling among Liberals that the Federation is becoming somewhat of a clique. . . . Putting, however, criticism of detail aside, I still assert, firstly, that the Federation should be independent of the official party Organization; secondly, that its annual general meeting should be more of a Liberal Parliament and less of a meeting called together to express approval of cut and dried resolutions." [2]

Even if it had wished to follow this advice, it was no easy matter for the Federation to do so; its connection with "official Liberalism" was too firmly cemented by Mr. Gladstone's powerful individuality, and then, however strong may have been the domineering spirit attributed to the " wire-pullers," they were sincerely convinced that it was a clear gain to the party to maintain close relations with the official leaders and to confine discussion to the arena into which these responsible chiefs could venture. But whatever may have been the motives for this policy, it none the less had the effect of giving an utterly wrong bias to the relations between public opinion and the party leaders under parliamentary government.

Parliamentary government reposes on a division of labour and an apportionment of powers between public opinion and the leaders, the rulers, — an apportionment prescribed by the very nature of both. While public opinion by a sort of volcanic process upheaves and hurls forth one problem after another, the party leaders who alternately come into office, the rulers, fasten on those problems the solution of which appears to them necessary and possible; they are not to meddle with the others, and it is a crime on their part to play with them. Taking up the questions which await solution on their

---

[1] *Truth*, of Jan. 2, 1890.   [2] *Ibid.*, of Jan. 9 and 16, 1890.

own responsibility, they must not shirk it or let their hand
be forced, no more than they may arrest or dam the current
of opinion which fertilizes the soil of every free political community. It is this which constitutes the real separation of
power on which parliamentary government rests, rather than
that mechanical separation which Montesquieu fancied he had
discovered in English constitutionalism, and which has since
been naïvely copied in various countries.

In getting their programme given them by the delegates
after having carefully composed it in private themselves
and adapted it to their aims and their resources, the leaders
of the party shifted the responsibility. In like manner, by
not allowing the representatives of the party, who had come
from all parts of the country, to speak on this or that
question because it was not ripe for solution and could only
hamper the leaders of the party who have to carry out
its policy, the managers of the Caucus inverted the parts
and consequently did away with responsibility. The judgment which they pronounced on the questions raised was
perhaps quite right in itself, but it did not admit of being
enforced as they enforced it. For instance, in 1891 the authorities of the Caucus would not allow a discussion or a division
on the "eight hours question," which was already stirring the
country. They alleged that from information in their possession (which they kept to themselves) only a few local Associations were in favour of the "eight hours." It is quite possible
that the question of introducing a compulsory maximum of
eight hours' labour in every industry was not ripe for discussion, and perhaps even that it may never become so from the
point of view of good sense. But the mere elimination of
the question was not a proof of this. It was only a means of
saving the leaders from the necessity of speaking out on the
question, as it was their duty to do if they wished to be true
to the spirit of parliamentary government, even if they found
themselves at variance with the majority of their party; it was
simply a device to avoid giving offence to any section of their
supporters, to prevent the loss of votes at elections, and to
enable them, while protected by the temporizing instructions
of the council of the party, to wait quietly to see which way
the cat would jump.

V

The effects and consequences of the complete identity which grew up between the popular Organization of Liberalism and the official leaders of the party, did not stop here. It was not only the general economy of parliamentary government which was disturbed; the concrete existence of the party, the free play of its forces and even of its feelings, was also affected by it. Having affirmed its community of interests with the official leaders on the Home Rule question, the popular Organization followed them so implicitly in this direction that it became a fixture there. It became engrossed, and made the whole body of Liberals become engrossed, in the single question of Ireland. For the parliamentary leaders of a party that is a logical and almost obligatory position to take up on great political questions. In contracting as it were to solve particular questions, the official leaders of the party stake their all on the result; they stand or fall by their definite programme. The party, on the other hand, cannot immure itself in a single question, however great the importance which it attaches to it. Representing, under the time-honoured system of party dualism, manifold and varied interests, it cannot sacrifice itself on the altar of one of them. Its government, its official leaders of the moment, have to play the part of scapegoat. The party which supported them in the country does not on that account abandon the beaten cause; it continues to keep it in view; but with the freedom of a body corporate unfettered by pledges, by feelings of *amour-propre*, by points of honour, it can relax any over-tension, retreat or advance a few paces, and while remaining true to itself *in re*, change its action *in modo*, and quietly create a quasi-new situation in which the old defeated leaders, released by the authority of sovereign opinion from the stringency of their former professions of faith, will be able to lead the party in new order of battle to combat and to victory. But if the party in the country completely identifies itself with the defeated leaders, if it follows them with all its baggage and intrenches itself with them in rear of the lost Bill, then its regular evolution becomes singularly difficult, if not impossible. The mutual pledges of the leaders and their supporters make them really each other's prisoners, like convicts fettered in couples, and even the example they set of reciprocal loyalty, edifying as it is in theory, fails to be so under the circumstances; for this feeling, when carried to its extreme limits in the relations between chiefs and followers, is apt to oscillate between sublime devotion and servility.

Having followed the example of the official leaders of the party in their immovable attachment to the question of Home Rule for Ireland, the next step for the popular Organization of Liberalism was to consider adhesion to Home Rule as the distinguishing mark of Liberalism, and not only adhesion to the principle of increasing the political power of the Irish people, but to Home Rule as it would be eventually proposed by the leader of the party. The Liberal creed having been set up in such a simple way with a profession of faith so easy of recognition, the notion of political orthodoxy penetrated the Liberal Organization from one end to the other, and with this notion its corollary of heterodoxy. All dissent on the Irish question was regarded within the Liberal Associations as a heresy in regard to which tolerance became cowardice and intolerance a virtue. This view was stated in almost so many words by the principal leaders of the Caucus, who proved far more intolerant than some of the official chiefs of the party, and were strongly opposed to all moderate and conciliatory language. Lord Rosebery, a member of Mr. Gladstone's last Cabinet and his future successor, was sharply rebuked by the President of the Caucus for having said that the Liberals would assume a grave responsibility if they let the split in the party become a permanent one. In the opinion of the President of the Liberal Federation, this "was not language that should be used" when one had a majority. Having proved by arithmetical calculation that the number of new Associations affiliated since the Home Rule crisis showed a clear gain of 25 per cent, he expressed indignant astonishment that any one should propose to them, as Lord Rosebery did, to "make a pontoon to bring over those members of the party who were standing on the other side of the gulf." [1]

The conclusion to which this language pointed was evidently

[1] President's speech at the annual meeting of the Federation, in November, 1886, at Leeds.

that it would be rather a deserving act than otherwise to widen the gulf, and in justice to the local Associations, it must be said that they did their best to bring this about. When the crisis of 1886 broke out, the withdrawal of the dissentient Liberals from the Caucus Associations was not complete; they had everywhere resigned the offices they held in the Associations, but in several localities they kept their names on the list of members, in the hope that when the Home Rule storm had spent its force, they would all be able to co-operate once more in the cause of Liberalism. But this did not suit the Gladstonian Liberals; they preferred to get rid of traitors at once, and they succeeded. As a general rule, the formal expulsion of the dissentient Liberals was not necessary; their position in the Associations was made so unpleasant that they were obliged to withdraw altogether. The same thing took place in most of the Liberal clubs. The mixed character of these establishments, which were clubs first and political organizations afterwards, would have allowed the Liberals of both persuasions to meet on the neutral ground of the dining-room and the smoking-room without being false to their political convictions. But the Gladstonian members, who were in a majority almost everywhere, thought fit to introduce the ordeal of the true Liberal faith, which consisted of Home Rule for Ireland, into the clubs as well. The dissentient Liberals were even ousted from some Associations in which they had a majority. By means of packed meetings the Gladstonians always put them in a minority; having once obtained control of the meeting, they carried resolutions hostile to the dissentients; and eventually the latter gave up the game. This is what would have taken place in the Liberal Unionist citadel of Birmingham, as Mr. J. Chamberlain, whom events had converted into a complainant against the Caucus, stated with indignation. But in places where the Gladstonian members of the Associations were in a majority, they had no need to resort to underhand practices, but displayed an honest fanaticism. In some localities, however, the caucuses in their weeded state contained sober-minded men of broad and lofty views, who did what they could to combat the sectarian and intolerant spirit of their fellow-Gladstonians, and it was owing to their efforts and their tact that the malignant attitude of the caucuses towards their old dissentient members did not become the rule. And it was the salutary influence of these persons that enabled some Liberal Associations to congratulate themselves " that the right of private judgment has not been called in question amongst us, and that no intolerance has been manifested towards the minority. . . . Looking to the future, we are in a far better position (for the reunion of the party) than the Liberals in many places, owing to the admirable forbearance of our party with the dissentient Liberals." [1]

The men who used this language would even be entitled to speak with less modesty, to contrast their own conduct with that of the Liberals not only in many but in most places; for the Associations which showed tolerance towards the dissentient minorities were few in number. All the other Associations thought that in acting as they did they were only in more complete agreement with the party leaders and deserving better of the Home Rule cause, but in reality they were working against it. It is not necessary to take sides for or against Home Rule to acknowledge that the Irish problem demanded a solution, whether in the direction of agrarian or political reform. But in view of the many interests, passions, and prejudices which the Irish claims evoked on both sides, the question was not one of those the settlement of which could be thrust on the country by a Ministerial majority of a few votes; it was more one of those cases in which the formal vote ought to express the assent of the national conscience conveyed in a spirit of concord and exalted justice. By envenoming the controversy, by embittering men's minds and exasperating differences on matters of opinion, the Associations prevented an understanding being arrived at. It is true that in so doing they were supported, and powerfully supported, by the great parliamentary leaders without distinction of party, who vied with each other in abusive language and rancorous imputations. But if the responsibility of the caucuses is lessened by this, it none the less remains, and whatever may be the share which ought to be attributed to them, they will always be chargeable with having helped to prevent or delay the solution of the Irish problem.

---

[1] Extract from the minute book of a Yorkshire Liberal Association.

VI

In any event, the caucuses might flatter themselves that they had secured the unity of the party, that they had set up a political conformity, so that henceforth there was only one fold and one shepherd. But it soon turned out that everything had to be begun over again. The whole body of Liberalism would not fit into the narrow groove of a single question of Home Rule. The spokesmen of several other Radical claims which made use of the name of the party or wanted to thrust themselves on it, held, and rightly enough, that if every Radical was a Home-Ruler, every Home-Ruler did not constitute a Radical. Far from consenting to keep in the background or to sacrifice themselves to Home Rule, they maintained that it was only by giving full satisfaction to their demand that the party of progress would justify its name and its *raison d'être*. The caucuses were destined to learn to their cost the old truth that one is always a reactionary in the eyes of somebody. It was, in fact, in this somewhat general and vague shape that the first signs of revolt against the Organization and the official leaders of the party appeared: they were not considered advanced enough, they were said to have kept a "Whig tail," and a pretty long one according to the thorough-going Radicals. The caucuses, in their anxiety to stifle all discontent, at first could only hit on the device of bringing out the old Whig implement, of opening the "grand old Liberal umbrella" under which all the elements of the party formerly gathered in a spirit of compromise, the favourite plan of the weak-kneed Liberals, whom the caucuses had been fortunate enough to get rid of in 1886. It was supposed that after their withdrawal the umbrella had been thrown into the dust-heap, but evidently it still had some wear left in it. All that was done was to lengthen the handle a little, and when mended in this way it was to serve as a support and a shelter to Liberals and Radicals of all shades whatsoever. This ingenious contrivance consisted simply of adding a couple of words to the title "Liberal Associations" and converting them into "Liberal *and Radical* Associations." Childish as this method of reconciling differences of opinion may seem, it was not wholly so in practice, since in some cases the Radicals were satisfied or appeared to be satisfied with it, while in others they cried out that it was robbery to take their name.[1] These latter were more numerous or at any rate more demonstrative, and they were destined to become more and more aggressive every day. Endless troubles and difficulties were, therefore, in store for the party Organization.

It had a foretaste of them as early as the year 1887, in London. As the metropolis was slipping more and more away from Liberalism, and had inflicted a crushing defeat on the Gladstonians at the last general election, the Organization decided to reinforce the Caucus in London. With this object it reorganized the local Associations of the various parliamentary boroughs into which the capital is divided, and, as a finishing touch, conceived the plan of combining them all into a central caucus for the whole metropolis, which should hold the representatives of every shade of the Opposition. The London workingmen's clubs not only declined to join the combination, but were opposed to the new London Caucus taking the title of Liberal *and Radical* Union, which its founders bestowed on it in conformity with the new formula of political chemistry. The representatives of the clubs attended the meeting held for constituting this *Union* to uphold the protest, and to claim for the members of the clubs the exclusive right to the appellation of *bona fide Radicals*. They moved an amendment to omit the words *and Radical* from the title of the Caucus. The matter stopped here; the holders of the meeting, true to the intolerant ways of the Caucus, would not allow the authors of the amendment a hearing, in spite of the efforts of Mr. John Morley, who was in the Chair. The protest, moreover, did not derive great importance' from the number of those who originated it; the Radical clubs, although they had some tens of thousands of members, did not represent any great political force in the enormous metropolis. But all these incidents were highly characteristic, from the state of feeling disclosed in the conflicts they produced between the irreconcilable Radicals and the Liberals of the official Organization, which the former regarded with profound distrust. The ultra-Radical Press was still more out-

[1] In some places, on the other hand, it was the "Liberals" who opposed the change in the sign of the Association so as to avoid all appearance of connection with the "extremists."

spoken on this occasion in stating the views of the *true* Radicals on the Caucus and its alliance with the official leaders of the party. "The Radical clubs," remarked the old organ of extreme popular Radicalism, "have a mission to fulfil which is certainly imperilled by absorption in the great Schnadhorst 'machine' . . .; the Brummagem machine will infallibly grind the Radicals to powder if they are not awake." Impugning the character and the past of the Liberal Federation, the paper showed that the "Caucusians" were only sham democrats, impostors. "The Caucusians know that if they avow themselves mere party opportunists, which they really are, the democratic fish would give their net a wide berth."[1] Other Radical organs, less violent in point of form, also considered the influence of the Organization a danger for Radicalism. The creation of the London central Caucus was, according to Mr. Labouchere, "merely an attempt to place all the London constituencies under the lash of the Liberal Whip. . . . What I want to see in fact," he concluded, "is a Radical party in contradiction to a Liberal party."[2] This conclusion exactly expressed the preoccupations and wishes of the advanced Radicals, and soon afterward it was realized to a certain extent. Under the leadership of the same Mr. Labouchere, a group was formed in the House of Commons which affected complete independence of the Whips and of official Liberalism and its leaders in general. These "new Radicals" often followed Mr. Gladstone, but they had no scruple about voting against him when they thought fit to pay this tribute to their Radical views. They undoubtedly enjoyed a good deal of sympathy in the country, but their Radicalism, which was essentially of a political nature and was prompted by politicians, was soon eclipsed by the social Radicalism which was beginning to rise above the horizon.

VII

The distrust of the Organization of the Liberal party and its official leaders, which the advanced Radicals professed and diffused throughout the country, coincided with the desire growing up among the working classes to use their newly acquired political power in improving their material welfare. As the

[1] *Reynolds' Newspaper*, Jan. 16, 1887.   [2] *Truth*, Feb. 25, 1887.

official Liberal party seemed to the leaders of the workingmen
as selfish and as insincere in their profession of devotion to the
popular cause, as much a tool of the capitalists, as the other
party, champions of labour despaired of political parties ever
promoting legislation calculated to bring about an economic
readjustment of society in the interests of the masses. They
thereupon conceived, or rather reverted to the idea of cutting
themselves adrift from political parties and of organizing the
labour contingents into an independent force for the conquest
of the Legislature, of accepting in the meanwhile social reforms
from whatever quarter they came, and of fighting every one
who happened to cross their path, whether they went by the
name of Liberals, Radicals, or Tories. The *labour party* formed
on this basis would adopt the same attitude in Parliament as
the Irish party under Parnell had maintained with such good
results to the Irish cause; in giving its support to the highest
bidder it would wrest one concession after another from the
rival parties, who were accustomed to sell themselves by auc-
tion, and so bit by bit construct the new social fabric. This
plan having been sanctioned by a labour Congress which met
at Bradford in 1888, the organization of a *labour party* was
forthwith set on foot throughout the country; Associations
with local branches, annual meetings of delegates, etc., were
formed on the model of the Caucus. Some old Organizations,
socialist societies, or ultra-radical bodies, in their turn exerted
themselves in exhorting the workmen to vote only for labour
candidates at all elections, whether for Parliament or for local
assemblies. The material success of the new Organization was
not very marked, in its early years at all events; the new Associations were far from causing uneasiness in the ranks of the
two great parties, and their annual congresses in no way possessed the representative importance which they tried to make
out by adding up an imposing total of adherents with a long
string of noughts. But the spirit which underlay this movement gained ground daily; the tendency to disregard political
quarrels, which kept parties alive, and to demand the improvement of their lot from legislation, extended among the working
classes. It invaded even the trades-unions, the professional
labour federations which carefully held aloof from politics and
had never made but one request to the Legislature, to the

State: Get out of our light, leave us alone to attend to our business! The old orthodox *Trades-Unionism* was driven back by the *New Unionism* with its socialistic spirit. The profound pity for the poor and needy which seized on the community and became, as it were, its public religion, gave life and impetus to the tendencies represented by the *New Unionism*, while a great upheaval of the lowest strata of labour, the London dockers' strike in 1890, was a solemn inauguration of its career.

This movement had not reached a high degree of intensity when several Liberals, who were, nevertheless, stirred by it, proceeded to interrogate their conscience and to ask themselves if their party really understood the needs of contemporary society, if it realized the new aspirations which were at work within it and if it cared to gratify them. The reply which they gave to these questions was in the negative: the Liberal party held itself out as the party of the masses as opposed to the classes (Mr. Gladstone's formula at the time of the crisis of 1886), but in reality it had not gained the affection of the people while it had alienated the middle classes; the official leaders, almost all of them survivors of an old order of things, were quite out of touch with the masses; the latter were indifferent to the political preoccupations of the leaders, they took no interest in Home Rule, to which these leaders were so attached; they would not follow them until the sterile controversies of party had been replaced by questions dealing with the people's daily subsistence; the party would only return to power on condition of adapting its policy to the requirements of the masses and of thus recognizing the transformation of the old into the *new Liberalism;* it was no use appealing to the party programme which met with unanimous approval at the last conference of the Liberal Federation; this programme was not the outcome of the deliberations of the conference, nor of any other representative assembly of Liberals; it was evidently the offspring of the small committee that meets in Parliament Street (the headquarters of the Caucus), and then no discussion of it was allowed, all the amendments were practically excluded; there was no great enthusiasm among the people for measures, no doubt valuable in themselves, such as Disestablishment of the

Welsh Church, the abolition of primogeniture, etc.; but, on the other hand, the masses feel that they have wants, and that a possible satisfaction must be found for them; these feelings are inarticulate, but "with the statesman rests the responsibility to devise and formulate those reforms by which, without violence to persons or shock to the principles of public morality, there may be compassed for the people a wider diffusion of physical comfort, and thus a loftier standard of national morality; this is the new Liberalism." [1]

But the measures which constituted the old Radical stock-in-trade, such as Disestablishment of the Church, abolition of primogeniture, etc., although they did not, as the "new Liberals" pointed out, arouse the enthusiasm of the masses, none the less still had their fanatical supporters. After the first intoxication of Home Rule had passed away, they all bethought them of their pet schemes and pressed them on the party Organization and the leaders. Each section demanded priority for its little or great reform, and each reform had its own group of members in the House and of voters in the country. The crumbling process which had afflicted the Liberal party for years past once more became conspicuous. The Caucus from the first undertook to root out this disease, and with this object, as we have seen, fell upon the moderates, whom it considered as the source of the mischief,—it was mouldy Whigs who stood in the way of the harmony of the party. The moderates had been got rid of, but complete unity was as far off as ever. Mr. J. Chamberlain, when he was master of the Caucus, had pointed out to the detractors of this Organization that they were wasting their time in opposing it, that the Caucus was like the fabled hydra, whose heads grew again as fast as they were cut off.[2] Now its adherents could see that it was the Caucus itself which had to face the hydra. New Radicalism, new Unionism, new Liberalism, were so many new heads added to those against which it had been long contending without possessing any resemblance to a Hercules. It was of no use

---

[1] Cf. "The New Liberalism," by L. Atherley Jones (*Nineteenth Century*, August, 1889); "The New Liberalism": a response by G. W. E. Russell (*ibid.* September, 1889); "Mr. Morley and the New Radicalism," by a "Socialist Radical" (*New Review*, 1889).

[2] Speech at Birmingham on the 5th of January, 1885 (*Times*, Jan. 6, 1885).

going on serving up Home Rule to the public. The Caucus
was obliged to admit in the end that the latter was not so fond
of the dish as in 1886 and in the years which immediately
followed it. Looking at the situation from the point of view
which was most natural to it, from an electioneering standpoint,
the Caucus came to the conclusion that the party could not go
to the country on Home Rule alone. Thereupon, unlike the
captain of a ship in peril, who throws all his ballast overboard,
the Caucus set to work to take in more. By piling up the
Radical demands in the course of two or three years, it managed, before 1892, to frame a lengthy programme which, in the
eyes of its friends, would last the Liberal party well up to the
end of the century, or, according to its opponents, to the end
of all time. In this catalogue of desirable reforms, the most
complete edition of which was laid before the annual conference of the party at Newcastle in November, 1891, and which
became historic under the name of the " Newcastle Programme,"
there was enough to satisfy, if not everybody, whom it is impossible to please, at all events a good many people. To some
the list offered Home Rule, to others the Disestablishment of
the Church and electoral reform, to others, again, local veto
of the drink traffic, the taxation of ground rents, the abolition
or transformation of the House of Lords, etc., etc. All this
was, perhaps, not very new; several of these measures, of older
standing even than Home Rule, had long been demanded by
the different sections of Radical opinion; but they now all
simultaneously received the solemn sanction of the supreme
organs of the party by virtue of a general undertaking which
conferred on each of these sections the benefits, coupled, of
course, with the obligations, of a mutual insurance. How and
when were they to discharge these reciprocal obligations and
to come by their own — the future alone could reply to this
indiscreet question. In the meanwhile all could indulge in
hope. Huddled together in the same *omnibus*[1] programme,
demands of the most varied character were required to combine and so ensure the unity of the party. The *omnibus* was

---

[1] The largest subdivision of the programme was proposed and voted at the
annual conferences of the Liberal Federation under the name of "omnibus"
resolution (Proceedings in connection with the fourteenth annual meeting of
the Federation, held in Newcastle on Tyne, pp. 8 and 92).

to take the place of the *old umbrella*, and with all the more success because it contained schemes of reform which met the social claims that had become so strong in the last few years. The Caucus, on behalf of the Liberal party, abjured as a heresy the old creed of *laissez-faire* and *laissez-passer*, and led it into the path of *State socialism*. The official chiefs of the party, who were accused of being " out of touch with modern Liberal thought," were really anything but socialist reformers. Some of them, above all Mr. Gladstone, were cast more in a Conservative mould, especially as regards social organization; others, bred in the rationalist individualism of the Mill school, held fast to their philosophic creed, and, so far as they personally were concerned. were even ready to sacrifice themselves to it; others again, being not much troubled with convictions, could not for that very reason feel any heartfelt attachment to or real enthusiasm for social reforms. But they were all obliged to adopt the programme of the Federation more or less explicitly, bound hand and foot as they were to the party Organization and forced to follow each other like the Siamese twins. Formerly the Organization, falling into line behind the official leaders, was dragging the whole party into the Home Rule question at the risk of cutting off its retreat and its supplies; now, suddenly shifting its sails to catch the new breeze, it was taking in tow the leaders, who were resigned, perhaps rallied, but not convinced.

Laying themselves open to suspicion, the Caucus and the official leaders had not disarmed the forces which confronted them, and especially those which were ranged under the banner of socialism. Their good faith was suspected far more than it deserved; every step they took in the direction of the new social demands was looked on rather as a snare or as a dodge to circumvent the voters. The alarm was, therefore, still sounded against "fossil official Liberalism," which took the part of stage villain played by the Whigs before 1886; "independent labour parties " were still formed, and workingmen candidates brought forward, who were destined really to give official Liberalism serious trouble, as was proved by the general elections, one after the other, in which independent candidates of this kind, without achieving any brilliant success on their own account, succeeded, in a good many constituencies, in detaching a sufficiently large number of votes from the Liberals to ensure their defeat by their Tory rivals.

VIII

Nevertheless the general election, which took place a few months after the adoption of the Newcastle Programme, ended in a victory for official Liberalism. The Liberals came back to the House with a very small and above all a very heterogeneous majority; it was more a collection of different groups whose varied aspirations and demands were entered in the famous *omnibus* programme of Newcastle. The members who represented these manifold and not always harmonious interests, none the less formed a compact array behind Mr. Gladstone on his return to office, which remained such during the whole of this Parliament (1892–1895). Invariably presenting a united front, it followed Mr. Gladstone steadily, impelled alike by fear and by calculation, or if the expression is preferred, by duty and by hope. The Liberal Associations which had returned the members of the majority and which held their re-election in their hands, were determined that they should vote obediently for Mr. Gladstone. This express obligation was reinforced by the agreement implied in the Newcastle Programme, which bound each group to vote — whether they approved them or not — for the measures demanded by the other groups, on condition that they did the same — the practice known in political slang by the name of log-rolling.

To carry out the agreement their common agent, the Ministry, prepared and presented to the House, with exemplary diligence, one measure after another intended to satisfy each group in turn. But it had great difficulty in passing its Bills; for not only was it confronted by an extremely numerous and very resolute Opposition, but not one of the important measures of the composite programme which it had received from the Caucus was backed by a body of opinion strong enough to overawe the Opposition and overcome the resistance of the House of Lords, where the Liberal government was in a minority. Refraining, for this reason perhaps, from appealing to the highest court, to the country, from submitting to it the questions in dispute, from taking its opinion specially on this or that important measure left in suspense, such as Home Rule or the Employers' Liability Bill, the Government thought it was cleverer to follow the plan of advocates who address their arguments to points of procedure instead of to the merits of the case. It impugned the attitude of the House of Lords, alleging that it hampered the work of progressive legislation, of reforms. All who desired these reforms, however different they might be, ought, so to speak, to club together their resentment against the Lords and presenting the semblance of having a common platform, already provided by the elaborate combination of the Newcastle Programme, give the Liberal Ministry a fresh lease of strength. In consequence the Caucus started a campaign in the country against the House of Lords and its legislative prerogatives, but without offering a clear and precise solution falling within the range of constitutional logic. The object, indeed, was rather to bring about a *state of feeling* in the country on which it appeared easier to reunite the majority of the electorate than on some definite legislative measures. With the same object the Ministry, in their anxiety to prove the wickedness of the Lords and the purity of their own intentions, went on zealously bringing in bills without any prospect of being able to carry them. They were aware that it was "ploughing the sands of the seashore,"[1] but they calculated that the defeat by the Opposition of all these bills, which promised so many things to so many people (and some of which, taken on their own merits, will perhaps, together with the administrative achievements of the Ministry, — the point need not be discussed in this work, — have a very creditable place in the history of English legislation and administration) would "fill up the cup,"[2] and make the exasperated electors go over in a body to the Liberal side at the next general election.

This expectation was disappointed. The masses did not boil over into wrath against the Lords, as indeed had been foreshadowed by the slight effect produced on public opinion by the stirring appeal which the Liberal Federation issued after the rejection of the Home Rule Bill in the Upper House. Worn out by its barren labour of "ploughing the sands," the

[1] Speech of Mr. H. H. Asquith, Home Secretary.
[2] Speech of Sir W. V. Harcourt, leader of the House.

Liberal Ministry, of which Lord Rosebery had become chief
since Mr. Gladstone's retirement in 1894, was obliged to resign
in 1895. And when the electors were asked to return a new
Parliament immediately afterward, the Liberal party found
itself almost as much split up in the country as it had been
in the House by the various demands for which it solicited
general popular support, relying in one place on local veto, in
another on the reform of the House of Lords, or again on Disestablishment, and so on. But the niceties of log-rolling, which
could be practised with a certain amount of success among
groups of an assembly, had not so good a chance of influencing
the bulk of the electorate, and the less so because the attempts
at fulfilling the promises of the Newcastle Programme had not
only given rise to disappointment among those who had placed
their hopes on them, but had also created apprehension in the
minds of a good many others whose interests were threatened
by one or the other of the proposed Radical reforms. The
result was that a certain number of desertions at the poll was
enough, in the precarious state of the Liberal majority, to upset
the balance of parties, and with the aid of the electoral system
in force which enables a small majority of voters distributed
over a number of constituencies to sweep them all off for the
benefit of the winner, as at a gaming-table, this Liberal reverse
was converted into a catastrophe. The cleverly concocted compound of the Newcastle Programme, this masterpiece of the
wire-pullers, instead of concentrating on itself a Liberal majority, helped to disperse it. After the event the eyes of the
great leaders of the party were opened; they were now of
opinion that the Newcastle Programme was too long to arrest
the minds and the consciences of the electors,[1] or they even
went so far as to regret having accepted this programme from
the hand of the Liberal Federation and to almost disavow the
campaign against the Lords.[2] These regrets were idle, the
phantom of unity which it was sought to retain by means of
the exorcisms of the Caucus was as far off as ever; all that
was left for the moment was a great historical party overthrown.

[1] Speech of Lord Rosebery at the Eighty Club, July 3, 1895, at the time
when he was making over office to the Marquis of Salisbury.
[2] Speech of Lord Rosebery at Huddersfield, March 27, 1896.

IX

While the Liberal party had to contend, during these years, 1886–1895, alike with the regular Opposition and the centrifugal tendencies in its own ranks which it endeavoured to overcome by devices of organization, the Conservative party had the good luck to find a more favourable battle-ground than that of its opponents, and to be well-nigh free from the anxieties caused by internal divisions. It will be recollected how "Tory democracy" had given a new direction to the Conservative party. The boldness and ease with which it had adopted this policy did not make the position of the Conservative party in its competition with the Radicals in Radicalism a less awkward one. The Irish crisis rescued it from this situation. It was a real windfall for the party ; while its old hand was left intact, it received a number of trump cards which enabled it at one time to pause and be more cautious in its play, at another to pursue the game with all the appearance of necessity and almost of decorum. Mr. Gladstone's attempt to grant Home Rule to Ireland allowed the Tories to assume the part of champions of the integrity of the Empire, to reappear in a Conservative rôle. They recovered their *raison d'être*, so to speak, and the consciousness that they had one gave them cohesion and buoyancy in the struggle for existence. There was no need whatever to revive them with the heroic remedies prescribed by Lord Randolph and his school. The beat of their pulse was once more spontaneous and normal. And they could flatter themselves that they were genuine Conservatives without reactionary tendencies. The best proof of this was their alliance with Liberals and even with Radicals, like Mr. Chamberlain, who joined their ranks to defend the national inheritance. To keep this alliance, they would make concessions to the policy of their allies, and assent to measures which would have seemed almost revolutionary to the Conservatives of the day before; but the extent of the sacrifices made would only be more striking evidence of their self-denial and boundless devotion to the great cause of the maintenance of the Empire. They would do evil for the sake of good; they would break with the traditions of the Tory party in order to preserve its ancient virtue.

VOL. I — Y

The Tory party having recovered its proper position, it was no longer possible to draw it on by a policy of dash; grand demonstrations against the leaders or *pronunciamientos* carried out with the aid of the popular Organizations were, for the moment at least, out of place and useless, even for urging Toryism farther on the path of democracy. Lord Randolph Churchill failed to grasp this, and he paid for his mistaken view of the situation. In the Salisbury Ministry, which came into office after the general election of 1886, Lord Randolph obtained the second place, not only on account of his personal weight but out of consideration for the urban democracy of which he was the acknowledged chief and which had contributed so much to the victory at the polls. His mere presence in the Cabinet with the rank of leader of the House of Commons evidently ensured democratic Toryism a large share in the counsels of the Government. But hardly had a few months elapsed when he suddenly left the Ministry on the pretext that it did not sufficiently consult the interests of the taxpayer in its financial policy. This retirement created a great sensation in the country, but that was all. The popular Organizations which had risen in Churchill's defence a few years before now kept quiet. What appeared to be in danger for the moment was not so much the cause of the people threatened by the aristocratic leaders, as the cause of the Union for which these very leaders had fought with so much distinction and success. The immediate future of the party being bound up with this cause, the provincial Associations felt instinctively that all they had to do was to rally round Lord Salisbury and his colleagues. And they did so in silence, leaving Lord Randolph Churchill to sulk in his tent. The leaders issued victorious from this incident, which looked like a grave crisis for a moment, and thanks to the success of their administration, which defied the onslaughts of the Opposition for years, they saw their authority and prestige grow daily higher in the party. Their brilliance, as well as the eclipse of the promoter of democratic Toryism, had the natural consequence of dimming the lustre of popular Organization which had just risen above the horizon opposite the leadership. Instead of being, as Randolph Churchill and his friends wished, the sun of the party's planetary system, the representative Organization became almost a satellite of the leaders. It performed all its movements and reappeared every year in the conferences of delegates of the federated Associations, but it was far from regulating the course of the party, even in appearance, as the Radical Caucus did. The resolutions passed at these conferences did not become *ipso facto*, and were not supposed to become, items in the Tory programme. While the delegates of the Radical caucuses formed deliberative, if not deliberating, assemblies, the conferences of the Conservative Associations, democratized as they were, only discharged consultative functions. The leaders, the official chiefs of the party, had the last word, and the popular delegates made no serious attempt to deprive them of it. A combination of circumstances favourable to the rise of the leadership was thus sufficient to show how great its strength still was, what a hold it still had on the public mind, how it swayed the imagination; in a word, how deep-rooted were the traditional influences of which the Tory party was the great depositary in the body politic of England. The logic of this situation, which Lord Randolph Churchill failed to appreciate, made a severe example of him; not only did he learn to his cost that it was not enough to pronounce against the leaders to make the people flock round him like Israel round Absalom, but when after leaving office he thought fit to occasionally remind his old colleagues in the Government of his existence by scathing criticism of their measures, the Union of the Conservative Associations, into which he had breathed almost a new life, repudiated him by turning him out of the Council at the annual elections of 1890.

But after all, in spite of the rise of the leadership and the eclipse of Lord Randolph Churchill, which showed the persistent force of the old influences, the latter were very far from being absolute masters of the situation. The impress made by democratic Toryism was too deep to be obliterated by them. Churchill's work did not disappear with him; by simple *vis inertiæ* the democratization of Toryism went on, quietly and unobtrusively, but without interruption. The progressive policy of the Salisbury Ministry was doubtless to a great extent due to the fact that it was kept in power by the votes of the Liberal Unionists. Consideration for this alliance not only prevented it from indulging in a reactionary policy, but it was even obliged to give proof of its Liberalism; for the Liberal Unionists, who were continually denounced by the Gladstonian Liberals as traitors to the Liberal cause, were anxious to show the country that Unionism was in no way incompatible with measures of a very liberal, broad character. Mr. Chamberlain, a thoroughbred Radical, who had parted company with orthodox or official Radicalism, was specially preoccupied with this. The Government met their views; it introduced one reform after another. The old Tories, who were too well disciplined to protest aloud, were in consternation, and, fastening on the most obvious cause, mentally cursed Mr. Chamberlain for leading the Tory party astray. In point of fact, the Salisbury Ministry, while listening to the advice of its Liberal allies, followed with no less alacrity the impulse coming from its own party fermenting under the democratic leaven introduced into it. This process did not go on as a matter of course, it met with many an obstacle in class prejudices, in the hierarchical spirit of the community, in the indifference and ignorance of the masses; but it none the less continued in an undemonstrative but unfailing way. Its principal centre and its prime agent was precisely the Organization of the party, the Conservative caucuses. So that in spite of the retiring part played by the Union of Conservative Associations, and its slight official influence, the local Organizations, by their daily, hourly imperceptible action, indirectly affected the policy of the party and the attitude of its chiefs. In fact, the mainstay of the Ministry in the House was now the Tory members for the large towns, most of whom represented the middle class and the workmen identified with the democratized Associations. The loss of power, in 1892, and the wish to obtain another and a more favourable verdict from the mass of voters was in no way calculated to alter these tendencies of the Tory leaders, nor to lessen the influences to which they were now subjected. The return of the Tories to power, which has lately taken place (in 1895) with the indispensable assistance of the Liberal Unionists, gives these influences a fresh lease of life.

We have now come to the end of the distance traversed by the English party Organization known by the name of the

Caucus. From its appearance on the scene of history we have followed its fortunes; we have pursued it in all its great manifestations, letting ourselves rather be guided by it, so as to discover what it would reveal of itself, with the liberty, of course, of seeing with our own eyes. Its career, up to the present relatively short, and above all the fact that in consequence of the method which I have adopted as being more scientific, we have only been able to watch the Caucus on the stage and on the move so to speak, have prevented us from giving a complete picture of it. But now that it has stopped, or rather appears to have done so to the observer obliged to stop himself, it may be possible to supplement the impression derived from the Caucus by considering it in a state of repose. After having observed it to a certain extent in its dynamic, we may now study it in its static condition. This is what I now propose to undertake by means of a systematic analysis of its component parts, of their co-ordination and their daily working.

THIRD PART

FIRST CHAPTER

THE MACHINERY OF THE CAUCUS

I

THE history of the establishment of the Birmingham Caucus which was the starting-point of the movement which we are considering, has supplied us with an outline of the machinery of the representative Associations. It will be remembered that according to the theory of the Caucus all the inhabitants of the locality belonging to either party assemble in public meetings to settle the affairs of the party, directly or through delegates elected at these meetings and constituting deliberative bodies outside those which owe their existence to the Constitution. Their duty and their work consist in upholding and developing in the constituency, and consequently in the kingdom, Liberal or Conservative principles, as the case may be, and in securing the election of Members belonging to the same party. The success of these Members at the polling-booth is intended to procure the party preponderance in Parliament, which again is to ensure the triumph of the principles of the parties styled Liberal or Conservative, supposed to be alone capable of making the country great and happy in times present and to come. The main, the real, business of the Caucus Associations thus amounts to manipulating the electorate in the interest of the party, with the pretension of doing this on behalf of and by the people. How do they set about it, how do they discharge the duty they have undertaken, and what is really the part played and the advantage derived by the people — this is what we are about to examine point by point.

Starting from the principle that the whole electoral population is divided into two sections, into Liberals and Tories, the organization of the parties expects that in each locality the

Liberal Association shall include all the Liberals, and the Conservative Association all the Conservatives.   This is the theory. The practice is very far removed from it.   In reality the Association embraces only a very small fraction of the "party." This is the first of the points which command the situation, and to find one's bearings it is necessary to take note of it at once.   The study of the daily working of the Caucus will consequently consist in ascertaining the reaction of this fraction on the whole, in considering their respective forces, the active power of the one and the resisting power of the other, the methods and mode of action employed by the former and their application.

We shall begin by studying the machinery of the Organization and the men who set it in motion.

The basis of the organization of the party in the boroughs is the ward or polling-district, where the local adherents of the party assembled in general meetings constitute the electorate of the Organization; from these original electors proceeds the representation of the party.   The delegates elected by the wards form the central Association of the electoral division, which is destined to be as it were the local parliament of the party with the executive committee for ministry.   To be a member of the ward Association or of the central Association it is sufficient, according to the Birmingham doctrine, to declare one's adherence to the party.   The practice in this respect, as well as in regard to several other points of organization, is not absolutely uniform.   In a good many places the new member must be introduced by one or two persons, or a formal vote be taken on his admission, or he must sign a declaration of adhesion to the Association and receive a ticket of membership.   In point of fact new recruits are warmly welcomed, and no difficulty is made about admitting them, especially on the Liberal side. Partly from a feeling of "confidence in the people" which they affect, and partly owing to certain easy-going ways which characterize them, the Liberals suffer every one to come freely to them, whereas the Tories, who are more particular, and who are still in their democratic apprenticeship, take elaborate precautions by admitting only members "duly enrolled," and sometimes by reserving to themselves the right to expel members whose political conduct may be held incompatible with the title of Conservative. They stipulate further, in their rules at all events, that the members of the Association are to respect the authority of the " recognized chiefs " of the party, etc. In spite of these grand precautions " traitors " creep into the Tory ward Organizations, who are abandoned enough to supply the Radical newspaper with reports of their meetings. When they are discovered they are expelled. The possession of a Parliamentary vote is seldom required as a qualification for membership of the Association. And there is hardly any limit of age; when the minimum age is stated it is fixed at twenty, eighteen, or even at sixteen or fifteen years, so as to enlist people as early as possible.

The statutory powers of the ward meetings consist in appointing their permanent committee (with as many members as they like), in electing the delegates to the central Association, that is to say to the " hundreds," and finally in nominating candidates for the annual municipal elections, in which the ward is the unit. The importance, however, of these ward meetings does not lie so much in this formal business, which, moreover, requires only two or three sittings a year, as in the relations which they establish among the adherents of the party. In the first place it is there that goes on the process of natural selection of influential persons destined to become leaders in their street or block. The managers of the Caucus of the division keep an eye on the rise and growth of these local influences; in attending the ward meetings they notice the good speakers, the ardent spirits, the men of action, and become acquainted with them. For it is they who will be the pillars of the Organization. Then the ward meetings are a means of maintaining cohesion, of keeping up party ties among their frequenters, just as they present an opportunity for making recruits. When there are no elections or statutory business on hand, members meet for the purpose of meeting, to be together. Sometimes the Caucus sends some one to make them a brief political speech. Sometimes it is the great question of the day or the passing of an important law which provides matter for discussion or conversation. Besides, the great familiarity of every Englishman with the procedure of deliberative assemblies and the imperturbable gravity with which he moves or seconds proposals, motions, amendments, almost

without an object, easily enables a meeting to kill the time
fairly decently. If the ward meetings are held, as is generally
the case with the Conservatives, in the public-houses, the current business is provided: drinking goes on. The public-houses
are to a certain extent the base of operations of the Tory organization of the ward. The latter is divided, for the needs of
the cause, into a certain number of sections with a public-house
for centre. The ward group holds its meetings by turns in
each of these ten or twelve public-houses where the people of
the neighbourhood gather round the small permanent group
which forms the nucleus of all the meetings. The publican on
his side tries to bring people to them for the good of the house.
He invites those who are not yet members of the Association,
offers to stand sponsor for them, and to procure their admission as members.

Important as the groundwork of the Organization of the
party, the ward association, in spite of its democratic constitution, really has an extremely narrow base; for its meetings
are very little attended. Of some twelve or fifteen hundred
electors in a ward only a very slender minority is affiliated to
the Associations. The others do not want to be on the list;
they refrain from displaying their political sympathies in
order not to lose customers in their business, or not to get into
bad odour with their master, who is on the other side; but the
majority of the non-affiliated consists simply of the indifferent, who do not care an atom for politics, at least between
the parliamentary elections. Even in places where the political pulse has always beaten strongly, and where the Caucus
has been a decided success, as at Birmingham, the proportion
of those affiliated to the party Organizations does not exceed
eight or ten per cent of the total number of electors. But, few
as they are, not nearly all of them come to the meetings of their
ward committees. In the beginning the ward meetings attracted
people in certain towns; in others the attendance of members
varied a good deal, until eventually the situation became the
same everywhere, that is to say, the ward meetings are deserted,
as the agents of the Caucus themselves admit frankly enough.[1]

---

[1] To the question if the ward meetings were fairly well attended, an Association secretary in a large town in Lancashire replied: "Yes, very well;
they could all get into this room (a very small one) just as the study of my

And it is in these meetings, which contain two to three per cent of the whole electorate, that the delegates are chosen who are to invest the Caucus with its representative authority. It has been my lot to attend ward meetings where there were not even twenty persons to elect seventy-five delegates. In these conditions the election of delegates is simply a farce. Generally, a list prepared beforehand is submitted to the meeting and voted in a lump. Often, to curtail the proceedings, even the semblance of a vote is dispensed with; the old list is adopted again. The inevitable result is that all the work falls to a handful of men, who are willing to attend to it. At their head is the ward secretary, who is the mainspring of the ward Organization. Gathering round him more or less active personages, whom he and the leading Caucus-men have singled out from the crowd, or who have become aware of their vocation themselves, he forms in conjunction with them a coterie, which manages all the political business in the district. Coming to an understanding beforehand, and always acting in concert, they are able to manage even meetings of some size without difficulty, and to have the last word in the choice of committee-men or delegates, who in consequence follow them implicitly. An artisan or small clerk by profession, the ward secretary knows all his men, he speaks their language, he has lived for years in constant contact with them, he knows how to lay his hand upon them. At meetings he speaks little or not at all, but it is he who inspires those who do, beginning with the chairman. At the election of delegates to the "hundreds," he "suggests" "good names"; and his list, settled beforehand, is generally adopted without modifications. He modestly leaves the addition of a few names to the wisdom of the meeting; if there are fifty persons to be elected, he gives only forty-five names. The secretary, as well as the chairman, is appointed by the meeting of the ward members, but in practice it is the Caucus which more often than not has "suggested" him in its turn. For the Caucus it is a matter of primary importance to have an adroit and energetic secretary

excellent colleague on the other side is large enough to hold all those who come to the ward meetings of his Organization." To keep up appearances several agents of the Caucus replied that the ward meetings were "fairly attended," but on enquiry in the town it turned out that there was room for the whole meeting on a sofa.

down in the ward; otherwise it is literally paralyzed, so far as this ward is concerned. For the Caucus the ward secretary is at once an agent for supplying information, and an executive officer. He receives instructions from the secretary of the Caucus; he is guided, controlled by him, responsible to him. The latter can always come and inspect the books of the ward, which are kept by the ward secretary, and in which is entered all the business relating to the Association and to the electoral matters of the locality. In a word, there is the closest possible co-operation between the ward Organizations and the Caucus; and it could not be otherwise. The Conservatives, who had, not without grave misgiving, introduced the representative principle into the Organization of the party, had thought proper, in more than one place, to exorcise the democratic spirit or, what was the equivalent of it in their eyes, the spirit of insubordination. By means of provisions in the rules which undoubtedly testify to a great faith in the efficacy of written or printed matter, they saddled the ward committees with the duty of " being responsible," of " acting under authority," of " referring," of " reporting " to the executive Committee of the central Association.

II

The delegates of all the wards, plus the chairmen and the secretaries of ward committees, constitute the Council or General Committee of the division (often known on the Liberal side by the name of " hundreds," the " 200 " or the " 300," etc.). Nevertheless this representative assembly is far from being derived in its entirety from the popular source, even in theory. In the first place, as we have seen in the Birmingham model, it contains besides the members elected in the popular gatherings, a certain number of *co-opted* members. The delegates have power to add to their number, in accordance with the oligarchic method of appointment of the old days, of the corporative system of the Middle Ages, which has been preserved down to this day in the municipal institutions of England.[1] In borrowing this feature from the municipal

---

[1] The Town Councils are composed as to two-thirds of members elected by the ratepayers, and as to the remaining third of aldermen chosen by the councillors themselves. The same system has been adopted for the County Councils established in 1888.

constitution, the Caucus was evidently not quite sure that the pure elective principle would suit it, although it was never weary of proclaiming its merits. The result proved that the creators of the Caucus were right. The Council of the Association has often been able to rectify the choice of the wards by means of the *co-optation* rule. Men who did not commend themselves to the ward politicians but who could render services to the party were admitted as *co-opted* members. Sometimes they were leaders, persons who brought with them experience of men and affairs, a conciliatory disposition and a balanced temperament. More often perhaps they were, and still are, important subscribers to the funds of the Association for whom a place is found in the Council as a reward for their liberality. The proportion of *co-opted* members varies in different Associations; it is 3, 5, or 10 per cent of the total number of members and sometimes reaches even a higher figure. A good many Associations, however, have given up *co-optation* in order to conform to the strict democratic doctrine.

Certain Associations, without having recourse to the expedient of *co-optation*, admit without election and as *ex officio* members people of position or large subscribers. Thus in several Associations (especially on the Tory side) the rules give a seat on their governing bodies to all the Magistrates, to the members of town councils and other local elective assemblies, such as School Boards, Boards of Guardians, who belong to the political party in question. To them are added, and on the same footing, the managers or other representatives of clubs, societies, and institutions which wear the party colours. There are also Associations which take into their councils and committees every one who pays a higher subscription, the minimum of which is fixed by the rules. This minimum varies from one guinea to a few pounds, but some Associations are ready to accept half a guinea a year. Certain Associations bestow on the generous donors even the title of Vice-President, which can thus be got for cash. Other Associations, without putting all the big subscribers in a lump on the committees, provide that this or that proportion of the committee shall be chosen from among them, but as their number is not large, the selection, if there is one, is very limited.

The Organizations resort to these methods of swelling their

budget because they are much in want of money. We already know, from the history of the Caucus sketched above, that the subscription has been practically abolished in most of the Liberal Associations. The Conservatives generally require it in their rules, even in very formal terms, but they too are obliged in practice to deviate from this strictness. Some Associations, while giving up compulsory subscription, stipulate that complete membership, especially the right of voting at meetings, shall be granted only on condition of paying the subscription, but this does not help them, for their adherents care more for their money than for complete membership. It will be remembered also that in several places an attempt was made, but without success, to require payment of the subscription at least from the members of the Council or Executive Committee. Practically payment is optional. Sometimes the number of paying members of the Council is one half, sometimes less; in certain Associations for one member of the Council who contributes a small amount there are nineteen who do not pay, and there are Organizations in which nobody pays. In places where the Organization does not work with great regularity, as for instance on the Liberal side in the constituencies of the vast metropolis, care is even taken to reassure the dignitaries of the Caucus. In the printed notices sent to inform them that they have been appointed members of the Council there is a memo to the effect that no pecuniary contribution is attached to the office. Under these circumstances it not infrequently happens that the caucuses depend on a few individuals for their pecuniary resources, wealthy men who supply the greater part of the income of the Organization of their party. Often half or more than half of this income comes from three or four or five people. The non-paying members are however supposed to contribute their share in the form of " work " which they are to bring to bear on the elector (by ways and means which will be explained later on). And it is in view of this " work " that they consider themselves fully entitled to refuse to pay anything, even a shilling a year only; they think that it is quite enough to make a personal without a pecuniary sacrifice.

III

Theoretically the Council or General Committee is the most important and influential body in the Organization. As this assembly is supposed to embody the mind and the will of the adherents of the party, it has consequently to prescribe its policy, to notify it to the great ones of the realm, the Ministers and Members of Parliament, for their guidance, and finally to select the parliamentary candidates [1] for whom the members of the party are bound to vote on the polling-day. But in reality the Executive Committee of the Association holds all the power. Composed, as we have seen, of the office-bearers of the Association (president, vice-president, treasurer, secretary), of the ward chairmen and secretaries, and of a certain number of leaders elected in the ward meetings or sometimes introduced by *co-optation*, the Committee includes the most active and influential men of the Organization. Not only does it set the machine in motion, but it regulates all the details of its working, it controls everything that goes on and everything which makes up the life of the Association and of its ward branches. The selection of the candidates practically rests with it. Sometimes this is formally entrusted to it by the regulations (on the Tory side). As a general rule the Association adopts the candidate, but the Executive Committee proposes him, and in most cases, not only *de facto* but even *de jure*, the Association cannot deal with a candidature if it has not been previously submitted to and considered by the Executive Committee. Even when it consults the Council before acting, it still dictates the latter's decisions. Containing all the leaders of the local branches to whose influence the delegates to the "hundreds" have become amenable in the wards, it is bound to carry with it the assembly, which moreover is too large to take its own line. Constituting an inner circle in the "hundreds," the Executive Committee is itself again too large to hold undivided power. Consequently an inner circle of the second degree is formed within it, at

---

[1] Occasionally, but very seldom, the name of the candidate adopted is submitted for ratification to a special meeting of electors convened *ad hoc.* Again, while giving the Council full power to choose the candidates, certain Associations require on these occasions a two-thirds' instead of a simple majority.

one time by a process of natural selection, at another by means of the rules which establish "parliamentary," "financial," "organizing" sub-committees. One of these sub-committees engrosses all the powers. For deciding delicate points and taking exceptional measures, in regard to expenditure for instance, which are sometimes shrouded in mystery, at election time when the decisive struggle is being fought, the innermost inner circle is even a necessity.

In the large towns the concentration of power in the hands of a few reaches its extreme limit, in spite of the autonomist doctrine of the Caucus, and exhibits in the most striking way its tendency towards oligarchic government. Since the last redistribution of seats in 1885, the large towns no longer form single electoral districts with a common representation for the whole borough, but are cut up into *Divisions* of almost equal dimensions, with a Member for each.[1]   To be true to democratic principles, the caucuses of large towns had to allow the new divisional constituencies the right of acting independently in the affairs of the party, a right which they had formerly asserted with such energy for the constituencies of the old type, the representation of which they had taken upon themselves. In consequence each *Division* obtained an autonomous party organization.   Nevertheless the old single Associations were unwilling to part with their power and tried to live on by the side of or rather above the new Divisional Associations.   The redistribution of seats was hardly passed when the leaders of the Caucus, and especially Mr. Chamberlain, looking to the future of the institution, recommended the preservation of the old organization for such action as concerned the whole town, while setting up an Association with the usual powers in each constituency.   Birmingham at once put this combination into practice by grouping the "hundreds" of newly created Divisions into one body of 2000, which to all appearance was simply a federation of independent units of divisional "hundreds."   Its powers were very vaguely defined: to give advice to the local Associations, to organize political meetings for the whole town, etc.   But almost everywhere else this plan met with a determined resistance in which the moderates and

---

[1] The Act of 1885, however, has not interfered with some urban constituencies which returned only two members.

the pure democrats agreed. The former were of opinion that the maintenance of a central organization would only perpetuate the dictatorial practices of the Caucus and prevent the growth of a spontaneous political life in the constituencies.[1] As for the "stalwarts," they were against a general organization for the whole town, out of democratic jealousy. In the face of this opposition the single Association has, in some towns, entirely given way to the new *divisional* Associations. In places where it managed to hold its ground, in the form of a *Union* or federated *Association,* or with the more modest title of *United Council* or *United Committee,* consisting only of a few representatives of local Associations, it had to encounter severe attacks from the autonomists at the beginning. But gradually, thanks to the healing action of time and above all to the excitement produced by the Home Rule crisis, which threw all other controversies into the background, the objections raised to the general Associations diminished in energy and persistency, and the latter asserted themselves and gained a firm footing, as if nothing had happened. In places where they had been abolished they were quietly started afresh, always with the modest duty of giving advice when they might be asked for it, of organizing meetings, etc. But all the essential powers of the new divisional Associations were soon more or less surreptitiously transferred to the *Unions* or *United Committees,* and before long there arose in all the large towns an unstable equilibrium between the mongrel general organization which wields real power, of course with the necessary formal precautions, and the Divisional Associations to which power belongs as a matter of right. Three, four, five, or seven *Divisions* are practically governed by a small party committee.

The Tory organization of the large towns has been landed in the same result, and with all the more ease and certainty because it was not, like its rival, upset by the crisis brought about by the change in the electoral system. The Conserva-

---

[1] The anxiety with regard to the Caucus was moreover not without its influence on the vote of the redistribution of seats. Moderate Liberals as well as a good many Tories in the House had, as it would appear, decided to adopt the system of splitting the large constituencies into a number of electoral divisions, in the hope that it would decapitate the Caucus. If Mr. Chamberlain's advice were followed everywhere, this advantage would be less certain.

tives, have not meddled with their old single Associations. By way of conforming to the principle of autonomy in the government of the party, which they now profess, they have conceded home rule to their adherents in the *Divisions*, but only on paper. Consequently, they have divisional Associations, with all the usual parade of presidents, vice-presidents, executive committees, etc.; but nothing is done in them without the advice of the general Organization, especially of its executive committee. According to the rules, sometimes they "shall" and sometimes they "may" consult it on important matters, but this practically amounts to the same thing, the option being really a duty.

IV

In examining the constituent elements of the Caucus, from the ward meetings up to its innermost inner circle, a passing notice only has been given to two persons, who are, nevertheless, the pillars of the temple of the Organization, — the secretary and the President of the Association. The secretary is an official appointed by the executive committee and working under its orders. His duties are of the most varied description. In the first place he is a sort of epitome of the ward secretaries. He performs on a large scale for the division or the whole town all the operations which the latter carry out on a small scale in their little respective departments. He gives them instructions, he assists them with his advice, he checks and supervises them; he is careful to get good secretaries appointed in the ward; he does his best to ensure the election by the ward meetings of good delegates to the "hundreds," active men and skilled in canvassing the voter; he looks after the uninterrupted working of the machine, he sees that the ward committees do not go to sleep, but act, that is to say, meet and hold forth for the greater glory of the party; he goes from one ward to another to attend meetings; in a large town he sometimes has more than one meeting an evening; he arrives, satisfies himself at a glance that all is going on well, and rushes off to another meeting; he encourages here, makes remarks there; he allays susceptibilities or local jealousies, he stifles or quells mutinies; he has constantly to display energy and tact; above all, he must not give himself airs, and he must keep his "head clear," — that is, not muddled by drink. Concentrating in his hands all the intelligence which reaches him from the wards or which he gathers himself as he goes along, he supplies the committee with the information of which it stands in need, and keeps the member or candidate, with whom he maintains a regular correspondence, posted up in the situation. To these functions of political newsmonger he adds those of tactician and consulting strategist if he is a bit of a philosopher, capable of drawing a moral from the facts which he accumulates, and consequently of pointing out the ways and means. He attends, in the interest of his party, to the electoral register, a highly complicated piece of work, as we have already seen; he argues before the Registration court in support of the electoral claims of members of his party and against those of his political opponents. He has many other duties which recur at more or less lengthy intervals, but which are none the less of importance. He organizes the great party meetings convened from time to time, the public demonstrations held on account of an important Bill or this or that political event, the receptions given to the big men of the party, who do the town the honour of bringing it their "authorized eloquence." He is master of the ceremonies at banquets of the party, umpire of sports organized under its auspices. At election time he is here, there, and everywhere. He has to set the "workers" going, to receive their reports, to give them instructions, to attend to the printing and distribution of bills and posters, to organize electoral meetings, to see this man, write to that, to settle endless details, to cope with endless incidents. Accountable to the Association, he is also responsible to the law, for he is generally the election agent, whom every candidate is bound by law to employ for the purpose of conducting the election in conformity with the enactments directed against bribery and corruption.

The perfect discharge of all these duties by the secretary is not of very common occurrence in practice, the burden is too heavy to be borne by everybody. It undoubtedly demands a natural bent and a long apprenticeship. The Caucus and the conditions which had brought it into existence are still of too recent a date in England for the type of a perfect secretary to be often met with as yet; but the process of reproduction of the species goes on and advances from day to day. The great difficulty of many Associations is their inability to afford a secretary, the expense is too great for their slender budget, and they are obliged to put up with the voluntary services of the "honorary secretary," who is one of their elective officers. He is not a "professional" but an amateur or a zealot of the party. Generally absorbed in his own business or profession, he cannot devote much time to the Association. Even if he has no work, if he is simply a "gentleman," he cannot be expected to put his shoulder to the wheel, which however is a *sine qua non* for the proper working of a party Organization.

The President of the Association, on the other hand, need not put his shoulder to the wheel. He is more a show personage. If the secretary's part somewhat recalls Figaro, the chairman has that of the heavy father in the play. He must be eminently respectable, very well known in the town, influential, and, what is always an advantage, pretty rich or at all events well off. The *name* of the President is a flag, a standard. It is his personal prestige, the respect and confidence that he inspires, which carry the members of the Association, the "workers," and keep them loyal and devoted to the Organization. For the voters who are outside the Organization, but whose votes have to be secured, the name of the President is also a sort of guarantee; for them it has the importance of the signature of the firm. But it is not enough for him to lend his name, he must exert himself personally as well. He has to show himself and speak on every occasion of at all a solemn description, at the annual gatherings of the Association, at the big meetings, etc. He opens the meetings and closes them by addresses in which he delivers himself with dignity of platitudes on the great cause, the old and glorious institutions, the unity of the empire, the union of classes (on the Tory side); on progress, on war against privileges and monopolies, on the selfishness of the "classes," and their odious resistance to all popular reform (on the Liberal side). Referring to this eloquence of the chair, a Tory Caucus secretary once defined the chairman as the "man who can tell the biggest lies." His respectability covers everything and adorns it.

The Tories, who pay marked attention to respectability, are

of course never at a loss for men qualified to fill this position
of pompous mediocrity. The Liberals have a good supply of
them too. It will be borne in mind that, at the time of the
Home Rule crisis in 1886, the hope was expressed that the
Caucus of the Gladstonian party would not be able to hold its
ground after having lost its respectable members, who had
become Unionists. This hope, as we know, has not been
realized; and, in so far as it was based on the desertion of
the respectables, it was, as may be pointed out here, not well
founded. For respectability has nothing absolute or individual about it; the somewhat inferior moral qualities and virtues
of which it is the outcome, or the generalization, however relative they may be, are found in every sphere of society. They
constitute, in every social organization, an inexhaustible store
which supplies, in the desired form and quantity, the wherewithal for equipping the men who serve as an example to
their fellows, who set them the fashion, who make them follow
in their train. It is, therefore, perfectly justifiable to parody
the saying, that one is always a reactionary in some one's eyes,
by the *dictum* that one is always somebody's ideal of respectability. When the respectable class has resigned or lost power,
its place is soon taken by the next succeeding layer of respectability, which becomes *the respectable one* with all the attributes attaching to its influence on the layers below it. There
may be an interregnum, but it is never of long duration.
Just as in society a great disturbance may displace the forces
revolving therein, but very soon these forces or others will
fall into position, and so long as the machinery is not broken,
it will continue to work with other men, with new respectables,
— perhaps not so well as before, — but still it will work.
When, in consequence of the Home Rule crisis, in 1886, the
respectables had withdrawn from the Liberal Associations, a
new category of respectables insensibly was evolved by or arose
within them, which became the fulcrum of the Organization of
the party. Besides, the Liberal respectables of a prior date
had not all withdrawn to a man; some of them had remained,
being held back either by their genuine sympathy for Home
Rule, or by their devotion to Mr. Gladstone, and by the difficulty of breaking old ties, or again by ambition.

However much the quality of respectability may preponderate in the President of the Association, it is not necessarily his sole title to the office. Sometimes he unites with it the qualification of a fighting politician. In accordance with his temperament and his abilities he directs the attack, leads the troups into action, or, as strategist, sketches the plan of campaign and organizes victory, in his study. If the President does not possess any of these qualities his place can be supplied by the honorary secretary, who under this more modest title is often the real inspirer and manager of the Association. A clever and hard-working paid secretary, an intelligent and energetic honorary secretary, and an influential and wealthy President form a trio at the apex of the Association which is the ideal of every party Organization.

V

The President with his qualifications of respectability and wealth leads the Association also from the point of view of social rank. He represents the well-to-do middle class which, owing to the well-nigh complete abstention of the aristocracy,[1] is almost always the superior social element in the party Organization. The numerical importance of this element is not great. It may be said of the middle class, especially so far as its upper strata are concerned, that it pays little or no heed to the daily life of the Caucus. All it does is to supply the party Organizations with a portion of their staff, on the Conservative side to a greater, perhaps even a preponderating extent, on the Liberal side in a lesser degree. But it is almost always the middle-class men who are the financial supporters of the Organizations. Consequently the power of the rich over the Associations would be immense if it were not diminished by their own indifference or their political lukewarmness. A good many of them in fact are satisfied with paying their subscription, from a sense of duty to their party or a feeling of self-respect, and attend only the big meetings of the party, for the pleasure of seeing their name in the paper the next day among the " influential and eminent gentlemen who were on the plat-

---

[1] On the Liberal side in very rare cases, on the Tory side more often, the members of the aristocracy consent to fill honorary posts in the Associations, but they do not take an active share in their labours.

form." Leaving the small fry of the Caucus to themselves in the daily existence of the Organization, the bigwigs appear on the scene when the parliamentary candidate has to be selected, and on these occasions they weigh more or less heavily on the Associations, especially in the Liberal camp, to such an extent that they may be considered the real masters of the Organization. In the Tory Organizations the inherited docility of their members prevents them from feeling this weight, while on the Liberal side the more timorous political views and the class feeling of the plutocrats naturally conflict with the more radical inclinations of the rank and file of the party. Nevertheless, there is seldom a rupture in the Liberal Associations, both because the rank and file are perfectly well aware that without the money of the middle-class members, the Association of the party, in one of which they are interested, could not be carried on, and also owing to the tendency of most of the members of the Caucus to gravitate in the social orbit of these middle-class people, a tendency which the latter carefully foster, as we shall see before long.

When one speaks of the bulk of the Caucus members, it is not popular masses that are really in question. Considering their enormous numerical preponderance and the democratic basis of the Caucus, it is they who ought to supply its main contingents and constitute its motive power; but, in reality, this is not the case. True, every Association includes many members who are workmen by trade, often even they form the majority in the "hundreds," but they are hardly *representative* of the working classes, who, taken as a whole, give the Caucus a decidedly wide berth. The ward meetings or the meetings of the "hundreds" and all that goes on there have absolutely no attraction for them. The consciousness of themselves, of their interests, of their wants, which for some years past has begun to take a more or less definite shape among the workmen, displays itself more in the sphere of social claims and makes even the most quick-witted of them look with distrust on the political Organizations which labour exclusively for the benefit of their respective parties or, as some say, of the capitalist class. The majority who think little or not at all cannot or will not rouse themselves from their habitual not to say normal condition of political indifference. In short, the general fact is that the great mass of workingmen come into contact with the Caucus at election time only.

Having thus dealt with the various social classes, all of which we have seen take little or no part in the Caucus, there remains only the lower middle-class to supply the framework of its organization; and as a matter of fact, it is from this class that the men who keep it going are mainly recruited. Shopkeepers, clerks, and superior artisans, this is the sphere from which most of the active members of the Caucus are taken. Their greater eagerness to join in it has a good deal to do with their moral position in English society. In the absence of legal barriers between the classes, the social life of England divides them in a harder and faster way than any legislation could have done. The gradations of wealth and of social relations, so long considered as almost physical lines of demarcation in England, are still far from having lost this meaning in the English society of the present day, engaged though it be in democratizing its institutions. The parliamentary Reform of 1832, and the great rise of industry and commerce from and after 1846, had thrown open the doors of "society" to the upper section of the middle class, to the manufacturers and the merchants. Those who came next to them in the social scale, especially the small tradesmen, the shopkeepers, were left out in the cold and treated rather as social pariahs. The shopkeeper was despised in the first place because he was only a shopkeeper, then because as such he was bound to have bad manners, and again because he had not even a decent religion; he was almost always a Dissenter, he attended the services of a man who was not a gentleman, who had not in his young days taken honours at Oxford or joined in athletic sports with young men of good family at Cambridge, like the Rector or Vicar of the parish. In proportion as political reforms made him the equal of this privileged order in the State and the levelling tendencies of economic life decreased the distance between them in society, the shopkeeper grew more and more anxious to step across the social barrier which confronted him, or, to use the English expression, to "force himself into society." The Reform Bill of 1867, by giving him the parliamentary franchise, undoubtedly raised him in the social scale, but the exercise of his electoral right was necessarily an isolated act: the opportunity of voting recurs only once every five or six years. The sphere and the duration of the activity offered by the Caucus was much more extensive: it set up a miniature parliament, the members of which were always in full view of their fellow-citizens and invested with powers of some importance, extending to politics in its higher aspects. The small middle-class man therefore readily availed himself of the opportunity of rising and he speedily managed to acquire a constantly increasing share in the government of the party Associations. It is by no means uncommon to see, both in England and Scotland, the caucuses of large towns controlled by men who only yesterday were nobodies, and whose claims to the distinction it would be very difficult to specify. Their office soon gives them a certain social position, even their name gains in syllabic importance, from the Tom Brown or Bill Smith which they were for the neighbours of their ward or street they blossom out into Thomas Robinson Brown, Esq., or William Wellworth Smith, Esq. Once raised to the rank of local notables they are ripe for municipal honours, and through the Caucus they obtain easy admittance into the Town Council or other local elective bodies.

In the Tory Caucus the lower middle class, important as its position is, plays a more retiring part than in the Liberal Organization. The Organization of the Tories having been pre-eminently centralizing and aristocratic in the old days, not only the lower middle class, but even the upper stratum of that class was left outside; it was therefore its turn to come in first, and it did so, as we have seen from the historical sketch of the *Tory Democratic* movement, partly by the channel of the new representative Organizations. Then the lower middle class is much weaker numerically in the Tory than in the Liberal camp, for the condition of social inferiority in which it was kept threw it into the arms of the party of attack, of the Liberals rather than of the Conservatives. Finally, there is a reason of another kind for the smaller importance of the lower middle class in the Tory Organization: to outstrip the Liberals, the Tories take a great deal of trouble to secure the workingmen and are ready to give the artisans who influence their surroundings a large share in the Associations.

VI

The station of life from which the great majority of the caucus-men are taken is enough to show that their intellectual standard is not a very high one.   For the most part worthy people, earning their livelihood honestly and laboriously as shopkeepers or in trades, they are generally devoid of enlightenment.   Their political horizon is extremely narrow, and they can scarcely widen it by common efforts and reciprocal influence, for the display and practice of which the Association should offer an opportunity, as the circle formed by the ward meetings is deserted by people of higher rank.   Called upon to produce or single out the men who are to govern the Organization of the party, they bring to the discharge of the task a criterion which presents a curious mixture of notions of respectability and political devotion.   Their aspirations in private life, their daily struggles of small tradespeople with the ambition of becoming a little better off and acquiring the dignity conferred thereby, incline them to look with respect and admiration on those who are a few steps higher than themselves. The common political creed enhances these feelings, and supplies, so to speak, a rational justification for them.   Consequently in the eyes of many a member of the ward meeting, the most eminent individual is the local bigwig who combines the requisite qualities of respectability with loyalty to the party, who has perhaps a narrow mind, but an open hand, who subscribes liberally to the local charities, and whom the "party can depend upon."   They "look up to him," to use the characteristic English expression, quite spontaneously, and are convinced that nature herself meant him for their chairman or president.   As regards the other leading members of the Organization, such a combination of excellences cannot, of course, be expected in their case, but they are bound at all events to display a quality which is all the more strictly insisted on, viz. political zeal.   The conception and estimate of this quality vary with the different temperament of those who form an opinion of it, presenting themselves especially under two aspects which reflect the mental condition of two main categories into which most of the frequenters of ward meetings are divided.   The one is composed of restless beings who court opportunities of acting, of holding forth, of agitating, on no matter what subject, and for whom this is not only a pleasure but a necessity. This category produces the militants, the fighting men, the orators. Endowed with an inexhaustible flow of words and with an imperturbable assurance, they intervene at every turn, and do not fail to make an impression on a good many of their colleagues. Side by side with them there is the calm and sedate section. Their political creed is more internal than external, and encompassing it with the uniform and regular devotion of a cult, they really mingle with it something of their Church religiousness, which is made up of a certain amount of sentiment and a good deal of ritual routine, the strict observance of which constitutes the just and God-fearing man in their eyes. Being attuned to this moral pitch, they are naturally disposed to consider the turners of the party praying-wheels, who are to be found in every Organization, as the most worthy priests of the political divinity. These are first and foremost the persons who attract attention by their assiduity; they never miss a meeting, they are always there as if on duty, one is sure to find them in their places, in the front row. They follow the proceedings of the meetings, and intervene in them with the regularity of automatons. Does somebody make a proposal which in accordance with established practice must be seconded by another member, one of this assiduous contingent rises as if touched by a spring, and declares with his most solemn air that he seconds it. Is there a motion to be brought forward or other business of a formal nature to be taken up, these personages can invariably be depended on. This alacrity and assiduity commend themselves to many of the frequenters of the ward meetings as much as the passionate ardour of the others; in their eyes it is unimpeachable proof of political zeal and the criterion of an " earnest politician."

These two main categories which the ward meetings put forward to serve in the " hundreds " and in the committees of the Organization, the restless and the staid members, supply the Caucus, the small group of leaders which arises within it, with a material which is most valuable because it is mouldable in the highest degree. Different and even diametrically opposed temperaments, they have this property in common, that they are ready to receive an impulse and not to give it. The former,

who are only too delighted to start, go off at full gallop at the
first touch of the spur, prepared to run down and trample on
everything which crosses their path. The latter, whose mood
is anything but adventurous and headstrong, are never safer
than when walking in the beaten track. Men of these types,
when brought together in fixed grooves and for a public object,
spontaneously create an atmosphere eminently favourable to
the growth of an uncompromising and inflexible political orthodoxy. But their orthodoxy, springing as it does from their
temperament, is not immured in an unchangeable creed, in a
series of unalterable propositions, to which the mind, with more
or less discernment, binds itself in perpetuity. It is rather a
mental condition, a constant inclination towards conformity
with the attitude of those who are supposed to be the depositaries of the faith. It is like a river-bed with steep banks
which receives and holds the streams descending from the
heights above. Unbending in its course, the orthodoxy is
variable as regards its contents. A fresh strong current can renew and change them to such an extent as to make the devotees
burn their idols of the day before, in the very name of this
orthodoxy. To take an example in the recent life of the caucuses : before 1886 all the Liberal Associations were opposed
to the Irish claims. Sympathy for Ireland in a public man was
an unpardonable crime in their eyes, as we know by the history
of Joseph Cowen. The question of self-government for Ireland could hardly be discussed even. In a large town of the
north, at the " Liberal 900 ," a member of Irish extraction one
day brought forward a motion in favour of Home Rule, and,
with the exception of his seconder, not a single person was
found in the whole assembly to support it. A few months
afterwards all the caucuses were fighting for Home Rule with
a veritable frenzy, and denouncing every opponent of the Irish
Bill as a traitor to Liberalism and almost to humanity.

When imbued with party orthodoxy, this twofold temperament, impulsive and inert, makes spontaneity and independence
of movement as well as the spirit of initiative and criticism out
of the question. All the more strongly does it kick against
criticism from others, against opposition. Opposition irritates
and offends one section like an obstacle which stops them in
their course; it destroys the peace of mind of the others by

exposing them to the risk of having to take their own line. Consequently, as we have also seen from examples of the intolerance and the uncompromising ways of the caucuses on many occasions, contradiction or free criticism had and still have difficulty in obtaining a hearing. A man who adopts an independent attitude or looks at things from his own point of view in the Caucus generally finds himself in such an extremely small minority that he only succeeds in making himself ridiculous. If he does not yield to discouragement himself, he is easily and quickly made to do so. The turners of the party praying-wheels of a higher rank in the "hundreds," the peremptory henchmen of the Caucus, make short work of him, and the rest add their Amen with the conviction of regular worshippers or of crowds which re-echo the cheer which has burst from the foremost ranks.

The caucuses, however, were and are true to the situation in looking on objectors as wet blankets, for a gathering of the "hundreds" cannot be a debating arena, it is too large for that. A collection of several hundreds of persons like that of ward delegates whose intellectual discipline and dialectical habits necessarily leave a good deal to be desired, sinks inevitably into a crowd, a mob. It is only capable of showing approval or disapproval and can never elaborate ideas. Consequently, as soon as the "hundreds" felt their way, they lost the quality of deliberative bodies with which they were invested by theory and became demonstrative assemblies.

This character of the "hundreds" naturally communicates itself to the eloquence of the speakers at these meetings, they aim more at effect and at strength of language than at the persuasive efficacy of argument. The elements of which the meetings are habitually composed help to pitch the key of the speeches: as the personages high in the social scale who belong to the Organization hardly ever come to the ordinary meetings, the rank and file can throw off all restraint and they give free vent to their ardour and expend it in language which is all the more forcible because as often as not they will have to carry out the wishes of the magnates who hold the purse-strings of the Organization. In addition to this, in the Liberal caucuses there is a special element which cultivates, by vocation so to speak, a vehement and aggressive style, to wit, the Nonconformist deacons and preachers, who are generally laymen with a small shop or in some other humble walk of life and who preach on Sundays or at religious evening meetings. Ranking amongst the most conspicuous speakers at the Caucus, they serve it with the sharp-edged oratorical weapons which they are accustomed to use against their professional enemy, the devil.

Given these intellectual and moral tendencies of most of the members of the "hundreds," so unfavourable to spontaneous and independent action, this obliteration of the deliberative character of great Caucus gatherings unable to stand the shock of ideas, and finally the organization of authority in the Associations resulting in "inner circles" formed by an unceasing process of filtration or natural selection, it is hardly possible for the "hundreds" to be really anything but registering assemblies, for their proceedings not to be arranged beforehand, or, to adopt the slang political term used to describe them, "cut and dried." In the ward we have already seen the ward secretary surrounded by his ring of associates concocting the business of the party behind the scenes. The same thing is repeated at every stage of the Organization; throughout it is regularly done by a handful of persons known in the language of the day by the name of wire-pullers. The ward secretary is their prototype who attains his highest development at the centre of the Caucus, where *the* wire-pullers, those who almost alone deserve this significant title, conduct their operations. They lean on the ward wire-pullers while they themselves are linked to the central London Organization as it were by electric currents which the wire-pullers of the Great Caucus set in motion in their turn. Thus the whole Organization eventually ends in being a hierarchy of wire-pullers.

VII

But being, as they are, of different rank and social position, what induces them to combine for common action ? What is it that impels them to draw near to each other, the middle-class magnates, the head wire-pullers, and the small fry of the wards? Where is the motive power which sets them going? It resides in the two feelings which between them generally fill the human mind — the feeling of duty and that of self-love. We have already obtained glimpses of this among the caucus-men when studying their temperament, their natural tendencies. The Organization fosters and develops these feelings so as to make them a living and acting force. To the solicitude for interests other than one's own, to the devotion to something higher than one's self which every human being feels the need of displaying, the political Organization offers the *party* for an object, as alone able to make the country, the nation, happy. And this premise being accepted by the elector through the fact of his joining the Association, the latter converts his natural feeling of duty into political duty, and having constituted itself the guardian thereof, extracts from it obligations towards itself. The members of the party higher in the social scale who are supposed to have political convictions, or even political knowledge, derive more or less spontaneously from them the stimulus to action on behalf of the party, the willingness to devote themselves to the work of the Organization, including even the least attractive jobs of the party; but for the average individual who forms the bulk of the Caucus contingents, the abstract notion of duty would not be enough. The Organization of the party supplements it therefore after the fashion of ecclesiastical Organizations, of Churches, which in order to keep the faithful in the proper path make them join in observances instituted for their sake. Similarly the Caucus inculcates their duty on its members by, to use a more profane term, regular performances. These are in the first place the periodical gatherings; then the extraordinary meetings on questions which come before Parliament or public opinion, or for the reception of a political personage who is visiting the locality, or of the Member for the constituency who is to make a speech; demonstrations organized in connection with an important event; or fêtes and entertainments. We already know by what we have seen in the first grade of the Organization, in the wards, what great importance the Caucus attaches to its members assembling methodically, how it encourages them to meet simply for the purpose of being together. The same system is pursued with regard to the

" hundreds." Every Organization which works well tries to
multiply the opportunities and pretexts for meetings, and their
frequency is one of the best proofs of its vitality. It is of no
consequence if the discussion does not, as has been pointed
out, fulfil the required conditions; the great thing for those
present is not to exchange ideas or engage in dialectical encounters, but to feel that they are a crowd, to lead each other
on, to rouse and excite one another.

The great difficulty which the caucuses experience in carrying out this mental drill is in the first place the apathy of the
electors, with which every political organization has to contend; but it lies above all in the fact that the normal duties
of the Associations do not take up enough time to adequately
serve the purpose. And it is partly from the natural necessity
of filling the vacuum, and not only from infatuation, that the
Associations do not rest content with the work of organization proper, but meddle with politics on a large scale. On
the pretext of giving expression to the ideas of the party on
the questions of the day, they had at an early stage begun
to seize every opportunity of sitting in judgment and pro-
nouncing sentence. At one time the subject is supplied them
by the attitude of the Ministry on this or that question, at
another by the conduct of the Opposition; sometimes it is
the speech delivered by one statesman, sometimes the Bill
brought forward by another. A meeting is held, a debate,
confined to what is needful or travelling beyond it, takes
place, and a resolution is solemnly passed. This performance
is one of the favourite pastimes of the caucuses. It helps
them to fill up their spare moments and at the same time
feeds within the members' breasts the sacred flame of the
party interests which they think are entrusted to their keeping. The passing of the resolution, which generally does not
mince matters, furnishes them and everybody else with evidence of their acuteness and their energy, and imbues them
with the pleasing consciousness of having discharged an important duty.

For even among the least self-seeking members of the Caucus
the preoccupations of *amour-propre* are closely connected with
the feeling of duty, just as with the general run of men the
two feelings are grafted on and intertwined with one another

when it is not the first which, as is more often the case, alone
supplies the sap and produces the plant. In like manner,
when it is not by the bait of a duty to be performed or by the
illusion of a duty, it is by procuring its members satisfactions
of *amour-propre*, which encourage or flatter their more or less
legitimate or more or less frivolous and vulgar pretensions
and aspirations, that the Caucus keeps a hold on its men.
These satisfactions of different kinds form a sort of scale, corresponding with the grades into which the staff of the Caucus
is divided. First comes the enjoyment of power, of influence,
of the pleasure of dabbling in important affairs. While very
fond of it themselves, the head wire-pullers, in order to succeed, are obliged to let the small local leaders have a taste of
it. And with this view they "consult" them, and by asking
their advice and their consent on matters generally decided
beforehand by a few persons, they give them the illusion that
it is they, the small leaders of wards, who are the real masters.
To the enjoyment of power often wielded behind the scenes
are added the visible distinctions which it procures or confers.
For the higher order of wire-pullers these consist of public
dignities, for some, perhaps, of admission to the House of
Commons, with the two magic letters "M.P." after their
name; but much more often it is two other letters, of more
modest appearance, which are the reward of a prominent local
wire-puller, — "J.P.," — which stands for Justice of the Peace.
For some time past, in fact, this honorary office has been a
sort of political current coin for recompensing party services,
and it is sometimes demanded as a due or even made a condition of the applicant's co-operation.[1] Although more common, the title of "J.P." cannot be very widely distributed
(the number of Justices of the Peace appointed every year
is barely a thousand), but for one person who wins the prize
there are five-and-twenty who hope to get it. The great object of the party Organization is, of course, to raise hopes

[1] In the towns the appointments of Justices of the Peace have always been
affected by political considerations, but party spirit did not run so high on
the subject as it has done for the last ten years. The appointments for the
towns were often made after taking the opinion of the Town Council. The
Town Councils are no longer consulted, and it is the recommendations of
the party Organizations which determine the choice made by the Lord Chancellor (who changes with the party in power).

in the breasts of as many people as possible.   Their version
of the classic *divide et impera* is: hold out hopes if you wish
to reign.

The dignity of J.P. is generally reserved, even in the
towns, where there is no property qualification for it as in the
counties, for the members of the well-to-do middle class which
lead the Organization of the party (the last Liberal Government raised several workingmen to this office).   To the others,
and especially to the lower middle class, whose important position in the Caucus we have noticed, the latter brings consideration in a less direct but very real way.   In examining the
social elements which go to make up the Caucus, we have seen
how the small middle-class man grows in importance, mounts
the social ladder in his own fashion, develops from Bill
Smith into William Wellworth Smith, Esq., or even becomes a
Town Councillor, thanks to the Caucus which introduces him
into public life.

Besides the influence, genuine or illusory, and the consideration which the caucus-man derives, or thinks he derives,
directly from his title of member of the "hundreds," the bulk
of his colleagues appreciate just as much the satisfaction of
being in good company within the Association, which perhaps
contains more than one person belonging to the upper ranks
of the middle class, and, generally speaking, leading men.
Hence the importance (exhibited on the occasion of the crisis
of 1886), for the Association of having some respectable members, — they are a sort of magnet which draws the *vulgum
pecus*.   And this is also why it has been noted that the personal
position of the President, with his qualities of respectability,
is all-important for ensuring the loyalty of the members to the
Association.

Even these motives, however, are of too abstract a nature
for many of the members of the Association; in their case
there is added the attraction of personal contact with the
local swells of the party, into which they are brought by
virtue of their position in the Caucus.   This contact arises,
perhaps, at very long intervals, and is not always direct; but
that makes it all the more appreciated.   To stimulate the zeal
of its "workers," the Association puts them in the way of
such meetings.   It invites them on certain days or gives them

a permanent ticket of admission,[1] to the great local club of
the party frequented by the richest, consequently, in their
eyes, the most eminent Liberals or Conservatives; and not
only by those who belong to the Association, but by a good
many others who do not deign to take an interest in the humbler work of the party, but who use the club for the sake of
the comfort and other advantages which it offers. The small
folk of the ward — office-bearers of the Caucus — can thus
breathe the atmosphere of this highly select circle, and, dressed
in their best clothes, sit in a good armchair and smoke their
cigarette on even terms with the real members of the club,
or even do so in their immediate society, "have a smoke with
them," and exchange a few remarks with them into the bargain.   Finally, from time to time the members are entertained
at receptions or parties given specially and exclusively for
their benefit, such as the "soirées," or "teas," which the President of the Association graciously offers in his drawing-room
or in his garden, or the *fêtes* and picnics organized by the Association.

All these satisfactions of *amour-propre* have the effect of
overcoming in people who are alive to them their indifference
or lukewarmness in regard to the affairs of the party, which
forthwith become their affairs, or of intensifying the zeal of
those who are "politicians" by temperament.   The honour conferred on both sections, the dignity with which they are invested, put them under obligations to the party, saddle them
with responsibility to its Organization.   It is this combination
of feelings that the managers of the Caucus trade upon.   And
if the Councils of the Associations are so large as to reach the
total of six hundred or eight hundred members and more, if
their numbers have been repeatedly increased it is due to this
calculation that, by bringing honours within the reach of a
great many people, their services are likely to be obtained.

It is true that satisfactions springing from gratified self-
esteem or from the fulfilment of public duties are not the
only advantages which the personages of the Caucus gain from

[1] Sometimes known by the name of "special membership ticket," notably
among the Tories who are fond of social demarcations and labels, and distributed particularly to the members of the Caucus who perform the important
duties of ward secretaries.

their position.   In the case of many of them this position gives them a gratuitous advertisement in their business; by their activity in the Caucus they form useful connections which they would not have acquired by other means.   Some of the members of the " hundreds " derive more direct and tangible profits from it by the orders which they receive from the Association itself. These are the printers and other trades-people, such as licensed victuallers and purveyors who contract for the *fêtes* and picnics of the Organization.   Finally, there is a class of members who make a little money in a still less indirect way.   The ward secretaries, especially among the Tories, are often paid a little and also get small perquisites out of the money allowed them for office expenses, etc.   A greater number, as will be seen later on, are paid by the day, at a modest rate, for the *work* done for the Association and the party.   Here again it is the Tories, much richer than their rivals, who spend the most money in this legitimate or illicit manner.   But when all is said and done, the members of the English Caucus who reap material benefit from it, in one form or another, are only a minority.   Most of the members of the hundreds, and of their fellow-workers in the wards, are governed by considerations which are more of a sentimental description.

The task of the wire-pullers, who are expected to satisfy and flatter the self-esteem of the caucus-men, has also its inverse side: no less care must be taken not to offend susceptibilities.   Not only is it necessary, as in every human society, to reckon with the moods, the passions, the individual idiosyncrasies, which now and again find full scope, but with the special touchiness which is the pendant of the very sentiments with which the Caucus inoculates these people in order to keep a firmer hold on them.   The more small vanities are flattered, the more they are inclined to raise their heads.   The caucus-man who takes himself seriously, or thinks himself of importance, is naturally jealous of his dignity, and prompt to take offence.   In the great towns the position of the wire-pullers of the Caucus in this respect has become much more delicate since 1885, in consequence of the subdivision of the Organization into several *divisional* Associations, because this transformation has increased the number of small important personages who have to be managed.   It appears that it is the members

belonging to the working class who exhibit the most susceptibility; always afraid of being trifled with and conscious of
the strength which numbers give them in the electorate, they
are more inclined than the others to be restive without rhyme
or reason.   To cope with the self-asserting members the wire-
pullers need a great deal of skill, tact, and sometimes energy
as well.   They, and especially the Secretary of the Organization, who is the drudge of these members, must often let people
talk without ever allowing them to go further, must not get
angry at the wrong moment, not provoke any one, and in general not be fussy.   It is the inevitable price to be paid for
the authority wielded by them over the members of the Association, just as the latter in their turn cannot escape from
the obligations incumbent on them with regard to the Caucus.
There is a tacit agreement between them, founded, like every
contract, on the principle of *do ut des*.   The one have the
uninterrupted enjoyment of the rights corresponding to these
obligations, in the form of manifold satisfactions which the
Caucus procures them, while the others, the managers of the
Caucus, receive on its behalf the return, which is the absolute
devotion of the caucus-men in regard to the Organization, or,
to use the proper term, *discipline*.   Here we have the gist, the
binding clause of the contract in question.   The long flowery
preamble, and the grand oratorical developments of the agreement about the influence of the masses, the autonomy of the
party, etc., as well as the commentaries made thereon by its
skilful expounders, only led up to this result.   There is no
difference in this respect between the Liberal and the Tory
Organization, except perhaps that in the former it is discipline
with phrases, and in the latter discipline without or with few
phrases.   The discipline, in fact, is almost military.   Once in
the ranks the caucus-man must obey orders and faithfully perform the part assigned to him, otherwise he is summarily dealt
with; he is flung back into the crowd from out of which the
Caucus had taken him.

Discipline, however, cannot be absolute in the Caucus.   First
of all must be deducted all those who are not amenable to it
by temperament as opposed to the majority who are naturally
disposed to submit to it.   Some of them, without exactly wishing to stop the coach, belong to the category of individuals

who can never be satisfied, and who instinctively run counter
to the general opinion. The others are men of really independent mind who find their way, although in exceptional
instances, into the " hundreds," and sometimes even spring up
in the executive committees. If these disturbers of the general harmony cannot be brought to terms or silenced, an effort
is made to get rid of them, and it is left to the ingenuity of
the wire-pullers to find the means of doing it. Both categories, however, are only a minority, sometimes a very small
one. The real question of discipline arises in regard to the
majority. Based as it is on the reciprocity of real or imaginary services or advantages, discipline here too cannot be so
perfect as not to be infringed. There can always be persons who consider that the reciprocity is not complete, that
the sacrifices which are demanded of them are too great. No
doubt the uncritical and sluggish temperament of the great
majority of the caucus-men, as already known to us, is not
calculated to make them keep their eyes fixed on the oscilla-
tion of the two scales, but on the other hand there is too large
a crop of local jealousies, petty susceptibilities, and vulgar
vanity in the Caucus for these not to show themselves. Accordingly the Caucus has its mutinies, which break out from
time to time in the wards, even among the Tories in whom the
spirit of subordination is however deeply rooted. The acts of
indiscipline or attempts at revolt sometimes assume a general
character, being committed in the name of principles, as for
instance was the case with the disputes between the head wire-
pullers and the *divisional* Associations of large towns. Sometimes, and more often, they do not go beyond personal dissatisfaction and pique breaking out in a trivial form, which reveals
only too clearly the smallness of mind and obtuse infatuation
of the ordinary caucus-man. For instance, a Chairman of a
local branch of the Association appears at a great meeting of
the party without his ticket, which he has obligingly given to
a friend; being refused admittance by the doorkeeper, who
sticks to his orders, he flies into a rage with the Caucus and
sends in his resignation. Another caucus-man leaves the
Association because his parliamentary candidate has not shaken
hands with him. But after all, these small incidents and the
quarrels of a more serious nature which arise in the Caucus are

rather the exception confirming the rule which makes discipline the basis of the Organization and the principle of its existence.

This intellectual and moral temperament of most of the caucus-men and the necessity of squaring them does not of course make the Caucus very attractive to men of delicate feeling, no more than its cut and dried type of proceedings has any charm for independent minds. When the machine of the Caucus began to work with a certain amount of regularity, the position of supernumeraries assigned to the great majority of the members of the Association soon struck men of an independent and thoughtful turn of mind, especially in the Liberal camp, where the Organization, being of older standing, developed to a greater extent at an earlier stage, and where the spirit of criticism and of doubt is more widely diffused. At the same time the small fry of the wards were continually rising to the surface. The consciousness of their isolation and the dislike of promiscuity felt by several men of higher position made them leave the Caucus, and, with the co-operation of events, in most localities a real deterioration in the quality of the staff of the Organization set in, including even the wire-pullers themselves, to such an extent that at the present time it often represents, according to the description of an honorary secretary of an Association, "anything but the cream of society."

The events which had contributed to this result were, as has been said, of a manifold kind. There was the Home Rule crisis, which served as a more or less plausible pretext to many people for withdrawing from active political life. Then again in the large towns there was the subdivision of the party Organization into several divisional Associations, which arose, as we have already seen, out of the establishment of single member constituencies. The friction which ensued on this occasion, especially on the Liberal side, between the new Associations and the general Association (of the town) deprived the caucuses of several wire-pullers of a superior intellectual and moral stamp. Some retired to their tents disgusted at the suspicion with which they were regarded by the politicians of *Divisions*. Others did the same because they considered that their position in the Organization was not good enough; after having dealt with the affairs of the party for the whole town they thought it a come-down to take the same place in a *Division*. All these withdrawals left the local element, that is the ward people, whom the mere subdivision of the Organization invested with a new and very considerable importance, in possession of the field. This transformation at once raised every ward leader from being tenth or fifteenth at Rome to being first in his village. Instead of one Chairman of Association there were now four, five, or seven, and a corresponding number of Vice-Chairmen, honorary secretaries, etc. This set of small personages admitted to a share in the management of the party, and full of their own importance, gave a marked impulse to a parochial spirit of a narrow, petty, and illiberal kind, measuring everything, men and things, by its own standard.

VIII

The description of the Organization of parties which has just been given was concerned with its predominant type as developed especially in the "parliamentary boroughs." The towns known by this name form, as we are aware, a class of electoral divisions distinct from that of the "counties." This duality of electoral constituencies is an outcome of the special conditions amid which popular representation grew up in England. When summoning representatives from the shires, which were from time immemorial the great local politico-administrative unit, "to serve in Parliament," the kings also singled out certain towns which were to return members to the House on the same footing as the counties. The boroughs which were the object of the royal favour became, at the end of the parliamentary elections, independent of the counties of which they geographically formed part. All the other towns were included in the "county constituency," composed of the geographical county minus the "parliamentary boroughs" situated within its area. When the Reform Bill of 1832 attacked the old electoral edifice, it not only lowered the voting qualification but it also effected a readjustment of political power between the towns directly represented in Parliament and those which were not so; by means of a "redistribution of seats" it gave a special representation to a good many towns which had become of importance, notably in consequence of the wonderful rise of industry, and disfranchised the insignificant and decayed boroughs (rotten boroughs) which had returned Members by virtue of their historic right. Stripped of their representation, these boroughs were "merged in the counties," that is to say annexed to the county constituencies. The further extension of the suffrage by the subsequent Reform Bills of 1867 and 1884–5 was effected on each occasion in the same manner: the qualification was once more lowered while several towns were raised to the rank of " parliamentary boroughs " with a special representation; or " parliamentary boroughs " already in possession of the franchise as well as " counties " obtained an additional number of Members, corresponding to the enhanced importance of their population, and this at the expense of small towns which were ruthlessly merged. Thus, in spite of the levelling character of the Reform Bills, the double type of electoral constituencies has been preserved: of " boroughs," that is to say, exclusively urban constituencies, and of " counties," *i.e.* rural constituencies with a more or less considerable addition of more or less important urban agglomerations. Even the introduction, in 1885, of the system of one-member constituencies, in pursuance of which each county [1] as well as each large parliamentary borough which had hitherto been single electoral divisions with a varying number of Members were divided into almost equal parliamentary *Divisions*, did not obliterate this duality. It is preserved not only practically by the difference in the economic and social conditions of the " boroughs " and the " counties," but also by the law, which gives the right of voting on conditions which are not identical in both.

The result is that the organization of parties in the " counties " is still, even since 1885, on quite a different footing to that of the " boroughs." The principal peculiarities which give the " county " constituencies their special character are the great extent of their area combined with the very unequal and sparse distribution of the population, the heterogeneous nature of the electorate, and the political youthfulness, not to say infancy, of the rural section of it, admitted only yesterday

[1] It is true that several counties were subdivided before 1885, but these subdivisions, to the number of two or three, were not yet single-member constituencies.

to public life — all conditions unfavourable to the growth of a robust extra-constitutional political organization. Nevertheless, the Caucus tried to introduce the "Birmingham plan" into the counties before 1885, but the experiment was not very successful. The Association started for each county on a would-be representative basis often amounted merely to a committee with its head-quarters in the county-town. Its members were gentlemen, landed proprietors, men in liberal professions, with a small sprinkling of trades-people. Instead of elective branches which the Association ought, in conformity with the doctrine, to have had in each locality, very often there was only one person who consented to look after the affairs of the party in a spirit of self-sacrifice. This person was a tradesman, a schoolmaster, occasionally a Magistrate. The members of the committees were assisted in the routine duties of organization by a few paid agents attached to the Association of the county and who went about from one village to another. The gentlemen residing in the locality did not take an active part in the work of the Organization. The Organization of the Conservatives was still less democratic. Their Associations were simply small committees which represented almost exclusively the old ruling classes. True, the Tories had "Workingmen's Associations" in the large villages with the squire as chairman and his steward as secretary. But the most obvious result of their political activity consisted of an annual dinner honoured with the presence of the local gentry. In small villages it was the clergyman and schoolmaster by themselves, or even one of the two, who represented the whole Organization of the Tory party. The work of checking the register, of attending to electoral claims, etc., was, as in the good old days, in the hands of a solicitor who made it over to his clerk. It must not be forgotten, however, that in spite of the great extent of the county constituencies it was easier, up to 1885, to deal with the voters in them, owing to their limited number.

The year 1885 opened a new political era in the "counties." The Reform Act, by lowering the qualification, added nearly two millions of rural voters to the electorate; every occupier of a cottage obtained a vote. Of course the labourer invested with full political rights forthwith became an object of deep interest to the Organizations of the parties. The Liberals, who had carried the extension of the suffrage to the rural masses, lost no time in proposing, through the medium of the Caucus, to complete it by conceding to them a voice in the management of the party, by means of representative Associations. Without denying the difficulties of applying the representative principle to the county districts, they expressed the opinion that " the organization could be brought to the same symmetry and perfection in them as in the towns," as Mr. Schnadhorst observed.[1] It must be said at once that up to the present time experience is far from having converted these expectations into a reality; it has only demonstrated more forcibly that the representative and elective principle has no inherent efficacy. No doubt the subdivision of the single constituency of the county into several electoral divisions has greatly facilitated the labours of the Organization, it is more easy to grasp the new *Division*, but even its more limited area does not present sufficient elements for an electoral extra-constitutional organization. In a good many parishes it is not only impossible to start an elective Association, but there is hardly the wherewithal for forming a small committee. One rural Division, for instance, has more than a hundred parishes, the majority of which possess barely forty or fifty voters apiece. Another Division is almost as familiar with political life and electoral strife as if it formed part of the Muscovite empire. There are Divisions in which there have not been more than two contested elections in the space of half a century.[2] In these backward districts, where stagnation and social tradition reign supreme, the position of the Liberal Organization was a peculiarly delicate one up to a very recent period, if it is not so still. If its adherents in the villages were demonstrative, they incurred the animosity of the representatives of the old ruling classes, almost all Tories. The economic condition of the small farmer or day-labourer is too precarious for him to wantonly jeopardize it by defying the squire and the parson. Often he has no habitation of his own, all the cottages belong to the landlord, who lets them without a lease and can turn out his tenants at any moment. Consequently in places where the

---

[1] *County Organization*, by F. Schnadhorst, Birmingham, 1885 (?).
[2] For instance, the Rutland *Division* has been contested twice since 1841. (See F. H. Macalmont's Poll Book.)

materials of a Liberal committee exist it is sometimes a very
knotty point to decide whether to form one or abandon the
idea in order not to expose its members to social ostracism.   In
a good many *Divisions* the Liberals consider systematic abstention the most prudent course, to prevent their most zealous adherents from becoming known.   The representative of
a Liberal Association, alluding to this position of affairs, described it as follows: "Our Association is a secret society."
Of course this state of things is rather the exception than the
rule, and even as an exception it is becoming a reminiscence of
the past.   When making my first rounds, in 1888–1889, I often
heard complaints of the political terrorism exercised by the
squire and the parson, to the extent that the electors were
afraid of attending the Liberal meetings or went to them by
night, one by one, like conspirators.   But during my last trip
to the country districts (in 1895) I was able to ascertain that
this was no longer the case.   The labourer has grown independent and makes no secret of it before the farmer, who accepts the new situation and placidly tells people himself on
market-day that so many of his labourers have voted "against
him," that is against the party he prefers.   It appears that
the incessant migration of young people into the towns with
which rural England is afflicted, and the agricultural distress,
have had a good deal to do with this small political revolution :
the number of agricultural labourers having perceptibly diminished, the farmer is glad to get any and takes good care not
to worry them about their "politics"; similarly the landlords,
who now have so much difficulty in letting their farms, no
longer intimidate those of their tenants who are inclined to
vote "against them."

The difficulty of forming regular party organizations in the
country districts is due in a greater degree to the absence or
the want of public spirit than to the intimidation practised by
squires and parsons.   It being impossible, for one reason or
another, to have village committees, the Organization of the
party falls back on secretaries, unpaid correspondents in each
place.   It is always some one who is well acquainted with his
locality and with the inner history of each of his neighbours,
"a knowledgeable man," as the phrase goes in some parts.
Without attracting attention, the correspondent watches the

political situation in his village and keeps the secretary of the Association informed of everything that can interest him. The latter controls him, sends him questions, gives him lists or other papers to prepare, or entrusts him with commissions of a less formal kind. In places where the Liberals have reason or think they have reason for apprehending boycotting on the part of their political opponents, the secretary of the Association sends all his communications to his correspondent by letter post, even when he wants to forward him a printed document, a circular, or a form. If the village is not far from the town, the correspondent himself brings the secretary the desired information on market-day, adding a basket of eggs or vegetables as a personal tribute. It is needless to say that as all the work of the party is entrusted to the correspondent, much discernment is required in selecting him. In this respect the Liberals exhibit more tact than their rivals: their correspondent in the village is the shoemaker, the tailor, the farrier of the locality, or an intelligent farmer, occasionally the postman.[1] Being a man of the people, this correspondent has the ear of his neighbours, he is " one of themselves," he can turn them round his finger, so that he makes a firstrate electoral agent. The Tory correspondent, on the other hand, is generally a " superior " man, the clergyman, the schoolmaster, a farmer, whose devotion to Church and State is unimpeachable and who is very good at keeping the books, but who does not " understand " the people. When the Tories form a committee of the party in the village their first thought is to put " a leading man " at its head. It is only in default of him that they fall back on an " intelligent workingman." Being still behind their fellow Tories of the large towns, they do not realize or they forget that not only is the hour at hand but that it has come.

If the parish cannot supply the groundwork of the Organization of the party, several of them are grouped together into local " centres," which thereupon serve as a basis for the Associations or district committees. Their delegates often hold their authority from themselves. Often instead of the district Associations there are only committees, which are also self-

---

[1] I have even been told (in Devonshire) of a policeman as one of the correspondents of the Liberal Organization.

appointed. The powers of these committees are sometimes exercised by party clubs which are to be found in certain villages. In parts of the country where either party is very weak numerically, as for instance, in the case with the Liberals in southern England or the Tories in Scotland, the rules of the Association themselves anticipate the impossibility of obtaining representatives selected by popular vote, and authorize the executive committees of the Associations to appoint the local delegates of their own accord.

All these difficulties of organization scarcely exist in the urban sections of county *Divisions*. Consequently the *divisional* Association generally has branches in all the small towns, and *à fortiori* in the larger towns, which sometimes form part of county constituencies. Some of these towns, which are " merged " boroughs, have even been familiar with the procedure of the Caucus for a considerable time, having possessed an independent Association before 1885. There are villages, too, which are in no way behind the towns as regards the development of the Organization of the party. This is precisely the case with rural non-agricultural districts. In the north of England as well as in Scotland, rural agglomerations are found, which are pre-eminently manufacturing and industrial. In several of these villages the inhabitants are counted by thousands ; and, in point of fact, they are more in the nature of towns.

But apart from these urban islets, the non-elective element (self-appointed or introduced under the rules), always fills a considerable place in county Organizations. Besides, the plutocratic element, that of the large subscribers, holds a still more important position in them than in the town caucuses. Consequently, wire-pulling becomes in a way a foregone conclusion and almost a legitimate proceeding. The activity of the wire-pullers operates in a more direct, a more patriarchal, manner, so to speak. They are not obliged to go through all the forms and ceremonies of the genuine town Caucus, although they have to sway their people by the same considerations, by appealing to feelings of duty and self-esteem, as modified by the surroundings. The subordinate wire-puller of the county Organization, who is the village correspondent of the Association, works on his neighbours by his personal and im-

mediate influence, and he himself is spontaneously affected
by the prestige of persons in the county town who have
assumed the position of wire-pullers, and who are adorned
with the titles of chairman or members of the executive committee of the Association.

But however far the counties' Organization may be from
theoretical perfection, it has none the less by its series of
branches, committees, and volunteer correspondents brought
about in the counties a certain decentralization in the management of the affairs of the party. And, what is equally
important, slack and defective as is the chain of the county
Organization, it is composed in the main of small people, from
the village shoemaker up to the tradesman of the towns, who
formerly held aloof or were pushed aside to make way for the
gentlemen.

These results have been obtained in a lesser degree in the
Tory Organizations; the Conservative county Associations are
often less democratic than their rivals of the other side, they
do not feel the need of it to the same extent. For it is not
only out of pure love for the elective principle that the Liberals
have introduced it into their Organization, but in order to get
at the new voter more easily; they have framed their machinery
with the special object of " reaching the masses." The Tories,
who are the heirs or legatees of the old order of things with its
time-honoured social relations which ensured the ascendency
of the landlords in everyday life, have more natural connections
in the country districts. There the squire and the parson form
the living nucleus of a political organization spontaneously
joined by all the country folk who have not, by their intelligence or by their interests and their cupidity, yet emancipated
themselves from their influence. True, in a good many places
the ground is undermined beneath the squire and the parson,
but the surface is still pretty firm. A landlord who deservedly
enjoys a good reputation is always followed, as in the old days,
by everybody, without reference to personal political preferences.
And then there are still many localities where the agricultural
labourers are so backward and so childishly naïve that the
Tory leaders have no need to stand on ceremony and to pretend to observe the elective principle in governing the party.
Hence there are Conservative county Associations which are

2 B

mere names. All the party work in the *Division* is performed
from a solicitor's office, which is the real laboratory of the
party. In it this lawyer and his clerks mysteriously manipu-
late the electoral business. In short, the old order of things
is still in full swing there. These oases are found mostly in the
south of England, in remote rural districts, or even within
the radius of old episcopal towns, where under the shadow of
the cathedral the whole population is half asleep and plunged
in some hazy dream of the past.

To ensure unity of action among all the *divisional* Organizations in the county, which may be necessary or useful in certain cases, county Federations or Councils have been started in
several parts of the country, on the pattern of the United
Committees or Councils of large towns. They have not attained
the importance of the general Associations of towns. The dis-
similarity of political conditions in the different parts of the
county and its large area are by no means favourable to the
formation of a strong central organization to take the place of
the *divisional* Associations, when the latter find it very hard to
cope with these difficulties, which are considerably less in their
case.

SECOND CHAPTER

THE ACTION OF THE CAUCUS

I

THE Organization of parties which we have been studying has disclosed to us a structure which may be described as ingenious; the living wheels of which its mechanism is composed are, we may admit, well co-ordinated and adjusted, and their regular working is fairly ensured. The forces which set them in motion are perhaps highly effective, and constitute a propelling power of an exceedingly strong yet very simple nature. Intended to fight the battles of fiercely competing parties, this Organization combines, it may also be admitted, all the essential conditions of success, by providing men accustomed to obey orders, well disciplined, and following freely acknowledged leaders, who in their turn possess in a high degree such qualities as energy, skill, and strategical and tactical ability. But, after all, this valiant army commanded by first-rate chiefs is really only a small battalion confronting the bulk of the electorate. How is it possible for such a handful of men to capture the formidable fortress of a well-nigh universal suffrage? This question, which naturally occurs to the mind, brings us to an examination of the various methods by which the Caucus reaches and acts upon the great mass of voters.

In the old days, when the electorate was far more limited, there was a gap in the constitutional wall which surrounded it; this, as will be remembered, was *electoral registration*, the keeping of the lists of voters, which was almost entirely left to private initiative by the authorities. It will also be recollected that the necessity of making up for the shortcomings of the State had even led to the formation of *Registration*

Societies.   Since then this wall has been repeatedly lengthened to take in an ever-increasing number of citizens.   But nothing has been done to repair the gap, and widened in its turn as time went on it was the first to let in the Caucus.   With the extension of the suffrage the interest of private individuals in *registration* became a still more pressing political need, and the Caucus Associations which ousted the old *Registration Societies* hastened to take up their business and at once found in it a sphere of legitimate activity and a source of influence.

To form an idea of this activity, and of the position which it gives the Caucus, it is indispensable to go somewhat closely into the details of the onerous task of *registration*.   The proper keeping of the register, which is of such paramount importance for the exercise of the vote, is really a most complicated piece of business.   The legislative provisions on the subject are contained in more than a hundred statutes, to which must be added a vast and obscure mass of judicial decisions.   The electoral qualifications alone, *i.e.* the conditions as to property and residence which give the right to be put on the register and to vote afterwards, are singularly numerous, varied, and confused.   In accordance with the usual practice of English legislation, which does not create anew, which does not make a clean sweep of old enactments, but patches them up or adds to them, every new Reform Bill which extended the franchise set up a new group of voters with special qualifications.   Thus to the several franchises which existed before 1832 the great Reform Bill added, in the boroughs, persons occupying rateable tenements of the annual value of £10, and in the counties, freeholders of the clear annual value of £10, copyholders of £10 per annum, leaseholders of the annual value of £10 when the lease was for sixty years, or of the annual value of £50 for a term of twenty years, and, finally, tenants at will paying not less than £50 a year.   The Act of 1867, while lowering the minimum of £10 to £5 for the counties, introduced new electoral qualifications by enfranchising, in addition to the persons qualified as above mentioned, in the counties all occupiers of lands or tenements of the rateable value of £12 and upwards, and in the boroughs all inhabitant occupiers of a separate dwelling-house of whatever value, and lodgers paying an annual rent of not less than £10.   The Reform Act of 1884 has introduced these last two categories of voters in the counties as well. By the same Act, construed in a very liberal way by judicial decisions, a vote has been allowed to service men (such as coachmen, gardeners, shop assistants living on the premises, etc.) not residing under the same roof as their masters. Legal opinion has conceded a vote also to sub-tenants of a house let or sublet in parts, even in single rooms, by a non-resident owner, without any condition as to minimum rent.

To these conditions which confer the franchise the law adds others for the exercise of the right, to wit, the payment of the poor-rate for the tenements the ownership. or occupation of which constitutes the electoral qualification, and the occupation of the premises[1] for a certain period, generally twelve months before the annual closing of the register. The voter who has changed his residence during this twelvemonth, while remaining in the same borough or, in the case of counties, in the same electoral division, retains his right to be put on the register if he is a householder; but if he is only a lodger *successive occupation* is of no use to him; the mere fact of removal into the adjoining building, into the next number in the same street, deprives him of his right of appearing on the register until he has spent the statutory twelvemonth in his new residence, so that he may remain without a vote for two years or more. In any case lodgers are only put on the register on their formal application renewed every year and supported by proof, while the other voters are entered in it as a matter of course once for all until proof is forthcoming that they have lost their electoral capacity or their right to exercise it. The franchise is lost by death, by promotion to the Peerage, and by naturalization in a foreign country; it lapses, at all events during the period for which the register is made up, by the loss of the property qualification, by change of residence beyond the permitted limit of *successive occupation*, by non-payment of the poor-rate, and by receipt of relief under the Poor Law.

Thus to bring a voter on the register or to keep him there in case his right is disputed it is necessary to establish a num-

---

[1] Except for owners in the counties, who are not bound by any condition of residence, and can come and vote even if they live abroad. These are the outvoters who have been referred to above (p. 147).

ber of facts and legal points which often give rise to doubt
and raise questions of great complexity. Has he the franchise
and on what kind of property or occupancy can he rest his
right ? can he claim it under such or such an Act ? can he appeal
to the law of King Henry VI in the fifteenth century ? is he
affected by this or that later statute ? — all occasionally very
knotty points. Is the voter on the register or applying to be
put on it an Englishman or an alien ? — the problem may be
anything but a simple one. The applicant is of foreign extraction and has never been naturalized; but that need not prove
anything against him, for perhaps he is a descendant of a
Hanoverian settled in England before 1837, when Englishmen
and Hanoverians were subjects of the same King. Does he
inhabit a "house" or not ? That depends. If there are several apartments or rooms all let or sublet, each of these tenants
"inhabits a house"; but if the person to whom they pay rent
occupies one of the apartments of the house in question, they
are merely "tenants" and can claim the franchise only as duly
qualified lodgers. The lodger's qualification is fixed at £10 clear
annual rent, but if the claimant takes the room furnished he
must prove a higher rent, but up to what amount ? It varies
with the importance of the borough. But apart from the appraisement of the rental qualification the simple capacity of
lodger, clear as it may appear, is often very difficult to establish
from the point of view of electoral law. Does the tenant share
his room with others ? Is his bed separated from the other beds
by a partition ? Can he use the room to the exclusion of every
one else ? For instance, a son living with his father can claim
the right to vote as a lodger, but if the door of the room has
no lock to it or if he has shared his bedroom with a visitor,
he has no right to a vote, for the room is not used exclusively
by him. The occupier of a "house," who is bound to prove
an occupancy of a twelvemonth, may have occupied several
dwellings one after another during this time, but if it is in
London the question arises whether the adjoining street into
which he has moved is in the same "borough" or not; if not,
he loses his right to vote, whereas at Birmingham or at Liverpool he may have moved from one end of the city to the other
without forfeiting his electoral privilege, for Birmingham and
Liverpool, although split up into several electoral divisions,

are each only a single city.   The receipt of parochial relief
by the voter or his wife or his children deprives him of a vote.
This is clear, to all appearances, but is the relief received to
be always considered as such ?   For instance, a voter troubled
with a drunken wife loses patience and turns her out of doors;
driven by hunger she applies for and obtains relief from the
parish; ought her husband to be struck off the register or
not ?   A voter suffering from the small-pox has been placed
by order of the authorities in the hospital set apart for this
disease, where he has been nursed and fed.   He has therefore
received relief in food, but then he was obliged to eat to
recover.   Can he be kept on the register ?

To these manifold questions and difficulties connected with
the application of the law on the franchise, of which barely
a few examples have been given, are added the endless formalities prescribed for the making up and revising of the register
of voters of every description, which in their turn entail in
practice numerous proofs of fact, arguments on points of law,
or simply pettifogging disputes.   As almost all the work involved in keeping up the register has, in the state of things
with which we have become acquainted,[1] been left to private
initiative, to the political parties, all three — proof, legal argument, and pettifogging — devolve upon the Caucus Associations.

II

Being anxious to get their adherents on the register, in view
of the election which may take place in the course of the year,
the Associations require to know, in the case of every voter,
all the particulars by virtue of which his entry or omission
can be claimed or objected to.   To obtain this information the
Association institutes a canvass, a general census of the constituency carried out by its members, who make their first appearance here in the capacity of " workers " of the Organization.
Each committee of a ward parcels it out among its members
by streets or sections of streets.   Over each block is set a
member of the committee (often called " captain " of the block)
to supervise the census taken by the canvassers, outsiders

[1] Cf. above, pp. 141, 142.

or members of the Association, both paid as a rule, but at a
very moderate rate, five or six shillings a day (this is one of
the opportunities of making money for the caucus-men which
were alluded to above). The canvasser goes to all the houses
in turn with the list of voters, to find out the inaccuracies or
errors which require correction and the additions which have
to be made. He takes down the surname and Christian names
of the householder with their exact spelling, the old address
of the man who has moved in, the new residence of the
man who has moved out, the date of each of these removals;
the letting value of all premises not used as dwellings, such as
shops, offices, warehouses; he tries to find out all the lodgers
and to ascertain if they have taken their rooms furnished or
not, the weekly rent they pay, their landlord's address, the date
on which they came into the house, etc. This census is a
work of great labour. A single house often has to be visited
more than once. On an average, three visits are paid to each
house. The lodgers make the canvass particularly difficult in
the large towns. An eminently floating population, they frequently change their address, and it is not always easy to discover their new abode, especially if it is a case of people who
flit from one quarter to another or are even in the habit of
decamping secretly. And they must absolutely be found,
for even if they are old voters, they have to be entered afresh
every year or at any rate it is necessary to prove the fact of
their removal into another house, which deprives them of the
right of being put on the register for the current year. All
the information collected by the canvassers and checked
by the local members of the Association is reported to the
secretary of the ward, who transmits it to the secretary of
the Caucus of the division. There, in the office of the Caucus,
the data supplied by the registration canvass are combined
with the particulars from the parish as to voters in arrears
with their rates and those who have been relieved under the
Poor Law, to become as many weapons for defending political
friends and combating antagonists. Every voter being invited
by the law to lodge with the Overseers of the Poor in the parish
who are entrusted with the preparation of the register, a *claim* to
be put on it if he has been left out, as well as *objections* against
wrong entries, the Associations, stepping into the shoes of the

individual voters, try to get as many of their followers on the register as they can by means of *claims*, and to strike off as many of their opponents as possible by means of *objections*. But how are they to know friends from enemies? This is ascertained in the course of the registration canvass, and is perhaps the most difficult part of its work. Besides the information mentioned above, the special business of the canvasser is to find out the voter's " politics," *i.e.* with which political party he is inclined to vote, and very often it is no easy matter to extract this from him. If the canvasser is a paid agent, a poor devil who wants to earn a few shillings, he has not much chance of being the recipient of these confidences. A neighbour or a business friend is in a much better position for this, but he is not sure of succeeding either. For some time past the Associations have been in the habit of entrusting these missions to the women who belong to the party Organizations and who manage to worm the voter's political opinions out of him more easily. But, after all, the " politics " of a good many voters remains a secret or a riddle, and they have to be entered in the third column of the canvassing-books which specify, firstly, say the Liberals, secondly the Conservatives, and thirdly the doubtful. The secretary of the Caucus always considers the " doubtful " ones as opponents, and he launches *objections* against them to get them struck off the lists on some pretext, good or indifferent. Sometimes a voter whose right has been challenged in this way writes an indignant letter to the secretary of the, let us say, Liberal Caucus, complaining of the attack made on him, a life-long Liberal, whose ardent Liberalism is beyond all suspicion, etc. The secretary writes him a humble apology and joyfully enters him among the voters on whom he can depend, *quod erat demonstrandum.*

The *objections*, numerous as they are, generally proceed from a single person acting as objector-general on behalf of the Caucus, whereas the claims have to be lodged by each claimant individually. Practically it is the party Association which, after having found out the person entitled to make the claim, draws it up. The Association sees that a printed slip containing all the details relating to the particular voter is handed to him; he has only to sign it and return it to the secretary of the Caucus, who forwards it to the Overseer of the Poor in charge of the register.   The latter takes down all claims and objections sent to him without adjudicating on their validity.   The decision rests with the Revising Barrister, who holds a registration court in each place every year for this purpose, and it is there that the rival caucuses have a regular fight over the names of the voters who are on or off the register.   They sift them thoroughly by starting all manner of possible and impossible objections to the qualifications of their presumed political opponents.   The very brief outline of the legislation on this subject which has been given above has shown how easy it is to raise disputed points.   The party agents devote all the resources of their professional knowledge to multiplying them in order to deprive as many persons on the other side as possible of the right to vote.   They leave no stone unturned. Nothing is more common for them than to object to the spelling of a proper name.   For instance, a man named John Thomson, a shoemaker by trade and a Radical in politics, has been put on the register as Thompson, with a *p* added.   The Tory agent applies to have his name struck off and succeeds, because there is no Thompson at the address given, the house is inhabited by another person called Thomson.   The slightest omission in the wording of the objection or of the claim may prove a fatal flaw, thanks to the highly technical view which the Revising Barristers and the courts of appeal take of these matters.   For instance, an objecting party while giving his exact address has omitted to state the name of the parish in which he lives ; at once he is put out of court and his objection against the illegal entry of perhaps hundreds of names effected by the manœuvres of the other side becomes *ipso facto* null and void.   Claims are lodged and objections made which are wittingly unfounded or are sometimes even fraudulent : to support a claim qualifying property is shown which in reality has never been occupied by the claimant.   The democratic Associations have in the matter of registration reverted to all the bad traditions of the old system and have even carried them further.   For instance, the plan adopted in former days by certain *Registration Societies* of starting thousands of objections, without rhyme or reason, has become a regular practice of the caucuses.   A citizen whose claim to a vote is unimpeachable is often obliged to go before the Registration Court and uphold his right to have his name on the register, which is disputed solely in a factious spirit. A voter of a cunning turn of mind defends himself by stratagem; he gets himself put on the register through the Association of the opposite party while taking care to let the secretary of the Caucus on his own side into the secret, so that neither Caucus disputes his claim. Not long ago in London (in the Islington Registration Court) a Revising Barrister suggested this mode of procedure in open court amid general laughter testifying to the easy indifference with which everybody looks on these practices.[1] Sometimes a similar course is followed by a voter whose claim is defective; for instance, a Liberal who has not completed his twelve months' residence tells the registration canvasser of the Conservative Association that he is a Conservative. If the Association finds out afterwards that he has not occupied the premises for the statutory twelvemonth, it takes good care not to draw the attention of the Revising Barrister to the fact.

Nor does this official raise all these points which may affect the right to a vote of his own initiative, the Revising Barrister is as a rule merely the umpire between the contending political parties. Although actually the representative of the Law, of the State, he is by no means the vigilant guardian of the public interest which is at stake. The fact that the suffrage was for a long time a personal privilege, the property of a few favoured individuals, has dimmed or obscured the notion of a vote as a public right exercised in the general interest. The intervention of the political parties, who flung themselves on the exercise of the suffrage to serve their own ends, has completed the conversion of the vote almost into a private right within the meaning of the civil law, a piece of property, benefiting however not the rightful holder of it, but the "party." When the right to a vote is challenged in the registration courts, it is the political parties who are the real litigants, and not the individual voters who appear in court only as witnesses to be cross-examined by the representatives of the rival cau-

[1] The following dialogue took place between the officials of the Court, the Revising Barrister and the Vestry Clerk. *The Revising Barrister:* "A wise man would send his claim through both parties." — *The Vestry Clerk:* "or claim through his political opponents." — *The Revising Barrister:* "and give notice to his friends." — *The Vestry Clerk:* "and use his opponent's conveyances at elections."

cuses. The caucuses, who wrangle over electors' rights for their own benefit, also make bargaining counters of them, as in the case of all property subject to litigation and compromise. Thus not unfrequently the agents of both caucuses, to clear the ground, "pair off," *i.e.* agree among themselves to withdraw an equal number of claims and objections on each side. Without having consulted the voters interested, they sacrifice their more or less well-founded rights, taking care only to see that the chances of the parties are equal. If a Revising Barrister is found to remind them that by acting in this way they allow persons to get on the register who, perhaps, have no right to a vote, or *vice versa*, the agents of the Caucus in their turn imperturbably remind him of the regular practice according to which all points are admitted on which the parties are agreed. When a party Association is taken unawares by the unexpected number of claims lodged by its rival, it sallies forth to search for fresh claims so as to be a match for the other side. The constituency is scoured in every direction to ferret out "political friends" who can claim to be put on the register. As long as it was supposed that they were not wanted, no heed was paid to them, no trouble was taken to make the exercise of their constitutional right easier for them, to give these indifferent voters the means of participating in civic life, to arouse their public spirit; it was only when the party was in danger that the Association set to work to hunt up new claims, just as in war-time on the approach of a superior force of the enemy a fresh levy of troops is hastily raised to procure combatants, to provide food for powder.

Thus, thanks to the complexity and intricacy of the law, to the confusion and occasional incoherence of the judicial decisions on the subject, and to the utterly selfish and unscrupulous activity of the party Associations, England still has, in spite of the great extension of the right of voting, equivalent almost to universal suffrage, an "artificial instead of a natural franchise," as has been more than once noted under the *old* régime.[1] A well-known Conservative election agent, whose double capacity of Caucus secretary and Tory clears him from all suspicion of hostility to the party Associations and of excessive partiality for the widest possible exercise of the vote, testi-

[1] *Blue Books*, 1868–1869, Vol. VII, § 1312.

fies to this state of things in eloquent language which breathes
an honest indignation : " The franchise has been made a mock-
ery and we must clear away the endless scandals of the Revision Courts. The law on the subject is a sealed book except to
a few, and those who are neither Tories nor Radicals — the
neutrals — political outcasts — suffer most, for the party agents
neglect to claim for them if let off the list, and if on, each side is
anxious to get them off, as neither side trusts them. The practical administration of the law should not be made the toy of
any political party. To get your right as a voter you have to
plead before barristers (many of whom apparently never take
the trouble to study the law) as if you are a criminal, or leave
it to party agents, some of whom delight to squabble indefinitely over procedure as absurd in practice as in theory — and
even then you are liable to be juggled out of your vote by legal
quibble. In any case the register, when complete, is a trophy
of party trickery and manipulation." [1]

The Caucus Associations through whom this " party trickery
and manipulation " is practised partly cannot help it, being in
a way driven to it by the law which makes straightforward and
open action a difficult matter. Interfering, as they do, in the
making up of the register, they render services to many a
voter who, left to his own resources, would never have been
able to make his way through the dense jungle of law and
judicial decision. But to a great extent the Associations are,
as we have been able to see, the deliberate authors of the
state of things which the Tory secretary rightly describes as
scandalous. For in it they try to find influence for their respective parties and discover a justification of their own existence.
On the pretext, made plausible by their own " trickery and manipulation," of helping the voter to maintain his right, the caucuses worm themselves into his confidence and mark out in his
very feelings, so to speak, the lines of their future action, of the
attempts which they mean to make on him when election time
comes round. The voters who have got on or kept on the
register with the help of the Association naturally feel under
an obligation to it. If they were old adherents of the party,
they are confirmed in their devotion to it; if they were holding aloof they are led towards it, connections and ties are

---

[1] Summary of a speech by J. H. Bottomley (*England*, 7th December, 1889).

formed between them and it.   To obtain this result, those who
are indifferent or neutral in politics are sometimes even made
to believe that the right of voting has been secured for them
by the exertions of the Association of one or other of the
parties, when in reality it has not been impugned by anybody.[1]
Other voters whose sympathies are entirely with the party in
general, are obliged to its concrete representative, the Association, for seeing that they are on the register, while not at all
anxious as to their right, and they get into the habit of looking
on the Association with a t.iendly eye and of listening to its
proposals.   In any event, whatever may be the effects on the
voters' minds, the annual campaign of registration gives the
Caucus an opportunity of converting it into a regular reconnoissance.   The Caucus penetrates into their conscience, pries
into their political opinions, in defiance of the secrecy of the
vote, and having ascertained their feelings towards itself, is
able to decide on the nature and the amount of the influence
which must be brought to bear on the voters in view of the
great battle on the polling-day.

III

The census of friends and of enemies having been taken, the
next point is to convert the latter, if possible, to keep and confirm the former in their friendly feelings and to decide the
"doubtful" ones and the waverers.   The only fair way of
doing this is to imbue them with a belief in the creed of the
party, in the excellence of its doctrines, and in the superiority
of its conduct over that of the rival parties.   The efforts which
must be made in this direction constitute the second great

---

[1] For instance, after the close of the registration proceedings, the secretary
of the, we will say, Liberal Caucus, writes the following letter to a number of
voters whose cases have not come before the Registration Court at all : " Dear
Sir, I have much pleasure in informing you that in spite of the determined
opposition of the Tories we have succeeded in keeping your name on the register."   The first impulse of the recipient of this note is to fly into a passion
with the Tories for having attacked him without any provocation on his part,
as he has no politics.   But when reason reasserts her rights, he reflects that
if the Tories wanted to deprive him of his vote, he must be their political
opponent, and if this is so it follows that he is a Liberal.   And by a process of
reasoning, the logical strictness of which is unexceptional, he thus arrives
at the conclusion which the secretary of the Caucus was driving at.

task of the Associations, that of the *political education* of the electorate.

The party Organizations supply this education in three forms: public meetings and other large gatherings, lectures, and political literature gratuitously distributed. Public meetings became from the outset the favourite resource of the caucuses. They corresponded with the idea of the Caucus that political progress could be achieved only by incessant agitation, and that agitating was educating the country. Besides, the old method of individual conversion seemed impracticable after the vast increase in the number of voters effected by successive Reform Bills, whereas meetings presented a ready means of carrying wholesale the masses who might have been attracted to them. They were to produce the same result as steam and machinery taking the place of individual labour in industry. In any event meetings serve to keep up a noise about the party, for the purpose of showing that it is alive and well. If only for this object, therefore, the Caucus tries to organize great party gatherings as often as possible without waiting for them to occur, as in the old days, more or less spontaneously and at irregular intervals. But to make a good show of the party's strength, which the meetings are intended to do, they must not only take place frequently but be a " success," *i.e.* get together an " influential platform," fluent speakers, and of course a large public. If the meetings were not held often, it would convey the impression that the party is losing ground; but if they are not a " success," the party is none the better for them, " it gives a bad tone to your party," as an expert has put it.

Practically the frequency of meetings varies a good deal with the localities. In small places there are not always large assembly rooms to be had; in others there is a want of go; in others again the reverse is the case, one meeting is held after another. Sometimes they are public in the strict meaning of the word, sometimes admittance is obtained only through tickets distributed by the Association. Ticket meetings are in vogue especially with the Tories, who have not yet quite outgrown their traditional distrust of the people. Their political opponents, however, undertake to provide them with an excuse for it; for when the Tories organize *public* meetings, these are often invaded by rowdies from the opposite camp.

It will be remembered with what success this device was practised at Birmingham under the paternal eye of the Liberal
Association.   The decline of habits of freedom which is becoming more and more a characteristic of great party gatherings
in England does not protect even ticket meetings from disorder,
especially at election time.

The success of the meeting depends first and foremost on the
merit of the speakers, especially in the absence of any great
political event or of an incident which happens to stir public opinion and to draw the masses.   The social position of the
speaker is an important claim to the attention of the public,
but his oratorical ability is far more so.   In the old days there
was no need to be an orator to make an impression on an English audience; all that it asked for was sincerity of tone and
common sense, which went straight not only to its homely
intelligence but to its heart.   Form was of no account; if it
was somewhat brilliant it even raised doubts as to the speaker's
straightforwardness; he was suspected of being like an actor
who has learnt his part and who wants to take in honest folk.
To gain the ear of the audience it was even not amiss to tone
down one's natural volubility a little, to approximate as much as
possible to the ordinary style of speaking, which Lytton Bulwer
has eulogized as follows: " Hesitating, Humming, and Drawling
are the three Graces of our conversation." [1]   But the extension
of the social refinement which is euphemistically styled culture
and, on the other hand, the advent of democracy have changed
all this.   In the course of the usual process of a surface civilization which develops the æsthetic feeling of the common herd
by giving them a taste rather for tawdriness and glaring tints,
and in consequence of the efforts made to win the new master,
the sovereign people, who is even more naïve and credulous than
imperious and infatuated, by oratorical devices, the rhetoric
of politicians has rapidly become a treat for the masses and
the clever speaker the popular favourite.   The thirst for political oratory is now really extraordinary in the country.
Some time ago Lord Salisbury advised his followers to train
themselves to be able to meet this demand, in the following
terms: " In these days, whether we like it or not, the power is
with the tongue, the power is with those who can speak, whether

[1] *England and the English*, Book II, Ch. II.

on the platform or in Parliament. I am not holding up this state of things as the ideal of political existence, but as a fact with which we are confronted now. I have known very distinguished orators who were perfectly incompetent men, and I have known very competent men who could not put two sentences — two grammatical sentences — together. But in spite of that fact, it remains still true that the desire for oratory, for speaking on every platform and in every portion of the country, is intense, and seems to be growing in intensity every year." [1]

The Caucus, on its side, helps to gratify this craving for oratory and to stimulate it. To some who are always dying to speak and who get excited and intoxicated with their own words, it supplies a pretext for airing their eloquence in the private gatherings of the Organization and then in the public meetings. To others the Caucus procures opportunities of hearing good speakers, or even celebrated orators, who come down to deliver a speech by invitation of the Association. A good many members of the Association join them, or even get elected to the "hundreds" simply for the purpose of having a good place at the large meetings. For them it is like having a box at the opera. Hence the importance for the Association of obtaining for its public meetings speakers who can make an impression, who can carry away the audience; otherwise people would not come to them.

The usual speakers of the Association are its own members, the President and other office-bearers, who are sufficient for every-day requirements, or even for special occasions in the wards or in small places of rural constituencies. Then comes the local M.P., the Member of Parliament for the Division, who is obliged to appear before his constituents as often as possible to make speeches to them. But the great attraction consists in the speakers imported from London, the "big guns." The Association communicates with them directly or through the central Organization of the party, which is far better able to induce speakers who are in great request to go down to the place. The local Associations always ask for an M.P. at least to be sent to them, if they cannot aspire to the honour of obtaining a Cabinet Minister or an ex-Minister. It is not easy with the best will in the world to procure them this last article.

[1] Speech of the 15th July, 1891, at the United Club.

for England has not yet got as far as some continental countries in which parliamentary government has had the effect that nearly everybody has been a Minister. English Ministers consist of two small groups of men who come into power alternately for a whole generation. They are therefore doled out to the popular audiences in the provinces. But plain M.P.'s are supplied to the Associations pretty liberally. It is in fact on them that the duty mostly devolves of satisfying the passion for oratory with which their fellow-citizens are afflicted. Formerly a Member of Parliament seldom spoke even in his own constituency; a special occasion was required for it, the annual meeting of an agricultural society or some other similar event. To go into a fellow-member's constituency and harangue his electors was considered almost a breach of etiquette. Nowadays M.P.'s do very little else; they are always talking, in session and out of it; no rest is allowed them. They are legislators in the second place only; their main function is to be commercial travellers for their party in the employ of the Associations. Next to the M.P.'s, Associations in search of speechmakers have a very valuable resource in the embryo politicians, most of whom, young men who have or think they have a career before them, are collected in London in special clubs with the particular object of providing the Organizations of their respective parties with speakers. We shall have an opportunity of reverting in more detail to these "speaking clubs" later on.

IV

However much the social and intellectual position of the speakers may differ, the eloquence which they contribute to the meetings has something in common which gives it a special stamp in spite of its endless variety. With but few exceptions their speeches are fighting harangues, the tone of them is polemical, marked by an aggressive ardour, and spiced with an ever-increasing amount of epigram. It is this last feature which is becoming the great attraction for audiences at meetings, and which in their eyes constitutes the true orator. The men who are gifted in a high degree with a slashing style of eloquence, the smart speakers, are at a premium on the platform. The thirst for applause is too great for them not to yield to the temptation to put themselves on a level with the audience, with its new ideas of the beautiful and also of the good. For at the same time that a smattering of culture was developing new æsthetic tastes among the masses in the manner just described, the progress of enlightenment was elevating their moral taste. Their minds began to be more keenly sensitive to every aspiration in the direction of justice and goodness; every lofty aim found a louder echo in their hearts; in a word, the faculty of moral enthusiasm had reached a higher point in the multitude than it had ever done before. But with the imperfect culture which the dawn of knowledge brought in its train, this enthusiasm lacked the moderating influence of judgment. Far from being guided by discrimination themselves, from undertaking the often thankless task of commending it to popular audiences, the speakers at meetings are inclined to trade on the new tendencies of the popular mind. Their language, breathing a spirit which sets the heart aglow, and interspersed with hits at their opponents, forms a highly seasoned dish which agreeably tickles the æsthetic and moral palate of their listeners. The platform speakers amuse and edify them at the same time. The anxiety to achieve this double result prevents the most cultivated orators from being careful in the choice of their expressions and arguments, and often tempts them not to be too particular even about the facts. Those who are on the highest rungs of the political ladder, the responsible statesmen, are not always able to resist this. The glare of the footlights dazzles them, and the immediate effect produced on the audience carries them away. More or less unconsciously they aim at the imaginations of their listeners; they try to make the springs of enthusiasm within them gush forth, to draw out their emotions, in order to enlist them in the service of the party. Through the oratorical electricity which they discharge on the masses, they steep them in the party spirit with which they themselves are profoundly imbued. This spirit, as it spreads by contagion through the assembled masses, inspires them with that feeling of being in the right which makes the disparagement of opponents a meritorious act, which lends a ceremonial dignity to the cheers and laughter that emphasize the words

of the speaker, and which, in perfect good faith, stifles contradiction whenever it ventures to raise its head. The great
increase in the number of meetings due to party necessities
tends to convert this style of eloquence into a canon and a
model. Being obliged to exert himself, that is to say his tongue,
too often, the speaker has not the time, even if he has the wish,
to think out his speeches, to prepare them. He is compelled
to almost improvise them. Having to prove unceasingly that
his party is invariably right and to crush the other side at all
hazards, he is forced to lay about him indiscriminately. The
inevitable result is that poverty of thought takes refuge under
strong language and that emptiness of matter is disguised by
rhetoric.

True, platform eloquence, as developed under the auspices of
the caucuses, marks a great advance on that of the hustings[1]
of the pre-democratic period. However hollow, claptrap, conventional, and sectarian the language of platform speakers may
be, it claims to convince the audience, it makes a show of
bringing forward arguments and facts, it states a case, it criti-
cises, it appeals to the moral feelings; whereas the hustings'
speakers, without troubling their heads about reasoning and
sentiments, tried to win the applause of the populace gathered
beneath them by the audacity of their language and by wit,
often of a vulgar kind, displayed at the expense of political
opponents. The platform eloquence of the present day is also
of a more elevated character than the old popular eloquence in
vogue at the time of great political movements, such as the
agitation of the years 1816–1819, or Chartism. But while the
comparison is in favour of the public meetings of our own day,
yet in itself it is perhaps not appropriate. The violent and
declamatory language of the Chartist orators, or of their predecessors, was simply the temporary and exceptional effect of
popular commotion let loose by misery and ignorance. Nor
was the hustings' style, which was of more regular and even
of periodical occurrence, a model for extra-parliamentary eloquence. In the public existence of those days the hustings'

[1] Before the introduction of the ballot, in 1872, candidates who stood for
Parliament appeared before the electors on a wooden erection called " hustings," which was put up for the occasion by the authorities in one of the principal public places.

period was a time of political carnival in which the proprieties of ordinary life were in a way suspended. The populace took its revenge for its political and social inferiority by often amusing itself at the expense of the candidates themselves, who were obliged to enter into the spirit of it. It was the price which they paid for their election. Their eloquence had to adapt itself to the mind and the mood of the crowds which surrounded them, and of course its level was not a high one. But this was of no consequence, and on a different platform to the hustings the same politician spoke a different language; he had another model of eloquence to follow, — that of the parliamentary arena. Along with all the profound changes which parliamentary eloquence underwent in the course of the last century of the pre-democratic era, it always preserved a certain elevation. It had its golden age, under the two last Georges, from Chatham down to Canning, in the period which constituted its "grand siècle"; it was then a grand style of eloquence, majestic and thrilling, aristocratic and refined. With the advent of the middle class it assumed a homely garb; it became a commercial, business kind of eloquence, not brilliant, but substantial and solid; in other words, honest. It still bore this character as it passed on to the platform when the questions of the day began to be discussed there, especially from the time of the agitation against the Corn Laws. John Bright appeared, and in speeches which were faultless in form poured the emotion which welled up from the depths of his inner being over the hard figures and the facts of the economic controversy which, in the mouth of Cobden and his lieutenants, appealed patiently and conscientiously to reason and to judgment. He made an epoch, but left no school; his oratory was not a "manner" which could be learnt. In a narrower field which was confined to the north of England, another great popular orator, Joseph Cowen, combined the old and the new style of eloquence in language marked by profound thought, full of startling imagery, clearly cut, of almost monumental conciseness, expanded on the one hand by the intense heat of the speaker's glowing democratic sympathies, and on the other by the abundance of ideas and facts which his speeches contained. But they were too polished and they pre-supposed far more culture and intellectual honesty than the platform admits of,

to become a model.   It was reserved for the illustrious rival
in eloquence of Bright and of Cowen, for Mr. Gladstone, to
become the master, the classic of the platform.   He took to it
rather late in life, after a political career of more than thirty
years, but he did so at the psychological moment when England
was on the eve of passing into democracy, and he brought
to it, besides his wonderful talent, certain special qualities
which particularly commended his oratory to the taste of the
masses and made it a sort of ideal.   Mr. Gladstone's language,
which was generally prolix, met the popular intelligence, which
lacks discipline and likes to be always returning to the charge
in its reasoning, half-way ; the consummate art with which he
marshalled facts and ideas and made them say just what he
wanted, turned the masses round and round like a top without
giving them time to reflect; the torrents of passion which,
springing from the depths of his sincerity and conviction,
flowed through his oratory, carried them completely away.
The majority of platform speakers followed this great model,
exaggerating especially its defects, just as shadows on the can-
vas of a master are transformed into coarse patches in vulgar
chromo reproductions.   Aided by the new conditions of English political life and under the auspices of the caucuses, who
have made themselves as it were contractors for public meetings, this chromolithograph oratory, with its verbiage, its facile
sophisms, and its real or simulated passion, has become only
too common and recalls the style of eloquence which has
grown up amid the democracy of America under the name of
" stump " oratory.[1]

V

However unfounded the claim of the meetings to supply
the masses with political education may appear, it cannot be

[1] In the west of the United States, in the midst of settlements run up on
ground barely cleared, stumps of trees served, during the first election campaign, as a platform from which the adventurers who solicited the suffrages of
their casual fellow-citizens harangued them with all the resources of an unscrupulous fluency.   In consequence, " stump " has become a term of political
slang, meaning mob platform, and the expressions " stump oratory," " stump
orator " became synonymous for political eloquence of a hollow, declamatory
and misleading kind, trading on the credulity and passions of popular audiences.   The word, however, is now used in ordinary parlance, without having
necessarily any invidious meaning.

absolutely disallowed; for, after all, scraps of information and
of argument do fall from the platform which may now and
then enlighten the audience on the questions of the day
and perhaps make them reflect on such matters. But the
extent to which these effects are producible can only be very
slight, not merely on account of the tone and character of the
eloquence of the meetings, but also because both parties are
not heard and those present being all, as a rule, of the same
persuasion see only one side of the shield. At meetings of
less importance it is often allowable to ask the speakers for
explanations by means of brief questions, but there is never
any discussion or debate. Dissentients may speak, that is
to say the chairman would allow them to do so, but the
audience will not listen to them. The tolerant frame of mind
with which in former days a statement of views manifestly
opposed to the general sense of the meeting was silently
and patiently listened to, is a thing of the past.[1] It is true
that the speakers of the different parties often reply to each
other in the respective meetings organized by their political
friends, and that their speeches, reproduced in the newspapers,
can be read and compared. But this publicity falls to the lot
only of speakers who have a national reputation and whose
sayings and doings interest public opinion; the speeches of
less important persons can find a place only in the local press,
where the speech of the political opponent is smothered in a
few lines. Even if the speech were reported at greater length
the reasoning of the speaker on the other side is, in this form,
only a piece of literature; it no longer has anything in common
with a gathering at which people argue face to face. After
all, the fact is that in the meetings it is a case of preaching
to converts, and that their sole object is to besprinkle the
audience with the magnetic party fluid, to kindle the ardour
which is smouldering within them, or, to use the favourite term
by which the leaders of the caucuses express their favourite
idea, to "raise enthusiasm," or at least to convey the illusion
of it to the public.

Here we have the dominant thought which prescribes the
choice of the speakers as well as the style of eloquence con-

[1] Cf. H. Jephson, *The Platform: its Rise and Progress*, Lond. 1892, Vol. II,
p. 319.

tributed to the meetings, and even the *mise-en-scène* of these gatherings. The great meetings organized by the Associations generally admit of a musical part in their programme ; songs composed for the use of parties are sung at them, with the accompaniment of an orchestra. The mere fact of singing at political gatherings is no novelty, but formerly it occurred only in times of great political agitations, and consequently the songs were then songs for a special occasion inspired by a cause, by a particular claim which had the power of stirring the heart. Of this kind were the hymn of the Birmingham Political Union demanding Parliamentary Reform, the Anti-Corn Law hymns, and the Poor Men's Songs composed on the occasion of the agitation against the Corn Laws. After 1868, especially under the auspices of the caucuses of both parties, political songs were introduced to serve as a liturgy, so to speak, to exalt, not so much a particular cause, as the church and the saints of the party, the great leaders on each side. At first there was a rather strong opposition to it, to wit, in the Liberal camp, where a good many were of opinion that political meetings were not "music-halls." [1] But people soon got used to it. In the extreme north of England and in Scotland singing was not a success ; the cold and more thoughtful temperament of the population does not lend itself sufficiently to it. The object of most of the songs is to foster general party virtues, such as devotion to and admiration for the leaders and a resolve to march shoulder to shoulder against the enemy. Sometimes stanzas composed for the occasion are introduced.[2] The

[1] It is not without interest to compare this protest, which proceeded from men belonging rather to the cultivated classes, with a similar manifestation of leaders of labour at a distant and memorable date. It occurred during the years 1816–1819, when, at the time of the political awakening of the masses which had led to so many public and secret meetings, a proposal was also made to introduce the stimulant of vocal music (Samuel Bamford, *Passages in the Life of a Radical*, new edition, 1859, p. 135).

[2] The following are some specimens of songs sung at meetings :

EARL BEACONSFIELD IS A REMARKABLE MAN

(Tune — *My Grandfather was a Most Wonderful Man*)

Earl Beaconsfield is a remarkable man,
The best one to lead the Conservative van ;
   *   *   *   *   *   *
Then flock to the *poll*, all Conservatives quick,
And make the Rads hold the wrong end of the *stick*,
Astonish the minds of great William and Bright,
As they see for themselves their deplorable flight ;

extracts given below prove that the lyre of the party Tyr-
tæuses is remarkable not so much for its poetic beauties as

> While Harcourt and Chamberlain, Parnell and Biggar,
> Look pale as a turnip, or black as a nigger!
> And give the best aid, as you certainly can,
> To Beaconsfield, who's a remarkable man,
> To Beaconsfield, who's a remarkable man!
> *   *   *   *   *   *
> Then fix him in office and keep out the Rads,
> And all the rough lot of Political Cads;
> Old England through them must receive no more hurt,
> Be snubb'd throughout Europe, and dragg'd in the dirt.
> Our true British Queen with her people so free
> Must be first of all nations o'er land and o'er sea!
> And so she will keep if the reign's not a span
> Of Beaconsfield, who's a remarkable man!
> Of Beaconsfield, who's a remarkable man!
>
> (*Conservative Election Songs*, Lond. 1880.)

THE UNIONISTS' SONG (*of recent date*)

(Air — *The Mermaid*)

Don't you think that the Radicals have meddled quite enough
With the Army, and the Navy, and the Church?
About 'three acres and a cow' they made a grand old row,
But they left the British workman in the lurch, the lurch, the lurch,
They left the British workman in the lurch.

Chorus

> For Harcourt and John Morley now may roar,
> And the Grand Old Man may crow,
> But we jolly Unionists will head the poll again,
> And the Radicals will all be down below, below, below,
> The Radicals will all be down below!
> *   *   *   *   *
>
> (Published by the *Central Conservative Office*.)

THE LIBERAL MARCH

> Men and Liberals! ye whose action
> Put to rout the Tory faction,
> Follow still the chiefs who led ye,
> Keep your ranks still firm and steady,
> In their ranks spread wild distraction
> Vanquished all their bands.
> Keep your swords still sharp and ready,
> Ready to your hands.

Chorus

> Shoulder press to shoulder,
> Onward march and bolder,
> Triumphs more we yet shall see
> Before we are much older.
> *   *   *   *   *

for the ardour of its sentiments.   The music of the songs is
taken in preference from well-known airs,[1] which flatter the

> Gladstone's government shall rule us,
> Men like these will lead, not school us,
> Tory Peers no more shall fool us.
>   We've a better way!
> Equal rights all shall be sharing,
> Equal burdens all be bearing;
> Each for all, for all each caring —
>   Hail the happy day.

THE GRAND OLD MAN

> O hark! O hear! how, far and near
> Through all this ancient land,
> The armies of Reform have made
>   Their last brave stand.

Chorus

> A grand old cause have we,
> A Grand Old Man.
> He knows the way to victory,
> The Grand Old Man!
> *   *   *   *   *
>   (*Songs for Liberals.*)

THE GRAND OLD STANDARD

> Rise, ye toiling sons of labour,
>   Crush oppression strong,
> Liberty and Progress brighten
>   At your thrilling song.

Chorus

> Raise it up, the grand old standard,
>   Flaunt the banners wide,
> Join the mighty march for Freedom,
>   Victory's on our side.

> Stand and view the glorious programme
>   Which is to be won,
> Loudly greet the grand old leader
>   Till his days are done.

Chorus

> See the Tories, they are nowhere
>   'Midst our force arrayed ;
> When the victory is over
>   Won't they look dismayed!
> (*Songs issued by the London Liberal and Radical Union.*)

---

[1] It appears that they are not always *popular* enough, and some time ago
an important London newspaper held forth gravely on the advantage which

ear of the audience and even enable them to sing in chorus.   If
everybody cannot speak, everybody can sing.   Moreover, they
are all allowed to join personally in the proceedings outside
the musical part, and to contribute to it in other ways besides
applause and shouts: voting goes on as well, and everybody
can lift up his hand; after every couple of speeches delivered
a resolution is generally put to the meeting, declaring, approving, or censuring something or somebody.   Finally, when all
the regular speeches are at an end, thanks are voted to the
Chairman of the meeting, on a motion made with more or less
brevity but always by a couple of speakers, the proposer and
the seconder.

For some time past it has become a common practice to hold
party meetings out-of-doors (open-air meetings), in a public
place, a garden or a park.   The masses are more easily attracted there, especially in the summer time, and the expense of
hiring a large room is saved.   In the field of religious propaganda dissent long ago popularized outdoor meetings.   The
great founders of Methodism, John Wesley and Whitefield,
deserting the consecrated places of worship and the respectable people who frequented them, preached in the open air,
amid the fields, to thousands of brutalized miners, and it was
there that they achieved their greatest successes by plunging
the assembled multitudes into nervous crises, by exciting to
the point of hysteria the religious enthusiasm which they
awakened in these rude and untutored souls.   Since then
preaching in the streets has become a regular feature of English life, as any foreigner taking a walk on Sunday can see;
but this has not made it more respectable, for it is addressed
to the dregs of the population collected from the street-
crossings.   The temperance propaganda, which is also carried
on in the streets, is addressed to the same social class.
Political outdoor gatherings, not having even the possible
excuse of saving souls, were in bad odour up to a recent date;
they had something at once common and revolutionary about
them.   True, in the old days, under the Georges, " county
meetings " occasionally assembled in the open air on a green;

would accrue to the Liberal and Radical Union of London from adopting the
air of *Two Lovely Black Eyes* for the songs.   *Pall Mall Gazette*, 7th April,
1887.

but their accessories were not so much vulgar as rustic, the
political life of the nation being at that time concentrated not
in the towns, but in the rural part of the country, in the
counties. These gatherings, at which freeholders alone could
speak, and which the rest attended only as spectators, were
almost official functions; they were presided over by the
sheriff. Occasionally, mostly at times of agricultural crises,
they discussed the economic situation and incidentally politics
as well.[1] It was only in the towns, amid vast agglomerations
of people brought together by the great outburst of industry,
that outdoor political assemblages, with their character of
menace to public order, came into fashion, when the first
mutterings of revolt were heard among the working classes.
The disappearance of great popular agitations, completed by
the extension of the suffrage to the urban masses, has deprived
gatherings of this kind of their revolutionary acuteness, while
the patronage bestowed on them by the party Associations,
anxious to attract the multitude, made open-air meetings if not
respectable, at all events acceptable. At the outset, many an
influential member of the Caucus, even among its founders at
Birmingham, felt scruples about encouraging them, but the
great organizer asserted that they were "excellent for raising
enthusiasm," and they let things take their course. Nowadays
no speaker or politician, even of the highest rank, would refuse
to address an open-air meeting; even the "last Whigs" are
obliged to submit to it to get at the masses, just like the
ultra-Radical speakers, ranting in public thoroughfares, who
are called and who humorously style themselves "gutter politicians." The Tories are not less ready to take to open-air
meetings.[2]

---

[1] Cf. H. Jephson, *The Platform*, I, 575, and the passage quoted from the
Lettres sur l'Angleterre, in 1825, by Staël-Holstein, the husband of Madame
de Staël.

[2] In the Tory party, but outside its official organization, a special league
has recently been founded to compete with the Radical propaganda in the
streets of London. This organization, which has taken the title of *The Constitutional Open-Air League*, is composed of workingmen, who on Sunday
"hold open-air meetings in places which were hitherto left to the Radical
and Socialist demagogues." Thereupon orthodox casuists raised the question
whether the Fourth Commandment was not broken by talking politics on the
Sabbath, to which other casuists triumphantly rejoined that there could be no
harm in preventing "a poor workingman from falling into the Socialist pit on

With the meetings are connected the party *demonstrations.* These are large extraordinary gatherings, the principal object of which is to convey an impression of the numerical strength of the party and of its enthusiasm. The display of these forces is intended again to stimulate the zeal of the rank and file, to give confidence to the leaders, and finally to carry away the waverers, to win them by the contagion of enthusiasm. The *mise-en-scène* here consequently comes before the oratory. Those who take part in the demonstration arrive in a procession with flags and banners, to the sound of drums and fifes. Special trains are organized to bring people from the neighbourhood at reduced fares. If the meeting is a particularly large one, improvised speakers address the crowd which has not been able to get into the hall, in another building or even on the staircase (overflow meeting). When the demonstration takes place out of doors, several platforms are erected from which the orators speak simultaneously. The voting of the resolutions is sometimes accompanied by blasts from a trumpet. Evening open-air demonstrations present an opportunity for lighting torches and marching with lanterns in the hand. The proportions and the programme of demonstrations, however, vary a good deal. Every meeting of exceptional importance assumes the character of a demonstration, even if there is no great display, so that it is not always easy to draw the line between a demonstration and a meeting; a "mass meeting," a meeting with "big guns" imported from London, fully answers the purpose aimed at by demonstrations. The peripatetic gatherings of the general meetings of the Grand Caucus with its thousands of delegates, or even of its district branches, belong to the same category. The great demonstrations, being difficult to organize and entailing considerable expense, are comparatively rare. To a certain extent they follow the lead of political events; when the latter stir up party spirit, or when the managers of the caucuses want to raise it to a higher pitch, the demonstrations serve to make it break out; sometimes, on the other hand, when a complete calm prevails, they are administered as a heroic remedy, to rouse

the Sabbath Day," and that the members of the League ought to continue to "go forth on the Sabbath to speak for their God, their Queen, and their country" (*England*, Jan. 1892).

an apathetic and sluggish constituency on which the ordinary stimulants of the Caucus have had no effect.

In the rural districts with their scattered population, utterly indifferent to politics, meetings have not been able to develop to the same extent as in the towns. Besides, it is not always easy to find a room, or, occasionally, an audience. Sometimes people are afraid of attracting notice by going to a meeting of either party, and of offending the landlord or the employer who holds different political views. But this is the exception. As a general rule, everybody goes to the meetings as they would to a play. For some time past the Organizations have tried to make the performance attractive as well as effective, especially by means of travelling vans provided with speakers. These latter travel about like hawkers or gypsies, in carts which serve them as a house and have a kitchen, bedroom, etc. The ringing of a bell or the blowing of a trumpet announces the entry of the van into the village, where it at once attracts general attention by its exterior, the ornaments, the flags, the portraits of the great leaders of the party covering the panels of the vehicle. A notice sent round from house to house invites the inhabitants to the meeting in the evening. Sometimes it is circulated by the village children, to whom handbills with pictures are distributed. The meeting takes place indoors, like ordinary meetings, with a committee or at all events a chairman who introduces the speaker to the audience, or out-of-doors on the village green. In the latter case the van supplies the platform from which the speaker addresses the crowd. He often illustrates his speech with pictures from a magic lantern: portraits of party celebrities or scenes relating to political events. The van is provided for this purpose with compressed gas and other accessories required for making projections on a screen. The meetings are not the only opportunity which the speaker has of carrying on his propaganda; he accosts persons he meets on the road, he stops before the smallest crowd. He calls on people to catechise them in private. At the meetings and on every other occasion he distributes political pamphlets gratuitously. This method of propaganda has a good deal of success in the villages, owing to the attraction of novelty which it offers and to the curiosity which it excites; but it is too expensive for party organizations, which are always in want of funds, to be able to make much use of it.

VI

Next to the meetings come the lectures, as an instrument of party propaganda. While the speeches at the meetings are by their nature more or less polemical, the lectures are supposed to be above all didactical. Being more *objective* both in form and substance, their aim is to instruct the audience on particular subjects connected with politics. This character no doubt should give the lectures the first place in the logical order of instruments of political education, but in practice they come far behind the platform. The number of political lectures delivered to popular audiences is continually decreasing in the country. This phenomenon is due to two causes: the party Organizations are sparing of lectures, and the public does not appreciate them enough, does not take to them. In fact, the share assigned to lectures in the labours of the official Organizations has never been considerable. The Tories have only recently become propagandists, at a time when, being unable to hold their own by means of "influences," they found themselves obliged to appeal also to the public intelligence. With the Liberals, on the other hand, lectures were formerly much in vogue, but when the Caucus began to take up the work of political propaganda, it directed its main efforts to "organization" and agitation by meetings, and thrust lectures into the background. This was the very point in which it differed from the Liberal Organizations of the opposite type, such as the *National Reform Union* and the *London and Counties' Union*, which held, as we are aware, that the future of the Liberal party depended, not on the management of voters, but on the development of political education in the true meaning of the word. "Ignorance is the mother of Toryism," exclaimed the organ of the *Reform Union*, "and the present generation is lamentably ignorant." [1] The *Reform Union*, as well as the *London Union* during its short existence, held one lecture after another, whereas the Birmingham Caucus (with its branches) started twenty or

[1] *Manchester Critic*, 24th January, 1879.

thirty meetings in which "enthusiasm was raised" for one
lecture. Having become, after 1886, master of the organization of the party throughout the country, the Liberal Caucus
has not changed its ways; it has even become more engrossed
in demonstrations and electioneering.

On the other hand, it is only just to point out that the very
moderate zeal of the caucuses for lectures is in no way stimulated by the public. There are not many people who care for
the political lectures which are provided: sometimes, it would
appear, the lecturers do not know how to *interest* their audiences; at others their language is above the heads of the public
which they address; or again their subjects are not happily
chosen. There is doubtless a large element of truth in these
explanations, but the great, the primary, reason which over-
shadows all the others is that by far the greater part of the
English masses are still unable to take an intelligent interest
in political questions. They lack the rudiments of culture
and the mental discipline necessary to concentrate their attention for half an hour on a subject outside the preoccupations
of their daily life. It is needless to add that there is a minority, very small it is true, to which this remark is not
applicable. There are exceptions, there are even exceedingly
brilliant ones. In Lancashire, and higher up in the north
of England, as well as in Scotland, workmen can be found
who possess a political culture very superior to that of many
a member of the House of Commons. But the vast majority
of the people have no interest in or intelligence for political
matters. Kept by the old ruling classes in ignorance, partly
by design, partly through neglect, they have been abruptly
"brought within the pale of the Constitution" by the calculations and the manœuvres of the parties, in their headlong race for power. After the event people saw that they
must "educate their masters," and they set to work to teach
them the alphabet. In this respect the Education Act has
produced important results, — it has spread instruction far
and wide in the country. The number of illiterate persons
has fallen remarkably low, but the intellectual standard of
the masses has scarcely risen. One might almost say that it
has rather declined; for they turn out a smaller proportion of
people who take a really thoughtful interest in politics than

formerly. In fact, there is more reading but less thinking, much less than there used to be. "Twenty or thirty years ago," as a veteran of the élite of the working class remarked, "the people read one book; now they only read ephemeral things." Even in popular circles where people plume themselves on advanced ideas, where they talk of principles, of rights, they read little or nothing, and confine themselves to retailing stereotyped phrases which have become common property. In its somewhat pathetic form, the following exclamation of an old working-man was only a true picture of the real state of things: "In my time, sir, no one talked of the 'Rights of Man' without having read Thomas Paine! Everybody who laid claim to be a Radical had read Paine, had read Ernest Jones." In fact, they were read and other authors besides. The fervour of the fiery American apostle and the lyrical effusions of the English agitator were far from monopolizing the people's minds; even the rigid dialectic of Bentham penetrated into these circles. Societies of working-men bought books wholesale at a reduced price, to retail them to their members at cost price. Clubs for study were formed, composed of twenty or thirty persons, in which political works were read and discussed, as, by the way, used to be done at a more remote epoch, full of gloomy memories for the people, during the years which followed the Peace of 1815, in the Hampden Clubs, the members of which met regularly once a week for reading and discussion.[1] At the present time the principal, if not the only, political pabulum of the great majority of the people is the newspapers, and even they are read in another way, and different things are read in them than used to be the case. Formerly, before the repeal of the paper duty in 1860, a working-man could not afford to buy a newspaper; the whole workshop subscribed, they took in a paper at a penny an hour; one of them read it, and the rest listened to him in solemn silence and with unflagging attention. Then the comments began; the cleverer ones discussed and explained the subject, and every one learnt something. Now, with the development of the cheap Press, a workman can buy a newspaper all to himself for a halfpenny, and can read it alone and take what he likes from it. Being full of

[1] Bamford, 7.

small items of news, the paper, instead of concentrating the attention of the reader, makes it flit from paragraph to paragraph, and in the long run brings more weariness than rest or food to the mind. As a rule, there is only one part of the paper which is read with serious attention, — the columns devoted to sport. The interest in sport, including betting, has become a regular endemic disease, which ravages the country. If people do not lose their money over it, they squander their capacity for curiosity on it; in the workshop sport is talked, during the meals which are eaten in common the last match is discussed, in the groups standing about in the streets of an evening or on Sunday football remains the topic of conversation, in nine cases out of ten. Not to mention the public-houses, the music-halls and concert-rooms in the large towns have their share in diverting the workmen from improving their minds. The conditions of labour in modern industry, to which the opponents of industrialism impute all the mischief, do in fact tend to the same result. Bound like a slave to his machine, isolated amidst the great mass of operatives in the factory, the worker is prevented not only from getting into touch with his comrades' ideas, but from having ideas himself, from thinking of anything whatever. After his crushingly monotonous day's work, he leaves the factory worn out, incapable of paying attention to anything that demands a mental effort.

Of late years no doubt the active Socialist propaganda has produced a certain intellectual awakening in popular circles. Economic questions are much discussed; they have become a subject of arduous study for many an artisan and many a small employé. Just as their predecessors of forty or fifty years back got as far as Bentham, they grapple with Karl Marx. But a different spirit animates the two generations, and it does not fail to produce different effects. The former, inspired by rationalist individualism, had no belief other than reason, and professed no dogmas which could prejudge its conclusions, whereas the men of the present generation, provided with a definite ideal of social organization, with the collectivist ideal, make this an immutable creed, and it is only within the four corners of it that they admit free enquiry, in which they indulge solely for the purpose of building themselves up more strongly in their faith. The one, if it is permissible to put it in this way, reflected the scientific spirit which emancipates and elevates, the other is imbued with the theological spirit which enslaves and degrades, the intellect.

This intellectual movement, however, started by economic problems, and confined to those problems, affects only a small fraction of the masses, a small sect. For the great majority, what has been said above of its intellectual condition still remains true. No doubt, the cheap Press and the political agitation carried on by the parties have brought into general circulation many facts and ideas which in their career have reached a number of people who before that never came across them. The questions of the day which divide the parties have consequently become much more familiar to the people than they have ever been, which leads a good many persons to say that working-men are now "well up in politics." But in the great majority of cases they assimilate the facts and the arguments by an absolutely automatic process, which is in a way thrust on them by the very conditions in which these facts and arguments are presented, and it is more by the senses that they take them in. Their want of intellectual discipline predisposes them still more than the other strata of society to the momentary and fugitive impressions of the feverish and agitated existence which is the feature of the age, and which has infected even the phlegmatic temperament of the English race. The paltry rudiments of culture diffused among the masses have rather been instrumental, for the moment, in developing a state of nervousness, of excitement, which at one time fosters a continuous dissatisfaction, at another, and more often, tries to find a vent in strong and constantly recurring sensations.

The character of the lectures provided by the party Organizations was by no means calculated to soothe this restlessness. The lectures being never *objective,* but being always intended, in more or less guarded language, to enforce the catechism of the party, the logic of instinct told the masses that it was not worth while beating about the bush, that it was better to strike home and hit hard than to bore them with a sermon. Turning almost invariably on party politics, and always with an apologetic purpose, the lectures harped on the same ideas, reproduced the same formulas. "They have nothing new to say," is a remark I have often heard. In contrast to this, the meetings with their fiery harangues, the demonstrations with all their accessories, offered the multitudes a show, a distraction, amounting to a kind of sport. The Caucus, which, being anxious above all to succeed, thought it more easy, looking to the intellectual condition of the masses, to "raise enthusiasm" than to appeal to reason, consequently found itself in perfect touch with the popular tendencies. Thus, through the connivance of the public and the Caucus, the form of political propaganda best suited for disciplining the mind and storing it has given way to methods which act mainly on the imagination, on the nerves; the quiet lecture-rooms are deserted for the exciting meetings.[1]

In the country districts lecturing is more developed and meets with more success, relatively speaking. As the newspapers are read but little or not at all by the villagers, and as political meetings occur only at rare intervals in rural localities, the Associations endeavour, with more or less zeal, to make good the deficiency by lectures, especially in the south of England. The quieter life and the absence of distractions among the village people make them more inclined for lectures than the townsfolk. At village lectures the audience is generally composed of adherents of both parties; curiosity attracts to them Liberals and Tories alike; but there is never any discussion, and it is very seldom that questions are put to the lecturer; from timidity or prudence, in order not to betray their political preferences, people hold their tongue. Sometimes the schoolmaster or some other strong-minded member of the party opposed to that of the lecturer ventures to draw attention to the "pernicious" doctrines laid down by the latter. But this is the exception; as a rule, there are no more manifestations of opinion at the lectures than at the meetings and the visits of the travelling vans. The mind of the rustics, like the soil which they cultivate, does not show the effect produced till later on.

[1] Making allowance for this state of things, the *London and Counties Liberal Union* resorted, in the last months of its existence, in 1886, to small stratagems to procure audiences for its lecturers; it requested them to advertise their lecture as a " political address " or even to summon meetings, with their usual accessories, for the delivery of the lecture, in which case the lecturer appeared in the disguise of a "Deputation of the London and Counties Liberal Union."

The lectures organized by the clubs, as well as by the Associations, are delivered partly by local amateurs, partly by persons invited from outside, and also by professional lecturers. The first and the second give their services gratuitously; the strangers are only allowed their travelling expenses, when they are not obliging enough to pay them themselves. The professional lecturers are paid. The Association of the constituency, the Caucus, contributes the fees, while the people of the locality in which the lecture is held defray the cost of advertising and the hire of the room. . As in the case of the meetings, the organizers of lectures on the look-out for lecturers communicate with them directly or through the medium of the central organizations. One of the obligations of the latter in regard to the affiliated Associations consists precisely in supplying them with lecturers, either voluntary or at all events paid. In the latter case the central Organizations act as registry offices. The big party Organizations, with regular lecturers whom they send, spontaneously or on application, to say a word in season, are: on the Conservative side, the National Union of Conservative and Constitutional Associations and the Primrose League; on the Liberal side, the National Liberal Federation and the National Reform Union (of Manchester), which from its first appearance had made the development of political education the aim and object of its existence.

In re-reading the above pages in proof-sheets, I note that since they were written, some years ago, the importance of the lectures given by the party Organizations, which I have had to qualify so much, has still further diminished; at the present moment they are at the lowest ebb. Even the activity of the Manchester Reform Union has become, in the matter of lectures, almost non-existent.

For some time past the Organizations have employed political educators of a different kind to the lecturers, — "political missionaries." Sometimes these missionaries are professionals, who work all the year, travelling from place to place to deliver political addresses or speeches at open-air meetings. Thus the Central Conservative Office has in its pay a group of "missionaries" of this kind. Sometimes, and more often, they are secret emissaries who have another regular employment and accept temporary missions for a few weeks. Generally workmen by trade, they penetrate into popular circles to advertise the party which employs them, to defend its programme in quasi-spontaneous conversations. The Liberals and the Conservatives both make use of emissaries, but with the latter this practice is, it would appear, much more developed and systematized. The *modus operandi* of the emissaries in the Tory organization is as follows. Sent by the representative of the Central Conservative Office of the district, the emissary arrives in a Division with a letter of introduction for the Chairman of the local Tory organization. This letter accredits him, gets him the assistance of this organization, and at the same time places him under its supervision. His chief who has despatched him hears about him from the local Tory Chairmen as the missionary gradually makes his way through the district. He never speaks at meetings, but works privately and incognito; he conducts his operations in public-houses, or wherever he can find a group of persons and start a conversation on politics as if by chance. He tries to challenge a Radical leader who is present to a debate, he fastens on the "bombastic Radical" of the village, and if he comes off best in the dialectical encounter, he destroys the latter's prestige and his political influence with his neighbours. Of course the missionaries are always sent into parts of the country where they are not known. After having discharged their mission, they return to their regular occupations. The party Organizations find a sufficient number of them to meet their requirements.

VII

After the meetings, the lectures, and the missionaries, which furnish methods of collective propaganda among more or less large gatherings of citizens, the party Organizations engage in individual political education by means of the gratuitous distribution of "political literature," that is to say, pamphlets and other printed matter relating to politics. The greater part of this "literature" is made up in London by the central party Organizations. A large number of copies being printed, the publications are sold to the local Associations by hundreds or thousands at a cheap rate. The latter have the "literature" distributed at the meetings which they organize, or sometimes, in the villages for instance, send them round from house to house. It has been stated above that this operation forms part of the duties of the itinerant speakers of travelling vans. Dealing with the questions of the day which divide the parties, or those about which they fought in the past, the pamphlets, whether they are reprints of speeches or of lectures by the party orators, or are written for the occasion, almost always have an electioneering twang about them. Finance, legislation, foreign politics, — every topic is treated not for its own sake, but to induce the reader to vote for this particular party and not for another. While some of these publications handle their subjects with more or less fulness and propriety in tone and form, the others are simply electioneering prospectuses, which, if they do not prove it, assert that every good thing comes from their party whereas the other party has never done the country anything but harm. Not that these pamphlets are wholly made up of general clap-trap, there are plenty of facts and figures in them, but they prove rather that there is a different history and statistics for the special use of each party. Figures are quoted to demonstrate that pauperism and crime become rife directly this or that party returns to power. Care is also taken to give these prospectuses an argumentative appearance by presenting them in the form of "70 good reasons why you should vote for the Liberals," but their logic is anything but strict! [1] Along with the pamphlets, which form the substantial element of the literature, a great number of leaflets are published, small sheets of two or three pages, intended for readers who would not be able to tackle anything of greater length or with more argument. The political question and its solution or the catch-word of the party are stated

[1] Thus, for instance, this last pamphlet, after having given "more than 70 good reasons," broaches the question why "the country is more prosperous under a Liberal than under a Conservative Government?" and replies as follows: "Because the Liberals, by a good policy, improve good times, and alleviate the bad; while the Conservatives, by a bad policy, make bad times worse. How is that? A bad policy produces uneasiness and want of enterprise. Uneasiness and want of enterprise produce depression in trade and want of employment. Depression in trade and want of employment produce an increase of Taxation, Debt, Misery, Pauperism, and Crime" (*Why I shall vote for the Liberal Candidates*, Lond. 1885, p. 11).

altogether *grosso modo* to make them sink more readily into the mind.

It is somewhat difficult to form an opinion on the effect of the "literature" distributed by the Organizations, but the assertion may confidently be made that it is far less considerable than the latter imagine. The pamphlets are little read. They are of use rather to second-rate speakers, who take their arguments from them. The leaflets are read a great deal, and some of them are liked. During the election campaign they are distributed by millions.[1] The productions of political iconography brought in during the last few years by the Organizations are also much appreciated, the coloured pictures with political subjects which not only take the eye but appeal directly to the emotions. Of this kind, for instance, are the compositions relating to recent events in Ireland, by means of which the Gladstonians represented the cruel conduct of the police in the pay of the Unionist Government, while the Unionists portrayed, with a similar abundance of chromolithography, scenes of assassinations committed by the moonlighters on tenants who had refused to join the Land League. The struggle of labour against capital, against the landlords, also furnishes subjects for pictures. They make a deep impression, especially on women, who know how to pass them on to the men with the naïve and passionate power of persuasion which Michelet has described with his poet's penetration.[2]

Beyond the "literature" which they manufacture themselves, and which they supplement by a few publications issued elsewhere, the Organizations of the parties do not offer the voters other resources in the way of reading. As a rule, in England the Associations have no libraries or reading-rooms. On the other hand, in Scotland reading-rooms established by the Associations are common. It is worthy of notice that it is the Tories who started the reading-rooms, and that the Liberal Associations have only followed their lead. In their efforts to emerge from the condition of a small minority, to which

---

[1] For instance, the central Liberal Organization distributed more than twenty-three millions of leaflets during the election campaign of 1895.

[2] See his chapter on "Le Prêtre, la femme et la Vendée" in *L'Histoire de la Révolution française*, liv. VIII.

they are reduced in Scotland, the Conservatives are more on the look-out for possible methods of propaganda.[1]

VIII

Thus when all is said and done, after having carefully pointed out all the forms in which the Organizations of the official parties distribute political education, or what they are pleased to call by that name, the result is that the amount of it which they provide is altogether insignificant, and that the little which they do give is poisoned by party spirit.   In any event, their supply is far below existing requirements, and the latter would have remained even more unsatisfied than they are, if they had not other aids at their disposal.   Of these some are of a political nature, and others not.   In the front rank we must place the Press, *i.e.* the organs of the parties, which the latter themselves consider as their most valuable auxiliaries. A good many representatives of Associations even hold that the Press explains political questions to the electorate so completely and satisfactorily as to make it unnecessary for them to take any thought for political education.   In reality it is only as a channel of political information that the newspapers contribute to the enlightenment of the public, and even this statement requires qualification.   But as for improving the political judgment of their readers, the great majority of the newspapers utterly fails to do so.   No doubt, if the standpoint of the Organizations is adopted, for whom the *education* of the voters consists in crying up the doings of the party in question to them, and in inspiring hatred and disgust for the opposite party, it must be admitted that, with a certain number of exceptions, the Press performs its task very creditably.   But that very fact evidently disqualifies it from discharging its real duty, which is to enlighten the reader.   This is above all the

[1] Of late, under the auspices of the political parties, circulating lending libraries have been organized which distribute books in the provinces free of charge. On the Liberal side this duty has been undertaken by the National Club of London, which sends boxes of books into the villages with permission to keep them for a few months. The Club has about a hundred boxes in circulation. The Association of the Conservative clubs recently founded in London follows this example. In each box containing thirty to fifty volumes there is always a certain number of works on politics.

case with the papers written for the masses, the evening journals especially, which, by dint of offering their public highly spiced stuff that tickles the palate of the multitude, have so far perverted their taste as to make them think every political article written with moderation insipid.[1] Of course the controversial violence and the habitual *parti-pris* of the newspapers disgust the more intelligent readers, and already the exaggerations in which the Press indulges are seen to turn against it. In fact, the public no longer has its old belief in the leading article, and the number of persons who systematically abstain from reading it, knowing beforehand that it is outrageously biassed, is rapidly increasing. People read the paper for its non-political news, and often vote with its opponents. I have frequently had occasion to note that in a locality where the Press of the party is prosperous, where, for instance, the latter has three papers with a good circulation to one of the opposite political persuasion, the party is beaten at the elections, sometimes badly beaten.[2] I have noticed similar facts in Yorkshire, in Lancashire, and in the Midlands, in manufacturing towns as well as in rural districts. The country voter often again has special reasons for distrusting the newspaper; he considers it "very clever," and is afraid of being taken in by it; he trusts more to intelligent friends or neighbours; he is sure that Jim, his pal, will not set a trap for him, will tell him the real truth, will show him exactly how to vote. Yet, if from a certain point of view the political Press is losing ground, it none the less remains a formidable power; if the voter does not take his politics from the paper, it confirms him in his party preferences or prejudices, and, by an action analogous to that of water dripping on a stone, keeps him loyal to the party; in any event the newspapers provide the parties and their organizations with a highly effective means of publicity.

[1] In a town in the east of England, where I found a newspaper edited with real regard for dignity in language and in controversy with opponents, I complimented the people of the locality on it. " Ah, sir, it would be better for us not to have a paper at all than to have that one! " " How so ? " " Why, it's not a paper; it's milk and water."

[2] The secretary of a caucus remarked : "While the only newspaper of our political opponents exists simply on the subsidies of the party, we have three and all doing well, but I will make a bet that these three papers have not secured us three voters."

Next to the Press, in the series of instruments of political propaganda other than the Organizations of the two great parties, come various political societies and associations, each of which pursues a particular object, either to bring about a certain legislative reform in the State, or to oppose it. Such, for instance, are the Land Restoration League, to obtain the nationalization of the soil; the Free Land League, to secure agrarian reforms of a less radical description; the United Kingdom Alliance, to pass prohibitive measures against the consumption of alcoholic drinks; the Liberation Society, to compel the separation of Church and State; the Church Defence Institution, to defend the Church against the attacks of the Liberationists; the Liberty and Property League, to resist socialistic tendencies in legislation; the Fabian Society, to carry on a Socialist propaganda, etc. All these societies stir up the country, appeal to public opinion by means of lectures and publications on the cause which they have at heart.[1] Unlike the official party Organizations, they are not hampered by a general party creed, do not make it a condition of adhesion to the ideas which they profess, but recommend the latter for their own sake, although in point of fact they are nearly all allied with one or the other party. In any event, however useful the intellectual action brought to bear by these societies may be, their educational activity none the less belongs to the category of selfish propaganda, so to speak.

IX

Several broadminded men have therefore come to the conclusion that political education, to be really worthy of the name and to answer its purpose, ought to be unconnected with any political Organization, and *a fortiori* with the Organizations of the regular parties. Attempts have been made to give shape to this idea. Thus, soon after 1868, when the

---

[1] The Fabian Society is specially remarkable for the considerable efforts which it makes on behalf of economic education by means of lectures, lending libraries, and correspondence classes, in which people are told what to read on a particular question, are given bibliographical and other notes, and are invited to send to the committee of the society a short paper, which is returned to them with corrections.

party politicians flung themselves on the urban masses who had received the franchise, like a wild beast on its prey, a few disinterested friends of the new voters founded a "League for the political education of working-men," which proposed, by means of classes, lectures, and debates, to give the men of the people a political culture devoid of party spirit.   But it did not meet with the sympathy necessary to make the undertaking a success.   Some time afterwards a few distinguished University men, with the historian J. R. Seeley at their head, gave their co-operation to the League which, under the name of "Social and Political Educational League," pursues its work by striving to "promote the formation of public opinion in reference to Politics, Government, Land, Capital and Labour, Finance, Colonies, and national well-being generally, upon the basis of History, Social Science, and Political Philosophy."   The League declines to favour any party whatever or to proselytize in any other way.   Its object is the cultivation of the political mind.   The principal mode of action of the League consists of lectures, which it provides gratuitously by voluntary lecturers (belonging mostly to the Universities of Cambridge and Oxford).   The audience is invited to put questions to the lecturer and to start a discussion with the co-operation of persons of different parties and diverse opinions.

The success of the League, however, leaves a great deal to be desired.   Apart from its good intentions, it is short of everything, of material resources, of lecturers, and of audiences.   The parties absorb all, — money, men of action, and the public.   The number of lectures which it manages to give declines rather from year to year.   Without having ever reached the figure of six hundred, it has fallen of late years below fifty.   The area over which the lecturers of the League conduct their operations rarely extends beyond London with its suburbs.   Having only absurdly small sums at its disposal, — from forty pounds to eighty pounds a year, — it cannot set up an organization of its own; in the matter of lecturers it has to be satisfied with volunteer helpers, and to find audiences it is obliged to apply to those who are already enrolled in other organizations, political, religious, or economic.   In the vast majority of cases it meets only with indifference.   The first look on the activity of the League, if not as a disloyal competition or an unwholesome propaganda of scepticism or political dilettanteism, at all events as useless; — for are they not engaged in "educating" the voters themselves, and, of course, in the best possible way?—the second are too prone to distrust all instruction given outside them and their regular friends, they scent heresy and heterodoxy in every quarter; the third are too preoccupied with their dividends when their interest in political questions has not been exhausted in the "politics" of the parties with which they are connected in their capacity of voters. In these conditions the University spheres which give the impulse to the undertaking carried on by the League, spheres foreign to the social strata upon which it wishes to work, add nothing to its strength, and the presence at its head of historians, of thinkers, of eminent scholars,[1] is not so useful to it as would be the patronage of the plutocrats and the politicians who are all-powerful in the electoral constituencies. But these latter would be the last to take an interest in a work of this kind, not excepting the official political leaders of the people, the Members of Parliament. Of 670 Members of Parliament, not half a dozen subscribe to the League. In fact, the object and the utility of its labours are beyond the intelligence of the majority of the Honourable Members. In their eyes politics is a race between two crews called Liberals and Tories; everything else dignified with the name is "philosophy," and is it necessary to make philosophers of the voters, when all they need is to know whom to vote for, for the Tories or for the Liberals, and in this respect they certainly get plenty of information and advice of an equally convincing and urgent character? Party spirit has not spared the lecturers of the League even, and in 1886 its managers had to weed them out and require from them a written engagement not to treat subjects from the standpoint of a particular party. It is the business of the League to combat party spirit, which has poisoned the whole atmosphere of English political life with its miasma, but it has all the more difficulty in driving it out because its lecturers generally address audiences belonging to the same party, mostly in Liberal and Radical clubs.

[1] The list of former Presidents of the League includes Messrs. James Bryce, A. V. Dicey, J. A. Froude, S. R. Gardiner, Frederic Harrison, T. H. Huxley, J. R. Seeley, Leslie Stephen.

The Conservative Organizations will not accept the services of the League.   In a few rare cases non-political organizations, such as co-operative or religious societies, apply to it.

X

After having exhausted the slender resources provided by the political Organizations and agencies (such as the Organizations and the Press of the parties, as well as the associations for promoting particular objects) and by the organizations which aim at political culture and are independent of the parties (such as the Social and Political Education League), there remains 'for the improvement of the *political education* of the voters a third and last resource, which is by no means the least important one.   This consists of the manifold organizations for the general culture of adults, in which more or less attention is paid to subjects connected with politics.   Besides the educational establishments of this kind, which give evening classes, such as the Mechanics' Institute, the University Extension groups, the Reading Unions, etc., which sometimes discuss questions of government, of history, or of political economy, or recommend books or chapters of works bearing thereon, special mention must be made of the popular societies, the members of which study in common questions of general interest, including, with letters, science, and art, political or social problems, of course on a somewhat modest scale.   In their meetings the members communicate to each other the result of their reading and their reflections in the form of essays or papers, which are often discussed.   The most common type of these associations for study is known under the name of Mutual Improvement Societies.   As a rule they are connected with the Church organizations.   To keep a hold on their congregations, or to recover it, the churches in England try to satisfy not only their spiritual needs, they have charge not only of their souls, but also of their bodies and their minds; they get up lay classes and lectures, wholesome amusements, gymnastic establishments, clubs and societies of various kinds for them.   Thus to a good many Nonconformist chapels, to Christian Young Men's Associations under the patronage of the Established Church, etc., there are often attached Mutual

Improvement Societies. Although free to all appearances in their inner life, and especially in the choice of the subjects of study, these societies submit spontaneously, so to speak, to clerical influence which does not fail to give a certain impress to their manners as well as to their mind, which is loth to venture into untrodden paths. But still the papers, on political subjects among others, read in them are none the less means of instruction. In Scotland these societies are found mostly in the villages; in the towns they have some difficulty in meeting the competition of music-halls and similar places of amusement. Having often an existence of their own, independent of the churches, the Improvement Societies, which sometimes affect the more pretentious title of *philosophical* or *literary Institutes*, recruit their members from all political and ecclesiastical parties. Liberals and Tories meet in them, and, keeping on the best of terms, observe perfect tolerance towards each other, even in political discussions, which under these circumstances produce excellent results for the members of these societies.[1] The communications received and the impressions gathered by the author on the spot when preparing this work are unanimous on this point.

XI

The debates which constitute one of the forms of intellectual training practised in the Mutual Improvement Societies are the exclusive object of other bodies, known in consequence by the name of Debating Societies. The origin of these institutions, which could only have arisen in a time-honoured land of liberty, dates from the eighteenth century. After having

[1] The Mutual Improvement Society in Scotland is sometimes the centre of enlightenment for a whole rural district. This was especially true of the past, of the first half of the Victorian era, as may be seen from the history of a society of this kind narrated in a small book called *An Aberdeenshire Village Propaganda Forty Years ago*, by R. H. Smith, Edinburgh, 1889. The society in question, the Rhynie Mutual Instruction Class, started in an out-of-the-way village with a dozen members, tradesmen and farmers, endeavoured to improve their minds, and, having arrived at satisfactory results, continued its labours zealously, trying "to train its members as writers and speakers." At the same time, through the agency of a correspondence committee, the Rhynie Society founded sister societies around it, forming a Union which published its monthly review.

played a certain part in the democratic agitation of the years
1793–1795 caused by the French Revolution in England, the
debating societies have again become a peaceful school of the
art of oratory.   With the development of town life which
followed the great outburst of industry, the debating societies spread in the manufacturing cities, where they attracted
members of the middle class, and in no small degree contributed to its culture and to the training in its ranks of men
who know how to speak in public, of debaters.   From the
middle class the taste for debating societies has descended a
few steps lower in the social scale.   In fact, debate gratifies
not only the love of free discussion, but also the combative
instinct of the English.   For them it is another sort of prize-
fight, a spectacle which procures violent sensations.   In several localities the publicans provide it, to increase their custom,
on market days, which bring in people from the neighbourhood; they give five shillings to a good talker, who *opens* the
debate.   In many large business establishments or factories
with a numerous staff, the latter form, side by side with a
chess club or a cricket club, a debating society among themselves.   The same thing takes place in certain religious organizations, such as the Young Men's Christian Associations, which
have debating classes.   But apart from these more or less private gatherings, there are many debating societies regularly
organized and numbering each hundreds of members admitted
by introduction and on payment of a yearly subscription.   In
all these societies there are periodically "political nights,"
i.e. evenings devoted to political discussion.

Of late years the old institution of debating societies has
given rise to a new and very interesting species, to the local
parliaments.   These are debating societies which confine themselves to politics and conduct their discussions in accordance
with all the rules and all the *mise-en-scène* of the House of
Commons.   The members fall into party groups just as at
Westminster.   They also have their leaders and their Whips.
The Cabinet taken from the majority is subject to the same
rules of ministerial responsibility.   The session opens by a
"Queen's Speech," announcing the bills which will be brought
forward by the Government.   The whole procedure, in a word,
is copied from that of the House of Commons, with the for-

tunate modification that the length of the speeches is limited. The great originality of these parliamentary debating clubs, which are not altogether unknown on the Continent, in Paris for instance, consists in the fact that the local parliaments are not composed exclusively of young men. Side by side with the latter may be seen grey-headed men, magistrates, sober tradesmen, manufacturers. In a parliament of the West End of London, I have seen a (morganatic) cousin of the Queen, a naval officer, on the Treasury bench, holding the office of First Lord of the Admiralty, while in a parliament in the north of the metropolis I have found a shoemaker discharging the analogous functions of Minister of War. Imitating their models at Westminster, the members put questions to the ministers, bring forward motions and resolutions, introduce bills, debate, attack, and defend with all the weapons of parliamentary warfare, reasoning, argument, flashes of wit, sarcasm, indignation.

No doubt the conventional character of their labours, which after all are only play, weighs heavily on the local parliaments; it lessens their value as instruments of *political education*, by accustoming their members to *play a part*, to strike an attitude for the gallery. And what makes things worse is that they have not even got to create their parts; for the pieces which they act are exactly the same as those performed on the great national stage of the House of Commons, and they simply copy the actors on that stage and imitate their gestures, their tones, making them still more emphatic if possible. Divided into closed and permanent parties, on the model of the House of Commons, the members of local parliaments take up a line beforehand on public questions, espouse a cause before they have studied it, and then try to become enamoured of it afterwards. In spite of these grave defects, the local parliaments are none the less a factor of political education which is not to be despised. They force their members to follow the political problems of the day, to deal with political facts and ideas, and they enable them to do this to a greater extent and with more freedom than there is room for in the caucuses. Besides, by bringing men of different opinions face to face to discuss both sides of a question, they give them the opportunity of knowing each other, and of finding out that their political opponents are not so black as the Organizations of the parties paint them for the requirements of their electioneering business. It is only to be regretted that the local parliaments are not as a rule very long-lived, for after a more or less brilliant career of a few years they die out. At one time, tired of their part or engrossed by their regular work, the leading actors retire and the companies disperse; at another time, after a few sessions, the Conservatives, who up till recently had not been in the habit of scrutinizing their own opinions or those of other people, are quite played out, so that the victorious Liberals are left in possession of the field, and the combat comes to an end for want of combatants; sometimes, again, personal feeling, questions of *amour-propre*, or social prejudices get in the way. The movement of local parliaments has therefore not attained the dimensions and the political importance which several persons predicted for it in the beginning. Some eminent men had hailed the new institution as destined to exert a stronger and healthier influence on the course of political life than "that Birmingham creation known as the Caucus," for "the new departure in the national political life has this most hopeful aspect,— it is a free, manly, and open educational movement." [1] Inside the local parliaments still greater aspirations for their future were indulged in: they would not only serve to train young people in debate, and to instruct members in the political questions of the day, but they would deliver their verdicts on the great political and social reforms, the consideration of which is demanded by the welfare of the country; like the federated Chambers of Commerce, the local parliaments would also form a federation of "chambers of politics," which would wield the same influence in the State as the former in commercial questions. [2] These hopes have not been realized, which is rather a matter for congratulation than for regret; for if in a free country the sources of political opinion ought to be of infinite variety, political authority can only have a single organ; in the matter of "chambers of politics" there can only be *the* chamber, the House established by the Constitution and formed by the

[1] Blanchard Jerrold, "On the manufacture of public opinion," *Nineteenth Century*, June, 1883.
[2] Speech of the Sydenham Premier, quoted *ibid.*, pp. 1088, 1089.

free suffrages of the nation. The Federation of Local Parliaments was created a few years ago (in 1892), under the name of National Association of Local Parliaments, but it wisely confines itself to the modest task of developing the movement and helping the existing and rising local parliaments by advice on points of procedure and organization, by forwarding them political papers, forms of bills and of ministerial declarations, etc. To prevent the local parliaments from dying out for want of combatants, the National Association communicates with the central party Organizations and informs them that in this or that local parliament the respective political party is breaking up, in order that the Organization of the party may, for the good of the cause, use its authority to stir up its political coreligionists of the locality and exhort them to take a more active part in the debates of their parliament. The National Association of Local Parliaments has secured the patronage of several leading political notabilities, with the Lord Chancellor at their head, who fill the posts of President and Vice-Presidents.

THIRD CHAPTER

I

THE propagandist efforts displayed by the party Organizations in the forms which have been examined are far from reaching the whole, or even the majority, of the electorate. Everybody does not go to the meetings, attend the lectures, and read the "political literature." It is not certain that the effect produced even on those who are drawn into them is of a permanent nature. What is to be done? Attempts were made to enlighten the political conscience of the voters, to act on the *zoon politikon*. This action proving inadequate, it is sought to make good the deficiency by appealing to the animal side of man, to his instinct of sociability, with the joys and pleasures which are connected with it, or which become enhanced by it. Being provided by the Organizations or through their agency, they are destined to produce an association of feelings between all those who are invited to share them and the political parties. As they can be enjoyed only by a number of persons assembled together, they supply the Organizations with an opportunity and a means at the same time of sweeping into this association and carrying the voters wholesale, in a lump.

Among the varied forms in which the "social tendencies of human nature are made subservient to the higher interests" of politics, the most important is provided by party clubs. The reader is aware of the origin of political clubs and will recollect that it dates from the seventeenth century, and that for a long time they were only friendly gatherings of people with the same political opinions, who met periodically to enjoy the pleasures of the table; that it was only with the founding of the Carlton Club (in 1831), and its Liberal rival the Reform Club, that clubs became genuine political institutions in which the head-quarters of the parties were established, from which issued the word of command for political circles in London as well as for the provinces.[1] The two great clubs gradually lost this position in proportion as a special organization with a central registration Association and local Associations grew up under the Whip of each party. The same fate overtook the clubs founded in the provinces on the model of the Carlton and the Reform. In truth, the part played by the great provincial clubs in the organization of the party depended more on the personal position of their members than on the fact of their belonging to the club, which was only the meeting-place of the local leaders. Being used as head-quarters by the latter, who met there to settle parliamentary candidatures among themselves, the clubs were included in the same disfavour by the advanced Liberals, who demanded the introduction of the popular principle into the management of the party. And in the midst of the controversy raised by the establishment of the Caucus, there resounded the cry among others: "Down with the clubs and up with the Caucus!"[2] Exaggerating the power of the clubs somewhat, the advanced party looked on them as a hotbed of anti-democratic "social influences," hostile to true Liberalism. At the present moment the official club of the party is the centre and instrument of the Organization only in places where there is no regular Association. Being the only collection of the adherents of the party, it is in that case just the body to take in hand matters of organization. In places where there is an Association, — and this is in the vast majority of cases, — the club exists side by side with it, at one time with an absolutely independent position, at another as its social branch, the executive committee of the caucus being the managing committee of the club and the secretary of the Association obligingly discharging the functions of manager of the club. On the Tory side the ties between the club and the Association are much closer, the clubs are always represented on the Councils and the com-

---

[1] *Vide supra*, the origin of political Associations, and of party Organizations, p. 145.

[2] *Times*, Aug. 22, 1878.

mittees of the Associations by special delegates, under the
statutes.   In reality it is even rather the club which pulls the
strings of the local organization of the party.   Associations
of course had been set up in accordance with all the rules of
the doctrine of representative Organizations, but it was often
done against the grain, and in a good many cases they are only
a make-believe.   Generally speaking, it may be said that in
the management of the Liberal party the clubs have given way
to the Associations; that among the Tories the Associations
have less political vigour, while the clubs are more powerful
than those of their rivals.

II

But throughout their varying fortunes as leading party
organs, the clubs preserved and developed their character as
places of resort for the members of the party, where the latter
associated on a footing of equality in spite of the difference in
their extraction and education, where by a daily contact they
spontaneously kept each other true to the political sentiments
which formed their connecting link.   The Carlton and the
Reform Club discharged this function on a large scale in the
capital, while their imitations in the provinces repeated it on
their own account by bringing together the local gentry and
the middle class and clothing them in the party atmosphere.
The Conservatives, being by their temperament more dependent on social surroundings, and consequently attaching more
importance to social ties, for a long time showed more readiness to set up clubs than the Liberals.   The Tories profited so
much by this that the Liberals, attributing with some show of
reason the success of their rivals to the co-operation of the
clubs, adopted the same policy, after 1874, with more energy
than before.   The Liberal clubs were not only less numerous,
but many a one had lost its active political spirit and had
remained simply as a social centre.   This was the case in
particular with the great stronghold of Liberalism in the capital, with the Reform Club.   The lukewarm Liberalism of the
Palmerstonian era made its political atmosphere much milder,
and of its great traditions the principal remnant is its old and
glorious reputation for good cookery, which artists from the

other side of the Channel had won for it, and which attracted
to it members without much reference to their political opinions. Consequently, "to infuse new blood" into Liberalism,
after several important clubs had been started in the provinces,
a new general centre for the party was founded in London,
in 1882, under the name of the National Liberal Club, intended, according to Lord Derby's definition repeated by Mr.
Gladstone, to serve as the great *exchange* of the Liberal party,
in which information and impressions as to the condition of
Liberalism in the country would pass between the members,
where the Liberals of the provinces would meet those of the
metropolis, where the leaders would receive deputations, etc.
In a few years the club has in fact attained this position, and
it is now in the first rank of English political clubs. If its
sumptuous premises are not quite up to the Carlton, it has
the greater number of members, as many as 6500 (including
country members, who amount to nearly 4000), and its annual
budget exceeds £70,000. This rapid success of the Liberal
club is accounted for *inter alia* by the fact that it has opened
its doors wide. The number of members being limited in all
the principal political clubs of London, the limit is fixed at a
much lower figure in the Tory clubs, while the subscription
and entrance fee are higher. Thus the Carlton Club has only
1600 members; but as against that more than 8000 candidates
are waiting their turn to be admitted, and it is the custom, as
in several large non-political clubs, to enter candidates at an
early age, in order that when they have arrived at man's
estate they may not have long to wait for a vacancy. This
applies also to the Junior Carlton Club, and will soon be the
case with their juniors, with the clubs of more recent creation.
As each of them admits only a limited number of members,
the Tory clubs increase to meet the demand. While the
Liberals have in the matter of big clubs, without counting the
old Reform and Brooks', now devoid of political importance,
only the National Liberal Club and the City Liberal Club,
the Conservatives have, besides the Carlton, which is still
their great politico-social centre, the Junior Carlton, the City
Carlton, the St. Stephen's, the Constitutional, and the Junior
Constitutional. The comparative paucity of members admissible, and the large number of candidates waiting to be elected,

added to the nature of the social sphere from which they are
recruited, have the natural effect of making the Tory clubs
more exclusive, of forming stronger ties between their members, and of spreading their *esprit de corps* even beyond them.
A man has not yet joined the club, he is still on the long list
of candidates; but while he is waiting for election he has caught
the tone which prevails in it, he has become imbued with the
sentiments which animate the members, he is already a link
in the living chain which they form in social and political
life.   The big Tory clubs in the provinces exhibit the same
character.   In the Liberal clubs this *esprit de corps* has never
existed, for want of conditions to keep it alive; there were
too many different shades of opinions and too much variety
in the social extraction of the Liberal clubmen, so that to
strengthen the bonds of union, to ensure the political loyalty
of the members of the club as such, it was necessary to depend
rather on the allurements in the way of comfort which it
offered them, and which after all are by no means irresistible,
as events had proved.[1]   Nevertheless, the Liberal clubs do
serve, although in a much smaller degree than the Tory establishments of the same kind, as a political cement for their
members, by keeping up the feeling of respect for society
which compels the individual to fall in behind his fellow-
men, which prevents him from taking a line of his own.

III

Whether they perform their part with more or less success,
all these clubs — the Carlton, the National Liberal, with their
provincial imitations — bring together only members of the

---

[1] When the divergences of opinion in the second Gladstone Ministry, between the Radical fraction represented by Mr. Chamberlain who had just
launched his "unauthorized programme," and his more moderate colleagues,
gave rise to apprehension that they might be followed by a formal split in the
Liberal party, a "member of the Cabinet of great experience and sagacity"
remarked: "I don't believe that there can be any break-up in the Liberal
ranks, because of the existence of our great political clubs; a man learns to
love his favourite club in course of time, and he will submit to anything rather
than to exclude himself from it." ("The Liberal Split and Liberal Clubs."
The Speaker, 1st March, 1890.)   A year had hardly passed when the Liberal
party was torn asunder owing to the Irish Home Rule Bill of Mr. Gladstone,
and in more than one "favourite club" there was an exodus of dissentients.

upper and middle classes, and present merely an improved form of the reaction of society which always gave cohesion to the ruling classes. But these classes are henceforth, from 1868 and 1884 onwards, but a small minority of political society. The reaction therefore can only be strictly local and the cohesion extremely partial; the great mass of the electorate remains outside. Consequently, immediately after 1868 steps were taken to bring the new popular voters into party clubs as well, and Liberal and Conservative "working-men's clubs" were started. The politicians had no need even to create them altogether. For ten years or so before this fateful epoch, under the inspiration of philanthropists of every shade of political or religious opinions, a movement had been in progress for organizing popular places of meeting and recreation of a more elevated kind than the public-houses. On the principle of rich men's clubs, small folk, workmen, shopkeepers, employés, formed societies, with unpretending premises, where for a trifling subscription of a few shillings a year the members could spend their leisure time in reading, in conversation, in games, and obtain refreshments, or even meals. Soon this movement received a powerful impulse in consequence of the establishment (in 1862) of a "Union of Working-men's Clubs and Institutes," in which persons belonging to the cultivated classes took the lead. Promoting and assisting in the formation of new clubs on the basis described, the Union had two great objects in view, — to make these clubs not only a factor of moral elevation, but an educational instrument, spreading enlightenment among the masses, and on the other hand to utilize them for drawing all classes nearer to each other, for levelling the barriers which divided English society. On a somewhat modest scale, it is true, these intentions were realized in more than one club, the promoters of which succeeded in organizing lending libraries, meetings for discussion, French, drawing, and music classes, in which "gentlemen," *i.e.* persons belonging to the cultivated and wealthy ranks of society, made not only pecuniary but personal sacrifices by coming down to the clubs to take part in the conversation, the reading, and even in the games of the labour members. The better class of working-men grasped the advantages of the clubs at once, but the great mass of the

people did not like giving up the public-houses, the result of
which was that most of the working-men's clubs had not a
sufficient number of members to make both ends meet and to
dispense with the pecuniary assistance of gentlemen philanthropists. Nevertheless the movement made progress, and
in a few years several hundred of clubs affiliated to the Union
were scattered over the Kingdom, always remaining perfectly
neutral from a political and religious standpoint. Referring
to this point, one of the patrons of the Union, Lord Carnarvon,
the eminent Minister of the Derby and Disraeli Cabinets (who
was on the Council of the Union with genuine Whigs, like
Lord Brougham, and advanced Radicals), remarked at one of
the annual meetings of the Union: "How far should politics
enter into the life of these societies? If they meant party
politics — politics which would give a colour and complexion
to the clubs — I should hold that to be a great misfortune. If
this politics were so to come in that clubs should be composed
of one side or the other — Conservative or Liberal — I should
hold that that was ruin to their system. But if by politics
they meant only to the extent that their discussion was in
common with political and social questions, that was different." [1] The "great misfortune" apprehended by Lord Carnarvon was already lying in wait for the working-men's clubs,
and before long, at the instigation of the politicians, most of
these clubs hoisted party colours. It is hardly necessary to
say that this transformation dealt a heavy blow at the original
conception of working-men's clubs. Instead of serving the
moral and intellectual welfare of the masses, promoted in an
absolutely disinterested spirit, they became party machines.
The parties seized on them to secure and extend their electoral
connection. Everybody who might have been attracted into a
club labelled Liberal or Conservative was to become their vassal from the fact of his habitually frequenting an exclusively
Liberal or Conservative circle which had been made pleasant
for him. A competition arose between the parties as to which
should start the greater number of institutions of the kind.
These efforts have attained extraordinary proportions during
the twelve years extending from 1883–1884.

[1] Sixth annual meeting of the Working-men's Clubs and Institutes Union.

IV

All over the country, even in the villages, there are now political working-men's clubs. In the large towns there are dozens of them. Their individual importance varies a good deal; some — that is, in London, and even in a few provincial towns — do credit to the spirit of co-operation displayed by English workmen; they are housed in their own premises, built for the purpose, and have as many as 1500 or 1800 members; the others hire a whole house, or simply two or three rooms, and have a hundred or even fifty on their list. Nor is the social standard of the members absolutely uniform; some are mostly filled by small middle-class people, shopkeepers, clerks, whereas the very great majority of popular clubs are really recruited from the class of manual labourers. A distinction of greater importance for the inner life of the clubs arises according as they do or do not allow the consumption of alcoholic drinks. In the vast majority of clubs, including nearly all the Conservative ones, wine and spirits can be obtained with even greater facility than in the public-houses, which are closed for part of Sunday and after a certain hour in the evening, whereas the clubs remain open later, and the whole day on Sunday. Consequently, drinkers highly appreciate clubs, and the scenes witnessed in them are not always of an edifying description. The complaints of their demoralizing action are numerous and very loud. It is not impossible that they are somewhat exaggerated, but in the main they are well founded. The managers of the clubs cannot even wish for less drinking to go on in them, for the bar is their great source of income. Yet there are a good many clubs in the country on a temperance basis which manage to get on without this resource. The fact is worthy of note; it is not, however, the rule. In the interest of the party, which is anxious to attract as many people as possible to the club, the subscription is fixed at a very low, often almost nominal, rate, and necessarily it is the bar and the games which keep the club in funds. The net profit from the liquors generally constitutes more than a third of the receipts,[1] and even with that the

---

[1] In the clubs of which I have examined the books, it amounted to 35 per cent, 40 per cent, and even, in Conservative clubs, to 50 per cent.

yearly balance-sheet of the club often shows a deficit, which
makes it dependent on the Organizations or on rich members
of the party, who pay the debts until they get tired of so
doing.   In addition to the full members the clubs generally
have honorary members, leading men in the party who subscribe a guinea or two a year.   Besides this, a good many
clubs are regularly subsidized by the Associations, or even
kept up by parliamentary candidates.   It sometimes happens
that working-men's clubs start up all at once in a constituency,
like mushrooms, just as they are apt to disappear suddenly
and simultaneously after, for instance, the local M.P. retires
into private life.   Their birth and their death were due to a
private individual.   There are seasons for the outburst of
clubs; it takes place especially after a general election and at
its approach.   The candidates who have just been beaten, or
who are going to enter the lists, cover the constituency with
clubs to prepare or retrieve their fortunes.   The great number
of working-men's clubs in existence, and the facility with
which new clubs of this kind are formed, is not due solely to
the co-operation of the party Organizations and the candidates,
they also multiply, thanks to the operation of the "tied-house
system," of which they accept the benefits and the obligations,
like most of the public-houses.   This system consists in rich
brewers letting the retail vendors have a certain quantity of
beer on credit, and not demanding payment for it as long as
the latter remain their customers.   The landlords of public-
houses are thus always tied.   In granting the same terms to
the working-men's clubs, the brewers procure them a great
part of their stock-in-trade, which they have all the less apprehension in placing at their disposal because they count on the
Organization of the party concerned or its rich members not
to leave the club in the lurch.

But the worst of all this, according to the party politicians,
is that the members of the working-men's clubs do not care
an atom for politics, that they join them simply for the sake
of the social advantages which these institutions offer them.
When hands are wanted for the various jobs which devolve
on the Organizations, as for instance electoral registration
work, or the election canvass or fetching voters to the poll, the
Association applies as a matter of right to the members of the

clubs of the party, but the latter turn a deaf ear to the appeal;
they prefer remaining in the bar, or in the billiard-room to
watch the performances of the crack players.   This indifference
of the members to politics is accounted for not only by their
crass egoism, but by a hazy feeling which they have that it is
not so much for their good as in the interest of the party or
of the parliamentary candidate that they are invited to join
these institutions, and they unconsciously meet the demands
made upon them with what is called in law *exceptio turpitudinis.*
The "earnest politicians" who belong to the club rarely show
their faces in it; the company is beneath them, the bulk of the
members being taken from the lower strata of the electorate,
and these on their side have a greater respect for the good
billiard-player or cricketer; it is he who gives the tone to the
club.   In some clubs there are groups of "politicians," who
work zealously for their party; but they could have done it
just as well without being members of the club.   The political
newspapers to be found in more or less greater number in every
club are little read, the reading-room is never crowded.   It is
often at the further end of the building, and before getting
there one is easily stopped in the bar or in the rooms for
games.   On more than one occasion I have happened to note
that it was not lighted of an evening, and that it was lit up
for the occasion, to show the room to the visitor.   The programme of every club includes lectures, but they are thinly
attended.   In the London working-men's clubs there are lectures every Sunday, but save in exceptional cases the lecturer
speaks to benches which are more than half empty.   Of several hundreds of members, barely two or three dozen come to
the lecture.   How often does it not happen that the lecturer,
who is generally unpaid, after a long and tiring journey in
omnibuses and trams, or even by rail, at last lands in the club
to which he has been invited, to find the room empty.   In
vain does the secretary rush from one apartment to another,
from the bar to the billiard-table, from the billiard-table to
the bagatelle-room, to entreat the members to go and hear the
lecturer.   After waiting for half an hour the latter begins his
address before a few scattered recruits brought in by the
unfortunate secretary, who is profuse in expressions of regret
and apology.   Formerly the lecture took place on Sunday

evening and was supposed to be the principal distraction of
the day of rest. Now it is generally moved back into the
forenoon or the afternoon, to leave the evening free for musical and dramatic entertainments, at which the families of the
members, women and children, are present. In a few large
working-men's clubs in London classical plays are performed,
Shakspeare, for instance, but in most of the clubs another
kind of repertoire is in favour, that of the music-halls; "nigger melodies" and comic songs are sung, to the great scandal
of the Puritans, who consider it a shocking violation of the
Sabbath.

If in the great majority of clubs "earnest politicians" disappear like a drop in the ocean of the indifferent, to make up
for it there are clubs the members of which are too serious
politicians, in which there would appear to be no other interest
on earth but that of militant politics. These are the ultra-
Radical clubs, somewhat few and far between in the provinces,
but numerous in London. Of course, with a considerable section of their members, the interest in the bar and the billiard-
room comes first, as is the case in every popular crowd, but
the "politicians" are a strong contingent, and it is they who
give the tone to the club. If the coherence of their ideas
and their political judgment are not beyond criticism, the
sincerity of their convictions, and in general their political
honesty, are undeniable. The most important working-men's
clubs of the metropolis belong to this very category. Several
of them have a large number of members and enjoy a real
prosperity. This enables them, and the uncompromising
fierceness of their Radicalism enjoins on them, to hold aloof
from the official parties, that is, from official Liberalism, for
which they have an unbounded contempt; for all its representatives are, in their eyes, simple reactionaries, and hypo-
crites into the bargain.[1] Of course they do not recognize the
Liberal Organization; they have their own, which is called the
Metropolitan Radical Federation, and which is at daggers
drawn with the Liberal Caucus.[1]

[1] The reader will recollect that the opposition to the establishment of a
special branch of the Caucus for the metropolis came from the Radical federated clubs. Cf. *supra*, p. 311.

V

Thus the working-men's clubs oscillate between two extremes; some are too much absorbed in politics, the others display an almost absolute indifference to them. The former being independent of the official parties, and the latter forming the very great majority of these institutions, the question arises — What is the use of them to the parties? It consists above all in this, that most of the members who do not know, and do not care to know, anything about politics vote unhesitatingly in accordance with the hints given them by the "politicians" of the club, or even by the best billiard or cricket players, to whom they pay a tribute of personal esteem and of good-fellowship in complying with their request to vote for the candidate of the party. Then the clubs supply the party Organizations with contingents for the demonstrations, which have become an amusement for their members like any other. Another service which the clubs are supposed to render is to "preserve young men" from political perdition. With the inexperience and innocence of their age, the latter might easily fall a prey to the opposite party, be seduced into voting with it by the example of their companions or by other influences, whereas if enrolled at an early stage in the clubs of the relatives or of the political friends who lay claim to them, they would be withdrawn from these influences and made to walk in the right path. This sort of prophylactic treatment by means of isolation is an equally important factor in the policy of the middle-class political clubs, in which it is in still greater request for keeping the rising generation in the political traditions of the family.

Altogether the services which the clubs known as working-men's clubs render to the parties by no means correspond to the efforts and the great pecuniary sacrifices made by the Organizations, by the parliamentary candidates or the M.P.'s and other party zealots to start these establishments and keep them going. The persons concerned are under no illusion on this point, and yet they go on with the game because it has been begun, and because with their eagerness of players they wait to see what may turn up, and, finally, because it would not be always prudent to throw up their hand and

make enemies of the members of the clubs, who have votes to
give at the elections. It is only when the financial or moral
difficulties become intolerable that they make up their minds
to sever the connection. It is from considerations of the same
nature that people are careful not to be outspoken with the
clubs, not to remind them of their proper functions and their
duty; in public nothing but compliments and flattery is
bestowed on them. Statesmen on a visit enjoying the hospitality of the big club of the party, and receiving deputations
from the others, lavish eulogistic epithets on them; they are
"admirable institutions," "beneficial," "full of hope in the
future," "a large portion of the intellectual and moral advancement which we all feel is going on around us comes
from the clubs."

Of the two historic parties, the Conservatives, who in private, just like their rivals, often speak of the working-men's
clubs in severe terms, have, perhaps, fewer reasons for considering them as of no account, and this, of course, in no way
from the standpoint of "intellectual and moral advancement,"
which is not a factor in the question. As the gentlemen's
club in the county town frequently serves the Tories as a
centre of organization of the party, in the same way the working-men's clubs supply them in a good many places with the
regiments for their army. The local branches of their Organization are very often represented solely by clubs, which in
their eyes have the advantage of not requiring to the same
extent the application of the principle of autonomy which is
supposed to be the basis of the "Associations," and, above all,
of providing by the development of "social tendencies" a
modus operandi alike more effective and better suited to the
traditions of the Tory party than the typical meetings of the
Caucus. The federation of Conservative clubs, the recent
establishment of which has been already referred to, is intended to accentuate the action of the clubs in this direction;
it tries to form subsidiary recreation clubs, as adjuncts to
established clubs, such as cricket and cycling clubs, and to
bring about the "interaffiliation" of clubs, which consists in
the member of an interaffiliated club enjoying rights of membership in all the other interaffiliated clubs.

VI

Inadequate for party purposes, the clubs might be of great value for the formation of public opinion in general, owing to their character of social centres where persons representing the manifold varieties of one and the same political temperament meet on neutral ground, and where divergences of view show themselves in the freedom of private conversation. But for this beneficial exchange of opinions to take place in the clubs two elementary conditions are necessary,— that there should be different views, a variety of shades of opinion, and that they should have free play. The existence of these conditions, already limited by the division into parties which lies at the root of political clubs, has been much impaired of late years. For a long time great political tolerance and a real breadth of views governed the selection of members, especially in the Liberal clubs (the Conservative clubs were inclined to be homogeneous by their nature) which took in the whole gamut of what is styled Liberal opinion, from the most timorous Whigs down to the very advanced Radicals. But the too close connection of the clubs with the official party eventually made them forget that a club is an organ of opinion and not of action, and they set up practically a rigid creed. The Home Rule Bill of 1886 was the starting-point for it. At the outset, when hostilities broke out in the Liberal ranks on the Irish question, the Liberal clubs proclaimed their neutrality. Having been dragged for so long at the heels of the Organization of the party, they were soon hurried into the fray. In London the old clubs, the Reform and Brooks', remained faithful to their traditions of tolerance, but the great official club of the party, the National Liberal Club, after having declared its neutrality, withdrew its declaration and threw in its lot with the particular measure which caused the Liberal divisions. The members of the club who belonged to the Liberal minority in the House of Commons would not consent to accept a toleration amounting only to a permission to take their meals or read the newspapers, and they resigned in a body. In the Liberal clubs of the provinces the majority of the party displayed still less tact, the dissentients on the Irish question were subjected to inquisitorial proceedings; they were expelled for having, for instance, consented to become an anti-Home Rule candidate.[1] The Liberal Unionists withdrew, but their number was often too great in a good many provincial clubs, when they were not in a majority as at Birmingham, for their departure not to seriously affect the financial position of these establishments, and in more than one case they had to be wound up. A certain number of clubs continue to take in both sections of the party, but the old cordial terms no longer exist.

The example thus set by the great clubs, the gentlemen's clubs, is certainly not calculated to encourage toleration and independence of opinions in the working-men's clubs, and the less so because, as a rule, the latter have been and are established for the requirements of the Organization of the party, or even to push a particular candidate. But even this does not constitute the great difficulty which the working-men's clubs have in becoming a centre of enlightenment, a laboratory of opinion. Even supposing that the party yoke did not weigh heavily on the working-men's clubs, their members, who have only a slight smattering of culture, would be unable to enlighten each other by their unassisted efforts; the club life in itself would be of little or no use,— several blind men do not make one who can see. Their eyes can be opened, their intellectual standard raised, and their political judgment improved only by the daily effective co-operation of men of a higher culture. The latter must make personal exertions, must come to the clubs and associate with their members, not in a spirit of condescension of superiors towards inferiors, but with the kindly feeling and the sympathy of the stronger for the weaker. Their unobtrusive presence would raise the moral tone of the club, their efforts would rouse the lethargic minds, contact with them would kindle the flame of intelligent curiosity. And perhaps there is no country in which this intervention of men of a higher culture would be accepted with greater alacrity and gratitude and with less class jealousy and suspicion than among the English working-men. But the maintenance of such relations with the working-men's clubs presupposes infinitely more good-will, self-sacrifice and disinterestedness than the

---

[1] Cf. the article already quoted, " The Liberal Split and Liberal Clubs."

politicians have at their disposal. In point of fact, the moral and intellectual welfare of the working-men's clubs has no interest for them, so long as they supply voting power, party combatants. Except at election time they never come near them, nor do they show their interest in the clubs in any other way; they think they have done their duty by them in signing a cheque. It is true that a good many of them, and especially the M.P.'s, even if they wished to maintain closer relations with the working-men's clubs, would not be able to do it. Their "stumping" engagements, their duties as commercial travellers for the party, occupy almost all the time not taken up by their work in the House, and it would often be anything but a welcome request to ask them to spend one or two evenings a week in the working-men's clubs of their constituency. The result none the less is that the clubs, being left to themselves except for party discipline, cannot be a factor of political culture for the masses. Like the gentlemen's clubs, but with somewhat different accessories, their sole mission is to cultivate party spirit in the bar and the billiard room.

VII

The clubs, which are the "social" counterpart of the Associations, serve, like them, as a permanent organization for receiving and keeping the adherents of the parties. But outside both there is also a vast floating electoral population, having no connection, even of a nominal kind, with the parties, and which, moreover, does not care a fig whether it votes for a Tory or for a Radical. To draw these voters out of their indifference, as well as to rekindle the ardour of the others, the Organizations offer their "social tendencies" satisfactions of an exceptional kind, just as in the preceding phase of their action, when they appealed to the intelligence, they had recourse to measures of a stronger description than those afforded by the routine of the ordinary meetings of wards or of Hundreds, which were suitable only for the initiated. These more heroic measures were the great meetings and demonstrations. In that case they had to deal with "brainy" people, and they treated them with high-sounding speeches. Here they are confronted by people of another kind, and instead of political meetings invitations are issued to "social meetings," in which people sing, dance, eat, drink, in which they amuse themselves in a number of other ways, and a political address, a bit of party claptrap, is slipped in incidentally between the acts to make it go down.   Experience had shown the managers of the Organizations that politics pure and simple were powerless to draw the masses after this or that party, that it was necessary to make allowances for the dispositions and tastes of men as they are in social life, that it was therefore advisable to "socialize politics."   The idea was that this result would be attained by a happy mixture of "politics and pleasure," offered to the inhabitants of towns as well as to country people.   "If," as a popular Conservative paper remarks in reference to the extension of this system to the country districts, "if we only give a little amusement to the rustic, the rustic will then drink in the instruction which we offer him.   Even as in a Kindergarten, instruction and amusement must go hand in hand."

So much for the theory.   As for the practice, it is of a still less abstract nature.   It consists in giving the people fêtes and entertainments calculated to amuse them, and consequently to advertise the party, or more particularly the candidate or member, who behaves so nicely to honest folk.   That is the object of all the varied forms of amusement devised by the ingenuity of the organizers.   Practice has not failed to sanction a certain number of them which have come into general use.   These are smoking-concerts, social evenings or conversaziones, fêtes, picnics, garden-parties, tea-meetings, etc.   The smoking-concerts, which, as their name indicates, are musical soirées at which smoking goes on, are particularly popular. Following the procedure of meetings a Chairman opens the evening with the gravity of the heavy father in the play by a short address, in which he expresses the hope that those present will derive as much pleasure as political edification from the proceedings.   After which the musical part is begun, consisting generally of songs or ballads or even comic ditties. Between two items of the programme is inserted a short political speech, very short, but humorous, making the public laugh, and of course at the expense of the political opponents. The oratorical interlude is performed by the usual representatives of political eloquence, beginning with the Members of the House of Commons. They speak either on the question of the day which is engrossing the country, or on the policy of the parties in general, without spoiling the effect of the comic song which has just expired on the lips of their artistic colleagues or of the ditty which will be struck up as soon as they have finished their political disquisitions. Thus passing from "two musical farces, with a political address sandwiched between," to a couple of monologues of "Irish humour" with the same interlude, and from these to short dramatic performances, the evening is spent to the general satisfaction, and, it must be supposed, to the greater welfare of the party.

The "conversaziones" and the "social evenings" are large evening parties, at which the programme often includes, along with the musical part and the political interludes, dancing, tableaux vivants, thought-reader's experiences, etc., besides the handing round of refreshments, which takes place in all the "social" meetings, and which is not the smallest attraction for many people. It is even the principal and only one in less important gatherings from which the artistic part is absent. The most simple type of "social" meetings are the tea-meetings, where a cup of tea and bread and butter constitute the only political stimulant. Being less expensive they are more common, and are often held even in the wards, where they serve to fulfil, on a small scale, all the purposes of "social meetings" in general.[1] In the summer-time picnics, pleasure parties in the country, and more or less distant excursions by rail or boat are organized. The Presidents of Associations, candidates, or other big-wigs of the party who have parks or large gardens, give political garden-parties in them, with a band, political speeches, and refreshments. To make a great hit a "fête" is organized, with a most varied programme of amusements; the ordinary attractions are reinforced by the performances of conjurers, acrobats, "contortionists," clowns,

---

[1] An Association has recorded an opinion on the usefulness of tea-meetings in the following terms: "They attract the young to our ranks: they enlist the interest of the numerous ladies who assist (in making and pouring out the tea) and of those who are present at the meetings, and they help in maintaining pleasant and cordial relations between members and their constituents" (Extract from the minute-book of a Liberal Association in the north of England).

by sports for men and women, with prizes, the whole preceded by a political part, after despatching which and shaking off the cares of State, the company indulges to its heart's content in innocent pleasures. These pleasures are enhanced by the presence of women. In fact, the organizers welcome them most warmly at all the social meetings, because they attract the men. A water-party or a picnic with good-looking young women is sure of success, as are the tea-meetings at which they sing; each of them ensures the presence at the meeting of several young men,— her brothers come as in duty bound to applaud her, her admirers for flirtation or amusement. And it is all so much gain for the party, as the young men get into the habit of walking in the right path. For this reason, in many localities women are in request even for purely political meetings, and a portion of the room is set apart for them; "but," as the managers of a caucus explained, "we encourage them rather to sit with the men." The other great attraction of a less æsthetic kind is the more than moderate cost of admission to these fêtes and entertainments. If it is an excursion, even less than the price of the railway ticket is paid; if it is a simple social meeting, "a social," as it is called for short, a ticket can be bought for a few pence entitling the holder to refreshments worth at least double the amount. The difference is paid by the Association, or by the candidate who is nursing the constituency for the next general election, or again by wealthy members of the party, who are asked to cover the deficit for the good of the cause. Thanks to their generosity, it is even possible to distribute tickets to poor people quite gratuitously.

Although committed out of election time, and often long before it, and perhaps even independently of the candidate, these acts of liberality none the less have in view the votes of the electors, and constitute *de facto* if not *de jure*, a purchase of votes in advance. The "social meetings" organized by the Associations have therefore not failed to attract the attention of the judges who try election petitions.[1] While admitting that the smoking-concerts, conversaziones, social

---

[1] In England it is not the House of Commons which adjudicates on the validity of contested elections, but the judges of the Supreme Court in accordance with the ordinary rules of judicial procedure.

suppers, etc., organized by the Associations are not in themselves necessarily illegal, the judges have laid down as a general proposition that they "are dangerously akin to corrupt treating," and that, in any event, "they tend to engender, on the part of those who are liable to be affected by such considerations, an expectation that they are going to get free drink, or practically free drink, at the expense of other people, and so to induce them to join these Associations, and in that way to join the party which these Associations are formed to promote." The judges came to the conclusion that the Associations were a source of real danger in this respect.[1] "People have a right to associate together in order to persuade their fellow-countrymen to adopt those views of politics which they are persuaded are the best and most wholesome; and so long as in doing that they resort solely to things which are likely to produce an effect upon the reason of those to whom they are addressed, no fault whatever can be found with their action; it is otherwise when they endeavour to go beyond that and to acquire popularity for political principles of a particular kind by endeavouring to secure the adhesion of those voters who take a less strong view of political matters, by addressing themselves not to their reason, but to less praiseworthy methods, by giving them treats and entertainments for the purpose of inducing them to join one or other of the great political parties into which the country is divided."[2]

The effect of the severe admonitions of the judges, "that the practices of the local Associations may be amended for the future," is and will be a long time in making its appearance, for the danger of coming within the arm of the law, of seeing smoking-concerts and conversaziones pronounced illegal, is not very great (they are only "*akin* to corrupt treating"), and the election petitions are not frequent,[3] while the "prac-

---

[1] Judgments delivered by the justices selected for the trial of election petitions (*Blue Books*, 1893, Controverted Elections, pp. 11, 81, 84).

[2] *Ibid.* 3, 81. Cf. the opinion expressed subsequently, after the general election of 1895, by the judges in the Lancaster and Tower Hamlets (St. George's Division) election petitions, where they take a much more lenient view of smoking-concerts (*Blue Books*, 1896, Controverted Elections, Part I, pp. 5, 6; Part II, pp. 10, 11).

[3] The cost of an election petition is too high — about £5000 on an average — for it to be resorted to frequently.

tices" referred to have become for "these local Associations"
an essential element of their action on the electorate.   Of
course their importance is not the same everywhere.   It varies
first of all with the latitude.   In the extreme north of England, and especially in Scotland, the "social meetings" have
much less success than elsewhere.   The Scot is too methodical
a being to take to the mixture of politics with amusements, and
too unsentimental to be moved by music, dancing, or tableaux
vivants.   The variation is not less considerable with the
political party.   It is the Tories who are past masters in the
organization of "social meetings" and in the art of making
them attractive.   The Liberals have had to learn from them;
while giving them credit for the fact that all beginnings are
difficult, it must be admitted that they have already made
considerable progress.   Their political relations, however,
with the Temperance party do not always permit them to give
their "social meetings" all the fulness that the latter have
with their rivals; to avoid scandalizing their teetotal friends
they are often obliged to fall back upon tea, whereas the Tories,
who are the political allies of the publicans, would be the last
persons to refuse their guests refreshments of a more stimulating kind.   But apart from the drinks, the Tory social
meetings hold out powerful attractions owing to the pains
which the Conservative organizations take with them.   It is,
in fact, one of their great preoccupations.   Not only do their
regular Associations devote themselves to the work, but also,
and above all, the innumerable branches of the Primrose
League.   Reference has already been made to the beginnings
of this League, founded by the members of the Fourth Party
as an engine of war of Tory democracy.   Later on, in the
chapter dealing with auxiliary party organizations, it will be
related how the League passed out of their control and became
an instrument, or at least an auxiliary, of the head-quarters of
the official party, and in what its activity and its rôle consist.
Suffice it to say in the meanwhile that the League is among
other things the great, the greatest, promoter of the "socialization" of politics, and that it performs its task principally
by constantly getting up politico-social meetings, with the
assistance of "entertainers" of the most varied kind, conjurers, ventriloquists, etc.   There is no end to the amusements

which it offers the public.   Great, immense, as is the success
of the League, it has nevertheless to be always making fresh
efforts in the same direction; for the voter is a frivolous being,
he soon gets tired.   "Our great difficulty," the representative
of a Tory organization confided to me, "is to keep them
amused."

FOURTH CHAPTER

CANDIDATES AND ELECTIONEERING

I

HOWEVER strongly the action of the Organizations may influence the minds and the "social tendencies" of the voters, its effect cannot be complete unless the liking for the party, developed in them by these efforts, centres in a concrete fashion on particular persons whom the Organization is anxious to get into Parliament — for that is its ultimate object. To bring about this result, the Association must obtain what is called a *good candidate*. Here, therefore, is a new factor added to those with which we are already acquainted.

But what is a good candidate? In general, one may say that it is the man who is likely to conciliate the greatest number of the predominating influences in the locality. As we already have an idea from the description of the modes of action of the Caucus, the influences which sway the voters are manifold. Party feeling, loyalty to the flag, while powerless to inspire all of them, is at all events capable of carrying a good many in each constituency. With some, more or less reasoned convictions lead them to prefer one party to the other. With others, devotion to the party is of a sentimental order; at one time it is merely the outcome of atavism, a tradition inherited from the family; at another simply a habit which has been contracted of hoisting certain political colours and which has become an integral part of their existence. These feelings are, perhaps, displayed only at intervals; overlaid by the political apathy which seizes on the majority of the voters between one general election and another, they nevertheless subsist in a latent condition. Idea or simple feeling, flashing brightly forth or smouldering under the embers of the last electoral battle, it is a sort of religion, resembling that of the Church, with its devotees of varying fervour, from the regular church-goers down to those who cross the threshold of the sacred edifice only once a year, to receive the communion on the day of the great Christian festival. The religion of the political party, in like manner, brings together all its followers on the solemn day of the poll, to make them communicate and to affirm their creed in the person of the candidate.

This quasi-spiritual need, this duty sanctioned by habit and decorum, makes the believers accept, for the particular occasion, the ministrations of the Caucus, which is, as a rule, ignored by the great bulk of the electorate. In fact, as we already know, the Association is in reality only a handful of men deriving their authority from a scarcely greater number of political co-religionists; its elective character proceeds solely from the sham elective procedure used in its formation; and its representative value is confined to the militant members of the party. But the Caucus has stepped forward as the officiating minister of the .party religion, as the guardian of the feelings engraved on so many hearts, and by that means, although made up of usurpation and convention, it acquires a real and almost legitimate power. The services which it holds may not be much frequented in ordinary times, yet the public is aware that they do take place, that the divinity of the party is glorified in them, and when the time for prayer arrives it knows where to go and where to look for the depositary of the creed, the orthodox candidate.

It follows that the first quality required in a candidate is that he should profess the creed of the party in all its fulness, and that his opinions should give complete satisfaction to the Caucus, which vouches for his orthodoxy. And since the latter is, as a rule, composed of the most ardent members of the party, the programme which the candidate has to endorse represents not so much the average opinion of the constituency as the views of the most advanced section. In fact, the creed of parties no longer consisting of fixed dogmas, the candidate must prove his adhesion to the political creed of the day, according to the latest quotation, so to speak; his political convictions must be "up to date." If, on the spur of the moment, a programme is issued, however voluminous, like the Newcastle Programme, the candidate must be prepared to subscribe to it

in a lump.   And if the Organization should think fit to add a
few big items to it, the candidate is bound to swallow these as
well.

Having set himself right with the general body of the adherents of the party, the candidate has to face the particular sects
which flourish in profusion among the voters.   One, anxious
to put a stop to the drinking which is a curse of the country,
wishes to prohibit the sale of spirituous liquors by law; another
has sworn not to hold its hand until compulsory vaccination is
abolished; a third believes that the solution of the social
question is to be found in "the restitution of the land to the
people"; another group of voters is mainly interested in the
strict observance of the Sabbath Day throughout the kingdom;
etc.   The followers of these various sects may lean towards
either of the political parties, and profess its creed in all sincerity, but their own particular claim is none the less in their
minds the point on which the problems of political and social
life converge.   Consequently, in constituencies where these
sects have many adherents the *good candidate* will be the man
who can give pledges and rally round him the greatest number
of these groups or the most important of them.   In other
words, the programme of the candidate must be as comprehensive as possible.

To urge the adopted programme on the voters, and to prove
that he is up to it, the candidate requires to be a good platform speaker; he must be fluent and copious, and quick at
repartee.   At a pinch, if he possesses all the remaining qualities in a high degree, eloquence will not be insisted on, others
"will speak to the people for him"; the Organization will
support his candidature with experienced orators who will
turn a flood of talk on the constituency.

But this is not nearly all.   The electorate is not composed
solely of believers and sectaries who can be won by professions of faith and programmes.   Perhaps they are only the
minority.   In any event, whatever their numerical importance,
there are always thousands of voters who in choosing between
rival candidates are influenced by considerations unconnected
with any notion of Liberalism or Conservatism or with any
programme whatsoever.   In one place workmen vote in a body
for their employer because he pays well, without caring a rap

whether he goes to the House to swell the ranks of the Tories or to reinforce the Liberals. In another, a rich man is voted for because he is rich, or because he has a reputation for generosity, because he subscribes handsomely to charitable institutions and signs cheques without hesitation in favour of every society and club which applies to him. Another large group is guided solely by influences springing from its religious claims or passions, which convert it into a single body with one "conscience," one will. To carry the votes of the electors belonging to these categories, it is the *person* of the candidate which is all-important. The qualities which he must combine in this connection are not the same in all cases, they are varied and manifold, but all of them may be reduced to a single term — *popularity*. The candidate must be a *popular* man — here is a new condition to be fulfilled by him, which is, perhaps, even more important than all the preceding ones, for the thoroughgoing party devotee himself is also a man swayed by less abstract and less general considerations.

The first postulate of the *popular* candidate is his position of *local man*, which ensures his being known to everybody. But often this is a drawback, or even a reason for disqualification. In his contact with local life he has, perchance, made many enemies. As employer of labour he has, it may be, aroused the discontent of his workmen, there has perhaps been a strike in his factory or his workshop, and thus his political prospects are spoilt beforehand, however great his political orthodoxy and however considerable the services which he has rendered to the party. In that case a stranger would be more acceptable, even if he were a lawyer, on condition, of course, that he has an aptitude for *becoming* popular. With good means the popular candidate should unite a reputation for generosity and for affable manners, and, in general, a sympathetic character or special qualities capable of impressing the ordinary voter in his favour. Among these special qualities there are some which one would never dream of requiring from a candidate in any other country. Thus a good "athlete," an adept at games, is a very good candidate; if he is a good cricketer, most of the cricketers in the constituency — and their name is legion — might find it difficult to resist the admiration with which he inspires them so far as not to give him their votes.

The combative spirit, which is a mark of the race, assigns almost a moral excellence to fighting qualities and, from a deviated ethical sentiment, the deference shown to the crack football or cricket player is in fact rather a homage paid to the character of the man. It is for the same reason that the platform speaker carries away the audience; telling blows are admired and cheered, whether they are delivered with words or with the cricket-bat. The candidate, therefore, must be a good talker, not only to win those who are able to follow his line of argument, but also those who pay attention only to form, without understanding, or wishing to understand, the subject-matter. The person of the speaker, his pluck, is capable of silencing political considerations in the mind of many a voter even with a relative amount of cultivation.[1] After all, it is only a question of degree, of more or less elevated æsthetic feeling; what forcible language is to some athletic feats are to others. Duller minds are attracted by still less stirring qualities in the candidate, by the simple attribute of "good fellow," which assumes so many forms in daily life, from a natural kindliness toward one and all down to a readiness to have a drink with everybody.

Thus the elements of the candidate's popularity with the voters are composed of a whole string of feelings suggested by his person or flowing from his character, apart from his politics. It is the action of man on man which asserts itself triumphantly here; living realities confront the conventions of politics, the artificial distinctions of parties. And the latter can win the day only by means of an alliance or a coalition with these live forces. It is no good defying them.

[1] I once told an Englishman an electioneering story belonging to the hustings period. The candidate on the platform, a very young man, looked almost a youth. A wag in the crowd called out to him: "Does your mother know you're out?"   "Yes," replied the candidate, "and on Tuesday [the day fixed for the poll] she will know that I am in."   "I would plump for such a man," exclaimed my interlocutor with cold-blooded determination.

A borough in Yorkshire, which had always been represented in the House by a Liberal, returned a Tory a few years ago. On visiting the town some time after the election, I made enquiry as to the cause of this change. The reply was that it was partly to be accounted for by the fact that the Tory candidate had contested the seat at four consecutive elections; a good many Liberal voters are supposed to have said to themselves: he is a plucky fellow, he deserves to win, and to have voted for him.

A conventional factor can never make any way if it does not throw in its lot, were it only as a parasite or by fraud, with a real force. Thus we have seen the Caucus climb into power in the rear of that great living force called party feeling, with which so many members of the body politic are animated. It matters little that in a good many cases this feeling itself has a purely conventional origin. Every notion which produces devotion, love, hatred, strife among men, is in itself a living fact and a real force. By appearing before the voters, who are inspired by party feeling, with a candidate who is the mouthpiece of it, the Caucus has seen its small battalion forthwith transformed into an army corps. This junction of two forces effected on the person of the candidate not being sufficient, in the majority of cases, to carry the election, the operation is repeated over and over again; by a series of simultaneous coalitions, invariably centring on the person of the candidate, every factor capable of joining in the fight — influences, social passions and prejudices, interests — is enlisted to win the constituency. Starting from a pure convention, the Caucus takes in blood and life at each contact with these realities. It selects as candidate a great factory-owner who employs thousands of hands; a rich brewer who has under his thumb all the publicans of the locality, who control their customers; or, on the other hand, a leader of the temperance movement, a respectable mediocrity, who is a tower of strength in the Nonconformist chapels, a man with a well-filled purse and an open hand; in a word, any one who, thanks to his personal position, is likely to poll a great many votes, and who, in addition to this, of course, is ready to don the party uniform. The more qualifications of this kind the nominee of the Caucus combines, the more closely will he correspond to the ideal of a *good candidate*.

The Associations, therefore, need all their sagacity to find their man; the occasion is one in which the skill of the wire-pullers of the Caucus is put to a particularly severe test. The task of selection is all the more difficult because the qualifications of the *good candidate* are not only of many kinds, but vary a good deal from one constituency to another, according to the relation which exists in them between social forces and political forces, between the nature and the composition of the former and the degree of intensity of the latter.   On a more level kind of ground, where the social influences or the particular groups are weak or few in number, the party Organization has more scope.   Party feeling having, in these cases, no serious rivals to speak of among the living forces, it becomes *the* living force, and bears away the crowd, like the wind which lifts the grains of dust into space and drives them straight before it.   Under cover of such a situation, the caucus can easily thrust on the constituency a politician pure and simple, a stranger with no local connection, a "carpet-bagger," whose sole claim is the confidence with which he has managed to inspire the leading members of the Organization.   In places, on the other hand, where groups and sects, each prosecuting their special claims, have to be reckoned with, the ingredients capable of producing the good candidate must be mixed with skill; they may not amalgamate, or they may perhaps be mutually destructive.   For instance, in a locality where the group of temperance men, who demand the prohibition of the sale of liquors, is very numerous, a brewer, were he the best "Liberal" in the world, the most generous of men, the most ardent of Nonconformists, will never be a good candidate for the Liberal party, which has long been allied with the temperance men, and the caucus which adopted him would probably be courting a defeat.   As against this, a temperance man, were he a Conservative to his finger-tips, is a bad candidate for the Conservative party, which derives its strongest support from the publicans.

II

In consequence the procedure laid down by the rules for the selection of the candidate, described above in the account of the powers of the Caucus committees, is simply a formality which just puts the finishing touch on the work of the wire-pullers — a work which has perhaps been a long time in preparation. But this formality accomplished by the Organization is in itself of great importance: it confers on the candidate an incontestable superiority over all his competitors of the same party; he becomes in truth the anointed of the party, and the Spirit of the party is "upon him from that time forth."   He is "the adopted candidate." Independent candidates may, of course, come forward, but he alone is considered the orthodox candidate. For this reason, therefore, and for another reason of a less doctrinal order, which will be mentioned later on in its proper place, it very rarely happens that independent parliamentary candidatures arise in the ranks of the party, in opposition to that which has been adopted by the caucus; and their success is still more rare. The prestige bestowed on the parliamentary candidate through the investiture given him by the caucus is one of the most striking manifestations of the influence which this factor, bred of conventions, manages to acquire in taking on itself the representation of the party in the locality. When grappling with the living forces of society, we have seen it bow before them and come to terms with them; here the formal forces have their revenge. It is their second triumph; their first was to impose on the candidate the programme of the Organization, which reflects only the views of a small group of militant politicians; in that case, however, they were dealing with an individual made of a special kind of clay, which is only too ready to be moulded, whereas the formal proclamation of the candidate of the party impresses the imaginations of thousands and places their wills under restraint.

Even the sitting member would not stand again if the caucus were to start another candidate in opposition to him. His position with regard to his party would somewhat resemble that of an excommunicated sovereign in the Middle Ages, whose subjects, so devoted to him the day before, are released from their loyalty to him. In practice, things rarely get so far as this. As a general rule, the sitting member is *eo ipso* the candidate of the Association for the next election; it recognizes his vested rights; even if he has proved his utter incompetence in the House or on the platform, he is not offered the affront of a notice to quit, unless his party orthodoxy is called in question. On this point there is no compromise. In the case of serious differences of opinion arising between the Association and the member, he himself gives up seeking re-election, if he does not wish to break with the party. If he were to appeal to the constituency, he would no doubt be in a better predicament than an independent candidate who had not been a member, but he would be very unlikely to obtain a

majority again; at the most he would succeed in bringing in
the candidate of the rival party, which would be the lucky
third thief in the fable; in any event, he would be the cause
of a split in the party, and party morality knows no more
odious crime than this.   The Caucus trades precisely on these
feelings to ensure the monopoly of its candidate; it relies on
the reprobation with which fomenters of schisms are viewed
by the general body of believers, and on the fear that the divisions in the party caused by them may benefit the candidate of
the opposite party, which presents a united front.   This being so,
the announcement of the candidate adopted by the Caucus puts
him, as it were, in possession, and has the immediate effect of
discouraging possible competitors, of nipping their candidatures in the bud.   To stop them more effectively, the Organization generally selects its candidate a good long time before
the election, sometimes several years beforehand.   This precaution offers certain other advantages besides: it enables the
Organization to connect its propagandist action with the name
of the candidate at an early stage, and gives the latter time
to prepare his candidature.   The Association itself profits by
it as well; as it does not receive many subscriptions, and is
always hard up, it cannot exist without subsidies from rich
political friends.   The candidate is marked out as the principal support of the Association, and the sooner it finds one,
and in easy circumstances, the sooner will it get out of its
financial difficulties.   The gifts which the candidate makes
to the Association sometimes run into respectable figures.[1]
When returned to Parliament, he continues his donations,
because he means to stand again.[2]   If he decides not to seek
re-election, the Association feels the effect of it at once; the
member, who was erewhile so demonstrative, begins to treat
it with marked coolness, and it is bound to find a successor
to him, not only for the seat in the House, but also for the
donations which he was in the habit of making it.   The anxiety
about ways and means sometimes makes the Association act
with undue haste and adopt a candidate who is, perhaps, not

---

[1] A good many candidates spend from £400 to £600 a year.   The average
amount of this expenditure might be fixed at £250 a year.

[2] There are, however, candidates and members who do not subscribe anything to the funds of their respective Associations.

the best available; the reason is that the stomach cries cupboard, and that somebody must be found with all speed to administer nourishment, or "keep the Association going," as is said in the political slang of the day.

The choice of the local candidate by the wire-pullers is arrived at, to a certain extent, by a process of natural selection. Often it falls on the President of the Association himself; for, as we are already aware, he has been placed in this position precisely for his qualities of "popularity," which make a good candidate. If it is necessary to have recourse to outsiders, the task is more laborious, unless the head managers in London recommend a candidate, and a strong one too, who is accepted at once. But if the Association has to find the man by its own efforts, it looks round and feels its way. It is not uncommon for it to open a sort of competition, applying to one person after another, getting them to state their political views, and coming to a decision after having inspected them all in succession. First of all, the wire-pullers examine them. Then the candidates for a seat in Parliament are invited to speak before the "Hundreds," and often at a public meeting into the bargain. The impression which they make on the audience is of great weight for the future of their candidatures; they undergo an ordeal similar to that of the tenor at trial performances on the provincial stage. The success obtained by the candidate at these rehearsals is the beginning of the *popularity* which he has to win. Even the candidate of local origin, who is well known already, has to give his mind to it; all the more is he bound to do so if he is a stranger to the locality, and this is the case with a large number of candidates, both in the boroughs and in the county constituencies. In fact, of the total of electoral Divisions, more than 50 per cent are represented by persons brought in from outside. The popularity of the non-local candidate has to be built up from the beginning, but this is not a very difficult matter, if, in addition to the aid of the caucus, he has a little tact and a good deal of money. Guided by the advice of the wire-pullers, the imported candidate will employ both to advantage; he will gain adherents by his engaging manners and by his munificence.

The interval, often of long duration, between the announce-

ment of the candidature and the election is actively spent in
doing this.   The sitting member's term has, perhaps, a
good long time to run, but the "adopted candidate" assumes
from that moment the part of the Lord's anointed.   He
attends all the important gatherings, from religious or
charitable meetings to outdoor shows at which performing
dogs are exhibited.   He tries to connect himself with all
the events which interest the local population, down to the
changes of the seasons almost.   He "identifies himself with
local institutions" by subscribing to them, by accepting the
title of honorary member of this or that society, of honorary
president of this or that club, of honorary vice-president of
this or that association.   In order not to do things by halves,
a good many candidates even belong to some of the numerous
benefit societies with the picturesque titles of "Ancient Shep-
herds," "Hearts of Oak," "Odd Fellows," "Druids," etc., all
the members of which call each other brothers, and meet to
enjoy fraternal feasts.   Generally, the candidate is obliged to
carry his "identification with local institutions" much farther
than he likes.   As soon as he takes this title he is beset on
all sides with demands for money; not an "institution" but
what requests his assistance for its "work"; churches, chapels,
hospitals, asylums, clubs, musical societies, societies for sport,
for all kinds of amusement, for every description of edification.   Every group of individuals who take it into their heads
to assume a collective title of some kind or other, to organize
themselves, even for the most fanciful of objects, tries to screw
a subscription out of him, by hinting that they represent
influential electors, people who have a vote.   It is nothing less
than a regular blackmail levied on the candidate, who would
deserve sincere pity if he had not laid himself open to it beforehand.   He is bound to submit to it in order not to make
enemies, and to increase the number of his adherents.   Besides this, he works the constituency, in concert with the
Association, on the approved methods, by means of speeches,
lectures, and "social" gatherings.   He gives political garden-
parties, at homes, he takes the chair at tea-meetings, he pays
visits to the workingmen's clubs, he attends the ward meetings, and speaks at them, as well as at the large public meetings organized by the Association.   In the rural constituencies

the task is a still more arduous one, if only on account of the way in which the voters are scattered over the country; the county Divisions, in fact, are composed of fifty, sixty, or even a hundred parishes. An active candidate visits them all, and, perhaps, more than once, and he does not confine himself to speaking at the evening meetings held in them; he goes from house to house, from cottage to cottage, to see the inhabitants individually, and to invite them in person to the meeting which he proposes to address.

III

Thus, if time allows, if the election does not come unawares, — owing to an unexpected dissolution or to a vacancy occurring during the term of the Parliament, — the ground for the coming election is prepared beforehand by the action of the Association and of the candidate. But in striving to create a current of opinion in their favour, they acted — however divided and differentiated the efforts may have been — on groups of voters, on masses. When election time comes at the close of which the voters are to record their votes, one by one, on the polling-day, the aspect of the political stage changes; instead of groups, of masses, it is the individual voter who becomes the protagonist. At the first blush, perhaps, the distinction will seem purely logical and not to admit of practical consequences; for are not the groups composed of individuals, and does not action on the one involve action on the other? It is not always so in reality. The inference which each one of the voters is intended to draw on his own account from the demonstration of the candidate's claims made to them in a body, often turns out to be beyond his moral and intellectual grasp. In that case the proof has to be presented in a still more concrete form, the quality of good candidate has to be brought home to each voter individually. Thus the Organization is confronted with the necessity of recapturing the voter, singly, of catechizing and exhorting him in private. This applies also to those who have never been reached at all by any of the forms of the propaganda set in motion by the Organization: they have not come to it, and it goes to them, to each one of them. At the decisive moment of the vote it knocks at every door to recommend its candidate.

These practices of the Caucus no doubt bring distinct recollections to the reader's mind; he has recognized in them the electoral canvass of bygone days, that instrument of the old order of things which was the most perfect mirror of it, and even more, its living soul. Having stepped in with the pretension of substituting the efficacy of principles for the baneful tyranny of social influences, the Caucus finds itself obliged once more to supplement the inadequacy of the former by the latter, and to resort, in this instance, to the action of man on man in its least dignified form. In fact, without the canvass the aspect of the electoral battlefields would be radically changed, a very large section of the electorate would not put in an appearance, and the political parties would lose many of their contingents. The most optimistic calculations put the number of electors likely to vote more or less spontaneously at 50 per cent. The proportion should perhaps be reduced to 40 or even 35 per cent to be nearer the truth.

Having lost none of its importance from the standpoint of the political parties, the operation of the canvass has become far more complicated. The extension of the suffrage effected during the last thirty years has increased the number of voters, that is to say, the number of persons who have to be hunted up; instead of 1,200,000 citizens who possessed the right of voting in Great Britain before 1867, there are now (in 1895) nearly 5,600,000. Again, owing to the *differentiation* of opinion and of social groups, the motives and influences capable of acting on the voters have multiplied in proportion. The *argumentum ad hominem*, with which the canvasser operates, has consequently to assume a variety of shapes unknown in former days. Besides, the parties have not at their disposal the old body of canvassers, which included, along with the friends of the candidate, paid agents. The law enacted in 1883 against corrupt and illegal practices at elections prohibited the employment of paid canvassers, for this was one of the devices for disguising the purchase of votes; it was customary to engage, ostensibly as canvassers, a number of voters ready to sell themselves, so-called "doubtful" voters who hesitated between the rival candidates, or else persons who, through the influence which they wielded over their relations and their friends, were able to secure a certain number of votes. Thus the canvassers must now be at once voluntary workers, numerous enough to cope with the large number of voters, and with as strong a hold as possible on all the varied groups of which the electorate is made up.

Being an elective body of numerous and unpaid members, the caucus is placed in a position to meet most of these new exigencies, to provide the staff suited for the canvass, in spite of the restrictions laid down by the Act of 1883. The members of the " Hundreds " and of their committees almost all turn into canvassers during election time. It is, in fact, the principal service which the Organization expects from its members, especially from those who do not lend it their name or their financial support. If payment of a subscription is not insisted on in the Associations, as we have seen, it is for the very reason that the non-paying members are supposed to give their *work* in place of it, to become *workers* of the Organization. They appear on the scene in this capacity on the occasion of the electoral registration canvass; but there the business is more of a mechanical kind, and may be entrusted, without infringing the law, to paid agents; in any event, it does not require a large staff. The real part played by the " workers " begins with the election canvass. With a view to this important and delicate " work," the wire-pullers, who arrange the composition of the " Hundreds " and of their committees beforehand, try to get experts into them. However, unselfish devotion does not supply the caucuses with all the assistance they need, and they think themselves bound to employ, in spite of the law, a good many paid canvassers, in the strictest secrecy of course. The importance of a more or less numerous body of canvassers is twofold: they bring to the caucus not only their " work," but also the connections which they possess in their respective spheres. Foremen of factories or workshops; active members of Trade Unions or other working-men's societies; followers of religious communities; representatives of associations for instruction or edification, such as Bible classes (for adults) or Young Men's Christian Associations, and other organizations of various kinds, bringing together a certain number of persons for some purpose or other; they are introduced, on the initiative of the wire-pullers, into the committees of the Association. Indebted for this distinction to the clever manœuvres of the managers of the caucus, and in no way to the suffrages of the masses who, as the reader knows, hold aloof, they none the less form, potentially, living links which connect the Organization with the various groups of the population to which they belong in their private capacity. The moment of the canvass (which, for some of these members of the caucus, is the beginning of the effective exercise of the authority supposed to be delegated to them) makes the power pass into action. Coming out as party canvassers, they deal with persons to whom they are no strangers, and who, perhaps, are in the habit of following them. At any rate, the Organization does its best to match the canvassers and the canvassed in this way.

A reconnoissance of the ground is made long before the election, during the annual registration canvass in which the *politics* of the voter are taken down as well as the details required for the revision of the register. With the help of the information thus obtained, the electoral canvass is started on the registration method. That is to say, each ward of the borough[1] is divided into small blocks made over to canvassers who, furnished with canvass books containing the electoral record of the locality, call on every one, without distinction of party, on this occasion with the sole and formal mission of obtaining a promise of the vote or, at all events, a flat refusal. The nature and the extent of the negotiations are endlessly varied. Sometimes they are limited to a simple exchange of a question and an answer, which the canvasser has only to make a note of, especially if it is favourable. At other times it is a long conversation, in which the canvasser has to display all his persuasive power or personal charm. If the voter has any scruples about the programme or the person of the candidate, it is the canvasser's business to overcome them, to prove that the candidate is the best of all possible ones, and that his programme is excellent in every respect. In case of partial differences, the canvasser dwells on the importance of the points on which the voter and the candidate are agreed and the comparative insignificance of the remaining ones. If the canvasser does not succeed in obtaining the

---

[1] In the country districts a systematic and formal canvass is less necessary, the sentiments of the voters are better known.

voter's adhesion, he asks him, at all events, to remain neutral, to abstain from voting.   The voter full of certain aspirations, absorbed in special claims, is made to believe that the candidate will be the best mouthpiece and the best champion of them; the canvasser gives pledges in his name, is lavish of promises in his behalf.   At the same time, he makes no scruple of abusing the rival candidate.   The charges, true or false, reflecting on the latter's public or private life, often due to the fertile imagination of the wire-pullers, find an obliging retailer and an authoritative commentator in the canvasser. If the voter claimed by the party shows a tendency towards independence, the canvasser recalls him to the right path by bringing before his eyes the dangerous incline on which he is venturing, and perhaps, also, the fate of backslider and renegade which awaits him.   If the voter is accessible only to considerations of a less abstract kind, it is again the canvasser's business to find the arguments suited to the occasion.

Thus, according to the degree of intelligence and morality of the voter, and the level of his own moral standard, the canvasser in turn argues, persuades, insinuates, promises, intimidates, or even goes farther.   He does not always succeed at the first attempt.   The voters styled *doubtful* in political slang, that is to say, those who have no party preferences or who have not given any positive pledge for or against, are canvassed several times over by different people.   Sometimes even before the local canvasser goes his rounds the "doubtful" ones are put on one side and are reserved for persons who have influence over them.   At the general meeting of the canvassers a personal appeal is made as to who shall canvass this man and who take charge of that.   If those who have accepted the mission do not succeed in extorting the required promise, fresh canvassers return to the charge.   It sometimes happens that a dozen visits are paid in this way to a single voter.   In places where the canvass is well managed, no voter is left unvisited, even if he has given a formal promise at the start.   If only for checking purposes, the Association repeats the canvass from house to house.   Sometimes it does not stop at this check-canvass, but resorts to a cross-canvass ostensibly made on behalf of the rival candidate.   For instance, a canvasser of the Tory Association appears as envoy of the Liberal Organization and asks for votes for the Liberal candidate; he notes the refusals with pleasure, and discovers among the consenting ones those who had promised the Tory canvasser to vote for the Tory while intending really to support his opponent.   In the boroughs where every one knows each other, a cross-canvass is almost impossible, but in the country constituencies, made up of a good many scattered localities, it can be carried out with impunity.   An element of uncertainty no doubt always attaches to the best-conducted and best-checked canvass: one is never sure that the promises made will be kept, if only by reason of the Ballot, the secret voting introduced in 1872, under cover of which the voter runs no risk of being convicted of breaking his word.   But if the people of the Organization know their business, they can calculate the loss beforehand with almost mathematical accuracy.   If in a constituency of ten to twelve thousand voters they cannot predict the exact result to within 150–250 votes, the Organization is considered very inefficient.

Still, the expected result will be obtained on one condition only: that of not leaving the voters to themselves on the polling-day.   A very large number of electors would vote *straight* when once they are inside the polling-booths, but if left to themselves they would not take the trouble to move, either from carelessness, or owing to infirmities or advanced age, or to save themselves further fatigue after a hard day's work.   To ensure their presence at the poll, the workers of both caucuses fetch them in carriages and take them there bodily.   This operation completes the work of the canvass after having been carefully prepared by it.   Each canvasser in the course of his visits makes a note of the voters whose spontaneousness cannot be relied on, takes down the time at which the particular voter is free and the place where he is to be found, the workshop or the factory, the tavern or the public-house, or his own home.   Those who have been left to their own zeal are also made to feel the spur of the workers at the decisive moment of the vote, to wit, those who are somewhat tardy in going to vote.   These laggards are discovered by the following method: on the eve of the polling-day the Organization sends each voter a card to obligingly inform him

of his number on the electoral list.   At the door of the poll-
ing-place stand agents of the Organizations, who ask each voter
as he leaves the room, after having voted, to state his number
or even to hand over his card.   The latter complies, and often
delivers his card to the agent wearing the colours of his party
before the assembled crowd.   The numbers which have come
out are communicated at very short intervals to the local
branches of the Association established, for the day, in each
voting section (committee-rooms).   There the names of those
who have promised their vote, but have not voted, are picked
out as the numbers are brought in, and they are fetched with
all speed.

The principal result of this very laborious operation of the
canvass, completed by the transport of the voters to the poll,
is to secure for the party the voters without definite political
opinions.   Real conversions from one political opinion to
another are anything but numerous, — the proportion of proselytes is, in fact, very slight; in certain places it is estimated
at one per cent only, exclusive of the, so to speak, professional proselytes, who always vote against the Government,
whatever its political complexion may be.   Among these are
the small struggling tradesmen, for instance, who hope for
better times under a new government.   If it is the Tories
who are trying to dislodge the government of the day,
they vote against it with enthusiasm from the widely held
belief that trade always flourishes under a Tory government,
although they are unable to explain this mystery of nature.
But the presence of the Tories in power does not prevent the
majority of this category of voters from pinning their faith on
the advent of a Liberal government.   Other electors vote
sometimes for the one, sometimes for the other party, from a
superior feeling of distributive justice, in order to "give them
a chance."   Without neglecting these groups, who, however,
are not numerous, the caucuses act mainly on the floating mass
of voters who inhabit the confines of the regular parties and
who vote on no system — to-day with the one and the next time
with the other.   In the electoral duel the main point is to
know which of the two rival caucuses will be the first to lay
its hand on the voters of this description, or, rather, which
will enlist the greatest possible quantity of them; for it is these

voters who, by their number, decide the issue of the electoral
battles.   And it is only by the canvass that they can be got
at; by it alone can the forces which they represent be mobilized.   From this point of view the canvass is more important
than the platform and the other modes of action, and in the
contests of the rival candidates the chances of success are to be
found rather on the side of the man who has a highly perfected
canvassing machinery to back him; it can often obtain the
victory for a candidate who is personally little known and a
poor speaker over a candic ite who is a man of mark, a good
platform orator, a pillar of the party, etc.   It is in this sense
that " everything depends on organization," that " organization
is everything."

   This exceptional part played by the canvass and the " organization " work which prepares and completes it makes it a sort
of keystone of the electoral edifice; everything is connected
with it, everything hangs on it, everything derives its value and
its practical object from it.   Association, candidates, workers,
the position of all is defined by the canvass.   The Association is important because it alone, thanks to its permanent
cadres, which include all the zeal, ardour, party fanaticism,
and political dexterity that exist in the locality, can provide
the regiment of canvassers.   It is by their number and not by
that of the adherents of an Association that the latter's power
is measured.   An Association with five thousand members and
fifty canvassers is of less value than an Association of five
hundred canvassers with no other adherents on its list.   The
more or less considerable number of canvassers may decide
the fate of the electoral battle not only in their own constituency, but in the neighbouring ones if they come to their assistance.   It, therefore, not unfrequently happens that an attempt
is made to lock up the canvassers of the rival party, to " keep
them at home " by starting a sham fight when there is no
chance of success for the party which resorts to this stratagem
and consequently no good reason for contesting the constituency.   For the candidate, the possibility or impossibility of
using the corps of canvassers settles the fate of his candidature
beforehand, and herein lies the second reason (along with the
fact that the candidate adopted by the caucus is alone supposed
to represent the orthodoxy of the party), the reason of a less

doctrinal order alluded to above, which prevents an independent candidate from having any chance of success: if he were to come forward in opposition to the nominee of the caucus, he would not get any canvassers outside his personal friends, all of them being already engaged, swept up by the caucuses of one party or the other. Even if the independent candidate managed to raise a battalion of his own, they would only be raw recruits facing an army of veterans.

This being the case the canvass confers, as a matter of right, peculiar claims on those who conduct it, especially on the "workers" who contribute their gratuitous services to the Organization. Being only too well aware of the importance of their part, these men claim an exceptional position in the moral hierarchy of the Organization, especially the working-men members of the caucus who compose the largest contingent of "workers." They refuse to concede this title to the big-wigs of the Association who take no part in the canvass, and, considering them as nonentities, call them, contemptuously, "ornamental members" or "House of Lords." This feeling is all the more readily accounted for because the task of canvassing is, in fact, often a highly disagreeable one. The canvasser is obliged to visit each of the voters assigned to him in their homes. Shopkeeper or workman, he can do it only of an evening, when he would prefer to rest after his day's labour. He has to go, maybe, into remote parts of the town, to wander about there in the darkness with a lantern. In this or that house there are perhaps big dogs ready to spring on the unexpected visitor. Their master does not always give him a better reception. The voter whom he comes to lecture does not care a fig for politics and insists on being let alone. Sometimes, on the other hand, the canvasser drops on a man who knows how to talk politics, and who, from a liking for the subject or simply to amuse himself, starts a discussion with him from which the emissary of the caucus retires, perhaps, defeated. Sometimes he has to put up with worse insults: he is snubbed, or turned into ridicule. These extreme cases, however, are not required to place the canvasser begging for votes too often in a humiliating predicament for a man conscious of his dignity, especially when it is borne in mind that over and over again he has to deal with people who are at the opposite pole to respectability. A good many persons, therefore, refuse to belong to the caucus in order not to have to canvass the "residuum." Nevertheless, in a certain number of places the principal dignitaries of the Association, beginning with the most respectable ones, set an example of duty; they canvass in person and even enlist their wives and their daughters, who devote themselves to the good cause by going from house to house with their sweetest smile to ask for votes. The consciousness of having discharged a great duty is not the only reward of the canvasser. Apart from those who, as the reader already knows, are paid in money, the bulk of the other canvassers are not swayed either by considerations of a sentimental order. The most important among the members of the caucus who "work," establish a claim to be brought on the Town Council by the Organization to which they have done good service, or even to be recommended for the honorary position of Magistrate. For a good many others the title of "worker" serves as a testimonial for getting one of the numerous small subordinate posts at the disposal of the municipalities in places where the party in question controls the Town Council. The small fry find their remuneration in the refreshments to which the canvassers are treated during election time on canvassing nights when they come in from their rounds.

If the party Organizations achieve a signal success with the canvass and if their most active members get some profit out of it for themselves, it is impossible to say as much of the electorate and of political manners in general. The voters are in many respects victims of the system of the canvass. In the first place, it is a source of great personal annoyance to them. As soon as election time begins, the voter becomes the prey of canvassers belonging to all the parties, of every condition and sex. The rule expressed by the saying "my house is my castle" is practically suspended during the whole duration of the canvass. There is not an hour in the daytime or in the evening when the voter is safe from the canvasser; the luckless possessor of a vote may be at dinner or on the point of going to bed, it is all the same to the worker of the Association. Just as the village peddler has all his travelling stock displayed on the table when he has barely crossed the threshold of the house, so the canvasser, without losing a moment, lays hold of his man and retails his claptrap to him.   It would be no use following the example of a voter in a metropolitan borough in whose window I have seen a placard with "No canvasser need apply"; the canvasser is a tenacious creature who is not to be got rid of so easily.

Interfered with in the proprieties of their private life, the voters are injured far more seriously by the practices of the canvass in their moral existence, in their capacity of men and of citizens.   The canvass is, in fact, a systematic attack on their dignity and their integrity.   Degrading himself, drain-ing, at times, the cup of humiliation to the dregs, the can-vasser degrades those before whom he lowers himself.   He strips them of the moral defence with which the Legislature has invested them.   By asking voters to give pledges in favour of this or that candidate, the law on secret voting is made a dead letter.   Won after a long and arduous struggle, the Ballot was intended to protect, in the political sphere, the in-dividual conscience against interested and corrupting attempts.   The canvass erects them into a system.   To extort the promise from the voters, the canvasser rarely appeals to their reason, whatever the official theory of the canvass may say, which represents the canvasser as a sort of travelling professor of political science, who brings it within everybody's reach by going from house to house to enlighten the civic faith of the voters.   In certain cases this may be true, though in an entirely relative sense: when he is confronted by an open-minded voter who wants to be convinced, the canvasser makes some display of reasoning, and does vouchsafe a certain amount of political argument and information if he has any.   But in the vast majority of cases, he addresses himself, not to the intelligence of the voters, but to their ignorance, to their credulity; he appeals to their least elevated and most easily roused feelings, such as vanity and self-love, which are worked on by low flattery, vulgar prejudices of class, of caste, of reli-gious sects, mean local spite, to the less reprehensible senti-ments of fear of the employer or foreman, of anxiety about the daily bread of the family, or, on the other hand, to shame-ful cupidity, to the base passions of personal interest.   When the canvasser does not act as an agent of corruption himself, he paves the way for it; he scatters its seeds among the voters as he goes along. Spreading demoralization around it, the canvass ultimately strikes at the whole political life of the country. Stepping down into the mire of the electorate, it lifts out of it elements which, left to themselves, would, for the most part, have remained in the depths of their civic indifference. It almost makes them the arbiters of the nation ; for when a large number of them shift from one side to the other, they turn the scales in favour of this or that political party.

IV

While conducting the election campaign with the time-honoured canvass, which it has developed and perfected, the Caucus not only does not abandon the new modes of action, of which it is the author or at least the responsible editor, but brings them up to the highest possible pressure. The most important of these methods is the stump; worked on parallel lines with the canvass, they complete one another. It would not be using too bold a metaphor to say that when election time begins every constituency is inundated with platform eloquence. From all points of the compass flock speakers of both sexes, especially at bye-elections (tolerably frequent in England), when they can be concentrated on a single place. The constituency is then literally invaded by two bodies of combatants containing a motley crew of Members of Parliament, "adopted candidates" of the district, secretaries and agents of neighbouring and distant Associations, professional lecturers, lady politicians, amateurs of every description. One and all set upon the electorate by speechifying from morning till night in covered enclosures, in parks or squares, in public places, at street-crossings, wherever and whenever a certain number of listeners can be got together. Eloquence is as much lavished on a small group of twenty persons as on a gathering of two thousand. Every evening there are several simultaneous meetings in different parts of the town, so much so that sometimes even the best-equipped newspapers run short of reporters for the speeches. In this monster concert the rival candidates are of course meant to take the part of first tenor. But if they have no voice, the position is by no means lost, others will sing for them; there is no lack of performers.

But candidates of this stamp are becoming rarer and rarer; they fail to get an engagement unless they are prepared to spend a handsome sum. Generally the candidates have a fair voice,— if not musical, at all events strong and shrill,— and they lead the stump in person with more or less *maestria*.

The immense oratorical efforts exerted during the election campaign are intended, not so much to bring conviction home to the mind as to strengthen the favourably disposed will, to provoke a thirst for victory, and drive it to the verge of passion, of frenzy, and to impress the crowd to the same purpose. The unceasing rattle of the torrent of words falling from the platform ends by plunging the more impressionable voter into a state of quasi-unconsciousness, in which he reproduces, like a hypnotized subject, all the gestures required; his head is crammed with phrases, with tirades, with exhortations, with invective taken in at the meetings, and it is almost a physical necessity for him to vent them on every one who comes near him. In a word, the meetings serve to turn on "enthusiasm," which is now more than ever the main preoccupation of the Organizations. Small gatherings, large meetings, demonstrations, torchlight processions, unharnessing of the horses which draw the candidate's carriage, all is intended to help to "raise enthusiasm" and to spread it by contagion. Many voters, in fact, are carried away by these material feats, which give them the semblance of power, of the superiority of numbers, the only one which they are capable of grasping. In reality the monster meetings and the demonstrations prove nothing at all; each party, aided by the experience of the local wire-pullers, succeeds in organizing "most enthusiastic" meetings, in getting "full houses." Even the overflow meetings, which seem to furnish such evident proof of the "enthusiasm" inspired by the candidate, are often only a deception. All the places in the hall are occupied beforehand by adherents of the party provided with tickets by the caucus, and when the interrupters and rowdies of the opposite camp arrive, another meeting is forthwith obligingly organized for them, and a few speakers held in reserve are told off to them, who "amuse" their audience while in the other room the candidate and his friends can talk at their ease, interrupted only by outbursts of "indescribable enthusiasm." The

rival party may produce the same effect.   Just as in the canvass the point was which of the two parties would be the
first to get hold of the indifferent voters, so here the whole
question is at which of the two fountain-heads of contagion the
latter will take a draught of "enthusiasm," and then follow
the fortunes of the supposed conquerors or "go for the winning horse," as is often said in England.   This turf expression, in fact, suits the occasion better than any other.   The
campaign of meetings, etc., which precedes the voting, no doubt
does plunge the population into a state of great excitement,
but the emotions aroused are decidedly of a rather sporting
character; it is not the consciousness of the public interests
at stake which produces them with the vast majority, but the
anxiety of the race-course.   Many a time at elections I fancied
myself more at the Derby (whereas on the Epsom Downs it
seemed to me that the fate of the State was being decided).
To the women and children the polling-day brings all the
excitement of a fair.   Standing in groups in the streets, with
rosettes or ribbons of the colour of the party to which their
husbands or their fathers belong, they shout, cheer, or hoot,
and wave their handkerchiefs as each election carriage goes by.
First of all comes the candidate, accompanied by his wife, driving about the town in an open landau, proceeding from one
committee-room to another like a general going along the
ranks when the battle is on the point of beginning.   Old and
young make themselves hoarse with shouting hurrah, with
giving three cheers for the candidate and another three for his
wife.   Then come the voters, who are brought up to the poll
often in their workaday dress, the butcher or the grocer in his
white apron, the chimney-sweep in his sooty habiliments.   On
the other hand, the horses and carriages are always made to
look smart, being adorned with the colours of the party and
with posters bearing final appeals couched in the tersest of
styles: "Vote for Smith and good wages," "Vote for Jones, the
working-man's friend," "Robinson and prosperity in trade forever."   The street urchins organize processions in honour of
the candidate of *their* party or against his rival, putting more
or less symbolism into the expression of their feelings.[1]   The

1 For instance, to show that the candidate of the opposite party, Mr. Smith,
an outsider, is only a carpet-bagger, the boys carry an old bag, taken perhaps

day must be made the most of, as on the following morning complete calm will once more reign, and the remembrance even of the election will fade away.

Side by side with the canvass and the stump an important share is assigned to "political advertising," which forms the last link in what may be called the trilogy of electoral action. The political printed matter completes the canvass and the stump by assuming a certain aspect of both. At one time it is meant, like the canvass, to act on the individual voter, and it consists of pamphlets and leaflets known by the generic name of political literature. At another it is addressed, like the stump, to the voters in a body, by means of posters. We are already acquainted with the nature of political literature. The principal distribution of this class of printed matter is made precisely at election time; small packets of it are forwarded by post to each voter, and stocks are kept in the committee-room for supplying all comers. Care is especially taken to circulate leaflets, among which a place of honour is given to sheets made up on the spot for the occasion, and containing appeals to particular groups of voters signed by personages known to them, manifestoes by the candidate, adorned perhaps with his portrait reproduced with more or less accuracy and art.

The posters in their endless variety of form and subject are a sort of quintessence of the election campaign, condensing and summing up the canvass and the stump for the least comprehensive minds. Solemn rhetoric, familiar language of the humorous order, rows of figures, sketches of sorts, caricatures with appropriate explanations, are all so many forms of instructing, arguing, attacking, abusing, slandering, of appealing to reason, to passions, to prejudices, to ignorance and credulity, of raising hopes or fears, of setting in motion egoism and personal interest. The latter is generally put forward in its most material aspect, reduced to its monetary expression, or to a still more primitive one when rudimentary minds and simple characters like the rural populations have to be dealt

out of the dust-heap, with the label " Smith's bag," in procession about the streets.

with.   As may be seen from the poster reproduced below,[1] the victory or the defeat of the candidate is presented to them as a question of more or less bacon in the household.

V

Does the appeal addressed to the voters' own interest dangle before them only the indirect advantages which are to accrue to them as citizens, as an ultimate consequence of their vote; or does it also include offers of direct and immediate personal gratification?   In a word, is corruption in the legal sense of the term resorted to in the election campaigns managed by the caucuses?   In the account given of their action some passing allusions or insinuations were made with reference to this subject.   They require an explanation.

It is well known that bribery has long been the general feature and the curse of English political life.   In course of time, and owing to the modifications introduced in the composition of the electorate, it changed its character, but it con-

---

[1] The following poster is from a rural constituency in Lincolnshire : —

WORKING-MEN
DON'T BE MISLED

C. (*name of the Conserva-* DEAR SUGAR
tive candidate) LOW WAGES
  LESS BACON

P. (*Liberal candidate*)
  CHEAP ALLOTMENTS.   FREE EDUCATION
  LOCAL MANAGEMENT OF CHARITIES

EVERY ONE WHO THINKS THAT A WORKING-MAN
SHOULD HAVE A
FAIR WEEK'S WAGE
FOR A
FAIR WEEK'S WORK
SHOULD
VOTE FOR P.
THE LIBERAL CANDIDATE.

Remember, if Mr. P. is elected, he will devote himself to IMPROVING YOUR CONDITION and that of the country generally.   There's no selfishness about Mr. P.   Be sure and put your cross against the bottom name on the voting paper.

tinued to exist in spite of the laws enacted for its prevention
or repression. As far back as before 1832, in the days of the
rotten boroughs, parliamentary seats were knocked down to
the highest bidder, or bought from the oligarchical municipal
corporations which were in possession of the franchise. In
places with a larger number of voters the latter were bought
individually, that is to say, those who were for sale. The
abolition of rotten boroughs and the extension of the suffrage
brought about by the great Reform Bill have generalized this
last method. The Corrupt Practices Prevention Act of 1854
(17 & 18 Vic., c. 102), with its minute provisions and severe
penalties, made no change in political manners. The new
and greater extension of the suffrage in 1867, which was to
make bribery difficult by reason of the excessive number of
persons who would have to be bought, has not been attended
with better results. On the contrary, the new electors belonging to the less fortunate classes have only swelled the contingent of voters who are ready to sell themselves. The effect
simply was that prices went down with a run, especially after
the Ballot Act of 1872, which, by introducing secret voting,
made it impossible to ascertain whether the voter who had taken
a bribe had really carried out his bargain, and therefore reduced
the value of the promise that was bought. The exorbitant
prices which used to be paid just at the close of the poll to
electors whose vote might turn the scale, have passed into the
region of history and almost of legend. But, on the other
hand, the milder or disguised forms of bribery, such as the distribution of silver coins and of refreshments in solid and liquid
form, or the fictitious employment of numerous voters under
the designation of canvassers, messengers, clerks, bill-posters,
etc., had increased to a considerable extent. In consequence,
at the general election of 1868 corrupt practices prevailed to
a greater degree than at all the elections of the preceding half-
century. The election of 1874, in spite of the first application
of the Ballot, was no purer, and that of 1880 surpassed them
both in illicit expenditure incurred by the candidates. It was
estimated at as much as £3,000,000.[1] This was the first
general election in which the Caucus, founded at Birmingham,
took part, and its participation was thoroughgoing, extending

[1] Cf. *Hansard*, Vol. CCXXIX, p. 1672.

to acts of corruption as well.   It will be recollected that on
its appearance on the scene the Caucus had announced, somewhat grandiloquently, that it was going to purify political
life, and it was undoubtedly sincere in its aspirations.   But
when brought face to face with reality, a number of Associations fell into the old practices.   In a good many places
the election-mongers of the old régime joined the caucuses and
slipped even into their executive committees, where they acted
as tempters and suggested recourse to the time-honoured
methods on pretence of making the triumph of the good cause
more secure.   Again, the "Man in the Moon,"[1] the classic
agent of electoral corruption, was only too ready to recommence
his operations and had no scruples about offering his services.
They were accepted more often, far more often, than was
desirable for the reform of political manners.   If the Conservatives of Birmingham were to be believed, the Liberal
Association of that town, the celebrated prototype of the
Caucus, had been the first to resort to corrupt practices.[2]   The
charge was not proved, perhaps because no opportunity had
presented itself of ascertaining if it was true.   But such
opportunities did occur in several other constituencies, owing
to the petitions presented against the return of members elected
in 1880.   The disclosures made at the hearings seriously compromised some Liberal Associations, as well as, by the way,
some Conservative Organizations.[3]   They also established the
fact that the Associations which dabbled in electoral corruption
were able, thanks to their collective and anonymous character,
to practise it under far more dangerous conditions than prevailed in the old days.   The masters of the art sheltered themselves behind the Associations with a coolness which had a

[1] At one place a mysterious person used to arrive with cash, known as the
"Man in the Moon," who approached at nightfall and was at once met with
"What news from the moon?"   The nickname of the "man in the moon,"
alluding to mysterious beings, came to be applied generally to secret agents
for bribery.

[2] Cf. the letter of the Vice-President of the Conservative Association of
Birmingham in the *Times* of April 21, 1880, in which he says: "This [secret
bribery and treating] has been done at all elections by the Liberals since they
introduced the Caucus into Birmingham, not excepting the late election."

[3] Cf. the enquiries into electoral corruption at Bewdley, Boston, Canterbury,
Chester, Macclesfield, Sandwich, etc. (*Blue Books*, 1881, Vols. XXVI, XXVII,
XXIX, XXXI).

dash alike of cynicism and of ingenuousness; for instance, having got the candidate and his election agent to sever their connection with the Association by means of official resignations, they quietly indulged in corrupt practices, in the belief that as the former had ceased to belong to the Association they could not be held responsible for its acts however illicit, or for the manœuvres of its numerous members.[1]

On the other hand, it is only just to point out that the Associations were still more often victims of the prevailing corruption; they were constantly exposed to interested offers and requests which they would have been glad to decline if they could have done so without endangering the success of their candidates. Many voters were in the habit of joining the Associations in the hope of establishing a claim to fictitious employment as messengers, distributers of handbills, etc., when the elections came round. The pretensions of a crowd of people who claimed to have "helped" or "worked" in the election had the effect of swelling the candidate's expenditure to an unheard-of degree. When, therefore, in consequence of the scandals of the 1880 elections, the Government submitted a new and much more stringent Bill against corrupt practices to the House, the Liberal Caucus gave very serious and useful help towards putting it into shape, and its co-operation was all the more sincere because the realization of the objects aimed at by the new Act was in its personal interest, so to speak. In the war which the Birmingham Caucus was waging on the moderate Liberals throughout the country, the Whigs, whose ranks had already been broken all along the line, remained standing here and there, thanks to their great wealth, which gave them the advantage at the elections over their poorer rivals of the Radical Caucus. The latter therefore might have been able to fight on more equal terms if electoral expenditure were reduced, spon-

[1] The report of the parliamentary commissioners on the Chester election establishes this peculiar good faith of the bribers: "It was arranged that the candidates and their agents should sever themselves from the Liberal Association with a view of escaping from responsibility for the acts of the members of so large a body. . . . The severance was thought so complete, and on the announcement of the dissolution of Parliament, a general notion seems to have been abroad in the city that the Liberal Association might bribe and treat without endangering the seats of the candidates" (*Blue Books*, 1881, Vol. XXVI, p. vi).

taneously or under compulsion, to a reasonable figure. The
new Corrupt Practices Act, passed in 1883,[1] made this possible
by the two great changes which it introduced: it prohibited
the fictitious employment of voters for the election campaign
and fixed a maximum amount of expenses beyond which a
candidate cannot go without being unseated.[2]   To enforce
these provisions, the Act added another innovation, a clause
forbidding the making of any payment connected with the
election otherwise than by an "election agent" formally
appointed for that purpose by the candidate and bound to
prove by his accounts that the election expenditure had not
exceeded the legal maximum.   Expenses incurred on behalf
of the candidate by any other person or body had consequently
to be entered in the election agent's account, on pain of being
treated as incurred with a corrupt object.

This provision as well as the general very severe tone of the
Act seemed to threaten everybody taking part in electioneering.   Some people hoped, while others were afraid that the
caucuses would not be able to work under the new law.   A few
Associations, which evidently had a heavy burden of electoral
sins on their conscience, were so frightened that they put an
end to themselves by dissolution.   But experience very soon
showed the groundlessness of both hopes and fears.   The
caucuses work perfectly well and, while continually sailing
very near the Corrupt Practices Act, do not run much risk of
losing the fruit of their labours with the unseating of their
candidate through their dubious practices.   For it is extremely
difficult to furnish legal proof of the candidate's responsibility
for acts of the Association which he has not instigated or known
of beforehand or which are not formally connected with his
election.   Strictly speaking, the candidate comes into being
only with the election period, whereas the Association has a
permanent existence, independent of the candidatures which
arise at indefinite intervals; it acts on the electorate perhaps
for years before the candidate is selected.   Can the latter be
made responsible for the previous doings of the Caucus, and

[1] 46 & 47 Vic., c. 56.
[2] This amount varies, according to the number of voters in the constituency,
from £350 to £920 in the boroughs, and from £650 to £1790 in the counties,
plus £100 for the candidate's petty expenses.

would he not be able to set up a convincing *alibi?* With all the more reason, can the expenses which the Association has incurred in preparing the ground for the eventual candidature be included in the maximum amount of expenditure allowed to the candidate? Without replying to these questions, the law has reproduced the old provision as to the candidate's responsibility for the illegal practices committed by his agents, while leaving the fact of agency to be determined by the courts in each particular instance. But the question of agency has always been one of the thorniest in electoral jurisprudence, and the collective and anonymous character of the Caucus Associations certainly does not make it easier to bring home agency to them in the absence of express provisions in the law. The very loose legal definition of the relations between the Associations and the candidates [1] has therefore not stood the test of experience under the new law better than it did before, and altogether the Associations, owing to their permanent existence, rather paralyse, to some extent, the effect of the Act than are held in check by it.

[1] The law omitted to give a stricter definition of the relations between the Associations and the candidates from the above points of view almost deliberately. During the discussion of the Act of 1883 urgent, even vehement, representations were made to the Legislature to take special measures against the caucuses. The attention of the Government was drawn to the fact that the Bill brought in by it did not touch the expenditure made by the Associations with a corrupt object, independently of the candidates, and previously to the election; that the draft contained no provisions against clubs started with an almost nominal subscription, and provided with billiard-rooms, dining-rooms, etc., with the sole object of obtaining the votes of their members for the party; a demand was made that the Associations, or at all events their managing committees, should be punished for illicit acts committed by the members of these Associations; it was actually proposed even that every candidate who came forward as the nominee of a political organization should be made liable to the penalties attaching to corruption. These proposals and several others of an analogous character, coming mostly from members of the Opposition and accompanied by virulent attacks on the Radical caucuses, coupled with the name of their patron, Mr. Chamberlain, who was a member of the Cabinet, had not disposed the Government to accept the amendments moved; it rejected them as useless or suggested that they should be examined at a later stage, no doubt in the belief that the Bill as it stood already increased the stringency of the law too much to be overloaded with fresh details which, perhaps, would not readily bear a legal construction (cf. *Hansard*, Vol. CCLXXIX, pp. 1667, 1670, 1686, 1687, 1695, Speeches of Stuart Wortley, Joseph Cowen, Cecil Raikes, Sir R. Cross; Vol. CCLXXX, pp. 392, 395, 597, 610–615, 1459, Speeches of J. Cowen, O'Donnell, Stanley Leighton, Randolph Churchill; Vol. CCLXXXI, pp. 311, 1133, 1142, Speeches of Lord George Hamilton and Newdegate).

This state of things becomes manifest in the application of the law, firstly with regard to the provision which places a statutory limit on electoral expenditure in order to cut off the supplies of corruption and which is consequently, as it were, the keystone of the Act. A considerable amount of the expenses which promote a candidature, but which having caused the legal maximum to be exceeded might have invalidated the election, can be incurred exclusively for the Association in the normal exercise of its functions. The Organizations can pass off illicit outlay in the guise of expenditure as legitimate to all appearance as, for instance, that relating to the making up of the register. The payment of "workers" at elections being prohibited, the caucuses can pay them in anticipation by nominally entrusting the future election canvassers with the registration canvass, remuneration for which is not forbidden by the law. In reality, in the vast majority of cases the number of registration canvassers is not unduly swollen, but in several places it is so, and sometimes even to a scandalous degree; for instance, hundreds of persons are engaged who are supposed to take the electoral census of an average-sized borough, or this operation is carried on throughout the whole year by instructing paid emissaries to call on the voters again and again on pretence of collecting information for checking the lists.[1] The Association can embark on preliminary expenditure for the benefit of the candidate with all the less scruple that the courts are very ready to accept the period in which it had been incurred as the criterion of "election expenses" and to limit it, if not to election time in the strict sense of the words, at all events to a lapse of time immediately preceding that period.[2]

Even before this very indulgent ruling was laid down subse-

---

[1] Cf. *Blue Book*, 1893, already quoted, pp. 84, 91, 92.

[2] "I am not quite satisfied that the constructive doctrine of agency is to be carried back to a period long before the actual contest is imminent . . ." declared one of the judges in his decision on the election at Haggerston (*Blue Books*, 1896, Controverted Elections, Part I, p. 30). Similarly in an election case in Scotland, one of the judges expressed the opinion that the incriminated period "was a period at least not much anterior, I will not say to the date of nomination, but to the group or series of events which immediately precede the nomination, and which, as we all know, begin in the case of a general election with the announcement of the Dissolution, and in the case of a bye-election with the announcement of the vacancy " (*Ibid.*, Part II, p. 36).

quent to the last general election (of 1895), several Organizations hit upon various expedients for establishing in a tangible manner the solution of continuity between their acts and expenses and those of the election period. Sometimes the "election agent" of the candidate buys from the Association its canvass books and other information constituting the material of war accumulated for years back, for the modest sum of five or six pounds, which he enters with scrupulous accuracy in the account of the expenditure to be eventually submitted to the authorities. Some Associations resort to a more radical device to throw the courts off the scent in regard to the continuity of the electioneering operations carried on before and after the election period; they lie low during the whole of this period; the moment it begins they "suspend their activity" and disband their followers, who fight as free lances. Acting inversely, but always with the same object of guarding against the danger of agency, of getting rid of the continuity in the acts committed for the benefit of the candidate, certain Associations come forward only in a semi-official way with their candidates before election time begins. They do not "adopt" a candidate beforehand, they only make "overtures to him in view of the next vacancy which may occur," and he, without giving a reply, visits the constituency repeatedly, under the auspices of the Association, in a series of meetings and "social gatherings" in order to feel the public pulse and make up his mind after full enquiry. The announcement of the election puts an end to his hesitation; he accepts and is adopted. Up to that time he was only a "prospective candidate," whose acts could not bind the "actual candidate," who is a different person in law. The latest judicial decisions have almost sanctioned this status of "prospective candidate" created by the party Organizations and enjoying every immunity.[1]

Thus, through the interposition of the Associations, disbursements for the election may not be considered as "election expenditure," and the candidate to whom they would be chargeable can be one without coming out as such.

The great preventive measure for the limitation of expendi-

[1] *Blue Book*, 1896, quoted above, Part I, pp. 7, 10 (Lancaster election); Part II, pp. 32, 36 (Counties of Elgin and Nairn election).

ture not having produced its full effect, the repression and suppression of actual corrupt practices has not succeeded either,
and here again the Associations have had, and still have, something to do with it.   At the outset, following on the elections
of 1885 and 1886, the new Act seemed to have the effect of
those marvellous remedies which act like a charm, but gradually it became apparent that nothing of the kind had really
taken place, that the forms alone had changed.   The traditional purchase of votes as a commodity, already on the
wane before 1883, has considerably decreased, but it still goes
on and not without the co-operation of the caucuses, although
it should be added at once that the Associations as such are
far from being an important factor in this method of corruption.   The Act of 1883 has no doubt purged the caucuses
of their corrupt elements, but there are still some remaining
here and there, sometimes even among the chairmen or other
high dignitaries of the Associations, who make themselves
indispensable by their great qualities as workers.   The "Man
in the Moon," although growing more and more rare, cannot
yet be classed among the fossil mammifers.   He is generally
taken from the ranks of third or fourth rate turfmen.   Regular
agents of the Caucus sometimes "work" in conjunction with
them.   For instance, of the cloud of caucus-men who descend
from far and wide on the constituency in which a parliamentary election is about to be held, all do not spend their time in
charming the crowd with their eloquence from the top of
waggonettes or in giving their assistance in the offices of the
local Association and in the candidate's committee-rooms,
some of them accept "special missions" — they go and "see
somebody."   They have no need to resort to the mysterious
practices of the "Man in the Moon;" as representatives of
Associations with a legitimate status, they attract no attention
even in broad daylight; like so many other politicians, they
have just come to "help in the election."

But the real changes have taken place not so much in the
character of the agents as in the forms and modes of corruption, changes to some of which the Caucus has contributed in
a special degree.   Corruption has become less direct, bargains
for the purchase and sale of votes have diminished and made
way for more disguised methods hinted at rather than expressly

stated. At the same time, the mode of operation has been altered: the individual corruption of former days, with the numerous special negotiations implied by it, has been succeeded, to a great extent, by wholesale corruption, so to speak, which the vast increase in the electorate has made well-nigh imperative. The two time-honoured types of English electoral corruption, bribery and treating, adapted themselves to the new state of affairs. Thus bribery has given way to practices which may be described as corruption by consequence, and of which the most refined is the betting which takes place on parliamentary candidates as on race-horses. A, partisan of a certain candidate, makes a bet with B that the candidate in question will be beaten; to win the bet B makes a point of voting for that candidate, Q.E.D. This ingenious plan soon became a lever for lifting a considerable number of voters at a single blow. A partisan of, let us say, the Conservative candidate promises a large sum to the leading man of the betting community in the event of this candidate being returned. The other thereupon lays on him in all the bets which he makes. Besides, the great authority which he enjoys among betting men makes them take the name of the Conservative candidate as an excellent tip; they hasten to back their leading man's favourite, and of course all vote solid for him, and try to make their friends do the same. The Q.E.D. is at once multiplied by the total number of all these persons, and a single "special mission" discharged with tact has been sufficient to bring about this result.

The election house-to-house canvass, which used to be one of the great opportunities for bribery, now constitutes only an indirect channel of corruption, it only affords a clue which will perhaps be followed up afterwards by the emissaries of the Organization. In the present day the unpaid canvasser, a member of the caucus, a devout partisan, often has too much respect for the law to offer money or its equivalent, but he makes a note of the voters who are open to particular attentions and gives their names to the wire-pullers of the inner circle. The latter find suitable intermediaries to determine these voters, perhaps by means of a drink or two, perhaps by some other civility. With this object a good many canvassers of the caucus draw up in the course of their visits a list similar to that which has been preserved for the edification of posterity by the trial of an election petition: "A wants change of air. B very favourable, but poor. C promises, but wants a little drop. D — wife wants liquoring up." [1]

Standing "little drops," "liquoring up" and other gratifications of the same kind (known by the generic term of "treating") increased in importance in proportion as bribery became more difficult to practise, but they could not, however, be carried out with advantage in the old rudimentary fashion. The voters being now too numerous not only to be bought, but even to be entertained one by one, treating called for a new *modus operandi* of a more comprehensive character. The plan resorted to by the party Organizations for "working on the social tendencies of human nature" happened to be admirably adapted to the new requirements, and they became, not generally, but often, an instrument of the collective corruption which the new cónditions of political life demanded. In the series of judgments on the election petitions of 1892, the judges have brought out very clearly the two terms of this equation, that is to say, the newly arisen importance of corrupt treating and the tendency of the party Organizations to practise it. "It must be borne in mind," says the judgment on the Hexham election,[2] "that treating is the particular form of corruption which can be practised with advantage at the present time. Now that the constituencies are so large it becomes impossible successfully to bribe. . . . But with reference to treating it is far otherwise; a very small amount is sufficient to procure a great deal of popularity, because there is in every constituency now, looking at the very wide extension of the franchise, a considerable number of men who do not make politics their serious business at all, or even attach much importance to one side or the other.[3] They are perfectly ready to vote for the man who is popular; and if by reason of treats and picnics and things of that kind you can produce a general feeling that the particular candidate is a good fellow, and that he is willing to give a poor man a supper

---

[1] *Hansard*, Vol. CCLXXIX, p. 1662.

[2] *Blue Books*, 1893, Controverted Elections (Judgments).

[3] Or, in the words of a Birmingham working-man, who summed up the situation to me in a more graphic way: "Politics is an abstraction, while a quart of ale is a tangible thing."

or a treat, or an entertainment of this kind and the other, and that gets generally spread over the division, an enormous amount of popularity is produced by that which, as against an Association which did not resort to the same sort of thing, would have a very large effect when the polling came to take place." [1] On the other hand, the Associations, while having quite a legitimate purpose, "are liable always to be diverted towards illegitimate means, and that is the danger of them." [2] The "social meetings" lavished by the Organizations give substance and consistency to this danger, not that, as the judges remark, smoking-concerts, conversaziones, etc., are in themselves necessarily corrupting, but because they "easily degenerate into corrupt treating," and attract corruptible persons to the Associations by the bait of refreshments. [3] While displaying great severity [4] towards Associations convicted of practices of this kind, the judges do not always push the proposition laid down by them to its extreme logical consequences, at one time declaring that this "practice of giving entertainments, picnics, dances, suppers, teas, sports, and what not, *would* certainly amount to corrupt treating *if* indulged in by the candidate," [5] at another, that the opinion cannot be endorsed that every act done by the Association and its immediate agents (after election time has begun and the candidate has been nominated) must be taken to be the act of the candidate, as if it were done by an agent of his. [6] So that, if the Association and the candidate only take care not to compromise themselves together too openly, to be prudent in their intercourse, it can screen him from the consequences of electoral corruption, even

---

[1] *Blue Books*, 1893, just quoted, p. 6.

[2] *Ibid.*, p. 81, Rochester election.

[3] *Ibid.*, pp. 81, 84.

[4] The later decisions, given on the election petitions of 1895, are not marked by this severity, and take a much more indulgent view of the smoking-concerts, in which the candidate or his friends of the Association supply drinks to electors who would eventually have to vote for or against him. "One has heard," says one of the judges, "even of very learned societies of whom it has been said that, with all their learning, with all the wisdom of their lectures, they would not entirely succeed, unless there was a little conversazione, ladies being present, and tea, coffee, and other amenities, which to these people are, perhaps, at least as agreeable as the beer is to the others" (*Blue Book*, 1896, quoted above, Part I, p. 95). Cf. the same *Blue Book*, Part II, pp. 10, 11.

[5] *Blue Books*, 1893, p. 11.   [6] *Ibid.*, p. 62.

should it expose a few of its members, and maybe the least important ones whom the judges perhaps would not have the heart to condemn, to the rigour of the law.[1]   The fact is, that neither the law courts nor the Legislature in England have been able to entirely divest themselves of the old conception which looked on a seat in Parliament, if not as a commodity for the Member's personal use, which has only to be honestly paid for, at all events as a prize which is competed for and of which it would be unjust to deprive the competitor who has won the race if neither he nor his agent have employed or caused the employment of fraudulent methods for outstripping their opponents. Matters of essentially public concern are influenced by considerations belonging to the private sphere, down to the legal procedure in electoral corruption cases, which follows the rules of the civil action where the beaten candidate is the plaintiff and his more fortunate rival the defendant.[2]

The cases of corrupt treating brought home to the Associations by the judges are not, it is true, very numerous, but that is because corrupt doings rarely see the light in England, proof of them being extremely difficult to obtain and the legal expenses of an election petition enormous, as much as £5000. Besides, in party circles it has never been considered quite fair to present these petitions; for the parties all more or less resort to the practices which come within the reach of the law, and they are not forgetful of the adage *hodie mihi cras tibi.* As for the authorities, it has just been remarked that they are in no way concerned if the parties interested do not come forward, even if the electoral operations were marked by the most shameless corruption.   This being so, the cases brought to light by the courts may be taken not as isolated facts, but as in the nature of types.

But apart from these cases, of rare or frequent occurrence, patent or not, which are liable to legal penalties, the Associa-

[1] Cf. (*Blue Books*, 1893, Vol. XXV, p. 85) the grounds of the judgment in the Rochester election, with reference to the responsibility of the representatives of the Constitutional Association, and of one of them in particular, Mr. W., " who has undoubtedly been — I will not say the catspaw, although I think I might almost be justified in saying it — but who has been the agent of persons behind, who are far worse than himself.   I hesitate to report a man who is in such a position as that."

[2] The " Public Prosecutor " has the right to intervene, but only in a collateral way, like a third party in a lawsuit.

tions certainly practise the collective treating, which easily evades the clutches of the law to a far greater extent, especially through the "social meetings" which they get up in the interval between the elections. From a legal point of view these but rarely contain the *technical* elements of a breach of the law; but as regards the demoralizing effects which they produce on the somewhat too "sociable" voters, the result is the same. At the approach of the elections the satisfactions provided for the "social tendencies" of this section of the electorate are already a thing of the past and cannot be detected. The Organizations go to work exactly like the domestic poisoners who administer arsenic in anodyne doses for months or years until they get the better of the gradually enfeebled organism; and then when the medical officer makes the *post mortem* examination, he finds nothing or next to nothing to set the public prosecutor in motion.

In a still more disguised fashion does the Association practise a sort of corruption on the voters from day to day and for years together, by procuring various favours for them, by trying to find them places, work, getting patients into hospitals, obtaining letters of introduction to persons who can be useful to them. The Association, in the words of a caucus secretary, is the "freemasonry of the humble voter." The distribution of help in money by charitable persons has for a long time past been often made to serve party purposes, especially in Tory circles, where an electoral following was secured by "a *judicious* use of charities." These practices have met with valuable support from the Organization of the Caucus, which in many places cleverly controls the dispensation of charity with a political object, by drawing, with its unerring professional knowledge, the attention of charitable coreligionists to needy persons, by getting lady adherents of the party to visit the sick poor, etc. Later on, the candidate of the party reaps this crop, discreetly sown by or with the help of the Association, in the form of votes at the election.

But the candidate does not always leave everything to the Association; he also often embarks on preliminary expenditure, to capture the voters in advance. "Prospective" candidate or even only candidate *in petto*, he quietly steps through the meshes of the Corrupt Practices Act and begins at an early

stage to load the constituency with his favours.   In addition
to the, so to speak, obligatory subscriptions to local charities
and others, which constitute "nursing the constituency," a
good many candidates, well supplied with the sinews of war,
present their constituents *in spe* with a park or a museum,
with land for building working-men's clubs, or grounds for
athletic sports, swimming baths, etc.   These tactics, which
have long been resorted to and are known as "salting the
constituency," are supplemented by concerts, evening-parties,
teas, and picnics provided by the Association.

Finally, passing from the material sphere to an apparently
more elevated one, the candidate and the Association unite in
an *ad captandum* operation which is the climax of indirect
and collective corruption, while quite beyond the reach of the
arm of the law.   This consists of the offers and pledges to
legislate in favour of particular interests, of a certain social
class or of a certain professional group.   It has often been
pointed out that these practices simply take the place of the
individual corruption of the pre-democratic era.   In fact, they
are another instance of a system of bargaining in which votes
are bought by promises which are not less corrupting because
they are often fallacious.   In vouching for these promises,
the party Organizations give the final touch to their share in
the disguised and wholesale corruption to the development of
which they had contributed.

VI

The electoral campaign, the principal phases of which I have
just described, occurs only once in several years, when a new
Parliament has to be elected (except in cases when a constituency has to fill up a seat unexpectedly, owing to the death or
resignation of the Member or his elevation to the Peerage).
But the Organizations by no means suspend hostilities in the
interval; not only do they perfect their armaments, and in
general continue their warlike preparations, but every year at
a fixed date they engage in contests with the enemy, which
are a sort of general rehearsal of the great battle of the parliamentary elections.   These encounters take place at the annual

municipal elections, in which local questions almost invariably give way to a passage of arms between Liberals and Conservatives. It will be remembered how the Birmingham Caucus by "widening the idea of Liberalism," developed this custom. The Caucus, however, did not make an innovation. The municipal elections in a good many English boroughs had for a long time, one might almost say from time immemorial, been tainted with political considerations. Under the old régime the oligarchical municipal corporations which possessed the parliamentary franchise were engrossed in their political privileges, which they turned to account, like a stock-in-trade, for the benefit of their members, and entirely neglected the municipal interests of their boroughs. They were purely and simply political machines at the disposal of a party or of a great family, of a patron, who bought them. The choice of the members of the corporation, the municipal administration, the current expenditure, even the control of the police which is supposed to protect all citizens indiscriminately, and the dispensation of public charity, were subordinated to the one idea of establishing or perpetuating the ascendency of a party or the political influence of a patron. The great enquiry made by the Royal Commission of 1834 on the working of municipal institutions threw a flood of light on the flagrant abuses of this system, of "this perversion of municipal privilege to political objects."[1] After the Reform Bill of 1832, which extended the parliamentary suffrage and abolished the pocket boroughs, and the municipal reform of 1835, which entrusted municipal administration to the large body of ratepayers, it became impossible to extract the parliamentary vote from the municipal privilege with the same facility, but the exploitation of the latter for the benefit of the former was far from being at an end. The municipal vote, even when exercised by a considerable number of electors, being easier to secure, owing to its smaller importance and its local limitation, the election-mongers, who were on the lookout for parliamentary suffrages, fastened on this vote, and

[1] Report on Municipal Corporations in England and Wales, *Blue Books*, 1835, Vol. XXXIII, p. 34, § 73. Cf. also §§ 76, 77, 121; Appendix, Part I (*Blue Books*, Vol. XXXIV), pp. 14, 440, 530; Part II, pp. 916, 999, 1033; Part III, p. 1958; Part IV, pp. 2094, 2111, 2174, 2486, 2498, 2499, 2538, 2547, etc.

in most of the boroughs they fought the municipal elections
on political lines, arraying the voters as Whigs and Tories,
and thus preparing the order of the parliamentary battles
beforehand.   In consequence it became the custom to bring
the electoral corruption, which was the great lever of English
electoral life, to bear on the municipal elections.   The voter
whose municipal vote was bought considered himself in a way
bound in honour to vote for the same political party at the
parliamentary elections, so much so that the rival party did
not even try to buy his parliamentary vote.[1]   The local election agents therefore had a saying that " £10 spent at a
municipal is better and more advantageous than £100 spent
at the parliamentary contest." [2]   Where the political parties
were evenly matched, as in Lancashire, for instance, politics
was the rule in municipal elections and with politics corruption.   On the other hand, in a good many boroughs politics
were not imported into the municipal elections, even in large
towns like Bradford, for instance; [3] but directly the plan of
municipal elections on party lines was adopted in a borough,
corruption took up its permanent abode there.[4]

The improvement of political manners began to tell on this

[1] " The bribe received at a municipal election is a sort of consideration for
his giving a vote to the same political party at the parliamentary election "
(Report from the Select Committee on the Corrupt Practices Prevention Act,
Blue Books, 1860, Vol. X, p. 16).   " You bribe a man at the municipal election,
and he has some sort of gratitude toward you, perhaps, or you expect it, and
you secure his vote at the general election " (Ibid., p. 259).

[2] From the evidence of the principal agent of the Conservative party, Rose,
given before the Select Committee referred to above.   The same witness said
in his deposition: " The real nursery of the evil (of corruption) is in the
municipal contests; and these oft-recurring contests have led to the establishment of what I might almost term an organized system of corruption in the
municipal boroughs throughout the kingdom, which provides a machinery
ready made to hand, available when the parliamentary contests arrive "
(Ibid., p. 90).

[3] Report from the Select Committee on Parliamentary and Municipal Elections, Blue Books, 1868–1869, Vol. VIII, § 2795.

[4] Cf. by way of example the deposition relating to Windsor, which states
how the borough, at one time " perfectly pure," even before 1835, under the
régime of close corporations, became corrupt in consequence of the introduction of politics into municipal elections: " The system of corruption was
introduced for the purpose of one political party getting the predominance.
I do not hesitate to say that I trace the whole political demoralization, if it be
so in our borough, entirely to that system affecting the virtue of the constituency " (Ibid., §§ 749–754).

state of things, and the habit of applying the divisions of political parties to municipal elections was growing less common and was, perhaps, about to gradually become extinct.[1] But at this point the Caucus appeared on the scene, and it gave the old practice a fresh lease of life; it raised it to the level of a principle justifiable by the general welfare and even to be founded on reason. "Political principle, where it is sincere," declared Mr. Chamberlain in his *apologia* for the Caucus, "is to a great extent a prevalent habit of mind — the Conservative being naturally inclined to keep things as they are for fear they should be made worse, and the Liberal eagerly embracing change in the hope of making them better. This permanent distinction shows itself as much in municipal as in national affairs; it affects our judgment and conduct whether we are considering the removal of nuisances or the disestablishment and the disendowment of the English Church. It should also be remembered that the exclusion from local affairs of the higher issue only leaves the door open to lower influences. If the battle be not fought on political grounds, there will none the less be party divisions, though these will turn on personal claims or petty local objects. Men are no longer chosen because they are Liberals or Conservatives, — in other words, because they belong to one or other of the great orders of political thought, — but because they are popular with a faction, or because they will promote some sectional object which interests an active clique; and in this way the administration of the affairs of a great community sinks to the level of an unintelligent and selfish parochialism."[2] The reader will recollect the success with which the Birmingham Caucus "widened Liberalism" by introducing politics into all the local elections, as well as the grievances of the Conservatives ousted from the town council. He will also remember that at the time of the foundation of the Liberal Federation several delegates who attended the open-

---

[1] ". . . The thing is breaking up rather more now; it is gradually getting less" (Report from the Select Committee on Parliamentary and Municipal Elections, *Blue Books*, 1868–1869, Vol. VIII, § 142).

". . . less political excitement in connection with the municipal elections in recent years; desire to enter the town council irrespectively of politics" (*Ibid.*, §§ 1053–1058).

[2] *The Caucus*, p. 19.

ing meeting took strong exception to the practice favoured by the Birmingham Caucus of converting the municipal elections into a political contest. But before long, at the instigation of the caucuses, the example of Birmingham was followed in most of the English boroughs, and with the same object of making municipal elections a preparation for the parliamentary elections, of setting up in the mind of the voter a psychological continuity between his municipal vote and his parliamentary suffrage. Under the old system it was established by means of the corruption which appealed to the feeling of honour and gratitude of the person bribed; for this peculiar ethics was substituted the no less peculiar logic that it was absurd to be guided by certain considerations at municipal elections and by other considerations at parliamentary elections. It is true that a number of good citizens who were outside the Caucus also preferred the political order of battle in municipal elections. They no doubt rejected Mr. Chamberlain's singular theory, according to which a man who wants to preserve the establishment of the Church of England cannot help wishing to keep the dirt in the streets and public places; they were aware of the fact, admitted even by a good many representatives of the Caucus,[1] that there are plenty of Conservatives who have very liberal ideas on the subject of municipal administration; but they held, in agreement with Mr. Chamberlain, that municipal elections conducted on a political basis would lift the contest above wretched parochial squabbles and personal jealousy.

These hopes were destined to disappointment. In the meanwhile each year marked a fresh stage in the custom which was transforming municipal elections into a battle of political parties. It often met with opposition; in not a few towns the Caucus had to return to the charge more than once before it succeeded in establishing it. On my first long provincial tour (in 1889) I found it already in vogue in all the chief places I visited from London northwards up to the Tyne country. At that time this was a sort of frontier between political municipalities and non-political municipalities.

---

[1] One of my correspondents among the representatives of the Liberal Caucus expressed himself as follows on this subject: " Many so-called Tories are quite as Liberal in local politics as some so-called Liberals."

Farther north, and especially in Scotland, the mixing up of politics with municipal matters was vehemently repudiated. There were barely a few Scotch boroughs which formed an exception. As a rule, people followed, as some of my correspondents or interlocutors phrased it, the "Scotch principle according to which local affairs ought to be considered as non-political."[1] If the Liberals are to be believed, the Tories, who were in a minority in Scotland, sometimes secretly infringed the rule by voting at municipal elections for their political coreligionists, but, at all events, in public no one put forward the Birmingham doctrine. At the present time (in 1896), after an interval of a few years, the situation is completely changed: politics in local elections are now the rule in all the important towns. And it is all the more so in England. To be successful, a candidate for the town council must be adopted and presented by the Association of the one or the other party.[2] It is true that a man who enjoys great local notoriety, or a working-man candidate in a popular constituency with somewhat socialistic tendencies, might enter the lists against the Organizations of the regular parties with better prospects of success than at the parliamentary elections, but these are exceptional cases which only confirm the rule. The Organizations sometimes also spontaneously refrain from bringing forward party candidatures when they are confronted with very respectable independent candidates, so that the election ceases to be in any way political, but this contingency is becoming more and more uncommon, and it is the Birmingham system which prevails.

Experience has not vindicated it but has proved that this method which, pushed to its extreme consequences, gives an ardent Liberal or a zealous Conservative the preference over a good and honest administrator, is rather destructive of healthy public life. While from some points of view the regrettable

---

[1] Some of my Scotch correspondents were almost offended when I asked them if they made a political fight of municipal elections, and they replied: "Politics are extraneous matter altogether at local elections, and do not affect such issues in the slightest degree."

[2] In the great majority of cases the rule is that the ward Organization selects the candidate for the town council. Sometimes the choice is made by the "hundreds," but in any event the executive committee of the Caucus has a hand in it.

effect of mixing up politics with municipal affairs, which is unquestionable, has not assumed a very grave aspect, at least for the moment, from other points of view it appears in a more threatening light. So far as the integrity of municipal administration is concerned, it may be said in a general way that municipal interests are not sacrificed to those of the political parties or of the politicians. This fortunate result is due to two causes, the salutary action of which is of uniform strength: the comparatively elevated tone of English public life, the vigilance of public opinion which strongly condemns all improper dealings with public money,[1] and secondly, the fact that the principal officials, the chiefs of the municipal departments, are appointed irrespective of all party considerations and solely for their special competence. True, the subordinate posts have become the electoral change which the councillors distribute to the adherents of the party, but being placed under non-political chiefs the holders of these situations forget their political origin when they cross the threshold of the town hall, and all the more so because they do not change with the majority of the town council. Thus in the office-rooms there are no political parties. It is not uncommon for Radical municipalities to have Tory employés in the principal posts. Generally men of large experience, of professional knowledge, these officers keep a jealous eye on the public money and, to a certain extent, make up for the incompetence of the members of the municipal assemblies. The latter, if not always competent to manage the affairs of the town, are generally honest, and their administration is not marked by flagrant abuses; in England there is no direct plundering of the municipal coffers, and it is not often that illicit profit is derived from them in indirect ways. Of course, as in all cases where large expenditure has to be incurred, contracts and orders to be adjudged, which naturally invite jobbing, as the flame attracts the moth, the possibility,

[1] Not long ago, in a very large town of the Midlands, a town councillor was suspected of having bought some land on the assumption that it might be wanted for a tramway line, and that he might be able to resell it to the town at a profit. The calculation did not prove well-founded, but the council none the less passed a resolution censuring the speculator. The result of this resolution was that the councillor who was the subject of it felt obliged to resign his seat and retire from public life.

or even the probability, of unduly swollen expenditure, by which private individuals benefit, is not excluded in English municipalities, but, all things considered, corruption is unknown in them.

Nevertheless, amid these eminently favourable conditions there appear symptoms which cannot be ignored or which are even of a decidedly disquieting nature. The rule which makes competence the sole test of candidates for responsible municipal offices meets with exceptions in practice. It gives way to the temptation which besets the members of the political party in a majority on the council to get places at all hazards for political friends. My enquiries, which have only extended in an incidental way to municipal administration, have none the less disclosed facts in connection with it which are much to be deplored. Thus, in the very heart of England, in two towns of the first rank, the one in Lancashire, the other in Yorkshire, the sanitary service is sadly neglected in certain wards which are conspicuous for their high rate of mortality and in which small epidemics of typhoid fever or other contagious maladies break out from time to time. The reason is stated to be that "an incompetent partisan had been appointed instead of a hygienist." In other departments a good many appointments of zealous party-men, little qualified for the discharge of their duties, have also been brought to my notice; some of them recognized their unfitness themselves and honestly acknowledged it by resigning a few weeks after their appointment. In not a few town councils the division into political parties introduced during the election campaign continues practically, if not formally, in the council itself, and the result is that the objections of the minority cannot be raised with advantage; for the political party in a majority, being inclined to look on criticism as a political manœuvre, invariably stifles opposition by a "party vote." Being practically unchecked, the majority plunges into heedless expense, — involves the town in too heavy a debt, perhaps.

Although cases of this kind are, it would seem, becoming more common, they are far from assuming a really grave aspect from their special point of view and compelling attention. But beneath them there already appears a general phenomenon, the gravity of which is much more incontesta-

ble — the indifference to municipal matters which is growing up among the citizens. They inevitably leave the
burden of their duty to the common weal to be borne by the
political parties who have monopolized local public life and
imported into it their purely conventional criterion, the blind
formalism of which, far from drawing out, tends rather to
repress all genuine and living interest. The first effect of
this state of things is strikingly manifested in the decline of
the intellectual and, to some extent, moral standard of the
personnel of the town councils. Instead of raising it, as was
promised by the advocates of "politics" in municipal elections, politics have lowered it, and all the more easily because
the first postulate of their thesis, according to which the
political character imparted to local contests would ennoble
them, would surround them with a halo of great principles,
was erroneous. For politics, while appealing to lofty principles, are not free from vulgar ambition and cupidity and petty
self-esteem, and very often only conceal them more successfully under the grand language of which they have such a
plentiful supply. Politics, to repeat another old truism, have
no virtue of their own; they are what the men who engage in
them make them. And the men who had to be busy in the
municipal elections were the men of the Caucus, the ward
people whose elevation of mind and character we are already
acquainted with.

Devotion to the party being, under the Birmingham system,
the first qualification for admission to municipal honours,
inevitably became before long the principal condition of such
admission. Too often these honours were simply the reward
of the most active "workers" of the caucuses. The men who
were competent to deal with public affairs, but who belonged
to the opposite political party, were shut out beforehand.
Among the adherents of the party the moderate men, the men
of business, shrank from going through all the nauseating
incidents of an electoral campaign conducted under the auspices of the residuum of their own party and under a running
fire from the residuum of the opposite one, and from donning the party livery for a contest with which politics
have nothing to do. The good citizens therefore, far
from being attracted by politics, were rather deterred by them

from taking part in municipal life. It appears that in this respect the situation has become much worse in the course of the last few years, in proportion as politics have penetrated more deeply into the municipal elections. On the occasion of my first tour in the provinces (in 1889), I pretty often heard it said that "good men (the Tories said "gentlemen") would not stand for the town council"; but on visiting the same towns after an interval of six years I was much struck by the tone of melancholy and sometimes of exasperation in which the effects of the introduction of politics into municipal affairs were spoken of. I no longer heard, as I formerly did, the specious argument that they created a purer electoral atmosphere, that they raised the character of the local contests, etc. In one of the most important towns of the kingdom, with a glorious municipal past, one of its leading citizens complained bitterly of the degradation of the town council, explaining that this was bound to be so "with the present system which limits the choice to members of the dominant political party. It is impossible for the quality of the members not to decline. In our council barely a third of the members are men of average ability; the rest are nonentities. Luckily, they follow their abler colleagues. But what will this bring us to? The only hope is that in twenty years' time the deterioration of the council will be such that the system will bring its own destruction; the sickened and disgusted population will rise in revolt." I will depart in this instance from the rule which I have adopted of not naming the towns referred to for facts of a general description; for the town in question is the very one which was the instigator of the introduction of politics into municipal elections, which revived this practice of the old régime and promoted it to the dignity of a principle of government. I mean the city of Birmingham. And I must add that the author of the remarks just quoted is by no means a discontented member of the minority, but a representative of the dominant party, and even more, one of the leaders of its Organization. The name having been given, I see no objection to completing the quotation by the sentences which contain, as it were, a synthesis of the working of this system at Birmingham: " At the outset Mr. Chamberlain, by his example and his prestige, induced a good many intelligent men to enter the municipality. But since matters have been left to the natural play of the system, it has only deteriorated municipal representation."

Outside the municipal council the mischievous effects of the system in question are not less felt both during the election period and after it.   The political importance attached to the municipal elections makes the contest particularly keen, as was the case in the pre-caucus era, but with this serious difference, that in the old days, when corruption was the great weapon at municipal elections, the fierceness of the combatants was that of *condottieri,* whereas now the Caucus sets bigoted partisans by the ears. It is less expensive and is always more effective to capture people's minds, even by fraudulent means, than to buy their consciences.   Corruption has not on that account disappeared from municipal elections; it fills a smaller place in them than formerly, as in English electoral life in general, but it is still practised enough to involve municipal candidates in an expenditure amounting to £200 and more in a ward of a moderately important town where the electoral machinery (offered by the Caucus) is ready to hand. In the majority of cases corruption is only a subsidiary or even an accidental resource; the principal incentive is supplied by party passion, which is never allowed to die out. From year to year, even when there are no parliamentary elections, the party fight is resumed on the occasion of the renewal of the town councils.   And there is more truth at the present time in the remark made in the great enquiry of 1834 into municipal corporations by a witness who was explaining the evil effects of politics always turned on even at municipal elections: "There is no cooling time." [1]   In the present day there is the Caucus to add fuel to the flame.   Animosity between fellow-townsmen has become a fixture; they are bound to fly at each other's throats in everyday life about their local affairs, because they happen to differ on certain questions which are being discussed in Parliament.

The representatives of the party Organizations are perfectly well aware of the effects of introducing politics into municipal affairs and they make no secret whatever of them.   But they are not at liberty to give up the system because it is eminently useful and even necessary for keeping the machine of the Caucus

[1] *Op. cit.,* Appendix, IV, 2499.

in order. It would get rusty for want of use, it would fall to
pieces if it were set in motion only once in five or six years,
on the occasion of the parliamentary elections; the zeal of the
"workers" would die out in the interval, and the discipline
of the followers of the party would grow lax. They must be
kept moving, be drilled continually, be made to rehearse the
part which they have to perform during the parliamentary election campaign. The annual municipal elections supply the
pretext and the means of "keeping the thing going." And
even if the leaders of the caucus wished to suspend party
animosity at the municipal elections, they are prevented from
doing so by their "workers," who look on these contests not
only as an opportunity for gaining distinction, for establishing claims, but, owing to their temperament, also find in them
a sort of moral gymnastics. It has happened many a time
that the leaders of the caucus have given up opposing an
excellent municipal councillor and very respectable individual
solely on account of his "politics," or have settled with the
leaders of the rival party to exclude politics from the municipal elections, and that these intentions and arrangements have
been defeated by the opposition of the "workers," who declared
that they would not "work" at all at the parliamentary election if a truce were observed at the municipal elections. In
this connection there is no distinction to be made between the
parties, no reason for incriminating, for instance, the party
which first introduced the Caucus; for one case chargeable to
the Liberal Organization I could cite another implicating the
Tory Organization; it is in the nature of the "machine."

The municipal election being considered as a preparation and
a weapon for the parliamentary elections, the interest of the
party Organizations in the former is generally exhausted with
the elections; they pay very little or no heed to the way in
which the municipal councillors discharge their duties, which
are in themselves non-political. Very different is the attitude
of the Associations towards those for whom they obtain a seat
in Parliament.

VII

The preponderating part played by the Association in the
election of the Member naturally gives it special claims on

him.   It is the Association which has to a certain extent *made*
the Member, and it is that body which is the recipient, in the
same proportion, of what the M.P. owes to his constituents.
Interposing between him and his electors, the Caucus not only
intercepts, so to speak, the deference which the electors have
a right to expect from their representative, but imposes on
him additional, or, at any rate, stricter duties towards itself.
The dependence of the M.P. on those who elected him was
pretty considerable before the advent of the Caucus; it had
been continually on the increase for half a century, since 1832.
Directly the great electoral reform had installed free opinion
in the place of aristocratic oligarchy, the former set up the
pretension of controlling the men who governed or legislated
in its name.   The very year of the Reform Bill witnesses
attempts at giving peremptory instructions to Members.
The electors of the city of London set the example,[1] which
is immediately followed in several large provincial towns.[2]
However, the movement does not gather strength in this
extreme aspect and practically amounts to a manifestation
more formal than otherwise, which only heralds the new
order of things.   But from year to year the control exercised by the electors over their Members extends with
the development of means of communication and of the
Press.   When there were no railways or telegraphs, and
when a letter or a newspaper took days and days to travel a
few hundred miles, and the cheap Press was not in existence
to keep the public informed of the sayings and doings of Parliament, the Member was, by the force of things, free from
the supervision of his constituents; he was a real plenipoten-
tiary and in a still higher degree than the diplomatist of the
days before the telegraph.   Steam and electricity in reducing distances had not failed to bring the Member under the
very eyes of his electors, and the penny morning paper, con-

---

[1] The "London resolutions" of the 17th October, 1832, are to this effect:
. . . Secondly, "That Members chosen to be representatives in Parliament
ought to do such things as their constituents wish and direct them to do " . . .
Fourthly, "That a signed engagement should be exacted from the Member
that he would at all times and in all things act conformably to the wishes
of his constituents deliberately expressed, or would at their request resign the
trust with which they honoured him " (*Annual Register*, 1832, p. 300).

[2] A. Alison, *History of Europe from 1815 to 1852*, Vol. V, p. 356.

taining the report of the sitting of the House which had finished overnight, enabled them to follow events in all their kaleidoscopic changes. The electors could now form an idea of the possible solution of the questions under discussion before the time came for taking a decision on them, and watch their Member to see if he took what seemed to them the right path. The next step with many electors was a wish to show him the way. The communications on this subject addressed to M.P.'s became more and more common; on the eve of important divisions they received letters, or even telegrams begging them to vote in this or that manner.[1] For a long time, however, the restrictions on the Member's freedom to do as he liked were weakened by the fact that he owed his seat, in a great measure, to his own purse and to the efforts of his personal friends, who swept up votes for him by fair means or foul. Besides, the pressure put upon the M.P.'s was only intermittent and irregular.

But when the second Reform Bill flung millions of new voters into the political arena, and ideas were more widely propagated throughout the country by the ever-spreading power of the Press and by other means, the electoral dependence of Members once more made a great advance: the growth in the number of voters who watched the course of events, with or without discernment, meant an increase of the number of judges whom the M.P. had to face in the person of his electors. But this salutary result, while imparting more genuineness to representative government, of which the jealous authority of public opinion is the very essence, was profoundly affected by the permanent electoral Organizations which were launched about the same time under the representative and democratic flag. They inevitably gave a rigid form to the new relations between electors and Members, which they directed into an uninterrupted and regular channel. Constituting themselves guardians of those relations, the democratic party Organizations assumed over the Members and even over the candidates for Parliament a formal authority, which tended to substitute the supervision of warders for the moral control of free opinion.

---

[1] Cf. Robert Lowe, *Speeches and Letters on Reform*, Lond., 2d edit., 1867, p. 89.

And as they disposed of the machinery, the assistance of which is henceforth indispensable to all those who court the popular suffrages, they were able to make themselves respected. It will be remembered that there was opposition at the outset. Powerful personalities, resolute characters, the Forsters and the Cowens, refused to bow to the yoke, but the great mass of politicians, who were not strong enough to resist, tacitly acquiesced in it. Then on the first important occasion, in the crisis caused by Mr. Gladstone's Home-Rule Bill (of 1886), the right which the Caucus had assumed over the Members was again challenged for a time, to wit, by the dissentient Liberals who appealed from the Associations to the electors. Whatever may have been the success of the Liberal Unionists at the poll, they were all turned out of the official Liberal party, and within its precincts the caucuses remained supreme. Their authority is now recognized and accepted, and they make the M.P.'s feel it to a degree and within limits which vary according to the persons concerned and according to the nature of the electoral obligations incumbent on or imposed on the Members.

The personal servitudes,[1] so to speak, of the Members towards their constituents are of three kinds: one affects the person of the M.P.; another his political influence; the third his political conscience. For the vast majority of electors the deference which the Member owes them consists of appearing before them as often as possible. Formerly the Member, after having shaken hands with almost everybody and kissed the babies during his canvass, was free for the whole term of the Parliament, and disappeared from the horizon until the next general election. Now, the electors, more impressed with their own importance, require the M.P. to descend from his Olympus and come amongst them. They insist upon it no doubt from a desire to keep in political touch with him, but especially from feelings of pride and vanity which delight in receiving the homage of persons who put in an appearance as at a court, as well as from a yearning felt by many a humble voter for material possession, so to speak. They want ocular demonstration that the Member really belongs to them; he

---

[1] We are already acquainted with the real servitudes; they consist of the subscriptions to the local institutions of public utility and to the Organization of the party, especially towards registration expenses.

must exhibit himself to them in flesh and blood, talk to them for hours together, exert himself physically and intellectually for them. And the Member had better not try to shirk it, the electors are not accommodating on this point — "he must come down," "we will have him." The Caucus tries to gratify them by inviting the Member to meetings or "social" gatherings which it organizes for this purpose, and all the more readily because this is for its own benefit: these performances of the M.P. stimulate the zeal of the members of the Association, rouse their "enthusiasm," strengthen their power of cohesion, apart from their usefulness in cementing the relations between the electors and their Member, and consequently in facilitating the task of the Organization at the next election.

Far more important is the share of the Caucus in the second servitude to which the Member is subject, and which consists in rendering personal services to the electors. The applications made to the M.P.'s in this connection are rather a new trait in political manners due to the extension of the suffrage and to the suppression of the coarser forms of electoral corruption. Giving his vote gratuitously, many an elector holds that it is only right that *his Member* should do him a small service when opportunity offers. England not being pre-eminently a bureaucratic and centralized country, the intervention of the Member in favour of his constituents has not the same weight as in certain countries of the Continent, but it does carry some. The fact remains that the M.P.'s are often appealed to for assistance, and from year to year in an ever-increasing degree. Their correspondence has attained alarming proportions in the last decade. A good many of these correspondents write to them on political questions of the day or on local business, but the majority address them about their private affairs. In most of these requests the caucus of the locality intervenes in one way or another. The caucus often backs up the applicant and gets him the ear of the Member. An elector who is in trouble invokes the good offices of one of the high dignitaries of the Association, of the President or Chairman, or if he is not acquainted with them he asks for the secretary's recommendation in his capacity of adherent of the party. If the elector applies direct to the Member, it is still the caucus which very often gives its opinion on his request;

for the M.P. asks it for particulars of the applicant, his position in the party, his political influence, etc.   Nothing can be
got out of a good many Members without the caucus, not even,
it appears, tickets for the Strangers' Gallery in the House of
Commons.   Whenever the caucus itself takes the initiative in
asking for a favour for one of its members or adherents, the
M.P. has of course to pay it particular attention.

But it is mainly in the sphere of politics, of the political
line of conduct to be followed, that the dependence of the
Member on the Organization shows itself in its strictest form.
To be adopted as a candidate, he has already had to give the
caucus guarantees of his orthodoxy, to subscribe to all the
items in its programme.   But agreement on principles is not
enough for the Organization, it does not allow the Member a
free hand in their application; he must comply with their
wishes on points of detail as well.   The zealots of the caucus
do not lose sight of him for a moment; they scrutinize his
votes; they weigh his words.   Composed of people whose
political faith is more ardent than reflective, the caucus is
almost always ahead of the Member in the matter of opinions,
and it often feels the need of stimulating him, of keeping him
up to the mark.   On important occasions the caucus does this
with some solemnity; it passes a formal " resolution " requesting the M.P. to vote in such and such a manner, to take up
this or that attitude.   However extravagant the resolution
may be, no Member can venture to disregard it.   He must
have it out with his Association, give his reasons and obtain
approval of them.[1]   The friendly relations which the Member
maintains with the big men in the local caucus make this
dependence less onerous; sometimes it is almost disguised
by the *entente cordiale* between the Association and its
nominee, but it none the less continues to exist intact and

---

[1] Some time ago, in connection with a measure of slight importance, but
which stirred up democratic passions, a Member who bears one of the most
illustrious names in the contemporary history of Liberalism, received from
his Association, like many of his colleagues in the House, an injunction to
vote against the Bill.   In great embarrassment he consulted an eminent
publicist, who knew his constituency : " What answer am I to send them ? "
— " No answer at all; that's the best thing you can do."   The advice was
followed.   " He could afford it," remarked the publicist in telling me the
story, " being the son of his father; but any one else would not have been able
to do it."

inexorable, ready to break forth at the first shock. The pressure put on the Member seems to the caucus-men all the more unobjectionable because they are not promoting any personal interest by it and think they are serving a cause; and all the more legitimate in regard to the particular M.P. because he owes his election to their disinterested exertions as "workers" made for reasons of the same order: having lent him their moral resources, they consider themselves entitled to a mortgage over his conscience. And as they have power to foreclose, the Member who wants to be re-elected cannot take a high tone, the instinct of self-preservation restrains him. From time to time he perhaps chafes at his bit, but he takes care not to kick over the traces; for, as I have often heard it remarked, "to quarrel with the caucus is to quarrel with the constituency." The times of heroic resistance have gone by; if the Member finds himself hopelessly at variance with the caucus, he quietly gives up the game, he does not seek re-election, at least in the same constituency, "in order not to go against his party."

Cases of serious difference on points of opinion and conduct are, however, becoming uncommon. Being no longer able to be master of his ideas, of his convictions, the Member is more and more inclined to do without them, or at all events to await an impulse from outside before giving them shape and consistency. The habit which he contracts of obeying this impulse makes it particularly easy for the M.P. to be converted to ideas of which he was or thought he was an opponent the day before. Hence in the last twelve or fifteen years the Caucus has been able on many occasions to record conversions, the number, thoroughness, and, above all, rapidity of which are sufficient to inspire a missionary with jealousy. Dragged at the heels of the Caucus, with but little space left for his own movements, the M.P. is getting more and more stripped of his old character of representative and becoming a simple delegate, a clerk. This is especially true of the Liberal party. In the Tory party more latitude is allowed to the M.P.'s; the Conservative Associations do not dictate their votes to them in a peremptory way. They refrain from this probably not so much out of philosophic respect for political freedom of conscience, as from a feeling of hierarchical deference which has lingered in Tory circles longer than elsewhere. But there, too, the new Organizations which hold the key of the constituencies have powerfully contributed to lower the prestige of the M.P., to make him docile and submissive. There are of course constituencies with a slack political life, in which the pressure put on the M.P. is confined to attacks on his purse, to frequent applications for subscriptions to "local institutions," but even there he is not safe from contingencies in which his political conduct would be challenged.

Like all servitudes, that of the Caucus has its compensations for the Member. Long before the Caucus there were always in every constituency some personages, very few in number, who exercised a commanding influence and were in a way the makers of the Member. Much freer with regard to them in his political conduct, he was less so in his personal relations, whereas now, thanks to the considerable number of the caucus-men and to the conditions of publicity in which their authority is exercised, the personal yoke of the M.P. is, perhaps, less burdensome in a certain sense. Another effect, and a more important one, of the new predicament of the Member is that the caucus in interposing between him and the electors serves him as a shield. It does not allow any faultfinding with the Member who enjoys its confidence within the ranks of the party. Independent criticism by isolated persons is stifled by the trusty followers of the caucus; organized as they are, they constantly mount guard around their man, preventing discontent from breaking out, baffling intrigues directed against the M.P. The latter reaps the benefit of this on the usual terms of certain despotic governments: less moral dignity but more security.

Such is the authority which the Caucus wields over the Member as far as its power goes. Seeing that the Caucus is not the sole factor of extra-parliamentary political life, that it is far from covering its whole area, it does not of itself exhaust the *outside pressure* to which the M.P. has been subjected since the extension of the suffrage and the development of the Press and of means of communication. Public opinion which weighs on the Member acts also through other channels, which are not always very distinct. Exposed on all sides, the M.P. feels every breeze, from whatever quarter it comes. An individual elector who writes in his own name to the Member to state his views on the questions of the day — and the case is not an uncommon one — is by no means considered as a negligible quantity by the M.P.; the latter will not throw his letter into the waste-paper basket. *A fortiori* any group, even if non-political in character and objects, commends itself to him, impresses his mind, and perhaps influences his conduct. Currents of opinions, as yet perhaps ill defined, do not pass over the constituency without an attentive Member trying to catch them and take them into consideration if need be. But however manifold and varied the influences brought to bear on the Member's mind may be, that of the Caucus is the most palpable and the most considerable. Whoever has a vote to give can press claims on the M.P., but the Caucus is his principal creditor; it holds the first mortgage over this heavily involved debtor.

FIFTH CHAPTER

THE SUPREME GOVERNMENT IN THE CAUCUS

WHILE generally superintending the party in the constituency and wielding in it supreme authority, which aims even at its constitutional representative, the M. P., the Association is nevertheless not an autonomous power. It forms part of a vast federation which extends over the whole country and which rises on the base of the local Associations with a central Organization in London for its apex. The Federation lives by them, but the force which it derives from them gives an impulse to each of them. The ties which bind them to the central Organization, as well as the nature and effects of the impulse which they receive from it, will appear from the investigation of the working of the great central party Organizations on which we are about to enter.

I

The Liberal Federation — which we will examine the first, as the most developed type of the English caucus system — has preserved, with a few unimportant modifications, the machinery with which it had been provided from its start at Birmingham: the deliberative power is represented in the first instance by the Council, or general assembly of the delegates of all the federated Associations and of the Liberal Members of the House of Commons meeting once a year and constituting the parliament of the party; in the second place, by the General Committee, formed on the same basis, but composed of a smaller number of delegates, its principal duty being to appoint the executive committee, with the power of giving it instructions from time to time and of bringing before the federated Associations the political questions and measures on which it is desirable to unite the party. The Executive Committee, which

manages the business of the Federation, is composed of some
twenty members elected by the "General Committee," plus
the President and the Treasurer of the Federation chosen in
the plenary assembly of the delegates.   Side by side with the
secretary's office, which is the driving-wheel of the Federation (and which up to the recent retirement of its celebrated
founder, Mr. Schnadhorst, was the Federation personified),
there is a Publication Department, already mentioned above.
Established for superintending the making-up and the distribution of the *literature* of the party, of late years it has developed
to a considerable extent; while continuing to publish pamphlets
and leaflets, it has become an office of political information
for the active members of the party.   It is a sort of literary
arsenal which supplies them with ammunition, for defence as
well as attack.   The speakers of the party, including the candidates, when at a loss for information or arguments, apply to
the Publication Department, which refers them to the existing publications, and especially to its monthly review *The
Liberal Magazine*.   Cleverly edited, this review gives, besides
the political events of the day, extracts from speeches, analy-
ses of Bills laid before Parliament, as well as of Blue Books
and other official publications with figures and statistics; replies to questions of correspondents; comments on speeches
and articles in the Tory Press, etc., all arranged with a view
to the interests of the party.   To arm its champions with
more direct weapons, the Publication Department supplies
the candidates of the Associations with the parliamentary
record of every Member whom they may have to fight.   These
records, which state, in the case of all important divisions, if
the Member has voted with the Ayes or the Noes or if he has
been absent, also comment on the vote itself, dwelling especially
on the pernicious nature of the vote of the rival party.[1]   At by-
elections the Department, having more time at its disposal,
gives the candidates of the party more extensive assistance; it
provides them with quotations, sometimes of a compromising

---

[1] The totals of the majority and the minority are accompanied by such
reflections as the following: "the minority (Tory) thus voting for giving an
exceptional privilege to landowners"; "the minority (Tory) thus voting for
crippling the powers of the Parish Council"; or, "the majority (Tory) thus
voting against a simplification of the law much desired by many working-
men."

nature, from the speeches of their political competitors ; it makes up with all speed "political literature" suited to the occasion and to the particular circumstances of the constituency, etc. Occasionally the Publication Department gives the voters explanations and interpretations of new, important laws, in the form of publications or even of replies to private letters.[1]

Besides its central committees and its London offices, the Federation has a dozen or so *district agents*, each placed at the head of a group of local Associations as supervisors and advisers on party organization. Being taken from among the secretaries of the local Associations, they have not enough authority nor leisure to wield any real influence.

Legally speaking, this Organization does not extend beyond England proper and Wales. Scotland has its own independent organization, formed on national lines, of the same type as the English one: the local Associations are combined into a separate Federation, with the title of Scottish Liberal Association. The strong particularist feeling of the Scotch has not yet allowed the National Liberal Federation to absorb the organization of Scotland, but the latter's co-operation can always be depended on.

Another provincial organization of the party established on a national basis is supplied by Wales; it forms, however, expressly a "divisional branch" of the National Liberal Federation. In England proper, there are also three or four local federations covering portions of the territory of the party Organization, and established for political reasons peculiar to each of the regions in question. They are: The London Liberal and Radical Union, which includes the 62 electoral divisions of the metropolis and its suburbs; The Home Counties Division, comprising the eight agricultural counties of southern England, known by the name of the Home Counties; and, lastly, The Midland Liberal Federation, recently created for laying siege to the impregnable fortress of Mr. Chamberlain, who commands all the Midland counties. But all the

---

[1] This was done in the case of the Parishes Council Act. Having published a Parish Councillor's Guide, the Publication Department invited readers to write to it for information, and this offer brought it more than two thousand letters. The Liberal Organization also got up district conferences for explaining the Act to the village delegates convened for this purpose.

federations just enumerated, being closely affiliated to the National Liberal Federation or even mere branches of it, follow its lead to such an extent that, so far as the study of the working of the central Organization of the Liberal party is concerned, they can all be brought under the N. L. F. with its office in Parliament Street.

II

The Federation has undertaken, it will be remembered, to serve as an extra-parliamentary organ of public opinion, to give it a voice and thereby force it upon the constituted authorities. Flowing from the electorate, the currents of opinion are to gather, in the first instance, within the local Associations representative of the party, to be finally united in the central Organization which is representative in its turn of the local Associations. While taking upon itself the second of these two successive operations, in the formation of public opinion, the central Organization has to help to bring about the first so far as is necessary for the better attainment of its object. In consequence, the Federation assumes a double part — local and national.

Acting locally, the central Caucus points out to the Associations, with the authority attaching to its position and to the experience of its staff, the best modes of action, offers advice on their formation, on improvements to be introduced into the machinery ; it gives opinions on the points of electoral law, so complicated in England, which crop up in the practice of the Associations. It does not wait for the local Associations to apply for its services, it forestalls them, it stimulates their zeal for the good of the cause; it constantly draws their attention to the necessity of being ready for the electoral contest, to the paramount importance of registration work, and to the need of unremitting application to the propaganda of the party by means of meetings, lectures, and distribution of *literature.* If the local Associations were full of energy, the intervention of the central Organization would be without pretext or object; but a good many Associations are deficient in ardour and even display an apathy which ill befits militant bodies. Some of them require to be constantly pushed on and stirred up; by their inaction they justify, from the standpoint of the interests of the party, the intervention of the grand Caucus, and drive it into exchanging the part of friendly adviser for that of regular monitor. It thrusts itself also on the other Associations, who are full of zeal, but often at a loss for means of action. The grand Caucus provides them with these in the form of speakers, lecturers, and *literature*, or even, on rarer occasions, money subsidies. There are but few constituencies who can supply all their own wants of this kind. The local speakers are not always numerous; anyhow, they have not always prestige enough to please the audience. Its critical taste requires speakers from London, real M. P.'s, at the very least. The central Caucus procures them for the local Association at its big meetings. It also supplies it, either gratuitously or more often at a reduced price, with the pamphlets and leaflets which form the literary stock-in-trade of the propaganda. It has a staff of lecturers at its disposal; it despatches the travelling vans over the country. Lastly, in case of need, the Caucus can even get the Association a parliamentary candidate, and, if the latter cannot afford to pay the election expenses, furnishes him, perhaps, with the sinews of war.

These services which the central Organization renders or is able to render to the local Associations only transform them with greater certainty into satellites of the big Caucus. It is the same when they are under no direct obligations to it, for knowing it to be up above watching over the interests of the party, they become imbued with a feeling of gratitude and of confidence towards it, which is only enhanced by the inertia peculiar to the majority of those whose existence is passed within a limited horizon. Thus, without legal subordination of any kind, there arise between the central Organization and the local caucus relations of authority and of deference.

The intervention of the central Organization in the choice of the candidates takes place at the present time under conditions differing somewhat from those of the old days, when the organization of the party, presided over by the Whip, kept a sort of depot of candidates. Now, as with the development and extension of the political market, direct relations between candidates and constituencies have grown up, London is not so often applied to for this article. Nevertheless, the part of intermediary played by the central Organization is still very important; one candidate out of two is recommended from London. The qualities which go to make a *good candidate* are so numerous, and are complicated by so many local conditions, that they are not easily found on the spot. When the party's chances of success are not very great, and there are no local amateurs — as the state of affairs is only too well known — ready to engage in a difficult or even desperate contest, the good offices of the central Organization are invariably appealed to. The rivalries and the local competitions which prevent the Association from agreeing on a candidate also demand the intervention of head-quarters, which assume the part of arbitrator.

It is of course difficult for the interposition of the London organizers to confine itself modestly to these duties. Instinctively inclined to extend the sphere of their action and of their influence, they try to go beyond the limits defined by the need of assistance felt by the local Associations. They are lavish of their advice, abound in exhortations, despatch one circular after another. But it is especially in the choice of the candidates that their anxiety to run the party manifests itself. The central Organization always has candidates to provide for, men who have rendered or are capable of rendering services of one kind or another to the party, and it seizes every opportunity of introducing them into the constituencies. It has no legal power, so to speak, to thrust them on it, for in law the Associations are independent; but by dint of clever manœuvring, of wire-pulling, it often succeeds in doing so. Keeping up a close connection with the local wire-pullers, it " suggests " an " excellent candidate " to them and makes them accept him. There have even been, it appears, cases in which the central Organization has brought regular pressure to bear to obtain the assent of the influential personages in the Association. Among the candidates provided for by the wire-pullers of the central Organization, and, for the most part, strangers to the constituencies whose interests they are called on to represent, there are eminent men who cut a very decent figure in the House in the discussion of general questions and who certainly contribute to the reputation of Parliament. But far more often the central Organization brings into the House mediocrities whose sole qualifications are their wealth and their willingness to yield a blind obedience to the party and its leader.   Amply provided with the sinews of war, they are not only formidable opponents for their competitors on the other side, but they can contribute handsomely to the expenses of the central Organization.

The latter always stands in great need of this, for its regular resources which figure in its official accounts are extremely limited : each affiliated Association has to pay an annual subscription of a guinea; in addition the official budget of the Whip contains a certain number of subscribers at four guineas a year.   The total of these receipts barely comes up to seven or eight thousand pounds; again, a good many payments made to these funds are only nominal, because certain Associations receive from the central Organization subsidies several times greater than their subscription.   In any event, the regular receipts, while perhaps sufficient for defraying current expenses, can never be adequate for intervening with effect in the elections.   It being impossible to provide all the constituencies with rich candidates, the Organization has to contribute more or less heavy sums to the election expenditure of the candidates who are poor, but whom it does not like to part with, either because they have special chances of carrying hostile positions and of swelling the ranks of the party in the House, or because they can be useful to it by their talent or their reputation, or, again, because they represent more or less uncommon types, as, for instance, " Labour Members."   Consequently, the electioneering fund of the central Organization must necessarily be a large one, and it is so more or less.   It is impossible to form an idea of its real resources, for both receipts and expenditure are kept a strict secret, into which a handful of persons only are initiated.   It consists of donations made by the candidates as well as the M. P.'s and other wealthy supporters, of whom many are more or less interested in establishing claims on the head organizers of the party. The Members do not require the assistance of the central Organization as much as the candidates, and the private patrons of the party have no need of it; but the Organization is able to procure titles for all of them when the party is in power, a knighthood, a baronetcy, or even a peerage. There is no Radical in England so austere as to be able to resist the temptation of a handle to his name, no more than his French congener can withstand the seduction of a red ribbon. If the generous zealot of the party does not himself care, or per-suades himself that he does not care, for the prefix of "Sir" to his Christian name, his wife is always dreaming of exchang-ing the homely appellation of "Mrs." for the two magic sylla-bles of "Lady."

While interfering often more than is necessary with the local Associations, the central Organization does not exert itself enough for some of them. Not being adapted for missionary work, but rather for pursuing the immediate and tangible success of the party, it is almost obliged to neglect the constituencies in which the chances of the party are *nil* or indifferent. It is unable to find candidates for these constituencies or speakers available for addressing their meetings. Leaving them to stew in the juice of their politi-cal infidelity, it directs all its efforts to the constituencies where the enemy can be dislodged or his majority, at all events, pulled down enough to justify raising a shout of "moral vic-tory" and impress the crowd by the noise made about it.

III

Next to the assistance given in organizing the constituencies for the contest, the second and principal duty of the central Caucus consists in ensuring the co-operation and the unity of action of all the contingents of the party. The Caucus under-takes to produce and establish these by means of its federative machinery. For this purpose it convenes the delegates of the affiliated Associations to periodical meetings, in which they have to settle the programme of the party, to recast it, to complete it, to express their views on the way in which the government of the country is being conducted; in a word, to take up a decided line with regard to everything that concerns the affairs of the State. These national assizes of the party are held once a year — sometimes in one, sometimes in another, provincial town. The meeting alone, independently of the de-cisions, important or not, which are taken, is a great event

in the organized party life; it is *the* "demonstration" to
which it treats itself and the country.   It attracts not only a
very large number of persons flocking from all parts of England, as many as two thousand delegates, but the "biggest
guns" which the party can command.   The great leaders of
the party — when it is in power, the Prime Minister, accompanied by some members of the Cabinet — do not fail to enhance the importance of these solemnities with their presence
and to procure their adherents the opportunity of affirming
their union in personal loyalty before it is vouchsafed to them
to realize it in the domain of principles and of ideas.   In this
last sphere an agreement is arrived at by means of votes, and
in no way by discussion.   The meetings of the delegates, supposed to form a parliament of the party, are not deliberative
assemblies; they simply register, ratify decisions taken outside them.   The Executive Committee brings up the resolutions to be voted, which it drafts of its own authority after
having ascertained the views of the local Associations.   At
the approach of the annual meeting the Committee invites
them to communicate their wishes, to be used as a basis of
the resolutions which it will lay before the general assembly,
where they have only to be "adopted or rejected."   The federative Associations cannot put any definite proposal on the
list of business, and the assembled delegates have still less
power of displaying any initiative.   In the view of the leaders
of the Caucus the sole object of the meetings of the delegates is to proclaim to the country what the party is agreed
on.   "It is not," explained the President of the Federation,
at the famous meeting at Newcastle, — "and I wish to be particularly clear upon this point — a meeting for the discussion of subjects;" the delegates, he declared, attend not to
express their opinions, but to ascertain what are the questions which the Liberal leader can take up with the certainty
of finding the Liberal party united as one man behind him ;
the subjects for discussion have been sufficiently elucidated
beforehand in meetings of smaller size and consequently
better suited for debating purposes, such as the General
Committee, not to mention the local Associations.[1]

[1] Proceedings of the National Liberal Federation, 1891, pp. 42, 43.   The
same declarations have been repeated on several occasions by the President of
the Federation.

This system of preliminary discussion, whatever may be its intrinsic value, has not worked in practice, because the General Committee is rarely convened, because its list of business is settled by the Executive Committee, and because the local Associations which send their delegates to the General Committee are not informed of the matters which are to come before it.[1] Similarly, the annual consultation of the local Associations to which the Executive Committee applies itself, and by which it pretends to be guided in drafting the resolutions which it submits to the big assembly of delegates, is not subject to the free control of the party: the replies of the Associations are not published; they are analyzed, classified, and interpreted in private; the power of the Executive Committee which undertakes this duty is therefore a discretionary one. And it is not even exercised with complete independence of mind. Owing to the constant preoccupation about the questions which the "Liberal leader will be able to deal with," the Committee is naturally inclined to eliminate the opinions, the views, the aspirations which are perhaps making way in the country, but which do not fit into the groove of the leaders. Hence the independent Liberals continue, with yearly increasing vehemence, to set forth the grievances against the central Organization which have been already referred to[2]; to wit, that the Liberal Federation, far from being the free organ of the opinion of the country, is dragged at the heels of "official Liberalism"; that it simply registers decisions taken by a handful of wire-pullers in Parliament Street; that all the resolutions are cut-and-dried; that discussion is stifled at the annual meetings.

The reproach which is continually levelled in certain advanced liberal circles against the Federation of being a creature of "official Liberalism," which they picture to themselves in the darkest light, rests on the fact that it is formally yoked with the factotums of the "official leaders." In fact, the central Organization has two sign-boards with the names of two different masters. It will be remembered that in the course of the crisis of 1886 the popular Organization of the party, having

[1] Since 1896, the list of business of the General Committee has been communicated to the local Associations a short time before it meets.
[2] See above, Vol. I, pp. 303, 304.

separated from Mr. Chamberlain, entered into a coalition with
the leadership represented by Mr. Gladstone and the other
official chiefs, and that this alliance, which brought the Caucus an accession of strength and prestige, was cemented by a
material arrangement which placed the office of the leaders,
managed by the Whip of the party and known by the name of
Central Liberal Association, and the office of the central Caucus, under one and the same general secretary. The independent existence of both organizations, which has lasted up
to the present day, is in reality a fiction (I have therefore in
describing them used the single term of central Organization). Living under the same roof, they engage in the same
work, under the same inspiration, not only in concert but
identically. The splitting of the official title only serves to
save appearances for acting now in the name of the one, now
in that of the other, and also for procuring certain funds more
easily. When it is necessary to work on popular feeling,
to bring democratic susceptibilities, passion, or duty, into
play, or when the routine of the organization proper is concerned, then the representative Federation signs the circulars or the instructions addressed to the local Associations.
When it is a question of "suggestions," which are quite outside the province of the Federation, or of cases *ad hominem*,
in a word, of matters which cannot bear the full light of publicity, then the central Association is supposed to speak or
exert itself. Thus the candidatures are hatched under the
wing of the central Association. It is that body which distributes the election subsidies to the champions of the party.
It also receives the secret-service money of the party, without
rendering an account of it, whereas the Federation has its
modest budget of receipts and expenditure audited by char-
tered accountants, and publishes the figures of it down to the
pence column. Being indivisible in the public mind, which
naturally takes its cue more from the real facts than from
formal distinctions, the influence wielded by this Organization
is all the stronger for it: having two strings to its bow, it carries, without their being aware of it, one set by the authority
of the leadership, and the other, which is refractory to it, by
the prestige of the democratic Organization.

It is evident that from the standpoint of electioneering preoccupations the party has every reason to be satisfied with this arrangement; that, events having brought about the existence within it of two central organizations, both possessing their own sphere in the political world, it is better that they should be united than that each should go its own way. But it is no less clear that it is difficult for two organizations, differing in origin and temperament, having to act through the same central organ, to be each perfectly free in its movements. Hence in practice the confusion of the relations between the "official leaders" and the popular Organization shows itself in a sort of irregular see-saw: at one time, as we have seen, it is the leaders who influence the acts of the Federation, at another it is the Federation which weighs upon the conduct of the leaders.

However this may be, the opposition to the present state of things in the central Organization is growing stronger, and has just invaded the precincts of the Federation itself. Emboldened or warned by the defeat of the party at the general election of 1895, voices were raised within it demanding that "the machinery of the Federation should be made more representative and more democratic."[1] To meet these requirements, some amendments were introduced into the statutes, with the object of making the committees and the Council of the Federation a little more accessible to the light of public opinion, but the practical import of these concessions can only be felt as time goes on. In any event, they have not succeeded in silencing criticism or allaying misgivings even among official representatives of the local Associations, who, at the last annual meeting of the Federation (in 1897), made declarations to this effect, the moderate terms of which gave them still greater significance.[2] The attempts in the direction of getting the Executive Committee chosen by the general vote of the delegates, and of ensuring full liberty of discussion for all

---

[1] Proceedings of the annual meeting of the N. L. F., 1896, p. 32.

[2] ". . . it was apparent that there was a certain desire for change in the ranks of the party and it was desirable that the Executive Committee should consider whether it was not possible to make that assembly the real Parliament of the Liberal party. . . . There was a feeling through the country that the Federated Associations had not so much opportunity as they ought to have to bring matters before these gatherings" (*Proceedings*, 1897, pp. 78, 79).

proposals emanating from the local Associations, have up to
the present been foiled by the opposition of the committees
of the Federation, whose position is still a preponderant one.

IV

This absolute power of the heads of the Federation, and their
allies the "official leaders," over the opinion of the party is
nevertheless considerably impaired in practice, for this twofold
and elementary reason, — that opinion can never be usurped
or held down.   When once it has reached years of discretion, opinion cannot be coerced; it surrenders, it yields to
seduction, it may be caught, it may be circumvented, but
always as an openly or tacitly consenting party.   On the other
hand, opinion is anything but steadfast and unchangeable.
Headstrong and fickle by nature, opinion cannot be brought
to take any course but that for which it has inclinations, at
all events of a latent kind.   No doubt these tendencies, being
of the moral order, can be and are fashioned or modified by
the force of the human will acting on men's minds.   The
different intellectual standard and political energy of the different societies offer a varying resistance to this action from
outside, but none escape it, while again opinion which has attained to some consciousness of its strength is never absolutely
passive.   It always obeys various impulses; at one time
spontaneous, at another external and more or less artificial.
It is at once a capricious despot and a docile slave.   Its
mouthpieces and its guides, in order to lead it, are under
the necessity of following it; they give it the impulse while
receiving it.

The present state of English political society implies this
twofold play of forces in a special degree.   As we have
already realized, with the great mass of the electorate independence of mind is far from being the predominant quality; an Englishman is always ready to look up to "superior"
men who impress him for various reasons.   But we have
also seen the progress which the democratic spirit had made
in the wake of the political and industrial transformation; we
have been able to note that if this spirit has not yet made
serious inroads on the national character, it has none the less

profoundly affected the political relations, by imparting to them an aspect of equality which speedily demanded formal recognition, beyond the limits of the Constitution. This was precisely the import of the movement of the Caucus. If, therefore, the passiveness of the majority leaves the men who have taken the lead in the Organization, the wire-pullers, considerable scope in the management of the party, they are no less compelled, as regards the use to be made of their power, to feel every inch of the ground on which they stand, to regulate their pace by the mood of their adherents. Consequently they watch the state of feeling in the ranks of the party; they follow the play of opinion to catch its decisive movements; they scrutinize, they appraise, they gauge, the needs and the aspirations which agitate the country, to enlist them in the service of the party, if need be, and to introduce them into its "platform." Amid the incessant fluctuation of opinion they are careful to distinguish the currents which may bring an accession of strength to their side, to note the claims which may win adherents for the party which is the first to admit them or which has sympathized with them in any way. This ultimate result is the invariable criterion which guides the wire-pullers. The genuine solicitude for the public interest, of which they are by no means devoid, inevitably clashes in their mind with the anxiety inspired by the next general election: being in charge of an Organization, they consider every political problem not only in its intrinsic significance, but also and above all from the electioneering standpoint. In this delicate task which devolves on the wire-pullers, the apparatus of the Associations with their successive delegations is but of little use to them. The clear-sightedness, the strategic divination and conception, and the resolution of the big wire-pullers point out to them their line of conduct in a far more unerring and peremptory way than do the Associations whose democratic forms and pretensions they use only as a screen for their operations. It is their own initiative, their perhaps intuitive penetration, that suddenly rouses a question which was slumbering in the political conscience of the nation, and makes an electioneering "cry" of it. It is their fertile brain that conceives and puts into execution tactical movements which can carry votes wholesale, by binding to the

party a whole social group, a whole "interest," through an
unexpected stroke which becomes a master-stroke when it
succeeds; as, for instance, the convening in the capital of the
kingdom, under the auspices of the party, of a congress of
rural labourers with claims and grievances to urge and also
votes to dispose of.

While following the trend of opinion, the big wire-pullers
nevertheless depart from it, sometimes unconsciously and
sometimes consciously. In the first instance, because it is
not possible to coincide with it exactly, its path being anything but clear and visible. The wire-pullers who follow it
are inevitably obliged to feel their way to a certain extent,
and are liable to deviate from the line in one direction or
another. Necessarily they complete of themselves the imperfect data supplied by information, without, perhaps, being
aware of it. But, on the other hand, they anticipate opinion
deliberately; sometimes the public interest, as they understand
it, or considerations of party strategy, bid them introduce into
the policy of the party elements which have not yet found their
way into its conscience or have not yet taken root there. Besides, with the great majority of voters nothing ever happens
to be implanted in the mind at the right moment, one is
always too soon for them. And yet, in all these cases, whatever may be the cause of the divergence between the real state
of the public mind and the policy decided on by the wire-
pullers, success is impossible without the assent or complicity
of opinion: if they do not meet with sufficient encouragement
from it, the problems or solutions put forward may damage
rather than promote the unity and cohesion of the party, and
even throw its ranks into confusion. To secure the agreement
that is lacking, or at least to present a semblance of it, the
central Organization undertakes, when time allows, what is
called the *education* of opinion on the matter. This process
consists of starting an agitation on the points in question.
The means of action are the ordinary ones of the propaganda
of the Caucus, only worked at higher pressure. The Organization, which is a fighting machine, likes to hit hard, and, above
all, to make a great noise so as to deeply impress the public
mind and imagination. It uses, on the one hand, the machinery of the local Associations by making them hold simul-

taneous meetings, vote resolutions, etc.; on the other hand, it acts by itself in addressing the public directly; it launches manifestoes; organizes great demonstrations with the foremost speakers of the party as chief performers, or stump tours of the great leaders of whom it constitutes itself in a way the showman; convenes special conferences of the local delegates, etc. — all this irrespective of the political literature devoted to the questions at issue and distributed in the usual fashion.

The agitation thus carried on from above does not revolve solely around great problems, of an organic nature so to speak, which constitute the platform of the party. While establishing unity by a common programme, in which are represented the various fractions of Liberal opinion with their claims to be realized at a more or less early date, the central Organization endeavours to produce the same unanimity in the party, and by the same means, on the questions of the moment, on the events of the day. Standing on high ground and observing the march of affairs, the Organization mounts guard over the interests of the party. It watches all the doings of the rival party and, on the first serious incident, gives the alarm for raising its adherents throughout the country.

V

By strengthening and bringing into prominence the unanimity of political sentiments within the party, the Organization tends *ipso facto* to exert pressure on the conduct of those who are outside its ranks, on the body of the voters in general, and eventually on Parliament, on the majority and the Opposition with their respective leaders. Indeed, the action is the same, it is indivisible, and it is only logically that it can be decomposed according to its objectives, which are manifold. For it is the property of opinion to grow like an avalanche. But besides the first impulse which starts it, there is, with regard to the human substance, another factor, to wit, the conscience of the living beings who constitute it and who require to see, to feel the mass gather and accumulate before they adhere to it. The sole object of the agitation carried on by the Organization is to demonstrate

this over and over again ; that is to say, to make the numerical strength of the party felt by all those whom it has
in view, beginning with its native surroundings which it
looks on as its private preserves, and ending with the upper
spheres of the rulers and the legislators.   In proportion
as it unfolds itself, the demonstration gradually increases
in volume and effectiveness.   To the factors which are striving on the spot, in each constituency, to close up the ranks of
the party and to make the "enthusiasm" in them more intense
and more conspicuous, the central Organization, extending its
operations above the whole country, brings its own prestige
with that of the leaders of the party who publicly connect
themselves with it.   Cleverly worked up with the leaven of
"enthusiasm," the various manifestations, inspired or directed
by the head wire-pullers and started in several places at once
or on a very large scale, are calculated to rouse the great
mass of the indifferent and the neutral throughout the country.
The appearance of a display of strength, obtained mainly by
the noise produced, impresses the waverers, the apathetic, the
men with no convictions, the cowards who always side with
the strong, and even intimidates avowed opponents.   If these
latter are but rarely converted, they can be easily made to
stand aside or slacken their speed under the bewildering din
of invective and threats of the popular verdict, which often
nobody can state or foresee.   The smaller the power of clearly
distinguishing the voice of the people to which everybody appeals, the greater the readiness to be influenced by the hubbub
amid which it is supposed to speak.   The great point is to
make the uproar as loud as possible.   For producing this
effect the caucuses are invaluable.   From the standpoint of
the London wire-pullers that is the *raison d'être* of the Associations scattered over the face of the country.   Being accustomed to obey the impulse of the central Organization, they
answer it as an echo answers the voice.   The wire-pullers can
thus open fire along the whole line at a given moment; they
"slip" the Associations to produce "national protests," "national declarations," "popular mandates."   The Associations
need not even exert their literary powers; often they receive
from head-quarters the actual draft of the resolution about to
be voted with enthusiasm.   In a very short time the post or

the telegraph will have brought back, in a lump, the resolutions voted, and then it can be said, in a tone of triumph, that the "country has spoken," that the "great voice of the nation has given forth no uncertain sound."

Opinion is thus turned out at will by the parties in proportion to the requirements of the war which they wage on each other, and of which it is the sinews. In the days when power was gained and kept by material force alone, it was the old-fashioned sinews of war which supplied it; and when cash ran short it was provided either by debasing the currency, or, later on, as civilization progressed, by issuing paper money. Nowadays, mercenary troops are powerless to uphold a government. Swiss guards can no longer protect a régime. It is by the play of opinion that policies are settled. But here again we find the leaders trying to obtain the new sinews of war as expeditiously as the old: they manufacture opinion just as paper money was issued, only by a much improved process. The Caucus with its branch establishments is the bank of issue of this new paper currency, which supplements and reinforces the operations of the other modern circulating medium of moral energy, the Press. The success of these issues is ensured by the very conditions governing the formation and play of opinion, in which reality and convention interpenetrate, engender each other, and blend into one another. By the mere fact of proclaiming views, whether genuine or not, you create them in others, nay more, you express the opinions of a number of people who have none at all and who hasten to acknowledge them as their own directly they are put forward. The source, the real nature and the value of the mass of floating views may not be discerned, at least not by the common herd. However, to keep to the language of finance, when put in circulation they are like the paper currency supposed to represent specie. The sole point is to get as much of it as possible taken up, in other words, to make the strongest impression on the crowd. True, the limits of the operation are marked by the relation in which the real, genuine opinion stands to the artificial, machine-made element which the aforesaid manifestations present. If the divergence between these is too great, the agitation started may fall flat and the wire-pullers perceive when too late that they had presumed too much on machinery, or, to revert to the currency metaphor, that they had made a larger issue than the market could stand in spite of its power and habit of absorption.

Subject to this reservation, the machine-made manifestations of opinion always take effect more or less. And what is more remarkable, they impose not only on the mob but on the party chiefs, so much so that the latter, Ministers or leaders of the Opposition, seek in them a stimulant for their energy and their will. Often, to "strengthen the hands of the leaders," the wire-pullers set the machine of the Organization in motion, and produce manifestations in their favour. At a signal given from head-quarters the addresses and resolutions voted by the local caucuses begin to pour in, all protesting their "unabated confidence," their "unswerving loyalty," their strong condemnation of their opponents, and urging the leaders to persevere in the course adopted, to pursue the enemy into his last intrenchments, etc. At the first blush it seems odd that the leaders, who know what's what, should attach importance to factitious demonstrations. If there is no logical reason why they should be impressed with manifestations brought about by themselves, there are psychological reasons, residing in the sensitiveness peculiar to men who are habitually before the public. It is a well-known fact that several artists who have earned undying fame on the stage had an imperious need of the accompaniment of the *claque* to keep up to their usual level of performance. In the present conditions of political life politicians, who are not always great artists, are still less able to dispense with this sort of applause. The organization of the Caucus supplies it, in this instance again concurrently with the Press of the party. The nervous reaction which it produces in the party leaders is, in their case especially, the effect of the play of the machinery of opinion, already repeatedly noticed; that is to say, of the branching off of the feelings to which its manifestation gives rise. Aroused at the instigation of the leaders, these feelings to a considerable extent lose their real character in their conscience as soon as they break forth. It is no longer the applause of the *claque* that the chiefs think they hear, but the beating of hearts which throb spontaneously and freely in unison with their own. In all sincerity they become, in a great measure, dupes of the illusion which they had helped to create, under the influence of the same reflex movement which runs through the whole of opinion, presenting, in the caprice and confusion of its undulations, its sole, unvarying phenomenon, perhaps its only rule, and which, after having swayed the multitude hither and thither, achieves its greatest triumph in the mind of the leaders. It is then evident that the greater the ease with which the leaders can set in motion the apparent play of opinion, the more easily is this psychological effect with all its illusory and chance character produced in themselves. The machinery of the Caucus has supplied them with both facilities in an unprecedented degree; for in endeavouring to enclose and dam up the vague and floating elements of opinion, it seemed to provide a means of gauging it without possibility of error. The history of the Caucus in England has shown us, however, that mistakes might none the less occur. It will be remembered how Mr. Gladstone learnt this to his cost, when he concluded from the noisy manifestations of the caucuses in favour of his Home-Rule Bill of 1886 that the whole of Liberal opinion in the country was on his side.

The pressure which the Organization exerts by bringing the force of opinion, which it is supposed to command, to bear on the great mass of the party, then on the body of the electors in general, and lastly on the leaders, attains its climax when it reaches the M.P.'s, the Members of Parliament belonging to the party. More or less indirect and moral up to that point, it here becomes, one may say, immediate and almost mechanical. The mode of procedure is the same: the central Organization in important cases sets the local Associations, the respective caucuses, on the M.P.'s. Singled out from the multitude, the Member finds himself alone with his Association and made to stand and deliver, so to speak. Holding his parliamentary mandate from it in the first instance, he is driven, by a feeling of self-preservation, more or less automatically into obedience, when at a signal from head-quarters the "hundreds" or their committee direct him to take one side or the other in the House, to vote for this or that. It will be remembered how successful the Caucus has been, on many occasions, in bringing refractory or wavering

Members to reason. Completely identified with the official leaders, the Organization exerts this pressure for their benefit, sometimes on the initiative of the Whip, both as regards the whole body of Members belonging to the party, in serious emergencies, as well as the individual M.P.'s whose loyalty has fallen off. It helps in this way to maintain discipline in the parliamentary party, "to keep them in order," that is to say, obedient to the leader, and gives the last touch to the unity of the party, which it constantly keeps in view from one end of it to the other, beginning with the lowest grade, the ward or the polling section in the electoral Division.

Developed and wielded behind the scenes, and being a sort of *occult power*, the influence of the central Organization is naturally not acknowledged to its full extent by those concerned; and sometimes even in spheres other than those of the wire-pullers there is a proneness to deny or underrate it. Some, whose personal position in politics protects them from all conflict or friction with the Organization of the party and keeps them at a distance from the wire-pulling manipulations, sincerely believe its influence to be less troublesome and less encroaching than it really is; whereas others put it below its real value from the feeling of lofty disdain by which people, more or less consciously, take revenge on the power of rank, of influence or wealth, which must, however, be bowed to when met face to face, and perhaps obsequiously. The truth is, that up to a very recent period the Federation profited largely by the unexampled influence of Mr. Gladstone's leadership, as a member of the great firm in which the illustrious chief was the senior partner; and that, on the other hand, considered in itself, the Organization reposes on an "unstable equilibrium," due to its having been in existence for so short a time, and, above all, to the varying source of its influence, which proceeds from the acquiescence of opinion. But as long as this is dammed up in the local Associations, the Federation is pretty well able to regulate the flow of it, at least in times of calm. In the hour of storm, when the national mind is deeply moved in a particular direction, the Federation would be powerless to breast the current, all its wire-pulling, all its prestige with the caucuses would be exerted in vain.

VI

Almost all that has just been said about the central Organization of the Liberal party is equally true of that of the Conservative party. There are, however, considerable differences both in form and substance. The machinery of the central Tory Organization is constructed on the same type: first of all, a federal assembly and a federal council which represent the federated local Associations, to wit, the *National Union of Constitutional and Conservative Associations*. The former meets once a year; the other is permanent. Both of them emanate, by election and through successive delegations, from Conservative opinion in the country as embodied in the Associations and the clubs, beginning with those of the ward or the polling section. But side by side with these popular powers there is another which is not elective and which holds a very important position in the head-quarters of the party, as is the case in the Liberal Organization. An analogous historical process has brought about the same dualism in both organizations. As long as the parliamentary leaders of the Conservative party held undivided sway in the country, they ruled it from London, from the Central Conservative Office managed under their authority by the Whip. When the democratic principle penetrated the provincial organizations and the latter were reformed or established, at the instigation of Lord Randolph Churchill and his friends, on an elective and popular basis, their central organ, the *National Union,* arose as a rival to the *Central Conservative Office* and disputed the management of the party with it. It will be remembered that the struggle between the leaders and the democrats did not produce a decisive victory for either, and ended by a compromise which divided the influence in the government of the party outside Parliament between them. The policy of the party remained in the hands of the leaders, while local organization had devolved on the popular Associations with their Union. The power formally conceded to the latter and upheld by the democratic tendencies of the large provincial towns, soon received, however, a formidable blow, caused by the fall of Lord Randolph Churchill. His split with Lord Salisbury and his colleagues on the Treasury Bench having turned to the advantage of the leaders, the star of the National Union paled and the Central Conservative Office resumed the reins of the government of the party with renewed vigour.

Following the arrangement adopted in the Liberal head-quarters, both organizations have been united in the person of a common general secretary; the head of the Central Office, known in ordinary parlance as the "chief Conservative agent," is honorary secretary of the Federation of Conservative Associations. But there has not grown up such a close connection between the two as that which exists in the Liberal Organization between the popular Federation and the leaders. The Tory leadership is still in the hands of supercilious aristocrats who dislike identifying themselves completely, even in appearance only, lowering themselves (to use an expression which reflects their sentiments) with the popular Organization. If they find themselves obliged to adopt a democratic policy, in order to meet the Radical competition, they indemnify themselves somewhat by their behaviour to the members of their party. They can largely afford it, considering the prestige which the leadership still enjoys in Tory circles. True, they are no longer able to disregard the new forces embodied in the caucuses of their party; they are bound to take them into serious account, even in matters of form, but after all their own strength still weighs heavy in the balance. The great leaders of the party and their agents of the Central Office are therefore only too ready to regard the Union with a certain condescension, as a not precisely subordinate but more or less auxiliary organization, good for helping in the rough work of organization proper. All the more important business is transacted in the Central Office alone, the representatives of the Union not being initiated into or consulted upon it. It is there that the candidatures are concocted, that decisions are taken on the personal rivalries and the divergences which arise here and there within the party, always, however, subject to the submissive inclinations of the constituencies concerned, where the new spirit of independence, developed with the popular Associations, assigns limits to intervention from above.[1] It

---

[1] The local resistance offered to head-quarters sometimes breaks out with a fierceness of which the old Tory leaders of the pre-caucus period, very recent, however, could not have formed an idea. An eloquent example of this was

is also the Central Office which receives the secret funds and spends them in the same way as its counterpart on the Liberal side. There is, however, a perceptible difference between the tendencies which inspire and direct the two head-quarters in their operations. In the selection of candidates whom it supplies to the constituencies, the Conservative Office shows itself less democratically inclined; it does not care about having "Labour Members," even for show purposes; while in the way of financial supporters it is not very fond of the plutocrats whom the Central Liberal Association welcomes so warmly. In order not to be under too great obligations to them, which would give a few wealthy men or parvenus special claims at the expense of the aristocratic element in the party, the Conservative Office has fixed a sort of sumptuary rate for their subscriptions; it does not accept more than £100 from a single person (except for special funds). It can easily practise such self-denial, because the vast majority of the large fortunes happen to be in the hands of the Conservatives.

supplied, not long ago (in 1895), by the attitude of the Conservative Association of Warwick and Leamington, where a Member had to be returned in the place of Mr. Peel, the Speaker of the House of Commons, on his elevation to the Peerage. By the compact concluded in 1886 between the Conservatives and the Dissentient Liberals allied against Irish Home Rule, they agreed to give up all electoral competition among themselves, and stipulated reciprocally for the right to select the candidate to fill the parliamentary vacancy according as the seat had been occupied by a political adherent of either section. Mr. Peel having belonged to the Liberal Unionist group, the Liberal Unionists of Warwick hastened to select a candidate of their own political complexion. The local Conservative Association started a Tory candidate against him, pretending that the compact in question, having been concluded by the leaders, could not bind it. In vain did the Central Office try to bring it to reason. The leaders, and notably Mr. Arthur Balfour, thereupon exerted their personal influence. It was of no avail. The Association replied by refusals couched in resolutions breathing an intractable independence: ". . . while admitting the great services rendered by Mr. Arthur Balfour to the Conservative cause, this meeting protests most emphatically against the recent pressure of the leaders of the party . . . against the exercise of this pressure as depriving the constituency of its constitutional right to return the member who may locally be considered to represent the political views of the constituency." The meeting, adds the *Times*, from which this quotation is taken, was stated to be of a most united and enthusiastic character.

An analogous case arose at Birmingham, in 1888, about the parliamentary vacancy created by the death of John Bright. And Mr. Balfour, then Secretary of State for Ireland, had to leave his post at one of the most troublous periods in the history of Anglo-Irish relations, and travel all the way to Birmingham to overcome the resistance of the local Tories.

Between the central Organization and the local Associations
of the Tory party there is an intermediate grade in the form
of Provincial Unions. England and Wales are divided for
this purpose into ten provinces (the metropolis, Lancashire
and Cheshire, Midland Counties, etc.). As for Scotland, the
Tory organization there is established on the same basis as
that of the Liberal party, that is to say, it is supposed to have
an existence of its own, and it also forms a national Federation with a council of delegates meeting in Edinburgh. Independent in theory, the Tory federation of Scotland gravitates
altogether in the orbit of the English head office, as is the case
with the Liberals. The Provincial Unions of England and of
Wales, created in 1886 in a spirit of decentralization, have
not succeeded in developing an autonomous life. The head-
quarters of the party were not anxious for them to take a high
flight,[1] and the Central Conservative Office has even managed
by a clever contrivance to get them into its toils. Over this
provincial organization it has placed agencies of its own, the
territorial jurisdiction of which exactly coincides with that of
the Provincial Unions. By offering them the gratuitous use
of their offices and staff, the agencies soon managed to get a
footing in the Unions, and they rapidly became the mainspring of the Conservative organization down to the electoral
Divisions. Without possessing any formal power in them, the
provincial agent of the Central Office nevertheless controls all
the local Associations in the Union, thanks to the fact that he
represents the Central Office not only with its prestige as organ
of the great leaders, but also with its resources of which the
Associations so often stand in need — speakers for the meetings, political literature, and last, but not least, money; an
Association which does not try to conciliate the agent of the
Central Office would not obtain any assistance. To this material power it adds the seduction of civility to the secretaries of
the local Associations. Thus, without even resorting to much
wire-pulling, the Central Office ensures the organization of the

[1] Thus, when it was proposed to give the Provincial Unions the management
of the work of organizing meetings and lectures in their respective districts,
the representatives of the Central Office opposed it, alleging that this extension
of the powers of the Unions " would weaken the hands of the central Executive " (Conference of the National Union of Constitutional and Conservative
Associations, sitting of the 22d Nov., 1887).

party a complete unity of management which makes all the threads converge in the London office and utilizes the popular Associations for its own ends, so as to get hold of the voters all the more easily. Possessing the reality of power, the Organization of the leaders looks on that of the popular Union as harmless and as even serving the purpose of "a safety-valve to let off the gas."

In fact, the Union of Constitutional and Conservative Associations is rather a show body, but it none the less has a certain demonstrative value. The annual conferences of the Union are held with the same display of representation as on the Liberal side; they also attract the attention of the whole country; the great leaders of the party attend them and speak at them. They enable the representatives of various elements in the party to come in contact, it is true, for a short time only. The "gentleman" element at first rather objected to sitting with the "paid agents" sent as delegates, the secretaries of the local caucuses, who had the great demerit of getting their living by work. Disliking the physical promiscuity, the gentlemen were by no means inclined to come into intellectual contact with them, to submit their ideas to their judgment and to listen to their speeches. But of late years the professional element, on the activity of which the electoral destinies of the party more and more depend, and in general the plebeian element, has increased in importance in the formal meetings of the Union. The professionals have carried a rule which con- .cedes to all the secretaries of Associations *de jure* membership of this parliament of the party Organization, without having to solicit their appointment as local delegates on each occasion. They command more attention; they are listened to when they speak.

As regards exchange of views, the conferences of the Conservative Organization offer more facilities than those of the Liberal Caucus, because there is more freedom of discussion in them; it is not stifled as under the Liberal wire-pullers in the meetings of their party. The material conditions are also more favourable in the conferences of the Conservative Union because they are much smaller than the meetings of the National Liberal Federation. But with this greater freedom of debate the decisions of the parliament of the Tory party are devoid of effect, as we are already aware from the historical account of the position created for the Union by the revival of the leadership after the fall of Lord Randolph Churchill.   Unlike the Liberal leaders, the chiefs of the Tory party do not consider themselves tied and bound by the resolutions adopted at the meetings of the delegates; these resolutions do not become *ipso facto* planks in the platform of official Conservatism.   In the course of the last few years the Union has more than once passed resolutions which would have most seriously embarrassed the leaders, if they had been obliged to comply with them — as, for instance, the motions indefatigably levelled against free trade, which might have threatened the alliance, so important for the Tory leaders, with the Liberal Unionists, Mr. Goschen and his friends, for whom commercial liberty is a dogma of their political creed. To denounce free trade was equivalent to denouncing the alliance and sending the Tory party adrift on the ocean.   The danger, therefore, would have been great if the Union had followed up its resolutions by starting an agitation in their favour throughout the country.   But it could only have done this through the federated Associations, whose local leaders are still under the spell of the prestige wielded by the big men of the party in London.   The manifestations of the Union nevertheless still inconvenience the official leaders of the party, and in order to "give them a free hand," attempts have been made to induce the conferences of the Union to confine themselves to the business of electoral organization proper, and not to take up questions of general policy, or at all events to discuss them without recording a formal vote.   They would thus be allowed to amuse themselves for a moment with great affairs, "to debate for a while," and then, like good children, they would give up their plaything.   The plan has naturally not found more favour with the delegates than it does with children; the standing orders have not been modified in this sense, but since then in more than one particular case the assembly has followed the procedure in question, by "deciding to allow the discussion to lapse without taking a vote."

If the influence of the Union is, for the present, of moderate importance in the management of the Tory party, if it cannot boast of *manufacturing* opinion like the Liberal Federation, nor of being able to force itself on the official leaders of the party, the Organization at the head of which it is supposed to be nevertheless does discharge, for the play of opinion, functions analogous to those which are the *raison d'être* of its rival of the Liberal party. Only the impulse comes from another point; it is not the Conservative Union which pulls the strings, but the Central Office. It is this body which has succeeded in laying hand on the new machinery of the party, and which makes it execute all the movements required for picturing the spontaneous outburst of the feelings of the party. At a signal given by the Central Office the local Associations vote resolutions on the policy of the day, send addresses to the foremost leaders to "strengthen their hands"; on the eve of an important division in the House it is at the request of the Central Office that the chairmen of the local caucuses telegraph to their Members to "vote straight." At the Liberal head-quarters the wire-pullers of the Federation, conjointly with the representatives of official Liberalism, make the machine go, whereas here the henchmen of the leaders alone set it in motion. The working of the Tory system therefore simply accentuates, gives point to the traits peculiar to both organizations, the government of which is really monarchical or oligarchical under a republican and democratic constitution, in which a wide and more or less popular base is crowned at the summit by the power of a few wire-pullers, forming together a quasi-organic whole.

SIXTH CHAPTER

I

ALONGSIDE or behind the regular armies of the party Organizations there are irregular troops as well, also formed into regiments and disciplined, but intervening only as auxiliaries. Among them the first place belongs to a variety remarkable alike for the exceptional importance of its effective forces and for their composition. These are the battalions of Amazons, party Associations made up exclusively, or to a great extent, of women, and offering them a field of political activity which they do not possess elsewhere and a sphere of influence which they had hitherto never enjoyed in the English State nor in any other country.

Under the Constitution of England women have always been excluded from political life. And it is in vain that a vast amount of erudition has been expended in trying to prove that they enjoyed the parliamentary franchise in the sixteenth and seventeenth centuries. In a judgment of the Court of King's Bench, of 1739, it was noted incidentally that women had no right to vote; for, according to the remark of one of the judges, "the choice of Members of Parliament requires an improved understanding which women are not supposed to have." [1] This, no doubt, was the general opinion. The mere idea of women politicians occurred to men's minds only at times of great constitutional disturbance; the public imagination had to be greatly unsettled by the force of events to conceive such a notion even with a malicious intention. It was, in fact, under this aspect that the political rôle of women was viewed, as is proved by the pamphlets and caricatures of the time of the Commonwealth in the seventeenth century, [2] and afterwards of

---

[1] *Modern Reports*, VII, case of Ingram *v*. Olive.

[2] In the collection of political pamphlets presented by George III. to the British Museum there is a small volume called "*An exact Diurnale of the*

the period following the great Reform Bill.[1]   And it was only in the second half of our century that public opinion regularly took up the question, which has since become one of the problems of the day, continually agitated in the country and frequently discussed in Parliament, but still unsolved.

However, women had not waited so long as this to descend into the arena and demonstrate or act in one fashion or another.   First of all, the women of the lower orders appear on the scene.   The popular societies founded about the year 1792 under the impulse of the French Revolution, in imitation of the Paris clubs, had members of both sexes, *citizens* and *citizenesses*.   In the secret associations which swarmed during the years 1815–1820 women attended the meetings in large numbers and, on the initiative of Bamford, were allowed to vote.[2] Before long their share in the movement became so considerable that Associations composed exclusively of women were formed with all the apparatus of committee-women, chairwomen, etc.   The Female Reform Society of Blackburn near Manchester took the lead.   It distributed a circular in the manufacturing districts inviting the wives and daughters of working-men "to form sister societies for the purpose of co-operating with the men and of instilling into the minds of their children a deep-rooted hatred of our tyrannical rulers." A deputation from this Society attended the Reform meeting convened at Blackburn, and presented a cap of liberty and an address to the assembly.   At the great meeting of the 16th of August, 1819, at Manchester, which gave rise to the " Manchester Massacre," two women's clubs arrived in a body with

Parliament of Ladyes, Printed anno Dom. 1647," with a vignette on the title-page representing the interior of the House of Commons with the Lady Speaker, Lady Sergeant at Arms, and the Lady Members on the benches (Collection of Pamphlets, an. 1647, E 386 310).

[1] A coloured print, of the year 1835, portrays a meeting of women engaged in electing a Member of Parliament.   Two candidates are before them, of whom one, Darling, young and good-looking, is in the attitude of a dancing-master, and surrounded by a bevy of pretty women ; the second, the *political economist*, of a more solemn than pleasant exterior, is kicking his heels alone in a corner.   " Do not vote for ugly old stingy " is inscribed on a board raised in the air, while Cupid or his representative holds up another appeal : " Vote for Darling and parliamentary balls once a week."   A reproduction of this print is inserted in the work, already quoted, of Grego, *Old Parliamentary Elections*.

[2] Samuel Bamford, *Passages in the Life of a Radical*, p. 134.

a white silk flag.[1] A few years later, at the time of the agitation for the Reform Bill, the women of the town of Birmingham, which was the head-quarters of it, made their little manifestation. Not to be behindhand, the Tories of Norwich also applied to the women, adjuring them to use their influence against the Reform Bill.[2]

The women of the upper ranks, of the aristocracy and the middle class, for a long time displayed no interest in politics save in so far as they affected their narrow circle or even the persons closely connected with them. Sometimes they are seen to exert themselves on their behalf as canvassers, but not often. One of these ladies, the Duchess of Devonshire, obtained celebrity by the zeal with which she canvassed for her friend, the illustrious Whig orator Fox; she even allowed a butcher a kiss in exchange for a promise to vote for the candidate whom she was patronizing. The political and social revolution effected in 1832 for the benefit of the middle class did not give an impetus to women politicians. During the Anti-Corn Law agitation the women of the Liberal middle classes no doubt co-operated zealously in the immense advertising work organized by Cobden's League, but they did not appear in public except at the banquets, at the teas of the League, where they discharged their traditional functions of presiding over the tea-table. In the election contests they did not intervene much oftener than before 1832; they are hardly remarked in the canvass.[3] Still less, of course, are they seen on the hustings. After a considerable time, at a period very near our own, they appear there occasionally for a moment to apologize to the audience for their husbands when detained by illness or business. The special aroma

---

[1] *Annual Register* for the year 1819, Lond. 1820, pp. 104, 106.

[2] In their appeal to the "ladies of Norwich," they expressed themselves as follows: "If ever you felt for the ruin and disgrace of England, and for the *miseries and depravities* of the obnoxious Reform Bill, you are called on by the most tender and affectionate tie in nature to exert *your* persuasive influence on the minds of a father, brother, husband, or lover; tell them not to seek filial duty, congenial regard, matrimonial comfort, nor *tender compliance* till they have saved your country from perdition, posterity from slavery" (Quoted in G. J. Holyoake's *Sixty Years of an Agitator's Life*, Lond. 1892, I, 29).

[3] *Blue Books*, 1835, Report on Bribery, p. 56. — Canvassing by women, however, spread to a certain extent, and in rural districts the wives or daughters of country gentlemen went about soliciting votes for their husbands or parents.

which pervades family life for Englishmen made them rather appreciate this display of conjugal devotion and give an indulgent reception even to the little puff which the wife occasionally, in the innocence of her heart, slipped in on behalf of her absent husband, when she vouched, for instance, to the electors for his political integrity; for, "knowing him better than any one else, she could say one thing, —that he always kept his promise."

After the advent of the democracy in 1867 the situation changed considerably, both in consequence of the propaganda of the political equality of women, which made signal progress, thanks to John Stuart Mill, and owing to the vast extension of the suffrage, which demanded new modes of action on the more numerous voters. The co-operation of women became of value, and at the general election of 1868 they took, for the first time, a very important part in the canvass. "The new class of voters," we read in a parliamentary enquiry of the year 1869, "were most tremendously squeezed at the last election," especially by ladies of the upper classes, who, by their social position, impressed the working-men, the shopkeepers, and other small folk who had just been invested with the suffrage.[1] At the same time another habit was introduced: women spoke at public meetings, at first to advocate the electoral rights of their sex, and afterwards on party politics. At the first meeting they did not venture to look in the face of the audience, who would perhaps have given them a bad reception, and they read their speeches, which, however, did not save them from the violent rebuke levelled at them from the House of Commons "of having disgraced themselves and their sex."[2] In the meanwhile, women obtained the right to vote at municipal elections (in 1869) and at the elections of school boards (in 1870). At the general election of 1880 they

---

[1] *Blue Books*, 1868, 1869, Vol. VIII (Report on Parliamentary and Municipal Elections), p. 228. One of the witnesses summoned before the parliamentary commissioners, speaking of the electoral pressure exerted by women, mentioned the fact of a countess who spent half a day with the keeper of a level crossing, trying to persuade him to vote her way. To understand the tenacity displayed on both sides, it should be added that the incident took place in Scotland.

[2] M. G. Fawcett, *The Women's Suffrage Movement,* in Th. Stanton's collection of essays, *The Woman Question in Europe,* Lond. 1884.

joined in the fray, with great vigour, as canvassers and as speakers at election meetings. Mr. Gladstone, although an avowed opponent of female suffrage, addressed a very sentimental appeal to them begging them to help him to combat and vanquish his Conservative rivals.[1] The appeal was responded to, but the Tories also found help among the women. They fought on both sides as free lances, as isolated combatants, without any organization. The Conservatives were the first to enroll the female contingents, and it was the Primrose League which served as regiments.

II

The reader will recollect the circumstances in which this Organization had been founded. The members of the "Fourth Party," headed by Lord Randolph Churchill, being anxious to emancipate Toryism from the aristocratic camarilla and to instil fresh life into it by bringing it nearer the heart of the people, hit on the idea of establishing a sentimental alliance between the masses and Toryism, by means of a League founded outside the orthodox organization of the party and appealing frankly to popular affections and emotions. The League was to cover the country with a network of brotherhoods composed of men deeply imbued with the honour and the glory of the fatherland, and united among themselves, under the auspices of the revered memory of Lord Beaconsfield, in the cult of the true Conservative principles of which the illustrious deceased was the champion and the propagator. The beginnings of the League formed with such lofty aims were unassuming. Recruits did not flock to it in large numbers. But in proportion as its ranks widened, the spirit of hostility to the aristocratic leaders which animated the small group of men of the Fourth Party, instead of gradually infecting the members, rather evaporated. The surrounding atmosphere was evidently charged with the feelings of respect and the traditional preju-

---

[1] "It would be," said Mr. Gladstone, "the performance of the duty the neglect of which would be in future time a source of pain and mortification and the accomplishment of which would serve to gild your own future years with sweet remembrances, and to warrant you in hoping that each in your own place and sphere has raised your voice for justice and has striven to mitigate the sorrows and misfortunes of mankind " (*Ibid*).

dices which have invariably constituted the essence of Toryism. Before long no flavour of heterodoxy was to be found
in the Primrose League, so much so that the official leaders of
the party had no reason to refuse it their approbation. In the
meanwhile, the League opened its ranks to women. This no
doubt was a grave departure from tradition; but considering itself not so much a political association framed on the
stereotyped model as a champion of "moral order" in the
political society of England, the League deemed it lawful and
expedient to summon all the living forces of society to the
combat. In fact, the League pretended in recruiting its adherents to disregard not only the distinction of sexes, but also
those of classes, of social stations, of religion, and even of
party. Founded for the propaganda of "Tory principles" and
in consequence entitled "Tory Primrose League," it now
dropped the adjective "Tory" everywhere and declared that
it devoted itself to the defence of religion, of the fundamental
institutions of the Realm and of its *imperial* ascendency. All
willing men obeying the call of honour, all patriots were
invited to rally under the banner of the League for the defence of the foundations of social order which at that time
(in 1884-1885) seemed to a good many people specially men-
aced by the Birmingham school with its weapon of the Caucus;
in fact, the League was to "supply the antidote of the Caucus." By their Conservative instincts and their deep religious feeling women were naturally marked out for a share in
this crusade, and by their mere presence they completed the
institution of the new knighthood; for was not the approbation of the lady the highest reward of the exploits of the
knight ?

However this may be, the admission of women into the
League made it a success. From that date (1884) the number of its members began to grow with astonishing rapidity.
The women carried the men with them, and in a short time
the ramifications of the League extended into the four corners
of the Kingdom, forming in less than ten years a formidable
Tory militia of more than a million, which surpasses the
regular army of the Tory party not only in numbers, but often
also in fighting strength.

I say Tory militia, although the League disclaims this epithet, and often puts the words "independently of party politics" at full length after its name.[1] Founded for the defence of the glorious principles above mentioned, the sole task of the League would be to instil them into men's minds, to propagate them. Its undertaking would therefore be simply "educational" without intervening in militant politics, or as Lord Salisbury expressed himself at one of its first annual meetings: "You are not confined within rigid party lines; you are not attached to members or candidates in any locality. You are the general missionaries of the principles which you profess, and, if I may say so without irreverence, you are rather the preaching friars of the message that you have to convey than the regular clergy attached to each particular district."[2] In reality this is not so, the independence of the League does not exist even in the attenuated form which the noble Marquis attributed to it. From the outset it identified itself with the Tory party in its "rigid lines." The division of the English political world into two sharply defined camps, and still more the vagueness of the general principles which the League has proclaimed, made it almost necessary for it to adhere to a particular line of conduct and to follow this line from point to point on pain of losing its foothold altogether.

Thus by the defence of religion the League understood not only the struggle against "infidelity and atheism," but also opposition to the religious neutrality of the public elementary schools,[3] even if this were demanded, as is the case in England,

---

[1] Cf. the numerous publications of the League, such as the *Primrose League Manual* (last edition approved by the Grand Council in June, 1894), *What is the Primrose League?* (Leaflet No. 86), etc.

[2] Annual meeting of 1886 (*Times*, of the 20th May, 1886).

[3] In fact, in a commentary on the principles of the League, from the pen of one of its high dignitaries, it is explained that the League strives to combat *secular education*, to oppose "those who would deprive our children of all religious instruction and all knowledge of God, as the so-called Liberal party on the Continent are doing to the utmost of their ability." It would appear that in the eyes of the League secularism and atheism are convertible terms, and that Christians who are not hostile to *secular education* are not sincere Christians: "All Christians have one point of doctrine in common, namely, that they believe in God the Father Almighty, Creator of heaven and earth; and if they are sincere, they are ready to defend that first principle against the Secularist and the Atheist, and to lay down their lives for it. They all agree that religion should be the basis of education and of government" (*The Primrose League*, by G. S. Lane-Fox, Vice-Chancellor Primrose League, p. 6).

by millions of Dissenters animated with the deepest religious feeling going to the point of bigotry. It is therefore not so much for religion as for the official religiousness enforced by the secular arm, of which the Tories were the traditional champions, that the League has gone to battle. As a matter of fact, the members of the League almost all belong to the Established Church, with a very small sprinkling of Protestant Nonconformists, of Catholics, and of Jews who join with them in professing the Tory creed. This close alliance of the League with the Anglican Church has even served its political opponents of the Catholic faith (especially the Irish Nationalists) as a pretext for asking the Pope to forbid Catholics to belong to this organization, which contains so many Orangemen denouncing Popery with all the virulence which is characteristic of them. The Roman Curia examined the question at length and finally decided against the opponents of the League.

The other great principle inscribed by the League on its banner — the maintenance of the fundamental institutions of the Realm — with no clearer definition, did not lend itself, in the way of action, to any special interpretation; for how are institutions maintained ? By never laying hand on them ? But in that case is there not a great risk of their being allowed to fall into ruin under the ravages of time? If, on the other hand, in order to preserve the edifice the injured or decaying parts must be renewed and constantly changed, it is only in particular cases that the question can be put, whether the change proposed is conservative or destructive, and it would be impossible before the cases giving rise to these questions had occurred to give an anticipatory and general answer to them and adopt it as an unvarying rule of conduct. Has not the policy of Tory statesmen themselves undergone an evolution? have they not themselves taken in hand constitutional changes which they had just declared to be subversive and sacrilegious ? In the matter of settled and comprehensive notions of conservatism there was and there is, in English political life, nothing but the firm of the "party" which goes by the name of Conservative. Consequently, the Primrose League, being anxious to do "conservative" business, has had no alternative but to hold fast to that firm by simply following the daily quotations ruling in the market of the "Conservative party," that is to say, devote itself to the maintenance of the institutions which that party will defend, and so long as it will defend them.[1] With some exceptions, this holds good of the third principle of the League, to wit, the maintenance of the "imperial ascendency" of England. Hence from the very start it fell into line, naturally and spontaneously, behind the Tory party; its branches speedily became a counterpart of the regular organization of Toryism, having the same territorial divisions, defending the same policy and placing their efforts, in the constituencies, at the disposal of the same men, of the local Members or the candidates of the party.

III

The organization of the League is elaborate and curious. It presents an odd combination of old bric-à-brac with well-contrived modern machinery. The first element symbolizes, it would appear, the preoccupations of honour and chivalry with which the founders of the League were imbued. Every adherent of the League of either sex, having signed a solemn engagement to defend religion, the Estates of the Realm, and the imperial ascendency of the British Empire, receives a special title according to the amount of his contribution — that of "associate" if he only subscribes the minimum figure, or that of "knight" or "dame" if he or she pays half-a-crown a year more, for the "tribute" credited to the central fund of the League. Entering the order with the grade of "knight harbinger" (at the time of the foundation of the League it was called "squire"), they can, after a probationary period of twelve months and for distinguished services, be raised to the dignity of "knight companion"; ladies fulfilling the same conditions are promoted to the "Order of Merit." With no other qualification than their devotion to the League they can, on payment of a guinea a year, be admitted, the men into the "Imperial Chapter of the Primrose League," and the women into the "Ladies' Grand Council of the Primrose League."

---

[1] One of the chiefs of the League in reality only admitted this when he said to me: "It cannot be asserted that the Primrose League is attached to the Conservative party, for there has been no Conservative party since 1867."

The members of the "Imperial Chapter," who are called "Knights Imperial," govern themselves by an elected council, at the head of which are a prior and two sub-priors, whereas the "Ladies' Grand Council" receives its presidents (extra-president and president) and vice-presidents from the hands of the Grand Council of the League. Each of these dignities is certified by a diploma and symbolized by special badges, to which are added various kinds of trinkets, brooches, and pins instituted for the use of the members.[1] These badges are worn at the meetings of the League and on other solemn occasions, as well as a bunch of primroses on the anniversary of the death of Lord Beaconsfield. In addition, special decorations are conferred on the most deserving members, from the "Grand Star," with its five grades, down to the simple clasps of honour. The lists of the decorated appear regularly in the official gazette of the League. All the members of various denominations are brought together under a hierarchy which extends from the remotest corners of the kingdom to London. Wherever there are as many as thirteen members, they can form themselves into a local branch or "Habitation," after having obtained letters patent for that purpose from the supreme authority of the League, which is called the "Grand Council." All the Habitations of an electoral division or of a county can group themselves into a divisional council or a county council. The delegates of the local Habitations, meeting once a year in London, form the "Grand Habitation," supposed to be a sort of Parliament confronting the executive power of the League, the Grand Council, at the head of which are a grand-master, four vice-grand-masters, with a chancellor and a vice-chancellor. The local Habitations also possess a whole hierarchy of dignitaries — ruling councillors or lady presidents, executive councillors, treasurers, secretaries, wardens and sub-wardens, each and all wearing badges distinctive of their offices.

It is these latter, the "wardens" and the "sub-wardens," who are the mainspring of the organization. The territorial area of each Habitation is parcelled out among them into districts and blocks, which they work systematically for the good

---

[1] Cf. the illustrated catalogue of the badges of the League, *The Authorized Badges of the Primrose League* (Publication No. 110).

of "the cause," that is to say, for the triumph of the Tory party at the next election. In places where the Conservative Associations are weak or non-existent, the League takes in hand the organization of the party. In any event, it aids the Associations in their task, and in this respect it is subordinated to the local Association. As soon as election time begins, the Habitation is obliged to place itself bodily at the disposal of the Association or of the Tory candidate. In the interval between the elections the League helps the Conservative Association of the locality in its daily labours, and especially in those of registration. Its members keep an eye on the removals and arrivals of voters in the district, supply the Association with particulars of the occupiers of the houses, and finally, by way of check and revision, conduct a regular registration canvass parallel with that carried on by the agents of the Association. The female members of the Habitation are specially valuable for the service of information, which often requires dexterity and lightness of hand. Having more leisure than the men and taking advantage of the privilege of their sex, which enables them to circulate among the population with more freedom, that is to say, without drawing attention to their capacity of political emissaries, the "dames" quietly work the constituency in a continuous fashion. As they go along, so to speak, they sow the good seed destined to produce a splendid harvest on election day. They "explain the principles of the League" in their application to the questions of the day; they lavish information on the lower-class voter recently admitted to political life to set the "lies of the Radicals" in their true light. Undoubtedly there are among the Primrose Dames women of a really superior mind, capable of discussing a question, and excellent speakers. But these are exceptions; the great majority is very far from being so qualified; which, however, is not surprising, looking to the character of the education which was vouchsafed to their sex down to a recent period. The reasoning of the Primrose Dames is therefore necessarily more of a sentimental order. It is too often reinforced, as is alleged, by arguments *ad hominem* of an entirely material nature, by small presents, of food or coal, and by promises to obtain work. The distribution of relief by the charitable institutions to which the members of the Primrose League belong is, it is said, practised and used by them with a view to the same object. The League, of course, indignantly repudiates these charges.

In addition to this familiar aspect of political education, the League also carries it on by means of lectures, of meetings, with speakers of the locality or imported from London or other large centres, and of publications, especially leaflets distributed indefatigably and with much method by the dames. The lecturing work is ingeniously reduced to a very simple form. The managers of the League in London have had a few lectures written on two or three subjects (the Primrose League, the British Empire), and send copies to the local Habitations, where they have only to be read. Often it is the clergyman of the place, who is almost invariably one of the pillars of the League, who performs this duty. Accompanied by very numerous projections from a magic lantern, which constitute the chief, if not the sole, attraction for the public, the lectures try to impress the imagination with the greatness of the fatherland, of the monarchy, of the time-honoured institutions of the country, of its colonial empire. The historical erudition introduced into these compositions is intended to serve the same object, by proving, for instance, that Queen Victoria is the direct representative of the oldest unbroken line of sovereigns ever known; tracing her descent from Fergus I, an Irish prince and founder of the Caledonian monarchy in Iona about the year 330 before the Christian era, which said Fergus is alleged to be descended in his turn from Heber, a notable Milesian who is supposed to have conquered Ireland and to have founded a dynasty there at a date contemporary with King David of Israel.

IV

Nevertheless, however considerable the number of lectures and of speakers who address the meetings so frequently held in the Habitations, as well as of the publications distributed in certain years by millions, it is not doctrinal propaganda which is the chief business of the League. Its real weapon, the one which always tells, is the social action which seeks

to realize "the union of classes," as opposed to the Radicals,
who are accused of only fomenting class dissension, who "set
class against class and man against man." The League throws
its doors wide open to persons of every social condition, down
to the humblest, — to small shopkeepers, to artisans, to day-
labourers, to washerwomen, to maid-servants, — and once
brought together the members of the upper and well-to-do classes
overwhelm them with civilities in order to prove to them in an
impressive way that the high-born and the wealthy "are the
friends of the poor people"; so that the flame of cupidity kin-
dled in the popular breast by the Radical agitators would die
out of itself. The League just supplies the common ground of
meeting and provides the opportunities for it. With this object
it has elaborated a whole liturgy for the communion of classes
by means of fêtes. The Associations have their *social meetings*
as well, but it is the League which is the great contriver of
them and which has well-nigh identified its existence with
them and raised them to the level of a political force, almost
of an *instrumentum regni*. Every Habitation organizes as often
as possible festive gatherings, rising from simple "teas"
to "high-class entertainments" and "fêtes." The "teas"
which are the most modest of the meetings, are also the most
common. Then come the concerts, the dances, the balls.
The "fêtes," which combine all these amusements, are often
adorned with small dramatic representations, — tableaux vivants, ventriloquism, conjuring, "Italian marionnettes," clowning, etc. The experience and the zeal of the organizers of the
Primrose League fêtes succeed in the difficult task of varying
the programme, as is proved, for instance, by the poster reproduced on the next page. In the programme of all the meetings of the League a place is always given to political eloquence, but it is never allowed to monopolize the audience;
long speeches are not tolerated. In truth, the addresses at
the entertainments of the Primrose League are rather an
aperitive, which does not even stimulate the appetite. Consequently, the speaker, even if he were a M.P., plays a somewhat retiring part in them.[1]

[1] A Tory M.P., in a very amusing book, gives a fancy and necessarily overcharged description of it, but of which the substance is true: "I am asked
to deliver an address to the members of a certain 'Habitation.' I appear at

Not to mention the attraction of refreshments supplied at
an exceptionally low rate, and which have drawn on the

what the lawyers call the *locus in quo*, in due course, and am welcomed by
the active and intelligent secretary (all secretaries have a prescriptive right
to be termed active and intelligent). 'Ah, Mr. Blank!' says he. 'How are
you? Glad you've come.' (As if it had not been an arranged thing for weeks!)
'Awfully busy, — capital meeting, — we shall have a roomful. They have come
to hear Melville Jones, you know.' 'So there is to be another speaker,' I say
to myself. 'Some local celebrity, fully prepared to cut me out and bring down
the house.' I hang about in a purposeless way for a bit, as it seems to be
nobody's business to pay me the slightest attention, and listen to what seems
to be a kind of tuning up behind somewhere. Presently the secretary passes
again. I hail him. He is a cheery man, with a pleasant wit. 'Walk up,
walk up, just a-goin' to begin,' he says with a smile, to intimate, I suppose,
that the Ruling Councillor is prepared to take the chair. I control my feelings
at this desecration of an occasion on which I am to deliver an oration that
may, metaphorically speaking, shake England to its core, and ask, as calmly
as I can, 'By the by, what is to be the order of proceedings?' — 'What! haven't
you a programme? Let me see' (scanning one that he takes out of his
pocket), 'I know you are down somewhere' (I should think so, indeed). 'Oh,
yes; here you are, between Letty Smith and Melville Jones!' — 'Between
Letty Smith and Melville Jones!' I repeat to myself, with inward bitterness,
and numerous suppressed notes of exclamation; then aloud, interrogatively
and plaintively, for I feel that there must be something very wrong somewhere,

---

PRIMROSE LEAGUE.   . . . . . HABITATION.

GRAND TEA AND ENTERTAINMENT.

ALBERT HALL, ...

Tea will be provided by ladies of the Executive Council and their friends
at 4.30, 5.15, and 6 o'clock.

Evening meeting at 7.30. Doors open at 7 o'clock.

Addresses will be given by the Marquis of . . ., M.P., Col. . . ., M.P.

A high-class and most amusing entertainment will be provided, consisting of

Juggling, Conjuring, Musical Grotesques,

Illusions and Delusions, Pianoforte Solos,

Comic Nigger Banjoist and Dancer.

Comic Donkey *à la* Blondin,

the funniest animal in the world.

Double clowning act, etc., etc.

Tickets for tea and entertainment, one shilling.

Entertainment only 3*d*. Reserved seats for entertainment, 3*d*. extra.

Tickets may be obtained of . . . .

GOD SAVE THE QUEEN!

Primrose League in a special degree the severe rebukes of the judges, already brought to our notice in the case of the Associations and their "social meetings,"[1] the gatherings of the League present many other powerful allurements of a less material nature. In the monotonous existence of the lower middle class and the populace they supply, down to the modest "teas," a distraction enhanced by a good many charms, of which the intercourse of the sexes is not the least. They afford young people a legitimate opportunity of meeting each other and of completing in the sphere of sentiment the rôle of "knights" and of "dames" which has been assigned to them for the defence of society. The union of sexes is thus added to "the union of classes." It has procured the League a great number of adhesions, perhaps as many as the "union of classes," which offers not only to young folk but to those of all ages one of the sentimental satisfactions most highly appreciated in England: the delightful pleasure of coming into contact with people of higher social rank.

By paying a subscription of a shilling or sixpence, one becomes the colleague of titled or simply rich personages, one obtains access to their drawing-rooms and parks, which they place at the disposal of the League for its meetings, and there the humblest can rub up against the great ones of the earth. If you only have a competency, leisure, and intelligence, you can even be made a sharer in the labours of the League and enter its "inner circle." You take charge of a district in the capacity of "warden" or "sub-warden," to conduct the political census, and this gives you an opportunity of reporting

'Miss Smith? So ladies are to speak, eh?'—'Oh dear, no. She sings; and a very nice girl, too. This is a sort of mixed entertainment; mixed, to match the company, don't you know' (and he smirks with satisfaction at his wretched joke); 'songs and speeches, and that sort of thing.' And it is for 'that sort of thing' that for weeks past I have taxed my brain for epigrams, antitheses, flowers of rhetoric, and so on! However, I am in for it now; so I pursue my enquiries, but without any real interest in the affair. 'And Thingummy Jones, what does he do?' I ask. 'Oh, he's our big gun,—capital fellow,—comic singer. Going to give us something in character, I'm told.' . . . I abandon all my high hopes of swaying by winged words the destinies of an empire, and deliver a scratch speech, huddled into fifteen minutes, to an audience dying to hear Melville Jones in his celebrated song, 'The man who went to bed in his boots'" (*Four Years in Parliament with Hard Labour*, by C. W. Radcliffe Cook, M.P. Lond. 1890, pp. 125–127).

[1] See above, Vol. I, pp. 438, 439.

and exchanging remarks on the results with the personages
who are at the head of the Habitation. With a little more distinction or wealth, a woman of the lower middle-class can take
her place, in the committees of which there is no lack in the
Habitations, by the side of titled ladies, perhaps marchion-
esses or even duchesses, and, seated in their grand drawing-
room, discuss the affairs of the Habitation on an equal footing.
If this does not fall in her way, perhaps she will be vouchsafed
the honour, at the innumerable fêtes of the League, of helping
the great ladies to make the tea and cut the sandwiches. Her
husband or her brother, the "knight" who spends his life in
selling mustard or candles, will receive his cup of tea from
the very hands of a "dame" who is a great lady. The dames
and knights who take the lead down in their country districts
are in their turn lifted into the London Olympus by the chain
of the organization, which connects the local Habitations with
the Grand Habitation and the Grand Councils. Every local
delegate is admitted to the receptions given by the exalted
ladies of the Grand Council on the occasion of the annual
meeting, and the honours are done to him by live duchesses
and Ministers or ex-Ministers. True, his share has not
amounted to very much, there were several thousand people
thronging the gorgeous reception-rooms, but still he carries
away a few shakes of the hand and a gracious smile or two.

Thus along the whole line of society enrolled in the League,
the self-love and vanity of its members, skilfully brought into
play, make them close up and fall into line behind a political
party, often apart from or independently of all political conviction. This is why the chiefs of the League, anxious to
make a wise use of their resources, are never weary of saying
to their dames: "Do not argue, take them in socially." That
is the watchword which sums up all the strategy and all the
tactics of the Primrose League. No doubt, politicians have
always traded on the enormous importance which Englishmen
attach to marks of outward attention from persons of a higher
social rank. During election time they lavished them on the
humblest citizen; a Lord Wharton would come and see Dick
the shoemaker to have a drink with him, and would ask his
wife about Molly and Jenny; in our own day, the working-
man or the small shopkeeper was courted and treated with

civil speeches and smiles in the course of the election canvass; but once the voting was over, they no longer existed for the more or less exalted personages who had condescended to notice them.   The lower-class voter was only too well aware of this, and on the next occasion he sometimes revolted.   The Primrose League stepped in and filled up this gap by ensuring through its organization a permanent supply of civil speeches and smiles.   They represented henceforward a market value which was all the greater because the recent law of 1883 made the time-honoured practices of corruption much more difficult and more dangerous, while the *social consideration* which the Primrose League undertook to provide, to meet the public demand, could be used as a safe means of electoral bribery.

The social influence which the League wields with so much skill does not serve it solely for attracting people to it and keeping them in the ranks of the Tory party.   If its opponents are to be believed, the League also uses social influence as a poisoned weapon against those who are not of its political colour, by the practice of "boycotting," which consists of making a solitude, in the matter of social relations, around the person or persons in question: no one will associate with them; no one will buy anything from them; no orders for work are given them; they are not employed in any way.   Terrorized in this fashion by the League, small folk of Liberal views are said to be under the distressing necessity of choosing between their political convictions and their daily bread.[1]   In the course of my investigations throughout the country I have met with complaints on this score in several places, but in several others the political opponents of the League declared unhesitatingly that they were not troubled with boycotting. In any event, boycotting is seldom the effect of a regular order.   In the small localities, in the country districts where people who have to earn their livelihood are more dependent than elsewhere, social pressure with a political object takes place of itself; the ground is all ready for it, and a politico-social organization like the Primrose League, which is always

---

[1] To protect the Liberal voters in the country districts from intimidation, a special League was formed, under the presidency of Mr. John Morley (County Voters' Defence Association), but it soon came to an end (for want of clients to defend, say the Tories).

in the breach, naturally cultivates it by the sole fact of its existence. It is not unlikely even that this state of things procures somewhat insincere adhesions for the League; that there are wolves in sheep's clothing in its ranks. But far larger is the number of those who, with no special sympathy for the League either, nevertheless join it without any social pressure: they simply want to amuse themselves, and at a cheap rate. For instance, in Lancashire, where the people are very fond of dancing, the subscription of 6*d.* or 9*d.* a year is readily paid for the right of joining in the dances of which the Habitations are so lavish.

V

The decisive share which "the union of classes" has in the activity and the success of the Primrose League, sanctions the preponderant part played by women who are the great engineers of this undertaking, alike by the privilege of their sex which makes the *dignus est intrare*, in social relations, depend on women or receive its full effect from their assent, and by the special efforts and the deliberate will which the Primrose Dames exert to win the good graces of those whom they attract into the League for the sake of the party. Having prepared the electoral ground by these daily and hourly labours, they supply at the moment of the election a very valuable contingent of canvassers who scour the constituency with an energy and zeal which know neither bounds nor measure; the cleverest of them deliver speeches every evening in favour of the Tory candidate; others perform the extremely irksome clerical work, — copy lists, address and distribute circulars. In every respect it may be said that the League rests on women ; it is they who keep it going and eventually ensure its success, although the number of members of the male sex not only equals, but even slightly exceeds, that of the women.

It would be a mistake, however, to infer from this that the influence of women in the League corresponds to the importance of their rôle. The women work, but the men direct them, especially the men in London. The women are only an instrument in their hands which they wield with skill and firmness, by turning to account in their case the same feeling on which the women trade themselves, — the snobbery which prevails from one end to the other of the social ladder. The Grand Council of Dames, which sits in London, has no real authority; each of its acts of any moment is submitted to the approval of the Grand Council composed of men. The Council of Dames is simply a decorative body serving as a pretext for subscriptions, a considerable amount of which goes into the coffers of the Grand Council.

It is not only to women, however, that the managers of the League leave so little authority; they govern the whole Organization in general in a somewhat autocratic fashion. The share of the local Habitations in the management of the League is still a very slight, not to say a fictitious, one. The assembly of delegates which meets every year in London (the Grand Habitation) is only a show gathering without independence, without a will. It is impossible for free speech to get a hearing there; it is stifled. All the power is in the hands of the Grand Council, which is to a great extent filled by co-optation. It is only with difficulty that an increase in the proportion of the elected members has been recently obtained. The Grand Council is not less strongly opposed to all extension of the individual life of the country Habitations, to the creation of provincial centres with a little autonomy. It holds that an organization supported solely by voluntary effort needs a highly centralized government.

VI

The success of the League varies with the localities. As a general rule, it may be said to prosper in the rural districts, where social influence is more powerful and where the population is more accessible to the special methods of propaganda of the League. Nevertheless, the towns also often afford it a good base of operations, especially in the lower quarters, the poor and ignorant inhabitants of which, in fact, supply the League with its largest electoral contingent. The north of England with its, up till lately, so numerous Radical strongholds and its hard-headed population was not amenable to the League. The local Tories themselves, in Northumberland, for instance, did not always look with favour on this organization which conducts politics "with dancing and feasting." They were afraid, too, that the League would absorb part of the money which went into the chest of the regular organization of the party. But since then the League has managed to extend its system into these localities, and in this or that large town where the Tory leaders had roundly declared that there was no room for the League, there are now seven or eight Habitations. At the present moment the League numbers as many as 2300 Habitations, with more than a million and a quarter members.

This wonderful success cannot, it is true, be accounted for solely by the fact that the League offers the English people distractions and gratifies its vanity. There are other and deeper causes, of which the reader may have already caught a glimpse in the foregoing sketch. In the first place, the Primrose League has really succeeded in levelling, to some extent, the barriers of classes which still attain such a height in England in spite of the democratic progress achieved. The class spirit, "the classicism, this curse of England," as old Bamford used to say,[1] made the small shopkeeper, the artisan, a social pariah whose sole touch was pollution. On this sore spot the Primrose League has poured healing balm; no matter if it is composed of coarse ingredients. From time to time it introduces the humble outsider within the circle of the "upper ten," of the possessors of "blue blood," and ensures him a courteous, if not a cordial, reception from them. The obsequious alacrity with which he seizes the opportunity of drawing close to them for a few moments, of getting a near view of them, of rubbing up against them with a feeling of beatitude on account of their rank or their wealth, is no doubt devoid of moral beauty. But beneath this snobbery, to which one may, if one is so disposed, apply the epithet of abject, is human dignity vindicating its too long neglected rights.

Again, political relations had, for more than half a century, in vain called for a social cement; all that they got was the artificial cement of party with its more and more perfected machinery. The Primrose League offered as a rallying-point for all men of good-will in every condition of life more general and more generous principles than the narrow and sectarian

[1] *Passages in the Life of a Radical.*

dogmatism of party; it wrote upon its banner the words: constitution, country, religion, without any epithet. Men's imaginations could not help being impressed, the hearts in which a desire for political fraternity was vaguely stirring, less conscient and less articulate than that for social fraternity, but not less real, were touched. Here, again, it mattered little that this was only an illusion, that in reality the League had farmed out inalienable principles to a party. In this case, and far more still in that of the union of classes, it was base metal which it offered instead of pure gold; but if you are not aware of it, is not bad money as good as genuine money? On the other hand, it is an acknowledged fact that in the long run spurious coin debases the market. In the moral sphere the effect is the same, — spurious moral coin degrades the national character. And it is permissible to enquire what the influence of the Primrose League is in this respect.

The grateful leaders of the Tory party, with Lord Salisbury at their head, are never weary of extolling the beneficent effect of the League on English political life. According to them, it has not only provided a most potent instrument for drawing together the children of the common country for the defence of their prosperity, but it has also developed public spirit and rescued the English democracy from the domination of the professional politician, by preventing it from sinking into the condition of a mechanically wire-pulled democracy.[1] No doubt the League brings together the "children of the common country," and even does so often, but with what object has been seen. The most obvious result of these meetings, the least debatable from a moral point of view, amounts perhaps to a certain softening of manners; for the lower-class Englishman, often somewhat brutal or of rough exterior, the meetings of the Primrose League, presided over by dames and "gentlemen," are a sort of drawing-room where he acquires a polish. The League's claims to gratitude for having quickened public spirit would be open to dispute if it were admitted that public spirit presupposes a consciousness of the public interest and unselfish devotion to the public weal. For the motive power of

[1] Cf. Lord Salisbury's speech of the 23d April, 1889, at Bristol, and of the 20th May, 1889, on the occasion of the sixth annual meeting of the Grand Habitation.

the League is utter selfishness on the part of the "superiors," who try to pick up votes by it, and on the part of the "inferiors," who join it for the sake of the greetings and smiles of these personages. The regular organizations of both parties are very far from being free from selfishness, but with the League it is undisguised, it hails people and entices them like passers-by in a public thoroughfare. No doubt the League has succeeded in lifting a good many voters out of their political indifference; it has laid hold of a large section of the new country voters invested with political power by the extension of the suffrage, and not prepared for it; it goes on mobilizing at each election contingents which, left to themselves, would never have appeared on the field of battle. But if they only blindly obey the word of command, as is the case with the ignorant portion of the electorate which the League brings up to the poll, they simply constitute what has been styled in America "voting cattle," from which the party derives a momentary advantage, but from which the honour and the future of the country suffer.

As to the merit ascribed to the League of preventing England from sinking into the condition of a "mechanically wire-pulled democracy," it has in reality all the less power of doing so because it is itself a machinery and, what is novel and unprecedented, a machinery which manufactures sentiments. By the steady movement of its special organization, working methodically and continuously, it is able to supply the market of the party with *social consideration* to order, so to speak. And, as in modern industry, it can easily find an outlet for its product at a distance by consigning, for meetings and fêtes, ladies of title to the localities which have no supply of them. Although advancing in the country by simple *vis inertiae*, the League is beginning to show symptoms of decay (this twofold phenomenon, contradictory in appearance, is not unknown in large organizations; it marks their culminating point). The receipts of the Grand Council, consisting mainly of "tributes" from the knights and dames of the local Habitations, are on the decline, while in a good many Habitations the ardour of the early days is cooling down. Liberal subscriptions were contributed to the Habitations to enable them to give fêtes and entertainments, a show was made of meeting people who had been habitually considered as inferior beings on equal terms; these heavy sacrifices were submitted to, but the game is beginning to pall. Nevertheless, the Primrose League still has a future before it, and a considerable part to play in English political life. A marked elevation of the intellectual and moral standard of the electoral masses combined with a real readjustment of the reciprocal feelings of classes, or a hopeless decline in the fortunes of the Tory party, would be required to deprive the League of its *raison d'être*.

VII

The appearance on the scene of the Primrose League, bringing an unexpected and extremely effective reinforcement to the Tory party, surprised the Liberals greatly, and before long they decided to use the same weapon against their opponents, to confront the Primrose Habitations with *Associations of Liberal Women*. Started in the north (at York) by isolated efforts, the movement gradually spread, and in 1886 there were already a sufficient number of Women's Associations to form a federation. The outline of their organization was borrowed from that of the Caucus; that is to say, it is established on a representative basis, by means of successive delegations, with complete self-government. The autonomy is twofold: not only are the Women's Associations not managed autocratically from the centre, but men have no power in them, for they are composed exclusively of women, unlike those of the Primrose League. Joining in the warfare of the political parties, the Liberal women set before themselves a loftier ideal than that which appeared to them to issue from the practices of the Primrose Dames; their aim was to work for political and social progress by adopting a moral as well as a political standard of action. Their propaganda therefore was to be directed not only towards men, towards electors who, by their votes, can assure the triumph of Liberal principles in legislation and in government, but was to be addressed especially to women, to arouse in them the public spirit, the interest in the common weal, which the want of education as well as the manners of the times had hitherto prevented them from feeling. As regards modes of action, the Associations were to appeal only to the intelligence and the moral sense.

Consequently, they have eschewed all the symbols and emblems, all the high-sounding titles, all the cheap display of badges and decorations, with which their Tory rivals have bedecked themselves.

The importance of the Associations formed by Liberal women varies a great deal from one locality to another. Some of them number as many as a thousand or fifteen hundred members, whereas others do not run to a hundred or even have only an intermittent existence. The great majority of the members is composed of wives of working-men, but the women of the middle class manage and, so to speak, keep alive the organizations. The aristocratic element is not absolutely wanting, but it is of small importance and cannot be compared with the troop of titled dames and of ladies whom the Primrose League can bring into line. The pecuniary resources of the Liberal Associations are consequently not considerable; provided by the donations of the well-to-do members, they are increased by the very modest contributions of the members belonging to the working class. The women of the lower orders, when they pay, do it with a regularity and a conviction which are all the more praiseworthy because the Associations cannot offer them the same satisfactions as the Primrose League. There is, in fact, a good deal of political earnestness about them which resembles the religious fervour of simple souls, and many of them have shown a real wish to learn, to obtain a glimpse into the mysterious region called "politics." The methods employed for "political education," which is one of the principal objects of the women's organization, are of the usual type: meetings, lectures, and distribution of literature. Their meetings have this special feature, that they are hardly ever large public gatherings, like those organized by the caucuses, but more of a private character and with an aspect differing according to the surroundings, from the drawing-room meetings down to the cottage meetings in the villages. In the former case, the members assemble in a lady's large drawing-room to hear speeches and political lectures delivered by persons of either sex; in the latter, the village women meet in a cottage or in a kitchen to hear a touring lady politician or to join in the perusal of a newspaper, interrupted now and then by the unruliness of the domestic

animals, which has to be restrained. Politics are often combined with women's work in the form of "sewing-meetings"
and others which are held periodically. But the most popular combination is, as with the Primrose people, the "tea
meetings" and other "social meetings," embellished with instrumental and especially vocal music. It will be seen that
the Liberal women have all the same borrowed from the Primrose League not only the idea of their organization, but also
some of their modes of action, within somewhat modest limits
it is true. Their teas and conversaziones are but a tame reflection of the fêtes of the League; no ventriloquism, Blondin
rope-walking, or greasy poles, no "union of classes" effected
by bringing together Duchesses and washerwomen. But, on
the other hand, the Associations of Liberal women have not
succeeded in raising the political propaganda to the moral level
which they had in their minds. It is only fair to admit that
very sincere and very serious efforts were made to carry out
the plans of civic education which they had formed. The
Associations or their Federation organized lectures and even
regular courses of civic instruction given by eminent women.
In a good many places energetic and devoted persons sought
out the women of the lower orders and imparted to them a
little political knowledge of the most rudimentary kind; with
this object they visited country districts, penetrating even into
small hamlets. Nevertheless, these efforts have not attained
great dimensions, being paralyzed at one time by the enormous difficulties of the undertaking, at another by the electioneering preoccupations which — save as regards the *modus
operandi* — absorbed the Liberal women almost as much as the
Primrose Dames.

The Women's Associations have, in fact, become a sort of
extension of the party machine. Like the Primrose Dames,
the members take a large part in the canvass, with this difference, that in the Liberal camp not only "ladies" but also
women of the lower classes are mobilized and sent into the
field; and these latter are by no means the least zealous. The
oratory of the female speakers is addressed both to women and
to men. They speak in assemblies composed exclusively of
women as well as in public meetings by the side of orators
of the stronger sex. In local elections, in which women have

the right of voting, it is perfectly natural that they should be appealed to; but often it is deemed advisable to do so even in questions of national politics, so as to influence men through them, especially when the question presents itself or can be presented in a moral still more than in a political aspect (for instance, to protest against the oppression of Ireland, or against the laws relating to the drink traffic, etc.). Relatively speaking, political eloquence is more highly developed and better represented among the Liberal women than among the Primrose Dames. The habitual weapon of the latter is the prestige of their social rank and of their wealth, so that it is enough for them to show themselves; whereas the Liberal women politicians, being often destitute of either, can only make an impression by their ability, their incisive speech, or their argumentative power. But even among the Liberal women the number of fluent speakers is not large; the proportion of practised orators, trained in the arts of the platform, is of course still smaller. There is a tiny group of them which stocks, so to speak, the whole political market. At the request of the local Associations or of candidates, the Women's Federation despatches its best speakers from London to all parts of the kingdom. At by-elections of any importance, they make their appearance, often arriving from a distance, in the train of the speakers of the party who invade, as we have seen, the contested constituencies, and they hold forth from morning till night to help to carry the Tory position. At a general election those of the lady speakers who have no husbands standing for Parliament also scour the country, visiting the points which are in the greatest danger. The other constituencies have to put up with speakers of local reputation, a good many of whom, however, are also imported from neighbouring districts. The Primrose Dames seldom travel far; they prefer to operate in their own neighbourhood, where they are known and where their name is a power in itself.

The assistance which the Liberal politicians of the fair sex thus render to their party, by canvassing, by speaking, or by helping the caucuses in the work of registration and in other ways, is by no means a negligible quantity, and it is assuming larger dimensions every year. Still, compared with that of the Primrose League, their work is much less effective; it brings in, so to speak, much less to the Liberal party than the League does to the Tory party: the Liberal women enrolled in the Associations are far inferior to the Primrose women in numbers and in social influence. Besides this, they are divided among themselves by the grave question of women's suffrage, which has naturally come more to the front since the parties have invited women to share in their political contests. Having the drudgery, many of them think they should have the honour as well, and they strenuously demand the political vote. When the Liberal Federation was formed, the most ardent women wished to make it a base of operations for their claims to the suffrage, but the majority, being concerned solely about the interests of Liberalism and the Liberal party, managed to thrust the question into the background by concealing it under a vague and general formula inserted in the statutes and making the promotion of "just laws for women" one of the "objects" of the Federation. The latter with its branches did in fact devote itself wholly to the party and, like a faithful servant, obediently performed for it all the work in its power. But when, in 1892, Mr. Gladstone declared energetically against the resolution submitted to Parliament in favour of conferring the parliamentary franchise on women, the revolt broke out. The champions of the political rights of their sex who succeeded in the meanwhile in "capturing" the Council of the Federation, in obtaining a majority there, came to the conclusion that they had had enough of blind submission to the party and its leader, Mr. Gladstone, who simply made use of them for their own ends. The moderate minority of the Council, or rather that loyal to the party, resigned in a body, and soon afterwards founded an independent organization, with the title of "National Liberal Association of Women," without any heed to female suffrage. A certain number of local Associations went over to the dissentients, but the very great majority (more than 400 Associations, with nearly 80,000 members) remained affiliated to the Federation. Thus there are now two organizations of women working on equal terms for the Liberal party.

The divergence on the question of the suffrage is not the only one which divides the rival sisters. Managed by women of the aristocracy and of the well-to-do middle class, full of combative ardour, the Federation has in its local sections a great number of women of the Nonconformist lower middle class, who, with the best intentions in the world, often display the temperament of aggressive virtue of which the Nonconformist sects are a hotbed. Their central body, the Federation, which considers itself not only as a party organization but also as a parliament of the sex, delights in "passing resolutions" on all sorts of subjects, and in raising questions relating to the sex, even of the most delicate kind, indulging, for instance, in public discussion of the necessity of passing a law against incest, of abolishing the supervision of women in cantonments in India, and then passing on to the question of vivisection, or to that of legislative measures against rural advertising, against the huge advertisements which "degrade our English country." The *National Association* of Liberal women has grouped around it steadier elements. It makes less noise, hardly indulges at all in the favourite pastime of the caucuses, which consists of passing hortatory, comminatory, or other "resolutions," but thinks more of the political education of its adherents and, what is better still, of that of its own general staff. It discharges this last duty admirably by organizing in its London office periodical discussions among its members, lectures on the questions of the day, delivered by the most competent persons, — Ministers in charge of Bills submitted to Parliament, eminent members of the assemblies where the problem is raised, publicists who have connected their name with the study of the question.

The third party which has been formed in consequence of the Liberal split caused by Irish Home Rule, the Liberal Unionists, who have in many constituencies an organization of their own with a central office in London, also possess an Organization of women (Women's Liberal Unionist Association), with sixty or so affiliated branches constructed on the same basis and working almost on the same lines as the National Liberal Association which has just been described.

VIII

Thus, in the never-ending struggle between the various shades of public opinion, or the various organized interests, not one of the combatants wishing to rank as a party thinks itself able to dispense with the aid of women. Excluded by the constitution from all participation in political affairs, kept at a distance from the forum by tradition and national manners, they are now entreated on all sides to descend into the lists in spite of the constitution and notwithstanding tradition. All the fury of parties was required to drive men to this extremity. It resembles the special levies, when the belligerents, decimated and exhausted but still eager for the fight, hunt up fresh food for powder to sate their rage. In order to cope with their antagonists, many people encourage, others, out of party devotion, tolerate, the intervention of women in militant politics, but the number of men who are frankly opposed to it, or who, at any rate, view it with scepticism, is still very large. It shocks the old-fashioned politicians, both Tory and Liberal, and does not always rouse the enthusiasm of the new generation. How often have I heard the following from the mouth of Conservatives and Radicals: "There is no good in women's electioneering." Several representatives of the organizations share this opinion, basing it often on the want of tact displayed by women politicians, who, through excess of zeal untempered by prudence, are easily led into acts of petty electoral corruption, on the Tory as well as on the Liberal side, or who in their canvass make such a dead set at the voter as to disgust him. Many voters not yet emancipated from the old notions and prejudices relating to the position of women, even consider it somewhat humiliating to be canvassed by a woman, who comes to lecture them on politics. Again, the husbands, in the lower class for instance, do not always look with favour on the political activity of their wives — sometimes from a certain sex jealousy, at others, owing to the time taken up by politics. Working-men submit to or even approve of their wives canvassing at a general election in which the fate of their party is determined for several years, but they do not see the necessity of their doing political work continually. In the middle class, where the women have more leisure, the time spent is not of the same importance, but the perpetual coming and going caused by the political activity of women, the series of committee meetings, of general meetings, of preparations for fêtes, may be very irritating for the husband of a lady president and make him "disgusted with all this business." Not a few people, too, are offended by the exaggerated energy with which women put themselves forward in election campaigns. In fact, the readiness of certain women politicians to lay hold of any weapon in the interest of their party and of the candidate, who is perhaps a near relation, has made them introduce unprecedented traits into electoral tactics.[1] However, not much attention is paid to grumblers in the parties, and all help is accepted from whatever quarter it comes.

As for the attitude of women in reference to their introduction into militant politics, it may be said, in a general way, that they showed much alacrity in responding to the appeal of the parties, more than they had exhibited in filling the position which the Legislature had assigned them in local administration, by conferring on them the right to vote for town councils and school boards (and by implication the right of being elected to these latter). Party politics, even in their extra-constitutional ways, evidently offered them a field of action which was more attractive, more emotional in every sense of the word, from the highest downward. The imagination of the woman with Liberal connections, animated, by education or contagion, with a wish, of a very vague and hazy kind perhaps, for the greatest happiness of the greatest number, and with a belief in the infinite progress of which "Liberalism" was to be the vehicle, showed her how to help the chariot forward by harnessing herself to that of the "Liberal party." For the Primrose Dames there

---

[1] As, for instance, the woman who accompanies her husband to all electoral meetings, and in the intervals between the speeches sings little songs to amuse the crowd, and whose music-hall recitations often achieve more success than all the speakers, and really win votes on the election day. If she is a good hand at rhyme, perhaps she will go so far as to lampoon her husband's competitor in one meeting after another. Some time ago, a lady, the daughter-in-law of a Liberal peer, who was helping her husband in his election campaign by fascinating the voters with her songs, introduced a stanza aimed at the Tory candidate into her repertoire. The latter, who was naturally vexed, wrote to the husband: "I am informed that Mrs. Z . . . lately sung at . . . the following: 'We'll put the Tories to the rout, and shove old X . . . up the spout.'" The heroine of the incident took upon herself to send this reply: "I have sung at . . . and other places, with great success, the following couplet: 'We've kept X . . . out, and put the Tories up the spout.' Yours truly, Y. Z."

opened the blessed prospect of saving souls from Radical damnation, of snatching from the monster of revolution and atheism the victims for whom it was lying in wait. The embroidery or the painting of the banners for the Habitation and its committee meetings offered the mystic languor of her dreamy soul and the ennui due to want of occupation that refuge which the embroidery of sacerdotal ornaments and afternoon services afford to the pious followers of the Church. Flinging themselves into the arena of public life, English-women were able to impart more intensity to their domestic virtues, their family devotion saw new and hitherto un-dreamed-of horizons open to it: here, for instance, is a woman who labours unremittingly from day to day to win her husband the favour of his future electors; another, from the moment election time begins, leaves everything, her home, her pleas-ures, delivers one speech after another, and by sheer energy carries off a seat in Parliament for her husband; a mother rushes about the country to address the electors, in one place for her son, who is entering political life, in another for her husband, or, again, for her brother. With many other women the motives which impel them into the arena of parties are of a less elevated kind; as in the case of many men, it is the glare of the footlights, the wish to shine and to show oneself off. Transferred to the political stage by women, these motives provide fresh pabulum for the *cabotinage* which is more and more invading English society and which casts a sort of shadow over that lofty and noble type of womanhood which is peculiar to the Englishwoman professing the maxim *nihil humani a me alienum puto*. Exaggerations are all the more readily indulged in because the interest of the good cause, that is to say, of the party, covers them with its moral authority.

SEVENTH CHAPTER

AUXILIARY AND RIVAL ORGANIZATIONS (*continued*)

I

AFTER the Women's Organizations, which second the regular Organizations in a general way, which are, if one may venture to use the expression, "maids-of-all-work," come auxiliary organizations entrusted with a particular duty, with speaking at party meetings. While having an independent origin and existence, these special organizations of speakers work for the political party with which each of them is connected. The prototype of these organizations is a Liberal society formed on the eve of the general election of 1880, when the Liberal party was about to deliver a decisive attack on the Tories, led by Lord Beaconsfield in person, by a group of cultivated young men of various shades of Liberal opinion. Brimming over with enthusiasm, they set forth throughout the country to champion the good cause by their eloquence. Their ardour and their talent contributed to the triumph won by the Liberal party, and they decided to found a permanent organization, which took the name of "Eighty Club," in commemoration of the general election in which they made their first campaign. Having only the name of a club, with no special premises, meeting now in one place and now in another (like the Cobden Club formed for the propaganda of free trade), the Society proposed to bring together the pick of the rising generation of Liberals for the service of the Liberal cause and for enlightening public opinion on political questions with a more thorough knowledge and in more elevated language than was offered by the ordinary rhetoric of political meetings. From time to time the Society was to invite statesmen of the party to come and expound their views to the juniors, who would imbibe the instruction of their elders and

qualify themselves to discharge their duty all the better afterwards. The plan succeeded, adhesions poured into the Eighty
Club, from young University graduates, from members of the
Bar; the leaders of the party extended their patronage to it,
and many an important political speech was delivered by them at
its meetings. The part which the members of the Eighty Club
took in election campaigns became of importance; they provided the party with numerous speakers and with candidates
ready to contest the Tory constituencies. This co-operation
with the official party, as well as the influx of members, a
good many of whom joined the Club precisely because of its
relations with the party Organization, soon obliterated its
primitive conception of an independent brotherhood of
preachers of Liberal doctrines. Caught in the toils of the
party, the Eighty ceased, by the force of circumstances, to be
missionaries of the faith and became ministers of the cult. The
crisis of Home Rule for Ireland which divided the Liberal party
brought out, in the Eighty Club as elsewhere, the incompati-
bility between the existence of an organized party and freedom
of opinion within its ranks. Obeying the logic of parties,
the Club, after some attempts at moderation and tolerance, turned out the dissentient minority.[1] After that the
Club only clung all the more firmly to the party and its official
leaders, defending their policy and nothing but their policy. It
became in reality a piece of the party machinery: it provides
the Liberal Associations with speakers for their meetings. The
Associations apply to it as to a registry office. The services of
the speakers are, however, given gratuitously. The Association, or in its default the Club, defrays the travelling expenses
only. An Association of speakers, the Eighty Club is at the
same time a nursery of candidates. The young members of
the Club,— and they form the majority,— by practising on the

[1] At the general election of 1886, brought on by the split, the Club left full
liberty to its members, but soon after the election it changed its attitude.
Mr. Gladstone having stated his views on the Irish question at one of the dinners of the Club, the Liberal Unionists selected Mr. Chamberlain for the purpose of expounding their point of view at the next dinner. The committee of
the Club opposed this. The general meeting of members to which the Liberal
Unionists appealed decided against them, and by a majority vote formally
embraced the policy of Home Rule. The minority was obliged to leave the
Club.

platforms, get known in the country to the local Associations and the central Organization, and by the oratorical assistance they render establish claims on them for being put forward as candidates. Having attained this object, that is to say, having got into Parliament, they remain members of the Club, with the additional duty of serving their party on the platform.

Having been obliged to turn out of the Eighty Club, the Liberal Unionists founded the Liberal Unionist Club on the same pattern. The Conservatives, on their side, have created a special corps of speakers under the name of "The United Club," which renders the same services to the Tories as the Eighty does to the Liberals, and it is also a piece of the machinery of the party. It might perhaps be noted that the United Club is not only a nursery of candidates, but a candidates' trade-union as well. The organization of the Tory party, the Central Office, being only too prone to select the candidates from a limited social circle, the aspirants who are not so well connected, but more intelligent, can, as an organized body, force the hand of the Central Office — now that platform eloquence is of such paramount importance in party contests — by the simple alternative: no seats, no speakers.

II

Along with the auxiliary organizations can be discerned others which are only allies. Independent by their origin and their peculiar aspirations of party politics, they nevertheless give their co-operation to one party or the other, according as it is favourable or hostile to the special cause which they serve. The principal of these special causes provided with organizations which ally themselves with the parties are connected with the Church and the public-house. The monopoly of the Established Church, which was long so oppressive for the Nonconformists, led them to form an organization for its disestablishment, while the mischief caused by drinking in English society, and especially among the toiling masses, gave rise to associations which strove to obtain from Parliament legislative measures against the sale of spirituous liquors. Threatened in their interests, the publicans in their turn organized themselves all over the kingdom. The Church,

though already possessing an organization in the clergy, reinforced it with a special defence institution. The Liberals
having always fought for freedom of conscience and the secu-
larization of the State, and the Anglican Church having been
from time immemorial the stronghold of Toryism, the two
organizations endeavouring the one to carry the Disestablishment of the Church, the other to defend it, naturally took
sides the one with the Liberal, the other with the Conservative party. Again the Liberals, having been the first to
espouse the cause of temperance in Parliament, threw the
publicans into the arms of the Tories, who were quite ready
to receive them. Thus by the force of circumstances there
has grown up a community of action between the parties and
the organizations in question, which, without being bound
to them, render them great services.

The association which demands the separation of Church
and State is called the "Society for the Liberation of Religion
from State Patronage and Control," or, by abbreviation, the
"Liberation Society." Founded more than half a century
ago, it has rendered some service to the cause of liberty of
conscience. Now that this is secured, it tries to deprive the
Anglican Church of its privileged position — without much
success, however. Being anxious to get a majority favourable to disestablishment in the House, it intervenes in all the
elections, and it possesses for this purpose a fairly developed
machinery in the form of paid agents, who each work up a district, and numerous unpaid correspondents scattered over the
whole country, almost in every parish. While keeping up very
close relations with the Liberal organizations which, by the
way, are full of their coreligionists, and very often belonging
themselves to the caucuses, the representatives of the Liberation Society try to get a candidate favourable to disestablishment brought forward, and once he is selected, they do their
best to ensure his success at the poll. Several Liberal
Associations, on their part, send delegates to the general
meetings of the Liberation Society; the ties which unite them
are, in fact, exceedingly strong, for, as Mr. Gladstone has
said, the Nonconformists are "the backbone of the Liberal
party."

The Tories, on their side, have a spontaneous ally in the

association for the defence of the Anglican Church, the "Church Defence Institution," founded in 1860 to protect the Church against those who wish to "dissolve that Union that has existed between the Church and the State ever since there was a united England at all, and to take away from Churchmen and from God Himself the money and buildings which for centuries have been set apart for His honour and service."[1] The Institution set to work to secure the co-operation of the clergy and the laity by forming local Associations of them, culminating through elected delegates in a Central Council. It succeeded in creating a considerable number of branches in the country, which have materially contributed to oppose the coalition of the Nonconformists and the Liberals. Still it has less intrinsic importance than its rival, the Liberation Society; for it borrows its principal force of action from the established clergy. The latter have even been recently made complete masters of the organization. By a sway cf authority the two Archbishops of the Church have transferred the chief work of the Institution to a small committee of their own creation, and placed all the branches of the Institution under the direct control of the Bishop in each diocese. Finally the Institution was altogether absorbed by the Archbishops' committee into an "Amalgamated body" of "Church Defence and Church Instruction" governed, under the Archbishops, by a Council and an Executive Committee which are only partly elected. By a curious innovation, which is a sign of the times, the Archbishops added to the local organization presided over by the Bishop a diocesan committee of ladies, with a central committee of their own in London under the wing of the Primate of the Church; and then by the rules of the "Amalgamated body" the direct representatives of each Diocese in the Council were made to consist one half of men and one half of women. Here again, as in the Primrose League, women are invited to fight the good fight for the defence of the old politico-ecclesiastical order.

The other organization allied with the Tories, the co-operation of which is much more direct, and certainly more effective,

---

[1] "What the Church Defence Institution is, and what it is doing," Leaflet No. 6, *The Church Defence Handy Volume*, 11 ed. Lond. 1895.

is the association of the publicans, the "Licensed Victuallers'
Association." Financed by the great brewers and distillers,
it has spread its net, not to say its web, all over the country.
It has divided the territory of the kingdom into districts, each
entrusted to paid agents, who supervise and stir up the publicans in the electoral struggle. The object is to return candidates who will oppose the measures aimed at the drink traffic,
or, what almost amounts to the same thing, to help to get
in Tory candidates. With but few exceptions the licensed
victuallers are all enrolled in this crusade, so that their influence, which is unquestionably great, may be brought to bear on
the voters. The publican is often far more the director of
his customers' consciences than the clergyman. The unedu-
cated man of the lower classes falls under his influence not
only through frequenting his bar every day, but because he is
often his debtor, without even being led into it by vice; in
small places the publican is also a sort of banker, a petty
usurer, and people are too often obliged to have recourse to
him. Indefatigable during election time, the publicans also
endeavour in the interval between the elections to make
recruits among the new voters who from year to year attain
their political majority; they try to swell the Tory register.
A considerable number of voters "put on the register" by
their efforts may turn the electoral scale in a good many
constituencies.

As a set-off to this, the Liberal party can depend on the
great temperance organization known as "The United Kingdom Alliance," which possesses many adherents throughout
the country. But it is an ally whose co-operation is sometimes dearly bought. Being for the most part enthusiasts,
who sincerely believe that it is in the power of Parliament to
put a stop to excessive drinking by means of laws, the temperance champions thrust their measures for prohibiting the sale
of spirituous liquors on the Liberal party as the price of their
assistance. To make things safer, the partisans of temperance
have attempted to "capture" the caucuses, and they have been
successful in a great many cases. Installed inside the Liberal
organization, they can force its hand all the more easily. But
as in the inflexibility of their virtuous ardour they do not make
sufficient allowance for national idiosyncrasies, they alienate

a number of voters from the Liberal party, and at the last general election (1895) they even managed to get it defeated. It is admitted, in fact, that "local veto" (which would give a majority of the inhabitants of each locality the right to prohibit the sale of intoxicating drinks) had a good deal to do with the rout of the Liberal party.

III

Among the auxiliary or allied organizations may be ranked also some which, while serving the same cause as the regular party organizations, endeavour, or have endeavoured, to attain an independent position, and, if the dream were possible, even to supplant the organizations in power. In fact, the growth of the Caucus on the one side, and of the Primrose League on the other, soon aroused emulation, with more or less ambitious aims, in the ranks of their parties. There was a great attraction in being able to pull the strings of an organization covering the whole country from London and to make it perform all the movements desired, and there seemed to be no great difficulty about improvising such an organization. Some attempts in this direction have been made in both camps, but they have come to nothing. The regular organizations have stifled them or have let the newly born organizations die of inanition. This is also the most practical way of getting rid of them, for the new organization generally comes forward with asseverations of its orthodoxy and of its ardent desire to serve the party with all its strength. The aspiration is such a pious one that the official Organization can only say amen to it. But to live and grow, an organization must, above all things, have money, and it is there that the old organization of the party lies in wait for the young one. It intimates to the zealots of.the party whose generosity is appealed to, that if they have more money than they know what to do with, they are at liberty to part with it, and as no one ever has a superabundance of money, the new organizations die out or vegetate for want of sustenance.

Among the organizations planned or actually created under these conditions may be cited two imitations of the Primrose League, the one Liberal, the other Conservative. The first,

"The Liberal League of Great and Greater Britain," tried to
bring about the triumph of Liberal principles "by associating
men and women of all sections of the Liberal Party" in
lodges of companions, provided with diplomas and badges and
governed by a "Central Lodge" and a "Supreme Council";
after having founded — in several cases on paper only — about
a hundred lodges, it became extinct. The Tory imitation,
"The National Conservative League," formed of lodges embracing all classes of society and having at its head grand
masters, a grand secretary, a grand treasurer, a grand librarian,
etc., still subsists. It also claims to promote the union of
classes for the benefit of the Tory party, and that without
going over the same ground as the Primrose League, by operating exclusively on the lowest social strata, on the dregs of
the population, which by their very nature escape the Primrose
Dames. It aims at procuring the return of Tory working-
men to Parliament. In the meanwhile, for the sake of their
"political education," the lower orders are enrolled in the
lodges, where they meet with gentlemen, nay with Lords,
who in the public-houses used as a rendezvous for the lodges
hobnob with them, call them "brothers," and make them
speeches on the superiority of Toryism. The Conservative
League possesses a certain number of lodges, especially in the
southern and western counties, but it is paralyzed in its
operations by want of money.

There is also on the Liberal side a large organization independent of the Caucus, of older standing even, and with a
somewhat glorious past. This is the National Reform Union
of Manchester, which was referred to at length in the historical
part of this work. It will be remembered that the Union,
which represented originally a political current opposed to that
of the Caucus, retired before the Birmingham Organization,
which had become the official mouthpiece of the party. Of
late years the Union has tried to recover its position and to
group around it the elements of the party most advanced in
opinions and desirous of emancipating themselves from the
"officialism" of the central Caucus, and it has placed its
organization at the disposal of the group of independent
Radicals in the House. But as it has not openly broken with
the party, and continues to co-operate with it at the elec-

tions, the official, orthodox organization, working in concert with the chiefs of the party, still takes the lead, and alone wields the authority and influence appertaining to a party organization.

Thus the experience of party organizations in England, although not very long, has conclusively proved that there is even less room for rival organizations within the limits of parties than in churches; that the party creed stifles or disables every independent organization; that an organization can preserve its independence of the two great parties in the State solely by placing itself outside them, in opposition to them. This has lately been done, as we are already aware, by the "Labour party."

IV

The reader recollects the circumstances in which the Labour party was formed, only a few years ago, for the purpose of assuming an independent and even hostile attitude towards the great parties. The workmen were invited to quit them because the Liberals, just as much as the Tories, represented the capitalist class, which exploits the masses politically and economically; it was urged that, having nothing to expect from the existing parties in the way of improvement of their lot, the workers should take their cause into their own hands. They should send Members of their own to Parliament as well as to the local assemblies, to fight the battle of the proletariate against the capitalist class.

The first part of this proposition is of less recent origin. For a long time the question of more direct representation of the masses in Parliament had been agitated; it was pointed out that they were not and could not be represented by gentlemen; that men belonging themselves to the working classes, and having lived their life, were alone capable of being their spokesmen, the interpreters of their wants and their aspirations. A few electoral organizations were even founded, with the special mission of getting working-men returned to Parliament (The Labour Representation League in 1874 and other associations), but they did not gather strength. The vast majority of the workmen remained indifferent, while some of their most influential representatives, who had themselves got into Parliament under the auspices of the Liberal party, were of opinion that it was not for working-men to treat popular representation from the standpoint of class distinctions; that they were more interested than any one in seeing these distinctions obliterated; that, having been brought within the pale of the Constitution, they were in charge of the interests of the whole nation, which included theirs, just as those of all the other groups of society.[1] Towards 1888 the tendencies towards "labour representation" took more definite shape,[2] particularly among the Trade Unionists, when a Labour Electoral Association was started, with branches in the country. Still this movement was not directed against existing parties or the capitalist class as such. Its promoters even disclaimed any intention of "setting class against class"; they simply wished to "bring the great manufacturers and merchants and the working-men together, to make them join hands and try to raise the poor and the miserable in the scale of society."[3] Their sole desire was "a leavening of the House of Commons with men having a thorough knowledge of the wants of the masses."[4] Even in the Conservative camp the question began to be agitated, and it appears that the luxury of a labour organization with the party label (National Conservative Labour League) was actually indulged in, which, as was to be expected, did not meet with the least encouragement from the leading organizers of the Tory party ("a chilling and discouraging reception," as the promoter of the League complained).

But before long the movement of labour representation and of a Labour party, which had sprung from Trades Unionism, was monopolized by the Socialists, who became particularly aggressive after 1890. The Labour party was to enter Parliament, not to demand various Radical measures there, but to carry out, by constitutional methods, the social revolution on the

[1] One of the most eminent members of the labour class, Mr. Thomas Burt, an ex-miner, on more than one occasion stated these views with real elevation of mind.

[2] This year was connected with the first "Labour Electoral Congress," held at Sheffield.

[3] *The Voice of Labour*, being the report of the first Annual Labour Electoral Congress, Southport, 1888, p. 21.

[4] Third annual congress of the Labour Electoral Association, at Henley, April, 1890.

lines of complete and absolute collectivism. Even the bourgeois Socialists of the Fabian Society, composed mainly of well-to-do educated persons and engaged in doctrinal propaganda, thought fit to tone down their temporizing policy, of which the name of their patron, Fabius Cunctator, was the symbol. Hitherto they had hoped to transform the Liberal party into a Socialist party by gradual infiltration, permeation, but party tyranny, which stifled every independent tendency and prevented advanced candidates from coming forward, made the task too difficult and left the primordial interests of Labour uncared for. On the eve, therefore, of the general election of 1892, the Fabians launched a manifesto in which they gave the Liberal party a bit of their mind and exposed its "hypocrisy"; and while fully aware that, looking to the great apathy of the working-men, there were at present not sufficient elements in the country for a Labour party which could dispense with the support of the middle class, they advised that labour candidates should be started against the Tories and the Liberals wherever there was a chance of their success.[1] The Fabians provided some candidates with the money required for election expenses, but the success of their protégés, as well as of the other independent and socialist candidates, was not very great; with but one or two exceptions they merely succeeded in diminishing the number of votes polled by the Liberals. This very relative success of the "independents" only increased their exasperation against the Liberal party, which was henceforth looked on as the great enemy of "labour," worse than the Tories; for to feelings of capitalist hostility towards labour claims it added the insincerity of professing sympathy with the masses. Pretending to be favourable to "labour" representation in Parliament, the organization of the Liberal party in reality tried to make away with it; the so-called labour members which the party possessed, and which it paraded, were not so much champions of the cause of labour as obsequious servants of the party, of official Liberalism, or, as Mr. Chamberlain put it, "mere fetchers and carriers for the Gladstonian party."

In this assertion, especially so far as it concerned the labour members, there was a vast amount of exaggeration. From

[1] Fabian Election Manifesto, 1892, *Fabian Tracts*, No. 40.

1874 genuine working-men had entered the House, being generally brought in by their respective Trade Unions; those of the miners, for instance, and others. In a dozen years there were as many as ten or twelve of them, all returned as professed "Liberals." By their intelligence and their character they almost all did credit to the social class to which they belonged, and some were even an ornament of the House of Commons. They intervened with zeal and devotion in the discussion of all questions relating to the toiling masses. Classed among the Liberals, they followed them in everything, according to the ethics of parties. But in their capacity of men who were not politicians born and bred, they were sometimes perhaps too eager to identify themselves with the party. No doubt it is always difficult for a man who enters a society considered superior to his own, and who tries instinctively to adapt himself to it, to avoid exaggerations. And how greatly must this difficulty of preserving one's personality be enhanced when the new society is a party which holds its man in an iron grip, which even goes so far as to change his conscience. In this particular case the difficulty was increased tenfold by the immense prestige of the leader of the Liberal party, and besides this, the party helped some of the labour members by defraying their election expenses (just as, by the way, it did those of so many other non-labour candidates). It is therefore possible that an independent observer may have been occasionally justified in paraphrasing, with reference to the Gladstonian labour members, the remark of the Patriarch, by saying: "The hands are the hairy hands of the people, but the voice is the voice of the party Whip." But, after all, the great crime of these members was that they were Trade Unionists of the old school, with more faith in individual initiative than in the tutelage of the State.

There was more foundation for the second cause of complaint; to wit, that the organization of the Liberal party was not sincerely interested in labour representation. In fact, whatever the official and semi-official mouthpieces of the party may say,[1] it gave its support only to those labour candidates —

[1] Thus, for instance, the *Speaker*, the semi-official organ of the Gladstonian party, wrote: " The Liberal party's organization is so free and so elastic, that no section of the party can truly complain of being ignored or excluded from

donning, of course, the party livery — who had undeniable chances of success, and who would have got in even in spite of it. As for the others, it graciously made over to them constituencies in which the power of the Tories or of the Liberal Unionists was such that any opposition candidature was doomed to failure. The tactics were the same as those pursued in some of the local caucuses, where the middle-class bigwigs who pull the strings of the Organization rewarded zealous workers of the labour class with candidatures for the Town Council in wards which were a stronghold of the Tories. In reserving the safe seats for non-labour men, the central Caucus acted not so much from class as from party spirit; labour candidates with perhaps very advanced and too personal opinions would not have offered the required guarantees of obedience to the party.

Having broken openly with the Liberal party, the champions of labour proceeded immediately after the general election of 1892 to organize themselves throughout the country, and founded the "Independent Labour Party," to oppose Liberals and Tories alike. Without including all the socialist and labour contingents divided among several organizations (two of which, The Fabian Society and The Labour Electoral Association, have been already mentioned), the I. L. P. really embodies the new movement in all its aspects. It raised the banner of "Labour" pure and simple, but enveloped within its folds a socialist programme of a most decided kind, briefly defined in its statutes as having for its object "an industrial commonwealth founded upon the socialization of Land and Capital," and expounded by one of the leaders of the party in the following terms: "It is the establishment of a state of society where living upon unearned incomes shall be impossible for any but the physically enfeebled; where the total work of the country shall be scientifically regulated and properly apportioned over the total number of able-bodied citizens; where class domination should be impossible by the full recognition of Social, Economic, and Sex Equality."[1] Attracting

its fair share of influence. All that talk about wire-pulling, the Caucus, the undue share of power possessed by local magnates, is sheer rubbish, born out of the ignorance of men who know absolutely nothing of the conditions of political life in the great provincial constituencies" (11th February, 1893).

[1] *What the I. L. P. is driving at*, by Tom Mann, 1894.

some by the rigid socialism of its programme, and others by the vagueness of its title of Labour party, the I. L. P. has recruited in the country, especially in the north, a certain number of adherents, not very considerable, but by no means negligible. Almost all of them belong to the working class, with a sprinkling of lower middle-class people earning about as much as artisans, and a few cultivated persons, among whom are found even University graduates. A larger number of persons of the well-to-do and educated class, without being incorporated in the ranks ⏉f the I. L. P., is with them in heart and mind. They are first of all the doctrinaire social-ists; then persons without economic attainments but highly sentimental, with a nervous sensibility which makes them look on the misery in the world with horror and on existing society with despair; and finally, as in every movement, dilettantes, not to say quidnuncs, who run after the last fashion, or what they believe to be such.

The working-class contingents are composed of two clearly defined sections: of a small minority of intelligent men, with noble aspirations, of excellent character, and of a very large majority of ignorant people, often taken from the dregs of society, of loafers, of social waifs and strays, of poor wretches who are open to one preoccupation only, — that of the stomach. And it is by appealing to their animal wants, by creating a feeling of revolt in their minds, that the I. L. P. attracts them into its ranks. A good half of the members of the I. L. P. are old followers of the Liberal organization; the remainder has been recruited partly in the Tory camp and partly in the circles which had hitherto, by their indifference, escaped the political parties. The losses sustained under these circumstances by the orthodox organizations, Liberal and Tory, were very perceptible, not so much on account of the number as the quality of the men who deserted them; they saw several of their "workers" go over to the I. L. P. To the great astonishment of the Tories, some of their old canvassers, who were by no means conspicuous in the routine discharge of the work of the Tory party entrusted to them, came out as speakers and agitators in the I. L. P. The Liberal caucuses did not experience any surprises of this kind; the men who left them were remarkable for their enthusiasm.

Having belonged to the Caucus for years, and having watched the plutocrats who led the Associations at work, they fancied they saw how the capitalist class duped the masses; taking an active part in the electoral business of the Caucus, they were initiated into the manœuvres of wire-pulling, to which they had even contributed in the sincerity of their hearts, for the greater glory of the "cause." When the new gospel of labour and of socialism opened their eyes, they saw that the god which they had adored was only a rude idol; and in the shame and disgust which overcame them, they were glad to find in the I. L. P. a refuge for their wounded souls and a sphere of action for their ardour and their desire to serve their fellow-creatures.

Moral enthusiasm is, in fact, one of the leading traits of the movement, and its ethical tendencies, the object of which is the raising of man and of society, give it its special stamp. They appeal with some to the intelligence, with the vast majority to feeling, and very often even to religious feeling. Whereas the socialist circles which arose in the old days, and which were recruited among the intellectual set, were generally composed of materialists and atheists, the great bulk of the I. L. P. are believers. The ideal pursued by the Labour movement is represented to them as a religious ideal, and an appeal is made to their religious enthusiasm to help to realize it. This religious conception has even found tangible expression in the organization of a "Labour Church" possessing a creed and provided with a cult. "The Church" has declared its aim to be the "realization of heaven *in this life* by the establishment of a state of society founded upon justice and love to the neighbour." It professes that "the Labour movement is a religious movement; that the religion of the Labour movement is not a class religion, but that it unites the members of all classes in working for the abolition of commercial slavery; that the religion of the Labour movement is not sectarian or dogmatic, but free religion, leaving each man free to develop his own relations with the Power that brought him into being; that the emancipation of labour can only be realized so far as men learn both the economical and moral laws of God and heartily endeavour to obey them; that the development of personal character and the improvement of social conditions

are equally essential to man's emancipation from moral and
social bondage." The services of the Labour Church consist
of the singing of socialist and Labour hymns, of a short
prayer, of the reading of passages from a work on religion
or democratic politics, and of a discourse on some aspect or
other of the movement. The Labour Church has not attained
large proportions; after a brief existence it has amalgamated
in some places with the I. L. P., while in others it exists
alongside the I. L. P. and in close connection with it.

The fervour which animates the adherents of the I. L. P.
makes up, to a great extent, for the intellectual poverty which
characterizes the majority of them. They display a keen and,
it might be said, almost thoughtful interest in their organization; one and all pay their pennies with a sort of ritual devotion into the chest of the party, which subsists only by the
contributions of its members. In this respect the I. L. P.
presents a novel phenomenon in the life of English party
organizations, in which, on the Liberal as on the Tory side,
a few wealthy individuals, headed by the Member or the
candidate, finance the Association. All that the working-men
voters belonging to the orthodox parties consent to give is
their votes, and even then, as we are aware, they want a good
deal of pressing to go to the poll; they must be fetched in a
carriage. They behave as if their interests were in no way
at stake. The I. L. P. are the only ones who "pay for their
own politics."

Another feature which distinguishes them, as well as their
socialist coreligionists, from other organizations, is their
ardour in promoting the political education of their adherents.
In the orthodox parties political education is talked about a
great deal, but, as we have seen, little or nothing is done for it.
The I. L. P. and the other socialists are the only parties which
systematically cultivate men's minds by classes and lectures,
by discussion, by readings in common. The activity which
they display in this respect has given an intellectual impulse
even to their opponents, by forcing them to study the economical questions which are so much talked about. The
propagandist zeal of the I. L. P. is indefatigable; it avails
itself of every opportunity to expound its doctrines, to enrol
adherents; it seeks them in the public parks, at the street-

crossings; it distributes writings of all kinds wholesale. The political education which the I. L. P. offers is, in truth, of a somewhat limited character; it deals only with economical questions, which are of course always viewed through the socialist-collectivist prism.

Their ethical standard is just as narrow; the unvarying criterion of political integrity is in their eyes unqualified adhesion to collectivism. Professing to disregard the insincere conventions of the social and political world, and to judge men and things by their intrinsic worth, they nevertheless oppose the election of Radicals animated with broad and genuine sympathies for the working classes, but not going to the length of subscribing to revolutionary collectivism.

Sectarian in their doctrine and in their propaganda, the I. L. P. are naturally autoritarian in their organization. The discipline to which the members of their associations have to submit goes beyond that of the Caucus which they abhor so much. A member of the I. L. P. or of the older organization, "The Social Democratic Federation," is never his own master. To be admitted into the I. L. P., a declaration must be signed by which the applicant pledges himself to have nothing to do with any political party and to vote at elections in accordance with the directions of the Organization. The local branch of the I. L. P. nominates the candidate for Parliament, but no selection is valid until it has been confirmed by the Central Council. In places where the I. L. P. does not run a candidate, its adherents have to regulate their conduct by the decisions of the central body, which "decisions are final and binding on the branches." The Social Democratic Federation asserts its authority over its members in still more imperative terms; it forbids them to take a single step in elections without having consulted the respective branch or the General Council, as the case may be. The candidates elected under its auspices must submit to the control of their local branch in regard to local affairs, and to that of the General Council for everything that concerns their parliamentary activity. The candidates are obliged to sign a form of resignation beforehand.

In the series of "methods" laid down by the I. L. P. for the realization of its aim, "the education of the community in the principles of socialism" and "the industrial and political' organization of the workers" are followed by "independent representation on socialist principles on all elective bodies," including local assemblies, town councils, school boards, parish councils, etc.   Even before 1892, but especially after that date, local assemblies became the objective of the champions of labour.   At the annual elections for town councils labour candidatures now occur regularly in most of the large towns; in several places the labour candidates have succeeded in getting on the town councils, as well as on the school boards, etc., and sometimes not without advantage to those bodies.   If they are not very competent to deal with municipal business (though in this respect they are in no way inferior to most of the councillors introduced by the caucuses), at all events they are resolved to keep a jealous watch on the money of the ratepayers and to throw the full light of publicity on the proceedings of the council, including those of its committees, the sittings of which are not public.

The efforts of the I. L. P. to get into Parliament have not been successful.   At the last general election (of 1895) it ran several candidates, but all of them were beaten, and most of them cut a very sorry figure at the poll — all the more so because the I. L. P. had made a great fuss before the battle, and had boasted that they would "smash the Liberal party." They did not smash it — far from it; but they cracked it in several places; their desertion has cost the Liberals not a few seats.   This is the only clear gain which the Labour party has to show.   Revolutionary collectivism does not as yet tempt the great majority of English workmen sufficiently for them to shake off their accustomed political apathy and leave the beaten track of the historic parties, in which they walk more or less automatically or are dragged along by methods which have an easy hold on them. . To rouse them from this indifference the masses lack the incentive of extreme poverty which the I. L. P. and their socialist coreligionists make so much of in their warlike appeals.   Nor are the jealousies which devour the various socialist factions better calculated to bring victory to their cause.   But if the hour of the I. L. P. has not come, and if its numerical strength is unimportant, it is none the less a factor in the life of English parties by reason of the dissolving effect which it produces on them. For by the sole fact of its organization it attacks not this or that party, but party loyalty in general; it loosens time-honoured party ties. In doing so it also demoralizes the leaders, who in their anxiety to keep their men, and through fear of fresh desertions, will not fail to stoop to concessions which they would not have made if they had listened only to their convictions or their prejudices.

EIGHTH CHAPTER

SUMMARY

I

Now that we have come to the end of our enquiry into the introduction, the development, and the working of party organization in England, we are at liberty to turn round and take a general survey of the route which has been traversed.

Introduced with the intention of making the government of the historic parties more democratic, the Caucus has succeeded in this to a certain extent, especially in the destructive portion of its work. Falling upon the leadership, which it regarded as oligarchical, it dismantled it and dealt a heavy blow at the old parties which were grouped around it; it powerfully contributed to overthrow Whiggism; it pressed the last life-breath out of expiring classic Radicalism, and helped to drive back old-fashioned Toryism. But it has been less successful in the constructive part of the task which it undertook. It has not been able to provide the parties with a really democratic government; it has created the forms of it, but not the essence. The soil in which the new institution was planted was far from being everywhere favourable to its growth, and it proved little more than an exotic. The political manners and customs of English society, taken as a whole, were not at all democratic; they did not require the development of the democratic principle to its extreme consequences with the rigour applied by the promoters of the Caucus. The extension of the suffrage to the urban masses, to the degree effected by the Act of 1867, came before its time, as one of its most ardent champions, John Bright, admitted by saying that it would have been better to accomplish the reform in two stages, at an interval of twenty years. True, this fact in itself presented nothing unusual in the history of political societies; in

a general way, it may be said that there is never any particular
moment in the life of a community when institutions are in
perfect harmony with manners and customs; sometimes the
one, sometimes the other, are in advance; there is always a
gap between them.   But that does not prevent the more
advanced community from developing, nor oblige the more
backward one to rush wildly ahead, if no attempt is made to get
the utmost out of the institutions.   By extending the democratic principle of the Reform of 1867, in all its legal strictness, to political life outside the Constitution, the Caucus
pushed this principle to its extreme logical limits, which happened to be far beyond those of the manners of the nation.   It
did not leave to time or the force of circumstances the task of
lessening the distance between too democratic institutions
and insufficiently democratic manners; it hurried on and tried
to substitute for the, so to speak, chemical process of permeation, of mutual penetration, the mechanical one of external
organization.   And it simply succeeded — with some exceptions
which will be pointed out later on — in bringing into glaring
prominence the contradiction between the capacity and the
power of the masses, a contradiction which can only disappear
gradually.

   The ex-ruling class, the middle class, confronted on the one
hand by its official dethronement, and on the other by the political incapacity of the masses, wished, both from ambition and
duty,— the duty of "carrying on the Queen's government," —
to reconcile this contradiction by dint of adroitness, by preserving in the management of parties the reality of power, of
which it had been legally divested by the establishment of the
Caucus.   And this English middle class, which had played a
glorious part in the conquest of public liberties and in the development of political spirit and civic dignity, now appeared
in a new rôle, of an anything but lofty character; pretending
to bow down before the masses, it let them say what they
liked, allowed them the satisfaction of holding forth and of
voting extravagant resolutions in the caucuses, provided that
it was permitted to manage everything; and to cover its designs it developed the practice of wire-pulling.   Being powerless, however, without the small ward leaders, created by the
democratic party organization, it undertook to corrupt them

systematically, to win them by acting on their "social ten-dencies." Invitations to "at homes," to garden-parties, to dinners with the big men of the party, free admission to gen-tlemen's clubs, methodically demoralized the leaders of the lower middle class and of the working class, by developing and fostering in them the abject snobbishness which infects social relations in England. Having given a democratic form to party government, in order to liberate it from "social influ-ences," the Caucus managed by the middle-class men itself appealed to those influences and borrowed from them the most disreputable part of their methods and conduct. The middle class often had good sense on its side and understood what was fitting in politics, but it was too faint-hearted to face the masses and it preferred to circumvent them by devices of management. Withholding from them the plain truth and offering them only the bait of gratification of self-love and vanity, it enervated and disgusted a good many of the best set to such an extent as to fling them into the sectarian but honest fanaticism of the Independent Labour parties, into the wild ideas of Utopia-mongers and collectivist agitators.

The development of the organization of the Caucus, however, presents yet another aspect, which tones down that which has just been described. The adroitness which the middle class was compelled to exert was in itself a homage to the power conferred on the masses by the Caucus. In fact, while keeping a firm hand on party government, the middle class was obliged, owing to the very constitution of the Caucus, to share its authority, in appearance at least, with the representatives of the lower orders. The mere play of this constitution brought out from the ranks of the people a number of leaders with a voice in the counsels of the party. Under the social conditions which prevailed in England a quarter of a century back, these men would not have been able to get so far by their unaided efforts; the Organization of the Caucus alone provided them with the means by admitting their right to share in the government of the party, in virtue of a prin-ciple, and no longer as in the old days when a few working-men members were put on the election committees for the occa-sion and as decoy-ducks. The more exclusive and oligarchical the political surroundings were, the more the admission, even pretended, of the multitude to power gained in value, and the greater the practical effect which it produced in party life. The Caucus, therefore, did democratize party government on the Liberal side, and still more on the Tory side and in the rural constituencies generally. The new Conservative Associations, which conceded a share of influence to the simple "workers," have served as a lever for the Neo-Toryism of the large towns called forth by Lord Randolph Churchill and his following; they have given shape and body to "popular Toryism," which was laboriously cutting a path through Disraeli's nebulous doctrines, the practical necessities of "dishing the Whigs," and the ambitions of the "Fourth Party" and of the Tory *tiers État ;* they have helped to install the *tiers* in the government of the party, to make the multitude an organic factor in it, and in general to impart to the rank and file of the party more freedom of manners, if not of mind. In the counties the new Organization has also helped to extract the practical consequences of the electoral Reform of 1885, by giving the masses a share in the business of the political parties side by side with the "gentlemen" who had hitherto managed it by themselves. If the reality of the power thus conferred on the masses was subject to much qualification from a political point of view, it was otherwise with regard to its social effect; for in social relations, where convention is paramount, form has precedence of substance, and external demonstrations take the place of genuine feelings, by providing, through the mere fact of their manifestation, the gratifications of *amour-propre* for which mankind in a social state has a craving. By the inherent force of its hierarchy and of its formal spheres of authority and influence, the Caucus has succeeded in raising the small shopkeeper and the artisan, who were kept in a state of inferiority by the manners of the nation, in the scale of society. Again, the methods which the Caucus, and its counterpart the Primrose League, had created for distributing "social consideration" at will and making it a sort of commodity put on the market, were in their turn instrumental in levelling society if not in making it democratic.

II

This distinction, which is often ignored by the common prejudice, appears all the more legitimate and necessary in the present case the further one proceeds with the enquiry into the effect of the Caucus on the improvement of the public spirit of the masses, which is the sole criterion of genuine democracy. At the outset the Caucus, which professed to appeal to the masses, succeeded in arousing, in several places, their interest in the public weal; it attracted men who represented the best elements of the lower strata of society, and it seemed to tend towards really widening the borders of the political community. But all this lasted but a single moment, just long enough to make it clear that the democracy inscribed on the standard of the Caucus was only a painted banner or a coarse sign. Independent and thoughtful people saw that there was no room for them among the small vulgar leaders brought to the surface of politics, or in the meetings and committees where everything was cut and dried by a little coterie which monopolized power by pulling the strings behind the scenes. Having repelled these men, the Caucus has contrived to attract only the enthusiasts, the bigots of the party, and the busybodies. The great mass remained outside, sunk in its apathy and its indifference.

To drag them out of it, the Caucus could devise nothing better than *organization*, which it ended almost by confounding with political *education*. For this latter it has really done nothing. The Associations have proved radically unfitted for serving as an instrument of political education; they have succeeded only in turning out electioneering machines. A servant of the party, engrossed by its immediate duties, the Caucus was not in a position to apply itself to the political culture of the masses, of a general and disinterested kind. An election broker picking up votes right and left, loaded with heavy omnibus programmes which promised the solution of all kinds of different questions, to please everybody, it was no more possible for it to make the public mind and conscience grasp all the problems raised than to devote itself to each of them or concentrate the attention of the masses on one of them to the detriment of the others. The Caucus, therefore, was naturally inclined, instead of bringing about an agreement of intellects, to resort to mechanical modes of rallying its forces and to keep its adherents together in an external and conventional conformity, by appealing not so much to reason, which analyzes and distinguishes, as to feeling; by preferring to stir up emotions which confuse the judgment and make a prisoner of the will. The followers of the party were all, in accordance with the shifting requirements of the situation, provided in a lump with a stock of convictions or political sentiments, which spared them the trouble of all personal exertion. Political ideas were introduced simultaneously into their minds, and they took them in collectively, by a single and undivided effort. "We now think in battalions," as a shrewd observer, a Northumberland workman, remarked on this subject. Lost in the crowd, even as regards the inner life of the intelligence and the conscience, individuality dwindled under the steady action of the Caucus, and in this connection, too, a levelling process took place, but of a kind which did not even possess the questionable merit of contributing to the enhancement of human dignity in social relations; its tendency was decidedly to lower the mind, in other words, to impair the moral dignity of man. In this work of obliteration of individuality, the Caucus was assisting a movement which began before it and was operating in every-day life independently of it. In the first part of this book it was pointed out how the social transformation inaugurated by the industrial revolution and philosophy, in emancipating the individual, brought about a levelling process which from many points of view seemed to have the effect of rather blotting out human personality. The unbroken progress of material civilization has powerfully forwarded this movement, not only by generalizing tastes and habits, but by forcing individuals to dissolve into crowds, for the better enjoyment of the benefits of this civilization, which can only be brought within their reach collectively. Intellectual culture in its turn tended to make men more like each other. It was no use for the somewhat rare survivors of the old order of things to bemoan the fact and to regret even the fierce insular individuality of bygone days; the inevitable process went on all the same, producing, along with beneficial effects, a certain

slackening of human personality.   This last effect of the play
of natural forces was intensified in the sphere of political relations by the elaborate action of the Caucus, which deliberately
aimed at stereotyping opinion, thus bringing down everything to a dead level.

Every attempt at asserting the freedom and independence
of political thought was now repressed; for every difference
of opinion was a blow struck at the unity of the party of which
the Caucus had constituted itself the permanent guardian.
The aggressive ardour of the Radical enthusiasts coincided
with the middle-class selfishness of the wire-pullers in stifling
opposition and the spirit of criticism in the Associations, and
they became in English society a great school of fanaticism,
of intolerance, of contempt for other people's opinions, and of
suspicion, which impugns the honesty and sincerity of opponents beforehand.   Political language, platform eloquence,
naturally grew all the more passionate and violent and full of
personalities.   Even when devoid of violence, the jealous and
irritable belief fostered by the Caucus produced an impatience
of discussion which more and more infected political life.[1]

Sentimental devotion to the party, which the Caucus kept
up as a cult, by saving its followers the trouble of professing reasoned political principles, released them from the
moral and intellectual discipline which principles impose on
conduct by riveting men's minds more or less tightly to definite
propositions and inspiring them with a resolve to look to the
efficacy of these principles only for the triumph of their cause,
without caring for immediate success and without stooping to
tergiversation or selfish compromise.   The Caucus, therefore,
by engrafting in men's minds rather a general feeling than a
creed of party orthodoxy, inclined them to the moral and intellectual opportunism which clutches at every proposal that
excites mental emotions and flatters the cravings and the
interests of the moment; it countenanced the transformation
of a policy of principles into a policy which "must give

---

[1] Cf. the remarks of Mr. Thomas Burt, the well-known labour member, in
reply to a labour leader: "One of the weaknesses — one of the dangers — of
the time is a certain impulsiveness and impatience of discussion.   Especially
is this manifest on labour questions.   Too many of our present-day reformers
seem to imagine that they are storming a rampart rather than reconstructing
a social system " (May, 1892).

quarterly dividends," to quote the graphic expression employed by a Liberal Caucus secretary to describe the new school of politics. The motto of "trust in the people," which the Caucus had adopted with affectation, as an absolute but external article of faith, almost forced on it the worship of what is popular and not what is just and reasonable.

These qualities of the Caucus made it in every respect an admirable vehicle for the new tendencies which the extension of the suffrage to the urban masses, in 1868, introduced into the life of parties, and in particular of the one which was to reap the most benefit from that democratic reform, of the advanced party, of Radicalism. Classic Radicalism, bred and nurtured by the Philosophic Radicals, which lived on the idea and for the idea, without caring much for parties, which, among a middle class enjoying its prosperity, represented the claims of right and justice and served as a moral leaven for that society, was dead. After 1868, Radicalism ceased to be a moral power and became a physical force. Being in a hurry to make its strength felt, it substituted discipline for philosophy and seized on the old party organization, which it found still standing, to make it its base of operations. It identified itself completely with it and turned into a partisan, a narrow partisan. Having staked its fortune, so to speak, on the party, and being bent on keeping it amid all the changes of events, Radicalism became opportunist. Having stepped off the solid ground of principles, it grew nervous, irritable, and intolerant. Standing in need of the multitude which upheld it, it took to coaxing; it led them on by soft words and promises when it had or knew of nothing more substantial to offer them, and it contracted demagogic habits. All these aspects of the new Radicalism, which became the protagonist of the political stage, were in a way materialized by the Caucus; it fixed them, threw them into relief, gave them body if not life, thus accentuating the outburst of formal and sentimental democracy which took place after 1868.

III

The important share which the Caucus had in the advent of this democracy will appear still more clearly if we pass from the study of its general tendencies to that of its methods of action, which have just been referred to.   To rouse the English voter from his apathy, to overcome the *vis inertiae* which constituted his conservative temperament and on which the time-honoured order of England seemed to rest, the Caucus erected political agitation into a system.   It composed a whole liturgy of meetings, with fiery harangues and energetic "resolutions," of demonstrations, travelling vans, political magic-lantern pictures, "social" gatherings, political fêtes, which were intended to keep the voter always on the go.   It entered on the same path as that other contemporary movement which undertook to impart religious feeling to the lower strata of the population by democratizing or vulgarizing religious practices, the movement of the Salvation Army, which, devoid of any theological idea, substituted physical demonstrations of faith and religious gymnastics for a creed, by means of a hier-archized quasi-military organization, with parades, with singing, with dancing to the music of drums and fifes.   Similarly, the Caucus, without losing itself in principles, tried to kindle and keep alive political ardour in its followers by "raising enthusiasm," to use the accepted expression.   The "sensa-tional" methods introduced by the Caucus into politics natu-rally developed a state of mind disposed to apprehend and resolve political problems by means of feeling, often of a generous but seldom of a thoughtful character.   They helped, so far as they were concerned, to change, if one may so express it, the English mind, which had for some time past been suffering from a spirit of unrest and feverish agitation, in con-sequence of the revolution in the means of locomotion and other improvements in material civilization, which have destroyed the equilibrium of the old life; of the moral progress which has made people more alive to the sufferings of mankind; and finally of the spread of a smattering of culture and an un-wholesome publicity, which have aroused hazy ideas or vague aspirations and produced a craving for morbid emotions.

   While raising political agitation to the level of an *instrumen-tum regni* and making it aim chiefly at men's imaginations, the Caucus has been led into giving an exceptional development to forms of action capable of lifting great masses at a single stroke; it has been induced to put wholesale methods, so to speak, in the place of, or, at all events, on the top of, methods *ad hominem*, in the shape of mass-meetings, demonstrations, smoking-concerts, picnics, and other politico-social fêtes which attract the multitude, and which even exert a new form of electoral bribery over it — collective bribery. But whether these performances are seemingly addressed to the intelligence, or whether they openly appeal to the cravings of the imagination or the stomach, their methods do not admit of any modulation. The action *ad hominem* of the pre-Caucus régime, which was most fully reflected in the election canvass, supplemented, in case of need, by individual corruption, was able to proportion the character and the amount of the efforts to be applied to the voter in each particular case. The Caucus, so far as the instruments of which it enjoys a monopoly are concerned, cannot operate in the same way. Thus stump oratory, platform eloquence, which is one of the greatest, or rather the greatest, resource of the Caucus for action on the mind, cannot vary its language; it can only sound one note, and that necessarily the highest, to be able to strike the dullest ear in the mixed audience which is being addressed. Without taking into account the diversity of temperaments, the stump administers the same dose to them all, and by spicing it as strongly as possible it tries to produce an identical amount of excitement in all. It is the same with the action on the "social tendencies" exerted by the Caucus and its vis-à-vis the Primrose League, with similar stereotyped means. Everywhere we find an utter want of flexibility and elasticity; there is invariably a rigid, uniform mechanism, regulated beforehand by cut and dried methods, which exclude all spontaneity of movement, and obeying a spirit of external conformity which resents all independence of thought.

The natural effect of this combination of forces is that all the political relations which the Caucus tries to bring about are dealt with in a mechanical way. Whether it is a case of manifestations of reason or demonstrations of political feeling, everything is turned out as in a Manchester factory or a Birmingham workshop. The machinery of the Caucus supplies public opinion wholesale, just as the machinery of the Primrose League and of most of the Associations produces "social consideration," for the consumption of voters who are partial

to it. If a pressing .need arises, if in the midst of a fierce
struggle the moral supplies of the leaders of the party run
short, a special consignment of opinion is forthwith ordered
from London; a simple telegram sent to all the Associations
of the party throughout the Kingdom is enough to make "the
voice of the country speak."   When it is no longer a question
of setting in motion large masses of men or procuring imposing
manifestations, but of a select body meeting in the assemblies
of the party parliament to draw up a common programme
or to modify it, it is always in a mechanical fashion that the
various opinions are made to agree; the divergent views are
either eliminated without discussion, or even stifled by the
quasi-material resistance which their authors encounter before
they have even entered the assembly hall; already in the
lobbies, in the smoking-room, they are overawed by the
compact mass of delegates, which crushes out individual
initiative or inclination, so much so that this effect and
not the facilities for exchanging views, for discussion, which
do not exist there, is regarded by the managers of the
Organization as the *raison d'être* of these great representative
gatherings.   Finally, and as a climax, even the individual
relations of confidence and esteem between man and man are
manufactured by the Caucus; it supplies the confidence and
produces the esteem with which a candidate or a Member
should inspire his fellow-citizens.   If the candidate is a
"carpet-bagger," unknown in the locality, the Organization
strives to "make him popular"; if, when he meets the electors, he is unable to impress them advantageously with his
talent or his competence, the Organization sends out its
"workers," who "speak for him" by flooding the constituency
with political eloquence.

IV

These effects of the dwindling of individuality and the
growth of formalism in political life, which have come to
light in each of the different aspects from which we have suc-
cessively considered the work of the Caucus, culminate and
are summed up in a way in the highest sphere of political
relations, that of the leadership.   This sphere had all the less

chance of escaping them because the leadership was the visible objective of the Caucus, and provided it with its *casus belli*. Having gone to war with party leadership, held by the representatives of the old ruling classes, the Caucus has not annihilated it — far from it; but it has subdivided it, broken it into fragments, or, if the expression is preferred, decentralized it; the leaders belonging to the upper middle class, the men of means and social position, have had to share their power with the crowd of small local leaders created by the autonomist organization of the Caucus. But, by working out autonomy and decentralization in too formal a way, with a multiplicity of subdivisions, in accordance with the strict logic of the democratic principle, the Caucus has succeeded mainly in bringing forward local mediocrity, and then installing it in the counsels of the party. The local man with limited views, who, left to his own resources, would never have been able to thrust himself on his fellow-citizens, has been hoisted up by the mere play of the machinery of the Caucus, automatically, so to speak. While these small leaders were rising to the surface, the old leaders, who were theoretically overthrown, but in reality still standing, saw their prestige decline, their influence diminish, and this twofold action produced a general levelling, which tended to shorten the average stature of public men, to make the type a poorer one.

The qualities which they had to prove the possession of, in accordance with the principles of the Caucus, and the means by which they were henceforth able to succeed, thanks to the methods of the Caucus, made this result inevitable. Unqualified adhesion to the official creed of the party having become the supreme political virtue which singled a man out for the confidence of his fellow-citizens in the discharge of every public duty, and his claims being made clear to them by the machinery of the Organization, which aimed especially at the imagination, the personal worth of the individual became of less importance. From the men of the ward meeting, in which strict observance of political routine or zeal as a "worker" marks out the "earnest politician," up to the parliamentary representatives, not to mention the town councillors, who are obliged to swear political allegiance, the virtues of public men became more and more formal and external, so to speak.

The deterioration of the men in charge of public affairs can be clearly discerned already; we have seen it break out more strongly in municipal life since the Caucus introduced party orthodoxy into it and placed its machinery at its disposal. Parliament has not been spared either; the choice of the Caucus, contrary to the promises of its founders, does not always fall on men of a class superior to that from which the national representation was recruited before the advent of the Caucus; the average of its nominees bears the stamp rather of mediocrity. The Caucus has by no means ousted the plutocratic element from Parliament nor from the counsels of the party. It needs it itself to provide for the upkeep of its machinery. Even the influence of social rank proved to be indispensable to the Caucus; being unable to turn out of its own mould genuine leaders who are raised above the multitude by some superiority, and who consequently command their respect, the Caucus has been obliged to accept, and often apply for, the services of the leaders of the old formation, while depriving them, however, of the feeling of dignity and responsibility imparted by the autonomous exercise of power. Although constituting an obstacle to the democratic eagerness of the popular and advanced element of the party, the middle-class leaders are carried along much farther than their real convictions and prejudices would permit of, through fear of still more impairing their authority, which they have to protect by devices of management, now that they cannot use it without any disguise. When all is said and done, the monopoly of the leadership, which the Caucus undertook to destroy, has only assumed another aspect; a little more divided and left much less to the natural selection determined by the spontaneous play of social forces, it is more *manufactured*, and it is more than ever inspired, if not solely, at all events in the main, by wire-pulling, with a diminution of responsibility for those who pull the wires. So that, if there were no danger in conclusions of a too sweeping kind, it might be said that the monopoly of the leadership which was held by the representatives of the old ruling classes tends to give place to a monopoly of wire-pullers backed by plutocrats.

In any event, the rôle of the wire-puller, and in general of the " worker " of the party, is growing; all the importance lost by social rank in party life has been gained by the "worker"; his zeal and skill are becoming a claim to the leadership. And this is all the more natural, and almost legitimate, because the methods developed by the Caucus have made his "work" not an improvised duty at the moment of the election, but a continuous occupation of an extremely absorbing kind, and demanding daily attention. The multiplicity, the variety, and the intensity of the efforts exerted by the organizations have made electioneering business exceedingly complicated; "it has become quite a science," as is said, not without complacency, by representatives of the party Organization; "it is now quite a business," say others, "and you must attend to it as to a business." To keep the small local leaders in working trim, they must be occupied; to rouse the masses from their indifference, they must be stirred up and stimulated unremittingly. "Political work" is never slack. In every constituency there is now a fairly large number of persons who are constantly thinking about "politics," intent on electioneering schemes; in other words, political professionals.

True, the type of these political zealots created by the ‚Caucus in England has not the objectionable features of the "professional politician" of other countries; he is not a parasite, who lives on society and makes politics a trade, often a low trade. The number of persons who live exclusively by "politics," although increased by the Caucus, is not yet a large one. They are (I am still speaking of the extra-constitutional sphere) the secretaries of Associations, the employés of the central and provincial Organization, the "missionaries," and the lecturers or other political agents. Even at a liberal computation they would hardly reach the figure of 2000 for the whole of England, with Scotland and Wales. Still they are becoming a marked body in the midst of society; the Caucus has given them a permanent status, and the "political agents" are beginning to form, if not exactly a separate class, at all events a guild. They already have a collective consciousness of themselves; they possess their professional societies, their benefit clubs. The best foretaste, however, of the professional politician is given rather by the small local leaders created by the organization of the Caucus. These men seldom make money out of their political situation, but most of them always expect some advantage from it, if not in cash, at all events in some other form. To a certain degree, comparatively slight, they can count on the public offices granted to the winning side for services rendered. These places are by no means numerous; the government service is almost free from the taint of party politics. But in the municipal administration the subordinate offices are too often distributed as a political reward since the Caucus has sanctioned the transformation of local elections into contests of political parties. The recent development of State functionarism, brought on, for instance, by legislation for the protection of labour, also provides some places which are sought and obtained by means of politics; thus a certain number of labour leaders, secretaries of Trade Unions, who are on the look-out for workshop and factory inspectorships, join the party Associations for the purpose of obtaining the posts to which they aspire by their assistance. Others among the small local leaders, who have no administrative ambitions, hope that their activity in the Organization will do them good in business, in their trade, or get them on in some other way. In short, without creating the regular type of "professional politician," the Caucus, to meet the requirements of election business, which it had made extremely intricate, has brought into the field and grouped in permanent regiments a whole contingent of small people, who devote themselves methodically to "politics" from more or less interested motives, which need not always assume a mercenary aspect to produce their demoralizing effect on public life.

The ultimate result, then, is that the Caucus, which aimed at hastening the democratic process in English political society, has succeeded only in a superficial, purely apparent fashion. The popular form of the party Organization merely enables the latter to penetrate deeper into the masses for the purpose of capturing them more easily, and not for giving them independence. The design which the Caucus undertook to carry out, of making the entire life of the people "an organized whole," of making "political and municipal life a consistent, earnest, true, and enthusiastic life, instead of a spasmodic electioneering impulse," has utterly failed. The Caucus has in no way helped to raise the tone of public life. **Far from** liberating it from unwholesome social influences, it has made its Organization, which cleverly superintends the process, an instrument of "social bribery" practised for the party's benefit. It has not increased material political corruption, but it has encouraged the deterioration of the mind of the electorate. The electioneering impulse is no longer "spasmodic," it is true; it has no doubt been transformed into steady "work," but performed by a special contingent of "workers," who only sow the seed of the "professional politician" more deeply in English soil; in society as a whole the political pulse does not beat quicker. On the contrary, in preventing the development of a spontaneous political life by its machinery, in offering a permanent obstacle to the free exercise of the judgment, the Caucus tends rather to enfeeble the public mind. It only strengthens political party passion. Blotting out independent thought and enervating the will and the personal responsibility of the voter, the Caucus ends in obliterating the individual, after having undertaken to establish his political autonomy up to the farthest limits of the extraconstitutional sphere. Attacking the old leaders as if they were an impediment to this autonomy, the Caucus has struck a blow at the leadership in general, by disparaging the qualities which constitute leadership in a healthy political community, that is, the personal superiority conferred by knowledge and character, and exalting the conventional and external qualifications enforced by stereotyped methods. In making these qualifications and methods an engine of government, the Caucus bids fair to set up a government by machine instead of a responsible government by human beings.

That is the final conclusion, the elements of which we have been collecting throughout this lengthy enquiry and patient analysis, and which, standing out with glaring plainness, throws a flash of light on the whole route which we have traversed. There we have what the Caucus democracy offers society disintegrated by the industrial revolution and the philosophic movement, the society in which the rupture of old ties has undermined the leadership and isolated the emancipated individual; to reconstitute a political leadership and embrace the individual and the community in a new existence, it offers a purely and grossly mechanical synthesis.

V

If we descend from the general sphere of political society, which we have just been considering, into the special field of the political parties, with which the latter are so fond of identifying the national existence, and which the efforts of the Organization have aimed at directly, do we find more satisfactory results? Has the Caucus kept the promises which it made of ensuring by its organization on a popular basis a real representation to the constituent elements of the party? Does it provide a means of gauging and eliciting their opinions? Does it succeed in bringing unity out of variety, amid the manifold contingents which it is its business to amalgamate, and in maintaining their cohesion, while at the same time reserving the party's freedom of action? The Associations of the Caucus cannot claim to be really representative of the party, the meetings in the wards, from which all the delegations of the Caucus emanate, being attended only by a handful of men in whom the diversity of social position and political temperament is far from being reflected. No doubt a considerable proportion of voters hold aloof from the Caucus, not because they disagree with it, but from indifference. In addition to this, the managers of the Caucus are careful to make allowance for opinion outside the Organization, and to a certain extent thus supply the deficiency in its representative force from their own store. But on the whole the channels by which this opinion penetrates into the Caucus are too narrow not to be obstructed by the element which predominates in it, and which is composed well-nigh exclusively of the vanguard of the electoral army. It is an almost general fact that the Association is more Radical than the mass of the party, more so even than the M.P. who has had to submit to its demands.

It follows in the first place that the Caucus is incapable of supplying a correct estimate of public opinion, of giving a more or less accurate idea of its tendencies and aspirations. And it has proved this incapacity more than once.[1] Besides,

[1] In 1880 the Liberal Caucus did not foresee the brilliant victory of its party; in 1885 it expected to win in the boroughs in which the Liberals were about to sustain a defeat only retrieved by the voting of the counties; in 1886

the too close relations of the Caucus with the official leaders of the party rob it of the independence of mind necessary for giving free expression to opinion. Sometimes they have shut its mouth on various occasions, when it was of importance to know the views of the nation, as, for instance, in the Soudan affair or the preliminary phase of Home Rule, at the beginning of the spring of 1886, before the party was irrevocably committed to that policy. At others the Caucus gave (as in the same Home Rule matter, a month later) wrong information about the state of opinion in the party, driving Mr. Gladstone further along the path of defeat. Thus, as a mouthpiece of opinion, the Caucus has failed, and is liable to fail, both the party in the country and its parliamentary leaders, by incorrectly reflecting the views of the former and offering the latter an inaccurate compass.

Being always apt to stride ahead, the Caucus forced the pace too much for average opinion, making the party compromise itself, if not by acts, at all events by pledges which it was by no means easy to redeem, and this was the case all along the line from the local Associations up to the National Federation. Goaded on by the Caucus, the party sometimes made abrupt transitions (opposed to Home Rule one day, it plunged headlong into it the next); in the space of four and twenty hours it found itself provided with new doctrines, with new articles of political faith, because its Organization had just adopted them, either of its own accord or at instigation from outside; at other times the same rigid orthodoxy which compelled the adhesion of the party held it as in a vice, entangling it in the pledges given by the Organization and hampering its freedom of motion. Nothing was left for it but to pay for the mistakes and the aberrations of its Organization.

Not being sufficiently representative of the party, either in its organization or in its movements, the Caucus has ensured cohesion in the party ranks, to the extent that this has been vouchsafed to it, not so much by its intrinsic force as by the feeling, common among the great mass of voters, of the neces-

---

it declared enthusiastically for Irish Home Rule, which the country was about to emphatically reject; then it brought forward the Newcastle Programme, which, after having rallied a small majority for a moment, burst up the party with a formidable crash.

sity of facing the enemy. Possessing permanent *cadres*, which enabled it to mobilize its contingents at a moment's notice, so to speak, the Caucus had greater facilities for grouping the adherents of the party around it. Unfurling the party flag, of which it had assumed the custody, it could almost always get its candidate accepted, by conveying the impression that it wielded real power over the electorate. The number of utter mediocrities returned to Parliament, not to mention the town councils, thanks to the Caucus trade-mark, appeared to confirm this impression.

In one respect, however, the Caucus increased the fighting strength of the party by its intrinsic force, by procuring the adhesion of many neutral or indifferent voters, who are outside the organization of parties, and who press heavily upon them, swinging between the two belligerents. The proportion of these voters is systematically diminished by the efforts of the Caucus. That is perhaps the most important result which it has achieved for the party, on the Liberal as well as on the Tory side. Both by its daily exertions and by the sole fact of its existence, of its permanent Organization brought to the doors of the people, the Caucus has popularized the title of the party, has imparted to the masses the abstract notion of it, which by its sweeping character gets accepted as a dogma and takes possession of the public mind by its intrinsic force, which is independent of the shifting aspect of men and events. This effect produced by the Caucus is all the more appreciable because the mental and logical process by which the popular mind manages to take in the abstract idea of the party is a very long one. At first it grasps it only under the concrete aspect of a man, of a leader; then the idea assumes the more general but still material aspect of the dwelling, of the castle (castle interest), with all those whom it contains, irrespective of their individual personalities. The owner of it, who wields the political influence of the locality, presents himself to the imagination as possessing a continuous existence through successive generations, as being only a single person, so that Hodge is incapable of distinguishing the masters of the house one from the other or from the building itself, which acquires almost an active property in his mind.[1] A further step is

---

[1] Cf. Richard Jefferies, *Hodge and his Masters*, 1880, Vol. I, pp. 269, 275–276.

taken in the process of abstraction when with the image of the dwelling is associated the notion of an office, the successive holders of which are conceived of only as a single person, like the prefect of whom the village mayor quoted by Taine remarked: "Monsieur le préfet m'a toujours conservé sa bienveillance quoiqu'on l'ait déjà changé plusieurs fois."[1] Then after the personal presentment of the idea comes the material symbol, which represents it to the mind by means of an outward token appealing to the senses, such as the colours which the parties adopt, and which in the eyes of the common herd become so inseparable from the notion which they embody that by changing the colours the notion itself is destroyed.[2] In the next stage the parties come to be denoted by abstract symbols, by material terms conceived in a figurative sense, one party being called the high, and another the low party. Lastly, the mind rises to pure abstractions, expressed by terms such as Liberal, Conservative. The intellectual level of society being anything but uniform, the successive party conceptions which come one after another in logical order still coexist in the electorate, some voters grasping the distinction of colour only in the physical sense and enquiring about a candidate: "What is he, blue or yellow?" others replying with dignity to the canvasser who asks for their votes: "No, sir, I never vote with the high party." But the number of people who vote, not less blindly and more spontaneously, for the "Liberal" or the "Conservative," is an increasing majority. Furthering the progress of enlightenment which makes mankind, who become the slaves of words directly they emerge from a barbarous

[1] H. Taine, *Le suffrage universel en France*, Paris, 1872.

[2] Before the advent of the Caucus in England, to decide between several candidates who offered themselves to the party, a test ballot was sometimes taken, and the one who obtained the most votes became the sole candidate of the party at the election. To enable the illiterate adherents of the party to make their choice, at Manchester, where Edward Jones and Milner Gibson were rival candidates, the idea was started of printing their names on the voting papers in different colours. At a test ballot between four Liberal candidates at Stafford, it was proposed to adopt the same plan, but the use of colours had to be abandoned because none of the candidates would agree to accept the colour of blue, for fear that some of the voters, being accustomed to see that colour hoisted by the Tories, would confound the Liberal candidate denoted by it for the occasion with them (Report from the select committee on parliamentary and municipal elections, *Blue Books*, 1868–1869, Vol. VIII, p. 526).

state, advance to more and more abstract expressions, the Caucus, by means of its machinery, has popularized the appellations " Liberal" and " Conservative," and under cover of them it sweeps into the organizations, in constantly increasing numbers, the voters who are known in them as " blanks," that is to say, those who are outside the stereotyped parties. The dream of the organizations is to get rid of the doubtful mass of floating voters altogether, so as to put an end to the periodical swing of the pendulum, which gives the victory now to one and now to the other party, each of them hoping, of course, that the pendulum will stop on its side.

And yet, in spite of the accession of " blanks," the organizations are not nearer the realization of their dream, for they have, and especially in the Liberal Organization, a vast deal of trouble to keep their old contingents together. The particular claims which contend with the more general designs in the party preoccupations, as well as the divergences of views on these schemes which arise within the party, are continually undermining its cohesion and threatening its unity. All the efforts of the Caucus to combat these tendencies have failed up to the present. At its start, the Caucus announced that it had a cure for the evil of the divisions in the party, a plan for making the general will of the party always prevail, and for silencing the special aspirations, the particular fancies, the crotchets, and the fads. In reality it rather encourages the sects by trying to win their good graces in order to obtain a majority. The Organization offers them a sort of exchange where they can sell their quota of support, and owing to the general rule that the existence of a regular market enhances or even creates value, the groups obtain an exaggerated importance. The natural obstacles which the bargaining of groups, so common in divided assemblies (log-rolling), encounters in a vast constituency composed of thousands of voters of varying intelligence and temperament, are overcome, thanks to the Organization, unless it can make sure of preventing the bargaining itself, when it is able to bring into the field a force large enough to intimidate the fomenters of schisms beforehand. Being anxious to get votes, and presuming too much on the electoral influence of the champions of the various special claims, the Caucus, especially in the Liberal party, which is the least homogeneous, was often too ready to come to terms with them and make the candidates adopt their fads. But on the election day the views of other sets of voters, opposed to one or the other of these hazardous proposals, asserted themselves triumphantly in a good many constituencies, and the party sustained a partial defeat, as in the boroughs in 1885, or a complete one, as in 1895.

The Caucus could not stop the divisions in the party for this simple reason, that it was unable to make divergent views not be so, and because divergence of views was an inevitable consequence of the divergence of interests brought about by the growing complexity of social relations. By the force of things the Liberal party was destined to feel the effects of this in a special degree. On its right wing was taking place a secession of the interests which conceived themselves endangered by its advance, while on its left wing the new Radical and Socialist claims were raising up malcontents and rebels. It was no use inviting them to take shelter under the "grand old umbrella," or asking them to step into the "omnibus" of the Newcastle Programme; it was impossible to huddle the centrifugal elements of the party into it and keep them motionless there, and the general election of 1895 furnished the most striking proof of the vanity of attempts aiming at securing the unity of the party by means of organization. This lesson was inflicted on the Liberal party, but the party which goes by the name of Conservative is in no way exempt from the same infirmity; in its case it only takes more time to break out. Most of the conclusions at which we have arrived as to the rôle of the Caucus, and its effects on English political life, have been supplied principally, but not solely, by the past and the present of the Organization of the party which goes by the name of Liberal; this is because that "party" represents the social strata which earlier attained to a more complete political development. But what the Liberal party is to-day, the Conservative party will be to-morrow, for in point of fact it is to-day what the Liberal party was only yesterday. The Conservative party is no longer the "stupid party";[1] it has got into touch with the age, its mind has

[1] This expression was applied to the Conservative party by John Stuart Mill, and commented on by him in the House of Commons in 1866 (*Hansard*, Vol. CLXXXIII, p. 1592).

expanded, and its old homogeneity has been broken; it is no longer the single block of bygone days.[1]

In its unsuccessful efforts to combat the centrifugal tendencies in the party, to pursue the cohesion and unity which were oozing away, the Caucus was confronted by the historical fact of the break-up of parties which had been at work in English political society for half a century. The appearance of two powerful party leaders, Disraeli and Gladstone, who, after the confusion which set in from and after 1846, succeeded in reforming two large armies, with fresh contingents supplied by the extension of the suffrage, gave the illusion that the old system of the dualism of stereotyped parties had recovered from its momentary collapse,— a breathing space in which parties, like armies exhausted by the contest, regain strength and reoccupy their positions. In reality there was no such thing; the process of differentiation of social relations, of interests, of aspirations, of ideas, which injured the classic dualism, continued with as much force as ever; that is, it developed the centrifugal tendencies in political society. And it is perfectly natural that the Caucus should have been powerless to stem the current. The means and the methods, mostly mechanical, which it adopted to obtain cohesion, doomed it to failure; for, once moral unity has disappeared in a community, no machinery, however ingenious, can restore it. And yet, owing to this very internal disintegration, the Caucus could only resort to factitious devices for reuniting the incongruous elements. This fact contains a new revelation, another flash of light succeeding that which disclosed to us that the Caucus tended to set up a government by machine instead of a responsible government by human beings. There we were contemplating the effect; here we meet with the cause. It is the task of trying to maintain the old unity on which the classic party dualism reposed, it is this hopeless task undertaken by

---

[1] To convince oneself of this, one has only to cast a glance at the majority which the last general election returned to Parliament, the largest Conservative majority commanded by an English Ministry for half a century. And in the most important legislative proposal of the following year (1896), the Education Bill, this formidable majority was not able to provide the government of its choice with enough votes to carry its clerical measure favouring the denominational schools; so great was the divergence of views in this party of which the Church was always the rallying-point if ever there was one.

the Caucus, which has forced on it methods leading to a
government by machine.

Not only has the Caucus not succeeded in healing the wounds
of the old party system, but it has even aggravated its evils.
Availing itself of the representative character to which its
organization laid claim, and of its position as authorized mouthpiece of the opinion of the party, it has assumed over its adherents powers which tended to develop party tyranny by giving
it a legal foundation.   To tradition and habit, which governed
the parties before the advent of the Caucus, it has added pretensions founded on right, on a mandate conferred, creating
formal powers on the one hand and obligations on the other.
There were, of course, wire-pullers and managers before the
"Birmingham plan" was introduced, but they derived all their
power from their personal position; now they are patented
in the name of the people.   There were also organizations of a
more or less rudimentary or developed character, Associations
more or less resembling the "hundreds" of the Caucus; but
being only free combinations of private citizens, it never entered
into their heads to set themselves up as a power before which
everybody — candidates,   individual   voters,   parliamentary
leaders — had to bow. On the pretext of representing the views
of the party in their integrity, the Caucus has assumed the
monopoly of them.   Sole depositary of its creed, it can apply
moral coercion to all those who come under the denomination
of the party with an effect equal to that procured by material
force; the power of intimidation is enough for it, and it
wields it.
    The first, the most tangible, result produced by this auto-
cracy of the Caucus was to put an end to the free competition
of candidates in the party; there are now only candidatures
of one kind, the orthodox ones, stamped with the Caucus trade-
mark; the others are doomed.   The loss of this freedom inevitably diminishes that of the electorate.   A party which
lives under such a régime is already half enslaved, and it
will have, perhaps, to use very vigorous efforts to recover its
liberty.   The compulsion implied by the approved candidature
is completed in the case of the individual voter by the behests
of party piety, which the Caucus is watching over and which

consists in voting obediently and blindly.   The voter who is
not refractory but simply thoughtful is regarded as an obstacle.
And with perfect good faith, from simple devotion to professional interest, a tendency arises, even in the governing
circles of the Organization, to look with envy on neighbours
whose voters do not exhibit this vicious propensity to argue.[1]
In fact, military discipline is the secret aspiration of the
"organizers," when they do not proclaim it.[2]   From the inexorable orthodoxy of the party which they represent there is
now no refuge but in open schism, such as the Socialist revolt
of the I. L. P., or again, perhaps, in the nationalist dreams
of a "Cymry Fydd," a movement of Welsh patriots inclined,
in the pursuit of their dream, to relax in the strict observance
of the Liberal creed.[3]   No independent or open-minded organization has been able to stand against the *regular* party organizations.   The rivals have been thrust aside by them; the free
organizations which drew near them drooped in their atmosphere, whether they were working-men's clubs created for the
moral improvement of the masses, or the "Eighty Club,"
founded in a moment of enthusiasm as a free brotherhood of
preachers of Liberal principles, or even the Primrose League,
which was intended by its promoters to introduce a fresh and
a freely flowing current into the stagnant waters of Toryism.
One and all have become in a short space of time simple annexes

---

[1] "In England," as was remarked to me in London, in a tone of annoyance, "they argue, whereas in Scotland they vote with enthusiasm."   Yet in
Scotland, I found that the wire-pullers envied their English colleagues, for
"the Scotchman is not like the Englishman; he goes his own way."

[2] In the office of a Conservative Association, one of the most important in
the Kingdom from its following in the constituency and its broad popular
basis, I was told as soon as I had stated the object of my visit: "You wish to
know about our Organization !   Sir, our Organization is a military organization; it is led by a general commander-in-chief, who is called President of the
Association, by so many brigadier-generals, who are styled Divisional Chairmen, by so many colonels," etc. . . .   The same thing, however, was said to
me elsewhere in fewer words: "Discipline above all," or "respect and discipline, that is our basis."

[3] This movement, of slight importance, has been started lately by Welsh
enthusiasts who hold that the English Liberal party, to which almost all the
Welsh members belong, makes use of them without giving them anything in
return, without serving "the cause of the Welsh people."   So, deviating from
the strict conformity of the Liberal party, the patriots of the Cymry Fydd look
on this party "no longer as an end, but as a means, and a means which can
be repudiated in case of need."

of the official organizations, in which the praying-wheel of the party is automatically turned.

VI

The preservation of stereotyped parties in the country, which the Caucus tried to effect by straining the system in this extraordinary way, was to ensure, in the long run, the best possible working of parliamentary government, which rests on the party system. Has this type of government, which has so long been " on its trial," really benefited by the Caucus? No doubt, by helping to sweep up majorities, the Caucus facilitated to a slight extent, for a moment, the duty of "carrying on the Queen's government." But at the same time its principles and its methods did still more to undermine the very foundations of parliamentary government. In the first place, the Caucus warped the representative principle on which parliamentary government reposes, and which consists in the personal confidence with which the Member inspires the electors, who trust to him to manage the affairs of the nation on their behalf. The Caucus invariably tended to eliminate, or at any rate to diminish, the personal element in the relations between the candidate and the electors, as well as in those between the Member and his constituents. The old committees, whose business it was to conduct the election campaign before the introduction of the Caucus, were the candidate's own engine, being formed on each occasion *ad hoc*, by him and for him, whereas the Caucus, by reason of its very principle, is an impersonal organization representing a firm behind which the individual shrinks out of sight and in which he becomes simply a more or less anonymous instrument of a "party." Under the auspices of the Caucus, the moral understanding which should arise between the candidate and the electors whose mandate he solicits is made up to a greater extent than in bygone days by the external party conformity; and as for the personal element which still remains in it, that understanding is brought about by the increasing co-operation of people other than the candidate himself, by the crowd of imported speakers, of "workers" of the party, who devote their energy and their abilities to inspiring the electors with confidence in the candidate.

The election over, the Member returned, once more it is party orthodoxy, according to the daily market quotation certified by the Caucus, which is set up as the criterion of the parliamentary conduct of the Member. If the M. P. is bound to his electors by personal feelings of devotion and affection, which come before party conformity, the Caucus, should a conflict break out, deliberately tries, as we have seen in the cases of Forster and Cowen, to stifle these feelings, to destroy the confidence based on the character of the man, in order to ensure the triumph of the conformity of which it is the self-appointed guardian and judge. Unable to use his discretion freely, and prevented from seeking his political line of conduct in his own knowledge and conscience, the Member ceases to be a representative and becomes a delegate, a subordinate. The régime of a widely extended suffrage, however, is moving in this direction of itself; when the number of voters becomes too great to allow of personal contact, from which the Member derives his inspirations direct and the electors their trust in his judgment, relations of confidence necessarily give way to formal pledges. The Caucus has only drawn the conclusions arising from this state of things while hastening it perhaps. Having stepped into the shoes of the electors, it drafts the pledges and sees that they are carried out. It is therefore inevitable that the Member should contract his obligations not so much to his electors as to the Organization, and that the feelings of responsibility due to the constituents whom he is supposed to represent, should be transferred to the Caucus, which stands closer to him. He assents submissively to all the conditions which the latter imposes. And it is in this way that the Radical tone of Parliament has, during the last fifteen years, risen abruptly above the level of the average of the electorate, and that the new type of English M. P. has been engendered, who is always ready to go ahead, without knowing exactly where he is going and where he will stop, or even if he will stop.[1] The result is

---

[1] A story is told of a candidate who, after having given one pledge after another at a public meeting, was asked by one of the audience if he was prepared to vote for the repeal of the provisions of chapter xx of the Book of

that the English Parliament sustains injury in the "two conditions which," according to Bagehot, "are essential to the
bare possibility of parliamentary government," and which are
"the extrinsic independence" of the representatives and "the
inherent moderation" which should prevail in the House. ·

The diminution of the responsibility, of the independence,
and of the dignity of the men returned to the House of Commons has not failed to impair the relations of the Members
with the party leaders such as Cabinet government presupposes. This exceedingly delicate instrument represents a sort
of see-saw, which works by a series of "actions and reactions
between the Ministry and the Parliament" (Bagehot), in which
the chiefs lead without commanding and the Members follow
without being dragged. The right and the power of the
Members to revolt at any moment against those who lead
them, and the authority with which tradition and the essence
of the party system have clothed the latter, maintained between both the equilibrium which ensured the working of the
government and preserved the freedom of the assembly. This
equilibrium is now destroyed in favour of the leaders. Formerly, especially when almost the whole House was recruited
in the same social sphere, the leader of the party was only
primus inter pares; now he is a general in command of an
army. He barely consults his staff, the front bench, and
practically confines his confidences to an inner circle of a
few lieutenants. All the rest of the army simply receives
marching orders. He no longer takes the advice, as formerly,
of this or that leading Member, who served as an intermediary
between the leaders and the main body of their adherents.
These intermediate ranks have disappeared.[1]

The leaders have mounted higher inside Parliament because
the prestige of the Members has been lowered outside it.

Exodus. "Certainly," he replied at once, without having even caught the
end of the sentence, "I shall have no objection." The hall was convulsed
with laughter. The candidate, disconcerted, bent over the chairman of
the meeting to ask him what was the matter. "Nothing," replied the latter
placidly, "you have only just pledged yourself to repeal the Ten Command-
ments."

[1] Cf. Montesquieu, *l'Esprit des lois,* Book II, Chap. IV, on the intermediate
ranks necessary in a monarchy to keep it at an equal distance from the despotic State and the popular State.

Raised above the levelled crowd of M. P.'s, the leaders now lean directly on the great mass of voters, whose feelings of loyalty go straight to the leaders over the heads of the Members. This last effect is due both to the action of the Caucus, which undermines the voter's respect for the M. P., and to other factors of a more general nature, such as the spread of knowledge and the development of communications and channels of information. Being more enlightened, the voter is more alive to his power of returning the Member, and at the same time he no longer wants the local representative to shape his political views by; thanks to the Press and to the telegraph, which place him, so to speak, in immediate communication with the great leader of the party, he can get his political supplies from him direct, just as, in the material sphere, he gets his stock of groceries, etc., in London from the "universal provider." Always requiring to look up to some one, the English voter naturally transfers to the great leader the respect and devotion which he no longer has the opportunity or the need of bestowing on the Member for the division. Here, again, the "intermediate ranks" to which Montesquieu refers are done away with or obliterated, the door being opened to a sort of popular Cæsarism, with which the great chief of the party has become invested. No doubt the highly magnetic personalities of Mr. Gladstone and Lord Beaconsfield have powerfully contributed to set up the Cæsarean supremacy of the leaders, but it was sufficiently developed by the situation which I have just described to enable their successors, who lacked the gift of impressing the popular imagination, to obtain the usufruct of this power over the masses. This being so, the elections have assumed the character of personal plebiscites, each constituency voting not so much for this or that candidate as for Mr. Gladstone or against Lord Beaconsfield or Lord Salisbury.

But this was not all; it was not only on the great occasions of going to the country that the leaders could take advantage of the popular loyalty, the current of which has been diverted towards them; they could henceforth use it as a propelling power in Parliament even in its daily life, and not only against their opponents, but also against their own adherents in the House who were not submissive enough, who exhibited inclinations towards resistance. This entirely new state of things has been brought about by the Caucus. Before its advent, under the old parliamentary system, the leader's only means of bringing to reason Members inclined to revolt was a threat of dissolution; and even that was available only for the leader of the party in power; the leader of the Opposition was helpless against his followers whose loyalty was on the wane. Now under the Caucus, and thanks to it, in both parties refractory Members are called upon by their respective Associations to fall in behind the leader, and they must comply if they want to be re-elected. Thus, in the intimate relations between the parliamentary chief and his followers, there has been imported from outside a regular intimidation agency, which makes the Members, for the nonce, simple puppets on the parliamentary stage.

The more or less discreet way — and it has not been at all discreet at certain periods — in which this means of pressure on the conduct of the Members of the House of Commons is employed, does not prevent it from being a recognized weapon in the arsenal of the leaders. If formerly there were a few extremely rare instances of attempts at extraconstitutional pressure directed by the leaders against the M. P.'s, they occurred only in the form of irregular appeals addressed to the masses in public meetings, and even then they were regarded as nothing less than a scandal and as an insult to the first principles of parliamentary government. When in 1866, in face of the cool reception given by the House to the Reform Bill brought in by the Liberal Ministry, Mr. Gladstone attended, in the parliamentary recess, a great meeting at Liverpool in order to influence public opinion in favour of the Bill, he was severely taken to task in the House, when it met again; "I say," cried a Liberal ex-Minister, who made himself the spokesman of his colleagues' disapproval, "it is unprecedented in the history of Parliament that a Minister should go down to the provinces and there endeavour to excite agitation in favour of his own Bill . . . and make a speech in disparagement of the House of which he is himself the leader." [1] Nowadays the pressure on the M. P.'s, exerted in a scientific way, is no longer a subject for scandal, and a leader

[1] *Hansard*, Vol. CLXXXVII, p. 1859, speech by Horsman.

who wishes to give them a sharp touch of the spur is no longer in danger of offending against the rules of decorum by compromising himself in person.

But all-powerful as the great party leaders have become, they cannot themselves escape the influence of the Caucus, especially on the Liberal side. Obliged to pay a price for the support given them by the popular Organization, they inevitably have to submit to its pressure themselves in their legislative functions, so that the freedom of movement of the parliamentary leaders is not complete either. The famous Newcastle Programme is and will long remain a conspicuous proof of this. Having accepted this programme from the " Liberal Federation " without enthusiasm, the official leaders of the party have since then dragged it about like a convict's chain.

No doubt the supreme power of binding and loosing, which belongs to public opinion even in the parliamentary sphere, still subsists, but the play of this great regulator is also impaired by the intervention of the Caucus. Indeed, opinion is supposed, apart from the elections in which it holds formal court, to supply the M. P.'s and the parliamentary leaders with a permanent source of inspiration, and at the same time to exercise a continuous control over them. Revealing itself independently of all constitutional channels, this twofold power guides and constrains at one time the leaders, when they are too timorous or too autocratic, at another their adherents, when too prone to obedience or, again, inclined to be restive. But to enable this power of opinion, which is eminently subtle in its nature and indeterminate in its essence, to make itself felt, there must be complete freedom for opinion to manifest itself in its varied and irregular forms and to come straight up to the doors of Parliament, and, for those who are in Parliament, the fewest possible impediments to the delicate task of catching the fluctuating views of the multitude. In interposing on behalf of opinion between it and Parliament, to demonstrate, to proclaim, or even to intimidate, the Caucus rather hindered their power of reciprocal penetration. It accomplished this sometimes through its anxiety to safeguard the positions of the parliamentary leaders of its choice; at others owing to the crudeness of its means for probing public opinion, to which it was reduced by the mechanical character of its organization and its methods. By developing sham manifestations of opinion, such as meetings and demonstrations arranged behind the scenes, capable of conveying rather a deceptive idea of the real views of the masses, the Caucus has introduced a new element of uncertainty into the gauging of opinion, and has therefore lessened its power of inspiring public men and, consequently, its power of controlling them (which in reality are one and the same thing and are distinguishable only in logic). The authority of opinion not being able to bear regularly and with its full weight on parliamentary relations, the equilibrium of party government, destroyed inside the House of Commons, has no chance of being set right from outside by the only power capable of doing it. Thus, through the intervention of the Caucus, the three great springs of parliamentary government — the independence of representatives, the elasticity of the leadership, and that of the relations between Parliament and public opinion — have been weakened, to the lowering of Parliament and the deterioration of its efficacy.

True, it is agreed, and rightly, that this result is the general effect of what is called, in ordinary parlance, the democratic movement. But it is always well not to forget that the "democratic movement" is not an entity; it is only an abstract term to denote the resultant of manifold forces which act in political society, under extremely varied and partly contradictory impulses. And it would be only possible to get a clear idea of the process which goes by the name of democratic by singling out the movements composing it. The Caucus has been one of them in England, and it has been so far from producing the effects referred to by itself, that even in the course of this work I have often taken care, in order not to distort the perspective, to replace the action of the Caucus within the general sphere of English political life, of the evolution of society, of humanity even. No, the Caucus has not had a monopoly in the deterioration of parliamentary government which I have just brought out, no more than in the other unquestionably genuine political effects which I have been led by my enquiry, in all honesty, to enter in its balance-sheet. The Caucus has, it is true, not invented them from beginning to end, but it has developed the elements of them; it has, in a way, systematized and crystallized them. In that, too, it has only lent a helping hand; for in the highly complex life of a community the varied forces which make up its movement resemble the contents of the solar spectrum, in which the colours composing the light each react on its neighbour. But just as these colours, which form so many shades, and which all blend in the whiteness of light, can be decomposed and clearly distinguished by every eye not afflicted with daltonism, so it is possible to assign their quota to the agencies at work in the community. No doubt this quota can never be defined with absolute precision, but the social investigator is in no way bound down to Shylock's bond: "Nor cut thou less, nor more, but just a pound of flesh;" for it is not matter that he dissects; he discriminates between movements vibrating in the social ether, the impression of which is to be conveyed to the intelligence. When the social undulations, after being long obscure, reach a certain degree of intensity, then they are brought together to make them more clearly perceptible to the intellectual vision, like rays in a focus, under the particular central image produced by the movement, which represents their source and which in reality is still more their reflector. Subject to this limitation, which is understood of every investigation into a living society, the "Caucus" has been in English political life the source and the agent of the effects described, and subject to this limitation again there is nothing to tone down in the picture drawn in these pages of its dissolvent action.

VII

The reality itself undertook to soften the lines of the picture. The Caucus had set out with the intention of pushing the democratic principle to its extreme logical consequences in the extraconstitutional sphere, but it was not really applied in all its logical strictness; it encountered various obstacles, most of which proceeded from the fact that the old social conditions of England had not completely disappeared and that the old influences were not annihilated. There are still plenty of them left. And while often representing what was least attractive in the old order of things, these conditions and

these influences assert, as against the Caucus, the power of
the living forces of society, which prevents the government
of the country from being a machine pure and simple, which
leaves room in it for the individual steeped in prejudice and
selfish calculation, but also subject to responsibility.[1] Wealth
still has a fascination for the English mind; a man who is
rich, and who makes a proper use of his money, has more
weight with the masses than men who represent nothing but
labels or formulas. Territorial influence is far from being a
historical reminiscence; at elections a good landlord is readily
followed, whatever his politics are, even in parts of the country
where the process of emancipation from the power of the landed
proprietors has made greater progress than elsewhere — in
Scotland, for instance. In the south of England the old
county families are still particularly looked up to, for the sole
reason of their antiquity. They are a sort of institution. On
the same ground the Church, in spite of the continuous weakening of religious beliefs, is still a living tradition, serving as
a rallying-point for many a man who has almost ceased to
have recourse to its ministry and who does not attend its
places of worship. The prestige of social rank has no doubt
declined, but a lord is still the figure invested with the most
charm for the public imagination; he is not even distasteful
to the Radicalism of the working classes, they "like a lord";
according to Mr. Gladstone, "the love of freedom itself is
hardly stronger in England than the love of aristocracy; as
Sir W. Molesworth once said to me of the force of this feeling
with the people: 'It is a religion.'" [2]   And it is not only to
gratify their imagination, but in daily life, for the defence of
their interests, the lower orders prefer a man of rank as leader.
Labour representation in Parliament, for instance, meets with
most obstacles from the workmen themselves; it is not the

---

[1] This point may perhaps be illustrated by the following passage from a
letter from one of my correspondents, an ardent young Radical of very
democratic origin, who bears a well-known name, and who was endeavouring,
as honorary secretary of a Liberal Association, to wrest a backward rural
constituency from the old influences: "The rule of Lords and squires or clergy
and farmers, harsh and cruel as it often is, is still tempered by many traditional feelings which the new 'wire-pullers and caucus-mongers' cannot
possess."

[2] "The County Franchise," *The Nineteenth Century*, November, 1877.

fact that Members of Parliament are unpaid which prevents
the workmen from sending comrades to the House, for a
pecuniary sacrifice of a halfpenny or a farthing a week submitted to by each of them would ensure the Member of their
choice an adequate allowance; but they do not care about it,
they would rather have a gentleman for their Member. The
hierarchical spirit, the class spirit, still lives in English
society; the English people has not yet ceased to be what
Bagehot called "a deferential nation," "politically deferential."

But the deference is not paid solely to rank or wealth. I have
mentioned among the claims which mark out a parliamentary
candidate for the suffrages of his fellow-citizens his skill as
an "athlete," as a cricketer. Many a non-English reader has
noted this, perhaps, with a pitying smile, giving thanks to
God that he and his are not as these men. Underneath its odd
aspect this homage rendered to the "athlete" by voters is in
reality a tribute to the moral qualities of the individual, to his
courage, to his energy, to his will; in a word, to the man apart
from and in spite of the conventional labels of "Tory" or
"Liberal." It is an exaggerated, distorted form of a general
tendency, inherent in the English mind, to consider his private
character, his conduct, in the public man. The value which the
Englishman attaches to these creates a feeling of esteem, almost
of admiration, even for the superficial moral qualities which
constitute "respectability," and which provide him with a
criterion, inadequate and narrow no doubt, but protecting
him from cynicism in his representatives and in himself, and
often forming a sort of barrier against adventurers, against
politicians of the baser sort. Mental superiority does not on
that account lose its rights in the Englishman's eyes; the
Englishman, and especially the lower-class man, bows down
before it without misgiving or jealousy, whether he finds it in
a man of higher social rank or in an equal. In the workshop the judgment of a comrade who is felt to be superior
influences all and is followed by all; this comrade is, perhaps,
a drunkard, but in his sober intervals his opinion commands
respect.

This almost innate respect of the race for the pre-eminent
qualities of rank, of character, and of intellect, makes the

Englishman particularly ready to accept the leadership of
men, without troubling his head about formulas and conventions. "I know no one," said an old Member of Parliament
to me, "so willing to be guided as an Englishman; and I
myself," he added, "I am quite willing to be led." Let but
the person of the leader inspire him with confidence, and he
is devoted to him for good, throughout, perhaps, the varied
vicissitudes of his fortunes. One of the men who has done
the most to destroy the old leadership, by introducing the
Caucus, has learnt this to his advantage and his glory; Mr.
Joseph Chamberlain, turned out of the Radical party on the
occasion of the Home Rule Bill of 1886, has defied all the
hosts of the enemy, including that of the Gladstonian Caucus,
by the sole power of his personality; by his sheer weight he
carried all the Midland counties at one general election after
another, in 1886, in 1892, in 1895, marching from victory to
victory; it was not so much a victory of Unionism as a triumph of leadership. A still more imposing spectacle has been
furnished up till recently by the enormous personal ascendancy
of Mr. Gladstone. In his proud and loyal devotion to the
leader, many a one of his adherents will not, even if he can,
put his person on one side in order to grasp the notion of the
cause which he defends, of the party which he leads.[1] Manifested with more or less intensity, according to the persons or
the circumstances, or subsisting only in a latent condition,
these feelings were a counterpoise or a check to the formal
authority of the Caucus. The extent of its power varied a
good deal in different parts of the country, according to the
greater or less amount of social leadership prevailing there in
its various aspects. In a general way it may be said that in
places where social rank and the Church have held out, the
Caucus, as representative of the formal authority of the party,
has had, comparatively speaking, little success, while in localities where the ground was more level its task has been greatly
facilitated.

Besides the exceptional prestige of illustrious chiefs and

---

[1] I asked a working-man at Birmingham what party he belonged to. "I
follow Mr. Chamberlain," he replied. "Then," I said, "you are a Liberal
Unionist." He merely repeated with an air of calm resolution, "I follow Mr.
Chamberlain."

the social leadership, besides the feelings of a traditional kind, the Caucus has had to face personal and local influences under yet another aspect, that of material interests, of preoccupations about "bread and butter," which on many occasions were even its accomplices in the struggle with the time-honoured social influences, owing to their power of severing the old ties which they find in their path. But in this dissolving process interests make no distinctions; they disregard all political conventions as well, whatever their origin and their pretensions, aristocratic or democratic, reactionary or revolutionary. Questions of labour, of wages, good or bad relations with the master, take precedence with many English workmen over all the political considerations which it is desired to impress on them, and alone decide their vote. With other electoral varieties, it is anxiety about their business, hopes or apprehensions raised by this or that legislative measure, which incline them to one or the other party on the polling-day. Interests of a selfish, occasionally perhaps even of a sordid kind, they present just as many living forces holding in check the formal force of the Caucus, which is often obliged to come to terms with them, or, if it cannot or will not do so, to court a defeat. We have been eye-witnesses, so to speak, of this; we have come upon the actual operation of these forces in the choice of the candidate, where we have seen a whole string of personal influences, local considerations of every kind, religious passions, social influences, private interests, collective interests of groups, rise in front of the Caucus; and the latter, having stepped on the political stage with the boast that it would sweep away all these "rotten influences" in a trice, has had to stoop to negotiations, to compromises, and to bargains, or run the risk of a defeat, and often of a crushing one, leaving somewhat overhasty reformers to once more reap the advice: *Et nunc erudimini*.

But in addition to obstacles coming from outside, the power of the Caucus is subject to limitations of an internal nature, which are due to the relative inadequacy of its *personnel* and to the slenderness of its material resources. Under universal or well-nigh universal suffrage, a political organization which aspires to capture it and hold its own amid hostile forces, of which the apathy of its own adherents is not the least, requires a great deal of money, or other resources capable of stimulating zeal, of remunerating services, of rewarding devotion. The English party organizations are not very rich, especially that of the Liberal party; the voluntary contributions in money which feed their budget are not excessive. The favours which the party in power can distribute are somewhat limited, consisting principally of honorary titles of different kinds, and of very few places, for the service of the State is almost entirely beyond the reach of the politicians. It is true that the English organizations raise the wind pretty largely with "social consideration," but the purchasing power of this currency, while considerable in England, has its limits. In this respect, again, the Liberal Organization is in a great state of inferiority to its Tory rival. This scantiness of material resources, which hampers the activity of the organizations, and the passive resistance of their environment, which is generally apathetic, inevitably paralyzes the energy of the representatives of the Caucus, especially in the interval between the elections. A good many of them, too, are prevented from displaying excessive eagerness in the service of the party machine by the comparative freedom of their mind, to wit, on the Liberal side, where there are actually paid agents who are restive even under the pressure of the central Organization, and who have not yet turned into perfect automatons. This is especially true of the agents who belong by their age and their education to the old generation. Thus, within the four corners of the Organization itself, the personal element, alike from its strength and its weakness, does add to the counterpoise offered to the machine of the Caucus by the personal, human influences of a general character which are at work in the community. At the summit of the political world, in Parliament, which is composed, in a still fairly considerable degree, of men belonging to the old political *personnel*, their character, as well as their position in the constituencies, also have the effect of deadening the blows of the Caucus. The final upshot, then, is that the nihilist work of the Caucus is attenuated in several of its logical consequences, that in the exercise of its power it is still subject to many servitudes. One cannot, therefore, give more than a qualified endorsement to the view of a celebrated English publicist, when he informs foreigners that the Caucus is enthroned on the ruins of the old British Constitution.[1]

VIII

But it must be admitted at the same time that among the divergent forces which have just been reviewed, those which hold the Caucus in check are, if anything, on the decline; that in their perpetual contests the chances are rather on the side of the centrifugal forces favouring the formalism and the mechanicalness which the Caucus tends to introduce into English political life under the auspices of democracy.

The personal influences of rank, of character, and of knowledge, which serve as a rallying centre in political life, which by their intrinsic force attract mankind and draw them into their orbit, find it more and more difficult to come to the surface. Many facts, both of a material and moral order, combine to produce this result. The steady growth of the towns, into which most of the population is flocking, makes the inhabitants strangers to one another; their contact is only superficial, and their power of reacting on each other is impeded. This general effect of contemporary civilization is aggravated in the great English centres by the habit which well-to-do people have of taking up their abode in separate parts of the town, in the " West End," for instance, in "residential suburbs," or even outside it, five, ten, or fifteen miles off. Manufacturers, merchants, rich shopkeepers, lawyers, doctors, — one and all desert the towns, spending only a part of the day in their offices or their chambers. The small folk are left to themselves, or are even confined to separate districts. Here, for instance, is a central ward of Manchester, in which, out of 2488 occupiers of tenements, there are only 13 who really reside there, who sleep there; out of the £230,832 rateable

---

1 " The Roman imposed his institutions with arms upon a conquered world; a willing world has adopted the institutions which had their original seat at Westminster. But the British Constitution now means little more than the omnipotence of the House of Commons. The immense edifice is still styled the palace; but the King who now dwells in the palace is the sovereign people, or perhaps rather, the sovereign caucus " (Goldwin Smith, *A Trip to England*, Lond. 1892, p. 120; a very remarkable tiny volume, intended to serve as a guide-book for American tourists visiting England, and giving a bird's-eye view of contemporary England in its monumental, social, and political aspects).

value of these tenements, the 13 residents represent only
£3286; in another ward, out of 1223 occupiers there are only
175 householders, the rateable value of whose dwellings does
not amount to more than £6923.   When they have made
their pile, the "better-class" people break even the slender
ties which attach them to their city, thus creating a still
wider gulf between them and the indigent classes.   Even
democratic Scotland does not escape this harmful process.
Thus at Glasgow middle-aged people can still recollect the
time when there was no West End, when rich and poor
lived side by side, mixed together, went to the same church,
sent their children to the same school.   The city was
composed of five independent boroughs, each of which had
its bailie and was a centre of local life.   At the present
moment there is far less intercourse between the various
classes; the West End has its churches and its well-equipped
schools for the rich, and the East End has its own humble
and modest ones for those who lack the good things of this
world.   Urban absenteeism, which had been conspicuous for
a considerable time,[1] is increasing every day, thanks to the
extraordinary facility of communication with the suburbs, and,
like its historical prototype, the absenteeism of landowners, inevitably produces mischievous effects, not only from the social
point of view, by accentuating the separation of classes, with
all its dangerous consequences, but also from the political
point of view.   It withdraws from the political service of the
community, from duties towards their fellow-citizens, men who
through their social position and their enlightenment would
be best equipped for the discharge of them.   But even those
who would like to put their shoulders to the wheel have now
much fewer facilities for impressing their neighbours, owing
to this material extension of town life, which creates huge
agglomerations where a man has more difficulty in coming to
the front, far more than twenty or five and twenty years ago,
were he even of the calibre of the men who arose, for instance,
in the municipality of Birmingham during the decade from

---

[1] Close observers directed their attention to urban absenteeism at a pretty
early stage. Thus in the Church Congress at Wolverhampton, in 1867, a
very elaborate report was submitted on absenteeism in the Midlands. See
the abstract of this report in the *Birmingham Daily Post*, 5th October, 1867.

1870–1880.[1]   And the reader is aware how greatly this difficulty of a natural kind, so to speak, has been increased by
the action of the Caucus.   To enter local public life you must
now have a passport from a political party, you must don the
party livery to serve interests with which party politics have
nothing to do; and even then, the excessive subdivision of the
Organization, created by the formal application of the democratic principle, transfers influence to the local mediocrity,
who wields it amid conditions little calculated to enhance the
prestige of the leadership.

The " deference," the supply of which in English society
seemed even larger than that of the coal below the surface
of England, is dwindling, and will assuredly continue to
dwindle, under the levelling process which has been at work
in England since the industrial revolution.   The democratic
Organization of the Caucus will continue to contribute to
this result in a marked degree, to undermine the hierarchical
feeling pervading political relations, even in the circles which
are most imbued with it, — in those of Toryism.   In all probability those Tories who flattered themselves that the democratic Organization introduced into their party would not lead
to serious consequences, that it could not prevail against the
old traditional feeling, will be undeceived.   The common mistake of the Conservatives is to deny or underestimate the
efficacy of political forms, as that of the Radicals is to exag-
gerate it.   Even sham representative assemblies are never set
up with impunity.   And in twenty years or so the old-
fashioned Tories, if there are any left, may be able to say to
the Liberals, from whom they borrowed the Caucus, like the
Turks to the Austrians who taught their old Serb subjects
European drill: "Neighbours, what have you done with our
raya?"[2]   To sum up, the political leadership, as a natural

[1] Perhaps the Birmingham of the present day would itself furnish proof of
this, if it had to begin over again.   Cf. *The Progress of Modern Birmingham,*
by Dr. Crespi, who says: " Birmingham is getting unwieldy, and its population is much scattered, but a generation ago it was a more manageable, and
in some respects gratifying, field for the display of great abilities than the
metropolis; a clever man was not lost in it; he was the common possession of
his townsmen, and within their easy reach.   It is open to question whether
any one will again make a great and general position in Birmingham " (*National Review,* May, 1889).

[2] Servia, after being conquered to a great extent by Joseph II. in 1788, was

link between the members of the community, founded partly
on tradition, partly on the legitimate action of one man on
another, on the confidence and devotion inspired by personal
worth, this leadership, which has already received so many
shocks, is likely to grow weaker still.

At the same time a shrinkage is observed, in social life, of
certain special sources the current of which served to unite
men into important groups, and, as a consequence, to provide
elements for the political leadership; as, for instance, the
solidarity of the great religious bodies.   This is giving way
under the action of tolerance and religious indifference, which
have made great progress in English society during the last
quarter of a century.   The passions and the jealousies of the
churches have lost a vast deal of their acuteness; people are
no longer, or far less, anxious to know if their neighbour goes
to church or to chapel; no attention is paid to it in social
relations.   This state of the public mind benefits Dissent, for
instance, greatly and legitimately, but it also robs it of its
social cohesion, which made it into a sort of freemasonry even
in political life, where it formed, according to Mr. Gladstone's
expression, the backbone of the Liberal party.   The joints of
this backbone are beginning to get dislocated.   In rural districts the old antagonism has still enough of its keenness to
maintain the cohesion, but in the towns the dissolving process
makes great strides, and is not a little helped by the social
ambitions which are infecting the richer members of the Nonconformist sects and making them keep to themselves amid
their coreligionists, even in the places of worship, which they
are prone to transform into chapels of a few select families.
Again, indifference to religion in general, which is increasing by the side of and in spite of the undeniable successes
achieved by the churches in the last half-century, contributes
in its turn to enfeeble the living forces of society and to
swell the conventional forces.

given back to the Turks three years afterwards by the successor of Joseph II.,
but during the Austrian occupation the Serbs had time to get a notion of freedom, to acquire independent ways, and the Ottoman commissioner who took
over the occupied territory, seeing a Serb detachment march out of a fortress
well armed, and manœuvring like the Imperial troops, exclaimed with mingled astonishment and alarm, "Neighbours, what have you done with our
raya!"

Moreover, a phenomenon is arising which is at once the effect and the stimulant of those which have just been described,—the political apathy which is creeping over society. "Politics is no longer popular" is the unanimous impression of people in the business. In spite of the economic commotions which are the peculiar feature of our age, material comfort is too great and too widely diffused among the English people for arousing their combative instincts, or even for keeping them interested in the questions which fill up the existence of the politicians. The middle class is retiring from the political arena, deliberately, so to speak, obeying alike its feelings of selfishness and its *amour propre* wounded by the political advent of the lower social strata. It looks as if this class had exhausted its ardour in the great battles which it fought one after another in the first half of the century. It has no longer any grievances to urge or claims to keep alive in the political and social sphere. The fire which burned brightly in the hearts of the preceding generations is but a faint gleam in the present generation. The threat of Socialist demands is not fraught with danger imminent enough to bring the middle-class contingents into the field, and it is loud enough to make a good many of its members still more timorous and to plunge them still more deeply into their selfishness. No doubt they still have a fine place in the political procession, but it is more by *vis inertiae* that they move in it; they have no impulse of their own, and even this automatic participation is decreasing; in the growing number of abstentions at elections they probably furnish the most considerable proportion. While the cultivated classes tend to turn aside from politics, the new strata of political society show no eagerness to fill the vacant space; public spirit is not developing sufficiently among the masses, to a great extent through the fault of the Caucus. At the same time that it assists the selfishness of the middle classes in discouraging their efforts by the democratic pretensions of which it has assumed the championship, it withholds from the masses real political education calculated to broaden and stimulate the mind; it keeps it back, offering them in its place a wretched substitute, which has the property of delivering them more easily into its hands. Thus is witnessed alike an abatement of interest in politics in the community, and a diminution of the moral and material facilities for the rise and the popularity of the best men and for rallying the masses around them, side by side with a decline in the readiness of the educated and well-to-do classes to come forward and put their shoulders to the wheel.

While these combined tendencies reveal the dawn of a separation of society as a whole from the small minority given up to politics, under a constitution which now denies hardly any one the power of exerting his influence on public affairs, in the narrower sphere of politics an important phenomenon is appearing: the political parties are more and more losing their distinctive characteristics. The political controversies which have of late set the two historic parties by the ears, however great the violence of the combatants may often have been, were not of a kind to mark a new line of permanent separation between them, or to prevent the obliteration of the old one which had been going on since 1846. The effect was that in the matter of principles, of policies, the two parties drew closer to each other. No longer representing clearly defined opposing principles, no longer having a monopoly, the one of progress, the other of reaction, the one of solicitude for the masses, the other of aristocratic or capitalist privilege, the parties as such tend to become simple aggregates, drawn together, by the attractive force of a leader, for the conquest or the preservation of power. In a word, parallel with the separation of society from politics, are seen indications of the divorce of politics from principles. When these last have disappeared, the only vital system of the parties will be a mechanical organization, all the more powerful the more it will be spread over the country, the more widely it will cover the constituencies with its network. In other words, the parties will live only by and thanks to a machine like the Caucus. The latter will not only have helped to drive back the living forces of the political community, to make a vacuum in it, but will also install itself in the empty citadel, and almost as a matter of right.

Stepping into the place of living society, the party organizations, instead of being an instrument, a means, will become an object in themselves, to which everything will be subordinated. Deriving their right to existence from more or less arbitrary conventions, from labels which will distinguish one from the other, the rival organizations, without even obeying sordid preoccupations, but from an instinct of self-preservation, will make all the relations of political life bend to the blind formalism of its conventions, in defiance of the real interests at stake. From this point of view the transformation of local elections into political party contests, and the deterioration of municipal government which it is already beginning to produce, offer a warning the gravity of which cannot be overrated. But in addition to this, the factitious character of the organizations will not allow them to command much disinterested devotion for long; people will serve them only in the hope of making use of them, on the basis of *do ut des*, and they will witness the development of an ever-increasing mercenary element within their ranks. In this connection the life of the Caucus has revealed an alarming symptom of late years; the voluntary aid given to the organizations is decreasing and being replaced by paid services, even when the law expressly forbids it, as in the case of the election canvass. There is no longer sufficient "enthusiasm" among the caucus-men of both parties; it is money which comes first, and this fact accounts to some extent for the great success at the last general election of the wealthiest party. No doubt the comparative slenderness of the pecuniary resources of the organizations is a fortunate obstacle to the development in their midst of the type of mercenary politicians, but it is not sufficient to allay apprehensions. The growing habit of distributing subordinate municipal offices as a reward for election work is there to confirm them. The measure, so often discussed of late, for giving a fixed allowance to Members of Parliament, is also somewhat calculated to foster these misgivings. The payment of Members would in itself be perfectly equitable and useful in enabling people of small means to enter Parliament, and all the less unjustifiable because, as things now stand, the title of M. P. is already a source of gain for a good many Members, procuring them advantages in business, well-paid directorships of joint-stock companies, so much so that not a few try to get into Parliament simply in order to forward their pecuniary interests. The difference between them and the legally paid Members would be, perhaps, that while the former make money out of their title of M.P. to provide luxuries for their wives and daughters, among the latter a certain number would get the daily bread of their family by their parliamentary position. But it is not less certain that payment of Members would provide the organizations which distribute seats in the Legislature with a war fund, the importance of which would not be measured by its actual amount, but by the rival appetites which it would excite, by the eager desires which it would let loose. The command of these large resources would give the organizations a formidable hold on the whole political system, and attract into their ranks, introducing many of them into public offices, men bent solely on personal gain.

By the side of these indications and hypotheses pointing to or foreshadowing the upward movement of the organizations which are forwarding a mechanical formalism, a few symptoms can no doubt be discerned which seem likely to hamper this movement, but their significance is still of a very relative kind. There are signs, at present slight, of a tendency among the voters to throw off the tyrannical authority of the party, to resent the attempts of the organizations on their political conscience. The agents of the Caucus begin to complain that "canvassing is becoming worse every year," "they will not tell their politics," "they object to be canvassed." The advance of knowledge develops a critical spirit in the electorate, while the decline in the standard of the caucus-men lowers the prestige of the firms which they represent, and the conduct of the rival parties suggests to many people that these parties are much of a muchness, one as bad or as good as the other. But very often it is these voters on their guard who withdraw from politics and leave the field open to the Caucus. The Socialist propaganda, in its turn, is systematically engaged in severing the old party ties, without, however, providing a refuge from party tyranny, for the socialist organizations, the I. L. P. or the Democratic Federation, imprison their adherents in a formalism not less, and even more, despotic than the old parties; in this respect the activity of the Socialists has only a negative value, by its dissolvent effect, as is probably the case with it in the general economy of contemporary social

life of which it stirs up the stagnant waters. By enticing
away the adherents of the organizations of the old parties,
and by introducing a fresh element of uncertainty into their
existence made up more or less of conventions, the Socialist
activity eats away these parties, makes gaps in them. An
analogous result will perhaps be produced by the break-up of
the great natural aggregations which is beginning to show
itself, — in Dissent, for instance. In tending to create a
vacuum for the benefit of the Caucus, this disintegration may
also be capable of producing a contrary effect, by dispersing
the disciplined contingents which were ready to ally themselves with the Caucus. But it is permissible to speculate
whether in this connection the forces which favour the Caucus
and those which create impediments to it will be evenly balanced; for the strength of formal and conventional forces
invading a community lies not so much in the fighting power
of their own contingents as in the weakness of those which
they tend to supplant.

In pointing out all the data and all the probabilities which
indicate that the democratic formalism of the Caucus, leaning
on the old convention of stereotyped parties, is launching
English society on the decline of government by machine, it
is not possible to consider the eventual consequences in other
than a more or less hypothetical way. For on this decline
there are still, as we have seen, many obstacles raised by the
old manners and customs of the nation, objectionable as some
of them may be in themselves from the modern standpoint,
and which the democratic institutions installed in the English
State have not yet obliterated. But there is already in existence a political community sprung from the very loins of England, its own flesh and blood, and which, left to itself in a new
world, has anticipated the development of the mother-country
by repudiating several of its habits and letting democracy have
free play, while keeping the substance of its political institutions. Pushing the representative and elective principle to
its extreme consequences, this new political society has at an
early stage permitted the rise within it of the Caucus, which,
implanted in its levelled soil, has had a long career, free from
the trammels which it still encounters in the "old country."

The circumstances under which the same social and political data operate in different societies being never identical, the experience of America cannot, of course, be decisive as to the future development of the Caucus in England. But it may, owing precisely to the relative diversity of the conditions, throw a powerful light on that development and on the whole problem of the organization of the electoral masses, by bringing out its effects as well as its pitfalls and its dangers, with more certainty and with far more fulness than could be done by the investigation of the English Caucus, which is still in the growing stage. We are thus brought logically to the study of the organization of parties in the great American Republic. And, following the plan adopted for England, I propose to examine, in their main outlines, the historical development and the working at the present day of the extra-parliamentary organization of political parties in the United States.

END OF VOL. I.